# TARNISHED GOLD

# TARNISHED GOLD

## The Record Industry Revisted

**R. Serge Denisoff**

*With the Assistance of*
William L. Schurk

Transaction Books
New Brunswick (U.S.A.) and Oxford (U.K.)

Library of Congress Catalog Number: 85-24556
ISBN: 0-88738-068-9 (cloth), 0-88738-618-0 (paper)
Printed in the United States of America

**Library of Congress Cataloging in Publication Data**

Denisoff, R. Serge.
    Tarnished gold.

    Bibliography: p.
    Includes index.
    1. Sound recording industry.    2. Music, Popular
(Songs, etc.)—United States—History and criticism.
I. Schurk, William L.    II. Title.
ML3790.D43    1986        338.4'77899'120973        85-24556
ISBN 0-88738-068-9
ISBN 0-88738-618-0 (pbk.)

*To the MTV Kids,*
*Gabriel and Arden*
*and*
*to Bonnie Jean*

# Contents

# Acknowledgments

This book is the product of the pestering of a number of people who liked *Solid Gold* and wanted at least a revision. Irving Louis Horowitz was kind enough to lead the chorus. The record industry itself played a large role in motivating the creation of this volume. The mechinations of the late 1970s and early 1980s begged for analysis rather than the descriptive nature of *Solid Gold*. Once again there are numerous industry people, media members, and others who consented to interviews and follow-ups. The Record Industry Association of America and National Association of Recording Merchandisers were helpful in supplying a great deal of statistical data. Roger Wise of Wood Cable Television taught me a great deal about his industry. Michael Walker provided a crash course on Satanism and backwarding of records. Doreen Lauer at MTV was most helpful, although I never did get an interview with Bob Pittman. The editors of the *Daily Sentinel Tribune*, (Bowling Green, Ohio), David Miller and Harold Brown, must be thanked for allowing me the freedom to pursue some stories the results of which appear in this work.

As always the secretarial staff at Bowling Green State University's Sociology Department provided invaluable assistance. Mrs. Pat Kane, particularly, performed a herculean task in typing and retyping a massive manuscript. Mrs. Kathy Hill equally helped. The Music Library and Sound Recordings Archives at Bowling Green State University are an essential resource for any writer on musical topics.

# Foreword

There is something transparently self-serving, not to mention rendundant, in a publisher serving as author of a special foreword to a book published under his imprint. Even if this circumstance is somewhat mitigated by the book and author under consideration being in the same general frame of professional reference to which I belong, namely, the community of sociologists, a sense of unease persists. Let me try to mitigate, if not remove this unease. Only under the rarest of circumstances and under severe prodding will I write a foreword to a work with which I am organically connected. All fourteen hundred Transaction Books are close to me in spirit, however they fare in the marketplace. Whether I agree with the premises and performance of each title or otherwise, each is a tiny slice of a vested interest no less than intellectual conceit.

Well then, why am I writing this foreword? The answers are several: let me be quick about the telling. First, R. Serge Denisoff may or may not have written *Tarnished Gold* otherwise. I was not about to have on my head any responsibility for a book that needed writing not being executed on my account. Second, I wrote the preface for the earlier volume, *Solid Gold*, thus knocking the props out from under many arguments with respect to writing another statement a decade later. Third, no matter how hard one tries for universalism in a publishing program, certain particular concerns, some may call it sentiments, play a larger-than-normal role in the evolution of a publishing effort. The sociology of culture and music is one such area for Transaction, and for me personally. Fourth and finally, this is one fine book, a work that could not be written by an economist for lack of musical scope, and one that could not be written by a musicologist for lack of economic depth. It takes a crossover figure like Denisoff to write expertly, feeling, on a crossover world of culture, business, technology, not to mention personalities linked to structures that most social scientists over twenty-four years of age only vaguely understand.

Denisoff's chapter on the political ideologies which attach themselves to rock and roll, and popular music generally, is as unsparing to the revolutionary Left as it is to the religious Right. The exaggerations, the hopes, and the organizational efforts to harness a mass culture to precise ends unravel at both ends of political-religious spectrum. The musical product itself proved in the past, and continues to function in the present, as too amorphous and ubiquitous to permit any sort of perfect fit. Culture neither shrivels and goes away under threats from fundamentalists, nor in the long pull of time does it become easily harnessed by ideologists. The empty efforts to do so are finely documented by Denisoff—with a quiet courage that the stuff of good scholarship is made.

What is so special about Denisoff's *Tarnished Gold* is his sense of the historical basis of current fads and foibles in popular music. Whether he is discussing the ratings system in popular music (going back to Martin Block and the *Make Believe Ballroom*, or the origins of mixed visual/musical presentations going back to Al Jolson and *The Jazz Singer*), Denisoff brings to his essentially sociological task a rich sense of history. This is not, I hasten to add, a fuzzy general history of society, but the quite specific history of the mass cultures within American society. If there is one aspect of music ciriticism that I find especially repellant it is the efforts of some to adduce a general moral theory of America by which to judge particular cultural events. Denisoff, much to his credit, avoids such easy, simplistic pitfalls, while at the same time, not falling into the opposite error of mis-placed concreteness, in which no general implications can be drawn. If music is not part of some sort of deconstructionist narrative that has an atomic reality totally divorced from the *cultural forms of society*, neither is it part of some sort of historicist mission to announce movements that are equally divorced from the *social forms of culture*.

Denisoff's work has a theoritical significance quite beyond social nar-rative. This is made clear at the outset, with a discussion of popular music that arrives at major findings. While the exact contents of the next wave of popularity are hard to predict, its physionomical characteristics can yet be broadly outlined: the clustering of tastes and styles, *i.e.*, electricism in place of purism; the ability to gain acceptance from a portion of the population beyond the vertical stratifications of race, sex and age that characterize so many smaller audiences; finally, the relationship between the *esoteric* needs of art and its capacity to relate to the *exoteric* requirements of audience.

Each of these elements not just in the successful marketing of cultural products, but more important, in the creation of a general theory of popu-lar culture. Denisoff's leit-motif is a theory as suitable for our day as the efforts of David Manning White and David Reisman and Herta Herzog were for the late 1940s and early 1950s. In this, one hopes that *Tarnished Gold*, even more than its less theoritically inclined parent, *Solid Gold*, will become a center of sober professional attention for the mavens and the doyens of popular culture in America—if in the odd chance they can lift their heads and hearts from the bottom line.

It may be asking for trouble, or at least for an additional prefactory assignment, but I somehow suspect that around 1990 we can expect a third volume in this series, perhaps under the title *Fool's Gold*, that will take as it point of departure the new linkages in popular music culture. The growing place of a print culture sitting astride a musical culture, which is paralleled by intimacies between video presentations and musical recordings, is the beginning of a new musicology no less than a new technology. As Denisoff shows, each has long and deep antecedents in American history, but stands as a qualitatively different form of media interaction as well as personal participation. MTV, what Denisoff refers to as the "new player in the game," is but the beginning, or rather the tip of a transformed popular music iceberg.

The last three sections of *Tarnished Gold* indicate that not just new forms of music are emerging, but new styles of art are mushrooming. Relationships between electronic games and electronic music, mixed-media presentations that offer sexual pleasures no less than musical insights, tie-ins between radio, quizzes, gifts, and purchases, all of these signify a volatility and an experimental capacity that, whether healthy or not (and who knows just what musical health means) betokens new musical break-throughs in the near future.

The carriers of the popular culture are young people. They are also the carriers of the technological culture presently centered around the computer. Relationships between technology and art are long-standing. No musical form could have emerged without corresponding transformations in the technology of instrumentation. The same is true now. What first appears as bizarre, atonal, unpleasant, may become part of the common culture. More likely, these experimental effects will be melded into the what Raymond Williams refers to as the "long tradition." Hence, the new finds its way through the interstices of the old, just as the old must continually struggle to maintain its integral place against new challengers. Harold Rosenberg's Tradition of the New is built into the marrow of Denisoff's music as commodity. If a new sensibility of American culture is to emerge, it will do so in considerable measure out of the materials fashioned in this substantial book.

IRVING LOUIS HOROWITZ
—RUTGERS UNIVERSITY

# Preface

*Solid Gold*, this book's predecessor, was written at a time when the study of the production of culture was in its infancy, especially when applied to the record industry. In the wake of the Woodstock Nation, Con III the music business was perceived by many as leading a generation down the road to either salvation or damnation. As a sociologist and journalist, I found both arguments flawed. However, the literature of the early 1970s was of little help. The few scholars in the area were basically analyzing the lyrics of Lennon-McCartney and of course the "bard" Bob Dylan. Numerous music publications such as *Rolling Stone* shied away from discussions of the business due to their dependence on "hip" corporate advertising. The trades seemed content as gross profits annually climbed. Consequently, *Solid Gold* was an attempt to describe the record business without getting involved in certain controversial areas. Several reviewers claimed that the treatment ignored the content of rock music (later treated in Greil Marcus's excellent book *Mystery Train*), which was and remains my intent. Content analysis and musical criticism are saved for my newspaper column and occasional academic journal articles.

*Tranished Gold* goes beyond the original volume of description to a more analytic and at times a critical posture. This approach was partially generated by the events of the past ten years and the industry's responses to them.

For several decades, beginning in 1955, the sales of the recorded product steadily climbed upward. In 1979 the "Great Disco Disaster," as Robert Christgau termed it, reversed the trend. The reaction to the crisis provides an interesting glimpse into the mind-set and economics of the industry as well as the electronic and print media that expose its releases. This period is fraught with contradictions, miscalculations, scapegoating, and corporate takeovers.

Music video especially (MTV) pulled the record industry out of the slump in the mid-eighties. Ironically, when the concept of a twenty-four-hour all-music video network was suggested, many companies considered the idea as "the stupidest thing ever heard." By Orwell's 1984, MTV was widely credited with saving a drowning industry. Music video, especially the MTV Network, has and promises to exert a profound influence on the music world. Some of these issues are raised in this book.

Then there is the rise of Tom Wolfe's Me Generation, the Yuppies, and the New Christian Right and its assault on the "makers of plastic ware."

Given its content, this work will no doubt raise some eyebrows and questions. Still, without questions there are no answers. One inquiry concerns the power of music, its manufacturers, marketers, and exposers. As noted previously, these questions and segments of the business need some kind of structuring if any serious fan, writer, or scholar is to make any sense of the unique world of the creation of commercial music.

Throughout this book there are a number of unattributed quotations. Many are drawn from unsigned press releases. Some are anonymous statements. Others are on "background," that is, the interviewees requested that they and/or their employers not be identified by name.

# 1

# What is Popular Music?

*Hey, Hey, My, My,*
*Rock n' roll can never die*

—©Silver Fiddle BMI

Popular music is like a unicorn: everyone knows what it is supposed to look like, but no one has ever seen it. Such music connotes a rhythmic idiom—songs, instrumentals, novelties, or what have you—that reflects the musical preferences of the people. According to this definition, popular music exists for the enjoyment of listeners within the general public; its alleged deficiencies mirror inadequacies in the popular taste. Neither of these definitions is appropriate.

Since the advent of the Beatles, Bob Dylan, Neil Young, and other intellectually acceptable artists, few writers have insisted that popular music is kitsch, déclassé, or somehow without merit. This is a quantum leap from the view of popular music presented in previous decades. Former U.S. Senator S. I. Hayakawa, for example, insisted that popular songs were "diluted, sweetened, sentimentalized and trivialized . . . the product of white songwriters for predominantly white audiences tending towards wishful thinking, dreams and ineffectual nostalgia, realistic fantasy, self-pity and sentimental cliches masquerading as emotion."[1] Popular music has retained many of these elements but it was not dismissed in its entirety, for the wave of high points of rock and roll such as *Sgt. Pepper, Dark Side of the Moon,* or *Highway 61 Revisited* are by no means representative of popular music.

The more things change, the more they remain the same. The components of popular music are in constant flux. Different sounds, personalities, and favorites dart on and off the music charts. Certain styles dominate specific historical periods. These are complemented by other genres. Even when the Beatles and other English bands ruled the charts, novelty songs and big-band crooners shared in the bounties of public acceptance. Popular music is not typified by any generic style. Marty Cerf, when at United

Artists, noted that just as "society is made up of many specialty, racial and mixed backgrounds, so is music, and the pop charts are made up of minorities." He continued, "On the pop charts you find 20 percent singles from albums; progressive albums 35 percent; rhythm and blues 25 percent; very straight middle-of-the-road and pop records 20 percent." A former Warner/Reprise promotion head concurred, "You look on the chart and all the records aren't the same." It is less than accurate to say that rock and roll or swing in the 1930s constituted the entire popular music spectrum of the time.

Quantitatively, popular music is a recognized product. The number of records sold is measurable and observable. Charts in *Billboard, Cashbox, Friday Morning Quarterback,* and *Rolling Stone* list what is being played on radio stations and in part selling in record stores. This amorphous market is quite distinct from others attuned to particular musical forms. Popular music is a much larger and eclectic idiom. It takes capriciously from specialty areas and momentarily provides an unfamiliar sound its place in the Top 40 sun. Popular music not infrequently is a blending of several specific musical forms. Rock originally was a wedding of country music and black blues. However, an important distinction must be made between the sum total of all musical forms and popular music.

Popular music is not just the sum total of all musical styles. It does not include all forms of music. If it reflected all the people's tastes, it would then have to include a multitude of styles and all of the esoteric genres enjoyed by hundreds of taste publics. This, of course, is not the case. Popular music is not beamed at all of the public but at a self-selected audience that elects what is called "popular" with its listening time and dollars. Popular music, then, is a specific subcategory of the entire spectrum of music; what is referred to in everyday language as "pop" is not ipso facto "popular." Popular music is a medium addressed to a particular segment of the U.S. and overseas public. Generally this audience consists of persons under the age of 34, but some preferences of people past that generational watermark do manage to sneak onto the pop charts. Still, popular music is primarily designed for people between the ages of 9 and 34, the courtship years, and whoever else cares to listen.

An ever-growing number of people seem to fit this latter group. Quantitatively, popular music consists of whichever musical style sells sufficiently to be deemed successful or representative of an exoteric audience. Success is determined by such indices of the music industry as radio play and over-the-counter sales. *Billboard's* "Hot 100" chart is based on 63 radio stations, 25 distributors, and 22 retailers. Consequently, sufficient purchases by the youth audience, the main consumers, define what constitutes popular music at any specific time. The actual mechanics of the delineation of the youth market arc highly complex. Adolescent and college tastes are not monolithic; they are shaped and influenced by numerous social forces around them ranging from age, race, marital status, and sex to geographical location.

### Popular *qua* People's Music

Any teenager who has heard the cry "You call that music?" can testify that some people—particularly parents—do not enjoy or even tolerate popular music. Feelings and attitudes notwithstanding, it is almost impossible to avoid popular music. Whether one is passing a record rack at the local mall or twisting the car radio dial in search of the most-up-to-the minute commuter report, it is usually present.

Popular music *is* everywhere. Some would call it a symptom of "noise pollution." Americans operate over some $7,661,115,000's worth of media vehicles ranging from tuners to television sets. Television in nearly all U.S. homes is increasingly focusing on music programming. Eighteen and a half million homes receive Warner Amex's Music Channel (MTV). The late Ed Sullivan, hardly a supporter of rock music, in the "now-for-the-youngsters" segment of his Sunday night show featured acts that appealed to his younger viewers but thereby alienated much of his older audience. He also presented singers liked Andy Williams, Dean Martin, or Doris Day, who appealed to older viewers. Owners of television sets are potential popular music listeners, but they are not necessarily consumers.

In 1955, 4,542 pop singles and 1,615 long-playing albums were released. In 1967 the record industry passed the billion-dollar mark in annual sales. In 1968, 6,540 singles were issued, and 183,000,000 singles were sold in stores, and to jukebox operators and other buyers. In that same year 4,057 long-playing albums (LPs) were released and grossed over $1 billion; 196 million LPs were purchased. An indeterminable number of bootleg records swelled this number. A decade later record sales peaked at $4.1 billion gross, no doubt aided by the staggering sales of *Saturday Night Fever,* which legitimately sold over 25 million copies. (The FBI estimates twice that number of sales if counterfeits are included.) With these figures the pop qua people's music thesis seems almost plausible because nearly every man, woman, and child *statistically* could have bought an LP and a large number of singles. This is not the case.

Beginning in the first fiscal quarter of 1979 record sales plummeted. As we will see, the industry blamed every cause under the sun. The objective fact was that the industry's growth was dropping a significant 11 percent per year. The heydays of the 1960s and the 1970s were over. In response record companies diversified and cut back, including the number of releases. The

Recording Industry Association of America (RIAA) reported the release of 2,630 new albums in 1982. Cassette titles numbered 2,710 (some observers believe that cassettes will outstrip albums), and 2,285 singles appeared in the same year. There were minialbums, midline albums—popular oldies, reissues, and new acts listing at $5.98. In total 5,375 new records were issued. Despite the product reduction, gold and platinum albums decreased in significant numbers. The boom year, 1978, had produced some 295 gold and platinum albums, and 71 singles had fared as well. By 1982 there was 40 percent drop in these successful and prestigious albums. Only 24 singles went gold, the lowest yearly total since 1966. Even more confusing was the fact that eleven recipients of the gold trophy were new acts like Stray Cats, Men at Work, and Tom Tom Club. The superstars did well, but not by previous standards. Fleetwood Mac, for example, could not repeat multiple platinums such as *Rumors* or Peter Frampton's *Alive*.

Prior to 1979 the volume of product had been a historic problem in the record industry. There were less than optimistic aspects of this flood of recordings. Murray Rose, president of an advertising marketing agency, once observed, "In a business that saw the release of 4,000 albums and 5,700 singles . . . , where only 10 percent even smelled 'break even,' you almost have to be an egomaniac just to think you can crack those odds."[2] More recently the "stiff" ratio was closer; 85 percent of the singles and 80 percent of albums failed to return their investment. Most releases never even get to the public. Only a small portion of the public usually buys a pop record.

The music industry itself places inordinate emphasis upon success as epitomized by the gold record, the success symbol. The gold record is awarded for the bona fide gross of $1 million and on the basis of units sold. The single far outsells the album, of course, because the price of the single is about two dollars in many parts of the United States and long-playing albums are much more expensive. In practice an album that finds about 502,000 buyers in the United States qualifies for the coveted gold record. An album is certified gold when net domestic sales of LPs and tapes valued at one-third list price amount to $1 million; a million albums sold garners a platinum record. Thus, at $8.98 list price, each sale counts $1.99 toward the gold record. Yet, considering the potential market, the figures are relatively small and certainly representative of only a small portion of the public. A baseball player with a batting average of less than 15 percent would not move past the first rung of sandlot ball. Record company executive Joe Smith underlined this point to *Rolling Stone:* "I'm talking business, because there are 70 million homes in this country, of that 56 million, i.e., 78 percent, have record players or some means of playing a record. Why should we jump up and down to sell a million records?"[3]

The notion of popular music qua people's music is further shaken by musical taste and preference surveys conducted over the past decade. Starting in 1977 Warner Communications published a study indicating a profile of the tastes and consumption habits of record buyers. Although methodologically exhibiting a number of classification problems (rock qua Simon and Garfunkel), it is one of the few surveys available not surprisingly rock the dominant preferred genre. However, it showed that as the under 30 taste group declines rock's share of the market had dramatically increased while overall sales drop 11 percent annually.

The National Association of Recording Merchandisers (NARM), which reported its sales figures in 1981, found rock and "pop" constituted nearly half the market, 49.8 percent. Country remained fairly constant, about 15 percent. For other than these categories, the numbers plummet; soul garners nearly 10 percent, showing little variance, but all other genres with the exception of children's records are below 5 percent. Pop music, then, is generally the province of youth.

### Popular qua Young People's Music

Popular music is virtually the exclusive playground of the young. A vast majority of the records sold in North America are purchased by young adults. In a Canadian survey 77 percent of the high school students picked rock music as their favorite idiom; only 11 percent echoed the tastes of their parents and teachers. When comparing generations on the variable of support for or appreciation of rock and roll as either their first or second choice, a significant 87.9 percent of those adolescents sampled made these choices: their elders followed suit only in 4 percent of the cases. In discussing the genres of show tune and classical, a combined 96 percent of the adults indicated a strong preference for this material.

Taste and record-buying habits are strongly influenced by age. Bubble-gummers or prepuberty females between the ages of 9 and 12 buy the lion's share of singles. After the age of 16, white youths begin to concentrate upon long-playing albums. Blacks, without comparable economic power, continue to buy singles for a longer period of time. As the courtship process begins, teenage males become increasingly involved in record consumerism. Record buying begins to decline at age 34, much to the consternation of retailers.

The question of adult membership in the popular music constituency is a thorny one. The passing of the statistical watermark of 30 does not push a person into the out-of-it category except in record-buying. People over 34 *buy* fewer popular records than do people half their age. Charts reflect this. Most acts on the Top 40, MTV, or the *Billboard* "Hot 100" are not performers known for their adult appeal. Nonetheless, radio programmers and record-company executives are aware that housewives who take care of the kids listen to daytime radio and occasionally buy a record. After age 30, the wife or mother makes most of the family record purchases. Although hard statistical data at this time are not available, the argument is that as more women enter the "pink-collar" world of commerce, fewer will be exposed to the so-called cookie-cutter material of daytime radio.

The type of music supported by housewives is called "easy listening" or "middle of the road" (MOR). It is a part of the popular-music idiom, but it is also a fairly small specialty area. MOR ranges from the piped-in Muzak heard in a dentist's waiting room to the soft strains of Lionel Richie or Barry Manilow heard on the car radio. MOR material frequently crosses over into popular music, yet a good deal of rock music is totally banned from easy-listening stations. "If I played Alice Cooper or Black Sabbath at 10 in the morning," said one MOR program director, "100,000 women would find another station. . . . I'd be looking for another job." Easy listening as it exists in the 1980s is generally a mix of traditional ballads and soft rock doing love songs. Some soft rock and novelty material also make their way from the Top 40 charts onto MOR listings. Nostalgia in the form of "golden oldies" is an important aspect of MOR radio, as it is in AM programming. AM stations will program "solid-gold weekends" to lure MOR listeners. The bait of nostalgia is designed to alter the stations' normal demographic profile of 9 to 24. By attracting older listeners, the station balloons its 25-to-49 category, and that is "where the advertising money is."

For record-company executives, easy listening is really a post-pop audience. The post-pop audience generally consists of people who have stuck to popular music of the kind they enjoyed when they were teenagers. A 40-year-old can easily "get into" a contemporary ballad when performed by Linda Ronstadt, Barry Manilow, or Olivia Newton-John and yet detest a "harder" version of the song. Indeed, many acts popular in MOR and "beautiful music," like Ray Coniff, Roger Whittier, or 101 Strings, have made it a practice to "cover" or copy the current hits in their more traditional styles.

The post-pop audience can and does buy 100,000 units of an album; attends night clubs and occasionally concerts: and watches its favorite acts on Johnny Carson's "Tonight Show." But, as Joe Smith indicated in *Rolling Stone*, one Jimi Hendrix record sold several million compared to Frank Sinatra's 200,000. Nearly all of the major record compaines, while exhibiting a few "easy-listening" artists, spend most of their time, money, and energy on performers who appeal to those under 34 because that cohort buys the majority of the records.

Popular music appreciation is along generational lines, but it is also not exclusively favored by all of the young. David Riesman, writing in *American Quarterly*, was one of the first post-World War II social scientists to explore the relationship of radio music to adolescents. The Harvard professor indicated that popular music was a monopoly industry that handed down material to the young, who accepted it without question. In his awareness of this alleged manipulative aspect of the music industry, he dichotomized the teenage audience on the basis of majority and minority taste units. The majority was characterized as an amorphous unit with rather uncertain tastes that reflected peer-group pressures. It typified what the author would term the conformist, "other-directed personality":

> Most of the teenagers in the majority category have an indiscriminating taste in popular music: they seldom express articulate preferences. They form the audience for the larger radio stations, the "name" brands, the star singers, the *Hit Parade,* and so forth. The functions of music for this group are *social*—the music gives them something to talk or kid about with friends . . . coupled with a lack of concern about how hits are actually made; an opportunity for identification with star singers or band leaders as "personalities" with little interest in or understanding of the technologies of performance or of the radio medium itself.[4]

Riesman delineated the minority group as small, comprising more involved listeners "who are less interested in melody or tune than in arrangement or technical virtuosity." He added that this esoteric group was commonly interested in jazz and blues. He could also have easily included in this group the folk music enthusiasts of Greenwich Village, Berkeley, and Harvard Square. A key to the recognition of this minority group was its dissent from mass-produced culture:

> The rebelliousness of this group might be indicated in some of the following attitudes toward popular music: an insistence on rigorous uncommercialized, unadvertised small bands rather than name bands; the development of a private language and then a flight from it when the private language is taken over by the majority group; a profound resentment of the commercialization of radio and musicians.[5]

The majority taste culture in the early 1950s was dominated by six major recording companies—Columbia, Victor, Decca, Capitol, MGM, and Mercury—that produced dreamy love songs and novelty and specialty numbers, which British rock historian Charlie Gillett pictures as featuring singers of "conventional expectations. . . their styles were bland, pleasant, and in effect suburban. The styles of female popular singers. . . were even more respectably pleasant."[6] The general tone of these styles and the songs reflecting them denied the physical nature of sex and expressed trite emotions about simple events with almost no reference to any shared experiences.

Until the serendipitous successes of Bill Haley, the Crew Cuts, and finally Elvis Presley, majority tases were defined and catered to by Tin Pan Alley, the American Society of Composers, Artists and Publishers (ASCAP), and the major record manufacturers. The minority and esoteric cultural groups were dependent upon specialty labels, which in a few instances were subsidiaries of the majors, such as Okeh of Columbia Records. Most were independent labels. Business people, in both cases, produced for the youth culture and the parents. In the majority category the popularity of the crooning style mirrored the tastes of the mid-1930s. Singers like Tony Martin, Johnnie Ray, Frankie Laine, Joni James, and Kay Starr, and quartets like the Ames Brothers, the Four Lads, and the Four Aces were musically closely related to the big-band crooners and quartets.

Only the minority, given their different overtones, in fact clashed with majority taste. Jazz clubs of the 1950s, peopled by Blacks, intellectuals, and college students, for many people remained in the historical context of dens of illegitimate behavior ranging from narcotics to prostitution. Rhythm and blues was considered "race music"—unsuitable for the white middle class. One religious publication claimed that "Rock and Roll [is] a Disease." Frank Zappa recalls, "They did everything they could to make sure their children were not moved erotically by Negroes."[7] When rock and roll dominated pop music, the minority of the early 1950s merged with a large segment of the majority to create a new plurality that the record industry could not or would not immediately accept. The quartets and crooners still led the music parade, but the tunes were changing and so was the audience, although not as drastically as Zappa would later suggest. Rock and roll did not constitute all of popular music, and even in the heyday of Elvis Presley not all teenagers were into his music, as many rock histories seem to imply.

In 1955 only one song, "Only You," broke into the coveted circle of the *Billboard* 25 top sellers from a minority taste category. The years 1956 through 1958, customarily described as the original rock and roll epoch, exhibited more authenic black rhythm and blues, although much of it was designed for a white audience. By 1959 the transmogrified product of the Philadelphia school and other pseudo rhythm and blues products joined the usual easy-listening fare on the *Billboard* charts. While Elvis Presley and "rock riots" were attracting news headlines and parental attention, the youth culture was not in fact following suit en masse. In a survey of Chicago high school students conducted by James Coleman in 1958, 43.5

percent of the girls and 45.2 percent of the boys chose Pat Boone as their favorite singer. Presley placed third, behind Perry Como, gaining 21.5 percent of the boys and a surprisingly low 17.5 percent of the girls. Studies of taste, while more supportive of the rock qua youth pop notion, did not indicate uniform adolescent backing of the new sound.[8]

If Coleman's Chicago sample was representative of national tastes, it appears that only half of the teenage market was then attuned to rock and roll as its favorite musical form. Another study undertaken during the same period, although not conclusive, did point to fragmentation of taste by peer-group influence and geographic propinquity, that is, neigborhood of residence. Even during the so-called golden years of rock, it is impossible to speak of a musically homogeneous taste culture.

Paul Hirsch and his associates, reporting a national survey conducted in the winter of 1969, indicated that the "widespread hypothesis of homogeneity of music taste preferences among teenagers is untenable."[9] Their survey, conducted by the Opinion Research Corporation, found that 18 percent of the teenagers preferred "message" songs such as "War, What Is It Good For?" and "Give Peace a Chance." The researchers also included so-called drug songs in this category. The "square" category, encompassing mood music, country and western, and classical music, polled 7 percent (N-560). With the categories set as they were, it is arguable that the Top 40 classification was favored; nonetheless, this sample does suggest that what is popular does not *in toto* mirror the youth culture. A study of collegians on the West Coast in the same year exhibited a parallel heterogeneity in musical preferences.[10] Measurements in the two studies were somewhat different: Hirsch and his colleagues labeled "square" to include jazz, classical, and others.[11]

The 1970s witnessed even a greater differentiation of musical tastes within the youth audience. Prepuberty girls continue to swoon over the current teen idol. Teenagers, three or four years older, have much different tastes, usually preferring heavy-metal bands such as Iron Maiden, Queen, Judas Priest, or UFO. People a few years older seem to fall into assorted taste groups. One group appears to be tied to established artists, in many cases "their early stuff," preferring the Rolling Stones or the Doors and the Who. Some remain wedded to quasi-country singers such as Charlie Daniels, Eagles, and Emmy Lou Harris. Still others prefer the reggae material personified by the late Bob Marley and a legion of imitators. Country music has made a significant dent in the pop music market. A majority of singles released remain country and western products. Indeed, some record companies seemed convinced that country and western music would become the dominant popular music style of the 1980s.[12] As usual they were wrong; *Saturday Night Fever* and *Urban Cowboy* created a passing fad.

Wesley Rose, one of the most powerful music publishers in Nashville, noted, "All that *Urban Cowboy* did was sell a lot of western clothes, hats and boots." The same can be said about the disco craze.

Not *all* young people and adolescents prefer popular music, but young people remain its major consumers. There is little doubt that popular music is largely the property of every passing generation and its particular preferences. However, the popular music audience over the past 34 years has not expanded considerably. This was largely a function of the character of the U.S. population in 1975. Sixty million persons were under the age of 25, a statistic that brought joy to the hearts and pocketbooks of record-company executives. The increase is also due to more over-30 adults staying with popular music. Despite this trend, popular music, especially the songs and acts supported by those under 30, is frequently the subject of generational conflict. Styles have changed over the years but the points of contention have remained remarkably similar. Jitterbuggers, whose music in the 1930s was termed "syncopated savagery," three decades later would label rock as a destructive force in society.

### Turn Down That Noise! Generational Conflict and Popular Music

Plato's often-cited admonition to the effect that music corrupts youth highlights the timeless quality of this generational struggle. It did not begin with Frank Sinatra, Elvis Presley, the Beatles, Mick Jagger, or new wave groups. Only the degree and form of generational difference appears to have altered. The folk culture featured its rhythms and play-party songs and courtship ballads primarily directed to the young. Elders had their own bawdy and drinking songs. The advent of the printing press and the ensuing rise of the broadside ballad further dichotomized songs suitable for children and those designed for their parents. The coming of industrialization and professional songwriters and publishers somewhat diminished the age cleavage because Tin Pan Alley produced material suitable for all—men, women, and children.

Sociologists Richard Peterson and David Berger have characterized the so-called Tin Pan Alley era as both monolithic and puritanical in nature:

> Tin Pan Alley procedures emerged in the 1880's on the wave of a rising popular demand for sheet music to be played on the home piano, the newly fashionable adornment of middle-class living rooms. To be acceptable for this market, tunes and rhythms had to be kept simple and rigidly uniform. *What is more, lyrics could not offend Victorian sentimentalities.*[13]

In this period the more earthy or deviant elements in the music were confined to jazz and country or "hillbilly" music. Following World War I, some elements of jazz were blended in recordings but the mixture rarely challenged middle-class conventions. As H. F. Mooney put it: "Commercial orchestras of the period around 1920-50 followed more or less the 'safe bet'—the aesthetic aspirations of the middle-class market—as did, indeed, most of the big Negro bands. They presented a music which despite solo variations emphasized precise, lush, ensemble harmony."[14]

The music of the depression era idealized the romantic love ethos of "June, spoon, moon," although some guardians of the public morality did object to a few songs from the Broadway stage such as "Love for Sale." Most popular songs were from the newly introduced talking motion pictures and radio. The songs were traditional both in content and style, even in the heyday of the fox trot. One apt description said they were customarily "orchestrated like symphonic tone poems," such as "The Night Was Made for Love." The classics were injected into the fox trot formula with "Tonight We Love" (Tchaikovsky) and "My Reverie" (Debussy). Big bands, like Freddie Martin's, simply "jazzed up" other well-known symphonic themes with great success. It was all good, clean, middle-class fare stressing self-improvement, which adults, who in fact were the major consumers, and adolescents alike could enjoy. The two generational units, it seems, were not attuned to the same aspects of the music. The songs played by big bands were lyrically, in the main, innocent; the rhythms, however, generated considerable generational conflict.

As with the rockabilly phenomenon of the 1950s, swing was a hybrid of a black musical style, jazz, with a style middle-class Whites would accept and purchase. It was also a musical form many adults perceived as "garbage," a sentiment their children often did not share. The deviant aspects of the music stemmed not from the lyrics but from the structure and the loudness of the riffs performed by Benny Goodman, Artie Shaw, the Dorseys, and Jimmie Lunceford, and the dance steps enacted by teenagers to "swing." William Allen White of the America First Committee attacked swing as "blood raw emotion, without harmony, without consistent rhythm, and with no more tune than the yearnful bellowing of a lonely, yearning and romantic cow in the pastures or the raucous staccatic meditation of a bulldog barking in a barrel."[15] A Barnard College professor termed the dance music "musical Hitlerism."[16]

The second objection went beyond the realm of musical taste or propriety into that of morality in the framework of the Puritan fathers. More than the music, the dance, given its physical nature, was subjected to attack. At one time the Spanish throne had prohibited the waltz for several centuries due to its supposedly immoral requirement that males and females actually touch. Centuries later the moral entrepreneurs of the 1930s viewed the fox trot and especially the jitterbug in a similar light.

According to Frank Zappa: "Our story [evolution of rock] begins in . . . the good old days, at the recreation centers, no Levis or capris please. . . . The kids would be holding onto each other desperately and sweating. The chaperon would come along and say 'Seven inches apart, please,' and hold a sawed-off ruler between you and the girl."[17] Jitterbugging at Benny Goodman concerts was indicated in the press as riotous behavior and roundly condemned by clergy, teachers, and parents. The focus of the condemnation was the timeworn symbolic figure—the fiddler. Throughout Puritan demonology, the fiddler was portrayed as a tool of Old Lucifer. In 1938 it was the jitterbugger who was performing the latest version of St. Vitus's dance while the devil fiddled. Satan, in this instance, took the unlikely form of Benny Goodman and the countless other big band leaders who paced the dances with riffs, interludes, and exhilarated solos. The satanic argument would reappear in the 1980s. Critic George Simon related the interaction between band and audience:

> There's nothing to match it today. The whining electrified guitars and the flabby-sounding electronic basses of the sixties have power, all right—they can virtually steam-roller you. But hearing big bands in person was completely different . . . they lifted you high in the air with them, filling you with an exhilarated sense of friendly well-being; you joined them, emotionally and musically, as partners in one of the happiest, most thrilling rapports ever established between the givers and takers of music.

The bandleader did not figure alone in the disapprobation of segments of the adult world. The bobby-sox idol, the young male band vocalist, was yet another target. Simon, in comparing the singers of the swing period to rock stars, recalls; "The hysteria that greeted boy singers during the forties almost matched that spewed on the vocal groups of the sixties. Mobs would wait for them outside stage doors. In the theaters they'd howl and scream—perhaps not as blatantly as the kids in the sixties did in the presence of their idols."[18] It must be remembered that the worried parents of the late 1930s did not have the comfort of historical comparison to quell their fears. In a delightful twist of irony the Tommy Dorsey band named its singing quartet the Pied Pipers. At one time it featured Frank Sinatra, who was later to become the symbol of the idolatry of the swing era. With swing the generational cleavage was established: "For the first time in American history teenagers were very much a social reality."[19]

World War II solidified this generation gap, leaving the adolescents on the home front as separate entities without young adults to serve as role models and with increasing buying power. Jitterbuggers, bobby-soxers and Victory Girls were all identifiable generational units within the populace.

The war years found radio a central source of immediate battle information and propaganda. Kate Smith and Gene Krupa, Bing Crosby and

Frank Sinatra—all appeared on broadcast marathons to heighten support for the Allies and to sell war bonds. Appeals by Sinatra and other teenage favorites were directly aimed at this age group. The tag "youth listening" began to appear in newspaper radio logs. One study undertaken during this time reported that "the pleasure of 72 percent of radio listeners under 30 in popular music is shared by only 22 percent of those over 50 years of age." Conversely, an observer reported, "Old, familiar music is more popular with older listeners."[20] While the nation was united in common cause, generational differences along cultural and a esthetic lines continued to increase.

The music of the postwar era was a retreat from the big-band era into the sentimentality of the ballad and the baritone crooner. Swing had, through the war years, become too complicated and "difficult to dance to!" The costs of studio recording and of maintaining a traveling band became prohibitive. By 1947 most of the big-name bands had been dismantled. Some bands continued but the world was, in jazz writer Simon's words, becoming the "property of a group of their most illustrious graduates—the singers."[21]

Following the war, popular music reflected what appeared to be an intra-generational appeal. In the late forties most of the top sellers were either studio bands or crooners. By 1950 the singers clearly dominated the charts. The *Billboard* top sellers of 1950 found 21 groups or individual song stylists in firm control of the chart. The remainder were either instrumentals or novelties. The Weavers' watered-down versions of folk songs, "Goodnight Irene" and "Tzena, Tzena, Tzena," and Red Foley's swing version of "Chattanoogie Shoe Shine Boy" were the only songs from a nonpopular base. Their swinglike arrangements made them totally suitable for the pop market. As reported by *Billboard*, the top ten singles of the early 1950s, a form predominantly directed to adolescents, found few songs not in the quasi-operatic style of the number-one songs. Only novelties such as Jimmy Boyd's "I Saw Mommy Kissing Santa Claus," "The Doggie in the Window," "St. George and the Dragonet," "The Thing," and several others broke the increasing monopoly of former band vocalists like Joni James, Eddie Fisher, Perry Como, Tony Martin, and Patti Page. The television show "Your Hit Parade" highlighted these years with four former band singers—Dorothy Collins, Gisele MacKenzie, Russell Arms, and Snooky Lanson—taking turns singing, after the drum roll, "the song that's Number One all over America!" The inability of this show to cope with rock drove it in time from the nation's television screens.

For many an adult, the popularization of rock and roll symbolized "overt rebellion," as did movies such as *Rebel without a Cause* and *The Wild One.* Yet, interestingly, neither used rock music in any manner.

*Blackboard Jungle* was another matter. Its theme was "Rock Around the Clock." Teenagers accepted the new genre as a symbol of their "new" status. According to Zappa: "I didn't care if Bill Haley was white or sincere . . . he was playing the Teenage National Anthem and it was so LOUD I was jumping up and down. *Blackboard Jungle* . . . represented a strange sort of 'endorsement' of the teenage cause: 'They have made a movie [*Blackboard Jungle*] about us, therefore, we exist.'"[22] Zappa's concluding phrase is taken from Camus's brilliant essay *The Rebel*, which in the original read, "I rebel—therefore we exist." Rock and roll, its black and country origins notwithstanding, was placed within the context of juvenile delinquency and "bopping gangs" that had attracted headlines in Los Angeles and New York.

*Blackboard Jungle* was a movie depicting the struggles of a teacher in an urban ghetto school. The transposed Evan Hunter novel was a classic statement of generational and social conflict—disrespect for tradition, authority, and learning—all values in especially high regard during the Eisenhower years. In the film even the musical tastes of the older generation are not spared. Richard Kiley, as the teacher, makes several futile attempts to reach his rowdy charges. One involved introducing his valuable collection of jazz and swing 78s to his students. Placing Bunny Berigan's "I Can't Get Started," on the phonograph, he explains the aesthetic of jazz. The students listen for a moment, then overpower him and proceed to destroy his entire collection. The theme "Rock Around the Clock" interdicts, underlining the rejection. As with the jitterbuggers and jazz fans, rock became the nexus of generational conflict, one that was eventually reified into struggle over the playing of the music itself.

Elvis Presley was the personification of evil for those who saw rock to be a force that was "inflaming youth." Unlike Haley, who was somewhat overweight and looked like everyone's "older brother," Presley epitomized the "bike hero." David Riesman presented the dynamic singer as generating a "a definitely 'anti-parent' outlook. His music—and he, himself—appeared somewhat insolent, slightly hoodlum."[23] The long sideburns, ducktail haircut, black slacks, and pink sports jackets were accentuated by the defiant curled upper lip and by the motorcycle. The overt sexuality of the singer's early television appearances only compounded his image as "child corrupter." Jack Gould, television critic of the *New York Times*, warned: "When Presley executes his bumps and grinds, it must be remembered by the Columbia Broadcasting System that even the twelve-year-old's . . . [sexual] curiosity may be overstimulated." Arnold Shaw recalled:

> Presley's impact was troubling to adults because his influence seemed more nonmusical than musical . . . . The intensity of teenage reaction suggested

that youngsters were responding to him for deeper psychological, emotional and social reasons. To them, he was in fact the first rock symbol of teenage rebellion—made so in part by adults because they did not like him, and condemned him as depraved. Anti-Negro prejudice doubtless figured in adult antagonism. Regardless of whether parents were aware of the Negro sexual origins of the phrase rock 'n' roll, Presley impressed them as the visual and aural embodiment of sex.[24]

Various campaigns and polemics were directed at the rockabilly star. One district attorney is quoted as saying, "Rock and roll gives young hoodlums an excuse to get together. It inflames teenagers and is obscenely suggestive." Evangelist Billy Graham, when asked about the singer, expressed a widely held opinion: "From what I've heard, I'm not so sure I'd want my children to see him." Listening to the songs popularized by Presley or many of the other rockers climbing the charts was another matter; the pop lyrics of the 1950s were usually innocent as the driven snow.

Donald Horton's content analysis of popular song lyrics of 1955, printed in fan magazines such as *Hit Parade, Song Hits, Country Song Roundup,* and *Rhythm and Blues* suggests the conflict was more symbolic than real.[25] Horton found that 83 percent of the lyrics in these song magazines dealt with boy-girl relationships. Of these, 39 percent addressed the traditional courtship theme; 9 percent, the honeymoon; 17 percent, disintegration of the relationship; and 30 percent, the "loneliness" syndrome. Lyrically, this is not far removed from the sentimental ballads and torch songs of the previous generations. They were, as writer Greg Shaw observed, more intense, emotionally direct, and aimed at the teenager as lover. Even the lyrics of the much-maligned Presley songs were simply reflective of the "boy meets girl, boy loses girl" snydrome.[26] Only his early Sun label covers, such as "Milkcow Blues Boogie" and "Baby, Let's Play House," evidenced verbal sentiments mirroring his "provocative" stage presence, and none of these was a hit. The late Gene Vincent, a Presley imitator, included the controversial Anglo-Saxonism in "Women Love," the flip side to his only big hit, "Be Bop a Lula." Still, the lyrics of the 1950s in the pop market rarely transcended the values of romantic love so popular in the dominant society.

The significance of the emergence of rock and roll and Presley as a superstar in the 1950s was fundamentally one of perspective and focus. The generational-aesthetic cleavage, as Zappa's paraphrase of Camus indicates, was solidified both by the condemnations of adults and the basic ineptitude of segments of the music industry and Tin Pan Alley. Statements such as "I know it's only a phase" or Frank Sinatra's portrayal of rock as "a rancid-smelling aphrodisiac" all were proven wrong. Riesman's "minority" of the crooner years in time seemed to become the majority—even for Mitch

Miller. Popular music—whatever it was—was "for the youngsters," to use Sullivan's tired introduction.

The conscription of Presley into the military and his ensuing image change from hoodlum to GI, coupled with the advent of "American Bandstand," defused much of the hostility to rock and roll. Dick Clark and his coterie of Philadelphia teenagers did little to offend anyone except rockabilly fans.

The payola controversy provided a forum for several congressmen and ASCAP, who disliked rock and roll, but it had little to do with teenagers' musical tastes (see chapter 5 on the payola hearings). The morality of Dick Clark, Alan Freed, and a host of other deejays was the issue. Some critics did maintain that rock and roll had bought its way into the hearts of the teenagers, but very few fans took this accusation seriously. *Billboard* replied to the allegation: "The cancer of payola cannot be pinned on rock and roll. Payola was rampant in the music business during the vaudeville era of the 1920s." The editorial went on to cite the generational aspect of the charge, indicating that the accusers were those who "sigh for the good old days, blame their plight on rock and roll, and construe that rock and roll is an outgrowth of payola."[27] Most of the industry concurred, and the hearings did not curtail the number of rock records being released. The rise of Chubby Checker and other go-go singers found adults joining teenagers in gyrating to the "twist," the "swim," the "frug," and other variations on that theme.

Beatlemania, prior to John Lennon's "more popular than Christ" remark, was received by adults as a continuation of the Davy Crockett and hula-hoop crazes. Signs saying, "Stamp Out the Beatles" and "Bach Not Beatles," were more in fun than in protest. "I Want to Hold Your Hand" or "I'm Happy Just to Dance" certainly lacked any of the threat or sensuousness of Elvis "the Pelvis" or the black rhythm and blues artists of the 1950s. David Riesman compared the Beatles to Presley:

> My impression is that the Beatles have none of this somewhat sinister quality that Presley represented for adults. They don't have the quasi-sexual, quasi-aggressive note that was present in Presley . . . it's very safe for a young girl to admire these Englishmen. Then, too, there are four of them, and there's safety in numbers.

The sociologist concluded this interview on the prophetic note: "If I were the Beatles' press agent, I'd work to have ministers and professors and the press all saying, 'Oh dear!'"[28] After the "Jesus remark" and *Sgt. Pepper*, ministers and professors would indeed say, "Oh dear!" but in 1964 even the Radical Right (to be discussed later) generally ignored the Beatles. One English psychologist ended a clinical report by expressing a prevailing attitude toward the Liverpool four: "'Beatlemania' is the passing reaction of predominantly young adolescent females to group pressures of such a kind that meet their special emotional needs."[29]

Only the association of rock and roll with the flower child phenomenon and the hippie movement revived outcries of "brainwashing" and "corruption." Much of the attack was ideologically inspired and a continuation of the Right's thesis that popular music was subverting the flower of U.S. youth for an expected Kremlin takeover. The charge that song lyrics were an open invitation to "turn on, tune in, and drop out" attracted more support. Sunday supplements ran headlines announcing, "Songs Have a Double Meaning." Nearly all of these articles focused upon two or three obvious examples and a number of songs open to various interpretations. The Byrds' "Eight Miles High" was reported to mean "high on LSD." Bob Dylan's "Mr. Tambourine Man" was characterized as "describing a dope pusher and a drug-induced dream."[30] The Association's "Along Comes Mary" and other songs invoking the name Mary were linked to marijuana. Later songs such as the Jefferson Airplane's famous "White Rabbit" were cited to support the pop-as-advocate hypothesis. The Beatles' album *Sgt. Pepper's Lonely Hearts Club Band* sparked considerable controversy after a *New York Times* reviewer decided that "Lucy in the Sky with Diamonds" meant the acronym LSD. Some segments of U.S. society took these allegations seriously, harassing radio stations that played "drug-oriented" songs. The bedroom-community sample in a British Columbia survey taken in 1969 indicated that the largest portion of both adolescents and their parents found popular music to be addressed to romantic love themes and love for humanity. A smaller percentage believed songs were topical and concerned with social protest.

Ironically, not one adult in the sample believed that the basic theme of popular music was drug oriented, despite a deep concern in the community over this issue. Fourteen (3.6 percent) of the teenagers, however, did believe that pop was advocating drug use. This clearly was not a major bone of contention between generations until 1970 and the drugola controversy.

A portion of the popular music of the 1970s can best be labeled punk rock, sometimes termed shock rock. Its lyrics are not terribly profound or protest oriented; the music is simple and loud. It is primarily a visual form. Shock rock challenged the norms of social etiquette. Performers appear to be championing those aspects of life that people consider perverse, deviant, and grotesque. Violence, homosexuality, transvestism, and infanticide all may be props in the act.

Rolling Stone Mick Jagger probably originated shock rock; he pranced about a stage assuming various poses and making seemingly "obscene" gestures. Ray Davies of the Kinks assumed a similar posture. Iggy and the Stooges expanded on this stage presence. Iggy would mimic sodomy with his microphone then leap into the audience, taunt, shout, and challenge the spectators. Writers labeled this punk rock, for it expressed social defiance in the most unsophisticated manner. One critic described it as embodying "the essence of a street gang."[31] It was giving society "the finger." In the context of the late 1960s, Iggy's act seemed to be "political." Critics merely assumed he was putting down "the system" in the usual Detroit MC-5 manner. He was not as intellectual as either the Mothers of Invention or the Fugs, but Iggy gained little popularity outside the Motor City area; the youth audience was not yet ready for shock rock right on the heels of the 1967 Summer of Love and the Woodstock Festival.

Alice Cooper, an all-male band, popularized the glitter version of punk rock. Some people stumbled into Alice Cooper thinking "she" was a folksinger with a repertoire of Child ballads; what they found was a band in homosexual drag. The music it played was high volume and unsophisticated. One patron leaving a Los Angeles night club told Ben Edmonds, "I've never seen anything like it. The very thought of it is enough to make me *vomit*. Alice Cooper . . . I thought it was gonna be like Judy Collins or something. It was the most revolting thing I've ever seen. You shoulda been there. . . ."[32] Revulsion became Alice Cooper's ticket to pop-music fame." Kinky sex and violence became important parts of the band's act. Former *New York Times* and *Billboard* critic Ian Dove described a typical Cooper concert:

> Alice Cooper went about cutting up mannekins, impaling babies, being laser-beamed (with James Bond film music in the background), being caught in a strobe-lit gang fight (shades of "Clockwork Orange"), singing to a boa constrictor, being guillotined (hardly a far, far better thing for the audience), wielding a 6-foot toothbrush and only in America—sending off stage for a couple of beers.[33]

In 1970 Alice Cooper's single "Eighteen" became an instant hit on CKLW, a 50,000-watt Canadian outlet that served as Detroit's favorite popular music station. Going to see Alice became the thing to do.

Several other acts either imitated or did variations on the Alice Cooper gimmick. A lesser-known veteran English rock artist, David Bowie, was repackaged by RCA Victor as a bisexual. A *Rolling Stone* writer labeled him "a brittle powdered flake of hermaphroditic humanity."[34] On stage Bowie continued Iggy's practice of simulated homosexual acts, this time with members of the band. After a major and expensive promotion campaign stressing Bowie's "deviance," a successful U.S. tour was launched. He has attempted to change this image. The latest versions of "punkitude" are found on MTV. They have been called "transsexual junkies" whose songs talk about violence in the subways, drugs, sex, and various forms of "thrill seeking."

Punk rock had many meanings. Arthur Kaye of the New York Dolls suggested, "People have the wrong idea about us. They think we're a bunch of transsexual junkies or something."[35] Some people see them as merely gay liberationists flouting the "straight" world. For some music fans they were merely a good rock band in the Rolling Stones tradition.

Outside its natural habitat of the concert hall or club, punk rock has encountered some opposition. Alice Cooper's appearance on the first "In Concert" found Lawrence H. Rogers II, president of Taft Broadcasting, calling his Cincinnati television station, after watching Alice for 15 minutes, and ordering the show off the air. Alice was replaced by an old episode of "Rawhide." A Philadelphia station postponed "In Concert" until 1:30 A.M., explaining its action as making sure "not too many kiddies would be watching the Alice Cooper rock program."[36] Nielsen figures indicated that although the show got excellent ratings, its audience was primarily under the magic age of 24. WABC-TV vice-president Bob Shanks complained to *Billboard*. "We must attract more than our target audience of serious rock fans in order to keep this show on the air. The hope here is that good rock has become acceptable to television viewers outside of the 19-34 age range."[37]

Two examples of differences of opinion regarding shock rock are the Ann Landers-Alice Cooper controversy and the Beach Boys flap of 1983. Ann Landers, the syndicated columnist, severely criticized rock singer Alice Cooper for some of his songs. Alice replied, "Kids know I am harmless. It's their parents that make me out to be some kind of monster." Teenagers seemed to agree. One wrote as follows:

> Ann Landers: I refuse to call you "Dear" because you have criticized the lyrics of rock 'n' roll songs. I am 17 years old and have grown up with rock 'n' roll. It isn't one bit dirty. It's the way people of this generation think and talk. Anyone who sees something filthy in rock 'n' roll lyrics must have a polluted mind.
>
> Some rock 'n' roll songs have a beautiful philosophy. They tell about being good to animals and neighbors and friends, and even parents and brothers and sisters.
>
> If you want to go after the real filth that people are hooked on, take a look at the soap operas. That's your generation—not ours. I bet you'll never print this.
>
> —A Former Fan[38]

Former Interior Secretary James Watt banned the Beach Boys from the July 4th bash on the Washington Mall in 1983. He contended the surfing group attracted "wrong elements," and Las Vagas singer Wayne Newton was booked as a replacement. The decision created a furor going all the way to the White House. The generation gap was obvious: rock, however mellow and nostalgic, versus a gambling casino lounge act. Ironically, on Independence Day, the Beach Boys, playing Atlantic City, outdrew Wayne Newton by 100,000 fans. Despite this overwhelming figure, other acts such as Charlie Daniels, Toto, Willie Nelson, Clash, Kiss, and even Bette Midler found themselves banned from concert arenas and auditoriums.[39]

Mr. Shanks's hope for a larger audience was dashed in 1976 with the advent of punk rock, later renamed new wave by media consultant Lee Abrams. Ira Robbins wrote: "What Americans saw (and heard) of punk was the safety pins through the cheeks, militaristic and masochistic clothes, crazily dyed and cut hair styles, mindless dancing, and rumors of violence." The Sex Pistols was the group viewed by most as the founder of this fad. Gallons of press ink was used to hype it as the savior of the stagnant rock scene. *Rolling Stone's*, Dave Marsh and even John Rockwell of the *New York Times* gave it high marks long before Warner Bros. released its first album. Its only U.S. tour was discontinued after a few appearances. For many people the group was a curiosity. Writers reported that many concertgoers left arenas in the middle of a performance. The Sex Pistols received little if any airplay, and its album fared poorly on *Billboard's* "Top LP's and Tapes" chart. Not even the Ramones, the premier U.S. punk band, broke into the top fifty on the trade journal's album listing. However, as Robbins continues, "their [the Sex Pistols'] very nature was self-destructive, nihilistic, and generally untenable, but, during their tenure, they were so powerful and influential that they caused sweeping changes in the rock world of the seventies that will undoubtedly last on into the eighties. . ."[40] The name new wave did last, but only the Clash was able to continue the material found on *Never Mind the Bollocks*, the only album of the Sex Pistols. Jon Sinton, then a Burkhart/Abrams executive, when asked what was new wave, said, "Anything that is new"—not a very precise definition. Elvis Costello, who physically but not musically resembles Buddy Holly, seems to be the only real transitional beneficiary of the punk-new wave fad. The label, however, still lingers more in Sinton's definitional sense than that of the Pistols or the Ramones.

*New Wave and New Music*

The reason for adult indifference to much of the shock-rock genre may simply have been lack of exposure. Most parents and the traditional guardians of public morality were generally unaware of the phenomenon. It was on exhibition only at concerts. If this totally unrepresentative sample of people interested in popular music is an indication, new wave remains a mystery to most people over 24. Considering the material and the stage acts of many shock-rock bands, only disinterest can explain the original lack of moral indignation leveled at Alice, Bowie, the New York Dolls, the Ramones, later the Sex Pistols, and now W.A.S.P..

In 1978, the peak economic year in record company grosses, rock music was confined to radio and concerts. The two short lived rock-music shows on television, "Midnight Special" and "In Concert," were broadcast long after the 11:00 P.M. news. Even late-night programming was mild. One ABC executive commented, "A lot of rock music is simply too sexy for TV . . . . The TV audience is not ready for any but the more tame breeds of rock." Artists, managers, and some record companies were not terribly excited about video. Manager Fred Kewley told a reporter, "They're afraid they'd [the acts] come across on TV as a pale copy of their real selves—and this kind of exposure would do their image more harm than good."

Another factor in the absence of rock music from television was money. According to Kewley, "You can do better . . . giving a concert in the boondocks. . . . A group can easily earn $25,000 for a night's work on tour and amounts over $100,000 aren't unheard of. That's far more than most groups could get from TV even in prime time."[41] The result of these diverse interests kept rock and television separated. Consequently, many adults were oblivious to the harder forms of rock as they watched "Happy Days" and "All in the Family."

Following the great record industry depression of 1979 and the success of the syndicated hour-long "Solid Gold" show on television, frequently aired during prime time, attitudes began to change on both sides. The record industry, faced with staggering losses, was looking for an alternative avenue of exposure because FM radio was growing increasingly conservative and music magazines were failing in droves.

Cable Television and the emergence of the twenty four-hour Music Television (MTV) Network (to be discussed later) changed the relationship between television and rock music. It also perked up parents concerning the presentation and content of rock, as cable operators were quick to discover.

In August of 1982, MTV appeared in a midwest university community. Roger Wise, of Wood TV, comments, "I've heard not only obscenity but . . . the use of instruments in certain fashions, and violent production techniques where it is backlighted and rear projected. But, yes, we've had some serious objections". The objections came not only from parents but also schoolteachers and even some university people. A typical letter to the cable company: "MTV is completely disgusting and a waste of our money. If people want to watch it they should pay extra. It is suggestive and offensive for young children." The same writer labeled the channel as basically a "negative influence." Other letters and calls to Wood TV "have been a little more frank than that." Unfortunately, the more adamant notes and phone objections have been lost. Wise said, "We've had some really tough letters and phone calls." Ironically, what the upset subscribers did not know is that MTV censors tapes submitted to it. David Bowie's beach scene in the "China Girl" segment was edited considerably. Most of the original clip found its way to the cutting-room floor.

Many adult cable subscribers object to the noise or volume level. One letter writer said, "It's distasteful . . . not pleasing to listen to at all." Another objected to the "crazy assaulting [of] the hearing of innocents." A lengthier note combined criticism of content and volume: "We do not see any value in MTV, only negative influences. We have small children and because of the loud volume of the program, children are attracted to it when flipping through the channels."

MTV is credited by many observers with giving birth to the new music, which is described as an outgrowth of punk and new wave. Jim Sullivan of the *Boston Globe* sees new music as containing a rainbow of musical styles such as rockabilly, soul, reggae, ska, and any other old form. It is danceable and features numerous technologically sophisticated devices like drum machines and synthesizers; bands such as Men at Work, the Police, Eurythmics, Culture Club, and Duran Duran are its most visible purveyors. The freshness of this sound is open to question. Older critics tend to see new music as nothing more than an old sound with a different label, and others view it as a marketing ploy to rescue an ailing record industry or as hype for MTV.

RIAA figures for 1983 lend some credence to the above position. Gold and platinum records once again declined in number: gold from 130 in 1982 to 111 (14.5 percent); platinum, 55 to 49 (11 percent). One writer suggested in the *Village Voice* that the figures would have been considerably worse had Michael Jackson and the Police been excluded. Stephen Traiman of RIAA observed, "The business is far from out of the woods."[42]

Columnist Erma Bombeck wrote, "I've seen hard rock bring a lot of parents to their knees."[43] All of this must remind the Presley generation of the parental cry, "Turn down that noise!" Numerous studies of generational conflict and popular music have found that it is caused by misinterpretation and lack of understanding rather than actual threat. Interest in popular music is customarily one of the first independent steps taken by a child. The first major purchase of many little girls is a record by the current teen idol. The taste preferences of teenagers are their own, not their parents'. Young people in the main view "their music" as just fun—"you can dance to it"—while adults may, as did Plato, impute more sinister motives.

Popular music is fundamentally an idiom of the young but it is not monolithically standard with all young people. Segments of the youth audience exhibit differing tastes and preferences. Only when these preferences coalesce can we say that a song is popular. The merging of these diverse tastes and preferences is in part the magical process that makes a song a "hit" rather than a "miss" or a "stiff," as unsuccessful records are called.

### What is Popular Music? A Definition

A frustrated concertgoer, after standing in line for nearly an hour, glared at the sign of the box-office window, "Popular Prices—Admission $15.95," cursed, and muttered, "Popular with who?" and left. The retort is fairly simple, of course: "Popular with the management." So it is with music. Record sales, taste, and social differences in musical preferences suggest that *popular* is a term that enjoys currency with those who produce and manufacture records and in the everyday vernacular but that is difficult to locate in the real world.

There are few definitions of popular music of any substance. Most writers join with Carl Belz in the sentiment that "any listener who wants rock (a segment of the pop of the sixties) defined specifically is probably unable to recognize it."[44] There is, of course, truth in this statement, but experience alone does not help clarify the maze called popular music. British writer Richard Mabey further defines popular music as being "concerned with participation, with parties, dances, outings, demonstrations and any other social gatherings where camaraderie and simple shared emotions are important. . . . The music, in fact, acts as a further binding force on the group, and the observed responses of the other members are a way of clarifying your own."[45] Popular music, therefore, is a cultural artifact shared by specific subgroups in the social order. Music may represent the taste of a subculture within a culture or that of a counterculture that exists in opposition to the dominant one. Jazz is a subcultural genre, and so-called new wave is perhaps indicative of another subculture, especially in large urban areas.[46] Mabey distinguishes pop music as a subdivision of popular in that it operates as a mode of communication to "satisfy teenage tastes." This refinement has considerable merit, for popular music does contain a number of sounds and styles that do not appeal solely to teenagers. Still, persons under the demographic cutoff point of 30 make up the major constituency for popular music. So popular music is not pop music but many parts of pop music are found in popular music.

Dean Tudor defines pop in a similar fashion with technology added:

[It] is a twentieth-century art form made available to the masses through records, radio . . . . As an art form it is in a state of constant evolution in which each generation redefines its own music. One's perception of popular music is based only on what is heard or what is available to be heard.[47]

A cardinal tenet in the record industry is the necessity for "airplay" or "exposure," that is, reaching the largest audience possible. Popular music is exoteric, supported by a majority of record buyers. The exoteric unit is by its very nature large and highly unstable both in taste and artistic personnel. The esoteric unit customarily, though not always, is small, stable, and relatively homogeneous. The jazz market, while containing many sub-genres, is a specialty field with an identifiable audience that record companies, concert promoters, and clubs service. Entrepreneurs have definite expectations in respect to this audience. According to one producer, few jazz acts sell over 40,000 records. Errol Garner's *Concert by the Sea*, Dave Brubeck's *Take Five*, Herbie Hancock's *Head Hunters*, and the George Benson concert album were pleasant surprises. Consumers of classical, romantic, and modern symphonic music equally constitute an esoteric taste unit, which responds in a relatively predictable manner.

Characteristic of esoteric genres is the homogeneity of consumers and their loyalty to specific artists and styles. Records on the country-music charts at one time remained there much longer than their Top 40 counterparts. Country-music performers have also exhibited a durability and staying power rare in popular-music stars. Ray Price, Eddy Arnold, and Bill Monroe are but a few of many artists with a firm faithful following. It was axiomatic that a country and western artist could live off one hit for 20 years. Jazz performers, at least those who are considered stars, also can command an audience for many decades. The classics are an even more stable market.

The larger the esoteric taste group, the less stability and predictability. In years past, country and western and so-called race music were aimed directly at specific audiences defined by geography and race. For many years country music was distributed only in the southern states. "Race" records were generally confined to the same geographical area as well as to stores in urban ghettos outside the South. The out-migration of white southerners and the growth in the black urban population expanded the audience for both genres. Therefore, although country and soul music remain somewhat esoteric styles, they appeal to relatively large numbers of people and also supply records that cross over to the Top 40 charts.

Crossing over, or "expanding the audience," involves an artist in one genre's appealing to a larger audience, that is, going pop.

Edward Eckstine, general manager of Qwest Records, estimates that Michael Jackson's "Off the Wall," which sold over 5 million units owes much of its success to white consumers. "My guess," he said, "is that half of the buyers were white."[48] Jackson's phenomenal success with *Thriller*, which sold 30 million albums, once again demonstrated his crossover ability. Charmaine Lanham, of the Nashville Bluegrass Music Association International, wants to follow the same marketing strategy: "We are trying to get the existing bluegrass community . . . to help promote bluegrass to the mainstream," that is, increase sales.[49] Esoteric taste groups are too small to go gold or platinum without moving into larger markets.

Middle-of-the-road (MOR) records are the ultimate extension of an esoteric genre tied to sex and age factors. MOR is predominantly the taste preference of married women over the age of 24. It is music that stresses nostalgia and styles of the recent past, and frequently enters the popular-music arena simply because tastes of many women in this category are not far removed from the dominant youth market. A number of artists are capable of appealing to both the MOR and college audiences. Billy Joel, James Taylor, Michael Jackson, Barry Manilow, Kenny Rogers, and Anne Murray are favorites. The larger the esoteric public, the more chance of its tastes entering into the exoteric world of popular music.

Because popular music is exoteric, the producer of popular music must address a generally amorphous, fluid, heterogeneous, and unpredictable collectivity of people. Popular music is, in fact, an idiom designed to cut across a number of taste cultures predicated upon age, education, class, geography, and race. Loyalties here are fickle. Consumer demand is difficult to measure because of the varied interests of those who constitute the audience. Yet popular music remains popular even if its internal parts change, as they frequently do. Some esoteric genres become exoteric or popular and then return to their previous status. Sociologists Rolf Meyersohn and Elihu Katz reported: "Every few months a new 'content' in the form of new hits flows through the same network of distributors (disk jockeys, etc.) and consumers (primarily teenagers and other radio audiences), while an occasional song may attract some distributors or consumers who are not regularly a part of the system."[50] Esoteric elements may enter popular music, such as "Amazing Grace," "Take Five," "Moritat," "Duelin' Banjos," and especially themes from motion pictures. However, they generally must take second place to the style of the period. The popular-music idiom, as a structure, remains the same with industry, promoters, cultural gatekeepers, and distributors, producing a "continuous cycle of discontinuous hits."

The discontinuity of popular music is an important element in its makeup relative to age. The songs and artists preferred by the so-called bubble-gummers and teenyboppers change nearly every two years. Heroes of the pubescent set have ranged from Fabian, Frankie Avalon, the

Monkees, and Donny Osmond to John Schneider or Rick Springfield. Chuck Laufer, editor of numerous teenage magazines and the proprietor of the now-defunct Partridge Family Fan Club, observed, "There *has* to be teenage idols, but the girls outgrow them. When they're 11 to 14, they can have a nice, safe love affair with somebody like Davy Jones, Bobby Sherman or David Cassidy. By the time they're 16, they're having dates and they don't need them anymore."[51]

By age 16 musical tastes are generally established. People outgrow an idol but not the style. The screaming girls who discovered Elvis Presley stuck with the rockabilly style through 1958, when their hero and his imitators disappeared from the scene; they did not flock to Dick Clark's army of pretty teenage vocalists. Consequently, popular-music fans are generally wedded to a specific style current in the idiom in their adolescence. As time progresses, taste publics loyal to a specific popular-music form proliferate to the point that within any two decades a vast number of rock fans can be identified, yet there is a vast difference between them. Only a few years can separate musical-style preferences. A 9-year-old may "like" her idol. A 12-year-old detests the idol and prefers a new wave band. Collegians have more esoteric musical preferences than secondary-school students. The success of many so-called easy-listening formula stations, which feature stylized versions of current youth-market hits and "oldies but goodies," further suggests that some carryover from adolescent tastes occurs especially during "drive time." Older people tend to prefer more traditional genres or none at all. People who were teenagers in the days of Glenn Miller still like crooners in the swing genre. Older Blacks have been reported to have tastes different from their soul-oriented adolescents.[52] Older country-music buffs attend fiddle conventions and mock the "modern country" musicians from Nashville. People who maintain a strong interest in any form of music after their courtship days are statistically out of the ordinary; their preference is usually more likely to be in an exoteric style than in an esoteric one. People in their sixties, seventies, and older, for example, can remain ardent country and western, swing, and symphonic buffs.

Age remains the crucial factor in popular music tastes but other social characteristics also have an effect. Sex and marital status complement age. Social class may be important; Hirsch observed that the sons and daughters of upper-class and lower-class parents exhibit more unique musical tastes than those in the middle class.[53]

The Warner Communication survey indicated that the highest percentage of buyers, those who spent the most money in 1978, were in the $10,000 to $15,000 income bracket. Those earning over $25,000 bought and spent almost half that amount. This appears to support Hirsch's contention.

Geography further complicates the situation. Polka fans are more likely to reside in Minnesota and Wisconsin than in New York City or Tennessee. Within the rock world itself geography plays a role; New York is the cradle of punkitude and new wave. This type of music is equally popular in Los Angeles and San Francisco. The Midwest is another matter. Detroit and Cleveland are entities unto themselves. As one fan observed, "In other cities rock 'n' roll is a hobby, but in Cleveland, it's a way of life." WMMS, Belken Productions, and the Agora nightclub are not tied to established artists; there are local artists like Michael Stanley who have little name recognition outside Cuyahoga County. Cleveland has also introduced or "broken" new artists such as Southside Johnny, the Cars, Fleetwood Mac, and Bruce Springsteen. The superstar acknowledged, "Cleveland supported me from the first";[54] few other major markets did. In the Southwest, Austin is an enclave unto itself. Other than Willie Nelson and Michael Murphey, the local favorites are unknown past the city limits.

Race has a great deal to do with musical preferences and record-buying habits. A composite of black and Latin music tastes would find a strong commitment in soul and ethnic material. Even in their early twenties, Blacks buy more singles than do Whites, who predominantly favor albums after 16.

Age is certainly the most important factor determining a person's allegiance to music. Race and geography further complicate the identification of taste units. These three factors help determine esoteric and exoteric taste groups and establish the individual's relationship to popular music. Some taste units are totally divorced from the Top 40 sound. Others, to their peril, contribute to the *Billboard* "Hot 100."

An esoteric genre that enters the popular-music arena must satisfy the demands of an exoteric audience while remaining unique to its original supporters. Its failure to accomplish the latter may lose it its supporters. Rhythm and blues, for example, was far from new when it was popularized in the 1950s. "Race" records had long been produced by promoters for consumption by a black audience. In 1955 portions of this minority taste unit entered the majority world of the "Hot 100." The envelopment of rhythm and blues by the pop market, in turn, watered down the original product, creating a vacuum into which a quasi-gospel sound labeled Motown and soul would enter.

The hootenanny craze and the folk-music revival followed a remarkably similar pattern. In the urban areas from the 1930s to The Kingston Trio in the 1950s folk music was an esoteric form generally catering to folklorists and some political "progressives" who interpreted the genre as a "cry for justice." *Sing Out!* magazine and recording companies such as Elektra and Folkways serviced this small group during the 1950s. The soaring success of

"Tom Dooley" changed the status of the music as well as its audience. The revival lasted approximately six years, undergoing two phases, and finally was overwhelmed by the "British invasion" and the defection of Bob Dylan. The excess of the revival in turn had so transformed the genre itself that many original supporters were driven to the entirely different esoteric blue-grass or country-and-western genres.

Although it is a minority or small portion of the total music audience, an esoteric taste unit is in fact a "fashion feeder"; it attempts to preserve its genre while remaining part of the crazy-quilt pattern of popular music. Rhythm-and-blues stations continued to broadcast "purist" material while many of their artists were being coopted into the white market. As some of the stars left, others with different sounds took their place. The Platters were replaced by the Supremes, and Smokey Robinson and the Jackson Five displaced the Five Satins and a multitude of other "street" groups. Folkniks, during the revival, generally disdained the revivalists and continued to collect Carter Family records and make "knowing" allusions to "old-time" country pickers such as the Stanley Brothers or the political folk group the Almanac Singers. Dylan, however, lured many of the politically oriented into the revival and then left them empty-handed in 1965. Still, although popular music feeds from and contains specialty esoteric genres, they also have an existence independent of popular music.

Meyersohn and Katz, when discussing the "fashion-feeder" aspect of esoteric genres, also maintain that the tenure of each in the exoteric or popular sphere is transitory. One genre in capricious manner replaces another. A genre never totally dominates the best-selling or most-played charts in purist form. The first rock era (1955-58) found nonrock selections placing number one. "Cherry Pink and Apple Blossom White" (1955), "Singing the Blues" (1956), "Love Letters in the Sand" (1957), and "It's All in the Game" (1958) were the top singles. During the second era of rock, English groups dominated the top position with "Satisfaction," "To Sir with Love," and "Hey Jude." The Monkees' "I'm a Believer" pushed the British "invaders" into second place in 1966. The rock revival (1964-68) was not a musically similar phenomenon. The basic rock instrumentation was wedded with numerous esoteric genres creating "hyphen-rock," such as folk-rock, jazz-rock, sympho-rock, ad infinitum. Once the genre experimentation was exhausted, rock moved increasingly into the visual arena. Arthur Brown and his "Flaming World" of pyrotechnics, hoisted masks, and eccentric costumes began what has been titled glitter rock. Other acts followed suit, especially with the advent of MTV and heavy metal.

During the 1970s and opening years of the 1980s, the record industry was racked by short-lived fads and false musical starts. It still clings to the "Third Coming" syndrome. First, Presley, then the Beatles. In 1970 James

Taylor, Cat Stevens, and other soft-rock singers were touted as the makers of the "new trend." Taylor was featured on the cover of *Time*—a kiss of death for many artists. Soft rock became a cult phenomenon, especially with college women.

Jimmy Cliff's "The Harder They Fall" signaled the possibility of a reggae trend. It was somewhat popular in the United Kingdom. Island, a major reggae label, quickly affiliated with Warner. The late Bob Marley, a reggae superstar, could not crack the mass U.S. market. Despite considerable promotional efforts, the Jamaican sound followed calypso into the esoteric category. As Kenneth Bilby noted, reggae was "only siphoning the residue left behind by the rock and disco industries."[55]

Punk rock, which received a remarkable amount of press coverage, was then confined to New York's CBGB and London night spots and never fulfilled its promised potential. Its aesthetic influence, now called new wave, did infiltrate the exoteric rock scene. (The reasons for these failures are discussed in chapter 3.)

The 2 April 1979 issue of *Newsweek* declared, "DISCO Takes Over." The lead paragraph of the article opened, "Roll over, Rock. Disco is here to stay . . . Americans are listening to a different drummer. . . ."[56] The academically oriented *Chronicle of Higher Education* titled a piece "Disco: A Sociologist Suggests Its Distinctive Sound Isn't Just Another Fad." Professor Richard Peterson concluded his analysis with the above quotation.[57] WABC in New York switched to a disco format and came out number one in the all-important ratings wars. Meanwhile, die-hard rock fans donned T-shirts emblazoned with "DISCO SUCKS!" Dennis Hunt several months later wrote that *Saturday Night Fever* "pushed the disco juggernaut into over-drive . . . the genre has been over its head and destined to nose-dive."[58] A $6 million industry—clubs, records, clothing, etc.—quickly was crowded out. Donna Sommer, the queen of the genre, virtually abandoned disco. The Bee Gees refused to record any more disco. WABC switched formats. Another trend turned into a fad within months.

The year 1982 was a period when country and new wave were considered top contenders. "New trend" Australian singer Olivia Newton-John topped *Billboard's* annual chart, and her "Physical" was the number-one single of the year; the theme from *Rocky III* followed. These findings once again show the diversity of pop music.

The existence of diverse genres and taste cultures makes popular music unpredictable, for every record must be directed toward a taste culture sufficiently large to promise a profit on the record. In a homogeneous taste culture such a return is relatively assured; however, a popular song must appeal to the parent taste culture as well as others. For example, the Blind Lemon Jefferson classic "Matchbox Blues" was originally recorded for a black rural audience. Another version, retitled "Little Wheel," by John Lee Hooker in the 1950s was directed at Blacks living in cities. The Carl Perkins's Sun label adaptation of the same song, "Matchbox," was a rockabilly piece aimed at the youth and country-and-western market. The Beatles' Mersey interpretation of the rock version transcended all of these boundaries, thus assuring its popular success.

It may not be coincidental that the few true superstars such as Presley, the Beatles, the Rolling Stones, Willie Nelson, Stevie Wonder, and Kenny Rogers all introduced hybrid musical forms that attracted diverse musical subtastes. Indeed, one operational definition of *superstar* may incorporate the ability to cross over or to place on charts other than the Top 40. The ability to transcend genres is a major determinant of popular-music success. Most popular singers in the esoteric sphere travel the road from success in one genre to the nebulous arena of middle-media in an attempt to maximize their exposure and in the process disassociate themselves from their roots. Michael Jackson, Kenny Rogers, Diana Ross, Roberta Flack, Donna Sommer, and Glen Campbell are but a few examples. Campbell's trek from country singer and studio guitarist to song stylist assured the success of his national television show. Johnny Cash, whose forte as more country than most popular music fans could take, failed dismally when he attempted a similar transition. Cash's style was too "purist" to hold the attention of a popular audience for long. His attempt to do "citified" or "uptown" material only alienated his original constituency. On the other hand, country artists like Willie Nelson, Waylon Jennings, and Dolly Parton did cross over quite successfully. Kenny Rogers moved from a dying pop and rock career into country, making himself a multimillionnaire.

The success of a given taste or style ultimately is determined by its popular acceptance in other taste clusters. Success depends on attracting support from either a small number of large taste units or a large portion of small groups. A single, such as "I Think I Love You" by the Partridge Family, by appealing to a significantly large portion of the "bubble-gum" audience, is an immediate success. Rick Springfield, then with a regular daytime television series, commanded an equally large segment of the same audience. The size of the late Presley's fan clubs and his multitudinous followers during his lifetime guarantee that all of his records will near the million-seller figure. Lesser-known and more esoteric artists are not afforded this cushion. Joan Baez's version of "The Night They Drove Old Dixie Down" relied upon a much larger number of groups, among them underground, country, and folk, to finally make the Top 40.

The problem for record-company executives is precisely how taste combinations operate. The comments of one advertising executive sum up the dilemma:

To be in the rock 'n' roll record business today, you've got to be a "total-crap-shooter" with a good instinct for money management. You've got to have enormous faith in your A&R people and your own ear. . . You'll have a better shot playing blackjack in Las Vegas with a stake of $10,000 using the house rules and an arithmetical progression money system.[59]

The late Amos Heilicher, prominent record retailer and rack jobber, commented in the early 1970s that the chance factor was declining, and picking a hit was becoming more complex. "At one time, 80 percent of our volume was done from 20 percent of our inventory. Now it's done from 35 to 40 percent of the product we carry."[60] At one point the Warner/Reprise bulletin *Circular* ran a headline announcing, "This Time the Big Trend Is No Trend." Passing years have not contradicted the announcement. In August 1980 the *New York Times* ran an article titled "Today's Pop—A Period of Pluralism," in which Robert Palmer wrote: "Country music will undoubtedly continue to make inroads into the commercial mainstream. But that movement won't affect the dedicated rock fans who follow the newest American and English groups and support a broad network of small. . . labels that's springing up both here and abroad."[61] (See chapter 3.) The diminishing pop music audience leads some observers to believe that no one trend will take over the charts.

The music industry is not quite as subject to Adam Smith's "invisible hand" as it would have others believe; nonetheless, the formula for a hit popular record remains elusive. Yet this element more than others distinguishes popular music from its nonentertainment sister conglomerates and also from the specialty labels that by and large know what their audiences want—at least most of the time. The very nature of popular music is dynamic change and all that that implies; however, it should be kept in mind that while parts of popular music are transformed, other properties remain relatively unchanged. The industry itself has not greatly changed over the years. Promoters, disk jockeys, critics, and other functionaries are not as fluid as the music and the artists.

Popular music is a whole that is different from the sum of its many diverse, static, and dynamic parts. With this in mind, one can attempt a loose definition of popular music. *Popular music is the sum total of the taste units, social groups, and musical genres that coalesce around certain taste and preference similarities in a given space and time.* These taste publics and genres are affected by a number of factors, predominantly age, sex, accessibility, race, class, and education. The definition of popular music is more a sociological than a musical definition. People select what they like from what they hear. The reasons for this selection are influenced by many factors, some of which have little to do with the aesthetic quality of a song or instrumental piece.

Record companies, much to their dismay, must orchestrate this demographic cacophony to earn a profit. Unlike the classics, blues, or jazz record company, the popular-music record company must deal with a mosaic of dissimilar genres and taste and age groupings. Kal Rudman's statement, "It is easier to get a bill through Congress than a record on the *Billboard* chart," is a correct assessment.

The following pages trace, beginning with the artist, the life cycle of a record from the studio until it reaches the "folks out there." The path of the artist through the record-company bureaucracy is hazardous. Few artists ever sucessfully traverse the obstacle course and achieve a hit record. Mere possession of talent hardly dictates success for a guitar picker, singer, or a band. The manager, producer, company, distributor, merchandiser, and the media also play roles in the scenario of a hit record or the success of an artist. In the best Horatio Alger tradition, it all begins with a stagestruck performer who, in acting out dreams of stardom, becomes another Paul McCartney, Michael Jackson, or Mick Jagger.

## Notes

1. S. I. Hayakawa, "Popular Songs vs. the Facts of Life," in *Mass Culture: The Popular Arts in America*, edited by Bernard Rosenberg and David Manning White. (New York: Free Press, 1957), p. 393.
2. Murray Ross, "The Record Business: What Makes It Run," *Record World*, 24 July 1971, p. 230. Also Henry Brief, quoted in "$2 Billion Worth of Noise," *Forbes*, 15 July 1968, p. 26.
3. Jann Wenner, "The Record Company Executive Thing," *Rolling Stone*, 8 July 1971, p. 34.
4. David Riesman, "Listening to Popular Music," in *Mass Culture: The Popular Arts in America*, edited by Bernard Rosenberg and David Manning White (New York: Free Press, 1957), p. 411.
5. Ibid., p. 412.
6. Charles Gillett: *The Sound of the City* (New York: Outerbridge & Dienstfrey, 1969), p. 10. See Howard Junker, "Ah, The Unsung Glories of Pre-Rock," *Rolling Stone*, 1 December 1970, pp. 46-47.
7. Frank Zappa, "The Oracle Has It All Psyched Out," *Life*, 28 June 1968, p. 85. See also Jonathan Kamin, "Taking the Roll Out of the Rock: Reverse Acculturation," *Popular Music and Society* 2 (Fall 1972): 1-18.
8. James Coleman, *Adolescent Society* (New York: Free Press, 1961).
9. Paul Hirsch et al., "A Progress Report on an Exploratory Study of Youth Culture and the Popular Music Industry" (Ann Arbor: University of Michigan, Institute for Social Research, Survey Research Center, 1971), p. 28.
10. R. Serge Denisoff and Mark Levine, "Youth and Popular Music: A Test of the Taste Culture Hypothesis," *Youth and Society* 4 (December 1972): 237-55. Also R. Serge Denisoff and Mark Levine, "Mannheim's Problem of Generations and Political Counter-Culture," *Youth and Society* 2 (September 1970):35-58.

11. A 1965 poll of San Francisco State College students supports these findings. David Brice notes that 43 percent of those questioned customarily listened to music classified as "general popular"; 24 percent, classical; 16 percent, folk; 11 percent, jazz; and 6 percent, rock and roll. These figures should be treated with care, considering the manner in which the data were gathered, the small size of the sample (N-100), and most significantly the time of the report. Rock music did not capture collegiate interest until the popularization of *Sgt. Pepper*, and in San Francisco until the local bands began to record. David Brice, "Students Favor Dylan," *San Francisco State Gator*, 1 October 1965, p. 1.

12. "Country Music Will Be the Music of the '80s," *Sentinel Tribune*, 7 January 1981, p. 5. Also John Rockwell, "Country Music Is No Small Town Affair," *New York Times*, 17 July 1983, pp. 1, 16.

13. Richard A. Peterson and David Berger, "Three Eras in the Manufacture of Popular Music Lyrics," in *Sounds of Social Change: Studies in Popular Culture*, edited by R. Serge Denisoff and Richard A. Peterson (Chicago: Rand McNally, 1972), p. 286.

14. Hughston F. Mooney, "Popular Music Since the 1920's: The Significance of Shifting Taste," *American Quarterly* 20 (Spring 1968): 68.

15. "A Sage Looks at Living," *Time*, 20 May 1940, p. 41.

16. Cited in J. Frederick MacDonald, "Hot Jazz, the Jitterbug, and Misunderstanding: Generation Gap in the Swing Era, 1935-1945," *Popular Music and Society* 2 (Fall 1972): 44.

17. Zappa, "The Oracle Has It All Psyched Out," p. 84.

18. George Simon, *The Big Bands* (New York: Macmillan, 1967), p. 35.

19. D. Duane Braun, *The Sociology and History of American Music and Dance, 1920-1968* (Ann Arbor, Mich.: Ann Arbor Publishers, 1969), p. 48.

20. Charles Siepmann, *Radio, Television and Society* (New York: Oxford University Press, 1950), p. 99.

21. Simon, *The Big Bands*, p. 32.

22. Zappa, "The Oracle Has It All Psyched Out," p. 85. John Sinclair, the creator of the concept of translove energy, the catalyst for the revolutionary potential of rock, also views *Blackboard Jungle* as the turning point in generational conflict (see ch. 7).

23. David Riesman, "What the Beatles Prove about Teenagers," *U.S. News and World Report*, 24 February 1964, p. 88. Also Jerry Hopkins, *Elvis* (New York: Simon & Schuster, 1971), pp. 141-47.

24. Arnold Shaw, *The Rock Revolution* (New York: Crowell-Collier, 1969) p. 16; Dave Marsh, *Elvis* (New York: Quadrangle Books, 1982), pp. 86-96.

25 Not all of the songs included in these magazines are in fact taken from the best-selling charts. Approximately 30 percent are not from *Billboard or Cashbox* reports but, rather, reflect the picks of the magazine editors.

26. Donald Horton, "The Dialogue of Courtship in Popular Songs," *American Journal of Sociology* 62 (May 1957): 569-78.

27. "Lame, Halt, and Blind," *Billboard*, 30 November 1959, p. 2. Also, "Ford Doubts Payola Made R&R Popular," *Billboard*, 9 May 1960, pp. 1, 27.

28. Riesman, "What the Beatles Prove about Teenagers," p. 88.

29. A.J.W. Taylor, "Beatlemania: A Study in Adolescent Enthusiasm," *British Journal of Social Clinical Psychology* 5 (1966): 81.

30. "Songs That Have a Double Meaning," *San Francisco Sunday Examiner and Chronicle*, 25 September 1966, p. 13.

31. Joe Fernbacker, "Days of Blood and Peanut Butter," *Punk Magazine*, 7 May 1973, p. 4.
32. Quoted in Ben Edmonds, "Alice Cooper Blows His Wad: Scenes from an Impending Conquest," *Creem* 5 (June 1973): 38.
33. Ian Dove, "At Alice Cooper's Show, Tunes Don't Get in Way of the Action," *New York Times,* 5 June 1973, p. 42.
34. Ed McCormack, "New York City's Ultra-Living Dolls," *Rolling Stone*, 26 October 1972, p. 16.
35. Robert Christgau, "In Love with the N.Y. Dolls, All-American Boys into Ultra-Decadence," *Newsday*, 18 February 1973, p. 18.
36. "Alice Cooper Rock Group Rocks Viewers," *TV Guide*, 9 December 1972, p. A-1.
37. Nat Freedland, "1st ABC Rock Special Ratings Spawn 3 More," *Billboard*, 9 December 1972, p. 6.
38. Ann Landers, "Singer Doesn't Suffer from Rock Lyrics," *Toledo Blade*, 5 December 1979, p. 40.
39. "Watt May Have Started Trend Judging Some Bands," *Sentinel Tribune*, 24 May 1983, p. 5.
40. Ira A. Robbins, "New Wave Music" in *Contemporary Music Almanac 1980/1981*, edited by Ronald Zalkind (New York: Schirmer Books, 1980), pp. 72-73.
41. Quoted in Max Gunther, "TV Can Be Hazardous to Their Image," *TV Guide*, 26 July 1978, p. 18.
42. Ibid. Quoted in Michael Goldberg "Few Million-Sellers in '83," *Rolling Stone*, 15 March 1984, p. 44.
43. Erma Bombeck, "Hard Rock Can Be a Decibel Ordeal," *Baltimore Sun*, 6 March 1982, p. A-9.
44. Carl Belz, *The Story of Rock* (New York: Oxford University Press, 1969), p. vii.
45. Richard Mabey, *The Pop Process* (London: Hutchinson Educational, 1969), p. 41.
46. Dick Hebdige, *Subculture: The Meaning of Style* (London: Methuen, 1979), pp. 90ff.
47. Dean Tudor, *Popular Music* (Littleton, Colo: Libraries Unlimited, 1983), p. xvii.
48. Steven Grover, "Record Buyers Remain Loyal to Black Music," *Wall Street Journal*, 25 September 1982, p. 1.
49. Michael Jensen, "Blue Grass Sheds Its Hay Bale Image to Enter Mainstream of Music," *Sentinel Tribune*, 6 September 1983, p. 5.
50. Rolf Meyersohn and Elihu Katz, "Notes on a Natural History of Fads," *American Journal of Sociology* 62 (May 1957): 595.
51. Leslie Raddatz, "Dear David—I Am 9 Years Old," *TV Guide*, 22 May 1971, p. 24.
52. See Charles Keil, *Urban Blues* (Chicago: University of Chicago Press, 1966).
53. Paul Hirsch, "The Structure of the Popular Music Industry: An Examination of the Filtering Process by Which Records Are Preselected for Public Consumption" (Ann Arbor: University of Michigan Survey Research Center, 1970).
54. Quoted in Robert N. Webner, "Cleveland: Rock Music Capital of the World," *Wall Street Journal*, 7 September 1979, p. 17. See Anastasia Pantsios, "History of the Cleveland Rock Scene," *Exit*, 5,12 December 1974, 9 January 1975; Grover, "Record Buyers Remain Loyal to Black Music."

55. Kenneth Bilby, "The Impact of Reggae in the United States," *PMS* 5 (1977): 21.

56. Barbara Graustark et al., "Disco Takes Over," *Newsweek*, 2 April 1979, p. 56.

57. Richard A. Peterson, "Disco! A Sociologist Suggests Its Distinctive Sound Isn't Just Another Fad," *Chronicle of Higher Education*, 2 October 1982, pp. 26-27; Hebdige, *Subculture*, pp. 90ff; Grover, "Record Buyers Remain Loyal to Black Music," p. 1.

58. Dennis Hunt, *Los Angeles Times* 13 January 1980, p. B-2

58. Ross, "The Record Business," p. 230.

60. Qutoed in John Sippel, "Major Retailers Prophesy Boom," *Billboard*, 12 August 1972, p. 1.

61. Robert Palmer, "Today's Pop—A Period of Pluralism," *New York Times*, 24 August 1980, p. D-21. Also, Jeff Hamilton, "Trying Too Hard," *Record*, January 1984, p. 12; Jim Sullivan, "Triumph of the 'New,'" *On Campus*, March 1984, p. 24.

# 2

# Emptiness in Harmony: The Artist

*You're a little insane*
*Playing the game for public acclaim.*

—©Tickson Music Co.

*God help the troubadour*
*That tries to be a star.*

—©Barracade Music

"You either have it or you don't." This simple statement is about talent, but talent alone cannot guarantee recording success. It all hinges on the performer's ability to persuade others to recognize their ability. Discovery and appreciation are mercurial events. An artist evoking encomiums from David Geffen may generate only yawns from Clive Davis at Arista or Berry Gordy of Motown. Talent is commonly defined as a natural or acquired ability or a natural endowment or ability of superior quality. This common and popular definition does not totally apply in the music industry. Talent is the *commodity* that has economic potential. Bar owners, nightclub proprietors, talent agents, managers, and the all-important record companies *define* who has talent. Omar Sadin, a nightclub owner in a midwest university town suggests, "I go and listen to groups all the time according to what I think . . . and like." But he adds, "Whatever I think doesn't really matter . . . *you can't make any money that way* . . . even if a band is very good it didn't really matter." Former manager Roy Silver asserts: "Talent is not sufficient." The artist must also have "the ability to perceive who's right and who's wrong; the ability to choose good people; ability to sustain performing regardless of emotional crises; to continue to work ahead because it's a long hard grind and continue to pay those dues. All those things have to be there. The talent aspect of it is not sufficient."

The people who transform the individual into a successful performer have to be professionals or plugged into the music industry. As manager

Ron De Blasio laments, "The material is accessible once it's heard; the challenge is getting it heard."[1] Talent must be recognized by someone in a position to bring further scrutiny to the musician. A band practicing in a cluttered garage is not considered talented unless it generates some excitement in people other than angry noise-conscious neighbors. If the band turns on enough people, it may eventually be brought to the attention of someone in a position to label it a peformer. Ry Cooder recalls, "They used to have party nights at the Ash Grove when people would get up out of the audience and play. And it seemed like when I was 16 I was good enough, and somebody said 'Get up, get up,' and they pushed me on stage. I got up and I was so scared I was petrified. I played and sweated and people laughed and clapped." This initial appearance did not establish the guitarist as a performer. He remained unemployed until later because no one in the audience treated him as a serious performer.

For aspiring artists, generating the label of performer, let alone star, is a monumental task. They must attract the attention of a sufficient number of people in a position to legitimate them as performers. Publicist Corb Donohue observed, "Anything that rises above the mire is a success. Anything that draws attention to itself and continues on without some sort of great preposterous hype involved is a success." The labeler, the guy who "can make it happen," is a person already within the music business, such as a manager, agent, executive, or producer. Veteran John Boylan, having produced Boston, Linda Ronstadt, and Commander Cody, says, " I want to find acts and, using my clout and leverage, get them the budget and the experience they need to make a world class record."

Preparation to become a successful performer is essential; an artist must be sufficiently developed to elicit a desired response. This maturing can occur only through performing, usually as local artists on high school or university campuses or as weekend bands playing in small towns. This is as true in the Midwest and Southwest as it was in the Cavern Club in Liverpool, the Exit-in in Nashville, or in a club in Hollywood. Many local artists, while dreaming of a break, rarely get it due to the lack of recognition. The few that do make it refer to this period as "dues paying." Ironically, the rare act that does get to national prominence following such a start only adds to the mythology of future stardom that permeates the dingy clubs and old ballrooms.

The odds against "making it" are enormous. Promoter-manager Bill Graham asserts that the chance of succeeding in the music business is approximately "a thousand to one." Only 17 new artists per year, it is believed, ever record a Top 40 hit, while in the same year 23 persons are statistically likely to be struck dead by lightning. (Of course, more people are exposed to lightning storms than try to achieve musical stardom.) With

odds so monumental, it is not surprising to find a good deal of misinforma-
tion and superstition surrounding the making of a star. Success almost
becomes a product of luck, time, divine intervention, or some other *deus
ex machina.*

There exist thousands of bar bands living on dreams and not much else.
The dreams come from the mythology of the music business. The transformation of a human jukebox into a superstar is a myth, but it does rarely
happen. Record "bizzers" scoff at the characterization "overnight sensation," usually commenting sardonically, "Yeah, she's been paying dues for
ten years."

America's road to temporary success was legendary. A deejay at a Boston
FM radio played "A Horse with No Name," thinking it was Crosby, Stills,
Nash and Young. Surprise! It was America.

The experience of John Cafferty and the Beaver Brown Band will only
fuel the dream factory. An 11-year-old band living off the fratbar East Coast
circuit, it found platinum wall hangings while still playing in clubs and
Greek gatherings where beer flowed. It originated in 1973, and did covers of
Top 40 hits and the oldies: Wilson Pickett, Fats Domino, Chuck Berry,
Mitch Ryder, and of course Presley. Like most bar bands, the five-member
group mimicked every star possible. "We kinda modeled ourselves after the
energy of the J. Geils Band," says Cafferty. "Every song was about 90 miles
an hour. For the first three years we were together I don't think we even
knew a slow song!"

In 1977 Michael "Tunes" Autunes became the sixth member of the band.
He was the only member of the unit to actually appear in *Eddie and the
Cruisers.* Autunes says: "They put a full-court press on me!"

The group paid its dues. "We played every bar you could play in Rhode
Island for a long time," said Cafferty, a slight sort of leprechaun with a Kirk
Douglas jaw and lengthy sideburns. "Then we branched out to Cape Cod
and Boston, and basically just stayed around the area for four years. Fi-
nally, we got a job in New Haven, Connecticut. Somebody saw us there."
Cafferty told a *Washington Post* reporter, "There's old show biz saying,
'You gotta be great every night,' because you never know who's in the
audience."

Cafferty recalls, "Kenny Vance was in the audience in the Other End one
night about nine years ago. He never introduced himself." Vance, formerly
of Jay of the Americans, brought about an association with Marty David-
son, which ended in the sound track to *Eddie and the Cruisers.* The film
critics were not especially kind to the film. Comparisons were constantly
made to Asbury Park's Bruce Springsteen. Others found the plot thin or
invoked the symbolism of the late Jim Morrison or the poetry of Bob
Dylan. Mired in the "teen scream" flood of summertime films, *Eddie*

grossed an unimpressive $4.7 million, which in film terms is a loss. The soundtrack album sold poorly, about 175,000 units, a figure that does not bring joy in the boardrooms of record companies.

Enter the infant world of music video and cable television. The film was a flop. Renting unsuccessful motion pictures to cable networks is a tried and true method of recouping at least a part of a producer's loss. Norman Hunter of the 152-outlet Record Bar chain indicated that the cable exposure for *Eddie* jumped sales from 12 units to 4,851 in four weeks. Cable television, regardless of the opinions of radio promo people, has an enormous impact on record sales. Cafferty and The Beaver Brown Band have their platinum record, thanks to HBO and the Movie Channel.

The question arises whether Cafferty and the band's postponed album will have the appeal of the *Cruisers* effort. Aside from its tunes, the group is faceless. As the few music videos aired indicated, Cafferty looks like a potential rock idol, but the resemblance to Springsteen and "Eddie Wilson" is hard to ignore. *Eddie and the Cruisers* created a large number of hit singles and MTV videos, such as "Wild Summer Nights," "Tender Years," and "On the Dark Side." As with America, can Cafferty and the Beaver Brown Band do it again? Can John Cafferty overcome the Michael Pare portrayal of Eddie Wilson. As a CBS publicist wrote, "To be continued."

A basic principle in the music business was articulated by Warner Bros. Records executive Stan Cornyn: "You can send it up in a balloon, you can put it on the Goodyear blimp, you can send it up by rocket, etc. If it doesn't have it in the grooves, it isn't gonna sell. You can't package and sell a piece of shit." Looking at the English development of rock, musician-writer George Melly wrote, "Some initial magic [must be] inherent in the group or artist in the first place."[2] This magic must be apparent to those exposed to it. Peter Yarrow of Peter, Paul and Mary evaluated the notion of magic in his performances: "In show business terms it may be my undoing . . . because I have the feeling you need at least an ounce . . . of mystique. There has to be a bit of a mystery and there is nothing mysterious at all about me." How artists are perceived by an audience is a critical factor in their success. However, before they can reach an audience, there are the ever-present dues to be paid. Not all people have the stamina, desire, or perseverance to travel the road to stardom.

### "Why Put up with It?" Artist Motivation

Joe Smith suggests an essential ingredient for success: "Something with the group that wants to make it too, in addition to making music. They want to make it. There's got to be some ambition in a group. You would think that everybody has it, but they don't. So many are willing to do that number and play three on bills with no people watching, things like that."

A reporter once posed the question, "Why would anyone want to go through the agony, against tremendous odds, to try to make it in music?" The obvious answer seems to be fame, fortune, and all of the fringe benefits associated with stardom. Most behavioral and social scientists who have pondered this question would agree with this commonsense notion up to a point. Artists are interested in the size of their bank accounts or at the very least an extravagant even if usually short-lived life-style. There exist at least three plausible hypotheses gleaned from scholarly works and the artists themselves: self-esteem, social mobility, and the music, and the three are frequently intertwined.

"If nobody helps us," says lead singer Rod Piazza of Mighty Flyers, "then we'll do it ourselves . . . whatever it takes we'll do it." "I'm a romanticist, sensualist and conceptualizer," emphasizes jazz saxophonist John Klemmer. "I want to present myself as a vulnerable soul through my music. It's always a risk when you present yourself to the public emotionally. In many ways, our American culture is afraid to feel . . . but as an *artist,* I'm willing to take it." The Go-Go's lead singer told a reporter: "Everyone treated us like a joke when we started. . . . Girl rockers, yecck, but we tried to ignore it . . . we knew we weren't very good when we started, but we also knew we'd get better."[3] They did.

Self-confidence is imperative for recognition. It is essential if a group is to survive the early stages of its career. Roy Silver explains, "You got to want to get out there and fight to turn them on. If I don't see that within the group, I will pass because I know that the odds are against your making it regardless of your ability as an artist and performer." As in the case of Bob Dylan, a former Silver client, it is the musician with self-generating motivation that survives the morass of semiprofessional popular music. Dylan, his hometown girlfriend recalled, "was sort of oblivious to the whole fact people were not turned on by his music. He lived in his own world, and it didn't bother him. There was this cat playing like they were clapping when they were really booing."[4]

Nearly all bands define their sound as being unique, almost as a protective device. Most artists become hostile and defensive at suggestions that their material is similar to that of better-known artists. Most seem to have forgotten their dues-paying time in barrooms, playing the most requested songs of the day, such as "Louie, Louie," "Stayin' Alive," or "Stairway to Heaven." A British rock musician objected to a review in the *Hollywood Reporter:*

> It said we were trying to sound like an American group. Like trying to analyze what we're about, and we're just trying to entertain people and

maybe make them feel good. We're not laying any numbers on anybody. . . . We've not borrowed from Chicago, we're not born from them, not consciously. We just got the band together, I wrote three songs, and there it is. . . . We can't possibly be doing a copy of anything. Colin Carter, lead singer of Flash, a spin-off of Yes, the progressive English band, concurred: "The main reason that people get too defensive is the fact that musicians have huge egos that they need to prop up on stage . . . so when they are compared to someone else, it is an affront to their ego."

Joe Smith elaborates on artist motivation:

I think the group has to believe it. You do run into monumental egos. The first time three girls scream in an audience some kids are stars right away in their own minds. I guess they believe they've refined it but that's crap. . . . I really think that anybody who has the guts to stand up on a stage and entertain people has got a quality that most of us don't have. An inner drive. Their ability to write songs and each song that they write, like James Taylor, is blood from the veins, and to hear it played and to sing it and try it on an audience and put it in an album wondering how somebody will receive it, those are things that you and I don't know about.

The very same quality needed to achieve fame may, after success, be an act's downfall. This contradiction most frequently manifests itself in the sphere of artist-company relations (see chapter 4). In the beginning self-esteem is imperative for survival and success. Teddy Bart, a Nashville television personality and author of *Inside Music City, U.S.A.*, describes the formula for success in the country music idiom as a mixture of "talent, desire, and perseverance." A healthy ego and self-esteem are essential for at least two of these elements.

At the outset, ego is important because it can carry the artist through difficult and sometimes unpleasant situations to the hoped-for first break. Ego or self esteem—high or low—is an essential variable in paying dues, being a human jukebox in a bar and putting up with uninterested audiences and music journals. Later this can cause problems. Billy James, once a publicist for the strife-torn Byrds, believes ego is one of the two prime causes for the dissolution of successful rock bands. Roger McGuinn's statement in *Fusion* about the original Byrds, considered by many critics to be one of the premier U.S. bands of the 1960s, is illustrative: "We just had a bunch of amateur musicians who couldn't play live. . . . Ah, Hillman was a good bass player. Crosby wasn't a hot guitarist. Ah . . . Michael wasn't a hot drummer. And Gene Clark . . . didn't really know how to keep time . . . at all . . . at all. . . . He was just spastic on the tambourine. . . . I'm glad he left, actually . . . I'm glad everybody left."

Rags to riches, or upward social mobility, as sociologists call it, is also an important factor in the quest for success. Tammy Wynette, when asked why so many great singers all came from within thirty miles of Tupelo, Mississippi, replied half jokingly, "Just to get out of there." Rock musicians have echoed this sentiment about other places or social conditions. Black musicians, especially, have found the entertainment business a ladder out of the ghetto. Gordon Friesen, former editor of *Broadside* (New York City), said:

> The black kids, and I'm talking of boys and young men, were continually forming and reforming quartets with the aim of somehow breaking out of the ghetto into the bigtime music world of records. They rehearsed endlessly, into the wee hours of the morning. It was generally on the streets, but not by choice. They were always begging for someone to provide them a place to rehearse in.

The desire to escape is not limited to Blacks. Country superstar Waylon Jennings explained, "It's kind of like they say sports is with black dudes. It's a way to get up and away from something that's bad. . . . I'll tell you what it is: either music or pull cotton for the rest of your life . . . you'll learn to do something if you've ever been to a cotton patch." Kids growing up in the shadow of Detroit factories have contributed to what became known as the Motown sound. Texas rock-and-roll band members have an equally economically deprived background. Other musicians have a more affluent background. The Carly Simons, James Taylors, and Art Garfunkels have some college experience and come from middle- and even upper-class backgrounds. The sheer expense of becoming involved in popular music in the 1980s almost negates the possibility that a "Johnny B. Goode" may emerge without either some economic cushion or tremendous drive to escape poverty.

The life-style of musicians and the community of musicians also are attractions at all levels of performing. Eric Burdon, of the reunited Animals, stresses that being a musician must be first and foremost:

> There is a very strong brotherhood of musicians, we talk about nothing else but music. A guitarist talks about nothing else but guitars, and when I meet a musician who talks about anything else but music . . . talks about anything else but creativity, I just avoid him because I know that he's no good, cause I know that he's playing a game, that he's being pretentious.

A promotional handout stated: "Nitzinger is a collection of purist musicians totally dedicated to their music and completely disinterested in the workings of the industry which supports them." The leader of the band, John Nitzinger, told the recording company, "When they are finished working out the details, and they tell us to come out and play, we'll be there. But all we want to do is make music."

Rick Springfield summarized the music-community attitude by saying, "When I get to the point in my show when I sing 'Jessie's Girl,' . . . I see 5000 people jumping up in the air and clapping their hands to a song I wrote. It's incredible, it's a great feeling."[5]

## Stairway to Heaven?

The three rungs of the ladder to potential exposure and perhaps success are starting bands, working bands, and recording artists.[6]

Starting or beginning bands are informal performing units without overt professional aspirations; these include high school groups and amateur entertainers of various sorts. The performers usually lack commitment and a high level of musical skill, and the dropout rate is extremely high. Initially they may play just for personal pleasure. High school bands such as Bob Dylan's quartet in Hibbing, Minnesota, begin as a lark and then start getting serious. Starting bands, are an important initiation and training ground for musicians, although they rarely last. Members come and go and regroup in amoeba-like fashion. A former member of the Raspberries recalls, "When you're young and try to play in a band together there are a lot of hassles coming about. Ego things and who wants to run the show and who doesn't and different outlooks. When you're young, it's hard to cope with things like that."

There are exceptions to the unfocused performing and shifting among groups, such as the Undertones from Northern Ireland. According to Sire Records publicity:

> John O'Neill and his brother Vincent had the idea of a group in their heads, along with Billy Doherty who used to live in the same street, and Michael Bradley, who was in Vincent's class at St. Peter's secondary school. They all had cheap acoustic guitars on which they had learned to play chords.
>
> Michael Bradley and Vincent learned at school, while Billy Doherty and John learned at Brooke Park activity center. Although they all thought about the group in 1974, it wasn't until late 1975 that they bought a small set of drums, a bass guitar, a microphone and two amps, through a loan company. Part of the reason for this activity was the addition of Feargal Sharkey, who was in Billy's class at St. Peter's, as singer. In the meantime, younger brother Damian had bought an electric guitar, so, Vincent was kicked out and Damian brought in.

The Beatles did the same thing to Pete Best, replacing him with drummer Ringo Starr.

They started practicing (and learning to play) and by March 1976 they had perfected about six songs. They played twice, once at a parents meeting in a scout hall and again at St. Joseph's secondary school.

After this they kept on practicing, first in O'Neill's house, then, through Michael's sister's boyfriend, they got a shed at the back of Mrs. Simm's house.

By the end of 1976 they had learned about 20 songs, and started asking around the pubs for bookings. All of the pubs refused, except for the Casbah. Up until then the Casbah had specialized in heavy metal groups, while most of the other pubs had country and western bands or groups playing "chart" songs.

The first night the group played it got a good reaction, although a lot of the audience thought it was good fun, but not "real" music, like King Rat or Toe Jam or National Dried, the local top "rock" groups.

They also played at local community centers and supporting showbands.

Some starting bands begin to take the avocation seriously and, like the Undertones, attempt to graduate to the second rung, working bands. Working bands can be subdivided into barroom acts and show acts. Barroom acts are strictly in the process of paying their dues, that is, acquiring the necessary musical skills and equipment, and most never transcend this level of "human jukebox." It is a secondary occupation or moonlighting for most performers, for only rarely can they support themselves from their music. Many give up in disgust, and others find nonmusical employment more remunerative. The attrition rate is high on this rung of the ladder, too.

The working band is simply an act that plays everything and anywhere to gain exposure and experience, not to mention money. Outside the recording centers—New York, Nashville, and especially Los Angeles—aspiring performers are wholly dependent upon being seen. This essential fact places employers in the role of talent arbiter and sometimes agent. They provide the first audition and the debut before a paying audience. The expectations of entrepreneurs vary, depending upon the market in which they do business. A nightclub owner may well be hiring background noise rather than talent. Frank Zappa began playing in go-go bars in Hollywood. Sly Stone performed in North Beach topless bars before becoming a rock star. Carlos Santana practiced B.B. King runs in the strip joints on Revolution Street in Tijuana. A good deal of dues paying is done in bars where the act is secondary. Working bands have many obstacles to overcome.

Working bands must have equipment that ranges in cost from $20,000 to $75,000. Jim Erikson, owner of a music shop, estimates the average to be about $50,000. He commented in 1983, "Dozens of bands have more equipment than the famous groups of five years ago." The irony is that a member of an average bar band or working band grosses two to three hundred dollars per night, and Erikson says most of the dollars are wasted: "There are lots of problems and they probably won't make it." Consider that a name-brand guitar like a Fender or a Gibson is around a thousand dollars. A bass runs twice that amount. Drums the same. Amplifiers, microphones, sound boards, lights, snakes or cables, power boosters, and the like escalate the total. Add to that truck rental or ownership; the days of the Volkswagen bus are over. Then there are support personnel to be paid.

Bar bands labor is under another burden in having to develop their own material. Club owners want familiar charted or Top 40 material. Omar Sadin, a Midwest bar owner, observed, "I rather they play new music, but you have a group of songs that all the bands play. The audience will recognize as soon as the band plays it clicks . . . like they say good songs never die." Most bands realize this fact. Greg Rankey, drummer and manager of Obsession, a heavy-metal glitter band supports this view: "Every bar band you find that wants to get hired is a cover band." This is a requirement for employment and in some cases survival. Obsession's repertoire is illustrative. Record companies are not looking for groups that sound like established acts and do the songs of established acts. "Who needs another . . . ," says one major executive. Consequently, "playing what people know they like" does not get a group, unless it is an exception, a recording contract—the ultimate prize in music.

## TABLE 2.1
### Song List, 1983

AEROSMITH
Lord of the Thighs
Sweet Emotion

APRIL WINE
I Like to Rock
Enough Is Enough

BLUE OYSTER CULT
Cities on Flame

DEAF LEAPARD
Let It Go
Rock off Ages

JOHN COUGAR
Hurts So Good

SAMMY HAGAR
I'll Fall in Love Again
Only One Way to Rock
Your Love Is Driving Me Crazy

DON HENLEY
Dirty Laundry

FOGHAT
I Just Wanna Make Love

JETHRO TULL
Locomotive Breath

JOAN JETT
I Love Rock 'n' Roll
Do Ya Wanna Touch

JUDAS PRIEST
You've Got Anotherthing Comin'
Electric Eye

FLEETWOOD MAC
Green Manilishi

KENNY LOGGINS & STEVE
   PERRY
Don't Fight It

**TABLE 2.1 (Continued)**
**Song List, 1983**

*LED ZEPPELIN*
Dancing Days
The Ocean

*JOURNEY*
Separate Ways

*LOVERBOY*
Jump
Lucky Ones
Hot Girls in Love

*LYNARD SKYNARD*
Saturday Night Special

*NAZERETH*
Do Everything For You

*ALDO NOVA*
Fantasy

*OZZY OSBOURNE*
Flyin High Again
Crazy Train

*PRISIM*
Don't Let Him Know

*RED RYDER*
Lunatic Fringe

*BILLY SQUIER*
Lonely Is the Night
Everybody Wants You
Emotions in Motion

*.38 SPECIAL*
Hold on Loosely
So Caught Up in You
You Keep Runnin'

*PAT TRAVERS*
Snortin' Whiskey & Drinking Cocaine

*ZZ TOP*
I Need Your Lovin'
I Thank You

*NEIL SCHON & IAN HAMMER*
No More Lies

*DURAN DURAN*
Hungry Like the Wolf

*BRYAN ADAMS*
Cuts Like a Knife

*RUSH*
New World Man
2112

*MEN AT WORK*
Overkill

*NIGHT RANGER*
Don't Tell Me You Love Me

*EDDIE MONEY*
Shaken

*JOHN WAITE*
Change

*VAN HALEN*
Pretty Woman

*STEEL BREEZE*
You Don't Want Me Anymore

*ROLLING STONES*
Brown Sugar
Start Me Up

*TOM PETTY*
You Got Lucky

*AC/DC*
Live Wire

*OBSESSION*
This Is One Time
Positive Ways
Tryin' So Hard
Possibilities
The Angle
Another Day
My Baby Likes It Hard

Several bar bands were quite candid about paying dues. Ex-Caliber, a midwestern band, noted, "Our own material, that's down the road." Moreover, "despite the fact there's a lot of material we do that we don't like, we play it." Peter Causino, drummer of the group describes paying dues. "You just can't jump into original music and expect people to buy it. You've got to work your way up to it . . . and hope the material is going to go over." Obsession's manager expresses the same sentiments: "We do write songs and we introduce them to the audience when they are really growing into the band. We play our own songs at the last set . . . we like to be called back so we play our songs."

**TABLE 2.2**

**Personnel Equipment List**

*DOUG BENROTH:* Guitar, Keyboards, Vocals
Gibson Flying "V" with Bowisn Tremelo Bar System
100 Watt Marshall Stack
Custom Built Effects Board Consisting of:
MXR Distortion Plus
IBANEZ 6 Band Graphic Equalizer
ADIA Flanger
DOD Chorus
CRY Baby Wha Pedal
DOD Analog Delay
HIEL Sound Talk Box
DOD Phase Shifter

*PHIL NEWTON:* Bass Guitar, Keyboards, Vocals, Flute
Kramer Duke Custom
Kramer Vanguard Special (Flying V)
Kramer Standard
Fender VI—Six String
Hangstrom—Eight String
Peavy—300 Series Amplifier
Peavy—8-10 Speaker Encloser
MXR Flanger
*Additional Instruments:*
Amstrong—Model 104 Flute
Roland—Model S409 Monophonic Synthesizer

*GREG RANKEY:* Percussion, Keyboards, Vocals
Pearl—Rosewood Finish Drumkit
6″, 8″, 10″, 12″, Concert Toms
12″, 13″, 14″, Mounted Toms
2—24″ Bass Drums
6½ x 14 Snare Drum
13″ Zildjain High Hats
16″ Medium Crash, 17″ Heavy Crash Zildjains Cymbal
18″ Medium, 18″ Crash Paiste Cymbals
22″ Ride, Zildjain
18″ Splash, Paiste
LP Brass Chimes
LP Cowbell
2—Drum Workshop Chain Driven Pedals
4—Pearl Boom Stands, 2—Pearl Straight Stands
3—Beyer Boom MIC Stands, 4—Beyer Straight Stands
2—Heavy Duty Atlas Kick Drum Stands

**TABLE 2.2 (Continued)**
**Personnel Equipment List**

*LARRY SWAIN:* Guitar, Keyboards, Vocals
Gibson Flying "V"
Gibson Les Paul
50 Watt Marshall Stack
IBANEZ Multieffects (Compressor, Delay, Chorus, EQ)
MXR Distortion Plus
*Additional Instruments:*
MOOG Opus 3 Polyphonic Synthesizer
Hohner International Electric Piano

**Group Equipment**

*MAINS, LOW END:*
•BGW 7000 Amplifier
•2—TL4050 Bass Bins, 2—15" speakers

*MAINS, LOW MID-RANGE*
•Crown DCA300
•4—JBL Perkins Cabinets, 1—15" speaker

*MAINS, HIGH MID-RANGE:*
•Crown DCA300
•2—Eastern Acoustic Cabinets, 1—12" speaker

*MAINS, HIGH END:*
•Crown DCA150
•2—EV HR90 Horns

*MONITORS:*
•4—EV Monitors, 12" speaker, 8HD Horn, 2—EV Tweeters, in each
•1—DCA150 Crown Powering Stage Monitors
•1—DC300 Carvin Powering Drum Kit Monitor
•2—BI AMP Graphic Equilizers, Model 210

*MICROPHONES:*
•4—SM 58 Shure
•2—AKG D 1000 E
•7—Shure Dynamic
•3—SM 57 Shure
•1—Shure SM 10 Headset
•2—AKG D 2000 E

*SNAKES:*
•24 Channel 150' Main
•14 Channel Medusa Whirlwind 100' Drum Snake

*LIGHTING SYSTEM:*
•4—PAR 64 1000 Watt Lamps
•12—Par 64 500 Watt Lamps
•6—Frenal 500 Watt Lamps
•8—75 Watt Rain Lights
•1—Altman 1500 Watt Quartz Follow Spot
•3—ETA 4000 Watt Dimmer Packs
•1—ETA, 16 Channel, 2 scene Controller
•1—50' 220 Snake
•1—220 Fuse Box Converter

Obsession has equipment worth $50,000. Loans and day work help pay for the elaborate machinery on the stage and off. Ex-Caliber's equipment cost some $70,000. Given the money individual band members earn, this is a remarkable amount. A band member said, "You've got to invest in yourselves and make yourselves sound good. Because if you get the best equipment, it's going to pay for itself." Maybe!

London Boys, a new wave band from Sylvania, Ohio, is a bit more sophisticated. Members are working on their own material but they do not lose sight of the demands of a barroom environment. Phil Hoffman, spokesman and informal manager of the band, explains:

> You've gotta write a lot of songs. I think most of the material ends up in the garbage, but by learning to do other people's songs that's how you learn. . . . You listen to some of your own songs over the years and all of the sudden you hit upon something that is in the vein of the audience. You never want to stray away from the function; you're there to entertain that crowd, I don't care what you're doing.

Another member of the group said,

> It's a good way to make money, it's a good way to test how you perform before an audience, and others' material is easily accepted. . . . And so you want to make sure in a bar atmosphere you want people to dance . . . and that is one sure way to do it. Then in between these other songs you can slip an original song in there while they're still on the dance floor and hopefully see if it works. The word *sneak* or its synonyms enter the conversation of many groups.

Most working bands realize the dilemma of playing clubs and earning enough money to pay expenses, to make the loan payment on the elaborate equipment, and to go about the day-to-day business of surviving. London Boys has invested much less than the other bands, a mere $25,000, but, for the members there is more to it. Hoffman outlined the band's goals: "We have to take in money so that we can keep going on projects such as recording, videos, and things like that, so we can have some actual tangible promotion to help us gain some connection with some of the bigger agencies and recording companies that are on the coasts New York or LA." Sarcastically adding, "The Midwest is not the place for it!" Hoffman's point is well taken. Bob Seger languished in Detroit for years prior to *Night Moves*. Cleveland's Michael Stanley Band still has significantly to break out of the borders of Ohio.

London Boys obviously has a game plan: a demo tape and a hoped-for move to the recording capitals. But it takes money, so London Boys and other bands concentrate on economics, dream, and continue paying their dues. The arena for dues paying goes beyond merely playing bars. High schools, university fraternity parties, and private social occasions are a source of income.

As Jim Erikson, a veteran of the working-band syndrome and now the owner of a music shop, suggests most dreams of success are just that: dreams. Take the case of General Store. The experiences of the now-defunct Los Angeles band illustrate the similarities of rural and big city situations, and also how acts may fold from the strain of competing demands.

The group began with five members, all of whom had had experience in other bands. Two guitarists, a drummer, an organist, and a bass player composed the group, and most members were in college. Only one had any outside income besides playing dates. Finances were to become a major problem. Believing that it might have "a chance at the big time," the group, using the bass player's past connections, hired a promoter who booked them to three nights a week at primarily fraternity parties. The band received from $50 for a four-hour gig to $150 for a one-hour performance as a supporting act on a bill with a headliner, less the promoter's 10 percent. The income was the group's sole and inadequate means of support. One guitarist could not afford to buy an instrument and was finally expelled from the group because he spent an inordinate amount of time borrowing an "axe" prior to each performance. One member spent over $2,000 on an organ. The band, according to one member, was "mostly in hock." Earning money and playing gigs became the immediate concern. "Money was all important. Payments had to be made." The group invested some $4,000 in equipment. The demand for playing dates became dominant. The group slanted its music to the fraternity scene in Los Angeles; most of its time was put into "getting it down so they don't complain." The group played standard popular pieces such as "Gloria," but mixed in with these party favorites were some country, blues, and folk pieces. However, the main thrust of the group was covers of current hits. The group had no time and mixed desire to develop its own style. "We were too eclectic," said one member, "not proficient in any one. Not good enough in any one area."

The fraternity-party scene disillusioned the group. Many "Greeks" were openly hostile toward the long-haired musicians, and when inebriated were even worse toward them. Some of the band's equipment was broken at these parties and beer was spilled on speakers and drums. The reaction of several members was open contempt. The guitarist turned his back to the college audience in Miles Davis fashion; "I refused to play anything that was requested, even if we planned to play it, . . . for a damn $50. Why sell out for that amount?" The situation was one of stagnation. The band was not improving because there was no time for improvement, so the members decided to take six months off and develop their own sound. The demands of economics again interfered; their promoter offered a $150 gig on New Year's Eve if they would appear using another group's name on a bill with the Standells and the Box Tops at San Bernadino. The attractiveness of this offer brought the unit to its subsistence posture. It continued to function for several months after its decision to forgo artistic growth. In March 1968, with only one of its original members still in the band, it played at a peace rally along with Big Brother and the Holding Company and Blue Cheer. Shortly after the group disbanded. The General Store career is not atypical.

The price of survival is a major obstacle to success. The ability to overcome unappreciative audiences, and the cost of electronic equipment, and daily sustenance is essential. Many groups have neither the commitment nor the ability to cope with these conditions. There are literally thousands of bands that never get past the third slot on a concert billing, even with the name of another more successful act. Perhaps the Achilles' heel of such bands is best summed up by the statement of one of General Store's guitarists: "I was willing to work, but I didn't like all this other crap." Putting up with daunting conditions is precisely what an aspiring act must do. Dues paying is exactly that.

The first step is getting to the record company. "Demonstration tapes are the calling card of the business."[7] Getting the calling card, or "demo," is not as simple as lore would have it. A member of Obsession wants to cut a demo, but "we don't have the money." Many demos are poorly done; some in garages, some in poorly equipped studios. London Boys went into a studio; the result came to nothing but more bills. Local producers do not always understand the ethos of the band. "He knew how to run the board, but he wasn't aware of the sound," says Phil Hoffman.

Those that do make that tape take the risk of the "over-the-transom," or unsolicited, demo tape that is either mailed to a recording company or to an agent. Such tapes are treated somewhat cavalierly, especially by thriving companies, but they do receive a hearing and a verdict is customarily rendered within six weeks. Recognition is another matter. Kenneth Funk of Baltimore's Primo group mused, "We get together . . . and cut demos. But what we really need is for someone to *notice us.*"[8] This fabled shortcut to the top seldom happens because submitters lack the experience to turn executives on. Still there are enough exceptions to keep the mythology alive.

During the punk mania of the late 1970s a trio named after an angel in the film *Barbarella* recorded a demo containing the song "Girls On Film." According to Capitol Records, it "fell into the hands of the Berrow [brothers]. . . . Impressed by what they heard, the Berrows agreed to manage Duran Duran and provided [it] rehearsal space in their club." Michael Berrow financed the group as it paid its dues. The result was an EMI-Capitol contract, and subsequent stardom due to exposure on MTV. The Doobie Brothers were picked up by Warner Bros. Records on the strength of a tape. According to a company spokesman, "An orphan tape arrived, devoid of hype or contacts. It was played and deemed worthy. The group was met with and signed shortly thereafter—the first time in company memory that a band was signed on the basis of sound and sound alone." The rarity of favorable outcomes after use of this attention-getting device generates considerable excitement and lore. Columbia signed Lacy J. Dalton on the basis of a demo. The Irish Undertones sent a demo to the Good Vibrations label in Belfast and were invited to record. They moved, in time, to Sire Records, distributed by Warner in the United States. Sire claims, "This is a true story." The Undertones, notwithstanding, for a majority of artists "There's a Broken Heart for Every Rock 'n' Roll Star on Laurel Canyon Blvd."—as the writer of the song, John Mendelsohn, knows from personal experience.

How are demos judged, if at all? Clive Davis, president of Arista, declares, "We listen to every tape that comes in. If the tape is good then we ask for a live audition . . . or when he [or she] is handled by a big name manager." A "big-name" manager enjoys considerable leverage with a record company. It may respect his or her musical judgment. More important, it is cautious in dealing with a manager who represents a successful artist with the company. Terry Knight, when managing Grand Funk Railroad, received contracts for two artists, both of whom "stiffed," that is, did not return the original investment or production costs. Still, as Billy James, co-owner of a small label at the time, noted, "We can't afford not to listen." Tales of superstars who got away are too numerous and painful to mention. If a near-miracle happens, the artist is offered a contract; most hopefuls are not.

Many who are rejected cut "vanity" records that are sold at public appearances. On rare occasions local stations air these self-produced records if the artist's regional following is significantly large. A handful are picked up by major labels if the "action" justifies the move. Heart and Boston were picked by CBS on the basis of local hits on vanity records. A & M signed the Police because they sold 6,000 units of their own record. This is, again, exceptional.

"Home tapes," performances of original songs recorded to highlight the artists' commercial potential, are another technique or chance at dream fulfillment. In the mid-1960s San Francisco bands provided Russ Syracuse, the all-night man at the Top 40 station KYA, with tapes, and he aired them (see chapter 5). Some twenty years later Baltimore became the capital of home tapes, or "garage tapes" as they are frequently called. "I've been overall very pleased by the caliber of the bands we've been hearing," observes Kelly Saunders of WIYY-FM (Baltimore). "Since the [home tape] feature started in April [1983] the station has played about 137 songs." Competitor WJHU integrates the tapes with the regular record rotation. Cobal, a local act, was number one on the station's singles playlist in September 1983. Saunders comments, however, "So far, I haven't been responsible for boosting anyone's career." The value of this type of exposure is questionable, according to musician Craig Hankin. "As far as what being on radio did for us, it was really nothing."[9]

Showroom or lounge acts tend to be in limbo in the music industry. Generally the musicians have developed their stage presence and obtained fairly expensive professional equipment. They capitalize on their musical dexterity and audience rapport gained while playing the hotel, lounge, and middle-class nightclub circuits. Such performers can make a living with current hits and all-time favorites, but they are unlikely to catch the attention of record companies, which search for artists with new and unique material.

Barry Di Biasio, formerly of Autumn, commented: "I'm sure there are a lot of rock bands being discovered, but I have *never* heard of it happening in a lounge. The old scouting thing, if they're out there, they're certainly not in the lounges, they're somewhere else."

A line in the television film *The Gambler* is, "You've got to read the room." Lounge owners, like their patrons, want familiar material. A spokesperson for Autumn said, "If we get a 21-to-35 audience, we're doing mostly Top 40 that night. . . . We sprinkle it with country or funk music, or whatever *they seem to be into at the time.*"

John Bridges, leader of the now-defunct Easy, observed, "There's nothing worse than showing up in a hard rock room and your first number played in a tuxedo is 'Tie a Yellow Ribbon Round the Old Oak Tree.' It turns off the room . . . very quickly." Not to mention the management. Di Biasio and Bridges agree that the function of a lounge act is to get people to "dance and drink." Perhaps their techniques differ, but the goal is the same. There are other similarities. Neither Easy nor Autumn crave road life. Di Biasio: "I don't like being on the road. I think the road gets to you. Bands break up because of that . . . really wears and tears on you." John Bridges: "Even the simplest things on the road, it seems, can be quite problematic." Superstars echo this sentiment. So why do it? Di Biasio: "It's a business thing, it's good money." Bridges, now an academic, put it more bluntly: "A capitalist operation, we were consciously out for nothing but money, as much as we could get. We were tired of doing our own thing and starving, of never having any money, or anything else." Here the consensus appears to end. Easy at one point in time had a chance at the "bigs." Autumn, at least one songwriting member, had a chance.

Lounge acts fall into three fundamental types. Some are attempting, usually without success, to climb the ladder to fame and fortune. Others have had their shot at it, and some of them made it for a while. Finally, a majority are stuck somewhere in between. Easy and Autumn are at the two extremes.

Easy Dance and Show Band was formed in the fall of 1973. Several members were veterans of Plant Life, a Florida-based band that experienced a brief unsuccessful fling with a CBS subsidiary. After the inevitable breakup, Easy appeared. The group was extraordinarily professional with promotional packages rivaling many of the major record companies.

Easy's marketing strategy involved an elaborate promo package including a color photo, biography of the group, list of material—these were fairly standard. It also issued the quarterly newsletter "Easy Stories," which discussed members of the band in a gossipy fashion and included an itinerary of where the act would be playing. The material was sent to a mailing list of customers, clubs, and booking agents. There was an answering service in Orlando. Needless to say, Easy played the better rooms and hotel chains because essentially it was more of a showroom band than a lounge act. Bridges: "That's where the really big money is." It was subject to the usual rigors of the road, internal personnel problems, marriages, divorces, breaking in new people, all of which partially led to the eventual breakup of the unit. Easy's fate is not uncommon. There are dozens of former recording artists on the same circuit experiencing similar problems.

Autumn, a Midwest tri-state lounge quintet, had been together for eight years, undergoing all of the pitfalls already described. Visions of "making it" are still alive and well. In the mid-1970s it cut a record for producer Tim Patterson in Toledo that received no airplay beyond northwest Ohio. Its "ace in the hole" was singer-songwriter Di Biasio. He says, "One thing I'm good at is writing and that seemed to be my in. I'm a good singer, but it's hard for singers to break into the business." He does not like the lounge act scene: "You write your way out." The Toledo record was based on Di Biasio's writing, according to Patterson. Beginning in 1979 songwriting awards began to flourish. Barry Manilow wanted his "Wild Chimes," which Di Biasio regrets not releasing to the star. He also won awards from the American Song Festival; Music City Song Fest, with "You Listened to My Heart"; Lyric Comeptition Ten; and several others. JMR Enterprise in Nashville has published three of his songs. In 1984 the long-awaited break appeared: "Just Another Night (in New York City)" was to be recorded by Atlantic artist Laura Branigan. Di Biasio hopes something will happen: "I can't see doing lounges going on 40." For modesty or the sake of group harmony, little is made of the writing during a typical show. "I don't do the original material until I can feel out the room. Then I'll *sneak* one in; if they applaud and they like it, then I'll say that was one of *ours.*" He is currently working for a social service agency.

Recording acts represent for most performers the Mount Olympus of the business. Recording acts have contracts and frequently perform on regional or national concert tours in an attempt to boost record sales. They are not necessarily superstars, who may be defined as artists whose concert appearances and records are considered guaranteed successes. Although superstars garner the vast majority of media attention, it is important to remember that nearly 85 percent of the albums released annually "stiff." Still, for most acts, record contracts are all-important. "That's why I am in the business," says the lead guitarist of London Boys. "I do want to record. That's the *ultimate goal*" (emphasis added). Achieving this goal is laced with difficulties: "A record contract usually proves to be one's most important career move," cautions superstar Kenny Rogers. "It can stall you, sometimes insurmountably, or elevate you, like a rocket, to some level of prominence." Rogers is a believable source; he reportedly earns over $20 million annually. He continues, "Don't look to make money on records . . . until you've had several major sellers back-to-back".[10]

This certainly qualifies the *Forbes* statement that "the fastest way to become a millionaire these days in the United States is to become a *big* rock 'n' roll star."[11] Superstars like Rogers are in short supply;[12] probably fewer than twenty artists fit the definition, especially in the 1980s.

A common complaint of artists about their recording contracts is "We were ripped off!" There may be a modicum of truth to this allegation. The record companies are in the catbird's seat in negotiating with working bands unless they have an established manager or legal adviser, or another company is bidding for their services. In many cases the artist functions as manager or uses a friend or "roadie" in that capacity. Neophyte artists usually sign a standard agreement. Bargaining with nightclub·owners is one thing, but record companies are the big leagues. Record companies have a legal department and the expertise. As one executive noted, "We've been here forty years, and we'll still be here long after the artist retires to Las Vegas lounges or the golden-oldies circuit."

An important aspect of a contract is the option clause, which gives the company control over the act for one to five years. The company has the power to renew its option annually. If the company is not satisfied with the act, it can drop it. Performers have no such power, except to renegotiate— usually at their peril. Contract negotiations, consequently, are of utmost importance, especially to the performer.

The stature of an artist, even at this fundamental level, greatly determines the terms of an agreement. The Doobie Brothers, who were signed by Warner on the basis of an over-the-transom tape, originally had little power in Burbank. Their chance for success was limited, for if artists have not demonstrated audience appeal by their third album, they are apt to be cut out of the catalog. Conversely, an act with proven audience appeal and professional management may receive a large advance and less cavalier treatment. For example, Warner advanced the Grateful Dead approximately $10,000 against royalties. To recoup, the company invested a considerable amount in promotion and was patient with the group, which did not produce a gold record until *American Beauty*, some five years after the initial contract was signed. Peter Banks, once of Yes, remarked, "They don't want to put a lot of money into a new band unless they make any money."

Companies also enjoy a psychological advantage. The artists want the recording contract after years of dues paying in dingy, noisy clubs and bars. The companies highlight "what they can do for the artists" usually in luxurious quarters; thick carpets, walls lined with gold and platinum records and autographed photos of superstars all impress the potential signees. Playing concerts rather than bars is the ideal. Doing one's own songs is a relief. A hit record is what dreams are made of. Consequently, arm-twisting or hype is rarely necessary. After the terms of the contract are partially explained—"It's a standard agreement"—the artists, usually in the absence of experienced management and legal advice, generally sign on the dotted line. Despite the plethora of "making-it" books, most of which are useless, working bands put their signatures to terms that may in time come back to haunt them. They rarely negotiate from a position of strength unless there is a bidding war.

Journalist and author Chet Flippo cautioned: "The record companies . . . deduct from the performer's income all production expenses . . . [and] most groups are obligated to do their first tours free—that is, the record company assumes the tour expenses, but also claims any profits resulting from the tour."[13] A popular heavy metal band such as Judas Priest reportedly barely breaks even on a U.S. tour. It hopes record sales the day after a concert will compensate.

Record companies, except on rare occasions, no longer subsidize tours. Larry Fitzgerald, one of Toto's managers, said, "The term 'tour support' really doesn't exist anymore."[14] The concert tour even for some former superstars has been a nightmare since 1979. Blame it on video games, cable television (MTV), ticket prices, or quality of the music, half-filled arenas are the rule rather than the exception. Some labels have been willing to "take a chance." One manager told *Billboard*, "At least the bands are getting shots. There's more willingness to experiment, especially in the heavy metal area." But there have been changes. As De Blasio suggests, "[It's] always going to be a problem in a conservative marketplace."[15]

The typical new artist is offered a royalty percentage of the retail list price, usually around 7 percent. Superstars get about twice that amount. It is rumored that Stevie Wonder, Motown's best-selling artist, receives 20 percent. Theoretically, 7 percent of a list $7.95 album is $1.14. At the 1983 list price of $9.98, the royalty should be $1.43. However, at the $7.95 figure, the artist actually receives 56 cents. A similar process occurs with singles. At $1.25 list the artist should get 20 cents or at $1.99, 27 cents; actually it is normally about half the above amount, 9 cents. Kenny Rogers explains this discrepancy, using the list price of $7.95.[16] Under a 7 percent contract, the anticipated royalties on 100,000 units total $56,000. But there are deductions even before the IRS gets into the act: the advance, usually $25,000 to $50,000; the promotion fees, which may be $10,000; and, prior to the industry's 1979 depression (see chapter 3), the tour shortfall. According to Rogers, *shortfall* refers to the company's subsidy of a tour, usually to promote an album: the difference between the amount earned on the tour and the tour's costs, which can run from $10,000 on up. Record companies also expect to be repaid for packaging that the company designed, perhaps about 6 cents an album. Video clips, also, are deducted.

## TABLE 2.3

| Gross sales: | $100,000 | |
| | − 10,000 | free goods |
| | − 10,000 | returns |
| Real sales: | $ 80,000 | |
| | $ 80,000 | sales |
| | x .56 | royalty per record |
| | $ 44,800 | gross royalties |
| Debits to record company: | $ 50,000 | advance (mainly for recording costs) |
| | 10,000 | extra promotion budget |
| | 10,000 | tour shortfall |
| | 6,000 | packaging costs |
| | $ 76,000 | owed to record company |
| Your income: | $ 44,800 | gross royalties |
| | 76,000 | owed to record company |
| | − $ 31,200 | TOTAL INCOME |

## TABLE 2.4
## Where the Money Goes

| $ | |
|---|---|
| .50 | to the distributors |
| .60 | for packaging |
| .40 | average pressing |
| .56 | artist royalty |
| .24 | 3% producer's royalty |
| .28 | mechanical royalty for a hypothetical 10 songs at 2 $^3/_4$ cents each, divided between publisher and songwriter |
| .12 | AFM health and welfare fees (1.5%) |
| .20 | advertising (5% of $4) |
| 2.90 | |
| 4.00 | gross income for each record sold |
| − 2.90 | costs |
| 1.10 | remaining for the company (well within the 30% margin it tries to maintain of the $3.50 left after paying distributors) |

Even after deductions, the company with the proper reserve clause can hold onto half the royalties left, to be applied to the next album's costs and possible "returns" (see Appendix II), unsold records. About 10 percent of the 100,000 projected sales are "free goods" given to record outlets to help promote the album. Then there are the "promos" sent to the media. The artist receives no royalties on free goods, promos, or cutouts. Using these figures, the artist owes the company at least $76,000. One performer lamented, "You can have a number-one record and still not earn a f - - - king cent!"

The artist owes $31,200, but the record company earned $88,000. The label makes $1.10 per unit at $7.98 list. Wholesale prices to retailers run about $4.00 to $4.56, depending on the volume of records purchased.

Album sales rarely create overnight millionaires. It helps significantly if the act writes its own recorded material and does concerts. Concerts can be money-makers and also stimulate record sales. But the artists are increasingly on their own. Managers and artists now complain that mechanical royalties are being withheld by some 25 percent of record companies. Production fees are dropping, thus cutting the availability of "name" producers. Finally, label budgets and advances have been cut except for the superstars.

### Social Characteristics of Recording Artists

The social characteristics of recording artists have been one of the most difficult aspects of music research. A major obstacle is inaccessibility. One doctoral candidate was not able to contact any performers until his project was advertised in an influential *Los Angeles Times* entertainment column. Even in this instance, the sample left much to be desired.[17] Academics with lengthy questionnaires and even tape recorders find it nearly impossible to get past the army of gatekeepers surrounding artists. In some instances a press card is of only marginal value.

Record companies, a potentially rich resource for scholarly research, are not terribly helpful. In the area of artist data, this resistance is not malicious or ill-willed; most companies simply have little in the way of archival material. If options are not renewed or the artist changes, labels and marketing materials, including biographies and photos, are discarded.

The usefulness of the print media as a source of artist data is badly tainted. Most accounts tend to feature "name" stars and the more sensational artists.[18]

Given these conditions—unavailability of artists, lack of industry cooperation, and media agenda-setting—obtaining data dealing with artists has been a major problem. In 1980 a study was done of recording artists, successful and unsuccessful. The methodology was quite simple. The two researchers did a content analysis of ten years of record-company biographies sent to one of the researchers, who is also a music journalist. The advantage was simply that failures were surveyed as well as successful acts. Here are some of the characteristics.

*Race*

As a category, race included ethnicity and nationality. This encompassed white, black, Hispanic, and native Americans and others. British- or European-born recording artists were equally sampled. Collapsing or folding of categories was done for statistical reasons.

### TABLE 2.5
### Race/origin of artist

| Musical style | White American | | Black American | | Other | |
|---|---|---|---|---|---|---|
| | N | % | N | % | N | % |
| Rock | 141 | 54.2 | 2 | 2.9 | 75 | 57.7 |
| Soul/rhythm and blues/disco | 21 | 8.1 | 36 | 52.9 | 6 | 4.6 |
| Easy listening | 11 | 4.2 | 2 | 2.9 | 14 | 10.8 |
| Country and western | 63 | 24.2 | 1 | 1.5 | 15 | 11.5 |
| Jazz | 22 | 8.5 | 26 | 38.2 | 19 | 14.6 |
| Classical | 0 | 0.0 | 1 | 1.5 | 1 | 0.8 |
| Other | 2 | 0.8 | 0 | 0.0 | 0 | 0.0 |
| Total | 260 | 100.0 | 68 | 99.9[a] | 130 | 100.0 |

$x^2 = 187.98$; df = 12; p. < .0001 ($n = 458$).
[a]Rounding error.

*Sex*

Male artists accounted for nearly 90 percent of the 667 performers. In the 1980s things are changing. Pat Benatar, Blondie, the Go-Go's, Madonna, Donna Summer, and Olivia Newton-John are important artists. A similar trend is occurring in country and soul music.

*Age*

The ages of only 35 percent of artists could be ascertained (mean = 32.6 years). For analysis, age was grouped into decades. Most of the rock artists are between the ages of 30 and 39, followed by 20 and 29. This same pattern is found for country and western artists. Soul/rhythm and blues/disco styles reverse the pattern slightly, with more artists between 20 and 29 than 30 and 39. Among jazz musicians, older artists (30-50 and over) predominate. Jazz musicians between the ages of 20 and 29 consist primarily of "fusion" players, making the effort to link jazz with rock and other styles.

*Education*

Level of education was calculated in U.S. standards for all artists. The biographies of artists who were not from the United States normally did not discuss education. Over 90 percent of the recording artists for whom educational information was available had at least graduated from high school. The numbers of artists become progressively smaller at each stage of higher education. The few individuals who had graduate degrees may have been involved in musical styles demanding more fluent "musical literacy" (such as jazz, big bands, or orchestral ensembles); or they may have held, or aspired to, positions as arrangers, composers, or studio musicians, for whom the ability to sight-read proficiently is most often a prerequisite to steady employment.

A final demographic variable was *geographic region*, which refers to the artist's community of origin. In those instances where an artist's family

TABLE 2.6
**Distribution of Recording Artists by Level of Education**

|  | *N* | % |
|---|---|---|
| Less than high school | 23 | 7.0 |
| High school graduate | 139 | 42.2 |
| Some college | 87 | 26.4 |
| College graduate | 75 | 22.8 |
| M.A. or Ph.D. | 5 | 1.6 |
| Total | 329 | 100.0 |

may have moved during his or her childhood, consideration was given to those areas wherein the artist spent formative years, and acquired education and musical skills and influences.

The one variable—and probably the most interesting variable—that was wholly unattainable using this method or any other was income. Artists with certified gold or platinum records hint at what their gross might be, but then there is little known about the clauses in their recording contracts. The same applies to concerts and publishing agreements. The closest one can estimate is by means of terms in contracts. The entire issue of royalties has evoked tremendous controversy in the industry ranging from the Beach Boys, the Mamas and the Papas, the Osmonds, Little Richard, Kenny Rogers, and ELO (Electric Light Orchestra).

### "On the Road Again": Touring

An act signed in the 1970s was put on tour coupled with the release of a record. Because a hit single is improbable, the tour was used simply to introduce the group to the "folks out there" and to stimulate record sales. The more exposure, the more recognizability and increased appreciation. Roy Silver's formula for the successful act centers upon this notion: "Air play means it's good. Audiences clap for *familiar* pieces." If there is no air play, "the audience adopts an 'I got to wait and see for awhile' attitude." Furthermore, "You have to expose the group continually, look for air play, press coverage, and the more things you can get to sock it home . . . to that

TABLE 2.7
**Musical Style of U.S. Recording Artists, by Region of Origin**

| | Geographic Region | | | | | | | |
|---|---|---|---|---|---|---|---|---|
| | Southeast | | Northeast and East Coast | | Midwest, Central | | West Coast, Southwest, Far West | |
| Musical Style | N | % | N | % | N | % | N | % |
| Rock | 14 | 19.2 | 74 | 65.5 | 40 | 53.3 | 27 | 29.0 |
| Soul/rhythm and blues/disco | 22 | 30.1 | 6 | 5.3 | 7 | 9.3 | 17 | 18.3 |
| Easy listening | 5 | 6.8 | 8 | 7.1 | 4 | 5.3 | 0 | 0.0 |
| Country and western | 29 | 39.7 | 8 | 7.1 | 15 | 20.0 | 30 | 32.3 |
| Jazz | 3 | 4.1 | 17 | 15.0 | 7 | 9.3 | 18 | 19.4 |
| Classical | 0 | 0.0 | 0 | 0.0 | 1 | 1.3 | 1 | 1.1 |
| Other | 0 | 0.0 | 0 | 0.0 | 1 | 1.3 | 0 | 0.0 |
| Total | 73 | 99.9[a] | 113 | 100.0 | 75 | 99.9[a] | 93 | 100.1[a] |

$x^2 = 95.24$; df $= 18$; $p < .0001$ ($N = 354$).
[a]Rounding error.

mass audience out there. 'They are good, they are good, they are good!' . . . so it ultimately sinks in." Besides the elusive Top 40 hit, touring is the best way to create a following. It is grueling, arduous work.

Bruce Dickinson, lead singer of Iron Maiden, commented, "If radio won't play us, we won't get down on our knees and beg." Steve Harris, bass player, adds, "We do know from the records we sell and the number of kids that come to our concerts, we got a big following." "Yes never actually had a hit single," says Chris Squire. "I believe that the live show is something that people remember," observes Adam Ant, "and talk about in a way they don't talk about records or videos." Ant might add that he has experienced problems translating his stage persona to vinyl.

Derek Sutton, manager of Styx, discussed a 111-city tour: It "will result not merely in ticket, but also in album sales. . . . Styx is grossly under-reported and grossly underrespected."[19] Feelings about the road are mixed. Record companies insist on touring because, it is estimated, a concert increases product sales by 10 percent in the local area. Terry Knight with Grand Funk proved this formula. Musicians have mixed emotions on the subject. "We all love being out there," notes Loverboy Matt Frenette. They must, having played 137 concerts internationally in front of 1.7 million people. The Marshall Tucker band is equally enthusiastic: "I can't play enough of them," asserts Tommy Caldwell. "The people put you where you are. Sure, we get road weary, but that's not an excuse."

Others including some very big or "monster" artists are not quite as fond of the road. One member of a British band said, "It's a real killer." Another added, "It's something you have to do if you're going to play music. You go into a group knowing that you have to travel and move around. You just have to accept it." Randy Bachman recalls his days with BTO and the Guess Who:

> The worst I can remember is 93 one-nighters in a row. And it's just no fun anymore. A job is a job. You tell me about a job where you work 20 hours a day for 93 straight days away from people that you're familiar with. . . . It's really hard on you, it's like being in solitary and working. Trying to look happy trying to groove with all these kids, it was such a false thing. It was unbelievable, going out there trying to be cool and happy while you're crying on the inside. It was really, really tense; emotionally, physically, mentally, *and sooner or later it catches up with most groups.*

The road is a series of one-night stands. The acts travel from one Holiday Inn to another between jet flights. "It's all so horrible," says Ozzy Osbourne, "flying around and around, landing again. The hotel room's the same, everything's the same, the walls. It drives me mad."[20] Each stop involves the usual meetings with local radio people, deejays, writers, con-

cert-hall managers, and record-company promotion men. The band generally plays its current album, introducing each song, "This is from our . . .,"
or "We'd like to do some song from . . . ." The songs, the reporters'
questions all rapidly become identical.

Other superstars equally dislike the demands of the road. The Beatles'
film *Hard Day's Night* hinted at the pressures placed upon the act. Keith
Richard of the Rolling Stones complained about the "hangers-on" who
clutter dressing rooms and make a general nuisance of themselves—representatives of small radio stations or contributors to obscure magazines.
"It's hard to fuss if they want to know what's going on or if they just want to
be around for a second-hand thrill." He also objected to the over-
enthusiastic audience reaction the Stones frequently received. At one point
the band could not play more than three of four songs before the battle
between fans and police broke out. "Chaos," he said. "Police and too many
people fainting. . . . We'd walk into some of those places and it was like they
had the Battle of the Crimea going on. People gasping . . . nurses running
around with ambulances."[21]

George Harrison told biographer Hunter Davies:

> Then came touring which was great at first, doing an even shorter, more
> polished act and working out new songs. But it got played out. We got in a rut,
> going around the world. It was a different audience each day, but we were
> doing the same things. There was no satisfaction in it. Nobody could hear. It
> was just a bloody big row. We got worse as musicians, playing the same old
> junk every day. There was no satisfaction at all.

The late John Lennon: "It's like the Army, whatever the Army's like. One
big sameness which you have to go through. One big mess."[22]

Very few artists enjoy the luxury of such superstars as Bruce Springsteen,
Fleetwood Mac, or David Bowie. Bowie told a *Sun* reporter: "The last tour
[1978] was emotionally and physically a bad time for me and it's taken this
much time [not to mention movies] to get myself excited . . . to want to go
and play in front of people again." One aspect of the "Serious Moonlight
Tour" as opposed to the previous cross-country tour, according to Bowie,
was the support system:

> It's a very sophisticated, top-of-the-line touring situation here. On the last
> tour, it wasn't as big—the tour itself wasn't as big, we weren't carrying as
> many people. This time, I think we're carrying in excess of 150 people just in
> our immediate group.
>
> So we have a lot of people taking care of a lot of things: people who cut our
> hair, wardrobe mistresses, people who take care of luggage, our own account-

ant, our own administration traveling with us, our own security. We have our own jet. Everything is well-planned and well taken care of.[23]

Bowie on the 1983 "Serious Moonlight Tour" was estimated to be playing to 2.5 million people, each of whom paid an average of $15.00 a ticket. Led Zeppelin, the Rolling Stones, and the Jacksons have all grossed in the millions of dollars, but the sums are not as monumental as they appear to be.

In the summer of 1983 Denver promoter Barry Fey despairingly commented, "It is the summer we can't wait to be over."[24] All over the country promoters echoed this sentiment. Only David Bowie, the Police, and the temporarily reunited Simon and Garfunkel made big concert bucks. Others did not fare as well; Linda Ronstadt, Joni Mitchell, Rick Springfield, Marvin Gaye, and a host of others played to half-empty arenas. It was said that the late Gaye had been losing $30,000 and $40,000 a night for promoters. Other "sure sellouts" also disappointed promoters. *Billboard* reported that stars such as Men at Work, Stray Cats, the Hollies (with or without Graham Nash), Asia, and even Robert Plant could not fill an arena.

Paul Simon, embarking on a 1983, $4.5 million concert tour, told an interviewer, "You make a lot less money than people imagine. Of course it's a lot more money than teaching school. But it's not as huge as people read about the grosses."[25] Frank Barsalona, a major booking agent, agreed: "Led Zeppelin . . . [came] from England, so the band also has an American manager who gets 5 percent; the American agent receives 10 percent, and the English agent, who hasn't even picked up a phone also gets 10 percent."[26] The band's regular manager gets another 20 percent, leaving the act 55 percent with which to pay the costs of one road manager, three equipment movers and their salaries, transportation, accommodations, and other expenses. At a concert grossing $31,000, after commissions and expenses the group is left with $5,900 for a night's work. Led Zeppelin was, however, a super rather than average act. Since this statement prices have skyrocketed.

Paul Kantner, of the Jefferson Starship, does not concur. "I've always wanted to stay away from that sort of big killer tour. We don't play [tours] that much. That's why we're still not crazy . . . you can only use so much money. . . . We're at the place I'd like us to be."[27]

For established artists the monotony of repeating their successes is one of the more boring aspects of touring and a consistent source of conflict. Peter Townshend of the Who is expected to smash his guitar at every performance. He feels it detracts from his musicianship. "The actual performance has always been bigger than my own patterns of thought. . . . I think with guitar smashing, just like performance itself, it's a performance, it's an act, it's an instant and *it really is meaningless*."[28] Yet, people come to see the Who smash their instruments after playing "My Generation"; it is the Who's trademark.

Paul Simon said, "I always felt weird on the road. I was in a state of semi-hypnosis. I went into a daze and I did things by rote. . . ." Moreover, "I didn't want to sing 'Scarborough Fair' again. I didn't want to sing all of those Simon and Garfunkel songs every night. When you've developed, it's harder."[29] The late Janis Joplin, in discussing the breakup of Big Brother and the Holding Company, said almost the same thing: "By the end we were shucking. We worked four, six nights a week for two years, man, doing the same tunes. . . . I was jumping and dancing and all, but I was lying, and I'd go off stage and feel like the world's biggest bullshitter."[30] Rick Nelson in "Garden Party" summed up this feeling: "If memories were all I sang, I'd rather drive a truck." Despite the sentiments in the song, Rick sang "oldies" until his death in 1985.

Corb Donohue voiced a notion widely held in the industry on established artists and touring: "As a recording artist, you have an obligation to your audience to at least be conscious of their desires. You've got to play your hit, whatever it happens to be. . . . If a person comes and pays money, which you are getting a piece of, to see you work and you refuse to entertain him, then you are turning your back on the obligation as a popular artist." An agent said, "If people drive 150 to 200 miles to hear your hit, you'd damn better play it." Established artists may use the tour to increase their audiences and their bank accounts; newer acts must use the same avenue for recognition.

A warm-up act is usually a "live" sound check that the headliner was too occupied or lazy to do at the traditional 4:00 P.M. time slot. There are pros and cons about being an opening act. The advantage of opening for a "name" band, as Doug Gray, lead singer of the Marshall Tucker Band, suggests, "is to make them play that much harder." Eric Carmen explained the problems of opening: "When you're a number-two act you really have to knock yourself out and knock out the crowd to get anything at all. It gives you a little bit of a challenge because if you can do really well you might be able to do better than the top act." Bass player David Smalley interrupted, saying, "The odds are against you; it's a definite disadvantage. The people know you're the opening act, the warm-up act, and they accept you that way unless you really, really knock yourself out and pull things off to the best of your ability. And then, possibly, I'd say maybe 20-30 percent of the time, maybe 40, they'll give you a break. But other times it's really a disadvantage. I don't like it." Professional bands accept these conditions as part of the job. The singer noted, "These people are more of a challenge than people who are really with you. . . . If you can get a crowd like this going, then you've really done something. Crowds like this make you work harder."

There is another side to the story. Audiences are frequently hostile. Bills are balanced with two styles of music, but the audience out front generally comes to hear only one style or group. Writer Jerry Hopkins observed, "Today in concert situations, up to one-third to one-half of the audience is entering the theater during the warm-up act's performance."

At a Beach Boys concert, amidst the James Watt controversy (see chapter 8) Firefall was the warm-up act. A goodly portion of the surfing-sound fans got up and walked around; obviously the mixture was all wrong. Even with a recording contract dues must be paid and support obtained.

The economic mechanics of touring have changed significantly since the glory days of the past two decades. Tours are expensive and record companies, now budget conscious, are reluctant to pay the freight. For example, the 1 October 1983 issue of *Billboard* headlined "Fewer Acts Planning Big Fall Tours" next to "Labels Fire Hot Product Salvo." The old formula appeared to be breaking down; touring does not a hit record make. MTV was selling more records than even major market concerts (see chapter 7). Promoters were complaining that *too* many big names were competing with one another. One promoter objected, "Many of the cities were overworked." Another commented, "There is so much choice out there and everybody is a bit jaded." Wayne Forte, a major talent agent, added, "The concert dollars are the same, but the number of shows are increasing." That is the problem. Ticket prices tend to run, depending on the size of the market, from $10.95 to twice that amount, limiting the economic capability of a youthful consumer to attend. Toss in the cost of overpriced refreshments and T-shirts, and attendance is even more expensive. Then there is the controversial issue of the quality of the music and the arenas. Shelly Schultz of ICM states:

> A lot of promoters will have to start making sure that it is as important to think about the comfort of those in front of the stage as of the artists back-stage, he says. There are a lot of venues where you can look at some very unhappy faces. You can see the same rough security guys, the same funky toilets and the kids being mishandled. And then you go to the summer venues, and there's no hassles. There must be a reassessment of what goes up in front of the stage.

Ironically, while tours were being cut back, promoters of the record companies were gearing up for the 1983 holiday season with gusto. Nearly every superstar was to have a release. This practice is common because the vast majority of record sales take place between September and the beginning of January. Touring is in part now being subsidized by other sources. Ironically, the same process that promoters have decried is now associated with the avalanche of "monster" albums appearing during the holiday rush. Beginning with the Beatles' white double-album record, companies have used *Bangla Desh*, *Kiss*, and other titles to crowd out the competition.

Since the 1980s artists have turned to large corporations to be on the road. One writer in the *New York Times* called it "three-piece suit rock." At one point the franchising of artists was almost totally tied to the teenybop idol; posters, lunchboxes, and every conceivable saleable item were advertised in *Fave* or *Tiger Beat*. The times and the economy have changed. In 1982 sales of T-shirts at concerts reached approximately $150 million. For example, superstars Hall and Oates on their 1983 tour sold such items as a nylon-satin jacket ($45), a sweatshirt ($15), a baseball jersey ($11), a T-shirt ($8), and an "official" concert program ($4) and button ($2).

Major corporations are subsidizing artists to promote their products. A short list of acts hyping nonmusical goods include Air Supply for Jordache; the Rolling Stones and Kenny Rogers for Jovan; ZZ Top and the Who for Schlitz; Hall and Oates for Canada Dry; the Charlie Daniels Band for United States Tobacco; and Eric Clapton for R.J. Reynolds.[31] The rationale of these and other corporations was summarized by Bill Graham: "It took the major corporations years . . . to realize who their audience was. . . . These are the people who buy jeans and stereos, and drink soda and beer. In terms of demographics it is a perfect audience." Air Supply reportedly sold out its records and *2,500* pairs of Jordache jeans at a Tampa shopping mall. Brewing companies have supported tours by not only the Who and ZZ Top but the Charlie Daniels Band, Iron Maiden, and a host of others. The reason is simply that 60 percent of beer sales are concentrated in the 18-to-34 demographic range.

There have been objections to the apparent merger of "Corporate America" and rock music. One group sees the alliance as totally the exploitation of the rebellious nature of the roots of rock, Presley and the Woodstock Nation. Critic Dave Marsh objected:

> Why have such companies as Miller, Schlitz, and Camel taken up sponsorship so heavily in recent years? Precisely because of the moral authority which rock holds for its listeners. It means something important for a brewery to acquire henchmen as powerful as Townshend, especially since one of the goals of all addictive substance manufacturers is indoctrination.

> Anyone who thinks that corporations don't censor the events they sponsor is dreaming. Hall and Oates are sponsored by seemingly harmless Canada Dry, which resulted in Scandal being dropped as opening act for their Philadelphia show because Scandal is sponsored by a rival ginger ale. I defy any sponsored group to attack alcohol, tobacco addiction or the conditions under which their product is made, on stage or on record.[32]

Ironically, *Record* magazine refused to run this column of Marsh's (see chapter 6). Conversely, Eric Clapton's affiliation with tobacco giant R. J. Reynolds created a minor outcry when *Money & Cigarettes* was released. A CBS executive told a reporter, "The whole Clapton thing shows how harmful these associations can be."[33] (R. J. Reynolds was picking up the tour tab that CBS was not willing to pay for.)

Touring is boring, but can be economically quite profitable especially for the so-called superstars. A few groups have *grossed* millions on the road. However, as Led Zep's situation indicates, agents, promoters, and a coterie of other people receive a large piece of the economic pie.

### With a Little Help from My Friends?

Management is one of the catch-22s of the music business. Most working bands do not have a professional manager. Phil Hoffman of London Boys, its unofficial manager, says, "We've never looked for a manager, or considered getting a manager the entire time of our existence." Yet, it is at the "working" level when an honest, knowledgeable manager can be most helpful. Decisions about direction, professionalism, and myriad dilemmas must be made.

Unfortunately, the better management agencies have clients more lucrative than bar bands, and the latter are not worth their time or effort. Ironically, it is in the developmental phases of artists' careers that management is important. The managers who do represent bar bands are rarely the cream of the crop, nor are they always very honest. Some will sign any performers on the remote possibility they just might make it someday—more or less on their own.

The contract below is an actual contract; the names have been changed to protect the not so innocent.

AGREEMENT

AGREEMENT made this _____ day of _____ 1984 and between GEE GOLLY PRODUCTIONS INC., Hollywood, California, and SUPERSTAR, USA.

NOW THEREFORE, in consideration of the foregoing and of the mutual promises hereinafter set forth, it is agreed:

1. Whereas Superstar agrees to the terms set forth in the ensuing agreement, terms for all services rendered (by Gee Golly Productions), a fee of 30% (percent) shall be paid to Gee Golly Productions.

2. Whereas Gee Golly Productions shall be the management company for Superstar, for a period of not less than 10 (ten) years, according to the date above, and ten years thereafter.

3. Whereas Superstar shall be held responsible for all of his own equipment.

4. Whereas Superstar gives Gee Golly Productions the full power of attorney, in the event of his absence, for the signing of copyrights, etc., etc.,

This agreement shall be binding upon and insure to the benefit of the respective parties hereto, and represents the entire understanding between the parties. If any part of this agreement shall be invalid or unenforceable, it shall not affect the validity of the balance of this agreement.

IN WITNESS WHEREOF, the parties hereto, have entered into this agreement the day and year first written.

Pat Carr of *Country Music* cautioned, "Choosing a manager is the single most important career decision a musician has to make. Pick the wrong man, and you may end up with holes in your shoes, howling creditors and a bundle of legal/financial problems difficult enough to send you back to pumping gas—and just when you thought that you were just about to move on to a house in Woodstock."[34]

Van Morrison, recalling the early days of his career, did not want to mention names or offend anybody in the business, but "it just put me in some awkward positions, because they were *unreal*—like lip-synching to the record on a television show. I can't lip-synch, 'cause every time I do a song I do it differently. I just can't sing any song the same way twice. Obviously it was what *they* wanted, but they didn't want *me*. They had some kind of singer in mind for that, but it wasn't me. I just couldn't do that kind of thing."[35]

A band with a large following and recognized potential for superstardom not infrequently experiences the same dilemma. The Grateful Dead, still one of the top road acts in the business, was given a contract by Warner and a $10,000 advance—$3,500 for signing; $6,500 when it sold 10,000 records. Two years later the band was $180,000 in debt. Of this $80,000 was wasted on the preparation of *Aoxomoxoa*, its third album. Jerry Garcia explained to *Rolling Stone* how it happened:

> See, our managers were Rock Seully and Danny Rifkin who were really our friends and they were a couple of heads, ole-time organizers from the early Family Dog days and they agreed to sort of manage us. . . . They weren't too experienced at it and we weren't too experienced at it and so all we really managed to do in that whole world was get ourselves incredibly in debt, just amazingly in debt in just about two years.[36]

The next manager of the Dead was dismissed for misappropriation of funds. Some five years after the Warner signing, the Dead was finally free of debt.

Elvis Presley, according to court transcripts and biographers, was either mismanaged or bilked out of millions of dollars. Tom Parker allegedly took 50 percent of the singer's income. An out-of-court settlement was reached in 1983; Parker agreed to discontinue his involvement with the Presley estate. Very few stories of this kind have a similar happy ending, for not many acts have the staying power and industry of the Dead or, occasionally, Presley.

Picking the right management and a willingness to work for exposure are essential for an act that aspires to success. Most companies' view of a marketable act hinges upon these two variables: the management and the direction of the agency affiliation, and the mobility and flexibility of the act. There is a love-hate relationship among the artist, manager, and record company. Rick Springfield remembered, "I'll never forget watching my shaking hand reaching to pick up the phone to say I want out."[37] Bruce Springsteen, Billy Joel, and others have experienced the same thing. Artists are equally unhappy about record companies. Peter Banks explained, "They don't want to put a lot of money into a new band unless they can see some return. As soon as they see a return coming in they start with the promotion. I think that was the problem with Atlantic. They sort of put us on one side. They had Led Zeppelin; we were on the bottom of the pile."

One of the difficulties is the size of the roster. A Warner publicist said, "We're overextended." Brownsville Station, one of a number of acts to leave Warner is still bitter. Cub Koda said, "When we went to Burbank and were playing at the Whiskey, we went down to the offices and never even got past the lobby. They didn't even know who we were. That's rough. And so you say, well what do you want to do, go around saying that you're Warner Brothers' recording artists, when it doesn't do you any good?"

Mickey Lutz: "I'll give you a good example of getting buried in the shuffle. When's the last time you heard a Dionne Warwick song since she signed with Reprise?" "Who?" answers Cub. "Exactly, now what about Moby Grape?"

Ray Davies of the Kinks told writer Bill Small, "Those guys are bastards, ain't they?" He went on to say Warner was "too big," causing the Kinks to lose their identity. The Kinks received no promotion until six months before their contract was up for renewal. They have done much better with Arista.

Managers of low-level acts frequently object to the unprofessional attitudes and actions of performers. One former manager of bar bands notes, "I can't get them to a photographer for a promo photo or to sit down and write a bio. Rehearsing and equipment problems are a constant source of difficulty. With one client I went through the misery of his two marriage settlements, x number of things he didn't need *or* afford."

Managers, whose philosophy is "What have you done for me today?" do not have many kind words for record companies. Dan Holloway of Plimsouls described Elektra/Asylum: They "want to see an indication of success before they do any work."[38] catch-22? One manager has observed that getting the record company "behind an artist" was his most difficult task. Publicity directors, especially at the larger companies, faced with competing demands from artists and agents, make decisions based upon "the bottom line," that is, based on profit or loss margins.

The executives at "Black Rock"—CBS—and Hollywood do not quite see it in the same terms. A former A & M executive outlined the problems with managers and agents:

> When they start trying to buck it [the company] then that's really hurting themselves. "What are you, crazy? Hey this isn't going to get you anywhere; it's not going to get your artist anywhere. And everybody's doing as much as they can for that particular artist and what else do you want us to do." We'll listen. If it's within the realm of possibility, we'll do it. But if it's not, forget it.

A & M, which prides itself on having a smooth-running, cohesive company, especially resents agents' unprofessionalism. The executive continued:

> We have gotten a lot of managers here that started in this office and moved on to graphics, and then promotion, and then to merchandising, and they've got a different story and a different approach to each department. But what they don't realize is that immediately after they've been in here, we call ahead and let the other department know that so-and-so's on his way over and the situation.

At every level from A&R (artists and repertoire) to marketing and publicity, an executive has a horror story about an agent. Some of these stories, as Dennis Killeen, once at Capitol, aptly stated, are cop-outs for some other company failure, but many have substance. David Anderle, an independent producer, tells of the agent who demanded to "mix" his act's record. One manager dealing with Capitol insisted upon designing his performer's jacket cover. Joe Smith observed:

> You sign an act, the management gets all over you, and it will make you crazy right from the start. Everybody's pushing and pressing and they create a law of diminishing returns right here. By their pushing, people respond less. By terrorizing kids who work here writing ads and things, they've now got those kids so they'll write crappy ads . . . and all the life juices will be sucked out of them. Roy Silver would say, "Hey, whatever you guys want to do, go do."

Conversely, a publicity director at Shelter Records noted that many agents are not "on top of it" because they do not follow the progress of their artists' records. More commonly, agents are seen as actually inhibiting the direction of performers' careers. Mauri Lathower, Capitol's former head of A&R, lamented,

> Managers are for the most part lame. Very unprofessional. . . . We just had a case of a group working at a club and the group should have been grateful that they were working. The group was so loud that people almost ran out; this was not a small club. And the manager says the club was wrong. And I say, "Hey, you have to adjust to the club. The club cannot adjust to you. You're not being professional about it." So what happened? You'll never go back there again.

Refusing to adjust to a club or not working in a club that is not "right" strongly violates the work-exposure ethic of the industry; the artist in question is no longer with Capitol. Yet numerous agents have done just that.

Some agents and management firms, such as Jerry Weintraub and Bill Graham, have been singled out as exceptions but, overall, performer management is a sour note to nearly everyone in the music business. Part of the reason is that many agents are neophytes. They lack the experience and the ability to communicate with business executives who are philosophically far removed. Bill Graham, since the days of the Fillmore, has screamed that agents and managers are not professional. Joe Smith again: "Many older people are promoters. . . . So if some straight kid isn't able to establish any level of dialogue with that, then he's less than a good manager." Attorney Richard Schulenberg also pointed to the communication problem of the artist and agent at Columbia Records: "You have the corporation being faced with this long-haired freak who mumbles jargon and whose language is incomprehensible to them saying that he's being ripped off because he didn't get paid for something and the company doesn't understand . . . is unable to develop the emotional understanding that that artist relies on us to support him." Because of these conflicts many companies such as Warner and A & M all insist upon professional management. Joe Smith: "Everybody used to have managers before, and then when you got rock groups, some kid who was their friend was their manager, and it didn't seem to be terribly important who managed them, if they had a hit or their records made it. But it soon became very competitive and good management made a difference."

Billy James describes a similar attitude, "Record companies now want to have as much support around the musicians as is available. By support I mean are they good live, are they professional live, do they have an employment agent booking for them, do they have a personal manager for advice and council and baby-sitting, do they have a bondsman, just how together are they." In the opinion of record-company executives, "It's the management's responsibility to get that act booked, . . . to get them working."

Most agents and managers, according to musicians and record-company spokesmen, are, in one voice, "incompetent" and "unprofessional." Some musicians might add "dishonest" to the list. However, as a CBS executive remarks, "If you're selling a million units at a lick, any album that comes out, no matter how much trouble you offer, for some reason you're not accounted to be a pain in the ass. If you're selling 40,000 units, and you're doing the same thing, no one wants anything to do with you, because you're not worth the trouble. Economics, again, is the deciding factor in who is and who isn't a pain in the ass."

Management since the days of the counterculture has become considerably more sophisticated, with corporate and copyright lawyers becoming an integral part of the industry—much to the chagrin of many industry executives. Also, many prestigious talent agencies, such as William Morris, no longer look down upon long-haired lead guitar players as freaks to be avoided. Still, the conflict persists over the same issue: money. The unprofessional roadies *qua* managers may be history, but the "new breed" repeats the same question, "What have you done for my artist today?" The cop-outs of the 1960s don't work quite as well in the 1980s; there are legal clauses to contend with by people who *really* know what they mean. Some artists resent the legalism of the current system. One commented, "Lawyers, company lawyers, what's that got to do with music?" Everything!

### Summary

The recognition of talent is relative and time bound. "The time of an act," to paraphrase Proust, "must have come" for it to be a success, at least according to many observers in the music industry. Dennis Killeen argues that the phenomenal success of America was one of timing. "Crosby, Stills, Nash and Young," he says, "didn't have a record out for a year and a half." The logic is that America filled the void. Elton John's Los Angeles success was explained in similar terms by Donohue: "The press and radio were so desperately looking for a super hero." The advent of MTV and the financial straits of the music industry created a new dimension of exposure for certain visually attuned acts. "Culture Club would still be in London dives," noted an executive, "if it hadn't been for Boy George *and* MTV." *Guitar Player*, a magazine addressed to amateur and professional guitarists, advised its readers:

> One of the most crucial factors of a group's success is timing. It is the most ambiguous as well as the most mysterious factor in music. If your group had entered the scene a little too early (the original Byrds) or a little too late (Dave Clark Five), your chances for survival were few. Whether or not you liked the

Top 40's groups or top underground stars of the day, you still studied their style and songs, not so closely as to let them completely influence you, but just close enough to know what their sound was doing on the market; whether it was rising on the charts or not. You also learned to tell whether or not a group would succeed, with reasonable accuracy.[39]

AM program directors at radio stations, especially those with formulas like the Top 40, generally support the notion of timing's importance, for they have only three or fewer vacant slots in their playlists and these are filled by different genres of songs. Three singles by folk-rock acts or Motown stars would find two of them being discarded. The mystique of timing and luck is weighed by many industry spokesmen against hard work and perseverance, in the best sense of the Protestant ethic, as the key to success. One writer said, "Horatio Alger is not dead, he is alive and well in Hollywood." Roy Silver, with a track record that lends credibility to his words, insists that "it's all very logistical. We want to make it into some great esoteric mystery mystique. Nobody wants to do the work." Silver's argument has considerable merit in that a group's longevity increases its probability of success. Recognition must occur in the early phases of an act's career. The leap from bar band to stardom is more a product of working than it is at the recording level.

The apprenticeship of the performers of popular music is long and arduous. Most begin in their teens with high school bands, later going on to clubs and college dances. Groups form and dissolve, and many fall by the wayside. To survive the rigors of the early years, performers must have the desire to make it, exhibiting many of the straight-world virtues lauded by Horatio Alger. As the act rises, the demands to work become greater. Landing a recording contract is but a small step on the way to success. Touring is essential, and the road is hard. Going from second place to the top of the bill also requires long, arduous work. Coupled with all of these demands are many conditions over which the performer has no control. As one experienced rock musician put it, "The only thing that we can control is our performance." The perception of the audience, media appreciation, and, indeed, timing and the state of the industry are all beyond the power of the artists. The artists are the product and the beginning of the chain. Their voice and sound constitute what is in the grooves. Before talent can be evaluated by the record-buying public the artists must go through a number of channels over which they have little or no authority, beginning with what many ironically feel is the major obstacle to stardom: the record company.

## Notes

1. Quoted in Paul Grein, "Shankman, De Blasio Tackle the Unusual," *Billboard* 7 March 1984, p. 31.

2. George Melly, *Revolt into Style* (Garden City, N.Y.: Anchor Books, 1971), p. 42.
3. Robert Hilburn, "The Go-Go's Going Strong," *ASCAP in Action*, Winter 1982.
4. Quoted in Anthony Scadato, *Bob Dylan* (New York: Grosset & Dunlap, 1972), p. 22.
5. Quoted in Maureen Orth, "He Prefers Rock to His Role," *TV Guide*, 17 July 1982, p. 30.
6. Portions of this section are taken from R.S. Denisoff and John Bridges, "Popular Music: Who Are the Recording Artists?" *Journal of Communication* 32 (Winter 1982): 132-42. Also see H. Stith Bennett, *On Becoming a Rock Musician* (Amherst: University of Massachusetts Press, 1980).
7. Quoted in Ronald Zalkind, *Getting Ahead in the Music Business* (New York: Schirmer Books, 1979), p. 12.
8. Quoted in Tom Nugent, "Battle of the 'Unknowns': Taking Notice of New Talent," *Baltimore Sun*, 10 January 1983, p. B-6. See Diana Sward Rapaport, *How to Make and Sell Your Own Record* (New York: Quick Fox, 1980).
9. J. D. Considine, "'Home Tapes' Can Put Local Bands on the Air," *Baltimore Sun*, 2 September 1983, pp. B-1, B-6.
10. Kenny Rogers and Len Epand, *Making It with Music*, (New York: Harper & Row, 1978), p. 114.
11. "The Rockers Are Rolling It In," *Forbes*, 15 April 1973, p. 28.
12. See Laurel Jeff, "A Rock Band Finds Stairway to Stardom is Crowded and Steep," *Wall Street Journal*, 21 April 1981, pp. 1, 20.
13. Chet Flippo, "Rock Journalism and *Rolling Stone*" (M.A. thesis, University of Texas at Austin, 1974).
14. Quoted in Parke Puterbaugh, "Concert-611 Blues! Long, Cold Summer," *Rolling Stone*, 15 September 1983, p. 45.
15. Quoted in Grein, "Shankman, De Blasio Tackle the Unusual," p. 31.
16. Much of this discussion is based on Rogers and Epand, *Making It with Music*, pp. 114-17.
17. William Goodykoontz, "Becoming a Star: An Interactionist Perpsective on the Presentation of Onstage Identity" (Ph.D. dissertation, University of California, Riverside, 1979).
18. See William York, ed., *Who's Who in Rock Music*, rev. ed. (New York: Charles Scribner's Sons, 1982). Also Brock Helander, *The Rock Who's Who* (New York: Schirmer Books, 1982).
19. Quoted in Tony Scherman, "Rock 'n' Retail: Styx on Tour," *New York Times Magazine*, 16 August 1981, p. 38.
20. Quoted in Robin Green, "How Black Was My Sabbath," *Rolling Stone*, 28 October 1971, p. 41.
21. Robert Greenfield, "The Rolling Stone Interview: Keith Richard," *Rolling Stone*, 19 August 1971, p. 29.
22. Harrison and Lennon quoted in Hunter Davies, *The Beatles: The Authorized Biography* (New York: Dell, 1968), p. 241.
23. Quoted in J. D. Considine, "'Moonlight' Tour by David Bowie Is '83's Big Event," *Baltimore Sun*, 26 August 1983, pp. B-1, B-2.
24. Quoted in Puterbaugh, "Concert-611 Blues!" p. 53.
25. Paul Simon, "Today Show," NBC-TV, 20 July 1983.
26. Quoted in Ritchie Yorke, "Pop Music—A Mecca for Money Makers," *Los Angeles Times Calendar*, 14 December 1969, p. 50.
27. Quoted in Rob Howe, "Jefferson Starship Tangles with the Empire Again," *Baltimore Sun*, 23 August 1983, p. B-1.

28. "The Rolling Stone Interview: Peter Townshend," *Rolling Stone*, 14 September 1968, p. 10. Also Dave Marsh, *Before I Get Old: The Story of The Who* (New York: St. Martin's Press, 1983).

29. "The Rolling Stone Interview: Paul Simon," *Rolling Stone*, 20 July 1972, pp. 3, 38.

30. Quoted in Michael Lydon, "Every Moment She Is What She Feels," *New York Times*, 23 February 1969, p. 44.

31. Michael J. Specter, "Rock Puts on a Three-Piece Suit," *New York Times* 2 October 1983, p. F-4.

32. Dave Marsh, *Rock 'n' Roll Confidential* 5 (October 1983): 1.

33. Quoted in Specter, "Rock Puts on a Three-Piece Suit," p. F-5.

34. Patrick Carr, "The Manager: Da Guy with Da Money," *Crawdaddy*, August 1972, p. 30.

35. Happy Traum, "Van Morrison: The Interview," *Rolling Stone*, 9 July 1970, p. 31.

36. Charles Reich and Jann Wenner, "The Rolling Stone Interview: Jerry Garcia" (part 2), *Rolling Stone*, 3 February 1972, p. 32.

37. Quoted in Orth, "He Prefers Rock to His Role," p. 28.

38. Quoted in Jeff, "A Rock Band Finds Stairway to Stardom Crowded and Steep," p. 20.

39. "On Making It," *Guitar Player* 4 (April 1970): 23.

# 3

# The Star-Making Machinery: The Record Companies

*Sell your soul to the company*
*Who're waiting there to sell plastic ware.*

—© 1966 Tickson Music Co.

Creating a hit record or a headline act is akin to constructing a jigsaw puzzle. Unless all of the pieces are in their proper place the effort is futile. Some of the most important parts of the puzzle are the province of the record companies and the large conglomerates that handle nearly every aspect of the business. Bhasker Menon, chief executive officer of Capitol Industries, views the record company as having three capabilities: "*manufacture* efficiently to get product to those who choose to demand it; *persuading* purchase by consumer and customer; and for lack of a better word is the capability of *management.*" The company makes records, distributes them, and attempts to motivate the "folks out there" to buy the "product," as records are called in the music industry. Over $4 billion's worth of product is sold each year. Stan Cornyn adds another element to the definition:

> A record company is truly nothing but a ticket seller. It can be a good ticket seller, . . . I don't go around singing. I've often had a feeling just because I'm interested in spending my life intelligently and fruitfully, of—and ticket selling is not my idea of being the most fruitful thing in the world—of doing it better than other people have done it before.

Records and cassettes—act, disc, record jacket, notes, lyric insert—are the tickets, and the record company sells them to the public. Record companies are first and foremost large business enterprises governed by laws of profit and loss. In fact, they are much more attuned to the canons of laissez-faire than their counterparts in the auto or steel industries.

Record companies lack the market control of their corporate counterparts, adroitly described by economist John Kenneth Galbraith in the *New Industrial State.* A record company cannot "control the markets that it is presumed to serve and beyond, to bend the *customer to its needs*."[1] Discs and cassettes are a discretionary item, a product a consumer buys with leisure funds. Records are also in competition with all of the other entertainment media. A publicist notes, "The people who work for record companies are really no more informed or enlightened in their tastes than is the general public." Cornyn believes "there is no formula." The lack of any sure guideline has made the industry as uncertain of success as any of its artists. Obviously the Capitols, CBSs, RCAs, WCIs, and MCAs will survive long after their current crops of superstars are gone. Still, very few billion-dollar corporations in the United States would openly compare their efforts with dice-throwing. Think of the stockholders! A former West Coast director of business affairs for CBS Records argues:

> Our industry is a classic example of crap shooting. When you win, you win big. You can afford to take a 70 percent stiff ratio. On the three that make it you more than make up your cost and profit on the entire 10. And if you spend on 10 records, say a million dollars, and 7 of these records earns back $50,000 but on the other 3 you earn back one million dollars, you still have a $100,000 profit over the million. That's still a 10 percent profit. I would think that is one justification why record companies can operate the way we do without having outraged anguish from the stockholders.

The crap-shooting analogy is widespread in the record business. Producer Phil Spector uses it. Joel Vance, a former Buddah Group publicist said, "The record business is a gambler's business . . . if you're not willing to gamble, then you shouldn't be in the business."[2] Murray Ross: "To be in the rock and roll business . . . , you've got to be a 'total crap-shooter' with a good instinct for money management. . . ."[3] In dice rolling, winners and losers emerge. So it is in the music business. At each level, the element of chance, the futuristic imponderable is present. Each segment of the puzzle must jell. Otherwise, the ticket becomes a loss in the $2.99 discard or "cutout" bin at Woolworth's or K Mart. The elements of luck and timing are enormously important, yet it would be a mistake to treat record companies as the innocent victims of the caprices of Adam Smith's "invisible hand." The companies' business orientations and philosophies greatly color their performances at the vinyl crap table.

A company's ability to succeed determines its status in the industry. This status in turn accounts for its approach to record making and selling. Several companies, partially because of tradition, are believed to be "majors"; other companies, due to their corporate birth dates or specializations are not. Nonetheless, some designations are commonly employed in the industry.

### The Majors, Independents, and the Others

Of the ticket sellers listed in *Billboard's International Buyer's Guide* there are three or even four categories that surface. These are not always easily definable types, yet there do exist some discernible characteristics that can be of some value in clarifying this maze.

Arnold Shaw characterizes the majors—the larger and most stable record companies—as possessing their own distribution systems and pressing plants, and enjoying a high sales volume. All are owned by conglomerates that are diversified in commercial enterprises other than music. The Radio Corporation of America (RCA) is involved in economic endeavors ranging from telecommunications to major appliances. The Columbia Broadcasting System is a multifaceted corporation deriving a majority of its profits from its broadcasting operations, but it also manufactures Fender guitars and Steinway pianos, and is involved in publishing. The ever-expanding Warner Communications, Inc. (WCI), owns a film studio, a publishing house, and cable systems and networks, as well as *Mad* magazine. Decca's reincarnation is the Music Corporation of America (MCA), whose forte is film—Universal Pictures and television production and distribution—and sheet-music publishing. Capitol Records, part of the London-based Electric and Musical Industries, Ltd. (EMI), oversees tape and disc manufacture as well as Merco Enterprises, a major audio-retailing and rack-jobbing complex.

The majors are high-volume enterprises exhibiting large artist rosters and a plethora of musical genres and catalog titles. It is common for a major label to list thousands of record titles as being available in conjunction with its current releases. The sheer size of the majors traditionally has been a key factor in their approach to corporate gambling: "The more cards you draw, the better your chances of picking aces."[4] A $100,000 to $200,000 gamble with possible winnings in the millions means little to a corporation like CBS Records, which earned $100 million in 1983, thanks to Michael Jackson. Parent companies in conglomerate structures readily subsidize such "uncorporate" activities for tax purposes, although as the stakes get higher the accountants become very uneasy. Accounting departments, fixated by a "bottom-line" mentality, crave stability and predictability.

Consistency and durability involve several strategies. A major label must avoid putting all of its marketing stress on one style of music, regardless of its acceptance at a given historical point in time. A so-called "trend" like disco can disappear literally overnight. Dwayne Witten, an Arizona distributor, writes, "Those labels which have survived over the years are the ones which built broad-based catalogs of all types of music, so that even in lean times they still have product that is in demand."[5]

The majors, with the possible exception of MCA, catalog a large number of musical styles—classical, country and western, jazz, middle-of-the road, soul, reggae, gospel, and even more esoteric sounds. During bad times in the pop market, a major may have to rely upon these other genres to keep sales up. Executive misjudgments about trends and external events make this imperative. Country and western, and sound tracks from stage and film have literally provided the economic foundation for several companies such as Columbia during periods of business miscalculations and ensuing sales slumps. Putting all of a company's musical eggs in one basket can be a disaster, as the pre-rock period aptly illustrated.

### When You're Hot, You're Hot

In the 1920s Columbia and Victor and their subsidiaries—which occasionally sold through mail-order catalogs—all but controlled the music market. A decade later Jack Kapp entered the fray with the Decca label, now MCA. Capitol in 1942 joined in, followed by Mercury and others. Four labels all but dominated the market prior to the Presleys, Berrys, Dominos, and other rockers.

From 1948 through 1955, four companies (Columbia, RCA, Decca, and Capitol) placed over 75 percent of the records listed on the *Billboard* top-sellers chart. By 1958 they had less than 36 percent of the market. The reason for this downturn was that the majors were not producing what record-buying youth wanted. White-owned black independents such as Chess, Atlantic, Imperial, and Vee Jay moved into the void.

The record industry during the early 1950s was characterized by company preeminence over artists. Singers had five-year contracts and were tied to the dicta of the record company. The companies determined style, song, recording dates, and in some cases the artists' stage names. Record companies took over what had previously been the function of the big band. Orchestra arrangers during the swing era put words and music together. Frank Sinatra, Helen O'Connell, and others came as part of the total package, along with Tommy Dorsey, Harry James, or Benny Goodman. The demise of the big band altered this relationship, with the balladeer becoming more dependent upon the record company for orchestration, material, and direction. The artists-and-repertoire (A&R) director became an increasingly important figure. He was, as David Lawhon of Capitol observed, "the man with the feel of the public pulse." He picked the songs the artist would record. Stan Cornyn, then employed by Capitol, described the power of the A&R director:

> The company would pick out 12 songs for Peggy Lee and tell her to be at the studio Wednesday at 8, and she'd show up and sing what you told her. And she'd leave three hours later and Capitol'd take her songs and do anything it wanted to with them. Her art was totally out of her—the artist's—hands. . . . That was a time when the artist was supposed to shut up, and put up with anything the almighty recording company wanted.[6]

Five or six A&R men dominated popular music during the early Eisenhower years: Gordon Jenkins (Decca), Art Talmadge (Mercury), Hugo Winterhalter (RCA), Ken Nelson (Capitol), and Mitch Miller (Columbia). All of these men were musicians steeped in either the classics or big-band swing. The most successful A&R director was the goateed oboe player whose songs appeared on "Your Hit Parade" and record-sales charts.

Mitchell William Miller was the prototype A&R man of the 1950s. A graduate of the Eastman School of Music, Miller became the highest-paid oboe player in classical music history. In 1947 John Phillip Hammond brought him to Mercury Records as a contributing A&R director. Producing Frankie Laine, he turned out successive hits: "That Lucky Old-Sun," "Mule Train," and "The Cry of the Wild Goose." Columbia Records lured Miller to its ranks with a contract for $25,000 a year plus expenses. At Columbia, Miller could do no wrong. *McCall's* characterized him as "The Man Who Makes Money Records." *Saturday Evening Post* introduced him in a feature story by Dean Jennings as "The Shaggy Genius of Pop Music." Jennings, who normally reported on movie celebrities, wrote, "Miller's snap judgment on hidden talent is almost as *infallible* as a Geiger counter."[7] Between 1950 and 1956, Columbia sold 80 million records with the Miller imprimatur. At one point he had eight songs on the *Billboard* "Top Ten," and defeated Columbia arch rival RCA in the pre-rock-and-roll 1950s, annually placing more songs on the top twenty-five sellers. His selection of a Pittsburgh night watchman's song, "Cry," for an equally obscure singer, Johnnie Ray, earned Columbia $2 million. He transformed Anthony Benedetto into Tony Bennett and moved 1,500,000 units of "Because of You." He revived the innocuous Confederate marching chant, "Yellow Rose of Texas," earning a gold record. Norma Jean Speranza became Jill Corey and sold millions of records on the basis of an over-the-transom tape. He did similarly good things for the Four Lads, Jimmy Boyd, Guy Mitchell, Rosemary Clooney, and the one-hit sensation, Joan Weber.

In a 1955 *New York Times Magazine* article Miller elaborated on his "keep it sexy, simple and sad" formula of success. Acknowledging that there are "still mysteries and miracles" to producing hits, Miller outlined the basic ingredients for successful records:

> 1. *Self Identification.* The song says to the listener what the listener has in his own mind but can't quite put into words himself. It speaks for him of his own love, or sorrow. It recalls nostalgically an episode of the past, sweet or bitter. Thus, the listener identifies with the song.
>
> 2. *Universality.* In articulating his own emotions, the song makes the listener aware that he is not alone, that the singer too has the same misery or joy. And so do the millions of other people who rush out to buy that song.
>
> 3. *Simplicity.* The ability of the listener to hum the tune, and to pick up the lyric quickly is essential.[8]

The ideal songs to reflect those elements were about love, "boy longs for girl, girl longs for boy" and optimism. In the same article, Miller defended the then-emerging genre of rhythm and blues. He felt it was a youthful reflection of a concern with the plight of southern "colored people" as well as generational rebellion: "I would rather have a teenager express his defiance of authority by listening to a rhythm and blues record than by going out and knocking someone over the head." This lukewarm endorsement was offset by a statement of concern over singers like Doris Day, Jo Stafford, and Tony Bennett singing in a style that once [belonged] wholly to the Negro singers."

The following year, according to several Columbia executives, Miller was offered a singer who was considered a possibility for the country-and-western catalog. He passed on Elvis Presley. Several years later, Norman Petty, a Columbia artist, approached Miller with a demo record. Miller told the instrumentalist, "Don't waste your time on a group like this; they'll never make it." He was wrong again. The group in question was Buddy Holly and the Crickets, and the song was "That'll Be the Day." Rock impresario Don Kirshner recalls,

> In those days Mitch Miller had a strong position in the business. If he turned down a song you were in trouble. I brought "Will You Love Me Tomorrow" to him and he turned it down. But I wouldn't accept that. I felt it was a terrific song and a sure hit if it was done right. So I gave it to the Shirelles (and Phil Spector) and it became No. One.[9]

The deviant and foreign strains of "Sh-Boom" and "Rock Around the Clock" were originally hailed as fleeting novelties soon to join "The Thing" and "How Much Is That Doggie in the Window." To cope with the new "fad," A&R began to cover compatible black music with the pop crooning style.

The practice of "covering", singing or recording other people's songs, is as old as the music industry. In the late 1940s it was common to hear four or five stylized versions of the same hit song by former band singers. In the early 1950s covering appeared to take on an exploitive aspect when mainstream crooners, much to the delight of music publishers such as Acuff-Rose in Nashville, began to take country hits and rearrange them in a middle-of-the road motif.

A number of Hank Williams's songs were covered by Tony Bennett ("Cold, Cold Heart"), Polly Bergen ("Honky Tonkin'"), and several other pop stars. Copying black material, however, added the dimension of racial exploitation. A *Los Angeles Times* writer noted: "The prevailing racism on white-owned radio stations could never permit a black blues artist the time to communicate his music to white audiencès. Only safe Negroes like Nat (King) Cole and Ella Fitzgerald were given that privilege. None of that 'dirty music' could be allowed to sully the ears of young white females."[10] This sentiment has been echoed by many diverse writers of different ideological persuasions, ranging from Eldridge Cleaver and LeRoi Jones to English rock writer Charles Gillett. Nonetheless, there are many more persuasive arguments beyond the racist charge.

Censorship has been popularly pointed to as a prime reason for the practice. Charles Calhoun's "Shake, Rattle and Roll," for example, was originally designed for a black audience. Bill Haley and Milt Gabler changed the lyric "You wear low dresses, the sun comes shining through—I can't believe my eyes, all of this belongs to you" to "You wear those dresses, your hair done up so nice—you look so warm, but your heart is cold as ice." Most white teenagers originally thought the song was about a dance. Gabler, the song's producer, recalled: "If any of the lyrics were double entendre I would clean them up. I didn't want any censor with the radio station to bar the record from being played on the air. With NBC a lot of the race records wouldn't get played . . . because of the lyrics. So I had to watch that closely."[11] (The Midnighters' very straightforward song "Work with Me, Annie"—followed by "Annie Had a Baby (Can't Work No More)"—was transformed to "The Wall Flower" by black singer Etta James and popularized by white vocalist Georgia Gibbs as "Dance with Me, Henry." The connotation given to the designation "rock and roll" by singers such as Teresa Brewer, Pat Boone, Georgia Gibbs, and the "Your Hit Parade" staff was one of partying. When Shirley and Lee sang "Let The Good Times Roll" or "Rock All Night," they did not mean "I Could Have Danced All Night." The sexuality in some rhythm and blues numbers perhaps justified covering, but a cursory examination of other songs copied indicates that it could not have been the sole consideration.

Many rhythm and blues songs by black artists that were copied did not contain "offensive" lyrics. Totally innocent songs such as "Dance with Me, Henry" (despite its origin) and "Ko-Ko-Mo" were covered. Nearly all of the majors, with the notable exception of Columbia, developed their own rhythm and blues and rockabilly singers when the sales of covers no longer surpassed the original version. When the Penguins' "Earth Angel" outdistanced the Crew-Cuts, and LaVern Baker surpassed Georgia Gibbs's "Tweedle Dee," then, as Danny and Juniors would later sing, "Rock and Roll Is Here to Stay."

During this period, Columbia used Johnnie Ray to cover a Sun recording by the Prisonaires, "Just Walking in the Rain," but did little else in the rock-and-roll genre. At a disk-jockey convention sponsored by Todd Storz, the father of Top 40 progamming, Miller launched an all-out assault upon the radio format and rock music. He lectured the 850 deejays assembled:

> You carefully built yourselves into the monarchs of radio and then you went and abdicated your programming to the 8 to 14 year olds, to the preshave crowd that makes up 12 percent of the country's population and zero percent of its buying power—once you eliminate pony-tail ribbons, popsicles and peanut brittle. Youth must be served—but how about some music for the rest of us?

> Does the demand for the record come because you play it first, or do the kids demand it because they heard it first on Top 40? If Top 40 is an election, will somebody please blow a whistle for the Honest Ballot Association. . . . The 75 percent of the nation over 14 years old is buying hi-fi record players in unprecedented numbers, setting them up in the living room, shutting off the radio and creating their own home-made programming departments.

Alan Freed, who reportedly originated the term *rock and roll*, replied to Miller with equal passion:

> It sounds like sour grapes to me. I believe Mitch knows little about rhythm and blues and native American music. He's always been classically minded and my feeling is that he's a musical snob.

> How can he talk out of both sides of his mouth? On the one hand he's condemning rock and roll. On the other he has such rock and rollers as Otis Blackwell, Leroy Kirkland and Jessie Stone doing writing and managing jobs. . . . Let's face it, rock and roll is bigger than all of us. As my personal protest against Mr. Miller's speech, I'm hereby banning all Columbia and Date Records from my show.[12]

Freed's threat was an idle one, for the Columbia roster had little to interest the rock jock. History, of course, has proven Freed the winner, for Capitol, Decca, MGM, CBS, and many others attempted to find country singers who could emulate the rockabilly style as well as rhythm-and-blues and urban-blues sounds. The attempt generally failed. In 1956 the majors' market share had dropped to 55 percent. Columbia enjoyed half of that figure. The remaining 45 percent went to the independents and specialty labels.

## *"Indies"*

The independent labels, or "indies," are the most difficult to define and the most confusing. Even Arnold Shaw shies away from attempting a definition. They are generally smaller in size, have to depend on others for the pressing of records, national distribution, and at times marketing. These smaller companies frequently match the majors in sales. In 1978 Robert Stigwood's RSO all but controlled the charts with singles and albums from the sound tracks from *Saturday Night Fever* and *Grease*.[13] Five years later RSO was absent from *Billboard's* listing of the top ten labels. Stigwood's label is classified as an independent, despite its moment in the sun, because it lacks the properties that characterize the majors. Still, some companies such as A & M, Motown, Arista, London, Fantasy, and others feature several musical genres, including soul, jazz, disco, and MOR, plus contemporary rock.

Historically, most labels began as independents—with the exception of Columbia and Victor, the pioneers in the industry. Only a handful reached the status of a major because most rose and fell depending on musical trends or absorption by a major. Warner Communications and MCA are unique examples of this upward mobility or change of status. Most independents do not change categories unless a large infusion of conglomerate money and chart success occurs.

## *Specialties*

Specialty labels concentrate on a given genre, usually with limited resources and a small roster of artists. Most of these labels have a unique focus such as the rhythm-and-blues companies of the 1950s and, of course, the yellow Sun label from Memphis, the cradle of rockabilly. During the 1960s and 1970s many of these minor labels were swallowed up by the majors or they contented themselves with a low-budget, limited-sales product. Few of these labels earn much money. Executives at Rounder and Alligator have called their activities "a labor of love," much to the dismay of their more commercial counterparts. Bruce Iglauer, president of Alligator, said he was happy to break even on a title. He wrote, "Our average sales vary from as few as 3000 LPs to as many as 30,000. Koko (Taylor) sells 10,000 copies." Koko is probably Alligator's best-known founding artist. A Rounder spokesperson, then a bluegrass communal company, shocked a panel of industry executives by saying, "We don't care if we make any money." Since that statement, Rounder obtained the U.S. rights to the recordings of guitarist Peter Green, a founding member of Fleetwood

Mac. Rounder's basic concentration still remains bluegrass and urban grass.

Specialty labels do not have the expenses or corporate demands of the majors or large independents. Alligator's costs, for example, are significantly less than those of the major labels. Iglauer provides the following cost breakdown:

Studio: $4,000-$9,000
Musicians' advance: usually around $5,000 for the whole band
Cover photo and design: $700
Color separations: $800
Jacket printing: $1,600
Initial pressing: $4,200
Promotional mailing: $1,500
Follow-up marketing, phone promotion, advertising, etc.: $8,000

This totals at the maximum around $30,000, about half of what a four-minute clip, produced by a major, costs for MTV.

It is tempting to dismiss these Davids competing with corporate Goliaths, but the impact of specialty labels has been economically and historically noteworthy. As writer Robert Palmer suggests, "The rise of rock 'n' roll in the 50's reflected a rise in the popularity of southern music . . . and of the scrappy independent record companies that were willing to record music New York based companies like Columbia and RCA had dismissed as noise."[14]

Rock music and jazz on specialty labels did affect the majors, and much of this music was of the cult variety. In the early 1980s Band X sold nearly 100,000 units. The Sugar Hill Company in New Jersey featured groups such as the Funky Four Plus One, the Furious Five, and Grandmaster Flash with some local success. Should a "Third Coming" occur in the music industry, the specialty labels are most likely to be the genesis of the trend. The Beatles' first American single was on Vee-Jay, not Capitol. Presley started with Sun Records.

Independent production companies such as Swan Song, IRS, Rolling Stones, 415, Grunt, Lone Star, Apple at one time, and others usually feature fewer than five artists. The Rolling Stones, Jefferson Starship, Led Zeppelin, all owned their labels and usually were distributed by major companies. Some majors like this arrangement, especially with artists who are viewed as unreliable, temperamental, and troublesome. One executive said, "They bring me the finished tape, we'll put it out. If not . . ." 415, originally a new wave label with Romeo Void in the beginning, according to Steve Seid, began producing "marketable products for insignificant sums [albums recorded for $3,000 to $5,000]," and was approached by major labels. In 1982 it signed with Columbia because "CBS is the best label." However, company President Howard Klein stressed the continuing independence of 415. The signing, he said, was "no sellout."

Independent production companies can enjoy a considerable amount of autonomy and irresponsibility. Several important ones, like the Beatles' ill-fated Apple and Phil Walden's Capricorn, went broke because of either mismanagement (Apple) or overexpansion (Capricorn, in Macon, Georgia). Walden recently revived the label. This type of operation is definitely a Janus type of structure.

### The Buckshot Theory of Record Releasing

The size and economic power of the majors traditionally has been a key factor in their approach to corporate dice playing. Unlike their smaller counterparts, they have greater resources to spend and consequently try more often to win big. Yet, despite the obvious advantages of size, the bonuses are not as decisive as one might expect.

Of every ten records released, only one or two are profitable. Thus large companies must produce massive amounts of product to sustain their corporate structure. Huge investments are made and must be maintained. A concentration upon proven talent, coupled with the 8 to 2 ratio, motivates the larger companies to treat newcomers indiscriminately, at the same time competing with each other for sure-fire sellers. According to rock historian Mike Ochs:

> They need that, they have to have that. Columbia owns all their own distributors. They've got like hundreds and hundreds of people employed, so that the guy in St. Louis works only on Columbia product. So to keep that kind of major overhead up, it's got to have a lot of superstars. They can't afford not to have like ten to twenty acts that sell a million out because they have all that *machinery that has to keep going.*

Joe Smith: "In this business you only need a few winners to make up for a lot of losers." Or in the words of Joel Vance, "Every record you sell, when it begins to pay for itself, is also paying for the records that don't make it." Another executive remarks, "A company the size of Capitol Records needs twenty LPs per month to support the overhead or 4,000 people get spooky." Capitol operates on what is called Formula 10. The company's marketing department believes that in 10 releases at least one should pay for the "stiffs"—those that do not return the initial investment. Other majors follow an identical philosophy. CBS Records uses a similar ratio, although publicly denying the practice. One title pays for at least eight commercial failures with luck or hype riding on the other. The key to the formula is the few superstars. Performers like Kenny Rogers, Michael Jackson, Willie Nelson, Stevie Wonder, Bruce Springsteen, and several others pay the corporate bills.

In the heyday of the Beatles, Capitol had nothing to worry about. If a record stiffed so what! The next Beatles effort would more than pay the rent and the salaries. This approach, while not endearing to the losers, did work for most companies until the ranks of universally acclaimed artists began to dwindle. The untimely deaths of Janis Joplin, Jimi Hendrix, and Jim Morrison, not to mention the demise of many star-quality bands made the sure-fire seller a highly desirable entity in the 1970s and beyond—especially for large companies with very high overheads. With these facts, only one conclusion is realistic: in the record business the established artist with a long list of gold singles or albums is in the driver's seat. Superstars get "what they want" says Bob Siner. Companies like WCI, RCA, MCA, and especially Columbia have invested vast sums of money in buying one another's fair-haired performers. CBS signed the Rolling Stones to a $28 million pact. Letting someone *else* take the risks and internal structural imperatives are the concerns that propel the star-buying machinery.

The majors have a dismal history in anticipating stardom and trend setters. Bob Rolontz (WCI) stated: "Trends are set by artists. Record companies can't make trends."[15] Companies tend to be basically *reactive*, rarely innovative; they will get "behind" an artist whose record is bulleting up the charts or sign an established trendsetter. At times they go after clones of a superstar or create one. In 1955 a former hawker for a medicine show walked into Mitch Miller's Columbia office and played a record for him. "Not bad," said the hottest producer in the business. "How much?" "Thirty-five thousand dollars," came the reply. "Nobody is worth that much money." Colonel Parker took Presley elsewhere.

Steve Sholes, a Nashville producer for RCA, signed Presley while complaining to friends his job was on the line. "Heartbreak Hotel" exonerated his stresses and anxiety. Capitol followed suit, acquiring Gene Vincent and Tommy Sands. Even Columbia went south, recruiting Johnny Cash as the "New Elvis." Later Ronnie Self ("Bertha Lou") became its "new hope." Liberty discovered Eddie Cochran and Jody Reynolds, and MGM transformed Harold Jenkins into Conway Twitty. RCA hoped lightning would strike twice and spent $100,000 promoting David Houston as the successor to Presley. Most of these singers lacked, at least for traditional A&R people, the professionalism attributed to the older crooners. Many record executives used this charge to validate their disdain of the new sound. Nonetheless, the ticket-selling function went on. Young teenagers were scooped up from the sidewalks of Philadelphia on the basis of their personal ap-

pearance and transformed into overnight idols on *American Bandstand.*
Some could not even sing. Bill Parson's "All American Boy" was recorded
by Bobby Bare and then played on the Dick Clark program as the real
thing. Echo chambers and other production devices became the rule. The
smaller labels still benefited from the majors' inability to cope with the
rock-and-roll phenomenon. The advent of the Beatles further complicated
the role of the major companies.

The success of the Beatles and a host of other English bands found the
major recording companies in the same position they were in in 1956,
when Presley was termed a passing fancy. This time the industry understood what was happening. Billy James described the climate of the time:
"There was nothing else happening in America then that anybody capitalized on. The Spoonful were in New York at that time but hadn't quite
gotten it together. The Airplane were in San Francisco, but hadn't gotten it
together. Those things were happening but nobody was into them." Billy
James and Terry Melcher introduced a new domestic rock group to Columbia Records, which had not experienced a "number-one" single in the
two years since Steve Lawrence's "Go Away, Little Girl," a middle-of-the-
road ballad. Billy remembers, "So we were lucky enough, the Byrds were
lucky enough to get with Columbia, to get me and Terry to appreciate what
they were doing, we were lucky enough, Columbia was hungry at the time."

The Byrds were joined by Paul Revere and the Raiders and a hundred
other bands aspiring to become the American "Golden" Beatles. The Electric Prunes, the Standells, the Vagrants, the Barbarians, Count Five, Shadows of Knight, the Mojo Men, and many others entered the race to record
one charted single or also-ran and then to disappear. Many of these bands
served as training grounds for some of the acts in the post-Monterey Pop
Festival era. All of them were minus the commodity record executives call
"professionalism." Critic and guitarist Lenny Kaye describes what A&R
confronted:

> Most of these groups (and by and large, this was an era dominated by groups)
> were young, decidedly unprofessional, seemingly more at home practicing
> for a teen dance than going out on national tour. . . . They exemplified the
> berserk pleasure that comes with being on-stage outrageous, the relentless
> middle-finger drive and determination. . . . And as these were kids who more
> often than not could've lived up the street, or at least in the same town, there
> was no question what even localized success could mean in terms of universal
> attraction. Elvis had shown us the first time around that rock's greatest
> strength has always been as catalyst, and with a whole new generation waiting
> out there to be worked on, there could be little doubt that something big was
> about to erupt.[16]

Bidding wars in the United States did not get going until the "Summer of
Love" when every company wanted an acid band from Haight Ashbury in

its catalog. The Grateful Dead and Jefferson Airplane had already been snapped up by Warner and RCA, although they really did not know what they were getting into. The second-generation bands did pretty well. Steve Miller and Quicksilver both got in the neighborhood of $75,000 out front. This in contrast to the Dead's standard $10,000. "We were signing most brand-new artists in those days," according to one president, "for five or ten thousand."[17] Monterey would change all of this.

The International Monterey Pop Festival began 16 June 1967, running three days and attracting 50,000 spectators, including most of the high rollers in the record industry. As most recall, their minds and checkbooks were expanded at that affair. Clive Davis, one of the bigger spenders, commented, "It all began for me at the 1967 Monterey Pop Festival." Here Janis Joplin, Jimi Hendrix, and a host of bands were discovered. The bidding for Joplin and Hendrix went well into the six-figure range; Davis signed Joplin for a quarter of a million dollars. More significantly, the high-stakes players discovered a youth audience that would change their marketing techniques and give rise to Craig Karpel's "hip capitalism."

Given the socio-cultural excitement of the music, most of the corporate bets originally paid dividends. "All this led," according to Davis," to a tidal wave of new music and, by no coincidence, to a happy explosion on Columbia's bottom line, jumping sales profits from five to more than fifty million dollars a year by . . . 1973 . . . I had sensed that Columbia had no choice but to change or suffer."[18]

Monterey and subsequent festivals, especially Woodstock, catapulted signing prices. Corporations and Wall Street money managers fueled the bidding wars for new and old talent. An opinion-making financial publication said, "Most *Forbes* readers may shudder at the sound, but today's popular music has pierced the Iron Curtain and made millionnaires out of dozens of performers and businessmen who have yet to see their 30th birthdays."[19] *Fortune* 500 members, such as Gulf-Western and Trans-America, entered the fray. The stakes, having grown tremendously, made established stars all the more valuable when some of the increasingly more expensive new acts did not pan out.

Clive Davis used good and bad judgment in luring people to Black Rock. Joplin proved to be a short-lived legend and gold mine. Columbia took a beating on Moby Grape, a highly talented San Francisco band, which suffered the ineptitude of the company's first psychedelic promo effort. Nobody believed the band was as good as advertised. Laura Nyro, Bonnie and Delaney, the Association, and Tom Rush were bad investments. A week after Bonnie and Delaney signed with the label, the stormy globe-trotting couple broke up.

Its San Francisco acquisitions were disappointments for Capitol. By the time the Steve Miller and Quicksilver albums hit the racks, the glamor of acid rock had peaked. They sold fairly well in the California Bay Area but not nationally. Executives at the Capitol Tower were unconcerned, however, because the Beatles continued to sell millions of albums.

Warner, having spent approximately $200,000 on Hendrix, very wisely picked up a number of artists who were leaving other labels in disgust. It got James Taylor for practically nothing after Apple closed its doors. Neil Young was a pretty good deal, too. Before anyone knew it, Warner had the strongest youth-market roster going, and most of it had been built on the rejects of other companies. Warner did a lot for people like Gordon Lightfoot, who floundered around on United Artists for a half-dozen records. Indeed, Warner talent in picking up secondary acts and making stars out of them was considered amazing.

Some companies passed on the festival spree. Capitol, MCA, RCA, and a host of independents abstained because of economic and industry positions. Capitol's decision almost proved fatal.

### Shakin' the Tower

The case of Capitol Records in the mid-1970s aptly illustrates the internal problems caused by a total dependence upon one act. The company had been founded in 1942 by songwriters Johnny Mercer and Buddy De-Sylva and record retailer Glenn Wallichs. Beginning with Paul Whiteman's "I Found a New Baby," the independent grew into one of the majors basically on the strength of such former band singers as Al Martino, Kay Starr, Peggy Lee, Les Paul, and Mary Ford. In 1961 most of the company's stock was taken over by Electric and Musical Industries (EMI), a British conglomerate. Through this association the label acquired the recording rights to the Beatles.

Ironically, the company's president, Alan Livingston, had originally turned the Beatles down twice because "English groups just weren't selling here in 1962." With the Beatles, Capitol adhered to the policy of having superstars carry the company, supplemented by the sporadic "one-hit wonders." The Beatles paid the bills, occasionally aided by an outsize hit like "Ode to Billy Joe" or the late Senator Everett Dirksen's reading of "Gallant Men." The "one shots" cost the company little money to promote and publicize. As the Beatles kept selling their usual 5 million units per release, the company began to "throw out" material. The occasional hit was nearly all pure profit, especially when the artist's advance money and studio costs were deducted from the royalty check. The roster grew to 247 acts. "As long as they keep going 'Yeah! Yeah! Yeah!' Capitol has nothing to worry about," so wrote *Forbes,* the financial magazine in 1968.

"People got lazy," commented Claire Brush, a five-year Capitol veteran. The Beatles required little promotion. All that was necessary was to tell the people a new album was out. An executive recalled, "What can you do for the Beatles except give them their billboard on Sunset Boulevard?" The affluence from Beatles product also allowed Capitol to buy and carry a number of so-called middle-selling artists, such as the Band, Steve Miller, Quicksilver Messenger Service, the Stone Poneys, Sea Train, and approximately fifteen other acts that sold in the neighborhood of 60,000 to 150,000 albums and returned a bare profit when advertising and production expenses were subtracted. In several cases, as with the San Francisco bands, the company bid excessive amounts to secure the services of unproven acts. The disbanding of the Beatles and the defection of the Beach Boys to Warner, along with a sales slump by country artists, affected Capitol both economically and psychologically, causing massive personnel and policy changes.

In 1967, enjoying the success of a $100 million fiscal year, Alan Livingston had told *Newsweek,* "It's impossible to be the leader for any length of time. Asking who's Number One is like asking what day it is."[20] Five years later, when Capitol's fortunes appeared bleakest, Mauri Lathower looked up at the ceiling and said,

> I could walk out on the Hollywood Freeway at rush hour, walk against the traffic, and not even get hit. That's how cold we are. There's no sense hiding it. It's just that we can't get tracked. I think the material is okay. Like Warner Brothers . . . when you've got things going for you . . . people like to go with winners.

Capitol was no longer the "hot" company. Promo men were not welcomed at radio stations by program directors eagerly awaiting the new Beatles or Beach Boys record. By 1972, Warner was the king of the mountain and Capitol was $8 million in the red. Its stock had dropped over the years from 63 to 6 points on the American Stock Exchange. Capitol's president aptly commented: "All things must pass." The sins of Columbia and Mitch Miller were being visited upon Capitol. Dick Schulenberg, then with Capitol, says: "They panicked . . . they started throwing things overboard, a lot of which they should have thrown overboard before. They may have overreacted, which once they came out of the cycle, may have put them into such a deep dive they may not be able to pull out." The roster was trimmed to eighty-one acts; executives were summarily dismissed. *Rolling Stone* asked, "What's Shaking at the Capitol Tower?"

After the Beatles disbanded, a series of misfortunes and management errors beset Capitol Records. To stem the tide, the company went over to the artist-development orientation, although it still takes occasional one shots with artists. Menon said, "I must assume . . . that a lot of very powerful balls . . . get flung onto this wall, and due to a lack of an adherent fall off." The adherent, of course, is company support and development. Menon ordered a cutback on the number of acts chosen and also a concentration on promising acts, such as the Raspberries, which was believed to have star quality. Continuing the off-the-wall analogy, he noted:

> I am a great believer in the concept of flinging the ball again, and flinging it again, and of trying a different groove [approach] and of throwing it by a different angle and so on. But that implies my most fundamental principle, which is I have a dedicated faith in this ball. Therefore, if the first or second or third didn't happen, I just refuse, I am too demented, to believe my faith is about to be shattered. This is an extreme way of putting it.

Mauri Lathower, then Capitol's director of A&R, had the unenviable task of supervising the rebuilding effort. The company wanted him to find other Glen Campbells or John Lennons. "You know," he says, "I stood on the corner of Hollywood and Vine for two days and three nights and not one Glen Campbell came by." More seriously, he added:

> When I was placed in this position about last October [1971] I simply had to focus on the new people. You're not going to have your quota busters. You're going to have to decide that you are going to have to do something with these people. There have been three people that I've been very happy with. There's a group called the Persuasions. Their first album was around 25,000 units, which is now almost 50,000. The second album is over 75,000. Or, there's Leo Kottke. He will never be a superstar, I mean that, because he doesn't create that type of excitement. . . . I'm sure he is a little unhappy because he feels his albums should be selling millions. Freddie King is excellent. You go to his performances, I mean they're standing up and screaming. But no album sales. It confuses me.

In an attempt to put the company in the black, the advertising budget was cut. Consequently, selectivity in which artist the company will back was exercised. The Raspberries received an extensive advertising campaign that culminated in a long-awaited Capitol top-ten singles hit, "Go All The Way." Groups like Flash, a spin-off act from 1972's most popular *Billboard* group Yes, Pink Floyd, and several other acts with superstar potential received similar treatment. Lathower turned down a number of groups for this stated reason: "We are not in a position at this time to audition and seek new talent and will not be until our roster is such that we can offer new talent an honest opportunity to succeed." By 1974 Capitol had regained much of its previous stature. In LP and tape sales it was again in *Billboard's* annual designation of the top-four companies. It also lucked out with Pink Floyd's *Dark Side of the Moon,* which has stayed on the *Billboard* album chart for over a decade, creating a historical milestone.

Capitol's experience, along with other unpleasant memories, have made the "throw-it-up-against-the-wall-and-see-if-it-sticks" or "buckshot" philosophy of the majors highly controversial. Many, including CBS, RCA, and Warner Communications (WCI), officially condemn the practice while actively engaging in star buying. Their efforts have shown mixed results. WCI singed Paul Simon, Elton John, and the Who for seven-digit figures. CBS lured James Taylor, the Rolling Stones, Bob Dylan, and the Beach Boys away from WCI. Electric Light Orchestra (ELO) and Pink Floyd also found their way to Black Rock following in the footsteps of Neil Diamond. RCA, especially after the demise of Presley, resumed star hunting. RCA chief Robert D. Summer motivated Diana Ross, Kenny Rogers, and Juice Newton to desert their former labels. Newton, by her own admission had vocal difficulties.

Buying superstars may be the safest bet in the popular music business, but it also presents its own set of built-in problems. An executive discussing Neil Diamond's reported $5 million signing with Columbia, cautioned, "The longevity of an artist might be five years. Now if he's already had four years of his career, extremely strong at selling records and being exposed, then maybe he only has a year left. . . . They [Columbia] may not just be able to do anything with him. He may fail completely on that label." There is that risk, but Neil Diamond is a star and his odds of success seemed good. The deejay still plays proven product rather than risking a job. Diamond's tenure at CBS was mixed. Several movie sound tracks such as *The Jazz Singer* sold well. In 1984 the artist was suing CBS, demanding the company release his recent tapes. Another executive, assessing the value of the Association to Columbia, said, "Rather then trying something new, they'll go with the Association record because they know the name—'They did "Windy" we'll see what their new thing is'—rather than taking a chance on a unknown." The Association was a sales disaster for CBS and disbanded in the early 1970s.

RCA's track record has been unimpressive. Rocky Laginestra, when heading the label, announced, "You don't create a Guess Who or a Jefferson Airplane overnight."[21] He then signed "Mama" Cass Elliot, the Everly Brothers, the Kinks, Lou Reed, and David Bowie. Bowie achieved superstardom. Reed's "Walk on the Wild Side" was a big hit record; the rest flopped. In 1983 Gary Kenton, a journalist and record company publicist, noted, "I doubt that they've [the companies] gotten their money back on any of the acts [superstars] signed in the last five years"

Artists, agents, and even company officials, all for different reasons and motives, decry the formula emphasizing superstars. "Artists are always notoriously unhappy with the company they're with, and I certainly believe they've had reason too, from what I've seen go down at most places," says one chief operating officer. Former manager Roy Silver claims that the major obstacle in the music business is getting "the record company behind the artist." Many artists feel lost at major companies. An industry executive observed, "There's no way of having 200 acts and keeping artists happy." "Do you know how many people from Columbia Records were here when I opened the other night?" asked blues singer John Paul Hammond. "There were none . . . not one person from my own company . . . they didn't bother to advertise either."[22] Ironically, Hammond's father was one of the most important producers in the Columbia hierarchy. Michael Lutz of Brownsville Station, an act that left the biggest-selling pop label for the serenity of a smaller company, said:

> WEA released like something like forty-seven, forty-eight albums in one month's release. And my God, let's say they hit over six, seven albums. Okay, six, seven albums and everybody goes, "My God, they're the hottest company in the world!" But what about those other forty-two acts? See, nobody ever hears about those forty-two acts. Everybody else forgets about those other groups.

Publicists and promotion people acknowledge that size and a substantial release schedule do hamper their abilities. Billy James recalls: "We used to complain a lot at Columbia when we would have twenty-five releases, and all of a sudden we'd have thirty for the Christmas release. Our feeling were that we couldn't do them all justice, the buckshot system. Throw them all out there, hopefully some of them will hit."

Another executive:

> The hardest job in a company like Columbia or RCA or Capitol is to convince their own people. Cause they are the greatest allies. If you get your own people turned on out in the field, they'll do their numbers vocally. I mean I can tell you about it and play the record and you'd get into it, imagine if there was forty people doing that all around the country. That's what you gotta do; you gotta turn your own people on and forget about what they think is good. No company can work on more than three or four recordings at a time anyway.

Publicists are especially aware of product volume. A Warner Bros. publicist exclaimed, "What do you do when Jethro Tull, Van Morrison, and other names are in town—all at the same time?" Other publicity and promotion people solve the size situation by pushing the acts they personally like as opposed to other acts. The artist in a publicist's disfavor may have only the usual bio-promo photo and review record mailing, unless a contract or agent dictate otherwise. Mike Ochs, formerly with Columbia, says, "It's a weird thing; it's a problem you get with the big companies. How do you get the whole company unified behind one act?" As for pushing groups, Mike continued, "I pretty much ignored the major groups. I figured any group that was big could afford its own publicist. I zeroed in on the people who needed the work . . . because they weren't selling then." Ochs's attitude did not sit well with the New York office. Despite the corporate imagery the top five companies were increasingly emulating the Steinbrenners and Autrys of professional baseball in bidding wars for the services of musical free agents. As in baseball, the longevity or "staying power" of an established performer is a riverboat gamble.

### Mergers: "Do You Wanna Dance?"

"Biggies become giants, giants become supergiants. Like stars feeding on hydrogen, as they grow they swallow up worlds, moons and asteroids," says Charlie Mitchell, former president of Takoma Records.[23] The process described is more technically called "corporate acquisition" or merger. The competition between record companies coupled with the infusion of conglomerate money found bidding for artists taking place on the floor of the New York Stock Exchange rather than in Los Angeles night spots. Some majors found it less expensive to buy up labels than to build up their own artist rosters and catalog titles in more conventional ways. The second week of February 1979, is a premier illustration: Capitol Industries-EMI, Inc., swallowed United Artists and its subsidiaries for an estimated $3 million and assumed a $32 million debt. Kenny Rogers, Crystal Gayle, and the jazz-oriented Blue Note label were just a part of the deal. Rogers, alone, had eighteen platinum records during his tenure at Capitol: RCA signed him for a reported $15 million in 1983, 40 percent of Capitol's total expenditure for UA.

The same February week MCA acquired ABC-Dunhill, a company with a strong country division and "name" artists like Jimmy Buffett and Steely Dan. The purchase was partially in light of the corporation's mixed track record with country artists Merle Haggard and Tanya Tucker and heated contract negotiations with Elton John. On the horizon were option renewal talks with John and the supergroup Who. Given the "star-wars" climate, MCA was apprehensive about the prospects with both acts, and its fears proved correct. The Who, with guarantees of $12 million, and John went over to WCI. As in the airline industry, it's cheaper to buy the entire company than individual artists and components. Robert Siner, former MCA president, noted about the defectors to Warner, "They'll have to sell a tremendous amount of product to recoup that kind of money."[24] Warner Communications may not be overly concerned, for it is prototypical in the corporate absorption merger game.

### "Worries about Warner?"

Wedding PolyGram to Warner would solidify WCI's dominant industry position. The ploy failed. This was a far cry from the giant's meager origins as a film company's music division.[25] After a decade of financial wheeling and dealing, involving Seven Arts, the Kinney Corporation, WCI emerged as a major force in direct confrontation with the industry front runner, CBS.

Warner Bros. Records at the start exhibited a roster of college-oriented folk artists and comedians. Bill Cosby reportedly accounted for over half of the label's annual sales. Reprise was purchased from Frank Sinatra. Warner/Reprise (W/R) had a strong middle-of-the road (MOR) flavor but was weak in the ballooning rock market. Dino, Desi and Billy were joined by the Grateful Dead and the Kinks. Warner Bros. purchased the small California-based Valiant label to obtain the Association, the opening act at Monterey in 1967.[26] That year Atlantic, a prestigious fledgling soul, rhythm and blues, and jazz company, was added to the fold for about $20 million. The acquisition also included domestic rights to Led Zeppelin, the Bee Gees, and the short-lived superrock trio Cream featuring guitarist Eric Clapton. Elektra was next, costing $10 million. The folk and California-rock label also processed Nonesuch, an "economy" classics line. The parent company's catalog now covered many musical genres and a common distribution setup, WEA.

Each unit was theoretically independent of the other, with separate executive offices in New York, Hollywood, and Burbank. Given the interchangeability of company heads, such as Jac Holtzman and Joe Smith, this paper separation seems more a legal maneuver than reality.[27] Joe Smith explained the arrangement: "The strength of this record company is in our branch distribution (WEA), which is monolithic, by the way. It has to be, it's one company, but it's being fed in by three separate philosophies, three kinds of attitudes. We're [W/R] the kind of laid-back hip company; Atlantic is funky; Elektra is very intense and sophisticated." He continues to further muddy the relationship in discussing the signing of artists: "We take a shot. The money's the same, who [which label] do you want? If we couldn't get them; we'd sure as hell try to steer them to Atlantic or Elektra, because they're our brothers. We're close to them." On market shares: "I'd like to finish ahead of them, but just ahead of them. I'd love them to be second. Ideally, I love to see our companies 1-2-3, with us number one; Atlantic number two. . . ." With the sibling labels, Asylum was added to the fold, in the background. Warner/Reprise, as Smith suggests, became the flagship of WCI and its distribution arm, WEA.

## "Meanwhile . . . in Burbank"

"Our philosophy," said Joe Smith, "has always been that we would rather go down in flames with an artist (like Randy Newman) than take a shot on a singles group that has a couple of single hits and no long-term staying power in the business." This may sound like a foolish gamble but is not, as Stan Cornyn indicates:

> We have a plateau theory that we will go from a smaller market to a bigger market, and a bigger market, trying to find a broader plateau. Randy Newman has stepped up a couple of plateaus. I think it will be a lot easier for him now to accelerate and accelerate. How far he can go nobody knows . . . we will not sign a polka band unless we think the polka band will have an appeal to the masses.

The Warner/Reprise ethos is traceable to Morris Ostin and Joe Smith, who, according to those around them, understood social trends like the rock revolution before their competitors. One event is cited by Cornyn, who in 1966 accompanied Mo Ostin to Haight Ashbury, where they viewed the Avalon Ballroom: "It was then the whole scene started to look up for Mo and myself . . . we got into an appreciation of that point of view . . . we understood it. It didn't uptight us too much." Presumably, it is this visit that made Warner aware of the Grateful Dead, a band instrumental in the Kesey Trips Festival that also transformed Warner corporate consciousness. Prior to the mad scramble for acid-rock bands, Warner snared the Grateful Dead, a group familiar only to street people and flower children. Their songs were long drawn-out improvisational artifacts. Smith told *Rolling Stone,* "With the Grateful Dead we learned there are other ways to sell records, like sponsoring a free concert in Denver. We learned you don't have to be on Top 40 radio, that there's a whole market in underground FM. We learned that posters mean something, that billboards mean something."[28] The Dead and other groups like them opened up new vistas for the corporation. With these techniques learned from the new culture, Warner set about packaging the Monterey sensation Jimi Hendrix. With the flamboyant guitarist another lesson was learned in the Burbank executive suite:

When we saw the numbers that those records could sell in, we said, "Wow, there's something here." You'd struggle with a middle-of-the-road artist to sell maybe 300,000 albums and have a major when you could sell 2 million Jimi Hendrix albums. Frank Sinatra never sold 2 million albums. Dean Martin never sold 2 million albums. I don't think there were too many artists who ever sold 2 million albums until this wave of "involving" records.

Having absorbed the economic value of the new culture, Ostin proceeded to find those artists suited for the 18-to-35 market. A promotion director explained, "We went after as many acts as we possibly could that we thought would relate to this age group or this type of music." Most market surveys of buying habits indicated the cohort was not attuned to singles but to albums. Warner's previous entree into this demographic unit was through Peter, Paul and Mary, and the Kinks, a band it totally misunderstood. Not surprisingly, the company courted many disaffected folksingers who were fleeing Vanguard and Apple or who had remained on the coffeehouse circuit long after the folkie revival was history. Andy Wickham found Joni Mitchell and signed her for $15,000. Smith and Ostin signed James Taylor from Apple; Neil Young, a refugee from the Buffalo Springfield; Gordon Lightfoot from United Artists; David Blue, formerly of Elektra; and Van Morrison of Parrot Records. They enlisted the interesting but commercially esoteric songs and voices of Van Dyke Parks and Randy Newman; neither was or is a chart buster. Newman considered calling one album *So Long, Mo,* believing he was to be dropped from the label at any moment. Unlike Tiny Tim, he has not been cut out, nor has Parks despite their most substandard ledger contributions.

The support of Newman has provided the company with an image of act building that is projected throughout the industry. Bob Regehr was quoted in *Billboard* as saying,

> I have to remember I'm working for the company by working for the acts. My greatest satisfaction is seeing an act break after we plugged along behind it for years, such as Alice Cooper or Randy Newman. In a way, that's even more of a thrill than when an artist is fortunate enough to hit it right the first time and take off immediately, as America did.[29]

Regehr's field personnel have a reputation with artists for providing excellent road service. "Everything from being at the airport with a limo to dope," said one competitor. The hip company image has helped Warner. Trade ads also have furthered this reputation. One announced the Van Dyke Park's album *Song Cycle* had lost $35,000. The ad read, "How we lost $35,509.50 on 'The Album of the Year' (Damnit)." The ad was both a hype for the record and the company. Repeatedly the message indicated, "It cost us $48,302," underlining the company's support for the artist. Parks was further lost when the copy stated. "We sell enough stars that we can afford a Van Dyke Parks."

*Rolling Stone* and other rock publications identified Warner Bros. with the "new" culture. Pushing the Mothers of Invention, the company told the readers of underground press, "Yes, Greater America may have Nixon, cold cream, and vacuum-packed lima beans, but we at Reprise are now allied with Frank Zappa and his Merry Pranksters." The hip corporate appearance has helped Warner considerably, attracting even more talent to its doors. Neophytes believe the company will give them a fair share of support and faith, as it did for Newman and others. Smith acknowledges, "One artist talking to another is far more effective than royalty points, dollars and so forth." Ron Saul added:

> Initially everyone gets a shot. But I think that's one of the great attributes of this company. I think that's why artists love us, speaking of us as the company, because we gave them a shot, we work with them and we continue to work with them. So many other companies, like you say, throw out the buckshot, they forget, they throw it out. Ninety percent of it is just mailed and nothing else is done other than being mailed.

Established artists wishing to back a winning horse also come to Warner/ Reprise. As Andy Wickham quips, "We are an efficient machine." In 1969 with the breakup of many of the super rock groups, popular music retreated to balladeers, writer-singers, and novelty acts. The Ostin-Smith philosophy of blanketing the youth market worked; Warner kept a solid foot in the acoustical field. In the wake of this success the Youngbloods, the Beach Boys, John Sebastian, Donovan, and Dionne Warwick signed with the company for then-unheard-of advances and royalty terms. The reason for Warner's attractiveness, according to *Rolling Stone,* was more than just corporate image. "There's still no inducement like good old-fashioned cash, and right now Warner/Reprise is rolling in it."[30] The Beach Boys at the time reportedly received one of the largest percentages and advances in the history of the record business. The Youngbloods, according to their manager, got "handsome and sizeable" economic rewards for signing. The company image seems to have been working, but not in the eyes of all observers. Competitors and disillusioned artists were critical of the formula or "hype."

Warner had made it in a big way and now was another CBS Records: a "laid-back" Columbia, throwing product up against the famous industry wall. Gary Buttice, then the Warner promo representative in Detroit, one of the most important markets, admitted that the company was primarily concerned with buying superstars rather than raising established acts into the million-sales superstar category. "They won't push new acts," Buttice said. This is not entirely true; Warner has promoted new artists. However, its most notable successes have been with acts with experience on other labels, either by signing promising artists or distribution deals with smaller or import companies. In the latter part of the 1970s and the early 1980s Warner top sellers were Rod Stewart, Fleetwood Mac, George Benson, Van Halen, Christopher Cross, Emmy Lou Harris, and teen idol Shaun Cassidy. Only Cross and Cassidy were entry-level performers with the label. Still, the company used *Billboard's* full back cover to promote artists, albums, and sometimes itself in a subtle manner. Most ads announced new records and those reaching gold or platinum status. Others were more image-oriented: "I have never seen a marketing campaign to equal the one Warners is putting behind *Superman*," signed by David Lieberman, and followed by "muscle in flight, on Warner Bros." A more typical full-color layout contained statements such as "Thanks To MTV For Letting People *See* Our Music," or "THE MUSIC SOLUTION: WARNER ELEKTRA ATLANTIC."[31] This fits well with the view of Lenny Waronker, president of Warner, that the success of his company is "based on a few acts. They weren't all the biggest sellers, but they certainly had a real effect on the *image* of the company . . . so when someone like Rickie Lee Jones decided she wanted to make a record, she knew that Warner Bros. would *understand her*" (emphasis added).[32]

Projecting the image of an artist-oriented, laid-back label has worked for Warner/Reprise. It has supported Randy Newman through thick and thin. He is still not a household name despite "Short People" or "I Love L.A." Many neophytes have fallen through the cracks or been lost in an avalanche of huge releases. Warner Communications, Inc., controlled a quarter of the record market by 1983. Its artist roster was cut, including Van Morrison. As one security analysist said, WCI is "beginning to emerge as one of the major companies in America, bar none."[33] Corporate image, superstars, and the occasional chart surprise made this possible in the music division of WCI.

### Artist Development

Smaller companies, whose sizes are determined by the number of acts and releases, place a greater stress upon the development of individual acts. A & M, is one model of this philosophy. "I think that A & M has taken advantage of Warner Bros.' mistakes," says Donahue, "and comes in as a much quieter . . . force in the industry." Another executive:

> It's family company. There's a tremendous interaction between all the departments on all levels. From stockrooms to president to vice-president to main-

tenance people. It's not a role-playing company. There are no shut doors, there are no high-level conferences. So in comes an artist off the street. We sign this particular artist. Then we get all together and pool our particular talents. We like an artist and we sign the artist and we deliver the artist.

The size of the company, which is located in Charlie Chaplin's old studio, allows for this kind of interaction.

Herb Alpert and Jerry Moss (A & M), a wedding of trumpet player and promoter, released a single titled "The Lonely Bull" in 1962. It sold 700,000 copies and earned $25,000 in its first year. Nine years later A & M grossed $56 million according to a company spokesman. On the basis of "The Lonely Bull" the company was considered a "one-shot" label; it had a gimmick. The Tijuana Brass sound dominated easy-listening charts while the Beatles controlled the *Billboard* "Hot 100"; in 1966 Alpert and the Brass sold 13 million LPs, surpassed only by Lennon, McCartney & Co.

The philosophy of A & M is based upon the Latin-sounding band. "There was no market for Herb Alpert when he first broke; he created his own market, and there's never been a waiting market for any act that we've put out." This formula was unexpectedly put successfully to the test with Sergio Mendes's Brasil '66, which earned A & M four gold albums. Until the pop festival at Monterey, A & M remained an MOR Company, appealing strictly to young adults and older people. It did have a few Top 40 acts. Tommy Boyce and Bobby Hart, who did the Monkees' instrumentals before Nesmith and company performed, and the We Five, but nothing to compare with the performers on the top festival stage. Only the unknown organist Lee Michaels could have qualified for the historical event. "As your traditional promo man I kept wondering why aren't there any A & M artists at this terrific event," Moss told Judy Sims.[34]

Following the historical Monterey gathering, Moss flew to England to purchase U.S. rights to Joe Cocker, the Move, Tyrannosaurus Rex, and Procol Harum, then enjoying the fruits of "A Whiter Shade of Pale." Cocker educated A & M, as the Grateful Dead would Warner. It discovered that pink champagne was not to be served during press parties for the underground media. Several untoward relationships with T. Rex and the Move further disoriented executive attitude. The company's experience with rock reinforced the artist-development ethos. The ideal label was a small one with talented artists. Jerry Moss: "We're perfectly happy hitting a lot of home runs with No. 1 artists." Another executive: "We don't break an artist on the first try, neither do we go raiding other labels for artists that aren't keeping their popularity to get that popularity on our labels. We've stuck with most of our artists for three, four, five albums, it's happened."

Unlike the majors, A & M is cutting its roster instead of increasing it. "We have about 65 artists . . . when we sign somebody we cut somebody, as a rule. We've never had a release bigger than ten albums; if we did we'd start getting nervous. You can't look after them. . . . We probably service artists, every artist, in a far superior way than anybody else."[35] The company cut its catalog from 300 to 250 titles and destroyed its closeouts to avoid competing with its new releases. More recently A & M got into the K Mart "cutout" bin business. The label prefers to convey a "family corporation" image and does so rather successfully, pointing to Peter Frampton, Styx, the Police, and Bryan Adams, primarily because of its lack of size in product and personnel. Small size has its problems, especially at the promotion and distribution level. One artist's manager explains:

> You go into, say, Philadelphia, and the jobber [independent distributor] there carries like A & M and ten other labels. So A & M can't exert much pressure on them. Like "X is coming in and we go to the local distributor that is handling A & M, and he's got two records in stock in the whole company. He's got two records in stock! "X" is doing a major concert there, like 3,000 seats, and he has only got two records. I mean, what do you do? You call A & M and complain, and A & M calls them and complains, but there isn't that much power.

There was an element of truth to the complaints about A & M distribution and the promotion system. Record-store managers said they were unable to get some A & M product. Jerry Moss, board chairman, acknowledged the situation, adding that the costs were prohibitive and would "sacrifice the development and marketing of talent."[36] The solution to the problem surfaced when A & M took its domestic distribution and promotion to RCA. Moss hoped people displaced by the move would be absorbed by Victor: "We'll see what RCA has and try to move people into the system." Moss's personnel layoffs stuck because Victor would soon be dismissing large segments of its West Coast media-relations people.

The RCA distribution pact has been fairly successful. Record stores do receive the product. The promotion and publicity functions are another matter, especially outside the twenty-five magic "major markets." A & M's media operations particularly in the southern and midwestern states leave room for considerable improvement.

"It's that [practice]," says a road manager, "all those high-priced PR firms going in Los Angeles and New York." Successful artists increasingly rely on their own publicity firms to coordinate Middle America tours. Artist development as manifested at A & M is a strategy applauded by majors and independents alike; however, few totally practice it. The majors track record is beset with stiffs that "should have made it" with the proper support. Major companies tend to be "reactive," even more so with little-known artists. Even A & M has its list of "get aways," such as the nucleus of the Electric Light Orchestra (ELO), Gram Parsons, Gene Clark, and country superstar Waylon Jennings. Deejay-comedian Don Bowman, who introduced Waylon's material to Jerry Moss, recalled, "They don't know anything about country."

Artist development versus star reliance were to be sorely tested in 1979, the beginning of the industry's "Great Depression."

## The Great Depression of '79: Cold Facts

In the spring of 1974 a young professor read a paper to a gathering of academicians interested in popular music. Jon Rieger warned:

> The development with the most profound bearing on the popular music industry as presently constituted is the changing age structure of U.S. society. For an industry that has tied its fortunes so heavily to the whims of the young and has profited so greatly in recent decades—*the adventure is about to end.* The number of young people in the U.S. during the next decade or two will decline, not only relative to the total population, but *absolutely.* The most recent projections indicate, in fact, that the age 10-24 will shrink by as many as six and one-half million by 1990. This cannot but have devastating implications for the popular music industry, for it is the young who buy the most records.[37]

There were few if any industry representatives in the audience to hear the gloomy forecast. A few months later *Popular Music and Society (PMS)* published an expanded version of Rieger's remarks. *PMS* was moderately read in the industry, but the article appears to have been generally ignored as sales figures continued to move upward. (Most music-industry executives place little credibility in academics, despite Rieger's analysis, as well as others', that RCA's video discs were doomed to failure in the pop music field. The Victor project folded in 1984, a $75 million disaster.) Demographic predictions, which were being taken note of by educators, criminologists, and others, went unheeded in the executive suites at WCI, CBS, and throughout the music industry, then toying with the commercial potentialities of reggae and a "punk" sound taking shape in working-class London pubs. In the mid-1970s executives coped with myriad messiahs; one just might lead to the musical promised land. Reggae, after Johnny Nash's "I Can See Clearly Now" and especially Jimmy Cliff's "The Harder They Come," became a contender.

The Woodstock generation was aging and mellowing into soft-core country represented by the Los Angeles-based Eagles, Jackson Browne, and Linda Ronstadt. Some authentic country artists—"the outlaws"— were garnering print media attention. Progressive rock, given its visual appeal, enjoyed a share of the market especially on the East Coast. Bruce Spring-steen, hailed "as the future of rock 'n' roll," became the superstar of the year with CBS's promotional campaign. He was not a trend starter. The success of *Born to Run* probably created more problems for the performer than he had ever anticipated (see chapter 4). Peter Frampton, using A & M's marketing strategy went platinum with the "live" album. This spanned a plethora of concert albums. Kiss all but dominated the teen market. *Creem* magazine featured the comic strip quartet on monthly covers for years. Disco, as *Rolling Stone* noted, "kept on growing, assimilating every-thing into its lifeless yet sexy, campy yet populist ethos. . . . It was a faceless, assembly-line music whose lack of star performers mirrored the every-body/nobody-is-a star equality-in-community of its dance-floor audience." Disco mirrored Tom Wolfe's "Me Generation" and Christopher Lasch's culture of narcissism. The *Saturday Night Fever* sound track predomi-nantly featured the Bee Gees. Despite predictions that disco would replace rock, it was merely dance-floor background noise.

The so-called punk movement in the United Kingdom spearheaded by the ill-fated Sex Pistols was a total U.S. disaster despite the massive pub-licity the group received. Lee Abrams, the media consultant, even gave the subgenre another name: new wave. The change in terminology did little to help the forebears of the British club scene. New wave in the 1980s would fade into a very generalized form. Ask ten people what new wave is and ten different answers are sure to follow. New wave—the ninth "British inva-sion"—was a musical Bay of Pigs.

*Newsweek* and *Rolling Stone* cover stories, a 20 percent share of *Bill-board*'s chart hits of 1978, and radio "numbers" or ratings fueled the ma-nia. A Polydor vice-president told *Newsweek*, "We're going through the most dramatic taste shift in popular music history. Disco is the pop music of tomorrow." Writer Robert Hilburn's assessment proved more realistic: "Disco is a temporary thrill—a night in a bordello."

The obituaries for reggae, disco, and punk were not premature. It is a trendy business. During the Me Generation of the 1970s the so-cioeconomic plights of Jamaican and lower-class youth had little ide-ological or cultural appeal. Young people wanted *into* the system, not to overthrow it. Program directors' (PDs) wholly concurred. New York critics notwithstanding, the Sex Pistols and CBGB performers did poorly. Disco suffered a similar fate. Performers rarely developed into stars. The Bee Gees viewed the *Fever* soundtrack as a one-shot, however profitable, ar-rangement. Donna Sommer used her sultry status to move into the Vegas and concert curcuit. The Village People faded into oblivion after several controversial hits such as "Y.M.C.A." and "In the Navy," an embarrass-ment to the Navy upon discovering the meaning of the song. Chart flashes such as the Blues Brothers, spawned by *Saturday Night Live,* and the top-fortyish the Knack were not trendy or even fad setters. They were one-shot sensations. The times appeared to be drastically changing.

In less than half a decade, Rieger's prophecy became a reality. The famous "we-must-be-doing-something-right" rationale took on a hollow ring. The first-quarter earnings statements of 1979 reported in *Billboard* indicated something was amiss—or very wrong. The U.S. economy was in recession, the record industry was entering a depression. A mini-panic ensued, duly reported by the financial press and the mass media. The news reports served to aggravate the situation further. Stan Gortikov, president of the Recording Industry Association of America (RIAA), characterized the response as

> demoralizing. The gloom and doom characterizations are contagious and tend to exaggerate genuine problems beyond their reality. They engender fear and they stifle hope. They encourage timidity at a time when positive actions and attitudes are imperative. Major journals, in their desire to turn a cutesy phrase, have said: "end to glory years" . . . "music is turning sour" . . . "blood baths" . . . "flaky, fadridden business." These are punitive portrayals.[38]

Clive Davis concurred, scolding Joe Smith for his statements to the national press. In an "open letter," Arista's chief executive officer began, "The profusion of national magazine articles trumpeting views of doom and gloom . . . is now alarming and potentially vastly damaging."[39] Blaming the messenger had little impact on the external realities. Bullish voices, in Wall Street jargon, were being drowned out by the record industry bears.

The waning months of the seventies experienced the predicted demographic peak of potential record consumers under twenty-five. The postwar boom had come of age, a fact almost totally missed or ignored by Robert Christgau's "bizzers" (industry personnel). Instead, a wave of euphoria prevailed, dominated by the disco mania and Robert Stigwood's *Grease* and *Saturday Night Fever* sales. Together the sound tracks sold 27 million copies nationwide in 1978. Pressing plants could not ship rapidly enough to meet the anticipated demand for the lucrative winter holiday rush. This zealousness, flying in the face of objective economic trends, fueled a pending crisis.

New Year's pundits analyzing the past year pointed to pervasive stagflation. The oil crisis had sent prices skyward. Automobile and retail sales had suffered. Unemployment was rising. Many record company executives had viewed their industry as recession-proof. "We thought we were safe from recessions, depressions—everything but success," recalled Joe Smith.[40]

Record companies had distributed millions of titles to retailers for the customary December sales spree. It never materialized. Merchandisers returned most of the product for credit. Retailers had overstocked and were shipping their losses to the manufacturer by the truckloads. Smith told the *New York Times*

> We had filled up the pipelines with major product in anticipation of a major selling period. . . . But it just never happened. In the record business the companies continue to own all the stock in a retail store—the only way we can be sure of getting exposure for new artists is to guarantee returns. Returns are usually balanced by super-star product, but this time there wasn't any.[41]

Even RSO had shipments of *Fever* and *Grease* coming back, including some that were clever counterfeits. In time spokespersons would use the counterfeiting and home-taping "dupes" (duplicates) as major culprits accounting or the decline.

The volume of returns should have been a warning, but the practice had been a vexing yet apparently insoluable problem for years (see chapter 4). Profit-conscious wholesalers and retailers had successfully resisted changes in return policies and frequently abused the policies. (The "They won't take the product, if they can't return it" policies prevailed only in record and book publishing; retailers generally are responsible for their buying decisions and "eat their losses.") Privately, executives cussed the so-called cherry pickers as shortsighted, ignorant, and out of touch with the times. This very attitude *justified* the unique return practices used in the industry. In *Billboard,* a company president blamed the "overshipping" problem on industry "self-indulgent gratification" in search of gold and platinum certifications rather than retailers' penchant to overstock. At best, this arrangement fitted C. Wright Mills's notion of a "coincidence of interests," in which both parties appeared to benefit from the policy at least temporarily.[42]

*Billboard* greeted the closing year of the decade with the optimistic headline "Holiday Sales Soar After Sluggish Start." Irv Lichtman wrote, "It was, after all, a Merry Christmas for the nation's record retailers." Representatives of large chains were quoted as elated because "we had the kind of resurgance you wouldn't believe," or, "I'm quite *certain* this showing will carry us into spring with *outstanding* business."[43] Only a few retail executives, such as Cleveland's John Cohen at Disc Records, reported a holiday sales decline.

Two months later the originators of those glowing quotations were changing their tune. One summed up the situation by suggesting the lack of star product and inflation were taking a "terrible toll . . . most people are going to make sure they have lunch before they buy a record." Lee Hartstone, president of Integrity Entertainment Corporation, added, "If the best the industry can do is give us two hit LPs (Bee Gees and Rod Stewart), it's pretty damn weak."[44] A softening market signaled returns in an industry already reporting profit declines. Walter Yetnikoff, CBS president, admitted business was "a little off," primarily because of returns.[45] WCI and CBS, with over a third of U.S. wholesale volume, witnessed a mild drop in their profit margins.

Record industry people viewed the downturns as seasonal or as a "market readjustment." Little was said about demographics. Only two *Billboard* writers implicitly acknowledged an age-group swing. "Audiences no longer leave the music scene to the kids down the block on turning 30."[46] They pointed to the "Hot 100" singles chart to support this thesis, citing the success of Fleetwood Mac, the Beach Boys, and Paul McCartney. A simpler interpretation was that as the rock market aged it continued to support acts from its younger days. Moreover, the staying power of Fleetwood Mac and the Jefferson Starship was a function of the increasing size of the over-30 contingent. Yetnikoff told a meeting of stock analysts: "I think . . . you can stand off on the returns, and I think we're going to do very well. We have a Paul McCartney record, a James Taylor record and a lot of other product coming out in the immediate future."[47] Both artists had adult appeal. This optimism proved false; midyear earnings statements by the majors were in the red. WCI Chairman Steven Ross characterizeed 1979 as "a period of relatively flat industry sales."[48] RCA and CBS concurred, pondering their losses.

Sagging profits generated some structural in-house cost cutting. Layoffs became commonplace, particularly in the creative and marketing departments. MCA, having absorbed ABC, combined personnel and plant facilities. Two hundred eighty to 300 ABC employees were displaced, including national publicity director Peter Starr. Capitol's acquisition of United Artists, and RCA's pressing-distribution deals with A & M plus 20th Century increased industry unemployment rate. Job overlaps had the employees of the merged company being pinkslipped. There were a few notable exceptions, such as RCA's Grelun Landon. "The dean of West Coast publicists" lost his fifteen-year position, along with 24 others who were let go. Casablanca terminated 25. In July CBS "axed" 53 people in middle-level positions, primarily in publicity and promotion. Bruce Lundvall explained the economy move: "This has been a bad year . . . in a difficult economy, and it was a helluva thing to let anybody go."[49] Within a month another 120 were removed from the CBS payroll. Reportedly, the former employees took to wearing "The Crash of '79" T-shirts.[50] Elektra "canned" 10; MCA, 30 more. The eventual casualty toll eventually reached around 600 victims in one year.

Members of the media, especially in secondary and tertiary markets, were displeased by these "economy" moves. Services, promotional and publicity material ranging from promo records to press packages, outside the twenty-five major markets were varied and unpredictable. Personnel changes only compounded the vexing situation. Familiar voices disappeared. Service lists were trimmed in apparently mindless fashion. Complaints frequently were answered with cold, impersonal form letters, some mimeographed. College radio staffers spent an inordinate amount of their free time attempting to get records to play on the air. "College radio is upset because of the potential lack of service," said a former RCA college consultant. "No one is at the record company to work with on promotions. Promotion men deal with . . . college radio if they have time." Music magazines became a dying breed as industry advertising declined. The survivors privately cussed at the new publicity people. One complained, "I don't know anybody, they're all gone. They won't return calls. The one's that do think they're doing you a favor by setting up an interview with the warm-up act." An editor lamented, "If this continues, we'll be out of business." Record retailers were not getting product for "in-store" play, a key tool believed to increase impulse buying. Shared advertising budgets were cut. Some of these charges were legitimate. The industry was targeting mass-media opinion makers at the expense of exposure in other areas. If John Naisbitt's megatrend argument of fashions swelling from the bottom-up is correct, the record industry was wrong. Some record executives contended these cuts were necessary.

"My eyes have been opened," said the late Neil Bogart. "No more T-shirts. I've made enough T-shirts to clothe a lot of people in this town. In the future, they can buy their own clothes."[51] Other fanciful marketing gimmicks were pared. Expensive press parties, ego-serving billboards, junkets, and other "goodies" were discontinued. Robert Siner: "If an artist asks us for a gold lamé jumpsuit, we're gonna ask him what it will do for his album."[52] Stan Cornyn added, "Record companies should concentrate on what helps to sell records."[53] Few questioned the wisdom of cutting the high-rolling frills associated with the rock world. Tour support was another matter.

Touring for years had been *the* alternative vehicle of exposure. Concerts sold records even when radio stations would not play them. Kiss, Deep Purple, Grand Funk, Judas Priest, and a host of others used the tour to ascend the stairway to stardom. Record-merchandising tours became an integral aspect of promoting product. Companies underwrote or sponsored tours. Escalating costs, as much as 400 percent, dampened companies' ardor and motivated a retreat—in some cases a complete withdrawal. A

CBS official: "We had to take a lot of artists off the road and concentrate on the ones that are the real killers live." Greg Geller, another CBS executive, told *Billboard*:

> We do not feel that tour support is an essential ingredient. Tour support is not the beginning and end—all that it was once perceived to be in breaking a new album. There was a period, about two years ago, that if you were a R 'n' R band, you felt that touring was absolutely essential in breaking you"[54]

The industry once again was banking on radio, which was becoming increasingly tight, to expose its product.

Ticket and gasoline prices were another consideration. Beginning, ironically, with the Woodstock Festival, artists' costs soared. Concert tickets became more expensive than record albums. Consumers were faced with a familiar and unpleasant choice: which concert to attend. One promoter told *People*, "They have to decide whether to see Frampton or the Bee Gees—not both."[55] Concert expenses, the gasoline crisis, and inflation drastically reduced the "bizzers" participation. As of 1985, tour support is based on ticket sales, merchandising, and cigarette and beer companies (see chapter 2). In Heller's best "catch-22" fashion this support is bestowed on the big-name artists whose endorsements have a perceived commercial value.

Some have called it the "Great Disco Disaster of 1979," attributing many of the industry's problems on the quality of music. For many critics "it wasn't in the grooves." Country rock fiddler Charlie Daniels encapsulized the dissent by observing "We've been discoed to death the last couple of years. I just can't tell one group from another."[56] The "disco-sucks" movement could not agree more. Disco was described by a plethora of rock writers as "mindless drivel," and they usually pointed to "Dance, Dance, Dance," or "Boogie Oogie Oogie." They overlooked such early rock classics as "Tutti Frutti" or Steve Allen's famous sarcastic reading of "Be Bop-A-Lula." The Little Richard and Gene Vincent hits were akin to "Staying Alive" or " Do Ya Think I'm Sexy." Still, a sizable portion of the youth market wished John "Ravolta's" music would disappear. Some industry people, usually in "off-the-record" conversations, concurred.

The pin-striped *Wall Street Journal* with a front-page lead announced, "Disco-Music Craze Seems to be Fading; Record Makers Glad." Pointing to a 4 percent market share, the financial paper predicted massive format changes and a rise in "new music" product.

Numerous factors were enumerated to account for disco's rapid fall from consumer grace. The key was a dearth of disco superstars. Disco mania flamed by *Saturday Night Fever* featured the Australian-born Bee Gees.

Other artists recorded "disco" tracks to sell a new album, including the Rolling Stones "Miss You." As jazz artist Herbie Mann groused, "Don't let your taste get in the way of reaching a broader audience." Rock and pop performers did not like doing disco. Disco, a dance-oriented idiom, was infertile ground for stars; of the hundreds of disco singers, only Donna Summer and the Village People enjoyed name recognition. "To make money in the record business, you have to develop artists who will have longevity in the marketplace, who will record hit after hit album," said a Capitol executive. "We developed a lot of hit disco records but very few disco hit artists with staying power. The problem is that most of the disco records sound alike and people who dance to these records in clubs don't even know who the artists are." Single hits, poor lyrics, a subcultural audience and just plain bad records all contributed to the fall. One writer blamed the record recession: "Disco . . . was undermined by the recent slump, which was mostly attributed to mismanagement and skyrocketing prices."[57] "Bizzers" took the opposite view: disco had done them in. Ray Caviano, Warner's disco person, told a reporter, "Companies tried to cash in on it by pushing bad disco records. Now we're coming back to reality from all that hype."[58]

"They actually believe their own hype," not teenagers, said one publicist.[59] Disco did appeal to an older audience. That, in part, was its downfall. Dancers quickly returned to other forms of exercise, such as jogging and aerobics, leaving disco a memory.

The revitalized "heavy metal" sound and other MTV offerings returned much of contemporary rock to the shrinking under-25 contingent. Those over 25 who are still musically attuned, appear—there are no hard data— to prefer concerts to records. Sixties artists received thunderous applause for recognizable hits; their current releases, if any, evoke only polite applause. At a Toledo concert Gordon Lightfoot's opening chords to vintage hits were immediately acknowledged. The *Shadows* and *Salute* albums got blank stares with a minimal response. The same phenomenon is evident at most concerts in the All American City (a marketing demographic designation).

The fading away of disco was not the anticipated cure for the industry's recession. A vacuum was created. Airplay and sales foundations remained for acts such as the disbanded Led Zeppelin, Billy Joel, and Eagles—hardly new discoveries. The Spartan approach of the 1980s, cost efficient on the ledgers, only underscored the overall lethargy in the industry and the U.S. economy.

Record companies schedule a preponderance of their releases to coincide with the resumption of the fall school openings and the winter holidays. Nearly 60 percent of product flows during a four-month span; 25

percent in the final five weeks. Greatest hits, "live," and double-record sets abound in this period.

Hoping for a turnaround if not an end to the dismal sales of 1979, companies cranked out all of the big guns beginning in August with Led Zeppelin's *In Through the Out Door*. From the Beatles to the Who, all were promised to retailers hungry for guaranteed hits. Fleetwood Mac's long-awaited double-record set *Tusk,* listed at $15.98, was released in the hope it would equal the sales of its multiplatinum *Rumours.* Warner was banking on this rushed album, along with Rod Stewart's *Greatest Hits* and comedian Steve Martin, to save the year for the label. The release of *Tusk* would bring about several unanticipated consequences.

*Tusk* reportedly sold 15 percent of *Rumours'* unit volume. A disappointing figure for accountants in Burbank; 2 million units as opposed to 12 million for the previous offering. The explanation for Fleetwood Mac's relatively poor showing stirred a heated controversy involving labels, tape manufacturers, broadcasters, artists, and consumers. Uninterrupted airing of albums and home taping joined counterfeiting as a causal culprit or "straw man" in the analysis of the depression, depending on the perception of the beholder: industry versus audiophile.

Unauthorized reproduction has been an expensive thorn in the financial side of record companies for decades. After years of unsuccessful lobbying, the industry was finally able to gain some legal protection in a majority of states and at the federal level against pirates or counterfeiters. The effectiveness of these legal sanctions has been questionable. In 1979 record labels lost an "estimated" $400 million to counterfeiters of legitimate hit records such as *Saturday Night Fever.* Beyond intensive public relations campaigns, labels were powerless in combating pirating. Home taping or "duping" (duplication) was viewed from a different perspective. Taping was legal, but *could* be taxed.

Duplication of sound dates back to the availabilty of the production-line tape recorder. Connoisseurs of symphonic and operatic music quickly found tape invaluable in obtaining complete broadcast masterworks. Most compositions were unavailable in record stores. The popularization of recorders made magnetic tape an inexpensive, secure mode of reproduction. Tapes did not wear or scratch, unlike disk surfaces. In the 1970s Congress legitimized over-the-air taping for noncommercial users. Despite this largess, reel-to-reel tape players remained a generally esoteric entertainment device. Consumer studies indicated many potential buyers considered tape "too inconvenient." People disliked cueing up a tape to find a favorite song, as eight-track cassette manufacturers painfully discovered.

Record companies overlooked the practice, concentrating on counterfeiters—pirates—and bootleggers. Pirates and "boots" constituted the predominant concern when contrasted to a seemingly minuscule band of tapers. In 1971 Stan Gortikov had told a congressional committee: "We in the industry certainly have known that such amateur practices go on in the home. We realistically recognize that no such enforcement is possible, and certainly none is intended." The industry's antiduplication war focused on protective legislation to combat unauthorized saleable discs competing with copyrighted prerecorded materials. The steady profits enjoyed by the companies negated any serious consideration of home taping. The "crash of '79" altered the state of benign neglect.

Home taping was perfectly legal. The 1976 copyright revision act permitted noncommercial duplication. As late as August of 1979, industry spokesman were debating duping as a potential revenue source, pointing to a German tax on taping equipment. Joe Cohen, a NARM vice-president, explained duping: "The consumer may be rebelling against poor record and tape quality which has not kept pace with hardware technology."[60] Cohen was partially correct but he did ignore the obvious. Mass production cassette tape decks and high record prices had escalated duping. Moreover, radio stations, aided by hardware stereo advertisers, began facilitating taping of new album releases.

"We in no way want to encourage home taping of albums," said a Leo Barnett agency executive, "We just feel that classical, rock, disco and jazz fans want to hear albums without interruption."[61] Ratings-conscious program directors viewed this as an audience-expanding vehicle. Many ran local newspaper ads announcing the album and the time slot it would be aired. Ken Buttice of Elektra/Asylum: "This has been going on awhile but now radio stations are telling their listeners to gear up their tape machines. That's what is starting to happen. It's getting serious."[62] Serious as the situation may have been, record labels were caught in a dilemma. Important stations such as WWWW in Detroit, WHPL in Baltimore, and Cleveland's rock bastion WMMS were playing entire albums. "Bizzers" depend on the goodwill of these significant gatekeepers for product exposure. Sanctions were out of the question. Friendly persuasion was the only tool available. It was ineffectual in opposition to higher ratings and advertising dollars. "What can they do?" asked one all-night deejay, "cut us off? We'll get the record somewhere"—probably at the nearest retail store. Retailers need airplay to sustain their volume. Harold Sulman at Arista aptly summed up the paradox: "We're definitely concerned about it. But I don't know what we can do about it."[63]

The sense of frustration was most accutely experienced by Warner Bros. Records. *Tusk* had become a favorite for "Album Hours" nationwide. *Billboard* quoted retailers as losing sales. "Playing *Tusk* in its entirety without a break . . . hurt our volume on this important album through the Midwest," lamented a chain operator. A southern retailer complained, "I lost 100 to 150 sales when WHHY [Montgomery, Alabama] played the album totally."[64]

Cassette demand more than compensated for *Tusk's* retail difficulties. A heavy desire for blank C-60 and C-90 cassettes was reported following radio ads that *Tusk* would be featured without commercial breaks. Recording artists led by Motown's superstar Stevie Wonder were appearing in ad campaigns for blank tape manufacturers such as TDK and Memorex. Duping was slowly becoming an industry *cause célèbre* and a rationalization for its rocky sales picture.

Within weeks RIAA issued a strong objection signed by myriad chief executive officers. The statement requested a cessation of uninterrupted airing of new releases. After chronicling the "abuses," the appeal stated:

> This overt action to foster home taping saps the lifeblood of the recording industry.
>
> Radio's encouragement of home taping is bad for radio too. It attacks the very resources of artists and recordings which are the corner-stones of radio's own programming and ability to attract audiences and commercial advertisers.
>
> A traditional and important interrelationship has existed to bind radio, recordings, and artists. That mutually beneficial rapport is worth maintaining.

The implied threat meant little to broadcasters. Obviously, record companies in the midst of a severe recession were in no position to sanction radio stations, especially in major markets. Like it or not, airplay was the key for product exposure. Many programmers explained that their occupation involved selling spots, not records, to advertisers. One program director repeated: "We play records to attract the largest possible audience. If it sells, great. If not, that's their problem. It's numbers that count; the hell with record sales." He went on to suggest that "people don't listen to a record and the radio at the same time." Record companies ironically agreed: "Kids who tape albums off the air," noted RCA's Chuck Thagard, "take listenership away from stations when they subsequently play back those tapes." RIAA's request was honored by the now-defunct RKO network; others totally ignored it. "Bizzers" transferred their anger to tape manufacturers and consumers.

The disappointing sales performance of Fleetwood Mac's new album energized the home-taping outcry; still the finger pointers lacked concrete evidence. The link between diminishing record sales and rocketing cassette purchases was a tenuous relationship at best. The opinions voiced had precious few facts to support them. Kent Burkhart, a consulting radio guru, told a journalist he would be "very surprised if a great number of listeners are taping."[65] He speculated that tapers were 2 percent or less of radio listeners, and promised a research survey. Burkhart then claimed surprise when 18 percent of the 18-through-34 age group in 13 states admitted taping albums off the air. He believed tapes were made to facilitate a purchase decision.[66]

The pink slips kept coming. WCI, A & M, Ariola, & MCA trimmed their personnel rosters. A & M fired 50 people. Warner, Atlantic, and Elektra/Asylum displaced nearly 45 employees. Ariola shut its West Coast operations and retreated to New York, cutting its staff from seventy-four to a skeletal crew of five. Industry belt tightening by the close of 1979 cost about 2,000 individuals their livelihood.

The year-end rush of "hit" product was dampened when CBS announced higher wholesale prices and a much stricter return policy. Retailers and wholesalers objected. A large "one-stop" operator complained, "CBS is our number one supplier, but the 20 percent returns policy restricts us." Others underlined that "defectives" accounted for 10 percent of records issued, leaving them only another 10 percent for unsold product. A CBS executive replied that the buyers will be forced "to accept the reality of the business and they will have to become real businessmen. Theirs has been a supported business, for too long." The company's general manager of marketing said wholesale "must adapt or change to gain more control of their accounts. Returns are much too high, it's been absurd and obscene."[67]

PolyGram followed suit, announcing a returns policy of 18 to 22 percent. A company spokesman claimed defectives constituted an insignificant portion of existing returns. RCA joined ranks: a 22 percent plan on returns was being put into place. Henry Droz, president of WEA, augered a policy alteration by suggesting "the concept of 100% returns is an unrealistic mode of doing business in the future."[68]

Caught in the throes of holiday planning, dealers found WEA's new returns policy more palatable. Beginning in 1980, the WCI distribution arm would impose an 18 to 22 percent limit. The cost would be dependent on volume and shipbacks, and those under the ceiling percentile would be rewarded. With reservations, most agreed with Sam Billis, a one-stop entreprener, "It sounds all right. I can live with it. Their stuff moves right out. Their salesmen don't come like CBS and PolyGram with quotas to load you."[69]

The distribution strategies by majors and others appeared well timed. In the midst of superstar releases, retailers were in a poor bargaining position. They needed the new product; especially, with holiday buying only a month away. Retailers grumbled, pointing to the Michael Jackson album as defective, but most expected strong sales. Ben Karol predicted a successful Christmas season.

Karol's bullishness had a hollow ring after the Thanksgiving weekend. A *Billboard* survey of retailers discovered a relatively flat market. Only a handful of top-charted albums showed any action, and multiple purchases were low. A Peaches buyer in Atlanta reported, "Fleetwood Mac and Stevie Wonder are selling okay but disappointingly considering they're superstar acts." The Nashville outlet for Camelot Records found *Tusk* "moving rather slowly." A chain vice-president: "Our volume is down. Except for several monster smashes . . . there's not much big product out there."[70]A four-day, last-minute Christmas rush partially reversed the sluggish pattern. (Significantly, the trade publications paid scant attention to a period where 25 percent of yearly volume is expected to turnover. *Billboard* ran a two-column sidebar minus a headline on 5 January 1980; highly unusual for the traditionally optimistic magazine.)

Having unleashed the big guns for the year-end sales push made the annual shareholder report look brighter. The industry coasted into the 1980s without much fanfare. The bottom line for 1979 was staggering. A twenty-five-year growth pattern had ended. Record and tape shipments in a twelve-month span went from 725 million in 1978 to 683 million; sales dipped from $4.1 to $3.7 billion. The CBS Records Group, the industry leader, reported a 46 percent drop in operating profits. Infinity and Capricorn Records were nonoperational. Capricorn filed for Chapter 11 bankruptcy. Phil Walden's miraculous Georgia-based company was $9 million in debt. The *Wall Street Journal* estimated 2,000 industry employees had been displaced. Artist signings with name labels in the last half of 1979 were down by 28 percent. CBS, on the other hand, offered Paul McCartney "one of the fattest royalty contracts" in music business history. The adage of "when in trouble buy superstars" remained in vogue. Signing the former Beatle promised to help the financial future of CBS but did little for the industry as a whole. "In his case going from one giant to another doesn't do much for the music or the customer," an observer commented. "All it will do is raise record prices. You watch." The unidentified spokesperson was prophetic. In passing months as volume declined, prices escalated a dollar. Copying the automotive industry, record "bizzers" raised prices on chart product; a few selected catalog items were reduced to $5.98. These lower-priced albums enjoyed a brisk turnover as the older rockers replaced time-worn titles. "Midline product has certainly been a boon to many of us," said a retailer. Price resistance was on the upswing in face of a faltering economy, and more significantly a lackluster music scene.

Disco and new wave returned to a specialty or cult status in spite of the money and energy the industry lavished on them. Karin Berg, Warner's A & R person, noted, "The new wave mania has passed. Other companies which used to laugh at it became berserk, and went out and grabbed everything. . . .[I] have become increasingly reluctant to sign anything."[71] Acts with a long-standing rate of success continued to create sales. Of the twenty top artists on the 5 January 1980 *Billboard* LP chart, only *two* were relative newcomers; Tom Petty was joined by Rufus with Chaka Khan. Three months later sixteen familiar names, especially Pink Floyd and Billy Joel, placed in the leading twenty. Only Pat Benatar would repeat her chart-climbing feat. Speaking to a group of stock security analysts, Walter Yet-nikoff remarked, "Customers still have a definite interest in 'must-have' records, though to a certain extent the list of 'must-have' records has diminished."[72] With soaring studio and marketing costs, record executives were hedging their bets. New-artist signings dropped. Option renewals for "marginal" performers became infrequent. The value of stars rose as their ranks shrank. Kenny Rogers, the Who, Diana Ross, Mick Jagger, and others switched companies for seven-figure advances.

Buying Yetnikoff's "must-have" acts in a soft, recessed market promised more "cost-management" programs. The money for inflated royalties had to come from somewhere. Marketing expenses once again came under fire, and those affected predictably reacted. Retailers strongly objected to various cuts in co-op (joint) advertising budgets and in-store audiovisual promotion. Letters flooded the trade magazines when direct complaints to the manufacturers fell on deaf ears. One correspondent grumbled, "Retailers are being penalized (less promo service and display material, smaller advertising budgets and tightened return policies) by the manufacturers for their loss of revenue while labels themselves are a large part of the problem. The artist, distributor and retailer are the ones taking the losses."[73] Segments of the media objected to being excluded.

After cutting service (promotional) lists to the bone, WEA announced enforcement of a two-dollar charge for 90-day-old releases. One spokesperson explained, "The policy is to prevent abuses or unreasonable demand on catalog. But we don't want to put the screws to radio people." This fairly diplomatic expression was more than countered by Ken Buttice of Elektra/Asylum. He told *Billboard*: "What we're trying to stop is the DJ at the boondocks radio station, who as soon as he gets records, gives them away to his family and then calls the record company and wants more." Rip Pelley, at the same label, stressed that the policy would not affect the larger broadcasters: "We're still going to sponsor station giveaways and be involved in any promotions we were involved in, in the past. If each individual DJ at a station is the programmer of his own show he's going to continue to receive service."[74] It was quickly noted that the "continued services" generally applied to the highly competitive, large urban regions.

Buttice's "boondocks" characterization of secondary and tertiary market stations was overly impolitic. Product service is a perennial sore point with programmers and journalists in the "minor leagues." It is an obsessive topic of discussion at broadcaster conventions. Trade magazine "letter-to-the-editor" sections abounded with unhappy media people, electronic and print, complaining about the lack of company service. Roy Kristofferson, WNBZ-AM (New York), angrily replied to Buttice's statements:

> Rural radio stations are the vagabonds of the industry. Many of us are starving for promotional product because "it's not what you are, but where you are." Small market stations . . . should not be fingered as the fall guy. If there is an overwhelming need to find a cause, WEA and many other record companies might look to the cities and perhaps internally to find waste.[75]

A midwest music critic for a news daily with a 50,000 circulation echoed these sentiments. Preferring to remain anonymous, he said:

> When I first started here I went through the usual channels. Promoters, concert hall people and record companies were called. The local concert people are pretty good although . . . can be a hassle. Record companies are something else. Some of them just plain lie to you, especially branch promo people.

Many secondary-market programmers dislike, sometimes despise, record companies, especially promotion people. A "heavy" program director and consultant said, "They complain about our operations. You should have been there when I was starting in the business. They wouldn't give me the time of day." The two-dollar catalog charge was minimal; however, the atmospherics surrounding the announcement only heightened the intense relationship between labels and media. Several radio stations rebelled by boycotting companies. WYER in Illinois put Motown on hold for lack of service. Jimmie Cole of KTIB wrote CBS: "I regret to inform you that because we have not received CBS product during the past 6 weeks, KTIB will no longer play or report any record bearing a CBS label." Most small stations just complained and purchased some product. Any semblance of goodwill evaporated—this at a time when exposure for new records and acts was scarce.

As industry executives pondered various strategies to combat the downturn, their Madison Avenue counterparts pored over the 1980 census data. Advertisers saw the U.S. population was aging and decided to emphasize the over-25 market. The result for broadcasters was significant. So-called Top-40 singles stations with a hot rotation of 14 to 16 tunes reprogrammed, stressing "adult" fare. John Lund of New York's WNBC-AM observed: "The music is going softer. There will be less harsh rock 'n' roll. You won't hear much of the B-52's or the Clash."[76] Advertisers' time buys, the mother's milk of electronic media, legitimized the older targeting.

In the opening three months of 1980, all were wrong. According to the influential *Blair Radio Report;* the most sought after age groups was the 25-to-54 group. Over 26 percent of paid radio ads were beamed at this generation. Lund suggested that the 25-to-34 bracket was "pivotal." The 18-24 collectivity attracted an insignificant percentage of Madison Avenue money. These findings got station managers' attention very quickly. The emphasis on advertising dollars by AM outlets relegated album exposure to the FM album-oriented (AOR) stations. The stength of AOR was the 18-to-24 demographic, with a bent toward the college audience. AOR, however, was commencing to reexamine its programming. Shifts in time-buying patterns are ignored only by comfortable noncommercial outlets, usually on National Public Radio (NPR) or campus outlets. Format alterations did not bode well for the record business.

A handful of "bizzers" saw this advertising ploy as an opportunity to bolster their MOR artists on the premise that rock fans would shift musical gears as they grew older. This assumption would prove highly suspect over the years.

Each generation coalesces into its own musical taste group. It has a pantheon of performers, songs, and styles. Big Country's Stuart Adamson's disparaging remark about rockabilly Stray Cats fans being "sexy 40-year olds" was partially correct. "The people who grew up on rock 'n' roll . . . now listen to country music," said Ed Salamon of WHN (New York).

The success of 1970s and 1980s nostalgia tours, such as Gary Puckett, the Association, the Turtles and "Happy Together" headlining Spanky McFarland, indicate 1960s rockers still enjoy *their brand of music,* which has little to do with contemporalia. Even a "Third Coming" would not divorce Presley, the Beatles, and early Led Zeppelin enthusiasts from their musical preferences.

There was some question as to the actual sales power of the mega-acts. The Beatles at the peak of their popularity saw Herb Alpert's Tijuana Brass sell more albums in 1966. Gary Puckett and the Union Gap, treated by most critics as a middle-of-the road bubble-gum act, surpassed the Liverpudlians in records purchased two years later. Whatever the empirical facts, the perception was the reality. Record labels were in good company as rock historians, popular culturists, and others used Presley and the Beatles—sometimes Dylan—to accentuate the music of the 1950s and 1960s.

In this stormy environment, RIAA and company executives resurrected the home taping issue, a topic that broadcasters, large and small, disliked: "I'm not in the business of selling records" responded a PD (program director). He might have added, home tapers listen to the station, increasing ratings in a very competitive market.

Duplication of any kind suddenly became "stealing" for *some* music business folks, regardless of the legality of home use. *Billboard* reported home taping paralleled piracy as *the* preoccupation in the executive suites. Addressing broadcasters in a full-page open letter, Joe Smith wrote: "For an industry such as ours, plagued for years by piracy, bootlegging, counterfeiting, and the effects of this year's inflation and recession, this can be the most dangerous threat thus far to our well being."[77]

A more reliable source of information was the Copyright Royalty Tribunal study of taping habits. The data provided the record industry with half-hearted support. The study indicated 40 percent of tapers increased their music purchases and an equal percentage bought less: a standoff. The only backup for the record makers came from the finding that approximately 70 percent of home recording respondents would not pay for music they could tape. Even this was muddied because a mere 35 percent of the sample copied entire albums. The study was inconclusive but provided ammunition for both sides of the question.[78] *Billboard* for 8 December 1979 headlined, "Cassettes Gaining the U.S." The matter was far from settled.

*Rolling Stone* entered the fray. The mass-market publication sided with the home tapers, many of whom were subscribers. Stereo hardware and cassette companies were substantial contributors to the advertising coffers of the magazine. The issue for 24 January featured 51 ads of a quarter half page or more. Only six plugged records; hardware and tape ads numbered 25, nearly 50 percent of paid material. In the same pages *Rolling Stone* reviewed the topic. After reporting the Burkhart and Copyright Tribunal findings, and editorial concluded:

> It seems then, that most home tapers fall into one of two categories: either they are taping an album to see if they like it (and if they do, chances are they'll want to spends seven or eight bucks on a higher quality recording [*sic*], or they are supplementing their record purchases. It's ironic that those who fall into the second group are the real fans—the same people who are helping to keep record companies in business.
>
> All things considered, it seems that airing entire albums on the radio does the record companies more good than harm. Should record companies seek legislation to ban this practice, as [Joe] Smith and other executives have advocated, it would amount to an attempt at censorship. There are many reasons for the current music business slump—to blame it on home taping is taking the easy way out.[79]

The editorial reflected the majority view of *Rolling Stone's* readership if letters are any gauge. In four months *Rolling Stone* followed up with a feature story, "Crisis? What Crisis?" The thrust of Robert Wallace's lengthy piece was that the record industry without sufficient facts was using home taping as a "smokescreen" for internal ills. Record prices, contended Wallace. "have finally risen too high." This was heady stuff for *Rolling Stone,* whose birth was financially midwifed by Warner, CBS, and others.

In the past Jann Wenner's journal had exercised extreme caution in covering the industry. Music publications, dependent upon record companies' advertising dollars, have been leery of biting the hand that feeds them. An open admission of hard times in the music world was believed to undermine the urgency and circulation of the magazine (see chapter 6). Other than *Rolling Stone,* few counterculture-based magazines survived the self-serving seventies.

Joe Smith and Stan Gortikov responded to *Rolling Stone's* story. Smith wrote, "When they develop the home photo copier that will enable everyone to knock off *Rolling Stone* without all those troublesome record-company ads, we'll save a seat on the plane to Washington." Gortikov raised the same photocopying point: "If you can so comfortably justify unbridled home taping of recordings then why don't you likewise allow the free use and duplication of any *Rolling Stone* copyrighted editorial feature?"[80]

A consumer simply commented, without the shaky analogies, "If the record companies hadn't raised the price of a disk by three dollars over the last three years, I wouldn't have to resort to airwave recording."[81]

Beginning with PolyGram, record firms adopted a cosmetic approach to curtail home taping. Retailers were informed that allowance or "co-op" monies would not be paid for ads that promoted blank cassettes. A vice-president for Chrysalis explained, "We make music available and why should we encourage consumers to tape LP's or radio? We don't make any money when they do."[82] Retailers were upset with the co-op policy, especially because it came on the heels of the returns edict. Sam Goody's and Korvettes, heavy-volume buyers, ignored the edict.

Tape manufacturers, gathered at the annual Consumer Electronics Shows, finally broke their silence. "When times are tough it's easy to blame somebody else," stated a spokesman for Audio Magnetics." "I don't think the record labels have done their homework." Al Pepper of Memorex: "Blank tape is not selling that much more. And where are the hard facts and statistics? Where is the research from record firms which shows that their claims are true? Blank tapes hurting the record business? It just ain't so." Correctly, he added, "They are alienating record retailers, radio stations and now blank tape manufacturers."[83] Other conferees recited the usual arguments, all denying any culpability in causing record industry problems. Sony's introduction of the portable Walkman falsely heightened "bizzers" concern. Other than from music publishers, the record labels found very little support.

Some industry insiders privately voiced reservations about the home-taping issue. One executive observed, "Gortikov and Smith are engaging in media overkill. Honestly, they make the industry look like a bunch of money-hungry bastards. People are price resistant in a recession." Pausing, "We're paying the price for punk and disco." David Geffen, insider extraordinaire, said on the record:

> It's hysterical. It's the reaction of people who don't know what the f--k is happening with their business and why they aren't making money. Instead of looking at the real source of their problems—lack of creativity and the ability to identify the right kinds of artists or the fact that they are recording too many of the wrong artists—they are saying the problem is home taping. It's not so."[84]

During the hardware- and cassette-tax debate, Geffen, when with WEA, recanted this statement.

The relationship between labels and independent distributors plus retailers was turning adversarial. At the fall National Association of Recording Merchandisers (NARM), meeting the product sellers vented their pent-up hostility. The nationwide economic recession was a prime concern; however, much of the discontent was aimed at the "bizzers" in New York and Los Angeles. Absence of industry planning, lackluster product, defectives, and return policies took center stage. Carl Rosenbaum of Flip-Side Records noted, "A lot of the lack of sales has to do with a lack of a lot of really good product to draw customers in." Another operator explained, "The industry as a whole has not been able to shift gears and react to changes in *taste* and *demographics.* The records being fed to them [buyers] are not necessarily what they want to buy at this point." Others grumbled about the pressing quality. One said, "Manufacturers tell us there's no problem with quality. But still there is a majority of returns [defectives] that are a problem. "The retailers pointed to the imports as demonstrating a demand for high record quality. Labels offered the relatively unconvincing argument that superior audio hardware "made" records sound bad by magnifying imperfections. Home tapers retorted, "The record industry's crying simply because we have found a dependable product in tapes. I've got a hundred-dollar cartridge, and I could just . . . when I spend eight bucks for a record that sounds like I'm using a nail instead of a needle."[85]

Retailers groused about the apparent flood of sound tracks. During the NARM meeting a quarter of the top-twenty albums were from movies. Noel Gimbel, a chain merchandiser, said, "Every sound track that comes out is the next *Saturday Night Fever.*" Some viewed film scores as "one-shot" items for atypical consumers. "People came in for *Saturday Night Fever* who I've never seen and won't ever again," asserted a Bowling Green,

Ohio, retailer. "One-shot" consumers are welcome, but retailers are in search of regulars—people who buy three or more titles a year. Music freaks with disposable income, as advertisers joined with retailers were quick to note, were entering their late twenties, thus leaving the marketplace, it appeared, to adolsecents and collegians with spotty cash flows or to "impulse" sound track buyers. These demographic fluctuations did little to instill a sense of confidence or security in an economically bedeviled industry.

Market analyst Harold Vogel of Merrill Lynch provided the industry with a contradictory growth picture. Sales would resume, he suggested, following the national economic recession. But the industry was faced with technological and demographic challenges: The shrinkage of the prime record-buying 14-to-25 age group by 7 million from 1979 to 1990 may be difficult for the industry to recoup.[86]

Stan Cornyn, testifying before the Copyright Royalty Tribune, added to Merrill Lynch's analysis. He cited skyrocketing production and marketing costs. The decline of "baby boomers," he claimed, made for "real problems on the horizon." "There's more than a recession going on right now in the record business. There's a transition to something that we're not sure what it is. There are so many variables we're grappling with . . .I have never seen anything like this before."[87] Cornyn, as always, presented an astute state-of-the art report while his industry peers were grumbling about the audiophiles and tape decks. Like Geffen, he would moderate his stance during the "Save the Music" foray.

The anti-home-taping publicity campaign was minimized, the reasons for which are unclear. The temporary low profile may have been caused by a severe shortage of allies. The labels realized little support from most segments of the music industry. Consumers rallied around prices and poor reproduction standards for all prerecorded music; cassettes were particularly criticized for limited selection, high list prices—a dollar above LPs—and sound performance. Moreover, as the *Rolling Stone* editorial indicated, the empirical data were unconvincing. Like scripture, the Burkhart and Copyright Tribunal studies could persuasively be used by either of the opposing camps. CBS and WCI commissioned independent studies of the taping "problem."

The legalistic shadow of the Sony Betamax case may have darkened a few executive suites in Hollywood. Disney and Universal had lost the first court battle over copyright infringement with video cassette recorders (VCRs), and the decision was on appeal.

A cursory examination of the evolution of the film and record industries suggests some major historical similarities. Both were struck by external assaults in the 1940s and 1950s. Television demolished the motion-picture studio system; rock and roll nearly destroyed the stranglehold of the major labels. Film studios shifted to independent distribution and producers; record companies followed suit. Studios enjoyed performance rights; music "bizzers" went after the same protection. The Betamax defeat definitely seemed to have ramifications for the record industry as well. It also served as a harbinger of the future when the judicial tide momentarily came in.

The film model for record executives has rarely been explored. Film was the dominant entertainment medium in the United States for decades. Marketing and distribution techniques were pioneered by the studios. Powerful in-house directors predated the A&R people of the 1940s and 1950s. Labels, either by their geographic propinquity or by scanning *Variety* and the *Hollywood Reporter*, learned quite a lot from filmmakers. Warner's Mo Ostin: "I've always tended to draw the analogy between film studios and record companies, and I've thought the ideal record company arrangement should be analogous to the movie studios in their heyday."[88]

The rise of entertainment conglomerates such as MCA, Warner, and Columbia Pictures created some interchangeability of executives and ideas. RCA and CBS with their television networks underwent the same corporate intermingling. Consequently, by the 1980s the worldview of both mediums was similar. One film producer told National Public Radio,"Music sells pictures as well as records."

In October of 1980 CBS Records issued its promised study, "Blank Tape Buyers—Their Attitudes and Impact On Prerecorded Music Sales." The study, based on a sample of 7,500 interviewees and 1,100 questionnaire respondents, alleged record companies were losing 20 percent of their sales, an estimated $700-$800 million, to tapers. The figures were derived from the assumption the average duper would have brought three more albums per year. The actual data, however, supported the notion that cassette consumers bought more albums than nontapers. Jerry Shulman, CBS marketing director, observed, "What the survey shows is that they would buy even more if it were not for home taping."[89]

The study revealed that a mere 20 percent of the sample taped from radio tuners; 30 percent borrowed albums to tape; and 40 percent of the tapings were made from the duper's own collection. Half of the sample reproduced for automobile use or portable units. Fifty percent gave credibility to the argument of Gene LaBrie of Maxell that "people are primarily interested in the best sound quality they can get for their money, not in the most economical way to build a musical library."[90]

The industry-financed study found that the heaviest blank-tape consumers were between 26 and 40, and annually purchased 100 million tapes. Rock-oriented "yuppies" (young, upwardly mobile professionals) also purchased high-priced digital or otherwise enhanced albums of their favorites, usually retailing at $15.95.

The findings were not as conclusive as Dick Asher, vice-president of CBS, would suggest. The widely reported loss of $700 million was a projection of what people *may* do rather than an empirical fact. The sound-quality issue was generally ignored in the study, despite the fact a quarter of the respondents cited audio excellence as their prime motivation for taping. The age factor was minimized. Still, Asher concluded that the survey "demonstrate[s] that home taping is among the most severe problems facing the industry. It is our hope that the industry will continue to seek out ways to cope with this problem." The 15-page report was mailed to the media, NARM and RIAA members.

The unspoken undercurrent in the home-taping controversy was demographic. Most music audiophiles concerned with superior sound reproduction were owners of expensive hardware units. They were not the stereotypical teenagers with a "boom box," and the portable Walkman lacks an input record capability. Sony street models are strictly listening devices. By taxing the hardware, the industry could indirectly tap into the cash flow from a demographic unit it was losing. Profiles of the owners of high-grade audio hardware suggest middle- or upper- class college-educated males, frequently with taste preferences in the speciality genres such as jazz and symphonic.

The year 1980 was trendless and economically flat year, tragically marked by the assassination of John Lennon on 8 December: "It was the negation of a spirit and life force that embodied just about all of what was great and important about rock music, about life."[91] Lennon's death had a stunning impact. One consequence, observable in subsequent record sales, was a retrospective appreciation of 1960s music. The tribute broadcasts, some lasting a week, rekindled interest in the Beatles. Other 1960s stalwarts reemerged. The Door's *Greatest Hits* was a platinum record; the Who achieved a similar award for *Face Dances*. AOR stations welcomed requests for oldies' sounds as they paralleled advertisers' concerns. Led Zeppelin's "Stairway to Heaven" was still the most requested cut. Some cynics suggested Lennon and Yoko Ono's *Double Fantasy* benefited from the mindless murder; it would sell 3 million units.

The RIAA results for the year found dollar volume exhibiting a slight rise to $3.68 billion from the 1979 total of $3.67 billion. This figure can be misleading because units shipped dropped by a substantial 34 million. Price hikes and less product was the bottom line. CBS and WCI received a bigger share of a shrinking market: WCI's music division posted an 11 percent gain; CBS reported a revenue rise to $1.13 billion from $1.04

billion in 1979, a gain of 8 percent. Veteran record executive Jay Lasker was prophetic:

> The record business is no longer an individual entreprenuer's heaven, it belongs to the really big guys, to the conglomerates, and this in itself influences a change in style and approach. . . . We are not in a different ball game. The overshipping of records, returns, discounts hidden discounts, deals, credit allowances, control of product and its packaging and the like, are all part of overall corporate strategies.[92]

Richard Harrington of the *Washington Post* aptly described the starting months of 1981, when a number of Lennon albums mixed in with new wave efforts ruled the charts: "The hottest new trend in the music business has *nothing* to do with music. Forget the rise of country, the death of disco, the mellowing of rock."[93] Harrington's slant was correct, the year had begun on the fading memory of Lennon's departure and a music scene without any sense of purpose or direction. A few outspoken music journalists were already expanding Don McLean's "the day the music died" ("American Pie") to link Lennon's fate to Buddy Holly's. There existed a handful of fairly obvious parallels; Holly's air crash marked the end of a mythologized music era, and Lennon's death appeared to symbolize a similar termination.

Radio advertisers during the first half of 1981 were primarily concerned with the 25-to-54 market. *Major Market Radio Sales* reported 32.2 percent of targeted time buys were aimed at the collectivity. Conversely, the teens generated only 2.3 percent. Ad placers, however, were hedging a bit by continuing moderately to address the 18-through-24 group. The figures read by broadcasting organizations clearly indicated buyers demanded the aging audience.

For broadcasters, expecially with an AOR format, the new economic realities posed a programming dilemma. Arbitron (ARB) ratings surveys— "numbers"—repeatedly found that the over-25 listeners were heavily into the adult contemporary and specialty sounds categories. Beautiful music, the dentist-office variety, had excellent numbers in most markets. These potential consumers infrequently bought records.

The specter of advertising "targeting" bode an ill wind for the record industry. Playlists and format changes usually followed directions hatched by Madison Avenue. Playlists were already tight and "horizontal," that is, appealing to all demographic groups. CHR (Contemporary Hits Radio) personified this broadcasting assault. As in 1967, when AM-Boss Radio blocked album play, the industry was desperately searching for an alternative vehicle for visibility. "Free-form" underground FM provided the answer in the late 1960s. Cable television would appear as the alternative of the eighties.

On 1 August 1981 Warner Amex's Music Television (MTV) became nationally available to cable operators. It was introduced as "a top 40 radio station [sic] broadcast from coast-to-coast with programming found nowhere else on the airwaves. . . add video to complete the picture." MTV was an expensive $20 million gamble because rock's relationship with television had been beset with horror stories. Company executives were somewhat elated by MTV's Bob Pittman's philosophy: "We'll be breaking the music for them [radio stations]. The exposure helps the music industry as a whole, because it's really lost its luster lately. MTV will be innovative and creative, and get people recharged about music"[94] On that note MTV was introduced as the "new" exposure flagship in the music industry.

The music channel would be treated like its audio counterpart. Labels would supply the video clips to be aired on the cable system. Video "service" was considerably more expensive to produce and supply. According to some insiders, the average 4-minute clip cost $15,000 to $30,000. Most clips originally consisted of concert footage and oldies kinescopes.

An immediate problem was that many well-known artists were nontelegenic. ("Talking" pictures had destroyed the careers of a host of silent film stars such as John Gilbert). The medium being the message, MTV and its imitators would rely on dramaturgical-theatrical rock bands to fit the format. New acts with footage discovered fertile ground to showcase their musical wares. MTV would have a significant effect. Some of the consequences would exhibit a Frankenstenish quality (see chapter 7).

The Rolling Stones September tour indirectly justified advertisers' concerns. The 20-city tour generated $25 million in ticket sales. *Tatoo You* was critically acclaimed the best album of the year. Jann Wenner, in a rare bylined *Rolling Stone* editorial, wrote: "Rock and Roll is here to stay if you want it. The Rolling Stones clearly want it, and judging from the success of their tour—so do we all."[95] The successful Stones tour on the heels of the Simon and Garfunkel reunion gave "bizzers" a moment for pause. Some critics labeled the Stones "the world's oldest rock band," and Simon and Garfunkel were considered a one-shot, concert-LP special arrangement.

Record executives seemed to be hopeful. The marketing and distribution changes apparently were functioning. The advent of MTV appeared promising. Gil Friesen, A & M president, claimed, "We've become a real business. Now the record executives are talking about overheads and costs like every other business man in the country." *Newsweek* declared, "There may never be another Elvis, but with sound management and new technology on the way, the record industry is confident that it can recreate some of his kind of magic in the marketplace."[96] Days after this article the judicial system would further underscore the claim of Doug Morris of Atlantic that the industry was "alive and well."

The U.S. Ninth Circuit Court of Appeals in October 1981 revived the dormant home-taping "vampire." Its 16-page ruling overturned the district court ruling in the famous Sony VCR case. The court found that Universal and Walt Disney studios were correct in insisting that video home recording was a copyright "infringement," and stated that manufacturers, ad agencies, and video retail suppliers were legally liable. It suggested that a ban might be considered or that a royalty payment could be assessed on each VCR sold. A ban, most observers commented, would be unenforceable, and because the 5 million owners of video hardware purchased prerecorded video cassettes, a royalty or tax levy per cassette and recorder seemed more economically appropriate.

Music industry spokespersons welcomed the ruling. Stan Gortikov saw it as legitimizing the RIAA contention that "copyrighted audio and video works deserved protection from all forms of unauthorized copying."[97] BMI's Elizabeth Granville viewed the ruling as adding "great impetus to the bill it would not ordinarily have"; [98] BMI was working on federal legislation to impose a tax or royalty on audio hard- and software. The court had handed the record companies a tax-levy tool more convincing than all the previous statements of indignation and surveys combined.

Hard on the heels of the Betamax case reversal Senator Dennis DeConcini sponsored a bill allowing videotaping for private use. Senator Charles Mathias offered an amendment requiring a royalty payment for video recording of any kind; his original amendment had ignored audio taping. Gortikov looked upon the amendment as a natural vehicle for filmmakers and record labels to exhibit a "commonality of interest." He expanded this view for *Rolling Stone*: "We felt that if we didn't get in there when there was this focus on copyright it would be a long time before another chance came along. That's why we opportunistically chose to get on the bill."[99]

Another holiday season came in the midst of gloomy unemployment figures. The prevailing attitude was "it looks pretty good, but we'll probably end up flat with last year." A dismal Thanksgiving weekend dampened the original 1981 retailing projections, but a late December shopping spree lifted the spirits of some retailers. A *Billboard* canvass reported a 7 percent holiday volume increase over the past year. Several retailers noted, "We compensated in cassette increases." The Rolling Stones in the wake of their highly publicized tour were the hottest Christmas item. Still, *Tattoo You* did not surpass the Kenny Rogers offering of 1980. A fast-moving title was RCA's *Hooked On Classics,* described as "vanilla pop" aimed toward 30-year-old listeners. Few would disagree with Bob Christgau's characterization, "The Bad Christmas of 1981."

Record companies promised "hot product" for the new year. Steve Holden, writing the annual *Rolling Stone* year-end wrap-up, pointed to a stagnation and closed the analysis soberly:

> Until the media find it profitable to promote a wider, more globally aware musical sensibility or until knowledge of it leaks through the radio-tv edifice to ignite the younger generation, American rock will probably continue to feast on its own past. It is a measure of our dread that it was far easier in 1981 to celebrate an old revolution than to prepare for a new one.[100]

Holden's revolution was not on the immediate horizon, but an uprising was brewing in English pubs, the New York headquarters of MTV, and record company legal offices.

Sales in 1981 dropped in dollar volume and units shipped. According to RIAA's original figures, units decreased by 50 million, and dollars showed a very insignificant swing dependent on the calculations. (In 1979 the RIAA altered its mode of calculating figures. The revised NPD methodology shows an increase of $11 million; the original methodology, a $5 million decline.) One set of numbers showed dollar volume below 1979 figures. Record producer Richard Perry told a reporter, "The recording business is sick but not terminal." The hit maker blamed the economy ("people aren't spending") and blank tapes, elaborating, "One kid buys an album for 7 dollars and a dozen of his or her pals copy the music on their cassette players for a dollar or two."[101]

Three Wall Street soothsayers expressed highly guarded optimism concerning the industry's growth potential. Harold Vogel of Merrill Lynch: "This business of music is not out of the woods yet in terms of its problems . . .there will. . .be tremendous competition from home video and the newer home arcade business." Dean Witter's Fred Anschel added, "There hasn't been anything really new to bring people into stores. With few exceptions, the charts have continued to be dominated by artists who've been around a long time." [102] They both predicted the worst was over. And about radio advertisers' continuing focus on the 25-to-54 age group as their "key demographic," Roy Lindau of *Market Radio* said, "This trend will continue in 1982 because yesterday's teens are in the . . . category." [103] So-called teen buys were down to a meager 2 to 3 percent of item purchased. Merchandisers echoed the New York blue suits.

Retailers complained vociferously about releases. The promised star product was absent. Talking to Leo Sacks, merchandisers listed their grievances. One chain operator lamented, "Major releases are still geared to the fourth quarter. No wonder kids are getting hooked on video games. There isn't enough new music to keep them interested in the record scene."

Others decried labels' "penny pinching" in advertising and wholesale pricing. Demographics, especially after the holiday season, were on the minds of many merchandisers. "Changing demographics can't be ignored. . .we're not reaching the soft-rock, MOR-oriented customer like we should," observed a rack executive. Roy Imber, president of 38 stores: "Streisand's *Guilty* and Kenny Rogers' *Greatest Hits* albums did extremely well with the 25-39-year-old consumer, and I don't think the labels are concentrating enough on the taste of this particular age group." [104] Labels again announced blockbuster releases by Kenny Rogers, Fleetwood Mac, Stevie Wonder, Paul McCartney, and others. Dealers' gripes could normally be dismissed as motivated by the scarcity of superstar titles; However, this time the surefire sellers were not moving as expected. Walter Yetnikoff said, "What we thought a couple of years ago would sell 150,000 might sell 50,000 now." [105] For whatever reason, star product was far below anticipated sales figures. *Tusk* sold one-sixth of Fleetwood Mac's *Rumors*. Queen, REO Speedwagon, Blondie, Peter Frampton, and others failed to repeat their previous successes.

Some entrepreneurs added Atari video games to their list of villains. Atari's role as scoundrel was paradoxical, for WEA would distribute the PAC-Man and Space Invaders cassettes. Retailers desired to cash in on the arcade video-game mania. Realizing the demand, WEA's Henry Droz attempted to balance these precarious scales. He said, "There will be complete separation of sales management and selling responsibility between our music and our Atari business. Music will not suffer." [106] Clive Davis discounted video games, claiming, "These games make sounds, but they don't create melodies. . . . You can't hum along with a video game or dance to its beat." [107] Davis did admit that lunch money and other discretionary dollars were being lost to Space Invaders. Droz and Arista's Davis appeared unconcerned, but many insiders were concerned. Warner's Atari connection seemed hypocritical, a bet-hedging ploy.

To complicate matters further, the nation's top weekly news magazines took dead aim at the music industry. The industry was unaccustomed to bad press, as its outcries in 1979 had exemplified. Jay Cocks of *Time* eulogized rock; "The thrill is gone" proclaimed the article subhead. Cocks blasted broadcasters and manufacturers for the debilitating decline of the rock culture. The bottom line was the catch-22 nature of the business. Discounting the effect of video games and home taping, he wrote: "With the record companies concerned mostly about making records that radio will play, and with the radio stations unable to play anything but what the record companies give them, the music may just have got lost in a lot of corporate second-guessing." [108]

*Newsweek's* Jim Miller provided a penetrating analysis of the state of the rock industry almost as a reply to Cocks. *Time's* "Rock Hits the Hard Place" was challenged with "Is Rock on the Rocks?" After detailing all of the familiar ills of AOR radio to the baby-boom generation, which was "more concerned with mortgages and babies than pop music," Miller closed on a cautiously upbeat note: "Rock 'n' Roll has a future all right, but . . ." the qualifier was a growing lack of sociocultural significance experienced by previous generations.

The two articles irritated many music people because neither author totally accepted the multitude of factors given for the "crash of '79" or the somnambulism of 1980s. Rather, both were expressing an overt sentiment, ignored by armies of insiders, that "it just wasn't in the grooves." A plethora of unthinkable propositions could follow from the news weeklies. In mass-communications jargon, "was it possible that the transmitters (labels and radio) sent out a flawed message unacceptable to millions of receivers?" The short-lived trends of the second half of the "Me Decade" lent some support to this argument. Moreover, the 1980s successes of revived 1960s artists added more credence to proponents of this view. Baby boomers were preoccupied with the rigors of suburban living, but the so-called midline reissues were the sales backbone of the early 1980s. The trend-conscious Jann Wenner practiced the unthinkable. *Rolling Stone's* pages were increasingly filled with articles treating politics, films, and other nonmusic subjects. Dylan's ode to the press, "You know something is happening but you don't know what it is do you Mister Jones?" did not include Wenner.

Broadcasters faced the same set of economic and population realities. The paths music stations chose were imperative. Making records outside the medium's format would create sure-fire stiffs or losses. The gastritis levels at record companies were further aggravated by the fragmentation of AM and especially by FM radio. AM Top 40 or Boss Radio was losing the under 25 crowd. AOR FM stations were experiencing a demographic identity crisis spurred by advertisers' demands and a generally unexciting music scene. Arbitron numbers in the first 1982 ARB "book" showed only a quarter of the 40 AOR stations in 20 major markets enjoying any ratings gains.

AOR staffers had experienced considerable ambiguity. Population trends and sales departments' demands could not be ignored. A broadcasting executive said, "We did shrink our teens by intent and we've improved the 25-to-49-year-old figures." A Cleveland program director echoed, "Oldies blocks on weekends is one way we reach women and 25-plus men . . . we play less heavy metal acts now." Don Davis in the nation's capital summed up the prevailing census-oriented viewpoint: "We're taking steps not to be just an 18-to-24 radio station; we're playing a wider list of oldies." He added, "The 25-to-34 group and women are by and large a *lost cause for AOR*" (emphasis added).

Hard rockers conceded the obvious, but clung to the position that younger listeners brought more. Rich Carroll asserted, "Advertisers may not think that audience is that valuable, but it is very valuable to the record community and radio industry. Those are the people who go to concerts buy the records and actively participate."

AM stations still courting "teen time buys" adopted a similar stance. Record companies pursuing the "youth market" had little choice. The labels went along because they shared a universal belief: "Once a person gets out of the 18-to-24 group, many go their different ways and it is extremely hard to reach them."[109]

Despite AM radio's low 22 percent share of the under-25 listeners, record company promotion people still saw it as a vital exposure tool, even with the emphasis on unprofitable singles. A CBS vice-president commented, "The lower demographic age group is still a big record buyer. They've really got to love AM to listen to it . . . (ouch) so a variable AM top 40 gets the same consideration as an FM station." Arista's Richard Palmese noted, "I look at ratings. I study targeted demos. However, if an AM station showed lower overall numbers but strong female penetration in the 25-34 group, and I was working product by Barry Manilow or Dionne Warwick, I would not ignore that information."[110] By implication Palmese was targeting an MOR market. MOR stations have "good numbers"; still, their listeners are very sporadic buyers of records. This was the dilemma for the record industry. Advertisers purchase time on radio stations with the "key demos." The population segment in the "key" group is notorious for its disc-buying weakness. A temporary solution by AOR PDs (program directors) was "fragmentation"—something for everybody--a conservative formula that appeared to irritate most listeners (see chapter 5). *Tune out* is a dirty term in the record business as well as in broadcasters' studios.

Atari sales were soaring. "Star Wars" and "Friday the 13th" buffs chose the box office instead of record stores as the place to deposit discretionary funds. Meanwhile, home taping returned to its place of prominence. The RIAA, among others, influenced some Senate leaders—including banjo picker and onetime recording artist Robert Byrd—to support Mathias's amendment. Mathias said the revised amendment "would extend . . . to include audio as well as video home taping activities in private homes."[111]

A large chain merchandiser cautioned, "Let's all be careful how we portray our situation, because the subsequent public reaction could be very negative towards our cause."[112] A top Sony spokesperson, Bill Baker, quickly counterattacked: the Betamax bill should not be confused by the music industry; home taping "is legal, by legislative history." Baker added that Gortikov was going to have to "overturn a practice that has been widespread for 30 years."[113]

In April sixteen organizations, led by the RIAA, formed the Coalition to Save America's Music" (CSAM). Broadcasters, retailers and, of course, equipment manufacturers were absent. Although a consensus was missing on royalty payments and their distribution, CSAM promised a vigorous public relations and legislative campaign for the amendment. The public relations push started immediately with the release of the long-promised, fifty-two-page report of the WCI survey of audio taping on the opening day of the spring NARM convention. NARM joined CSAM; the reason for this union has never been satisfactorily explained.

Annual taping losses, according to WCI, reached $2.85 billion, or an astounding 78 percent of annual industry earnings.

The survey, reportedly based on a sample of 2,300 respondents, indicated a majority taped to avoid buying prerecorded tapes: 45 percent of duplicators absorbed entire albums; 33 percent recorded individually owned material; 34 percent used borrowed records and tapes; and 21 percent taped off the airwaves. Another finding was that, demographically, the key culprits were not allowance-bound adolescents but young adults: the 20-to-34 age group accounted for half of the sample's tapers and for 69 percent of complete albums duplicated. By implication, the group could afford a royalty tax.

A House subcommittee traveled to Los Angeles to hold hearings. Representatives of the Home Recording Rights Coalition (HRRC) and CSAM appeared. Charles Ferris of HRRC restated the hardware manufacturers' position: home taping was legal. CSAM brought in big guns like former presidential adviser Alan Greenspan, who testified that home taping had occasioned an industry loss of $1.05 billion the previous year; Stan Gortikov, who read the WCI study's conclusions; and A & M's Jerry Moss. Using three albums, Moss illustrated the decline of "hit" product unit sales: *Frampton Comes Alive* sold 6.8 million copies in 1976; *Breakfast in America*, 4 million in 1978; and the Go-Go's *Beauty and the Beat* had not yet, in 1982, turned over half of Supertramp's successful *Breakfast* album. He blamed home taping for the decline and predicted an ominous future.

In a later Senate hearing opera star Beverly Sills challenged Senator DeConcini, and was joined by Jack Valenti of the Motion Picture Association of America, actor Charlton Heston, and naturally Stan Gortikov. Gortikov told the panel, "We know that home taping is destroying the value of our copyrights, jobs, careers, creativity."

The hearings received wide media coverage, especially the star witnesses. Still, the legislation was bottled up in committee. CSAM mounted a massive mail drive to support the Mathias amendment. One bulletin read: "We need grassroots support for this bill, mailgrams, letters, personal calls all directed at *ten key Senators,* asking their support." A packet of pamphlets, postcards, and testimonials accompanied the appeal. And HRRC, buoyed by the Supreme Court's acceptance of the video recording case, reinterated its strong opposition to a tax: "Hollywood being paid twice for the same use."

Jack Wayman of the Consumer Electronics Group was rapidly emerging as the leading spokesperson for the anti-Mathias forces. He told *Billboard,* "Now we're going after audio" because "the Supreme Court is a win for us."[114] True to his word, Wayman fired off a lengthy critique of the WCI study to the trade paper, which had become the debate's arena. He disputed attribution of the drop in sales of prerecorded units to taping; instead, the economic recession and "the onslaught of the competing video revolution" were the dominant factors. "The record industry reacted defensively and retrenched, thereby compounding its problems." Wayman restated the charges of shoddy product, poor marketing, and merchandising techniques. Readers of the trade paper were all too familiar with the issues addressed.

Wayman raised another matter, however, one rarely discussed by CSAM: "It is estimated that at least one-half of all tape recorders are used for non-copyrighted taping." Here, using WCI data, he scored a point. The Mathias amendment did ignore homemade videos and a multitude of uses for tape recording ranging from interviews to wedding ceremonies. The remainder of Wayman's article took an "industry-heal-thyself" posture rather than "pleading in the halls of Congress for new and inequitable taxes."[115]

The battle of the surveys resumed with the Electronics Industries Association (EIA) report. As with its predecessors, the findings could be used to buttress arguments on both sides. The sample consisted of 1,018 telephone interviews with users of audio tape over age 14. A bare majority, 52 percent, made tapes of non-music-oriented subjects. The study supported previous findings that frequent music dupers bought more prerecorded material than minimal users. Tapes from individually purchased records made up 51 percent of the sample; 49 percent came from broadcast or borrowed sources.

Several criticisms of the EIA report surfaced. Congressman Robert Kastenmeir suggested the questions might be biased. The pollsters had not asked if taping substituted for purchase. Nor had the study gauged the volume of lost unit buys. Gortikov noted the study supported CSAM's contention that a majority of tapers were duplicating records and tapes;

EIA countered that 52 percent were not music related.[116] After thousands of research dollars, none of the special-interest surveys had transcended the Copyright Tribunal data. Home taping was increasingly taking place as cassette sales soared, and prerecorded cartridges equally exhibited a higher volume in sales despite admitted title and audio quality limitations. On the other hand, the fairness of a usage tax and the actual dollar losses to labels plus music publishers were estimates at best. The decision on which of the two special interests would prevail was in the hands of 535 elected lawmakers.

One inescapable result of the debate of the coalitions was predicted by Joe Bressi: "public reaction could be very negative." If public opinion on the home-taping issue could be measured by youth-market papers and magazines, the readers were overwhelmingly unsympathetic to the woes of record companies. One widespread perception involved self-righteousness as a smokescreen for economic self-interest, an attitude most prevalent among active consumers of prerecorded music.

Top artists remained silent. Tom Petty earned a *Rolling Stone* cover story by objecting to a proposed dollar increase on his about-to-be-released *Hard Promises.* He explained, "Fighting the record industry—that ain't romantic, man. That's *survival . . .* it may look romantic, but I really ain't Robin Hood, man."[117] Petty's survival plan worked. Other artists disagreed, but only in private. One confided, "He's grandstanding. He works on a higher split [percentage] than the rest of us." Record buyers appreciated his stance.

As RIAA executives concentrated on congressional lobbying another anxiety-provoking Japanese import was on the horizon: record renting. A retailer in Japan began the rental plan in 1980, copying the merchandising methods used with video cassettes. In a matter of months 800 outlets appeared. The Japan Phonograph Record Association (JPRA) saw sale losses of 20 to 60 percent. Moreover, the JPRA estimated that 90 percent of the rented albums were taped.

Stateside, Rena's Rent-A-Record, a Toronto-headquartered firm, led in the new retailing technique. With four franchise stores, Rena's reportedly was doing a brisk business. A Providence, Rhode Island, outlet operator said, "I've rented 20,999 LP's thus far"—a figure based on one year's volume. So-called mom-and-pop stores copied Rena's marketing gimmick. Music Odyssey in Los Angeles was renting a new record for one dollar. Other retailers charged more; $2.50 per thirty-six-hour rental was normative. Nearly all of the practioners justified the approach in light of high record prices. A San Jose renter: "For music afficionados, it seems, there really is a way to beat the high cost of listening." In Omaha a retailer explained, "Because the labels were asking such hellish prices." Joe Smith told *Newsweek,* "We have got to stop this before it becomes an epidemic."

The rental phenomenon was short-lived but served to fuel further the antitaping forces.[118]

As the storm clouds gathered, the media were rerunning the doomsday scenarios of the "new crash of '82." A front-page *New York Times* article by Robert Palmer received considerable attention. The thrust of the piece was that the slump of 1982 was ushering in the end of an era. Palmer outlined the woes besetting the industry, and cited the obligatory villains of home taping and arcade games in addition to the conservatism of AOR. He noted that bored rock fans might accept the music of new artists if they were exposed to it, but "AOR stations do not play the new material."[119] Palmer assigned the labels some blame for the slump, and said that independent companies were releasing music with a vitality unheard on AOR stations. He closed by quoting a superstar manager: "The big companies have reacted by cutting back, trimming their staffs and their budgets . . . that means it will take even longer for the industry to get healthy again, because what's going to be cut first? . . . The new acts, the future of the industry." A touch of the "Third-Coming" syndrome.

*Billboard's* editorial staff reacted within a week. The august *Times,* a widely admired model in print jounalism, was a national opinion maker too important to ignore. The trade paper described Palmer's article as "realistic, if down beat." Most of *Billboard's* wrath was directly aimed at the *Los Angeles Herald Examiner's* conclusion: "The summer the music business died." The rebuttal was applicable to the *Times*:

> No newspaper considered the emerging significance of cable TV's growing role as an alternative channel for exposing music . . . [or] how the business has started to take potential 'problems' like the rise of cassette tapes and actively seek new business. . . . It would be naive to overlook the severity of the problems. . . . But it's equally naive to transform current transitional pains into an epitaph."[120]

CBS Records Group enjoyed good chart position in 1982. The profit picture was another matter; revenues declined by 15 percent the first quarter. "The troubled consumer economy and an expected low level of major record releases caused a loss," said CBS. The second quarter improved to a 2 percent downside figure. In August a major firing and company restructuring was announced. Three hundred staffers, the largest such cutback since 1979, were pinkslipped, including nine vice-presidents. Nine branch offices were closed. CBS was tight-lipped about the dismissals, speaking only of "the realities of today's marketplace." CBS radio advertising buys plus co-op advertising monies were reportedly halved.

*Rolling Stone* continued the journalistic assault. Kurt Loder and Steve Pond's lead sentence read: "The U.S. record industry is in the worst shape in its history."[121] The authors dutifully eleborated on the companies' hard times, then pointed to "poor management and the increasing burden of extravagant long-term recording contracts" as the main culprit. They also brought up a subject close to readers' pocketbooks: high prices. Citing the opinions of retailers, Loder and Pond said that adolescents in a recessionary period could not afford the $8.98 list price, and consequently record stores were poorly stocked—a situation compounded by the labels' return policies. They neglected to mention the negative credit-line policies that had been effectuated in late 1979. The close was somewhat conciliatory: "There are no quick-fix solutions to the record industry's problems, but not everyone is panicked yet. Records and tapes *are* still selling after all."

*Rolling Stone's* issue of 16 September contained a well-written and researched special report, "The War Against Home Taping," advancing three main points: the record companies loss claims are "greatly exaggerated"; company-sponsored surveys are "distorted"; and factors other than home taping caused more damage to the record industry.[122] Author Michael Schrage examined each of the Save America's Music claims, and refuted most of them. For example, "In essence, the record industry is saying that its best customers are its worst enemies." Or, "ironically, Sony's basic Walkman—probably the one piece of audio equipment that's sparked the greatest desire to home tape—would be exempt from royalty under Mathias . . . [bill on taping] because it does not record."

Despite several glaring omissions, Schrage's provocative report served to characterize the Save America's Music drive as an economically motivated power play. Most *published* letters to the *Rolling Stone* supported its conclusions. Jim Oliver of San Diego sarcastically wrote, "What if we all got together and bought just one copy of a record, then pass it around."[123] This *ad absurdium* retort was joined by others that evinced little sympathy for the record companies. Even the one published pro-Mathias letter was primarily concerned with the harm done to "artists and producers who get cheated out of the fruits of their labors."

Predictably Stan Gortikov submitted a rebuttal. The RIAA's president rarely missed a media opportunity to advance the cause. (Several executives again privately expressed reservations over the publicity overkill.) Gortikov, not surprisingly, labeled the report "slanted, distorted and unfair."[124] He declared that home taping was hurting everybody, including the duplicators. "If fewer songs are written, performed and recorded, home tapers are losers, too." However, because *Rolling Stone* admitted cassette recording does cost sales, "why dispute those realities with other conflicting distortions throughout your article?" *Rolling Stone* replied, "We stand by the reporting, analysis and facts in our article." Gortikov's response was unpersuasive because the record companies were ranked alongside the oil cartels and James Watt as exploiters in the minds of many *Rolling Stone* readers. Save America's Music was beginning to sound like "Save the Record Industry." This was poor public relations, and another case of shooting oneself in the foot. A broadcast vice-president observed, "Their home taping fears are overplayed."

Throughout the home-taping debate *Billboard* had presented a journalistically balanced coverage. Serving the *entire* music industry and upholding reportorial standards, the paper was generally neutral. The *Rolling Stone* report, however, motivated the "Bible of the industry" to offer its opinion. Embracing the spirit of copyright law, *Billboard* sided with the labels:

### In Defense of Copyright

Last week's "special report" in *Rolling Stone* on "The War Against Home Taping" attacks the music industry for attempting, through legislation, to retrieve some of its losses by a royalty on blank tape and recording equipment.

This goal should not come as a shock to anyone truly concerned with preserving the concept of copyright. *Rolling Stone*, once known as a music paper, missed the point.

The principle is simple. If not for copyright, there would be no business of music. Creators of words and music and, yes, of recordings, must be allowed to benefit from the public consumption of their works. This provides the incentive for creators to fashion new works, those very essentials that keep the wheels of the industry turning. Billboard has always supported this principle.

Anyone who ponders the current state of the industry must be alarmed that even as more and more prerecorded music reaches listeners, the sales of recordings decline.

No one can say with certainty how much of the slump in record sales is due to home taping. But those who insist home taping does not work to abort precorded sales are just as myopic as those who blame all the ills of the industry on home taping.

No more than ordinary common sense tells us that some percentage of sales is lost when people are able to appropriate copyrighted property with impunity for the price of a blank tape.

As technology provides ever new ways of delivering music to the consumer, it becomes even more important to fix the responsibility of the user, or his supplier, to pay something to the piper. Both are bound by a fragile, but necessary, umbilical cord—and the fortunes of one impact the fortunes of the other.

A fair royalty on blank tape and recording equipment is therefore essential if the inequalities are to be redressed, at least in part.

An indefinite free ride may hasten the day when a more sophisticated music delivery system will no longer provide a message anyone cares to hear—even at no cost.[125]

The Mathias amendment continued to crawl through Congress shadowed by Sony's appeal to the Supreme Court. For some legislative members the pending Court decision was welcome, for politicians are expert vote counters. Audiophiles and VCR owners already numbered in the millions. (One congressman pointed to the author's tape recorder and said, "You wouldn't want to pay a tax on that would you?")

Aiming at the upcoming holiday season, Chrysalis Records released Pat Benatar's *Get Nervous* album. An accompanying letter signed by Jack Forsythe, the label's promotion vice-president, warned that the songs on the record "were selected and sequenced by [company] employees . . . resulting in a musical compilation copyright *owned* by the undersigned." In nonlegal language Chrysalis was claiming that airing the entire album—"tracking"—was a copyright infringement because the label had ordered or sequenced the cuts. This was a bold tactic because the "compilation right" is considered a judicial vagary, but more important was a possible confrontation with radio programmers. Other labels stood aside, expressing their admiration for the independent's courageous move to curtail home taping. A & M's Gil Friesen was typical: "I'd like to do what I can to support Sal Licata. He really stuck his neck out. The problem is, we just put out our new Supertramp album."[126] One program director saw the maneuvers as desperation: "They've been cold this last year; they are vulnerable. They need this record very badly." Whatever the motivation, the Benatar material was noticed. It would go platinum.

Radio station DC-101 in the nation's capital banned the Benatar album. "We can't let record companies program this radio station," said Don Davis. "They can't dictate how and what I put on. When they do, I just won't play their product."[127] A war of words quickly erupted. DC-101's music director snapped, "I get my pay check from them, not Chrysalis Records." Chrysalis President Licata: "Radio has been dictating to us for too long . . . I don't want to blow off any airplay, but when you're talking about airing an album in its entirety, and killing sales through home taping, we have to take some kind of stand." *Billboard* surveyed broadcasters nationally, discovering most objected to programming dictates. Some sympathy was expressed for the fear of taping. A Chicago programmer summarized: "We're not here to provide a home taping service. . . . But we're not going to be held up by the record companies."[128] As in past confrontations with the omnipotent medium, a label found itself in a Don Quixote posture. Particularly an independent label with limited clout. The

Chrysalis-DC 101 standoff proved to be another unsuccessful battle in the war against the home taper. Without federal intervention, the labels remained powerless to curtail the dupers.

Buried in the rhetoric was a kernel of reality. The *New York Times* and *Rolling Stone* were correct. AOR was conservatively airing the "safe" records. Led Zeppelin's "Stairway to Heaven," a 1971 album cut, was the most hotly rotated FM song in the country. The music appeared stale. The recession and competing idioms such as arcade games were eroding adolescents' discretionary purchases. Some label "economies" did more harm than good. Marketing cutbacks did cut off retailers and exposure media at the knees. Conversely, the quality improvement of prerecorded cassettes was a wise move. *Billboard's* positive acknowledgement of rock video would prove an understatement. Other than by broadcasting sales departments confronted by hard-nosed advertisers, the key structural dilemma went unnoticed. The prime record-buying segment of the population continued to lessen in size, a statistical trend that remained unaltered.

A demographic shakeout was witnessed in 1982. Jay Cocks was correct in proclaiming the death of the "rock culture" as it had been understood in the 1960s. Disco had momentarily postponed the inevitable. *Saturday Night Fever*, with its unprecedented sales, fostered an illusion. When disco faded the gray light of dawn revealed a highly unpleasant reality. The WCI study of 1978 had reported that 23 percent of the 25-to-34 group still occasionally brought a record, but its favorites were disappearing. In informal surveys at Bob Dylan and Rolling Stones concerts, patrons made it quite clear they preferred "the old stuff." Dylan's new material literally drove concertgoers out of the venue. Jim Miller: "No rock star can hope to have that kind . . . [Elvis, Beatles] of impact. The experimentation of the Beatles mirrored the restless questing of a generation in revolt. Today, such a restlessness is confined to the margins of America's youth culture."[129] The industry's task was to win back the heavy users in the youth market, win them away from video games and repeat viewings of sci-fi plus "chop-'em-up" movies.

There were, of course, strategies available to the industry to rejuvenate the youth market. However, the crusade against home taping, if successful, was to be the magic elixir or cure-all. The "not me but them" psychological projection helped many "bizzers" to sleep at night, especially the true believers whose considerable weight and prestige were on the line.

The events of 1982, inside and outside the music industry, created fertile soil for change. Out of the darkness a "new," more promising era seemed to be dawning. The difference between ideology and reality was finally too great to overlook. Labels were forced to devise or at least partially alter traditional strategies. Superstars were still very attractive. They may not match the sales of *Saturday Night Fever* or *Rumors,* but a triple or even double platinum record supported many corporate expenses. They also were still welcomed by strictly formatted AOR stations. However, the post-1979 years had clearly demonstrated superstars were finite in their sales potential and longevity.

Most of the economic practices that are taught to M.B.A.'s had failed to resurrect the industry. New directions, as Mo Ostin suggested, needed to be tested: "I think the problems must rest with the music, and will be solved by music people. If you believe in the future of this business, you've got to bet on the music."[130] Lenny Waronker, Warner's new president, concurred, adding that the label should return to artist development as practiced in the late 1960s. Artist development had been pragmatically declassé among the majors since 1979. The opposite was normative as signings plummeted and rosters were drastically cut. Waronker's argument was a variation on the "Third-Coming" thesis. "There are a lot of young bands, a lot of experimentation going on," he told the *New York Times,* "sooner or later, one of these new bands or several of them, are going to catch on in a big way and sales will start going up again." CBS's Al Teller pointed to video rock as the genre to accomplish this feat: "MTV will play videos by bands most radio stations won't touch, and that really helps us break new artists. It may also have the effect of liberalizing radio."[131] The assessment was on the mark, although somewhat belated. A year prior to Teller's remarks *Billboard* reported that video music affected record and tape purchases. New acts were the chief beneficiaries.[132]

MTV was the rescuer on the Hegelian white horse. The music channel appealed to the magic demographic minus-25. As Seattle merchandiser Ms. Kopecky aptly stated, "While the MTV universe is small, it's heavy in record buyers." If she was correct, a larger universe should mean more buyers.

The record companies promised the usual array of super product for the 1982 holiday season. The Thanksgiving weekend was rescued by video games. A chain reported sales up by 10 percent because of the high demand for "Donkey Kong." Record and tape sales were pictured as "flat" compared to 1981: "Records and tapes are down 10 percent this year, but video games more than made it up."[133] The annual last-minute shopping spree once again saved retailers. Video games, cassettes—blank and prerecorded—were major sellers. Men at Work and two Motown artists, Marvin Gaye and Lionel Ritchie, were the leading sellers.

Industry observers called 1982 at best an "odd year." Robert Palmer of the *New York Times* wrote, "Pop was a game called Survival of the Fittest." Jack Valenti (MPA) told ABC News, "The record industry is in a near state of collapse." Dismissing the home-taping campaign, Ken Tucker suggested,

"The reason they weren't selling many albums was that their product just wasn't very exciting." Most year-end analysis applauded the emergence of some new acts and stronger efforts by "name" performers. MTV was widely credited for the success of Duran Duran and Men at Work, as well as the rockabilly Stray Cats and Human League. Critics' evaluations are taken with a grain of salt by label executives; RIAA unit-shipment and especially dollar figures are the bottom line.

Platinum and gold albums dropped in 1982. The million-unit sellers shrunk by 11 percent, while the golds went down by 20 percent. One positive note was seven "new" acts that garnered the platinum wall hangings; Men At Work, Stray Cats, the Go-Go's, and four other neophytes accomplished the prestigious feat.

RIAA sales and shipment figures were rarely disputed except in award certifications prior to returns. The trade association, reacting to criticisms, altered the policy. Its 1982 findings raised a furor. Figures provided by *U.S. News and World Report* showed a unit-shipment decline of 7.4 percent between 1981 and the reporting year.[134] Three weeks later RIAA's official report presented a drop in units moved: *594* million to *576* million, an estimated *3 percent* drop. Dollar volume according to its numbers lessened by only 1 percent: $3.63 to $3.59 billion. This was a marginal dip, disputing the pandemic aura of gloom in 1982. The fly in the ointment was RIAA's statistical methodology, which had been changed. By the new methodology units moved in 1981 were 635 million, and dollar volume was $3.97 million, figures that work out to much larger declines than the 3 percent stated. Then there were the *U.S. News and World Report* numbers.

RIAA credibility was tarnished. Accusations of "cooking the numbers" appeared at the very same time Congress was examining the home-taping issue. "Obviously we're in the home taping battle, and they would say, hey, we're trying to make things look worse than they are," Steven Traiman stated. The RIAA executive director's argument did not persuade outsiders and insiders. "How's the U.S. record business doing?" asked *Rolling Stone's* Kurt Loder. "Don't ask unless you can make sense out of its latest misleading and contradictory answers."[135] Shulman, chairman of the association's research committee, angrily noted the trade group was advised "to make clear that the comparison between the figures . . . was somewhat of an 'apple and pears' issue."[136] Officially, RIAA seemed oblivious to the problem, issuing a statement reading in part, "Many industries . . . have altered methodologies from time to time. . . . Our industry is fortunate that the new availability of NPD data makes available the most valid statistical base it ever had." The faux pas underscored the fragile nature of the RIAA accounting procedures. A revised news release on 20 June showed recalculated 1979-82 numbers. However, the earlier annual figures stood, distorting the 1978-79 comparison.

The apparent tempest in a statistical teapot had its significance. Many industry plans and projections are based on RIAA reports. One example: "These figures dramatically portray the troubled economic circumstances of our industry," said Gortikov. He was correct. Remedies for these "troubled circumstances" affected all aspects of the music industry and consumers. The myriad self-inflicted wounds and negative external factors began to gradually diminish in 1983.

On the darker side, WCI's 1982 corporate profit-and-loss statement was discouraging. Blame was placed on a "worldwide slump in the music industry, which is in past due to adverse effects of unauthorized home taping." As if to emphasize the state of despair, WCI announced a major organizational shake-up at Elektra/Asylum (E/A). The companies' West Coast brass would be moved to New York; a reduction of 80 Los Angeles employees occurred. The Nashville operation was absorbed by Warner Bros. Records, which kept the E/A people and dismissed its own. E/A lost 40 percent of its revenue to Warner with the transfer of the country roster. One staffer told *Rolling Stone,* "Lots of people think WEA is going to turn into WA."[137] E/A was to occupy space in Atlantic's Gotham headquarters.

The profits of CBS, the other major corporate entity, dipped. The losses were attributed to organizational restructuring because CBS artists, new and old, were enjoying good chart action and sales. Walter Yetnikoff predicted a measured upturn: "You get the feeling the really big hit may be coming back. I think we're starting to see those bigger numbers again. . . . I think Men At Work will hit five million, and Michael Jackson [*Thriller*] will be way, way up."[138]

Home taping still beclouded segments of the industry. In an address at Columbia College, Gortikov stressed, "Personal piracy, or home taping is every bit as sinister as commercial criminal piracy. It's acceptable on the surface—everybody does it. But it is not a victimless crime."[139] Many proponents of the Mathias legislation were resigned to leaving the matter in the hands of the federal governmeent. Several months later the senior senator from Maryland restated the Save America's Music argument: "The public is consuming just as much music as ever [sic]; it just buys less of it, and tapes more of it."[140] Because sales appeared to be growing, led by Michael Jackson's *Thriller* and the *Flashdance* sound track, the home-taping "crisis" appeared to lose some of its urgency. Even Gortikov conceded industry losses would not be "substantially offset, but [it was] a step in the right direction." WCI attempted to keep the issue alive, claiming that in 1982 fifteen of each seventeen Asia albums were taped by consumers. It maintained cassette recording of the debut album had cost WCI $5,955,000 or 794,000 units. But taping was losing its cause célèbre status. RIAA statements and trade paper commentaries on the issue waned dramatically.

Hit product was returning to its prerecession status. Top-charted albums, according to WEA's Henry Droz, were "hitting numbers we thought might no longer be attainable." Nearly all labels with top sellers concurred. An MCA spokesperson said, "We are getting more sales volume than a year ago, but it's all predicated on product at the top."[141] Most hoped the enthusiasm for superproduct would trickle down to catalog titles. The recovery was being led by the superstars, some by creations of MTV. The superstars were getting Blacks and women back into the stores. Age data showed that the 10-to-34 age group's consumption of recorded material either remained static or declined. The 35-plus category increased its participation, a figure influenced by sound-track sales and, again, *Thriller.* Just as *Saturday Night Fever* had skewed 1978 sales figures, *Thriller* skewed 1983 sales figures.

"We had a very strong first six months in '83," recalled Roy Imber of *Record World.* "Michael Jackson and *Flashdance* had a lot to do with that, because they were bringing in people who were not the normal record buyer."[142] Megaplatinum albums transcend traditional age and ethnic classifications; both albums enjoyed an equal split between white and black consumers. Few artists or albums possess the universal magnetism that propels them into the *Guinness Book of Records.*

The preslump buyers appeared to be returning. The marketing philosophies of the years prior to the "crash of '79" reemerged. Reliance on superstars and rumblings concerning a "new music," reminiscent of the 1970s took hold. A flood of star product was released for the summer: *Loverboy,* a solo Stevie Nicks effort, and Police's *Synchronicity.* A coordinated campaign with MTV was devised to promote the album and the Police tour. Other sales contenders were Joan Jett, Human League, and Flock of Seagulls. None of these newcomers matched the volume of its maiden albums. Men at Work's *Cargo* couldn't surpass *Business as Usual.*

The dog days of August 1983 showed that *Thriller, Synchronicity,* and Def Leppard's *Pyromania* were carrying vacation-period sales. One retailer told *Rolling Stone,* "The top five or ten records are doing well, but after that, records just aren't selling."[143] The shaky recovery was undoubtedly the result of a handful of artists, a reality that shored up the "superstars-pay-the-bills" thesis. Stephen Holden asked, "Which records, if any, will keep the momentum going" after Jackson, the Police and the *Flashdance* score?[144] The labels answered with the Rolling Stones, Lionel Richie, Stevie Wonder, Prince, Paul McCartney, and a host of others. Managers of new artists were finding labels reverting to past policies. One artist's lawyer observed, "I haven't seen any significant change from the peak years of 1972 to 1978." Another attorney concurred: "When you put that much money into one artist, you're risking your ability to acquire the new acts needed."[145]

Talk of a "midline" crisis further escalated the value of platinum sellers. The less-expensive midline albums had helped retailers survive during the slump. Now, fewer catalogue titles, artists' resistance, and higher prices were drying up the budget market.

Record sales declined, but not industry profits. Prerecorded cassettes began to outperform albums. Cartridges transcended LP sales by 13 percent; 236.8 million C-60s were shipped as opposed to 210.4 million records. Demographics were a key factor. Heavy-metal groups, such as Quiet Riot, Scorpions, and Def Leppard, sold more tapes than records. One explanation offered was that "there are a lot of kids out there racing around in cars, and they're listening to hard rock." A WEA spokesman elaborated: "Generally, it's been the market with wheels." Walkmans also were primed at the youth market. Russ Solomon of Tower Records suggested that older consumers were sticking to albums. "I don't see any reason for people who buy music for their home to buy cassettes," he said. "The quality isn't as good, and tapes don't have the convenience of albums—the selectability and graphics."[146] Although country fans and "one-shot" consumers somewhat altered the demographic equation, youthful music buyers were moving in the direction of cassettes.

For labels this technological transformation was a two-edged sword. Ads such as WEA's "Why Our Cassettes Sound Better" or CBS's "See Red" did not solve the sound-quality issue. Graphics on miniature plastic boxes lacked the appeal of album covers. (The value of graphics, especially album art, is discussed in chapter 4.) Nonetheless, company tape purchases did improve the profit picture going toward the essential year-end holiday weeks.

In the wake of a good summer merchandisers were fairly buoyant before the 1983 Thanksgiving weekend, and this time their bullishness proved correct. Major chain sales were up by 5 to 30 percent, the best reported gains in a four-year period. Print advertising and MTV were cited as major contributors. "Television has helped us with new acts and with establishing superstars, and perhaps most importantly stretching longevity of albums," said a chain operator whose sales jumped 30 percent.[147]

The holiday boomlet was equally fueled by superstar product and relatively new faces: Culture Club, Quiet Riot, Duran Duran. All had received repeated MTV airing. The Police after a MTV super promo campaign was in third place, following *Thriller* on *Billboard*'s 17 December 1983 "Top LP's" chart.

The year 1983 ended on a cautiously upbeat note. As one insider observed, a "faint whisper of sanity" was surfacing. Joe Smith in leaving Elektra/Asylum, under curious circumstances, said, "We were all just in shock over the last couple of years; every day something else would come along and just knock you for a loop. It's very hard to all of a sudden switch off a crisis mentality when this business had gone through every previous economic up and down showing at least some kind of growth."[148] Smith's farewell statement proved prophetic; CBS and RIAA figures estimated a 3 to 5 percent dollar incease in 1983. However, established superstars, particularly Michael Jackson, and MTV discoveries carried the modest surge. In its annual report RIAA noted, "A few superstar releases have brought much excitement to the prerecorded music business, the overall unit volume has not significantly improved. The pervasive and escalating problem of home taping is still affecting the industry."[149]

The continuing unit decrease could easily be explained by the $9.98 list price, as well as the shrinking demographic pool of music buyers. "What these people have in part overlooked," wrote Jay Coleman of Rockbill, Inc., "is the power of the consumer with limited financial means." He aptly summed up the 1979-82 period: "For an industry of such alleged high rollers, we have really been shooting a very bad game of craps."[150]

Two years and two months following the RIAA's success in wedding audio taping to the so-called Betamax tax bill, the Supreme Court ruled on Sony's appeal. In a five-to-four decision, home videotaping for private use was deemed legal, and off-air taping was not deemed copyright infringement, as Universal Studios and its allies had claimed.

The Court basically tossed the issue back to Congress. In an election year a perceived "anticonsumer" bill had a "snowball's chance in hell" of passage. Representative Kastenmeier, an industry ally, cautioned, "Congress will not be disposed in light of the Court's decision, to act on legislation calling for the imposition of royalties on home taping." Gortikov urged Congress to "take a fresh look at this ncw [sic] technology." Hal David of ASCAP and George Weiss of the Songwriters Guild echoed this sentiment. Most press accounts saw little if any hope of legislation protective of industry. A *Billboard* article reported that such legislation "will not be a high priority for any but the truly courageous members of Congress."[151] A few grumblings continued to appear in print, but the Court at least for the moment had defused the issue. The record industry's track record in Washington was unimpressive.

Five years after its disco issue *Newsweek* ran a slick cover story proclaiming a newer trend. "Britian Rocks America—Again," the cover promised, with a Janus-like color photograph of Culture Club's Boy George and Annie Lennox of the Eurythmics. Seasoned writer Jim Miller concluded the lengthy piece with, "So Roll Over, America. Forgot about nostalgia for the earnest pop optimism of the 60s and face the era of cramped hopes and wild style. Here comes the rock and roll of 1984."[152] The invaders were a mixed bunch led by Culture Club, whose sound has been described as "recycled Smokey Robinson" or "torchy American schmaltz and classic Motown," or simply "new music." Boy George's drag-queen appearance made the group a natural for the visual demands of cable television. The new music included a revived, perhaps more outlandish, version of heavy metal popularized originally by Led Zeppelin and later Deep Purple, which was listed in the *Guinness Book of Records* as the "world's loudest rock band." AC/DC, Scorpions, Iron Maiden, Twisted Sister, Motley Crue, and Quiet Riot continued the style in the 1980s. *Billboard*, with its usual optimism, described the style as "molten-hot metal flares anew in fad-defying fling at pop success."

The "British invasion," according to most, was targeted at the under-21 market. Bill Graham declared, "Teenagers want that sound." Quiet Riot's manager Warren Entner observed, "Traditionally [it] has appealed to the 15-18 year old male audience. This year [1984], it's reaching both a younger demographic and going further into the 20s, and the audience is far more mixed male/female."[153] Heavy metal does enjoy a broader generational appeal, given its musical evolution, than the new music. Most of the new music was dismissed as 1980s bubble gum. Older rock fans took to "Boycott Boy George" buttons. "It is ironic," wrote Jim Miller, "to watch these older fans grimace at the new bands. But the kids love it."[154] Both sounds were manifestations of MTV with their reliance on the visual. As an Elektra executive acknowledged, "Video is the key to success. . . you get a Motley Crue on MTV and you get exposure immediately." MTV is the channel of choice for most adolescents.

Some observers have pointed to the latest British invasion as mere media and industry hype. Discussing Miller's *Newsweek* article, Dave Marsh, while supporting heavy metal, wrote, "The British invasion is supposed to indicate that we're experiencing a revolution in American pop music taste . . . HOOEY."[155] John Kalodner of Geffen Records: *"Time* or *Newsweek* will do a cover story on it, and then we'll know the trend is over." Meanwhile, record companies were signing proponents of power chording as fast as possible. The "British invasion" may be due to Anglophobia, MTV, or a quiet desperation by the industry for some musical sense of direction. It could be all of these. "Bizzers" and media gatekeepers are comfortable with trends that create a temporary sense of security. In 1984 some veterans again were willing to make the new music or heavy metal *qua* popular music statement.

Demographically, record producers were following in the footsteps of their moviemaking media counterparts. Film studios in the 1980s targeted the adolescent high school market with sci-fi extravaganzas like *Star Trek* and *Star Wars*; cosmic dreams like *Conan, Indiana Jones,* and *Superman*; teen fantasies in *Porky's*; and also the low-budget horror sagas. All of course, made for profitable signals. An added bonus was that teens thought nothing of going to the same flick a half-dozen or more times. Teenagers are Hollywood's bread and butter. Concert promoters and record manufacturers were competing for a piece of the same economic action now that video arcade business had flattened by 60 percent.

Invasions can be as successful as the Normandy invasion of 1944. The Beatles did it twenty years later. Punk and new wave were failed attempts. The verdict is still out on *Newsweek's* cover story, but the chart action of 1984 suggests a guerrilla war more than it does another D-Day adventure.

The "Great Disco Disaster of '79" followed by Christgau's "Bad Christmas" of 1981 is a history of miscalculation, denial, finger pointing, and social change.[156] It was a severe test of marketing strategies and value systems, as well as a demonstration of the seeming capriciousness of the music consumer.

*Saturday Night Fever* had postponed the inevitable. Punk, later euphemistically called new wave, was the seed of a potential trend that never materialized because of the resistance of AOR stations. After the fallout there was little excitement left. The remaining artists were losing their aging constituency. The shrinking adolescent window was immersed in other pursuits. In the midst of these demographic shifts radio stations adjusted their playlists in a conservative direction. Firing marketing personnel and blaming a "Nipponese conspiracy" of home taping only focused media attention on the obvious slump. Both moves were a public relations fiasco. Warner Amex's MTV has temporarily reversed the decline. Playing executive musical chairs, like moving professional football coaches around, does not bury old cherished ideas or change an organizational structure that, to paraphrase Stan Cornyn, rarely plans beyond tomorrow's luncheon.

Rock and roll may never die, but neither have ragtime or cowboy songs. The canon of "when you're hot, you're hot" dooms those resting on their conservative formulas and aging superstars to failure. One never knows when there really will be another "Third Coming," if ever. Record companies will still try to create one, aided by the media looking for "a ticket to ride."

## NOTES

1. John Kenneth Galbraith, *The New Industrial State* (Boston: Houghton Mifflin, 1966), p. 6.
2. Joel Vance, quoted in Jody Breslow, "New Releases: Quantity and Quality in a Gambler's Market," *Rock*, 5 July 1971, p. 14.

3. Murray Ross, "The Record Business: What Makes It Run," *Record World*, 24 July 1971, p. 230.
4. Breslow, "New Releases."
5. Quoted in "Breaking the Dump Cycle," *Billboard*, 22 September 1979, p. 15.
6. Stan Cornyn, address presented to National Association of Record Merchandisers, Los Angeles, 27 February 1971.
7. Dean Jennings, "The Shaggy Genius of Pop Music," *Saturday Evening Post*, 21 April 1956, p. 69.
8. Quotations from Mitch Miller, "June, Moon, Swoon and Ko Ko Mo," *New York Times Magazine*, 24 April 1955, p. 19.
9. Quoted in Stuart Werbin, "Monkees Man Does 'Fillmore on the Air,'" *Rolling Stone* 7 December 1972, p. 10.
10. Mike Greshman, "The Blues Once Black, Now a Shader White," *Los Angeles Times Calendar*, 19 January 1969, p. 37.
11. Quoted in John Swenson, *Bill Haley* (New York: Stein & Day, 1982), p. 52.
12. Quoted in Ren Grevatt, "Pro's and Con's Have Their Say on Miller's K.C. Speech," *Billboard*, 24 March 1958, p. 14.
13. See "Rock Tycoon," *Newsweek*, 31 July 1978, pp. 40-47.
14. Robert Palmer, "New Bands on Small Labels are the Innovators of the 80s," *New York Times*, 6 September 1981, p. D-17.
15. Breslow, "New Releases," p. 15.
16. Lenny Kaye, liner notes, *Nuggetts* (Elektra Records, 7E-2006).
17. Clive Davis, *Clive: Inside the Record Business* (New York: Morrow, 1975), p. 78.
18. Ibid., p. 6.
19. "$2 Billion Worth of Noise," *Forbes*, 15 July 1968, p. 22. Also see Mike Gross, "Music Rumbles—Wall Street Tumbles," *Billboard*, 6 December 1969, pp. 1, 8.
20. Quoted in "Capitol Gains," *Newsweek*, 27 February 1967, p. 59.
21. Quoted in "Money Man on Leave," *Forbes*, 15 January 1972.
22. Quoted in Ed McCormack, "John Paul Hammond: They All Want to Suck His Blood," *Rolling Stone*, 23 November 1972, p. 20.
23. "Little Labels and Their Survival," *Billboard*, 5 May 1979, p. 22.
24. Quoted in Laurel Leff, "Once a Free Spender, MCA Gets Tough, Trying to Make the Record Business Pay," *Wall Street Journal*, 25 June 1981, p. 23.
25. Steve Pond, "Warners-PolyGram Merger Shocks Record Industry," *Rolling Stone*, 18 August 1983, p. 40.
26. Press release, "An Original Returns: The Association Back Together," David Fishof Productions, North Dakota.
27. See Charlie Gillett, *Making Tracks* (New York: Dutton, 1974, pp. 279-81; Steve Chapple and Reebee Garofalo, *Rock 'n' Roll Is Here to Pay* (Chicago: Nelson-Hall, 1977), pp. 201-9.
28. Quoted in David Felton and John Morthland, "Will Warner Bros. Corner the Market?" *Rolling Stone* 2 April 1970, p. 14.
29. "He Handles a Lot of Chores for Acts," *Billboard*, 14 October 1972, p. 10.
30. Felton and Morthland, "Will Warner Bros. Corner the Market?" p. 14.
31. Ads in *Billboard*, 7 April 1984; 26 December 1978.
32. Quoted in David Gans, "New WB President Optimistic about Industry's Prospects," *Record*, May 1983, p. 18.
33. Quoted in "Worries about Warner," *Newsweek*, 16 August 1982, p. 52.

34. Quoted in Judith Sims, "Record Industry Profiles: Two Lonely Bulls and How They Grew," *Rolling Stone*, 12 October 1972, p. 14.
35. Quoted, ibid., p. 16.
36. Quoted in Ed Harrison, "Exit Is Shock to Indie Ranks," *Billboard*, 27 January 1979, pp. 1, 100.
37. Jon H. Rieger, "The Coming Crisis in the Youth Music Market," address presented at Popular Culture Association meetings, Milwaukee, 3 May 1974.
38. Quoted in "Music the Answer to Industry Fears, Asserts Gortikov," *Billboard*, 8 September 1979, p. 8.
39. Clive Davis, "An Open Letter to Joe Smith," *Billboard*, 25 August 1979, p. 16. Ironically, Davis outlined five serious industry ills prior to "crash" news analyses; see "'Business' Not a Dirty Word," *Billboard*, 14 April 1979, p. 22.
40. Quoted in "The Blues in Vinyl," *Newsweek*, 13 August 1979, p. 67.
41. Quoted in John Rockwell, "Record Industry's Sales Slowing after 25 Years of Steady Growth," *New York Times*, 8 August 1979, p. C-23.
42. See C.W. Mills, *The Power Elite* (New York: Oxford University Press, 1956): Also John Sippel, "Marketing Execs Mulling Answer to Profit Falloff," *Billboard*, 6 January 1979, pp. 3, 75.
43. *Billboard*, 6 January 1979, pp. 1, 71, 82.
44. Irv Lichtman, "Retailers Bemoaning Poor Product Flow," *Billboard* 3 March 1979, p. 14.
45. Quoted in "CBS Corp Earnings May Drop 40% to 50%—Backe," *Billboard* 24 March 1979, p. 9.
46. Irv Lichtman and Paul Grein "Over-30 Set Keeps Old Musicians Young," *Billboard*, 28 April 1979, pp. 3, 88, 89.
47. Quoted in Roman Kozak, "Yetnikoff Vows CBS Records to Up Profits," *Billboard*, 17 March 1979, p. 9.
48. Quoted in "WCI's Income Disappointing," *Billboard*, 21 July 1979, p. 16.
49. Roman Kozak, "CBS Cuts 53; Portrait Label Absorbed," *Billboard*, 7 July 1979, p. 3.
50. "The Summer Turns Bummer. . .," *People*, 10 September 1979, pp. 65-79.
51. Quoted in "The Blues in Vinyl," p. 67.
52. Quoted in "The Summer Turns Bummer," p. 71.
53. Quoted in Rockwell, "Record Industry's Sales Slowing," p. C-23.
54. Quoted in Roman Kozak, "Attitudes at Columbia A & R Modulating with the Times," *Billboard*, 17 May 1980, p. 5.
55. "The Summer Turns Bummer."
56. Quotes from "Disco Takes Over," *Newsweek*, 2 April 1979, p. 57.
57. Dennis Hunt, "Disco Declining but Not Dead Yet," *Los Angeles Times*, 13 January 1980, p. B-2.
58. Robert D. Summer, "There Is No Last Wave," *BG,* 12 December 1981, p. 16.
59. Quoted in "Record Sales Led by Rock Musicians," *Los Angeles Times* 12 December 1969, p. 32.
60. Quoted in Irv Lichtman, "U.S. Industry Stirred by Home Duping Impact," *Billboard*, 4 August 1979, p. 29.
61. Quoted in John Sippel, "Dealers Deplore FM Airing Complete LP's," *Billboard*, 3 November 1979, pp. 1, 14.
62. Quoted in Cary Darling, "Labels See No Answer to LP Play," *Billboard*, 3 November 1979, p. 14.
63. Quoted, ibid., p. 14.

64. Quoted in Sippel, "Dealers Deplore FM Airing Complete LP's," p. 1.
65. Quoted in "Off-Air Tapings to Be Surveyed," *Billboard*, 3 November 1927, p. 3.
66. Doug Hall, "Entire LP Taping Substantiated by Burkhart Study," *Billboard*, 1 December 1979, p. 1.
67. Quoted in "Tighter Returns in Effect at CBS," *Billboard*, 8 September 1979, p. 10.
68. Quoted in Paul Grein, "Tighter Returns Plan Teed by RCA-A&M," *Billboard*, 27 October 1979, p. 1.
69. Quoted in John Sippel, "WEA Returns Policy Pulls Optimistic Reaction," *Billboard*, 1 December 1979, p. 14.
70. Quotations from Paul Grein, "Holiday Sales Suffer Below Par Launching," *Billboard*, 1 January 1979, p. 6.
71. Quoted in Roman Kozak, "Signings Off 28% in '79 Second Half," *Billboard*, 19 January 1980, p. 14.
72. Quoted in "Hotter Than Ever Before," *Billboard*, 22 March 1980, p. 8.
73. Rip Shepherd, "Commentary," *Billboard*, 5 April 1980, p. 10.
74. Quotes from Doug Hall, "WEA's Novel $2 Promo LP Policy Gaining Acceptance," *Billboard*, 15 March 1980, p. 3.
75. "A Reply from the Boondocks," *Billboard* 5 April 1980, p. 10.
76. "Listeners Older So Where Are the Records?" *Billboard*, 17 May 1980, p. 25.
77. Quoted in *Billboard*, 27 October 1979, p. 25.
78. Doug Hall, "Entire LP Taping Substantiated by Burkhart Study," *Billboard* 1 December 1979, p. 1.
79. "Editorial," *Rolling Stone*, 24 January 1980, p. 16.
80. "Letters to the Editor," *Rolling Stone*, 6 March 1980, p. 6.
81. *Rolling Stone*, 21 February 1980, p. 8.
82. Quoted in Roman Kozak, "CBS, Chrysalis Ban Blank Tape $," *Billboard*, 21 June 1980, p. 93.
83. Quotations from Jim McCullaugh, "Blank Tape Makers Call Ban Paranoid," *Billboard*, 28 June 1980, p. 35.
84. Quoted in Robert Wallace, "Crisis? What Crisis?" *Rolling Stone* 29 May 1980, pp. 17, 28.
85. "Letters," *Rolling Stone*, 28 October 1982, p. 6.
86. Quoted in Roman Kozak, "Analyst Analyzes Industry," *Billboard*, 14 June 1980, pp. 8, 78.
87. Quoted in Jean Callahan, "WB's Cornyn Tells Tribunal of Cost Fears," *Billboard*, 12 July 1980, p. 4.
88. Quoted in Sam Sutherland, "Waronker Eyes Basic Approach," *Billboard*, 13 November 1982, p. 80.
89. Quotations in George Kopp, "Home Taping Costing Cos. $700-$800 Million," *Billboard*, 11 October 1980, p. 69.
90. "Scapegoat for Lagging Sales," *Billboard*, 26 July 1980, p. 18.
91. *Rolling Stone Rock Almanac* (New York: Straight Arrow Publishers, 1983), p. 307.
92. "It's a Whole New Ball Game," *Billboard*, 28 June 1980, p. 16.
93. "Rock Music Products Big Business Trend," *Toledo Blade*, 15 February 1981, p. G-3.
94. Laura Foti, "MTV Cable Channel Exposing New Acts," *Billboard*, 15 August 1981, p. 3.

95. "Time Is on My Side," *Rolling Stone*, 7 January 1982, p. 7.
96. Quotations from "Record Companies Turn for the Better," *Newsweek* 12 October 1981.
97. Quoted in Jim McCullaugh, "Shock Vibrates Through Industry," *Billboard* 31 October 1981, p. 114.
98. Quoted in Irv Lichtman, "Appeals Decision Viewed as Impetus for Tape Levy," *Billboard*, 31 October 1981, p. 15.
99. Michael Schrage, "The War against Home Taping," *Rolling Stone*, 16 September 1982, p. 61.
100. "Look Back with Longing," *Rolling Stone*, 24 December 1981, p. 22.
101. Vernon Scott, "Pop Record Sales Take Strong Downturn," *Sentinel Tribune*, 12 January 1982, p. 5.
102. Quotations from Sam Sutherland, "Analysts Peer into 1982," *Billboard*, 16 January 1982, p. 45.
103. Doug Hill, "Advertisers Are Continuing to Target Older Audiences," *Billboard*, 16 January 1982, p. 19.
104. Quotations in "Dealers Say Big Acts Could Relieve Blahs," *Billboard*, 27 February 1982, p. 62.
105. Quoted in Jim Miller, "Is Rock on the Rocks?" *Newsweek*, 19 April 1982, p. 105.
106. Quoted in John Sippel, "Atari Games Via WEA Get Late June Bow," *Billboard*, 5 June 1982, p. 3.
107. "You Can't Hum a Video Game," *Billboard*, 20 February 1982, p. 18.
108. "Rock Hits the Hard Place," *Time*, 15 February 1982.
109. Quotes from Doug Hall, "AOR Nears Crucial Crossroads," *Billboard*, 22 May 1982, p. 65.
110. Quotations from Leo Sacks, "Labels Still Targeting AM Outlets," *Billboard*, 8 May 1982, pp. 1, 22.
111. Quoted in Bill Holland, "Betamax Bill Adds Audio Clause, Fee," *Billboard*, 13 March 1982, p. 72.
112. "Blank Tape—Dealer Dilemma," *Billboard*, 27 February 1982, p. 12.
113. Bill Holland, "Song Executive Attacks Industry Anti-Tape Lobby," *Billboard*, 20 March 1982, p. 3.
114. Bill Holland, "High Court 'Betamax' Review Won't Deter Solons, Lobbyists," *Billboard*, 26 June 1982, p. 74.
115. "Home Taping: Scapegoat," *Billboard*, 10 July 1982, p. 14.
116. Laura Foti, "Home Taping Issues Probed in EIA Study," *Billboard*, 2 October 1982, pp. 1, 15. Also Stanley Gortikov, "Blessings on Their Survey," *Billboard*, 9 October 1982, p. 16.
117. Steve Pond, "Tom Petty: A Rock and Roll Hero Keeps Fighting On," *Rolling Stone*, 23 July 1981, p. 43.
118. Quotations from "Record Albums Take a New Spin," *Newsweek*, 23 August 1982, p. 54; John Sippel, "Survey Finds LP Rentals Still Grow Slowly in U.S.," *Billboard*, 24 July 1982, p. 8. Also "Record Industry Fears Advent of Rental Plans," *Sentinel Tribune*, 13 March 1982, p. 5.
119. "Pop Music's Heyday Said to Be Waning Amid Falling Sales," *New York Times*, 14 August 1982, pp. 1, 14.
120. "The Sky Is Not Falling," *Billboard*, 28 August 1982, pp. 3, 52.
121. "Record Industry Nervous as Sales Drop Fifty Percent," *Rolling Stone*, 30 September 1982, pp. 69, 78, 79.

122. Schrage, "The War Against Home Taping," pp. 59-67.
123. "Letters," *Rolling Stone*, 28 October 1982, p. 6.
124. Ibid.
125. *Billboard*, 18 September 1982, p. 5.
126. Quoted in Sam Sutherland, "Label Monitor Album Tracking Row," *Billboard*, 13 November 1982, p. 72.
127. "Chrysalis Warns on Airing of Entire LPs," *Billboard*, 30 October 1982, p. 1.
128. Doug Hall, "Radio Reaction Mixed to Chysalis Tracking Move," *Billboard*, 6 November 1982, pp. 1, 18.
129. Miller, "Is Rock on the Rocks?"
130. Sutherland, "Waronker Eyes Basic Approach."
131. Robert Palmer, "The Top Record Industry Is Under Electronic Siege," *New York Times*, 28 November 1982, p. H-24.
132. Jim McCullough, "MTV Cable Spurs Disk Sales of Artists Aired," *Billboard*, 10 October 1981, pp. 1, 68. A 1982 article reported similar findings; see "Survey Finds MTV Strongly Affecting Record Sales," *Billboard*, 11 September 1982, pp. 3, 60.
133. Quoted in John Sippel, "Games Help Boost Thanksgiving Sales," *Billboard*, 11 December 1982, p. 68.
134. Gordon Bock, "Why Recording Industry Sings the Blues," *U.S. News and World Report*, 21 March 1983, p. 66.
135. "Sales off a Little. . . No, a Lot." *Rolling Stone*, 26 May 1983, pp. 51, 53.
136. Quoted in Is Horowitz, "Statistics Snafu: RIAA Scored," *Billboard* 30 April 1983, p. 60.
137. Steve Pond and Andrew Slater, "Elektra Cuts Staff for Move East," *Rolling Stone*, 3 March, 1983, p. 42.
138. Quoted in Sam Sutherland, "Yetnikoff 'Reasonably' Optimistic," *Billboard*, 19 March 1983, p. 61.
139. Moira McCormick, "RIAA Chief Hits Home Taping," *Billboard*, 22 January 1983, p. 5.
140. Charles Mathias, "Preserving Creative Incentive," *Billboard*, 14 May 1983, p. 10.
141. Quotations from Paul Grein, "Sales Peaks Rising for Hit Albums," *Billboard*, 28 May 1983, pp. 1, 66.
142. Fred Goodman, "Dealers Expect Late Spring Upturn," *Billboard*, 9 June 1984, p. 1.
143. Quoted in Steve Pond and Kurt Loder, "Summer Sales Surge Gives Record Business a Boost," *Rolling Stone*, 1 September 1983, p. 43.
144. "Christmas Comes Early in Pop Music," *New York Times*, 11 September 1983, pp. 4-31,32.
145. Quotations from Paul Grein and Sam Sutherland, "New Acts: Labels Play It Tight," *Billboard*, 8 October 1983, p. 70.
146. Quotes from Jeff Leisch, "Cassettes Now Outselling LPs," *Rolling Stone*, 24 November 1983, pp. 59-60. Also, Steven Rea, "Compact Cassettes Are Soaring in Popularity," *Toledo Blade*, 18 December 1983, p. E-2.
147. John Sippel, "Chains Give Thanks for Sales Booms," *Billboard*, 10 December 1983, p. 71.
148. Paul Grein, "What Made Joe (Smith) Go?" *Billboard*, 12 March 1983, p. 63.
149. See "RIAA On '83: Units Flat, Shipment $ $ Up 5%" *Billboard*, 14 April 1984, pp. 1, 64.

150. Jay Coleman, "The Faint Whisper of Sanity," *Billboard*, 2 April 1983, p. 10.
151. Quotations from Bill Holland, "High Court Betamax Ruling Costs Doubt On Taping Bills," *Billboard*, 28 January 1984, pp. 1, 67, 76. Also, Nancy J. Schwerzler, "Ruling Doesn't End Videotape Dispute," *Baltimore Sun*, 18 January 1984, pp. A-1, A-6; "A Long Complicated Story Researches a Judicial Climax," *Billboard*, 28 January 1984, pp. 67-76.
152. Jim Miller, "Britain Rocks America—Again," *Newsweek*, 23 January 1984, p. 57.
153. Quotations from Ethlie Ann Vare, "Heavy Metal '84" (Spotlight), *Billboard*, 14 April 1984.
154. Miller, "Britain Rocks America," p. 50.
155. Dave Marsh, "Anglophobia," *Record*, May 1984, p. 64.
156. See Robert Christgau's brilliant "Rock 'n' Roller Coaster," *Village Voice*, 7 February 1984, pp. 37-45.

# 4

# Inside the Record Company

*If you want to have a hit you*
*gotta make it fit so they cut*
*it down to 3:05.*

—©1974 Tinker St. Tunes BMI

*You cheated, you lied*
*You said that you loved me.*

—©Balcones Publishing Co. BMI

Sometime during negotiations, more likely after a contract has been signed, an artist is afforded a grand tour of the record company on which he or she visits all of the departments and is introduced to the people who will be working on the record. Through a maze of corridors, offices, and cubicles, the hopeful is shown the innards of the "support" unit. Some facades are more lavish than others. One company has its personnel in quarters across the street from the Warner Bros. movie lot. The Capitol Tower, which casts its shadow over the corner of Hollywood and Vine, is spacious and seemingly well organized. The CBS Group at Black Rock and WCI labels located in New York's Rockefeller Plaza are austere and businesslike. Outward appearances are frequently deceiving. Still, companies need to maintain an image.

The new artist is escorted from the A&R department, which discovered him or her to meet the marketing head, who relates a myriad of ploys, campaigns, and gimmicks that have been devised to create a million seller. The graphics departments make equally spectacular claims. The performer will be introduced to people in the promotion and publicity sections and will find their stories are no less heady. In Los Angeles the larger companies may even ferry their new acquisition to Santa Maria or Northridge to view their pressing plants. All of this is designed to impress the artist with the company's power, energy, and commitment. Few companies take the artist through the accounting department or their distribution outlets, although they outweigh all of the creative divisions in wielding corporate power. The division heads that the artist meets on the tour essentially represent three dominant organizational entities that operate independently of each other while at the same time ideally striving for a common goal: production, marketing, and distribution qua sales.

Production—where the buck begins—encompasses all of the support functions necessary to give birth to a successful sound. This includes discovering an artist, getting him or her into the studio, and producing a single or an album. Once a tape is edited or "mixed," the other two divisions come into the picture. One attempts to create an image; the other delivers "sound" to the consumer.

Marketing (publicity, promotion, and graphics) receives the mixed session tape and devises a plan to expose the record. It will call upon advertising executives, market analysts, publicists, and promotion people, as well as those in charge of album covers, buttons, badges, and in-store displays. This division will map out an advertising and selling campaign to "hype" the record. It must consider the type of audience to which the record will appeal. This is translated into "media approach," album cover design, video clips, all of the things deemed necessary to make the total package attractive and commercial.

Distribution and sales is the least glamorous part of the record company. It is also the most important. Here the bottom line of profit and loss that is so feared in the industry is determined. Additionally, this division is directly concerned with manufacturing.

The finished record is shipped to distribution centers owned either by the company or independents. Company-owned centers are called branches. Independents that stock records from several labels are called subdistributors and one-stops; they are wholesale houses that service record stores and jukebox operators. Some are also rack jobbers that supply retail chains, department stores, supermarkets, and various other outlets where their place of business is set up.

After 90 or 120 days the accounting department determines if the record is a winner or a loser. The cold printout figures pulled from a computer are a matter of life and death for the artist. Failures become cutouts.

### Come Together, Over Me

Bhasker Menon describes the record-company president as occupying a position similar to a symphony conductor. With figurative baton in hand, he must coerce and cajole disparate instruments into working together so as to have a chance at a hit record. A smooth, highly integrated company helps but does not guarantee a successful profit-earning record. Conversely, few acts get a chance at the vinyl crap table when there is internal squabbling. Roy Silver aptly summed up the problem: "Getting the *entire* record company behind you is the hardest job in the music business." The "symphonic" direction is complicated by the number of organizational parts in a record company, each with its own specialties and values. Some unifying values exist, certainly, but others simply divide company employees. One long-lasting conflict has been described as "art for art's sake" as opposed to "art for profit," or "creativity" versus "accounting." These clichés bear some resemblance to truth but lack the essential economic ingredient. Records, artists, and even record companies rise and fall strictly according to the bottom-line, profit-loss principle. Creative persons may pay lip service to this dictum, but they rarely accept it. The artist's desire to use the studio for "just a few more" hours to create the "perfect sound" generally runs up against the wishes of the producer who has another act coming in or is afraid of the accounting-department executive, who is totally concerned with keeping costs down.

An industry observer told *Billboard,* "Bookkeepers don't understand the delicate relationship that exists between the merchandisers and the creators of the music business."[1] This is "a traditional rivalry in all industry," says Billy James. "There are some people who say that because this is show business there is a greater degree of openness among the various departmental functions. Sometimes that's true, sometimes it's not. Often there are producers who could just as easily be making shoes as records. So the conflict does exist." Promotion people expect the A&R people to give them something that will sell. Examples of distrust abound. The sales people at Columbia viewed senior producer John Hammond as "some kind of a joke." They allowed him to sign Bob Dylan and Bruce Springsteen to the label merely to humor him, and the two succeeded despite the bookkeepers.

Martin R. Cerf, when at United Artists, fought a protracted battle with the accounting department over the packaging of the Legendary Masters series, two-record sets by such stars of the 1950s as Eddie Cochran, Fats Domino, Jan and Dean, and Ricky Nelson. Referring to the accounting department, Cerf protested, "They would rather put out superpacks [economy-line records for supermarkets] than Legendary Masters series because they see a greater profit. . . . Sales people think this group of people who buy records are a group of mindless nubies, that they have no idea what they're doing. And it's not true." Legendary Masters eventually sold over 200,000 units and received critical acclaim throughout the industry. Not all of the creative people were allowed such luxuries. Billy James has kept for years a two-line memorandum written to him by a Columbia

Records executive: "We are not interested in signing Lenny Bruce. Thank you." For him, it is a perfect example of the myopia of the Columbia bookkeepers.

A Capitol executive called this curious organizational format the *cop out*, meaning that someone else down the line is responsible. *Buck passing* is a more common term. For Bill Graham, the villain becomes the immature performer

> who was two years ago working in a coffeehouse, whose education is limited, who is nontrained in music. Success came so quickly, more quickly than the growth of a valid personality, that he didn't know how to handle it. He takes advantage of the audience, knowing they'll accept anything he does, whether it's good or not. A group will come on stage, tuneup for 20 minutes, then do nine versions of their hit and be accepted as a god.[2]

Billy Squier blamed producer Kenny Ortega for the failure of his "Rock Me Tonight" video clip. "I think 'Rock Me Tonight' is a very demonstrable case where the director let his perception of me overrule what I was about," said Squier. "I'm not perceived as a pop star, I'm not in *16* magazine, I'm not a teenybopper idol. I'm much grittier than that." And he lost that in the clip. Ortega replied: "If anything, I tried to toughen the image he was projecting . . . both the editor, Peter Sternlicht, and I became so frustrated by our lack of involvement that we insisted our names be omitted from the credits. Let there be no doubt, "Rock Me Tonight" was a Billy Squier video in every sense. If it has damaged his career he has no one to blame but himself."[3]

Fear of failure, because of the great odds, permeates the record industry at nearly all levels. Artists distrust their managers and producers, while at corporate levels the A&R department may accuse promotion of laxity and not "getting behind the record" when the record of A&R's artist does not sell. At yet another level, the West Coast office of a company may be greatly at odds with the parent New York office. Record companies almost universally condemn rack jobbers—at least in private. "Our business is not corrupt," exclaimed a character in an episode of a television show dealing with the record industry, "just everybody in it." The word *unreliable* is more accurate than *corrupt*.

In the everyday world of the record industry corruption is not the norm, but the divisions between departments frequently require that informal arrangements be made to accomplish internal goals. For example, a publicist had arranged for one of his artists to be interviewed for a major rock magazine. The publicist contacted field people who were in another department. Nothing happened. As the date for the interview approached, the reporter attempted to confirm it with the publicist. The long-distance call was transferred to the head of promotion when the publicist was *coincidentally* in the man's office. The promotion director was duly embarrassed and the interview was saved. Another illustration of this informal method of "pulling" in one direction is the use of a "plant" in the trade papers. Publicists and promotional people frequently place anonymous items with journalists from *Variety* or the *Hollywood Reporter* that are designed to motivate others in their company to get behind a program or artist they consider important. The item "X is considering moving to a new label" generally means someone or a publicity-promotion department wants more company support or money.

The size of a record company greatly intensifies interdepartmental copouts. The size of corporations, where most communication is either by long-distance telephone or memoranda, adds to the structural differences. A & M prides itself on its open-door policies. Bob Garcia says:

> I've got to be able to walk into anybody's office and say, "Hey, this is wrong." And they can say, "You're full of shit." But if I can explain why it's wrong, then we're in agreement. . . . For me to walk into a vice-president's office does not require setting up an appointment, or going through secretaries, but being brave enough to speak my mind. That's how this place seems to work. A lot of things are consummated right here in this lot [A & M]. People standing out and talking, screaming and yelling a lot, but it gets done.

The New York "home-office" phenomenon is seen by many in Los Angeles as exacerbating the conflicts inherent within record companies. Columbia, RCA, and Elektra have headquarters in Manhattan. The three-hour time lag between coasts is of very real concern to RCA and Columbia because all major decisions are made in New York and much of the action takes place in Los Angeles. Bob Garcia observes, "It's very difficult for the New York home office to understand what happens out here." A former CBS artist development executive said:

> No matter how much we use the telephone, it's still 3,000 miles away. You come in here and call in the morning, and its lunchtime in New York. You wait for them and they're tied up. Then you go to lunch and that's when they call you back. So you adjust your eating or social habits accordingly to make sure that you get through to them when they're available because they're certainly not going to adjust their habits for us.

The time lag creates many frustrations. "Getting answers to things" is a major problem. Royalty advances in many cases have to be cleared with the home office. Responses to artists' requests are frequently held up because of the communication lag. Delays upset temperamental artists. David Anderle, a former Elektra A&R director, comments, "The West Coast-East

Coast situation is deadly." Discussing an artist he is independently producing for RCA Victor, he says: "I'll work for her. I'll definitely work with her. But I cannot do for her the things I'm doing with the other people I'm working with strictly because she's on RCA and strictly because I don't know who to go to." The key reason is the two-coast dilemma. "The power decisions are made in New York; they're not made on the West Coast. [You have] the situation where you get the local head of A&R to say yes to something, and then if it's really a major issue you go through that period of waiting again, the phones and the whole thing."

While the two-coast situation is of consequence, the bureaucracy of large corporations—getting to the right people for decisions—and the unique personalities of company heads further complicate the situation. RCA's president may be remote, but he does delegate some authority. At Columbia several employees felt that Clive Davis, prior to his dismissal, worsened the situation. "The problem is Clive," said one employee on the verge of quitting.

> What Clive really should do is he should have a counterpart on the Coast that would be able to act immediately, that would be able to make those kinds of decisions, rather than always having to go through New York for anything major. Like on a publicity thing, . . . I have to clear it through New York. It's a problem. I don't know why he doesn't do it unless it's giving up part of the power.

He adds, "At times we feel like a farm club." In many respects the West Coast office was just an outpost.

MCA executives in New York complain about a reverse situation. Nearly all of the company's business is conducted on the West Coast; however, record-company business does not start, in earnest, until 11:00 A.M. West Coast time, which makes it after lunch in New York City. Reportedly, many of the conflicts that sprang up over the promotion and later production of *Jesus Christ Superstar* stemmed from this distribution of authority. The addition of Nashville offices and studios by many companies has further contributed to the time-geography split.

To dismiss the lack of company integration as solely a product of size and time zones would be misleading. Small companies with a high level of communication and integration have many of the same problems on a departmental level. Even artists at A & M like Styx accuse the family company of lack of support. Although some accusations no doubt are camouflage for artist bumbling, the structural problems become even greater when one actually begins placing sound on a record.

### The Producer

The individual with whom the copout process begins but rarely ends is the producer. In the plant or studio the creativity and talent of an act are tested and transformed into a commodity to be bought and sold in the marketplace. In the studio, acts "sing and make noise on instruments." This 48-track "noise" is preserved on tape, later to be broken into stereo channels. Frequently neither the record company nor the act is happy with the result, but each blames the other for the undesirable outcome. "No one starts out to make a bad record" is a favorite industry statement. A Capitol Records executive said, "Elements of the industry can blame their failures on the manufacturing blokes—the operations systems." This sentiment is widespread. Performers frequently blame unsuccessful albums on producers, a complaint echoed by promotional personnel as well as the media cultural gatekeepers. Critics in *Rolling Stone, Record, Rock*, and other rock journals have lamented about how a "producer screwed up a good artist." One veteran program director attributed the large number of stiffs to the complexity of sessions and overproduction, where a number of tempos and styles are "jammed onto one record." The producer, according to a "bizzer," is "the element between the artist and the record company." He selects the music and judges the sound. He is the most important person from the time the artist enters the studio to the time the session tape is delivered to the pressing plant and to the marketing people. After that the success of a record is out of his control.

As with nearly all aspects of the record business, the role of the producer drastically changed during the sixties. In the heyday of Mitch Miller, the producer—then called an A&R man—went through hundreds of songs selecting just the right one. A recording date was set up. Arrangements were contracted. The singer walked into the studio and left three hours later, after creating a completed master tape. The function of the engineer was to reproduce what occurred.

Stereo, which allowed for two tracks, altered the role of the engineer. Les Paul and Mary Ford had already used "overdubbing," with two tracks being fed into monaural track, and the Alvin and the Chipmunks records produced by Ross Bagdasarian for Liberty used a similar technique.

Rock and roll's ascendency both altered and staggered studio methods. Many professional studio people considered the new genre to be a noisy fad. They did not understand it and treated it with contempt. Using two channels, they simply reproduced sound. Thus, engineers with little if any musical background became producers, interpreting on tape what had happened in the studio. A veteran A&R man, a studio musician during the introduction of rock music, recalls, "I was still playing at that time when Fabian and them came along. Everything was done in the key of E because that's open-string guitar. All guitar players played in the key of E because you didn't have to take any lessons because you could play three chords and that't all you had to have." One engineer, when asked his opinion of a tape, answered the producer, "I'm sorry, man, I turn my ears off on playbacks."[4] A & M producer Creed Taylor told Gene Lees, "I once saw an engineer cutting a master [the final tape] while reading the *Wall Street Journal*. He had the sound turned so low you could hardly hear it. If anything went wrong, he wouldn't know it."[5]

John Phillip Hammond, George Goldner, Shadow Morton, and Phil Spector were the ablest and most important producers of the pre-Beatle era. Spector, especially, transformed a fundamentally simple idiom into spectaculars rivaling those of D. W. Griffith and Cecil B. DeMille in cinema. Spector characterized his production as "little symphonies for the kids." His magnum opus, Ike and Tina Turner's "River Deep, Mountain High," cost $22,000 to make, an unheard of amount for a single in 1966. Although a critical success—one writer classified it "a 'rushing, mighty wind' the Bible talks about"—it was an economic failure. The best record Spector ever cut was a stiff. Embittered, he withdrew from the business, returning as the Beatles' producer of *Let It Be*. Even his monumental "Wall of Sound" could not uplift the role of the producer; most remained technicians, merely editing sound from the studio and doing little to embellish it.

Stereo appeared in record marts in 1958. Most of the releases were "ping ponged": the "bottom"—rhythm (drums, bass)— on the left channel; the "top"—vocal, lead guitar, horns—on the right. As program director Gary Shiver indicated, "So stereo often did not put you in the center of the performance, but it added . . . another canvas for the creative mediator of recorded sound."

The growing sophistication of recording tape and multitrack stereo equipment coupled with various combinations of overdubbing or "mixing" signaled a breakthrough. The Beatles' clever exploitation of this equipment with the aid of EMI staff producer George Martin did more than anything else to legitimate and bolster the technical status of the man behind the glass. The producer became the man who could, at John Lennon's request, hire a large orchestra and concoct a final chord with an Indian tamboura and the sound of a hand hitting the strings inside a piano to create "A Day in the Life." Richard Goldstein, the New York critic, reacted to *Sgt. Pepper*: "It reeks of horns and harps, harmonica quartets, assorted animal noises, and a 41-piece orchestra. . . . An obsession with production, coupled with a surprising shoddiness in composition, permeates the entire album."[6] The impact of *Sgt. Pepper* "behind the glass" was staggering. David Anderle: "It took a lot of producers many years to find out that they could not all make *Sgt. Pepper*s. They all tried. God knows we had a year and a half of some of the weirdest sounds on record. Everybody trying to make *Sgt. Pepper*." Unlike Spector, who received credit for "You've Lost That Lovin' Feelin'," George Martin found his success attributed to the Beatles.

The artist was afforded an editorial control he had not previously enjoyed. Reflecting on the change, veteran producer Jimmy Bowen said:

> The record producer's role has changed. It used to be he was an A&R man. His main responsibilities were to find hit songs, properly cast them for the right artist, call in an arranger and book the musicians. It was a casting job, almost—a putting together of music.
>
> Back when I worked with Frank Sinatra, Dean Martin and Sammy Davis Jr., these people were singers. They weren't writers/artists. They didn't get deeply involved in the music of the session at the session.
>
> The record producer for today has to be a totally different animal. He needs to have song sense. But it's no longer an era when he has a meeting and says "Here, artists, are your songs." We're in an era when the people who sell the most albums are the artists who are doing their own music. The producer's job—although it is quite extensive—is basically to help the artist get his music on tape. The producer should fill any gap the artist has musically, but he shouldn't dominate.[7]

The acid-rock phenomenon further altered the producer-artist relationship. For most rock bands of the period, producers were straight technicians with little musical understanding but immense technological know-how. Marty Balin, then with Jefferson Airplane, complained, "RCA's conservative. It's run by older men who really don't have anything going in rock and they were so desperate to get into it . . . when we started doing our material, they were very confused by the lyrics."[8] Nearly every Jefferson Airplane LP was released only after bitter arguments between the band and the company. Jerry Garcia recalled the Grateful Dead's first Warner Bros. album: "The first record was like a regular company record done in three nights, mixed in one day. . . . So we weren't surprised when it didn't quite sound like we wanted it to."[9]

The bands hired their own producers, many of whom knew little more than the performers. The record companies, sensing a new trend, dismissed a number of staff producers. One A&R vice-president explained, "Let's say for instance that you've got four staff producers working for you and you're giving them weekly salaries, and the last three acts you've signed have come in with other producers or want other producers. They don't want your people." The spiraling costs of signing, recording, and promoting acts further pushed many companies away from staff production to independents who could produce or at least record an act.

Beginning with the late Goddard Lieberson of CBS Records, company executives said, "There's a parallel between records now and the movie business. Today, Hollywood finances productions by independent producers, and merely distributes the films. That's what's happening in records."[10] Jac Holzman and a score of others held the same viewpoint. The companies became Stan Cornyn's "ticket sellers," and A&R departments were transformed, in Mauri Lathower's terms, into "service organizations."

Independent producers became the rage. By the 1980s most charted material was attributed to independent producers or to the performer. The self-produced act generally used a token engineer or friend as a producer. A dejected Phil Spector described that period:

> The groups said, "Well, we don't want to do anything, except make our own records. We don't want studio cats because they can do everything we can't do, and they represent something hostile to us." They go to the record company saying, "Listen, we want to do our own record and that's it. . . ." The group has its own material and has its own ideas; its own thing, so the *producer has become no more than an engineer.*[11]

"The idea of having somebody there in the final analysis is to have a sounding board—somebody with a different viewpoint. That can be incredibly important," observed Capitol's A&R director Ray Tusken.

The Grateful Dead use a producer in this fashion. "He's an ear. He translates the band's wishes to the engineer." Jerry Garcia and "whoever cares" mix the recorded tapes into a master. Some self-produced tapes have motivated many industry people to believe that the dictum "the lawyer who defends himself has a fool for a client" should be posted in all recording studios. The stories of waste and misuse of studio equipment are folklore in the industry. The Beach Boys reportedly filled a studio with sand from the local seashore for effect. The Mothers of Invention made an album tripping on LSD. Many bands have spent incredibly large sums on producing albums that did not sell. Todd Rundgren, both a performer and an independent producer, thinks that most performers tend to confuse their "art with their life-style" and consequently "do not know the bounds of their own act."[12] David Lawhon agrees, attributing the abuses of self-production to the lack of training inherent in rock bands, the flexibility of equipment, the absence of written musical scores, and the "nonprofessional nature of contemporary performers."

One symptom of unprofessionalism cited by numerous industry people (usually off the record) is alleged excessive drug use in the studio. Andy Wickman, a staff producer at Warner Bros., asserts that drugs distort performers' hearing, thus muddling the ability to distinguish between illusion and reality while playing and mixing records. This accounts for the high cost of recording, he says. Wickman, once the house hippie, now labeled a "closet fascist" by some artists, does get some nods of agreement even from those who ideologically oppose him. Another producer said,

> I think he's had some bad experiences first of all. If a guy has to smoke a joint to get there, fine. If another guy has to take an upper, fine. I've had incredible problems with people on acid in the studio . . . but my biggest problem is with booze. I've had more bad sessions with alcohol than any other kind of thing. . . . A lot of people absolutely don't want any kind of smoking, or anything going on in their session. They're just so afraid of it themselves.

The laissez-faire attitude toward substance use does not apply to those inside the booth. David Anderle cautions,

> The engineer and the producer have to watch what's going on. The engineer . . . is in front of all those machines. If somebody lays down a good take, boy, it better be on the tape tomorrow. It better be exactly the same way you're hearing it. . . . Sometimes you can run into problems if the bass player's on downers and the drummer's on uppers.

Self-produced groups do not have this corrective mechanism. The tempo of the Grateful Dead's first album was too fast because members of the band were on dexamyl, a diet pill with an amphetamine base. "So we played some hyperactive music . . . the tempo was way too fast. We were all so speedy at the time. It has its sort of crude energy."[13] Sense distortion is not the only problem inherent in self-production. Ted Templeman at Warner adds, "I was an artist [*Harper's Bazaar*] for a long time and I couldn't produce my own records. You can't be as objective. You need someone to say, 'Okay, that's it. That's the take we want.'"

Templeman defines the role of a staff man: "He's responsible for the recording part of a performer's career. That entails money, watching the budget, submitting the budget, getting budget approval, having the right studio, being able to direct material and finding out what is the best environment for an artist to work in." The staff man's loyalty is first and foremost to the company. "I'm a firm believer in that I'm being paid by a company. I usually don't work under a situation that I live on an override from the production of an artist. I'm paid by the company a salary to do A&R as well as production." The producer is loyal to those who pay his salary. Staff producers in most cases are expected to give their fealty to the company. On the other hand the independent producer, who normally receives 5 to 10 percent of an artist's record gross, places his loyalty with the performer. While Warner does in fact attempt to combine the best of these economic arrangements, its staff people are essentially tied to the company. Templeman claims he would take a pay cut rather than work anywhere other than Warner/Reprise.

Many record companies have discounted the value of loyalty for the savings of independent production. As service organizations they are now predominantly concerned with merchandising, distribution, and promotion. The Beach Boys, Rolling Stones, and many others are now responsible for bringing in finished or master tapes. A&R then does the paperwork, making sure that the record licenses are in order, doing all the mechanical work to see that the artist gets proper payment. After that the A&R department ideally serves as the artist's aide de camp. It contacts the art department, which then evolves a concept to highlight the tape. Frequently this is a problem because art work takes longer to process than the disk. "You can make a disk overnight. Art takes weeks for color collections." Here the famous buck-passing process quickly enters the picture. "There is usually some mistake about label copy or liner notes," said Mauri Lathower, adding, "We sit through the hope that we can get and put it all together." The art department quickly answers that the hang-up is the kind of acts A&R signs, not graphic work. A&R's shepherding a record through a company is quite a chore, for nearly every step involves a similar conflict. This has been compounded by the growing number of independent production agreements and contracts giving artists control.

Depending on the artist involved, independent production deals may be treated with less vigor and enthusiasm by A&R people. However, for those in the executive suite and the accounting department, these arrangements help control excessive studio costs or unreliable and capricious artists or producers. Commenting upon the Beach Boys, then with Warner and considered by many to be the industry prima donnas, Joe Smith said if they do not "deliver the record we'll keep the doors open this month." Ironically, Smith, when with Elektra/Asylum, gave the Eagles a rhyming dictionary to encourage the delivery of an album.

Not surprisingly most of the volatile acts are increasingly finding themselves in a pay-on-delivery basis. The Beach Boys, Grateful Dead, Jefferson Starship, and many others have independent production arrangements with their record companies. A number of "name" producers have tried their own labels; Bones Howe, Richard Perry, and Michael Chapman are but a few. Independent production has escalated into a host of small record labels that are distributed by a major record label. Grunt Records (launched by the Jefferson Airplane, now Starship) and a number of other labels claim to have ultimate freedom over the entire record package with the advantages of large distribution systems controlled by the majors.

Artistic freedom is cited as the major bonus of independent production. Many independent producers and, indeed, record companies see CBS and RCA as a labyrinth or maze in which one has to go through five executives to get a decision on even the simplest matters. Lenny Waronker, president of Warner Bros., disagrees "No one ever forced a staff producer to work with someone he doesn't fit with. There's fantastic creative freedom, . . . [they] never told a producer here to delete a cut from an album. They don't dictate policy. That's the only way an A&R staff can work."[14] Nonetheless, few staff producers fare well in a dispute with a "name" performer; the higher echelons of a company almost always side with the artist. One producer said, "It's pretty much up to the artist, here at Warner Brothers, if the artist isn't happy and he has something, I think the company is going to stay with the artist." Independents also claim staff men are grossly underpaid. To counter this charge, Warner has developed profit-sharing for its people; other companies are not so generous.

Despite artistic control, independent production is a high-risk business. There are ten independents making "big money," and "any producer who doesn't score within 34 of the Top 100 in a twelve-month period is in trouble." A staff man, while enjoying more security, must also know that a poor in-house chart showing can get him fired. Still, a staff position is a bit more secure, when available, than independent work.

### Behind the Glass Lightly

All producers go through fairly standard procedures that are colored by their relationship to recording companies. The producer's major function is to orchestrate, through the taping and mixing, the sound that will eventually become a record. Todd Rundgren defines the role of the producer as "anything you have to do to make the record meet your professional standards." This may involve arranging, engineering, and even playing on a record, as Phil Spector did in his glory days. The producer does everything he can to accentuate the strong points of the act in the studio. David Anderle sees himself as a mirror of the artist: "If the artist is performing and I'm not reacting, then he feels something wrong with it. So he can use me as an alter ego." This process—the birth of a hit record or star act—begins in the studio. The copout philosophy also begins both in front and behind the glass separating the control room from the musicians and singers.

Nowhere is the cost-creativity conflict more apparent than in the studio. The man in the middle is the producer. Studio costs can be astronomical. Village Recorder's studio D rented for $20,000 per week; in 1978 Fleetwood Mac occupied the facility for six months. Kendun Recorders in

Burbank was planning a rate of $30,000 per week. "Superstars are demanding all the latest electronic toys. A super studio allows the big city operator to compete with the exotic vacation studios often in the countryside that boast of saunas, showers, kitchens and complete privacy plus state-of-the art equipment," explained Kent Duncan.[15] These deluxe facilities obviously are beyond the reach of less-marketable artists. Platinum artists are budgeted at $300,000; the top budget for less-marketable acts is in the $80,000-or-less range. "It's tough to make an album for $40,000, but you can do it," noted a former Doobie Brother turned producer, Jeff Baxter. "I'll have to engineer or overdub myself and not use someone whom I'd love to. Budgets make me work faster—and I get better and quicker with every project like a surgeon honing his skills." Not all producer's share this view. Phil Spector had the Ramones bassplayer redo a bottom track for nearly 12 hours. Even Bob Margouleff, known for his work with Stevie Wonder, says, "Don't use studios as a place to create. Use them as a place to perform." A studio rents for $125 (cash) to about $200 market rate or per hour, that is, about $2.50 per minute, not including engineers' fees and the cost of hiring "sidemen." Studio musicians are paid $320.00 for a session of two hours and fifty minutes in the nation's five recording centers. Top session men in Nashville, Los Angeles, and New York can earn over $100,000 a year if they work the "four-a-days" six days a week.

"With smaller budgets you cut the fat," says Baxter. "Everyone gets more for their money." "Time means money," declares producer Garry Sherman, "The more time we save and the more we accomplish in a given time period, the more money we've saved, the more we've earned."[16] The artist, although frequently unaware of it, generally pays for studio time because record companies subtract the cost from the artist's royalty payments. Independent producers either follow suit or see their percentage of the act's earnings diminish.

Package independent production deals encounter the same problems with costs because the producer is assigned a given amount for X number of albums to be delivered. Mike Curb admits, "One of the hazards an independent producer faces is to discover that his budgets are cut because the company has to pay high talent and production fees so the producer's promotional allowances is cut."[17]

From an accounting standpoint, the fast-paced three-hour session producing a single or even an album is ideal. This is how it was done in the days of Mitch Miller. However, the vast potential of the 16- to 48-track board and the temptation to spend extra hours, even days, in the studio become a seductive force. Paul Simon told Jon Landau, "A lot of times I don't do anything but sit in a studio for an hour or so. . . . I like the studio to be a home, to be comfortable, and then I think, 'I'm talking to this guy, and if I talk . . . for two hours that costs $300.'"[18] Simon simply avoided looking at his studio expenses, which have run in the neighborhood of $50,000 to $100,000. But few performers have the status Simon enjoyed with his record company; he was then a superstar. An act that sells 80,000 albums per release cannot afford to indulge itself with lengthy stints in the studio—but many try.

The producer is the timekeeper and in many cases the controller. He is the policeman with one eye on the wall clock. Costs, from rents to musicians' fees, are all contingent upon the clock. Creativity, however, is not measured by this yardstick. David Anderle states:

> The quickest way to turn an artist off is to remind him how much money he's spending at a time when he's right on the verge of creating something. . . . But at some point you have to go up and say, "Hey, Manny, that's it for the night, we're just wasting time, it's money down the drain." And it is our money that somebody's putting up. . . . There has to be discipline. An artist does need guidance, especially in a studio. Somebody has to supply that discipline. Somebody has to say, "Okay, let's go home 'cause we're wasting time and money.'"

Todd Rundgren, having worked both sides of the studio glass, agrees: "People when they first get in the studio aren't aware that every hour they spend in the studio is another 140 bucks. They'll just keep going in there, and in a month the bills'll come in and they'll have spent $20,000 in studio time alone, and still not even be finished."[19] The Grateful Dead reportedly wasted over $80,000 on their early albums.

Artists, on the other hand, believe musical quality is more important than dollars. Leon Russell, Paul Simon, and many others laud producers Terry Melcher and Bob Johnston for their "rich man's approach" while decrying the three-hour session that produces a record regardless of the quality of the sound. Ike Turner, referring to Tina Turner's "River Deep, Mountain High" on the *Pop Chronicles*, said, "The only record I've heard that could come close to that record is a record by the Beach Boys called 'Good Vibrations.' I think these are the two records that I've heard in my life that I really like." "River Deep, and "Good Vibrations" are believed to be the two most expensive singles in recording history. The Beach Boys' song also failed to reach the *Billboard* "Top 10." Worst of all, "River Deep" was the most expensive stiff ever produced in the Top 40 arena.

Performers and producers firmly espouse artistic freedom over record sales, but no one is sure where artistry ceases and economic irresponsibility begins. "On the last few albums I've done," says hit-maker Richard Perry, "I've rarely gone beyond three takes."[20] "That's a critical thing," suggests Anderle, "you're sitting there on the one side of the glass and you know that it's not quite there yet and musicians are starting to tire. The tricky decision for the producer is to force several more takes or close the session and start anew the next day." Many successful producers avoid taxing musicians because it generates tension that inhibits rather than enhances creativity. At this moment the primary role of the producer is reintroduced and his loyalties are challenged. Several takes more may capture the desired sound, but another three-hour session is expensive. The final judgment is the producer's.

To avoid these taxing, problematic situations, producers have become "psychoanalysts with rhythm", using all manner of theories to understand and manipulate the "feel" of a session. Nearly all believe that some kind of psychological orchestration is necessary for a successful record. Don Gant, a producer at MCA comments, "Personality is as important as ability. You have to make people feel relaxed . . . joke, laugh, and make everybody feel comfortable." Ted Templeman: "Sequence and pacing are really important." To achieve the proper "feel" Templeman employs five engineers, each of whose experience and temperament fit a particular act in the studio. Barry Gibb produced Kenny Rogers and Barbara Streisand with the philosophy "There's no point in using a producer unless you're prepared to be pushed a little bit. You've got to get a camaraderie going and both the artist and the producer work for that. We meet in the middle and it works." He admitted Kenny Rogers "would get unhappy about things . . . the full spectrum of emotions came out of the guy." Anderle uses a more encompassing technique. His musicians and singers are friends. He considers Rita Coolidge to be "like a sister." From then on it is simply a matter of making the performers reach a plateau. "I think that's why we have so much fun in our sessions. I just can't get a musician, contract him to come and play a specific part. I make him become part of the session . . . and if the drummer is unhappy or the bass player is unhappy I want to know about it. . . . He's going to have to contribute to the music."

Manipulating the emotions of musicians at recording sessions is critical. The techniques vary depending on the artist. A producer told Donna Summer "If you think you can sing as good as Chaka Khan, you're gonna have to prove it." She performed best under stress. Other artists require different tactics. "You have to get the artist relaxed so you can get spontaneous performance." One observer described Quincy Jones as being "so modest and cool you wind up doing exactly what he wants, no questions asked. That's why his records sound so relaxed. He's the ultimate mood-maker and the most skilled manipulator in the business."[21]

Cutting a record when everything is properly "mixed" is fairly routine. A producer sits at a control panel with an engineer and separately records the various instruments to be used. It is only *after* the music is on tape that the configurations take place. Having achieved the sound he believes to be the best performance possible, within budgetary limits and other factors, the producer then mixes the tapes.

There are, of course, many variations on the theme. Echo, equalizing (softening or bringing up parts), and reverberation that are mixed into the final recording. Some instruments can be further amplified. If the producer wishes, he may mix in a lush violin or even a symphony orchestra. After the tracks have been executed to the satisfaction of all, the material is edited or mixed. At this point decisions are made that help determine the fate of the recording. Here the artistry of the producer is all important but still not dominant, for many performers are given a veto power on the mixing of their tapes—and some later regret not having exercised the option to participate in this critical stage.

The first mix is in the head of the producer or artist. Ted Templeman:

> First of all you do a basic track. You have drums on, say, five to six tracks, piano maybe on two, three guitar tracks . . . and you're using a lot of tracks on four instruments, but that's how you're creating the magic that is missing because maybe you can't see them. Then you go from there . . . it's got to be in your head . . . the producer does have to be a creative person. That's why a lot of engineers aren't really producers.

The Raspberries' gold record "Go All the Way" was taught to members of the group although only its writer, lead singer Eric Carmen, knew the total concept for it. "None of you guys will really know what the song's supposed to sound like until it's recorded and all mixed. Then we'll know how to play it," he said. "Nobody could really conceive of that, except I would be able to hear it in my head, being the writer of the song." The late Tom Wilson: "The producer paints on layers of technique, deciding in the process the type of echo to use, the number of tracks . . . and the choice of overdubbing and equalizing devices."[22] Volume, tempo, clearness, or fuzziness of one or two tracks all are determined at this point. Other sounds are added if needed. Anderle attempts to make the song as real as possible: he will "throw in a pedal steel with a lick, or maybe a violin here or something, anything that will enhance the music and give it something that will turn people on."

The artist should then have the final say. Anderle, as well as many other producers, insists that the performer accept this responsibility. "An artist has to tell me he's happy." Other producers, either due to inexperience or pressure by a company's rush to get the record out, may mix the record without consulting the artist. The consequences are predictable. The failure of the record will be laid at the feet of the producer because he mixed the record, at least in the mechanical sense.

A producer, in mixing a record, also must consider the tastes of his projected audience. A single is mixed differently than an album. The emotional impact of the single must be immediate, and its length should fit AM airplay formulas. Albums can be a bit more subtle. "Stairway to Heaven," Led Zeppelin's "classic," is an FM staple. It's too long and starts too slowly for Top 40 airplay.

During the mix-down the realization of radio reality impacts upon the producer. The song or instrumental must have a "hook" or an attention-getting device. An infectious opening is ideal. Every producer attempts to recreate the magic Kinks, CCR, or Deep Purple sound, which attracts the listener's attention during the first four bars of the cut. Beethoven perhaps pioneered the technique with his *Fifth Symphony*, and it still works, as ELO aptly demonstrated. Producers are well aware that music directors are sent enormous quantities of listening material. Consequently, as veteran producer Frank Jones indicates, "You always look for that hook. Be it either in the lyrics or in your arrangement, and that's where you find in many cases. . . . Nashville musicians are so creative they come up with some very imaginative sounds."

Top 40 or "Hot Hits" programmers frequently follow the lead of the mid-1960s KHJ and listen to only three or four seconds of a record before deciding if it is a "hit pick." Producers of albums, such as Templeman, deny pandering to the reviewing habits of program directors, however; Templeman always places the strongest song as cut one, side one on an album. "That's because the program director will head that first. That's just common sense. It probably wasn't necessarily the best as far as the total concept, but I owe it to the artist to give him that." Anderle and his artists, Rita Coolidge and Kris Kristofferson, continuously discuss the manufacturing of a hit single. "Once in a while," he admits, "we may learn to add something. Maybe we put strings on this, the AM market would have more of a chance of playing it. When we're cutting songs with Mark, we're not embarrassed to use words like *hook*. . . . It's a matter of saying here's the song, here's how we laid it out." Capitol Records laid out the single "Question" by overdubbing a heavy Kinks-like bass line introduction that was absent from the album version.

Some performers believe that there is an overemphasis on the hook. Waylon Jennings, who coproduces and writes many of his own songs, said, "If a big beat complements that song, then use it. If a kazoo complements that song, we got just as much right to use that as anybody else. Or horns or anything. But *don't use them* just in order to make it where it will get played in certain areas." Once again, we find the conflict between artistic concerns and record sales.

Producers and A&R departments include other extraneous factors in the mix of records. The channeling of a record is determined by the idiom to which it is addressed. Mauri Lathower says, "There are times we'll mix a single differently for the radio stations than the copies we sell or the marketing copy." This practice assures the company that listeners will hear the entire record. Radio stations receive monaural singles or type B monos on which two stereo tracks are condensed into one. The reason for this policy is that with two channels it is possible to lose a track in transmission. The highs and lows from the rhythm section can be lost, or even the vocal. To accommodate stereo broadcasters, many singles sent to radio stations now have the same song in both one track and two tracks on different sides.

Time is a very important factor. Radio programming is governed by the "Hot Hits" or other format that allots a certain amount of time for a song and no more. The producer must be aware of this policy. Many good records have failed because producers disregarded the time factor. Phil Spector's "River Deep" is believed to have failed because it contained 40 seconds more music than the average Top 40 single. Another Spector production, "You've Lost That Lovin' Feelin'" by the Righteous Brothers, almost suffered a similar fate when program directors discovered that the time listed on the record was incorrect. Although it caused public service announcements (PSAs) and news stories to be cut short, "Lovin' Feeling" was Spector's biggest success. Very few other records have successfully deviated from the dictates of time scheduling. The Beatles' "Hey Jude" was the longest single to reach the *Billboard* "Hot 100." Don McLean's "American Pie" was originally shortened from the album version; only listener demand garnered the entire song air play. Most songs longer than 2:37 or 3:05 minutes have been cut down to meet the radio time requirement.

Yet another consideration facing the producer is that few bands are evenly balanced between instruments and vocals. The producer generally determines emphasis between the two on the basis of market. Many A&R people believe easy-listening stations prefer lush arrangements on which the listener, probably doing housework or driving to work, need not concentrate. Lyrics are incidental, the instruments provide the background noise. The same philosophy is true for heavy metal bands as Quiet Riot, whose energy and high volume are all-important. On the other hand, for the college youth audience, lyrics are not totally to be disturbed by complex arrangements that overshadow the singer. These, of course, are general rules of thumb balanced out by synthesizing both down into a single channel, thereby orienting a song into two markets, it is hoped. Michael Jackson, Prince, Neil Young, Lionel Richie, and the Oak Ridge Boys have successfully appealed to the youth, adult-contemporary, and even easy-listening markets, but it is tricky business and artists are wise not to stray too far from their audience bases. Richard Sterban of the Oak Ridge Boys: "A crossover record for a country artists is kind of like a bonus. It's nothing you can depend on" (referring to "Elvira"[23]). Willie Nelson's version of "Stardust," after selling 2 million copies in all demographic units was widely criticized in Nashville circles. Linda Ronstadt, George Benson, and a legion of others have disaffected their original fans by crossovers. A producer must be mindful of this dilemma.

Producers are increasingly specializing in certain types of artists. They are viewed as being especially effective in reaching a particular taste public. Some producers do not like the labels. Jim Steinman, who has produced hits for Meatloaf, Bonnie Tyler, and Barry Manilow, objects: "I'm less obsessive about images, and more concerned with hits." He added, "They want me to do Black Sabbath, and I want to, because the idea of doing Barry Manilow and Black Sabbath in a five-month period is so cool."[24]

Like artists, producers are categorized by others and themselves. Richard Perry said,

> I've come to recognize that this [established acts] . . . is my ultimate strength. That's why I'm very enthused by the focus within the industry on tried-and-true artists. All of my success has been with that type of act. I've come to realize that my greatest asset is being able to take an artist that has a track record. Whether they're hot or cold at the moment is not important. I can work with these acts more efficiently and effectively because they're pros.[25]

Perry is one of the few producers in the industry who can successfully adopt this stance.

Producers rise and fall with trends and fads. Indeed, some producers cannot work with certain artists either because of personality factors or because of the act's style. Anderle who concentrates upon solo artists, commented: "As a producer my biggest failure is working with a band. I have problems working with multiple personalities." Andy Wickman sees himself as the Roger Vadim of the industry, concentrating on producing female vocalists. He will, however, undertake "everybody but underground artists," who in his mind are mirrors of the "plastic Orwellian" state of the United States. Templeman preferred rock music bands, such as Little Feat or the Doobie Brothers, because they had "a lot of quality rhythms and strong percussion." George Goldner thrived in the 1950s on a cappella New York street-corner groups. Jeff Barry carried on this tradition, and is now being called in the industry the "maker of Top 40 hits." Spector originally worked with female artists. Bones Howe, a former engineer, did especially well with his knack for overdubbing voices with vocal groups like the Association and Fifth Dimension. The list goes on.

A producer can do little with some artists. For stage bands, the studio is a prison rather than a tool for creativity. Gary Duncan, of Quicksilver Messenger Service, makes a comparison: "Playing something in a studio means playing for two months. Playing live, a song changes in performance. In a studio you attack things intellectually; on stage it's all emotion."[26] Cub Koda, a member of Brownsville Station, further explained the difference between the studio and the stage. "There's a lot of groups that the first thing they do is they go into the studio. They don't even worry about live performance, they master the studio and sometimes they come out with good stuff. Us, man, we're dragged out of high schools, we're dragged out of basements . . . we learned everything we know on the stage." The group's lead singer adds, "Obviously you can't have all the charisma that you have in a live performance, particularly with us, because you've got the visual thing as well. You're seeing the music as well when you come to hear us play, so to speak, but you can't get that on an album. We're trying to get as close to it as possible."

For many bands, getting "close" has proved to be an impossibility. A vinyl or even a video clip or cassette rarely can condense the excitement of a club or concert performance for the home listener. The visual and sensual aspects of a "live" performance are elusive. Records by the Grateful Dead have generally disappointed critics and fans, yet "Dead-heads" travel literally thousands of miles to their concerts. Video clips have assisted some groups to overcome this problem, and the MTV clips frequently are better than the albums. In a studio or a soundstage the producer or director provides feedback, but many artists simply cannot function without an audience. As a result many acts become flat on recordings, especially when they are asked to play the same tracks over and over again. The psychological tricks used by those behind the glass sometimes fail to generate excitement.

The producer's art of mixing all of the ingredients into a salable commodity borders upon alchemy. Formulas exist but few are either foolproof or consistent. The magic that made Phil Spector a "teen-age tycoon," as Tom Wolfe labeled him, an overnight millionaire, failed him after "River Deep." For the sound to be in the grooves, a right number of elements must jell. Once the master tape is delivered to the A&R department it is immediately put on trial. The type of economic and psychic energy the record will receive is determined at this point. An A&R department that believes in a record will try to get the rest of the company behind it. A lukewarm response will generate only a minimum of effort. It is true that most companies give everything "a shot." The kind of shot is originally determined by A&R, which hopes (and prays) the emotional contagion will carry over to marketing.

## Marketing: Buttons, Banners, and Hype

From the time Vance Packard's *Hidden Persuaders* and Milton Meyer's *Madison Avenue U.S.A.* dominated U.S. best-seller lists, advertising executives have been seen as sorcerers armed with motivational research and other magical potions with which to inveigle the average consumer into purchasing anything from toothpaste to presidents. There is considerable doubt in the record industry about the magical qualities of marketing. Murray Ross, president of Ideal Planning Associates, once wrote in *Record World*: "The techniques of marketing and merchandising in the music industry are the most underdeveloped of any billion dollar industry . . . no giant industry can survive and prosper where marketing and merchandising planning is the least dynamic component of its total sales efforts."[27] An industry publicist remarked, "If a PD in the Midwest says we don't know what's going on with his people and their daily lives, I partially agree with him."

Joe Smith, holds that horse-and-buggy marketing techniques permeate the record industry: "Marketing is an industry problem. . . . It's a problem of how to get out goods out to as many places as possible . . . that's the next challenge for us. To penetrate the market and get music in more homes, there's equipment to play it." Until the 1980s penetrating the market was a relatively standardized operation. After World War II the basic desire has been to "break the record on radio." This task has dominated a majority of industry marketing efforts. "Radio has to be looked upon as your key," said producer Frank Jones. Sixty-three percent of album purchases were influenced, according to A. C. Nielsen, by radio exposure in 1983. The difficulties of getting air time have motivated companies to look elsewhere for exposure. Cable music video channels, despite the costs, originally were accepted by most labels. Even the skeptics eventually jumped on the bandwagon. They *had* to.

It is axiomatic that every album warrants an 8- by-10-inch glossy photo and a "bio." Prior to the "crash of '79" other "goodies"· accompanied product. Buttons, badges, and T-shirts were relatively inexpensive, and companies produced these items as a matter of course. The T-shirt with the logo of the record company and the name of the act is now a historical artifact. T-shirts were worn to one press party, then discarded. They are not designed for durability; after one or two washings the colors usually faded away. Deejays and critics probably had drawers full of T-shirts sent by record companies. Several companies actually keep on file the neck sizes of important critics and programmers. (While preparing a mailing of a Hot Tuna gold-and-red shirt in time for a local concert, an RCA secretary asked, "Is J. R. Young a medium or large?") With these shirts went a plethora of toys, notebooks, balloons, cans, cups, and shaving mugs—gimmicks designed to lend something special to an artist or his album.

Capitol Records, Warner Bros., and Mercury were perhaps the most ingenious gimmick creators. One Pink Floyd LP, *Atom Heart Mother*, was accompanied by a pink balloon shaped like a cow udder. Hurricane Smith's "has a lot of gusts" was inscribed upon a raincoat sent to deejays and critics. *H.R. Puff 'n' Stuff*, also from Capitol, had a gigantic mobile that brightened the day of many a record gatekeeper's child. Mercury Records mailed out Rod Stewart coffee cups and Uriah Heep candles. A & M sent out a wristwatch to commemorate a Joe Cocker tour. The actual impact of these goodies was illusory; however, a well-planned gimmick, as in the case of the Raspberries' scented sticker, brings fleeting notice to the album. After that, "it has to be in the grooves." One reviewer commented, "The gifts are fun, but really don't make a helluva lot of difference. I can't stand Hurricane Smith, and a wind-breaker is not going to change that. . . . But I did listen to the album." For Capitol's marketing people the mission was accomplished; the writer's unfavorable response was laid at the feet of the gravel-voiced Smith. New marketing and merchandising techniques became the key in the 1980s. Many companies started creative services sections that attempt to pioneer new methods of giving their record "a shot." Video clips were the new mode of exposure.

"All you've got to do is make some good music that people feel good about," observed Elektra/Asylum's chairman Bob Krasnow, "and market the hell out of it."[28] With a good sound, an attractive record and a projected audience a record company makes certain decisions. The first involves the amount of promotion and publicity money to be spent on a specific album or act. The amount frequently is determined by the act's contract and also by its status in the industry. A new act is the most difficult to market, so many companies give only a marginal shot to the act's record. If signs are good in the field, then more capital and effort will be expended. An executive explains: "With a new group you have to be *reactive*. You have to be very attuned to what's going on in Des Moines, Atlanta, and Peoria, because from there you're going to get feedback. Based upon that feedback and things growing or targeting your market, you hopefully can make big things happen." Some kind of movement or action must occur for the marketing push to go into high gear.

The most vexing problem for a marketing department is acts selling 100,000 to 200,000 units. These marginal acts are corporate "judgment calls." Clive Davis lamented about a group he personally enjoyed, "It's a bottom-line decision." The Band, Styx, and even the Grateful Dead disappointed a number of labels, despite expensive marketing campaigns. Still, the potential is there. The argument made by an artist's manager, "If you'd just do a little bit more," is a tempting and convincing one at least once. It gives the act a feeling that it is being supported, as well as makes the marketing department look good in the eyes of the rest of the company.

Artists rarely think their companies are doing enough for them. A strong marketing campaign may offset this attitude. Bobby Goldsboro renewed his United Artists contract because of its biographical family-album mailing to radio stations. Marty Cerf recalls, "When he [Goldsboro] saw this," pointing to an elegant album with a gold-lettered red cover enclosing pages of pictures and the performer's previous recordings, "all of a sudden how could he refuse to sign? This was right on the verge of going to Columbia, which has very large friends down in Nashville. Some of his closest buddies are with Columbia." United Artists may have regretted the move.

While catering to the psychological needs of the artist, a good campaign may generate company support. "People," says Dennis Killeen, "have to be able to see what you're doing from a retail standpoint. It's important to them, it's important to our people." Consequently, keeping the artist and the artist's management happy is important until the label can make a final decision. No artist-development person likes the prospect of a marginal act's moving to another label and "making it." Warner has more than embarrassed a number of marketing divisions with its "discard" campaigns. "Sure it makes them look good," commented a disgruntled executive, "and it makes us look bad."

Major marketing campaigns usually appear in times of bad company financial reports. Capitol's Raspberries push, the *Born to Run* CBS Springsteen campaign, and Warner's *Tusk* promotion all occurred at a time these labels desperately needed a "monster" record.

The Raspberries was the brainchild of its lead singer, Eric Carmen, who talked drummer Jim Bonfanti into a collaboration. Bonfanti was previously with the Choir, a group with the hit "It's Cold Outside," as was Wally Bryson who joined next. The Raspberries was formed in the belief there exists a "teen-scream" cycle that recurs every eight years. After the appearance of a *Time* magazine story, the Raspberries intentionally set out to be the next Beatles. Appearance, stage presence, and even the music were linked to the English quartet. The name Raspberries was chosen by accident when the band was searching for a simple nonpsychedelic label of the 1965 era. As with all bands, one of the original members did not fit the "concept" and was removed because he "lacked charisma." David Smalley, a former Choir member then in the jungles of Vietnam, was invited to join the band with a letter saying, "Practice."

Once assembled, Carmen and the others practiced nine hours three nights a week. He says: "It wasn't too hard on the fingers, but terrible on the voice." The band played anywhere it could in the Cleveland area, members writing own songs and reviving early rock-and-roll songs in the Beatles' tradition. The band signed and stayed for a year with a New York management firm that did nothing for it. It sent a demonstration tape of two songs, "Come Around and See Me" and "I Saw the Light," to many producers, including Jimmy Ienner. Ienner hated the songs but liked the Mexican obscenities at the end of the first: "Anyone with that much guts must be good." Upon seeing the band, he became the "fifth Raspberry." Ienner invited eight record companies to see the band at J.B.'s in Kent, Ohio, the very place that launched the James Gang. Capitol, in search of a replacement for the Beatles, outbid its rivals and signed the act.

Capitol mounted massive advertising and promotional campaign, but the Raspberries' first single failed to generate the desired response. Named after the band, the album was average, its cover featuring an early Beatle-like cover pose and a pungent raspberry-scented sticker. Jokes about the "stinking record" served to push the group into gatekeepers' and retailers' consciousness. Dennis Killeen explained:

> A group no one's ever heard of before, like the Raspberries, you do a smelly sticker, you do something a little unique. When a package of 10 of those albums hits any bin in any store, it's going to smell like raspberries. The consumer is going to catch on to what's going on. Reviewers are already talking about the package itself, in print, on the radio. DJs are saying, "My God, this thing smells like raspberries," on the air.

Even years later, copies showing up at thrift stores still retain the odor. Capitol also placed a trade ad with the scented sticker. At the Capitol Tower one day in May was designated Raspberry Day. Buttons, balloons, banners, and stickers were everywhere. Raspberry ice cream was served to visitors and the staff. That evening a press party introduced the group to the media. All of these devices brought immediate attention to the act. Subsequently, on a tour sponsored by Beechnut Gum, the Raspberries were on the same bill with the Grass Roots.

For Capitol, the Raspberries was a sheer gamble. In May 1972 its advertising budget was less than $50,000. Many executives were not sure "we're going to get it back." The support given the act was contingent upon external events. An executive said, "With the Raspberries, we've taken the attitude of 'if the stations go on it, we will support it.' In other words, if KHJ could go on the Raspberries record, we will buy some spots and tie in with dealers to tell people it's available because you're maximizing your impact there. That, then, becomes expensive. Initially the banners you see, the ice cream, all that hoopla, is a minimal kind of thing." Making the Raspberries a well-known Top 40 act did fulfill Killeen's fear of high expenses: "Making 'Raspberries' a household word, . . . it's going to cost you a lot of money." However, as publicist Heidi Robinson added, "Raspberries are one of the more important acts on the label. . . . They have commercial potential and that's all that matters."

The company reportedly spent over $150,000 on the band. Herb Belkin, the vice-president in charge of A&R, observed, "I think light-weight rock will be it . . . anyway, I hope it does because we've got a . . . lot of money tied up in these guys."[29] "Go All the Way," described by Carmen as the "I Want To Hold Your Hand" of 1972, was certified "gold" in November of that year. The promotional campaign became more elaborate. The band donned mod white suits in the finest Beatle tradition of 1964. Capitol announced in 1972 a "Win the Raspberries Rollswagon" contest. Entrants were eligible to win a mini-custom limousine with stereo equipment and tapes. The company placed a million entry blanks in over two thousand racks and stores, part of a package of displays, pictures, and posters of the group and the car. The contest was announced in a teenybopper fan magazine, *Stars*, to maximize the appeal to the 12-to-18 female age group.

The Raspberries' initial triumphs are largely attributable to the ingenuity of the marketing department at Capitol Records. The scented sticker attracted considerable attention. The professionalism of the band as well as the timing was equally important. In 1972 Capitol was searching for "new Beatles." The Raspberries' stated aim to follow in exalted footsteps helped the band, but continued use of gimmicks hurt it. Carmen observed, "Our most obvious problem is having people think we're some kind of contrived Madison Avenue project."[30] Spending too much money in fact can be as hazardous as spending none. For the Raspberries it was.

The story of Moby Grape is legendary in the record industry, although the experience of the ill-fated San Francisco band is not unique. Moby Grape was one of the stellar Bay Area acid-rock bands. It was locally as popular as the Grateful Dead, Jefferson Airplane, and Big Brother, and the Holding Company and some believed the group was superior. Enjoying the fruits of a nearly suicidal bidding war, the group signed with Columbia Records. In conjunction with the beginning of San Francisco's "Summer of Love," Columbia launched a massive promotional campaign to cash in on flower power. The Beatles' "All You Need Is Love" and the Airplane's "Somebody to Love" were selling well. Scott McKenzie's invitation dominated Top 40 airplay: "When you're going to San Francisco be sure to wear some flowers in your hair."

The Moby Grape campaign opened with a gala press party on the East Coast and a concert for 1,500 members of media and "flower children" at the Avalon Ballroom. Journalists were flown in from various parts of the country. That day five singles and an album were simultaneously released, something unheard of, especially for a new act. The unprecedented move reportedly demonstrated Columbia's commitment to the group, but it was also a classic example of Columbia's buckshot theory of promotion: the singles were so good that a disk jockey had only to air any one of them and a monster hit would result. All of the singles were on the album, along with "Make It If I Want To," "Ain't No Use," and "Lazy Me." The trappings of Haight-Ashbury were visible. The singles were housed in separately designed and colored sleeves. Color photos were used on the albums and there was a poster inside the jacket. A special logo or insignia was prepared for the campaign. A manual for promotional people was devised. Full-page ads ran in all of the trades and teen magazines. *Billboard* announced, "Columbia Gives Moby Grape a Whale of a Buildup." At least 100,000 advance orders on the album were reported.

With the exception of the single "Omaha," which reached an unflattering 88 spot on the "Hot 100," the Moby Grape campaign ended in economic disaster. Albums and posters were recalled because of Don Stevenson's "offensive" raised middle finger. After the Avalon concert, members of the band were charged with possession of drugs and contributing to the delinquency of two teenage girls. Neither the arrest nor the cover controversy account for the poor response to what was a critically acclaimed album. The post mortem was simply that Columbia's then extensive $100,000-plus advertising expenditure frightened disk jockeys and others away. One program director recalled, "Nobody could have been *that* good." Other companies relate similar tales of overfinanced advertising campaigns that failed.

The fact that a Raspberries campaign momentarily succeeded and an equally intense Moby Grape hype failed underlines the difference between advertising and hyping. A hype is simply a marketing campaign that oversells, but the line of demarcation between the two is almost totally obscure. "There are lots of mysterious elements," says Dennis Killeen. "For some artists, for some careers, it's important not to seem you're hyping it, because indeed it's the hype that you're going to turn off the people you're trying to reach which ultimately are the consumers." With an overselling job, people assume "the group doesn't have any talent and this is the only way that can promote them when talent should be able to stand up by itself."

Bruce Springsteen is a classic example of Killeen's point. Jon Landau, later to become the singer's producer, called him the "future of rock and roll," a description the artist would later disavow. But, in 1975 the stock of CBS in the rock world was falling fast. Many of Clive Davis's signings had not panned out. Joplin was gone. Dylan had moved to WCI, later to return. Disco was enjoying its first wave of national popularity. Rock was in a general state of malaise. Columbia's need for a superstar and the overall musical climate contributed to the controversial *Born to Run* campaign. Henry Edwards commented in the *New York Times*:

> This decision was prompted . . . because the record company executives knew their business depends on the creation of new sensations every year. Accordingly, they have to promote *somebody* . . . the decision to gamble on Springsteen must have taken note of the fact that in this time of record-industry doldrums, the return of the middle-of-the-road . . . and the popularity of disco music, there is a large potential rock music audience which feels neglected. In such a climate, the very derivativeness of Springsteen's music, and the throwback quality of his punkish persona have an irresistible appeal—both for younger rock music fans who were discovering their own new stars for the first time as well as older nostalgists hankering for the return of the days when rock music was considered a "challenge to the establishment" and rock performers were looked upon as symbolic rebels.

Edwards's somewhat oversimplified description possessed a grain of truth. His main thesis, "if there had not been a Springsteen, the media would have made him," was entirely off the mark, but the conditions were there.

CBS did spend around $250,000 hyping the album. Manager Mike Appel did insist that cover stories accompany interviews. Critics were flooded with concert tickets. Glen Brunman, the CBS publicist behind the campaign, told Dave Marsh, "Everything I said was designed to push people to see him. But only because I knew he could back it up. Which he did."[31] The appearance of the rock singer on the covers of *Newsweek* and *Time* the same week raised some eyebrows—only presidents and popes get this kind of coverage. Syndicated columnist Bob Greene's analysis was, "The real thing is hype." Shep Gordon, the creator of Alice Cooper, said, "This is one of the greatest hypes ever seen executed. *Time* and *Newsweek* together. I've tried for it my whole life. This is the finest promotion job I've ever witnessed. Springsteen? Forget him. What's he have to do with it? . . .[He] has absolutely nothing to do with the reality of this. What wonderful hype. I am so envious."[32]

The damage from the hype charge was minimal as compared to the damage from the Moby Grape hype. The Edwards and Greene pieces were *after* the fact. However, the charge did tarnish what was otherwise an astonishing marketing campaign. In concert Springsteen was as good as the press indicated. Unfortunately, his albums—at least the nonbootlegs—were not.

CBS did learn from the excesses of the original promotion of Springsteen's *Born to Run*. The Black Rock machinery geared up for *Born in the U.S.A.* in May 1984. The drive began with 350 kits sent to field personnel. It contained an LP cover and the usual T-shirt. Listening parties were arranged in the eleven major markets. Tapes were made and aired prior to the release date of the first single, "Dancing in the Dark," on 7 May. A video clip of the song was planned, to be produced by Hitchcockian director Brian De Palma, and a problem arose. Springsteen originally walked off the set refusing to do a dramatic "concept" clip; he preferred a concert clip scheduled to be shot in Minnesota during his tour, after release of the album.

Posters abounded in record stores and branches. A ten-minute concert video of "Rosalita," taped originally in 1978, was made available to MTV. Brunman's "live" strategy continued.

A month later *Born in the U.S.A.* shipped platinum. CBS's Al Teller praised the singer, not the promotion: "He's one of our superstars in every sense of the word. He's had a profound influence over music for the past decade and he's an important fixture in American rock 'n' roll." Jim Fusilli in a story for the *Wall Street Journal,* "The Selling of Bruce Springsteen," credited the artist with the album's success: "It's debatable how much the success of [the album] owes to the Columbia campaign and how much can be explained by the fact that it's the first album in two years—by perhaps the most influential white American rock artist since Elvis Presley."[33]

Ironically, the Asbury Park singer was given some unforseen help from fellow CBS artist Michael Jackson: the media favorably compared Springsteen's tour to the highly publicized Jackson "Victory tour." The point was repeatedly made that the rocker, whose tickets cost half of the Jacksons' price, was playing to appreciative sold-out audiences, and the Jacksons were not. The Jacksons' Phoenix concert was cancelled because of poor ticket sales. The album charts reflected the differentiation; *Born in the U.S.A.* was strongly outselling the *Victory* album, which had been released at the same time.

Warner's marketing of *Tusk* by Fleetwood Mac had also run into some unanticipated events. *Tusk* was viewed by Burbank "bizzers" as the potential savior of the 1979 season when the disco disaster was beginning to appear on accounting ledgers. On the basis of *Rumours'* multiplatinum performance, the English band was the hottest act in the Warner stable and a good bet to salvage the otherwise flat sales year.

*Tusk* was reportedly produced at Village Records over a period of six to nine months. The cost overruns exceeded the studio expenses of most superstars. It was completed in the mid-1979 period, with "rushes" on individual cuts being provided to the band. Bob Merlis, Warner's publicity chief, said "It's one of the few groups to get samples of the records during the middle of runs, whereas most just listen to the test pressing and approve that."

To orchestrate the campaign the label hired a youth-oriented ad agency, Geller, Federico, and Einstein. Fleetwood vetoed the idea, fearing the band "was being oversold," and the campaign was returned to an in-house status. An elaborate graphic and in-store display was evolved. Warner developed a motorized floor display, with a silk-screened image of the dog prominant on the album cover.

Bob Merlis garnered considerable publicity in *Rolling Stone*. Sally Rayl did a sidebar story on 23 August, quoting a source: "I think the whole record business is awaiting an album like this to get people back into the stores."[34] Retailers, as trade paper surveys indicated, were anxious for a blockbuster for the holidays.

A hour-long, "making-of-*Tusk*" rockumentary was filmed for distribution to television stations. Most of it was concert footage, complemented by cinema-verité footage by award-winning filmmaker Tom Spain. This aspect of the marketing strategy was a forerunner of the Michael Jackson *Thriller* drive.

The original game plan was to ship 3 million units around the middle of October. However, the "best laid plans. . . ." On 3 October, two weeks prior to the release date, the RKO chain of seven radio stations began airing the 20-song set. The release date was pushed back to the eighth of the month for radio and four days later for merchandisers.

Mick Fleetwood picked the title song as the single, USC Trojan marching band and all. Bob Regehr almost apologetically said, "That was Mick Fleetwood's idea. I think what he had in mind was to pique people's interest." As an omen of things to come, the single had to be recalled because it was defective and re-pressed. This entailed a week's delay.

The initial shipment of *Tusk* was less than 2 million units at a list price of $15.98. There was price resistance; many retailers were selling it at $13.98, and some merchandisers used it as a loss-leader at $11.98 to $9.98.

Broadcasters nationwide found *Tusk* and Led Zeppelin's *In Through the Out Door* ideal promotional vehicles to boost ratings. Major AOR stations began airing the two albums in their entirety, sometimes without commercial interruptions. These "happenings" were dutifully announced a week in advance on the air and local newspapers. *Billboard* reported a "heavy surge in blank tape sales, especially C-60 and C-90 packages when stations advertised in advance they would be programming the two-record *Tusk* in its entirety."[35]

Press coverage was mixed. *Rolling Stone* published an "insider" piece by Steve Pond and James Henke, "Fleetwood Mac, LP Gets Big Push," prior to the release date and later, "Tusk Is Tops in Most Stores." The actual *Rolling Stone* lead review by Stephen Holden generally praised the album, but cautioned, "On a-song-by-song basis *Tusk*'s material lacks the structural concision of the finest cuts on *Fleetwood Mac* and *Rumours*."[36] In November *Tusk* reached fourth place on the *Billboard* album chart and then began its descent. It had peaked too soon. The release did create several Top 10 singles, the title song and, several months later, "Sara." Warner privately considered *Tusk* "a loser." Members of the band seemed to agree as more solo albums began to surface. A "live" album set appeared in December of 1980.

*Tusk* did eventually earn a platinum record but overall it was a disappointment. It sold fewer than 2 million units; poor when compared to *Rumours*. An analysis of the campaign suggests that the basic flaw was in promotion. The RKO leak and the midnight home-taping broadcasts certainly contributed to the problem. The defective 45 or single was in the province of distribution. Graphics and publicity receive high marks for the aborted campaign. Menon's admonition remained valid: all the pieces have to work together for a successful outcome, even with outside interference. However, each of the three components in the "exposure" business has its own unique set of problems beginning with the graphics department.

### Graphics: Promotional Tool or Headache?

Prior to the golden year when the record industry enjoyed its first billion-dollar sales figure, marketing generally consisted of the promotion of air-play, trade-paper advertising, and store displays. The displays usually were large colored posters of a grinning band leader with a horn or his favorite vocalist. The 78-rpm singles came in brown grocery-bag jackets with a listing of the companies' other records. Album covers either showed the toothy artist on the front or a painted portrait or photograph of a pinup girl. The advent of the long-playing record provided more space for artistic design, a fact not immediately recognized. The cover of Columbia Records' first LP, released in late 1948, had on it a depiction of a large marble pillar as well as the name of the composer and the title of the album. The most prominent elements of the cover were the company name and logo, and the catalog number. After this construct was used on some two hundred albums, it began to prove rather unsuccessful—the LP was altering record merchandising.

The sealed LP brought a halt to the traditional practice of "listen then buy." No longer would record stores allow the patron to hear a record prior to purchase; the cellophane album skin prevented such an amenity. Art departments attempted to soften the effects of the new practice by using the cover to sell the record. The covers of the easy-listening albums of Jackie Gleason or Art Van Damme left no doubt about the albums' purpose. Couples in their mid-twenties were pictured sitting in a penthouse suite overlooking New York, with a martini glass and desirous expressions. Mood music was the sound of seduction. Albums designed for collegians also stressed the sociability aspect of music. Taking a cue from *Life* magazine, folksingers and pop quartets were portrayed on their album covers dating, drinking (soft drinks, of course), and dancing. Covers of surfing albums were typically taken directly from Coca Cola ads. Following the lead of paperback novels, many album covers had little to do with the contents of the record. As often as not, the artist on the front cover was superimposed over a fashion photographer's backdrop, and a testimonial to the record appeared on the back cover.

These marketing techniques reflected the nature of the 1950s LP audience. Adults, not teenagers, purchased most of the more expensive records. The best-sellers were either from motion pictures or the Broadway stage. Soundtracks contained familiar tunes, and a cover with pretty girl and a title were enough to make the sale. Jazz and classical records such as Columbia's Masterworks series could be pushed with a tombstone on the cover. These specialty items frequently contained extensive liner notes by aficionados like Morton Gould, Leonard Feather, or Ralph J. Gleason.

Teenagers were the fans of popular music. They purchased singles they had heard on the radio or perhaps in the record-store booth. Many a corner record store or mom-and-pop outlet in the 1950s was an after-school hangout. The arrival of teenage rock idols Elvis Presley and Pat Boone saw record advertiser borrowing from fan magazines and placing a color photograph of the idol on the jacket. Originally this was done with EPs (extended-play 45s with four cuts) containing previously released material for the most part. Buy the record, get the picture. In time the practice was expanded to Presley's singles. The record became an attractive item and it frequently advertised his latest movie—Colonel Parker rarely missed a promotional opportunity. The pop albums addressed to teenagers either lacked liner notes entirely or were synthesized statements of adulation revealing that Paul Anka, Fabian, or Frankie Avalon favored certain kinds of dates, food, clothes, and cars. Photos and liners were selling points because most of these albums contained only one Top 40 hit, already mass consumed by fans, and 10 or 11 filler songs.

Even the Beatles' first album was a prototype of 1950s packaging. The cover featured them against with a dull brownish-yellow background, and the back listed the songs and announced, "Introducing The Beatles" and "America's Greatest Recording Artists Are on Vee-Jay Records." In a matter of several years the Beatles would be instrumental in altering marketing patterns. Their albums were generally presentations of 10 to 12 hit songs, half of them on the singles charts. From the sheer economic standpoint, their albums appealed to a vast number of singles-buying teenagers because each could be had for the price of four 45s. The Beatles, more than any other act, moved teenagers into the album market.

The rise of LP sales among teenagers was also helped by the emergence of the San Francisco Haight-Ashbury counterculture, which rejected Top 40 material as irrevelant. Many local favorites were not on singles. Rock music was, for the flower children, a total media experience—light, sound, volume, and all else that constituted a "trip." Records not possessing these qualities were regarded as "lame." The Jefferson Airplane's first release was highly criticized for not mirroring its stage presence. The first issue of the *Oracle* described Ralph J. Gleason's liner notes as a "company hype." To reach this new market, album covers for "acid" bands begin to exhibit posters from Fillmore rock concerts. The Grateful Dead's first album cover was in the language and layout of Haight-Ashbury posters.

As the 1967 "Summer of Love" was in progress the Beatles released *Sgt. Pepper*, which many have cited as the album that made the cover as important as the recorded material itself. The Beatles extended the theme of the album to the cover, and the "total-package" idea was born. In fact, although *Sgt. Pepper* accelerated the total-package syndrome, it is the Beatles' *Yesterday and Today* cover that should be credited as the trend setter. Capitol's censorship of the cover delayed implementation of the concept for several years. The company had held back two songs from each of the Beatles' early albums, and released them in *Yesterday and Today*. As a reported act of protest, the group designed a cover depicting themselves in butchers' gowns in the midst of cut-up dolls and slabs of meat, meaning that Capitol had dismembered the group's previous albums. Record programmers who saw the original cover objected, and all copies of the album were recalled. Most fans never saw the cover, but they did see and like *Sgt. Pepper*.

The *Sgt. Pepper* album cover encouraged others to design their own covers to enhance sales potential and to make an artistic statement. Unfortunately, few recording artists matched the Beatles' ingenuity in the graphics area. Referring to the *Sgt. Pepper* era, Ron Coro, art director for Elektra/Asylum, recalled, "Things were brought to an extreme two years ago. Everything that could be done was done. Now things have turned around: photography plays a more important role. People realize that you don't have to spend a lot of money to have a successful album cover."[37] An exception may be Roger McGuinn, who (after *Yesterday*) used the cover of the *Notorious Byrd Brothers* to express his contempt for David Crosby by showing three members of the band and a mule, the mule a replacement for Crosby.

The message cover and the total package became a source of conflict between artists and their record companies. Company executives were not willing to follow psychedelic posters into the realm of sexual and political explicitness. Moby Grape's first cover was changed to remove Don Stevenson's defiantly pointing middle finger. The MC 5's liner notes were changed

Stan Cornyn (Courtesy of Warner Brothers)
Bob Garcia (Courtesy of A & M Records)
Bhaskar Menon (Courtesy of Capitol Records)

**Joseph Smith (Courtesy of Warner Brothers)**
**Quincy Jones (Courtesy of A & M Records)**
**Robert Summer (Courtesy of RCA)**

**Herb Albert (Courtesy of A & M Records)**
**Mitch Miller (Courtesy of NBC)**

David Bowie (Courtesy of RCA)
Bee Gees (Courtesy of RSO)

**Raspberries (Courtesy of Capitol Records)**
**Alice Cooper**

to remove John Sinclair's closing comments. Nearly all album censorship fights have been won by the record company. Stars like Jefferson Airplane, Blind Faith, Jimi Hendrix, Rolling Stones, Country Joe and the Fish, and Alice Cooper have all lost to the censor. Because of a dispute between the Rolling Stones and London Records, *Beggar's Banquet* was not released for six months, and then only with a white cover and black script lettering. The object of contention was a photograph of a public bathroom the walls of which were covered with inoffensive graffiti. In time Jagger gave in, but London Records lost the war. The Rolling Stones left and formed its own production company.

Only John Lennon and Yoko Ono's first album triumphed, in part, over the censors. *Two Virgins* showed the couple standing nude on the cover, and Capitol in the United States and Polydor in Canada refused to distribute it. Finally the album was distributed by Tetragrammaton Records, but in a brown paper bag. The publicity generated by these cover controversies rarely has hurt sales. *Two Virgins*, an aesthetic and critical disaster, no doubt benefited from its brown cover.

The Rolling Stones' dispute with London reportedly did affect its album's sales, which originally had been scheduled for late summer release. Jagger's reluctance to accept a change delayed the release until mid-December, one week before the Beatles' long-awaited two-record set. Sales of the Stones' outstanding album were definitely adversely affected.

The Rolling Stones did not learn from their experience. In June of 1976 a Sunset Strip billboard and magazine ads depicted a bound woman, legs spread, hanging from a pipe. Women Against Violence Against Women (WAVAW) joined by the California chapter of the National Organization for Women (NOW) vociferously objected to the graphics of a "trussed-up, beaten, and bruised woman straddling the cover" with the caption "I'm 'Black and Blue' from the Rolling Stones . . . and I love it."[38]

Several months after the appearance of the Stones' ad and billboard, WAVAW initiated a boycott against WCI because of its "gratuitous use of sex violence and violence against women in record advertising when rape and battering of women are common occurrences." Julia London during a street theater rally in 1977 indicated that "offensive" covers were marginally on the decline. Nearly two years into the boycott *Billboard* surveyed art directors at major labels and found that a vast majority of LP covers were innocent; it "is minimal, if at all." There were two dissenters. George Balso of Phonogram and producer of the Ohio Players covers said, "A little of everything goes. We're mirroring what's happening in our society. We don't innovate. We're the mirror and we reflect." London disagreed: "It blows me away to hear record companies claim that sex and violence are going out. If anything, violence in album graphics is becoming more of a problem."[39]

To document her position London published a lengthy analysis of graphics in *Victimology*, a journal addressed to issues of rape and physical abuse. In the article 17 covers and record company ads were featured, accompanied with a page-and-a-half discography of "unacceptable" LP covers. She noted, "The majority of record purchases are made by young people between the ages of 14 and the mid-twenties and that more males buy rock records than women, the implications of the debasing portrayal of women are quite obvious." London described the WAVAW campaign against WCI, and characterized WCI as attempting to "discredit WAVAW and NOW, to evade the issues and to repair WCI's public image. . . . WEA executives have been issuing contradictory and misleading statements since June 1977."[40]

Nearly two and a half years following the Stones' *Black and Blue* graphics the twenty-five-chapter WAVAW and WCI reached an accommodation. WCI issued a statement opposing "the depiction of violence against women or men on album covers and in related promotional material and [opposing] the exploitation of violence, sexual or otherwise, in any form." David Horowitz, now MTVN's CEO, said, "By publicizing this policy, WCI is acknowledging that the commercial use of visual and other images that trivialize women victims is irresponsible in light of the epidemic proportions of real life violence against women." The threatened boycott appears to have been successful—at least temporarily. Joan Horowarth, the spokesperson for the feminist group, seemed satisfied: "We look forward to increased receptivity from other companies as a result of the step taken by the WCI record group, one of the most important leaders in the industry."[41]

The graphics controversy had been tempered but not solved. In 1984 the Scorpions would revive the issue with its *Love at First Sting* and the hit cut "Rock You like a Hurricane." Wal-Mart, a major retail chain, objected to the cover. The album was recalled by PolyGram after selling a million units. A member of the heavy metal group, singer Klaus Meine, objected: "It may look like we are [sexist] . . . but we all like girls, women. We never think of them as sex objects." *Kilroy Was Here*, a Styx album, found its "warning label" "BY ORDER OF THE MAJORITY FOR MUSICAL MORALITY THIS ALBUM CONTAINS SECRET BACKWARD MESSAGES" removed from U.S. distribution.

The value of album covers and graphics in general is dubious. Although no hard statistical data are available, few consumers appear moved to purchase an album on the basis of a cover, especially at $9.95 list price. Informal polls of university students over a five-year period seem to show that less than 1 percent of the collegians sampled bought a record strictly on the basis of graphics. Album art can be magnificent, but covers have not significantly evolved since the head shots of the late 1950s.

Assuming album covers do not sell product and that they can create a host of headaches, why do the labels go to all the trouble? Several executives, off the record, point to artists' egos and the graphics departments. "They give Grammy's for albums covers," said one "bizzer." Another marketing executive suggested, "*Sgt. Pepper* and *Physical Graffiti* were the models. Everyone wanted a jacket like those two. What the acts forget is that the Beatles and Led Zeppelin could afford the most exotic art work they wanted. The graphics cost more than the vinyl inside the package." At Capitol an executive remarked, "It's ego, just like the billboards on the Sunset Strip. They don't sell records, just show the artist we care." Another executive at Capitol, Roy Kohara, partially supported his colleague's view on album art, especially in dealing with gatefolds;" Although we do have requests by some artists for them, when it's justified we will give gatefolds, but only then." Phonogram's outspoken George Balos summed it up nicely: "The artists feel the double LP is more prestigious." This point is underscored by the fact some of the most elaborate graphics frequently appear inside the gatefold jacket, as with ELO's *Blue* album. A plastic skin prohibits the potential consumer from viewing the art work unless the album is purchased.

"Gatefolds," are not terribly popular with art directors. Cost is a factor, as Atlantic's Bob Defrin noted: "We have found that the double LP cover is just not practical and it costs twice as much as the regular LP." Bill Levy at Polydor objects to the price and size of the package. "If you can get 25 LPs in a bin, when you're dealing with a gatefold that number will be cut to fewer than 18. Everybody gets hurt in this type of deal except the shipping company."[42]

The decline of product has heightened the quest for unique eye-catching covers and displays. Capitol's former advertising director said, "In an industry where product level goes up and up and up and up, it's becoming more and more difficult, as it is for the consumer, to call attention to something you feel deserves a chance or deserves special merit." Ideally, this would entail the development of a special campaign for each act, but obviously not all receive such treatment. Only an act regarded as potentially "hot" gets a *complete* shot.

In store displays and elaborate full-color ads in the trade papers, album covers do not appear especially effective as marketing tools, except to enhance the ego of the artist and the image of the company. Graphics are an attention-getting device; however, it is the electronic media that actually sells records.

## Promotion: Working the Record

In a survey of Florida high school students, George Allen Booker found that 54 percent of his respondents listed the disk jockey as the most important influence in the development of their musical tastes.[43] Veejays, at least in the eyes of promotion directors, enjoy the same impact. Atlantic's Vince Faraci: "The video may be a good concept, and work well as an image-maker, but the record goes nowhere without a radio base."[44] Culture Club's Boy George commented, "Our record was number two even if MTV wouldn't accept the video clip."

Despite the artists' dues paying and record-company mixing and hype, it all comes down to getting stations to play a record so a sufficient number of people can hear it. It is hoped that some of the listeners will like it well enough to buy it. The more people who hear a record, the greater its chances for success.

Originally the problem of exposure was sheer volume (see chapter 5). Top 40 and FM stations were deluged by dozens of labels with thousands of singles and albums. The "crash of '79" stemmed the flow. Now programmers are complaining about quality product regardless of the quantity. The record has to be "good" or "hot" and fit the "image" of the station. Some artists are pigeonholed to the point that a number-one single and album on the *Billboard* charts could not generate airplay in certain formats.

Some superstars are gone or fading. In 1984 a broadcaster asked, "After the Jacksons and heavy metal, what's next?" The promotion director must aim his product and efforts to those program directors and deejays who might be receptive to new product. When all is said and done, the interaction between the promotion and publicity departments of the recording company and the keeper of the playlist makes or destroys a record or an artistic career.

A majority of program directors believe that record companies do not appreciate their business. A West Coast PD said, "The record people don't understand that the competitiveness in the radio business is such that people cannot listen to two radio stations at one time. I can go and buy a Columbia album and an Atlantic album, but I can't . . . listen to more than one radio station at a time." Radio is an either-or or zero-sum situation. Only one station can be on top in the ratings. Promotion directors, with different degrees of empathy, are aware of this situation. A Warner executive said,

> They want to be sure they're playing the right music. One bad rating and usually the program director or music director is out of a job. And that's the terrible thing about it. If the industry was a little more secure in terms of

positions held and the ratings were not so important—which again, it's the life of that industry—then I'm sure there would be a little more room to play a little more than we have. It's difficult to walk into a major station in a major city and ask the music director to go on an unknown record by a group. . . . His job may be at stake if he makes the wrong decisions too many times. When he puts on a record, it's usually because it has started to break in another area.

For security, most PDs attempt to get "behind a record" rather than "get in front of it." The record company obviously wants to move the station in front.

The fundamental problem for acts is that the perceived interests of radio-station program directors are antagonistic to those of the record company. Especially in the major markets, radio is a tremendously competitive business. The competition historically has been for higher numbers as measured in the Arbitron (ARB) ratings polls. On the basis of these numbers advertising contracts are awarded and withheld, and profits and losses result. Large numbers alone have not been sufficient because advertisers have become more sophisticated and concerned with the social characteristics of audiences. For example, an advertiser of skin cream is more interested in a 9- through-18 audience than a 25-through-34 audience— which is most attractive to brewers and to appliance and automotive manufacturers. As in television, failure to achieve the proper numbers results in the cancellation of advertising and consequently formats and radio personalities. Any well-trodden avenues to higher ratings are welcomed. If youth is the targeted audience, safety is the CHR format; if the 24-to-49 age group, AOR or AC. There are many variations of course, depending on markets. Markets are compiled on the basis of size and income. Most record companies consider the ten highest in population as majors: New York, Los Angeles, Chicago, Philadelphia, Detroit, Boston, San Francisco-Oakland, Washington, D.C., Pittsburgh, and St. Louis; the last two are replaced by Newark and Cleveland on buying ratings. Stations in major markets can be more esoteric because a sufficient number of people may be attracted to specialty stations. AOR FM stations traditionally pull the 18- to 24-year olds, much to the delight of stereo manufacturers and other advertisers seeking to exploit the college and young-adult set. In smaller, secondary-market cities, the large-numbers philosophy is hooked to demographics.

As Bill Drake indicates, "Picking records will be determined by what occurs . . . the criteria will be the same to find out what records *please the most people.*"[45] The record companies' goal is to get *their* records played on the station. The station in turn wants to air only records that are established hits. Program directors customarily tell promotion men, "We're not in the business to sell your records. We're in the business to entertain, to get listeners, not to sell your product," or, "When it's on the charts we'll play it," or "I'll take all the Prince records you got." In view of this attitude, it is safe to say that more recording careers die in a program director's office than anywhere else. The task of converting the PD is to get around these copouts, and it is the task of the promotion director and field representatives.

*Under-Assistant Promo Man*

The promotion department is not particularly popular with recording artists or producers, given its failure rate with records. The Rolling Stones early in their career wrote, "Under-Assistant West Coast Promo Man," one sentence of which runs, "Sitting here and thinking just how sharp I am, I'm a necessary talent for every rock and roll band." Richard Robinson, author, deejay, and producer, portrayed promo men as "a breed apart, resembling human beings, but living lives based on plastic being the true essence of good. To say, therefore, that the promotion man is, of necessity, jive is simply to state a sad fact of life."[46]

Despite the disapprobation hurled by Robinson and the Rolling Stones, to the company the promo man is the pulse of the people. He is closest to the street. His sole function is to get precious airtime for his records, which is no simple feat, given the amount of product available and tight playlists. Promotion departments use standard techniques of selling: visits, calls, artist biographies, and sample copies. Occasionally, the promotion man is assigned to escort a touring act from station to station. Beyond this is the shady area of goodwill, described thus by one Detroit program director: "The game of the promoter is to get you obliged, be it through exclusives, dinner, theater tickets, or what have you."[47] The "what have you" is a sticky subject. Various favors are frequently exchanged in some markets, and none in others. Some stations consider plastic bags containing "grass" or coke inserted in an album jacket a token of goodwill. A bottle of Chivas Regal or J&B is still welcome. The soul-music market, which is nearly identical to the Top 40 milieu of the late 1950s, is the most susceptible to under-the-table promotion. Small black companies vie with the majors for airtime. Payola is an important promotional technique with soul radio stations, and because of this situation many industry executives do not accept soul charts as accurate. Kal Rudman at one time refused to have a soul section in his tip sheet, saying, "I started the whole R&B thing, and I want no part of it."[48]

Most professionals consider themselves corporate executives and consequently frown upon activities that are openly beyond FCC rules or other prohibitive regulations. However, there is a gray area wherein certain questionable practices occur—practices also seen elsewhere in the world of commerce—all designed to promote airplay.

Many program directors view the unflagging attention of promo men as an occupational hazard. Some AM stations allocate one afternoon a week for promo men, who are given a quarter of an hour to present their current product.[49] Other stations have quota systems that balance product from the various companies. More rigid stations demand that product be mailed to their libraries for review; most of these copies are never played. A Midwest music librarian, has a huge cabinet full of singles that are kept for six months and then donated to a local university library. He plays no record unless it is charted, despite calls from promo people "who come on like long-lost friends." He resents their approach, preferring the more objective fact sheets. Most program directors interviewed regard promotional literature as useless unless it correlates with *Radio & Records* or *Billboard*. However, not all assemblers of playlists are negative. One declared, "I love the promo people. I find them not only very interesting to talk to, but they give me valuable amounts of information. . . . They can provide me with what other stations are playing, which is knowledge they all pass around." He does caution, "The promo people are always very uptight. They get very frustrated if you don't add one of their records. They get their butts chewed on big time. Lots of pressure on those people."

All record companies have similar promotional ploys but differ in their approaches, depending on the individual company emphasis. Singles companies are not like album companies, yet the goal of both is still "getting the needle on the record."

The singles company has a distinct advantage in exposing its product, for nearly all radio media will play singles. Album cuts are more selectively treated; PDs do not have time to listen to hundreds of album cuts just to find a few that might please their audiences. As Bill Roberts commented, "If he [the PD] listened to every record that came in, he would go mad." Album companies therefore are at a disadvantage in exposing their material through the AM channels. They are faced with greater obstacles to overcome, although predominantly singles-oriented companies are dinosaurs. One executive at Warner noted, the "dollars are in albums, not in singles." The company has developed various techniques by which either to circumvent or entice the traditional AOR program director, aiming directly at the new alternative media. Stan Cornyn explains:

> We've had to work harder. We've also had a lot of artists who are not about to have singles successes. The basic folk artist ain't going to go pounding through on the Top 40 radio. Therefore, at a time when FM was just a glimmer, I personally and several of this company rushed in and said, "Hey, where have you been? This is neat. We love you." I remember someone would

rumor that an FM station would be cropping up in St. Louis, and I would try and find that station and give them advertising money for the time that they were on the air because we needed them so much.

Warner did in fact fill the coffers of media, radio and press.

In addition to going around the traditional radio gatekeeper, Warner developed innovative means to hook the program director. Its promotional philosophy is to collaborate with the radio stations. In approaching the CHRs, AORs, and Top 40 outlets it attempts to complement their playlists:

> Say they've added four records that were up records. Most likely, they would be looking in terms of programming balance for a downer record. If you happen to have a downer record as opposed to an upper record, both equal in terms of priority, you better be pushing the downer record first and talking about the downer, saying, "Hey, you added three up records. I'm sure you're looking for a downer record." Then right away they are more receptive.

Another technique to get to the program director is through the use of advertising:

> We will give our promotion people the monies necessary to be able to walk into a station and advertise a product. So that . . . they not only talk to a music director or program director about what kind of music he should be programming but can walk down the hall, up to a sales manager or the general manager of the station, talk to him about fixing an advertising program, and then go back to the program director and incorporate these two things. This makes them much more professional and vital to the total successful operation of the radio station and not just a delivery boy.

The buying of advertising has increasingly become a promotional tool. Television spots provide the record company a minute in which to expose its acts before potential radio audiences without having to go through the program director's screening process. Theoretically, with enough advertising revenue a company can break an act in this manner. Clips feature one or more cuts on an album followed by an announcement of the title and the closing, "on Warner Brothers Records." There is sufficient precedent to believe that spots are going to accelerate both on radio and television. Warner originally experimented, especially in England, with television advertisement for Deep Purple.

The validity of spots has perhaps been best illustrated by the metamorphosis of two commercials into popular songs. "We've Only Just Begun" was originally a theme for a California savings and loan firm; the song earned the Carpenters a gold record. The New Seekers followed this success with "I'd Like to Teach the World to Sing (in Perfect Harmony)"—a Coca-Cola commercial.

Some labels will provide records by big-name artists, prior to release date, to favored stations in exchange for a spot on a playlist for other acts. It is an approach that carries hazards; slighted PDs from other stations may retaliate. However, the exclusives practice does take place, especially in major markets. In its heyday KHJ in Los Angeles received product "hot off the press" many hours and even days before its competitors. Record companies justified the practice, saying. "If 'HJ gets on it everyone else will anyway."

Companies lacking a hot hand must work harder to break their acts. Perhaps the most spectacular example of this has been the media campaigns undertaken by Bill Roberts and Martin R. Cerf. "American Pie" by Don McLean was the biggest record of 1971. Although Roberts and Cerf give McLean all credit for its success, their promotion of the record had a good deal to do with it. As Roberts indicates, "American Pie" had it in the grooves: "Without a doubt it stood out in everyone's mind. . . . It was just one of those songs that stands out." In preparation, Cerf wrote a letter to the rock press announcing its impending release, advising that recipients should not trade it in at Aaron's or Goody's before listening to the title song. This is an unusual but effective message; the trade-in practice is openly engaged in but rarely discussed, especially in promotion copy. At the same time a McLean recording of the song was being aired in the New York area as a public service announcement, creating—it was hoped—a built-in market. Tapes of the album were sent to progressive FM stations in areas where McLean was known either through his college concerts or his stint on Pete Seeger's ecology boat, the *Clearwater*. His acceptance on FM radio, particularly in the Chicago area where he was appearing at the Quiet Night club, hastened issuance of the album.

Roberts and Cerf envisioned "American Pie" as a hit single on AM radio. There were two major problems: the AM program director and the artist himself. "American Pie" is eight and a half minutes in duration, violating the 2:37 or 3:05 length so popular with AM programming. The second problem was McLean's anti-record-company attitude; he was veteran of the *Broadside* (New York City) folk-protest scene. McLean was anti-establishment, and Top 40 radio is as free-enterprise, as dog-eat-dog as any of John D. Rockefeller's early oil companies. Roberts, in time, persuaded McLean to "go around to the radio stations and meet some people with [him]." He was never able to get McLean to explain the message of "American Pie." This problem was minor in contrast to breaking an eight-and-a-half minute folk song on AM radio.

According to Cerf, United Artists ignored many of the traditional avenues. At first it went *around* the Top 40 PD to the progressive stations by means of a two-week national tour of FM stations and a mailing. Also, "We didn't buy one ad. We didn't buy one T-shirt. We didn't buy one button. We went after it as straight AM product. It was a lot of money." United Artists then alloted the largest album expenditure in its history on "American Pie," at least $100,000. Cerf recalls, "It was the greatest success this company ever had, but had it not been, it would have been the greatest expenditure on a flop we ever had." Nearly all of the money went for AM radio spots, again going around the program director to the people. Mike Stewart, then United Artists president, personally ordered the field men to break it. "Mike would have looked bad if it bombed," admitted an employee. College radio play was arranged. This was all prior to release of the shortened singles version. "It was," says Cerf, "a totally planned committed promotion . . . we totally committed ourselves. We tried to develop it and sincerely tried to bring it in." The album and the single sold nearly 5 million copies. A number of attention-getting devices had been utilized, and many of them are history.

In the summer of 1971 United Artists introduced a 7-inch scale miniature of the 33 $\frac{1}{3}$ album with a full-color, deluxe design down to the printed dust cover. The announcement said, "It's something the radio stations have been demanding for some time. . . . With new acts . . . we must find as many areas as possible to promote the groups, for PDs and DJs just simply don't have time to dredge through 45 minutes with every new act that crosses their desk." The experiment, which failed, was fundamentally an attempt to get around the barrier between people and the albums. The minialbums contained four cuts from the parent album that the United Artists staff believed to be the most salable. Another technique developed by Cerf and Roberts was direct promotional mailings to record-store personnel, not just the dealers. Coupled with their innovations was *Phonograph Record Magazine*, which was a full-scale, *Rolling Stone*-size rock paper. All of these tools were used to reach consumers if the gatekeepers were uncooperative.

As the number of stiffs produced yearly painfully illustrates, most records fail. Not unexpectedly, much of the blame for this is placed squarely at the feet of the radio industry. Joe Smith says, "Most disk jockeys today, even program directors, they talk the same lengths, they're all doing Drake, you go across the country with very few exceptions. They're all doing 'the good guys,' boss radio. How many stations tape [the top station] in this town? . . . They tape it and copy it exactly."[50] Bob Hamilton argued, "If you do not get a record on KHJ in Los Angeles, then you're sunk in the entire area."[51] Smith goes on to stress that PDs are guided strictly by charts. About their promotional records, he says, "They don't play [them]."

Sixty-eight percent of the stations once queried by *Billboard* replied that they listened to "every record sent to them." There is little evidence to support this figure. Most stations do not review all new material. Program directors, Smith says, will use "any cop-out that [they] can use to tell you that [they're] not going to play the record until you break it nationally." With a gleam in his eye, Roberts tells the story of the music director who says, "That is the worst record I've ever heard," and then throws it in the waste basket, exclaiming, "That will never be played on this radio station!" Six months later, the same record is number one nationally. This does not happen very often.

With few exceptions, radio programmers are viewed as ranging from formula puppets to tin-eared idiots capable only of reading the Tuesday-morning issue of *Billboard*. Program directors frequently reply that if the record companies manufactured "decent" (hit) songs they would play them. Because of capriciousness of "play for pay," the record companies have virtually no control over programming, but they can blame their field men for not working hard enough on product. Many home-office executives privately lament the shortcomings of the branches and their promotional staffs in the field. Some of this is buck-passing, to cover domestic office problems, but some charges have some validity. Interviews with touring acts frequently are messed up, as are other dealings with local press and broadcasters. A southern field branch of a company renowned for its promotional staff frequently fouls up media relations. These difficulties stem primarily from so-called communication breakdowns, but some blame can justly be placed upon the shortcomings of individual field people.

The confrontation between promotion and program directors is complicated by the variable of geography, that is, X number of promotion people have to "turn on" Y number of program directors. This process of "spreading" further weights the odds against the recording company. As one record-company executive noted, "So we turn on a PD in one station in Phoenix. It's not enough." For a record to be a hit, a sufficient number of radio stations throughout the country must get on a record. Ideally, several stations in major markets can break a record. The tremendous power of WABC was built on the simple fact that it was a prototype for hundreds of others. Even now heavy airplay on a handful of stations charts a record. Bob Hamilton holds, "Forty-two radio stations in the country sell all the records."[52] At these stations promotional people are falling all over themselves, but in this type of market each company is usually allotted 15 minutes a week to present its new product. Consequently, some companies—especially WEA and Columbia—have taken to "surrounding" major markets by focusing upon secondary outlets. To make an impact upon the Cleveland market, a record company pushes a record in Cincinnati, Dayton, Columbus, and other cities in the area. Columbus is especially important because many advertisers use Ohio's capital as the prototypical U.S. city. Success in Columbus is a strong promotional selling point. To succeed in spreading, a coordinated promotional drive of equal magnitude must be mounted. Each field man must accomplish his individual mission. The odds against good fortune are tremendous, especially when nonprimary cities are emphasized. Two breakouts in 25 major markets is a formidable task. Five or ten advances nationally just to move these two stations in large cities is even more unlikely, considering that secondary market are usually guided wholly by charts. The life of the under-assistant promo man is not an easy one.

Breaking a record through radio involves certain factors. Company support is essential. For a maiden act, the album has to be "worked," to be singled out for promotion, but few are. Video clips on MTV and hot singles are important. This may motivate a music director or PD to explore an album for more material. The only certainty for the recording company is a single or album by a superstar. However, only a handful of artists can guarantee airplay; Prince, Neil Young, Michael Jackson are rarities. Even Jackson's *Victory* LP was pulled by a number of AOR stations because of poor audience response.

"You can't ride with a Rod Stewart the rest of your life at a record company . . . or the Rolling Stones either, for that matter . . . that is, they might be around, but you must break new acts to replace the others who won't be or just in order to expand."[53] It is the new acts that are the most difficult to break, barring some serendipitous events. Consequently, the promotion departments of record companies must try to "hook" program directors with their product. The volume and quality of records and the competition between companies renders this an exceedingly difficult task. The number of stiffs in the industry is a reflection of this interaction.

Ideally, the superstar with a single is the best bet for success with a program director, but albums are where the dollars are. More people spend *more* money on LPs than singles. An album by a prominent rock group usually sells in the neighborhood of 1 to 2 million copies. At $8.98 or $9.98 a copy, it can be readily understood why the most profitable companies are album oriented even though they experience more problems than the singles companies do. Warner, rather than issuing *Zuma* or *Decades*, could release Neil Young singles, but Young's constituency is in the LP rather than singles market. The same is true of Jimmy Page and many others. Given the difficulties of dealing with formula radio, especially the AM variety, the recording companies have attempted to open up other avenues. Warner economically assisted the growth of FM progressive radio. Spots, *Billboard* ads, and packaging innovations have all been efforts to go through or around the program director to the potential consumer. After all, the name of the game is record sales, and record companies, as Stan Cornyn noted, are the ticket sellers.

## Publicity

Publicity departments do not deal with the news media as their promotional counterparts do. In the late 1970s most of the majors integrated the press-oriented company component into the marketing operation.

The actual value of press coverage is often at the center of polemics, which flared with particular intensity with the release of Bruce Springsteen's *Born to Run.* Henry Edwards wrote in the *New York Times,* "Many lavishly praised performers and albums proved incapable of winning large scale public support." Robert Christgau gave considerable credit to the rock-critic establishment, located in New York, for the success of the album, which was "a rare instance of a rock musician who owes much of his stardom to print support." David Marsh in his best-seller biography *Born to Run* is a bit more moderate, giving the artist's concert appearances and airplay credit for the press attention "Still," he adds, "the press had played a very important role for Springsteen, nurturing his talent when everyone else seemed to have given up."[54]

Record companies in varying degrees do believe in the value of the press, particularly in the major markets and the news weeklies. "The press does sell records. A public relations campaign can have a lot to do with the success of artists who sell in the range of 100,000 to 200,000 records." Mike Gormley of A & M continued, "Any kind of exposure is important. We just had a two-page spread in *People* magazine featuring Pablo Cruise. I see that as equal to two ad pages. And at $20,000 a page, that's $40,000 worth of free exposure." Gary Kenton, a New York publicity person, noted, "Favorable reviews keep an artist afloat without major airplay. (See chapter 6.)

Depending on the label, an artist is given a "publicity plan" based on in-house interviews and the company's perception of market potential. The CBS Group's strategy involves projecting "the ideal image," tour information, the number of review albums to be mailed, "press angles," and a methodology to achieve these goals.[55] It is a strategy used by most of the majors in different ways but the goal is identical.[56]

Majors frequently have presented fairly elaborate publicity campaigns for some artists such as Springsteen and Capitol's the Knack. Other artists get the basic essentials also utilized by companies' smaller competitors.

Upon release of an album those fortunate enough in the print media to be on the "service" list receive the album, an 8-by-10-inch glossy photograph, and a "bio" (biography) that should be read with a grain of salt. One critic observed, "Artists' quotes are the real value of those things. The historical accuracy of the rest of it is questionable." A & M during Doreen Lauer's tenure outlined press service:

*Press Kits:* For each new album, we write, update, or rewrite a biography about the artist. The bio and an up-to-date photo comprise our basic press kit, which we mail to reviewers with the review copy of the album upon release. Press kits are also serviced to our promo men in the field and anyone else who works with the artist. We make these kits available to any press person who needs information.

*Bullets:* Each week we stay up late on Thursday nights to gather the week's hottest news and put together this information sheet for a Friday mailing, so that it hits the mailboxes on Monday morning. It goes to everyone on our press list, everyone at A & M, all managers, and public relations firms, as well as some record retailers and radio stations. The percentage of information reprinted is . . . well . . . astonishing. Should you have anything you'd like to share about one of our artists, please don't hesitate to call us and we'll spread the word. Likewise, please use anything you read in "Bullets" to inform your readers. If any of our short "Bullets" items pique your interest, let us know and we'll be glad to help you gain more specific information.

*Tour press kits:* Often, for major tours, we make up special tour press kits using itineraries, artist profiles, posters, or whatever else seems appropriate. If you do not hear from us first, and an A & M artist is due in your town, please feel free to contact us for information and/or a possible interview.

*Test pressings:* Often, we have test pressings, in advance of an album's release date. If one of our artists is of particular interest to you, let us know and we'll send you a test as soon as one is available.

*Photos:* A & M artists are photographed in concert whenever they appear in Los Angeles, and live photos are always on file for your use should you need them. We have two of the finest concert photographers in the business (Neal Preston and Andy Kent) on retainer and they keep us supplied with top-quality shots. We also have a studio on the Lot for publicity photo shootings. If you need an exclusive shot for an article about an A & M artist, let us know, we can usually supply one in the time it takes to make a print (If your needs are color we'll have a transparency duped as fast as possible).

*Interviews:* Our department has traditionally set up interviews with press in Los Angeles, New York, and on the road. If you would like to obtain an interview with one of our artistts (either on the phone or in-person) let us know and we'll do our best to set it up.

In return for "service" a critic or journalist is expected to submit "tear-sheets" or copies of a review or feature story dealing with the company's artist. The value of tearsheets is described by A & M:

We love getting them. While we do employ a clipping service to help us gather them, often they arrive long after the fact. We encourage you to keep in touch and sending us your tearsheets is the best way of doing it. Your reviews and stories are immensely helpful to our promotion staff, other writers, and, of course, our artists themselves. In some cases, we may ask permission to reprint them for mailings or inclusion in our press kits.

Critics who ignore tearsheet requests quickly find themselves dropped from the service list. "Money reviews," or those that can be included in ads and press kits, are important to the publicity departments.

Prior to the "crash of '79" press parties were almost an everyday occurrence in the two media capitals. Rod Stewart's infamous $42,000 gala put a damper on the practice. Occasionally parties such as Prince's *Purple Rain* bash are given on a more economical basis. Grelun Landan, the dean of West Coast publicists, outlines how a guest list was put together during his RCA days:

Invitation lists: From my end, when I have the deal to run—not always in this spot—I look at what the budget will be and what we can accomplish with it most effectively short range and long range, both radio and TV, and press plus buyers, behind-the-counter-people and whatever . . . trade and consumer media.

If there's any kind of a hook and legally okay, I go for TV news/feature programs. If we are lucky that no other hard news is breaking, we have had an excellent percentage of getting remote crews out.

Mediaprint: Here, I always want the five trades (unique in that Hollywood has two daily papers)—*Variety, Hollywood Reporter, Billboard, Cash Box, Record World* [now defunct]. . . . We need instant print for the act plus longevity, so we go for straight coverage plus features and magazine pieces for later. Again, if there is a hook, I'll go after the *Wall Street Journal*, teen publications, wire, undergrounds, street talkers, the two major dailies, outlying dailies in the market area, *Time, Newsweek,* whatever has a chance of some print projection. That's the theory.

We are lucky here in that we work closely with our promotion and marketing people and have common goal situations, many of which are not ideal. We work with the artist management, which means we can cover with agents, TV-motion picture production types (depending as always on the act).

I try to cover demographically for the benefit of the artist and the company. Sure, we cover college papers and college radio students. . . . We have a seminar each month (summer excepted) for colleges in our studios where we present live radio programmers, jockeys, artists (not limited to RCA acts), managers—whatever is of interest and we also cover a spectrum that embraces top 40, country, middle of the road, R&B, FM. Our promotion people set these up and we all have a hand in it.

The grand finale, of course, is that we have no set lists, which I believe lock you in. For an opening at a local spot like the Whisky or the Westside Room, you go different routes. For a concert, it's something else.

In general, I try to avoid parties where everyone saw the same people the night before and will see them the following night. Inbreeding.

At the same time, because of the record company concentration here, you can be drawn into a rivalry sort of thing that does no good so far as spending for results goes but, rather, falls into the ego pattern of making a small puddle splash a bit and that's all. The club owners and others are anxious to have the record labels spend insurance loot and, in some cases, it is an actual subsidy, which also applies to concerts, etc.

What you are covering is an ever-changing program of sorts which expands and contracts as budgets and concepts change. If you are trying to break a new act [album] you think differently than if it's the umpteenth time around. The partygoers are fat cats here in Hollywood in that they have been able to pick and choose luncheons, dinners, entertainment, and whatever because of the plethora of parties.

A percentile profile is a tough thing as each event is tailored as much as we can make it. A press selection which covers effective media for now and later, ditto radio and TV, ditto buyers, ditto street opinion makers.

Each of these things/events should try and persuade people to our point of view in the most favorable manner and also (alas, also) motivate them into expressing this. That's what it should all be about anyway.

Nearly all of these events occur in New York and Los Angeles. On rare occasions an artist will have a company-sponsored party while on tour, especially in major markets as Cleveland or Detroit.

The interactions between publicists and the print media are less high pressured than promotion. Many publicists are former critics and understand the limitations of space and the market in which a newspaper or journal is located. With a national news publication, the audience demographic has to be respected. *Hit Parader* is almost strictly heavy metal, as is *Creem.* Publicity people compete for space while promotion fights for airtime. The nebulous "power of the press" relegates publicity almost to a support system for promotion.

"One indication of our status with the record companies," said a writer with a weekly column, "is that nearly all of the product that comes in has been on the air for at least two to three weeks. Maybe the *Stone* gets tapes and pressings, I sure don't."

After the marketing arms have been set in motion, distribution takes over getting the product to the merchandisers. The argument, again, is that marketing must have gotten exposure for the artist and the record if it is going to sell.

## Distribution: The Bottom Line

Once the artist has done "his thing," the producer has delivered the tape, and marketing has developed its package, success is determined by the consumer's walking into a store and saying, "I'd like to buy the record." All of the mixing, hyping, promoting come to naught if the clerk responds, "Sorry, it hasn't come in yet." The demand-supply imbalance has vexed record company executives for decades. With the infusion of large conglomerate assets, they are working on what may be the "solution." Ironically, it is based on the prototype of the depression years when Decca, Columbia, and RCA directly distributed and wholesaled their own records, many of which were retailed for 35 cents.

The rise in popularity of singles, released by an ever-increasing number of labels during the 1950s, gave birth to a new type of wholesaler; the "one-stop." The one-stop stocked all labels, allowing the jukebox operator to transact all his business in one store. The coin operator paid a small convenience charge of three to five cents on each record he bought, and record companies gave the one-stop a 10 percent discount for selling their singles. Many retailes later found this a quick and efficient way of obtaining records.

Originally the one-stop came between the record company and the jukebox operator, but later it evolved into a major wholesaler and middleman between the record company and retailer. Simultaneously with the emergence of the one-stops, the majors gave birth to "multiple distribution," a merchandising concept that has been the nexus of the distribution controversies of the late 1960s. Irwin Steinberg, once president of PolyGram, defines this technique as "the flow of goods from manufacturer to consumer through *more than one* channel."[57]

The introduction of the record club by Columbia, followed by Capitol and RCA in 1958, found majors shipping to their own branches, "one-stops," and the newly formed mail outlets. The record clubs originally placed the three majors in the role of record retailer, allowing them to sell directly to the consumer and bypass the cost of the middleman. In 1962 the Federal Trade Commission responded to the objections of retailers and accused Columbia Records of creating a monopoly by distributing only its own artists. In 1971 the clubs made available artists from other labels, but the move has not resolved the highly controversial practice of giving clubs favored pricing status.

Many retailers believe that clubs purchase albums at less than a dollar per unit; retailers and wholesalers must pay nearly five times that price. One retailer expressed a sentiment widely held by those who compete with record clubs: "I'm no attorney but there are some laws being broken along the line. . . . How can some of these large companies sell to dealers, sell to racks, yet still be in the record club business? . . . Some of these large corporations are wearing many hats, and one of these days . . . the government is going to come and take a good look at some things that are going on."

The traditional record-club membership numbers less than 9 percent of the market, according to a WCI study. "Our members are somewhat older," says Stanley Narus of Columbia House, "say, late 20s compared to people in their early 20s. And perhaps because of that, they don't even like going into the stores." RCA's Record and Tape Club director, Robert Gordon: "They aren't trend setters. . . . So they like to buy a product from us, which . . . already has had a chance to prove itself in the marketplace." He estimates RCA record club members to be in their thirties with an average income around $15,000 to $20,000 per year; in 1981 this was slightly above average.[58]

The clubs' increasingly small percentage of total volume has stilled but not eliminated much retailer criticism of these operations. One obvious objection, besides pricing policies, is that club members rarely walk into the merchandiser's place of business. The "impulse buy" is thereby hampered.

"Free-standing" stores or the local record shops are also faced with the discount chain stores, which are stocked by rack jobbers. In 1952 in Philadelphia Elliot Wexler started Music Merchants, the first rack jobber in the United States. The rack jobber extended to supermarkets, drug stores, and variety shops the convenience of a retail record shop; people no longer had to go to a downtown record shop to buy a record. Originally racks carried only budget items, but in time expanded to top-selling albums. The rack jobber set up a four-and-a-half-foot Friedman rack as near as possible to the flow of shoppers in a store. Music Merchants eventually failed, but the idea was picked up by David Handleman, a health-and-beauty-aid rack jobber in Detroit, whose racking was a complete success. Jules Malamud, then the president of the National Association of Record Merchandisers, recalled,

> The rack jobber solved the mystery for the public of where to buy a record. They made it easy. When I was a kid I was a record buff. In those days Ella Fitzgerald, the Mills Brothers, Nat Cole were popular. You'd have to walk around and go to a store that sold radios or something and try to find a record and they'd say they'd order it for you and maybe they ordered it for you and maybe they didn't. But, I wanted to hear it. When you love something and you have your girlfriend with you, you wanted to listen to a certain song. You wanted it that night. So what the rack jobber did was they really made it easy for people to buy records.

RCA Victor was the first major company to realize the importance of racks. The company produced a "60 years of greatest hits" album at a very low cost especially for the rack. Somerset Records produced budget records designed especially for the rack, wholesaling records at 93 cents to the rack jobbers who in turn sold them for $1.98.

The immense volume power of the rack provided the jobbers with the same purchasing power as the one-stop. They were officially subdistributors purchasing albums from the company at a 10 percent discount. The tremendous volume of the rack accorded them with yet another benefit from the record companies: a 100 percent return privilege. This practice was altered in the early 1980s..

Rack jobbers quickly outstripped mom-and-pop retail stores. The convenience of the rack, the volume discount, and the stocking of only fast-moving product gave the rack jobber a major advantage over the retailer who paid more and carried less-popular catalog items.

The bigger rack jobbers quickly became preeminent in volume. In the early 1960s they enjoyed a third of total record sales; by the early 1970s, nearly 80 percent. From the supermarket the rack jobbers moved into discount stores like Arlans, K Mart, or White Front, further boosting their economic power. Much to the dismay of record manufacturers, rack jobbers began to cross over into more traditional retail areas.

Department stores, which had previously purchased product directly from the companies were courted by rackers, who offered to take over the responsibility of following musical tastes. No longer would the retailer be required to wrestle with the world of Top 40 radio, and many found this a welcome relief. Malamud explained:

> In a 5 & 10 cent store like Woolworths they did not know how to sell records. They didn't even have a buyer of phonograph records. They left it up to a girl who made $25 a week. A guy would go in and buy her a box of candy or something and say, "Hey, buy some records," . . . so they were constantly loading these stores with bad records. And these chains were not dumb. The manager of the store came and said, "Hey, you bought these records and they didn't turn into dollars, get rid of them. They didn't pay the bills." So the rack jobber came and said, "Look, I'm an expert. Now I'm going to set up a record department for you. Give me 20 square feet [or whatever amount of space he says] and I'll decide what goes in there." The rack jobber said to the department-store owner, "We will guarantee that everything gets sold, and if it doesn't we'll replace it with salable merchandise.

Jack Geldbart recalled: "So out rode the White Knight. The rack jobber came and offered to the retailer a single source of supply, a way for the retailer to hold a single company responsible for his entire department, a way to minimize the perils of an extremely volatile and perishable product."[59]

Many rack jobbers knew little more about the record business than the beleaguered appliance manager in a department store. Ross Halamay, a veteran record salesman for Decca and RCA, as well as a rack jobber during the 1960s, comments: "Many racks gave the representative carte blanche. They gave him a figure to work with. It was up to him to turn those into dollars. He was doing a job for them that they possibly couldn't do for themselves."

The rack jobber was also aided by the nature of the 1950s record market. Records stayed on the charts much longer. Audience loyalty was greater. As one rack jobber put it, "*Sound of Music* was great for a year and a half. Now, this was great for the Handleman Company. They couldn't make too many mistakes there." The invasion of department stores and retailers by rack jobbers led record companies to try to coerce rackers with threats of cutting them off or withholding product. But by then the rack jobber had become the major merchandiser of the recording industry's product.

Ironically, the record industry gave the rack jobber the power. The 10 percent discount provided a distinct advantage over the traditional retailer. The 100 percent return privilege allowed the racker to err without penalty. The racker could easily walk into a department store and make outlandish promises, and then subsequently return any stiffs or "schlock" product for top-selling artists. Cushioned, the rack jobber stocked entire record departments in many chains and department stores, which placed him in even more direct competition with the retail specialty shop. The White Front, K Mart, or Woolworth's record departments in many instances paralleled the specialty store. At this point the role of the rack jobber was difficult to define. Was he a wholesaler? A retailer? A distributor?

Shemel and Krasilovsky, in their industry handbook, only hint at the source of the troubles: "Although there is little argument about the functions of a distributor, which is the first link in the chain of distribution headed by manufacturers, some distributors *simultaneously* operate as rack jobbers on the side and service locations that undersell their regular dealer customers."[60] Prior to the so-called rock revolution, this confused mode of record merchandising was generally tolerated, but the expansion of the LP market through the unorthodox avenues of "free-form" radio and the underground press created an awareness of the anomalies of the distribution and merchandising systems. The industry, according to David Lawhon, "woke up one morning to find the rack jobber in control of the market," as the decisive merchandiser of albums.

In 1965 there existed three fairly well-defined distributors and sub-distributors. The record companies were the direct distributors. MCA,

Columbia, and RCA enjoyed close direct distribution with their branches. Subdistributors, who bought product at a 10 percent discount, were the one-stops and the rack jobbers. The youth market and the rise in popularity of long-playing albums had an important effect upon each of these outlets. One-stops servicing jukeboxes moved into the album field and in effect began to compete directly with rack jobbers. Rack jobbers in many cases expanded their activities to service jukebox operators. In time, rack jobbers and one-stops became indistinguishable; they performed the same functions. Rack jobbers, merged with one-stops, now service jukeboxes, stores, supermarkets, and even own their own record chains: *ergo,* they are independent distributors.

RCA Victor celebrated this wedding in 1969 by classifying rack jobbers as wholesalers and lowering prices for them. Smaller jukebox-oriented one-stops and retailers were not happy because their larger competitors were getting records at cheaper rates. One-stops servicing *only* jukebox operators had to pay more to the manufacturer; they would either have to absorb the cost to remain competitive or pass on the increase to the opeator. Retailers were no less happy when chains, owned by racks and large one-stops, could get records at least 10 percent discounted. The record companies reasoned that racks controlled 80 percent of the market and preferential pricing would only encourage further buying and distribution. Norman Racusin, a company vice-president, explained to *Billboard*: "As part of our total approach to the record business, our objective is total balance in distribution, in selling and promotion and most of all in product. Our planned additional distribution points will give us the balance we need to maximize retail exposure."[61] With this move the terms *dual distribution* or *multiple distribution* began to dominate the trade papers. In fact, racks became competitive with the companies' own franchised distributors.

Small independents and previous RCA distributors objected violently. One franchised branch perceived the action as "a strange move and a serious mistake. It takes away a distributor's customers and gives him additional competition." Another franchised branch said, "We took the line several months ago and invested about $300,000. Now the racks in our market are to get the same price and have the same privileges as distributors."

Most observers labeled RCA's move as an explicit recognition of the state of the industry. Jac Holzman explained: "It is inevitable because the responsibility for promoting records has fallen increasingly on the manufacturer. The distributor has too many lines . . . when the manufacturer took over promotion the handwriting was on the wall."[62] The rise of multiple distribution underlined the problem the RCA move was aimed at. Subdistributors, prior to the mid-1960s, directed most of the "person-to-person" promotion of records, calling on program directors with the latest single. The proliferation of labels that occurred during the rise of rock and roll drastically cut subdistributors' abilities to "plug" the voluminous amount of product. Even single-line franchised distributors or branches were more apt to push established artists. A "key manufacturer" observed in *Billboard*: "The independent distributors have too many lines. They cannot attend to all. They pay attention to only the hot product and much product is not getting adequate exposure in retail outlets. As a result the cutomer over 25 years of age becomes alienated. He finds a concentration of top hits."[63] Henry Brief said, "The distributors already have so many labels they need another like they need two heads."[64] Even one of RCA's unhappy discontinued distributors concurred with this assessment. Jim Shipley of Cleveland said, "RCA had too do something. . . . The pure independent distributor is obsolete. . . . Nobody needs two middlemen. There has been an integration or merging of functions."[65]

Yet, selling directly to racks did not satisfy the record companies' desire to merge functions. RCA's version of "multiple distribution" treated only the distribution problem, not promotion, but the move was the death knell for the previous modus operandi. Sam Sachs prophetically told *Billboard*:

> Dual distribution, if carried out fully, can lead to a marketing structure built along the same lines as the cosmetic industry, in which the manufacturer does all the advertising, promotion, and marketing, and then sells to any retailer or wholesaler who can afford to buy this product, and all at the same price.[66]

The shift to multiple distribution, while expanding the record company's retail outlets and increasing sales, ignored another problem. Rack jobbers do not do across-the-board promotional work. They sent few field people to radio stations and do not escort artists to meet program directors. They merely sold records in their racks and retail outlets; the recording companies were left with the exclusive responsibility of breaking records. The trade papers carried more and more familiar complaints from dealers, program directors, and executives. A headline in *Billboard* announced: "Chaos Hits Radio on Disk Service." Claude Hall, then the paper's authority on radio stations, reported, "A vast number of radio stations are asking the record industry to by-pass present distribution channels—the distributor and the rack jobbers and their local and regional promotion men—and service them directly."[67] Station managers throughout the country accused rack jobbers and others of not "servicing" them. The operations manager at KFOR (Lincoln, Nebraska) said, "The distributors are extremely erratic." Bill Tanner of KACY (Ventura, California) urged manufacturers to "go around the racks somehow and make the product available in the market. As it is now, there's no reason to play it if they can't buy it." Several weeks later small record companies were protesting: "It is imperative that small labels find a good distributor who can collect their company so that they can continue to promote new releases."[68]

In September 1970 twenty-five of the most powerful executives in the record industry rate distribution and merchandising as the industry's major problem, even above the inflation then badly cutting into sales. William Gallagher accused the rackers of displacing the small retailer and then failing to recognize the "responsibilities they have inherited. Too little consideration is given today to the music buyer who likes to browse and be motivated by other than the top 20 or 30 chart-busting LP's."[69] Jay Lasker concurred, suggesting that companies must circumvent the rack by educating the public. Jac Holzman continued the indictment: "Rack merchandisers, because they are not aware of the music on esthetic and social levels, often do not recognize a hit until it is highly placed on the charts. As a result they buy too much too late." The cost of returns was rising.

Returns are records that do not sell and are sent back to the manufacturer for account credit. Forty percent of all records released were being returned. The returns procedure cost the manufacturer from 27 to 45 cents per unit of one album or five singles. The actual amount is based on the cost of shipping the product and the paperwork necessary to keep the accounts in order. In 1972 rack jobbers shipped back $189,000-$750,000 in merchandise. Record manufacturers prefer to reduce such costs as much as possible, and in 1979 they did.

It is fashionable in the record industry to blame returns totally upon the rack jobber. Jules Malamud, on the other hand, says that returns are not solely the fault of the merchandisers. He acknowledges that in the beginning "some of the rack jobbers didn't have good personnel, knowledgeable buyers, and they bought wrong." The 100 percent return policy covered the mistakes. Malamud:

> I don't think the answer is 100 percent return because in a sense there are a lot of rack jobbers that are not as good as the Heilichers and other people. They don't buy right. What really pisses them [the record industry] off is when they [rackers] order cartons of albums, don't even open them up and put them out, and then send them back. That's been done." He cautioned, "The reason that a record doesn't sell is because it doesn't really have it in the grooves. A rack jobber's not a genius. All he can really do for the companies is really expose that product.

Bob Thiele predicted future trends: "The majors have always had good distribution. I believe it's going to be tougher than ever for the independent company to obtain proper distribution. The distribution pattern of Warner/Reprise, Atlantic, and Elektra shows the way of the future." Racks and independent distributors, reasoned manufacturers, took few of the risks and gained much of the profit. "The manufacturers said, 'The hell with you, we're going to take over our own distributing. We'll open our branches, and we in turn will create our acts and market our acts, and promote our acts, and develop our acts through our branch system.'" A branch is simply a distributorship owned by the record company; it performs all of the functions of the independent but only for the company. According to a Warner Bros. release, "A branch works on just your own product, not on a lot of companies. . . . A branch can also hire long-haired freaky people who frequently listen to new music. A branch need not hire pudgy cigar smokers who are really into the Ink Spots."[70] (The majors in the 1970s increasingly began to distribute and promote smaller labels.)

Branches were not an innovation. In the early days of the recording industry Columbia, RCA, and Decca all relied exclusively upon their own company-owned distribution centers. During the 1950s, with the rise of the independent record company, "sub-distributors sprang up to perform the same functions as the branches." Decca and others, believing it an economy move, dismantled their branches, transferring their distribution accounts to the independents and the one-stops. Capitol and Columbia hung onto the branch system. RCA both maintained branches and used independent one-line distributors. Some of RCA's branches, however, were frequently linked to appliance franchises and did not effectively sell records. Nonetheless, a 1967 *Billboard* survey found that companies with branches provided radio stations with the best service and information. Capitol, Columbia, and even RCA Victor earned 59 to 58 percent excellent ratings. A & M, with the one of the most popular promotion directors in the industry, Don Graham, placed only fourth, with a 47 percent excellent rating.

Much of Columbia's success over the years has been attributed to its branches. Columbia executives brag that they can place a record in most record stores nationwide within a matter of days. Billy James credits the introduction of the Byrds and "Mr. Tambourine Man" partially to the branch system. He says: "Columbia's branch operation was a major factor, they wanted to get behind somebody. We were able to communicate to them that [the Byrds and "Mr. Tambourine Man"] were something they could get behind. It had nothing to do with money, it really didn't."

The sheer magnitude of product rendered the old system in which a distributor handled four to eight labels as basically ineffectual. However, prior to the infusion of conglomerate funds and the pursuant amalgamation of companies, branches were economically out of reach of all except the majors, for a company must do $50 million to $60 million in volume to maintain such an operation. The Kinney Corporation (now WCI) merger with Warner, Reprise, Atlantic/Elektra, and many smaller labels made the formation of Warner-Elektra-Atlantic Distributing Corporation (WEA) possible. Seven national branches close to major markets, with 30 promotion men, distributed all the labels as well as a number of smaller companies. Columbia handles Epic, Scotti Bros., and several others in addition to its own product. In 1972 RCA and MCA returned entirely to branch operations. MCA continued to carry independents as rack dealers but took over the promotional and distribution functions. In 1973 only two important labels still relied primarily upon independents: A & M and Motown. A & M, with a small catalog, believed that the independents was the ideal vehicle for its records. Jerry Moss, a former promotion man, regarded a self-employed distributor as much more open to the profit motive than branch managers. This was a minority view in the industry that would switch in the 1980s.

In the mid-1970s the majors began either to purchase smaller labels or enter into distribution and promotion deals. WEA and the CBS Group exhibited considerable rosters of labels at their branches.

### Major Label Branch Distribution

*CBS*
Columbia (Cleveland International, ARC-Columbia, Park Lane, Odyssey, Accomplice), Epic, Portrait, Blue Sky, Caribou, Jet Kirschner, Life-song, Nemperor, Philadelphia International, T-Neck, Tabu, Unlimited Gold, City Lights.

*RCA/A & M*
RCA (Victrola, Bluebird), A & M (Ode, Horizon), Free Flight, Grunt, Hologram, Pablo, Road-show (Nature's Music), Rocket, Salsoul (Bethlehem, Different Drummer, Dream, Free Spirit, Gold Mind, Tom N' Jerry); Solar, 20th Century-Fox, Tortoise, Windsong, Arista Ariola.

*MCA*
MCA. Motown, Source.

*Capitol*
Capitol, United Artists, Blue Note, EMI-America, Harvest, Angel, Seraphim, Melodiya.

*WEA*
Atlantic, Atco, Big Tree, Cotillion, Little David, Rolling Stone, Swan Song, Nonesuch, Jazz Fusion, Elektra/Asylum, Elektra/Curb, Warner Bros., Warner-Curb, Warner-RFC, Warner-Spector, Whitfield, Bearsville, Dark Horse, ECM, Island, Paradise, Sire.

*PolyGram*
Capricorn, Casablanca (Chocolate City, Oasis, Parachute), Phonogram (De-Lite, DJM, Lone Star, Mercury, Monument, Smash, Sound Stage Seven, Vertigo, Zappa), Polydor (Charisma, MGM, Spring, Verve), RSO (Curtom), Deutsche Grammophon, Philips, Archiv, Festivo, Privilege.

Other than A & M and Motown, the "indies" were left with specialty labels and cutouts.

One-stops serviced retailers whose credit lines with the major labels were not established, or whose volume was too low. In 1979, when the independent arrangement was in for a shock, a retailer paid a wholesale premium of 22 cents per unit.

In January of 1979 A & M resumed the flight from independents to the majors. Alpert and Moss signed a pact with RCA; *Billboard* announced "Exit Is Shock to Indie Ranks." "It's like a death in the family," said a Cleveland distributor. "I've never seen such upheaval in my life."[71] The same week United Artists merged with Capitol. The $100 million distribution system was getting nervous. Five of the larger distributors even suggested funding some new producers and their smaller labels, but nothing came of the proposal.

*Time* labeled it the "jukebox blues," and the independents had a severe case. Coin-operated machines had declined from a half-million units in 1976 to 320,000 in 1982, and these were predominantly located in southern taverns, causing a writer to observe, "The once proud symbols of teenage America may now be on their way to becoming just collector's items and sources of nostalgia."[72] Even the foundation of the "indies" was diminishing. Independent distributors, except for those also in retailing, were being squeezed by the majors, by their mergers and by branch arrangements with high-volume individual labels.

In 1983 Chrysalis joined the CBS branch system, followed by Arista and Ariola, which linked up with RCA. It was estimated that the label led by Clive Davis and Ariola constituted 30 percent of volume of the independents. Some distributors threatened legal action. One of the larger companies, Schwartz Bros., did file a $5 million breach-of-contract suit. Pickwick's Jim Moran said his company was "no longer viable."[73] Motown was the only "hot" label still in the "indie" fold. In mid-1983 Motown entered the MCA branches. Legal action again was resorted to; this time $3 million in exemplary and punitive damages were sought by Big State Distributing and Schwartz Bros.

The independents essentially were returned to the role of wholesaling small and specialty labels plus blank tapes, accessories, and cutouts. Some focused on stocking major chains and suburban malls; a chain like K Mart will buy 2.5 million units of a title, which is very lucrative for the rack jobber servicing the national merchandiser. Despite this major realignment some of the problems persist. Artists and smaller labels can get lost at branches as well as at subdistributors.

The "crash of '79" found majors retreating. Many branches were consolidated; for example, several labels in Detroit transferred the actual distribution outlets to Cleveland. CBS moved its operation to New Jersey, leaving a sole promotion person to work the Great Lakes region.

By the mid-1980s one-stops and independents saw a brighter business climate that was partially due to an upturn on sales in the retail sphere. This was bolstered by the improving economy. One rack jobber-one stop was actually charging and getting $9.49 for a hot title. Rack jobbers and retailers had to become more responsible. Late payment can result in the withholding of hot product by the majors.

The record companies' most potent weapon is the "hold." Every 90 days distributors and retailers receive bills from the manufacturer. It is to the companies' advantage to have quick payment; it is not in the interest of the retailer or racker to comply. A retailer or racker may easily have much of his cash locked up in stock, and may be unable to pay at the time requested. The record companies motivate the jobber to pay through a hold: refusing to ship newly released records until the retailer or racker pays the bill. A Capitol executive stressed the positive aspect of hold: "Big sellers bring in outstanding accounts from retailers."

From the retailers' perspective, the hold is a bothersome and generally ineffective method of soliciting payment. A racker who services a major California chain of discount stores explained. "You must pay in 90 days or be placed on hold, but this puts the record company in a bind, because no product moves at all." The hold, in fact, does not accomplish its purpose. Rather, as one retailer remarked, it only makes him buy the record from another source.

> If you have the bucks to pay, the product is always available. Let's say tomorrow Carly Simon comes out with a new album. Now, what do you do if you're on hold? So you've got to get that product some way, don't you? Now, you might not be able to come up with $2,500 to pay yourself off hold the following morning, so it's important to have sources and resources, so if you can't get it here, you can get it elsewhere.

The "elsewhere" is either from other racks or one-stops, and thus the hold system is rendered relatively ineffective.

The withholding of product is further compounded by the shadier areas of record distribution. Although certainly not as newsworthy as payola, considerable wheeling and dealing occurs under the distribution and merchandising table. Not all of it can be pinned on rack jobbers, whose ethics are constantly questioned by the more "respectable" corporation record executives. To fill their quotas, record salesmen make various arrangements with rack jobbers. For example, a salesman may persuade a rack jobber to buy a stated quantity and then, after the salesman's deadline has passed, the records can be returned. This is a rather prevalent practice, as Malamud indicates:

> They will wine and dine the rack jobbers, romance the pants off of him, build a relationship with the guy, and say, "Hey, you gotta do me a favor. If I don't make the quota, it's my ass and they're gonna fire me or I'm gonna be low man on the totem pole." and the guy feels bad. I think it's stupid business, but it does go on. And so what happens is first thing you know they say to the guy, "If it doesn't sell, I'll give you a return authorization."

A former rack jobber described a company that used advertising in a more sub rosa fashion. A major company had a sales quota, and by the twenty-fifth of each month one of its sales people would come in and tell the racker, "If you do this, I'll give you this [amount of money] in advertising." The racker recalled, "One large manufacturer came in right on the twenty-third. The deadline date came in about the twenty-fifth, and we bought some budget albums. He gave me a full-page ad, and I didn't even have to run the thing. He just told me to send him a charge back . . . but I didn't have to mail in tear sheets."

In many parts of the country other company representatives, who have considerable access to product, have been known to sell unmarked freebie records at a discount to retailers, pocketing the proceeds of the sale. The discarding of promotional records by media people (see chapter 6) is pale in contrast to the "reps'" operations. In all, as Bhasker Menon and many other company executives admit, distribution and merchandising remain the chief barriers to the introduction of new artists and their music.

Grelun Landon calls rack jobbers "cherry pickers"; they carry only what is a proven success. Yet, as Ron Saul indicated, "Remember! The name of the game is breaking an act." This is a mammoth obstacle for record companies, especially in areas where radio stations are equally governed by "getting behind" *Billboard's* weekly ratings. Bill Roberts said:

> He buys just the hit recordings. The ones that are in the top 50 of *Billboard*. The big problems we run into are the secondary markets, which are the means we use to break a new product, usually. Where it's racked, there's no way possible that you can get your recordings into that market. Because the rack is the only one who can expose them into the shops. What you have to do is basically forget about that market.

There is no way that record companies can compel rackers to buy new product. Bhasker Menon explains, "Because the rack jobber says when you get it on the charts then I'll stock your record." There is economic security in the *Billboard* charts. It is only wise business to go with a winner. Rackers live by the dictum of "I'm in this business to make money. Period!" There is an equally convincing reason for the racker's reliance upon *Billboard*: most rack jobbers are not of the current generation. They may wear contemporary clothing, but their musical tastes are of another era. Joe Smith: "They're so remote from it. They're still waiting for the next Sinatra album because that they understand. They don't know who Black Sabbath is or who they represent. Black Sabbath represents a certain kind of music. They don't know how to buy. We need exposure and they won't touch it." Regardless of the disdain record companies have for rack jobbers, they cannot afford to ignore them. Record executives have tried numerous techniques to pry the racker away from his *Billboard* chart, ranging from incantations to unavailing coercion. A Capitol executive believes rackers do not depend solely on charts, and that an effective salesman can move a racker: "It may mean a few extra advertising dollars. It may mean asking a favor. It may mean *whatever* it means in the business." The most obvious "whatever" has been to entice the older-generation businessman to appreciate the "new sounds."

"Act your age," Stan Cornyn told a gathering of the National Association of Record Merchandisers (NARM). "Talk to the rock generation, without fear or prejudice. Try being curious, not know-it-all. Act your age by *listening*." Admonitions like this are expressed semiannually at NARM gatherings as well as numerous meetings sponsored by record companies. Jack Gelding advised, "Know your product—what you are selling and where. The long-haired kids have made us all a lot of money. Take the time to understand the music you sell and, more importantly, know your demographics. . . . Know the market, not old philosophies."[74] Such advice has largely gone unheeded. Many rackers got up and left as a rock band began to play at a NARM meeting. This lack of appreciation is a major problem; companies sorely need the merchandiser to do more than just stock records. The former president of Atlantic, Ahmet Ertegun, says, "There is a great challenge to the NARM to expose new artists because the 'now sound' may not be . . . tomorrow. It's very important to be aware of changing musical tastes. It is our responsibility to keep aware of what the public wants."[75]

As might be expected, Jules Malamud takes issue with the one-sided indictment:

> Smith and Menon and all those guys, they're not completely wrong but they're not completely right. . . . It's a dual blame. There are rack jobbers who

are bad buyers and there are manufacturers who have very bad policies. And the combination of the two creates the problem. Every week Warner Brothers and Capitol have to go out and sell the records, and they got to sell them to the same people. It behooves them to make better buyers out of some of the companies that are not too good.

Rack jobbers believe they know what the public wants. Their income is derived from providing the public with what it wants. One prominent racker told *Billboard*, "Businesses last longer than acts."[76] Like radio programmers, rackers are not in the business to expose new artists from Capitol, Columbia, or Warner. Indeed, the larger rack jobbers, such as Handleman, may have *more* accurate figures of consumer preferences than the RIAA or *Billboard*. They use computerized daily sales reports of records that have actually walked out of their stores with the consumer, and record-company statistics are based upon the number of records *shipped*, not sold.

The RIAA certifies a record as gold or even platinum on shipping figures. Only after a minimum six-month period, when returns and promotional materials are deducted from the amount shipped, can an accurate figure be reached. Corb Donohue notes, "It's based on speculation more than facts." Rack jobbers, of course, are aware of this and are consequently quite skeptical of record company statements about an act's being "hot" unless *Billboard* supports this claim. Many observers even question the accuracy of trade charts. However, not all of the rack jobbers are wedded to the charts. Ross Halamay maintains that 76 percent of the racks are tied into only "key product." Others, especially those in the discount stores, must by necessity carry large amounts of catalog. Those servicing smaller retail outlets have a similar demand. Where persuasion fails, other less high-minded techniques have been used, generally with little if any success. Rack jobbers have been approached with discounts of "buy a hundred and get six free," knowing that the rack will take only a certain number of so-called key records and that a few new acts may receive some exposure. The use of advertising as an inducement is helpful. Companies are known to offer to pay from 3 to 8 percent of the purchase order for ads that plug both their records and the store. This amount varies depending on the size of the distributor or region.

### Cutouts: The Games People Play

An important part of the rack jobber's role results from the high percentage of unsuccessful records or "stiffs." Eighty-five percent of the albums released annually stiff. "When a pop record fails to break even" said Harry

Brief, "it usually is a total loss."[77] The record industry gives its mistakes to the rack jobber to dispose of or bury.

Asks Malamud,

> You know what he is? He's an undertaker. It's a necessary evil. Nobody likes undertakers but you need them because when people die somebody has to . . . and that's really terrible work to do . . . but you need an undertaker and they make a lot of money. A schlock dealer or a cutout company really is not the kind of company that has real love for the music or feel. They'll sell anything. They'll sell dirty old socks or anything. They sell whatever the market will take.

The cutout allows the company to regain part or all of its loss. Merrill Rose, a wholesaler and major retailer, alleges, "I know a label dumped $4 million, and maybe they were able to salvage $1 million to $1.5 million of their investment. . . . A large proportion of releases are instant cutouts. There is no reason to destroy them. The manufacturers are entitled to realize some return on their mistakes."[78] Cutouts are records that are discontinued in the company's catalog. A notice is sent to retailers and wholesalers announcing the recall and the period of time allowed for the return of the cutouts.

The returned cutouts are then wholesaled to rack jobbers; the return to the company on a cutout is usually less than a dollar. Lenny Goldberg, once a buyer for Ampex, a New York rack, declared, "LPs are made available at prices like 50 cents to a dollar each and are resold on $1.00, $1.25 and $1.50 lists."[79] If the rack cannot get that price he will lower his sights. "You gotta keep going down the level with these cutouts until you get some dollars out of it. Before it is a zero." Ross Halamay maintains, "You can always get rid of something at 57 cents or 99 cents." Racks are ideal for this mode of operation. Stocking only the "quick movers," the jobber does not have a more specialized catalog stock to compete with. He can keep shifting these "bargains" from one chain to another, lowering prices on slow movers as he goes. A similar rationale is at work in stocking and selling so-called budget records of ten cuts from $1.99 to $3.99.

The practice of deleting albums from the catalog is not entirely beneficial. For the artist, the cutout bares the stigma of failure. Warner/Reprise announced one cutout order with the apt title "96 on Death Row!" "This death sentence for 96 has its humane side," said *Circular*. "No one has accused Warner/Reprise of producing a classic every time at bat; many of the bombs were schlock the day they were born."[80] It was not in the grooves.

Cutouts are the product of disillusionment. "When we think we've taken our best shots and haven't had encouragement to go on with it," states Joe

Smith. "When there's a kind of apathy, none of our promo men say, 'Hey, they're great,' no radio stations, the group doesn't shake up anybody in their personal appearances." He adds, "I don't think we've turned out many artists with less than two shots, or an album and a few singles, just to see if we can stir up some interest." At Capitol, similar philosophy exists: "Their appearances aren't making it. It's an attitude, when you just don't think you can do anything more with it." Capitol will not cut out "*unless* the first album and everything falls apart . . . because there are energies [psychic and economic] that went into promoting it and we [A&R] have told our force that this is a good group."

The retail impact of cutouts is a matter of concern. A & M has accused its competitors of dumping cutouts that compete with new releases. An MCA vice-president of sales acknowledged, "Many retail record shops, in order to compete with the record stores selling cutouts, are now trying to buy cutouts themselves to sell, which takes away from the space devoted to selling new product."[81] Ira Moss, president of the defunct Pickwick label, attacked manufacturers for creating a marketplace of "deep confusion and instability." He told *Billboard*, "These manufacturers see only the quick buck . . . and hurt the industry as a whole." His concern was generated by Pickwick's competitive stance with cutouts. Pickwick records usually sold for $1.99 or more, and some cutouts, found in the same rack, cost less. Moss, however, has no easy solution. "Tighter A&R control perhaps," he said.[82]

At one time, an independent record-distributing company offered albums originating at Atco, Bell, Buddah, Decca, Kapp, Dot, Paramount, Liberty, Motown, Roulette, RCA, Sun, UNI, and Warner Bros. for one dollar. Albums from Cotillion and Elektra were available at slightly higher prices. Name acts such as the Temptations were available for 50 cents wholesale. Such cutouts, retailers believe, unfairly compete with their merchandise in not only in pricing but availability. "Labels are being run by accountants who, with their computer printouts, are cutting out product regardless of regional activity," wrote Dwayne Witten. "If it hasn't sold 'x' amount within the last six months, get rid of it. Cut it out or dump it. And the catalog that remains is not being pressed to meet the demand."[83]

The editorial pages of specialty rock magazines—"fanzines"—abound with similar denunciations. Epic Records has received many condemnations for its treatment of old Yardbirds albums. MGM cut out much of its early rock music catalog including the Velvet Underground recordings, but due to consumer demand this material was reissued. Many collectors spend hundreds of hours annually searching through racks for the oldies that manufacturers deemed worthless. Record-shop owners prefer they spend this time in their stores.

Cutouts also involve a considerable bookkeeping problem for retailers. Termination notices are sent to record stores with a notice of six to eight weeks to return the cutout records. The dealer must then receive an authorization to ship back the items so as to receive exchange credit. Some companies mail these notices with the hope of sticking the dealer: "I've seen . . . X put out a cutout list and on the date of the letter they'll have January 15, and when you receive it it's already January 27. And they've given you 30 days to get it back. Some companies do this deliberately so they go on the books saying they've given you the satisfaction of a date, and you must move very fast if you have a sizeable amount of this product."

Artists, retailers, and fans, joined by music publishers, have repeatedly attacked cutouts. Manufacturers, they charge, are avoiding payment of mechanical royalties. Al Berman of the Harry Fox publishing agency alleged that music publishers' percentages were decreased by the sale of discontinued merchandise. Rack jobbers countered, blaming artists for excessive royalty fees and urging the continuance of cutouts.

Artists, especially, dislike cutouts because they are ego deflating but, more important, they mean reduced and sometimes no royalties. In fact, a bargaining chip used by some companies to keep artists from label-hopping is the threat of cutouts. Cutouts compete with newer full-price releases. ELO's defection to CBS from United Artists saw the latter dumping its entire ELO catalog just as ELO's Columbia material was hitting the stores. RCA used a similar tactic with Willie Nelson. Ironically, as the crossover country singer's popularity soared, the same albums but with different titles and packages reappeared. It is impossible to estimate the number of sales both parties lost due to the cutout product.

Cutouts remain very much a part of the industry. Record companies can recoup losses through the use of this technique in light of the number of failures. Cutouts also keep the rack jobbers busy.

Distribution and retailing constitute a major barrier to the success of a record. Only the radio station program director is a greater obstacle. If this decision maker airs a record long enough in the proper market, it will make the *Billboard* charts and the racker will have no choice but to stock it. After all, he is only "in the business to make money. Period!" Repeated air play is an effective method of introducing a new act; however, it is also the most difficult.

### Notes

1. Quoted in Mike Gross, "Music Rumbles—Wall St. Tumbles," *Billboard*, 6 December 1969, p. 8.
2. Remarks by Bill Graham at Second International Pop Music Festival, Monterey.

3. Quoted in Paul Grein, "Squier: I Was Clipped by Clip," *Billboard*, 24 November 1984, p. 36; "Assessing Blame," *Billboard*, 5 January 1985, p. 8.
4. Gerry Sherman, "Mixing the Right Ingredients," *Billboard*, 9 December 1967, p. 37.
5. Quoted in Gene Lees, "Music Business Maverick," *Hi-Fi*, May 1969, p. 116.
6. Richard Goldstein, *Goldstein's Greatest Hits* (New York: Prentice-Hall, 1970), p. 148; George Martin, *All You Need Is Ears* (New York: St. Martin's Press, 1979).
7. Quoted in Ed Morris, "Producing Country Artists Is a Balancing Act, Says E/A's Bowen," *Billboard*, 11 July 1981, p. 52.
8. Quoted in Ralph J. Gleason, *The Jefferson Airplane and the San Francisco Sound* (New York: Ballantine Books, 1969), p. 84.
9. Quoted in Charles Reich and Jann Wenner, "Jerry Garcia: The Rolling Stone Interview, Part Two," *Rolling Stone*, 3 February 1972, p. 30.
10. Quoted in "He Makes Music Pay at CBS," *Business Week*, 7 October 1967, p. 107.
11. Jay Rudy, "Phil Spector Interview," *Jazz and Pop* 8 (January 1969): 26-27.
12. Quoted in George Uhlman, "Record Producers: The Lure of Independence," *Rock*, 14 August 1972, p. 31.
13. Reich and Wenner, "Jerry Garcia," p. 30.
14. Quoted in "Lenny Waronker and the Burbank Sound," *Circular*, 14 June 1971, pp. 3-4.
15. Quoted in Eliot Tiegel, "$20,000-$30,000 Cost for Week in Studios," *Billboard*, 2 December 1978, p. 91.
16. Quoted in "Budgets Tight, Creativity Up—Producers Agree," *Billboard*, 19 September 1981, pp. 56-57, 61. Also, "Sherman Spins Time Saving Tips," *Billboard*, 23 December 1967, p. 16.
17. Mike Curb, remarks at 2nd Annual International Music Industry Conference.
18. Jon Landau, "The Rolling Stone Interview: Paul Simon," *Rolling Stone*, 20 July 1972, p. 38.
19. Uhlman, "Record Producers," p. 31.
20. Quoted in Paul Grein, "Perry Preference 'Music/Know Best,'" *Billboard*, 12 September 1981, p. 6.
21. Quoted in David Rits, "Quincy Jones . . .," *Rolling Stone*, 12 April 1984, p. 47.
22. Quoted in Ann Geracimos, "A Record Producer Is a Psychoanalyst with Rhythm," *New York Magazine*, 29 September 1968, p. 60.
23. Quoted in Tom Davies, "Oak Ridge Boys Love 'Elvira,'" *Toledo Blade*, 26 July 1981, p. F-3.
24. Quoted in Christopher Connelly, "Producer Jim Steinman's Total Eclipse of the Charts," *Rolling Stone*, 2 February 1984, p. 41.
25. Grein, "Perry Preference," p. 6.
26. Goldstein, *Goldstein's Greatest Hits*, p. 118.
27. Murray Ross, "The Record Business: What Makes It Run," *Record World*, 24 July 1971, p. 230.
28. Quoted in Jon Pareles, "The Pop Record Business Showing Signs After 4 Year Slump," *New York Times*, 28 November 1983, p. E-20.
29. Quoted in Michael Jaye, "They're Light Weight Title Contenders," *Rolling Stone*, 18 January 1983, p. 16.
30. Ibid.
31. Quotations from Henry Edwards, "If There Hadn't Been a Bruce Springsteen Then the Critics Would Have Made Him Up," *New York Times*, 5 October

1978, p. D-17. Also, David Marsh, *Born to Run: The Bruce Springsteen Story* (New York: Delilah Books, 1979), p. 117.

32. Quoted in Bob Greene, "The Real Thing Is the Hype, Brother," *Chicago Sun Times*, 24 October 1975, p. 10.

33. Jim Fusilli, "The Selling of Bruce Springsteen," *Wall Street Journal*, 2 July 1984, p. 12.

34. Quoted in Sally Rayl, "Fleetwood Mac Double LP for Fall," *Rolling Stone*, 23 August 1979, p. 13.

35. John Sippel, "Dealers Deplore FM Airing Complete LPs," *Billboard*, 3 November 1979, p. 14.

36. Stephen Holden, "Fleetwood Mac: Putting Together a Golden Moment," *Rolling Stone*, 13 December 1979, p. 77.

37. Paul Grein, "Cover Art," *Billboard*, 17 February 1979, p. 8.

38. Julia London, "Images of Violence against Women," *Victimology*, 1977-1978, p. 519.

39. "Women Protest Album Covers Again," *Billboard*, 10 September 1977, p. 14; Jean Williams, "Less Sex and Violence Pledged for LP Art," *Billboard*, 18 November 1978, pp. 1, 19-20.

40. London, "Images of Violence against Women," p. 521.

41. Ed Harrison, "Women and Warners Forgive and Forget," *Billboard*, 17 November 1979, pp. 3, 73.

42. Williams, "Less Sex and Violence Pledged," p. 20.

43. George Allen Booker, "Disk Jockey and His Impact on Teenage Musical Taste as Reflected Through a Study in Three North Florida Cities" (Ph.D. dissertation, Florida State University, 1968), p. 79. Also see Algin Braddy King, "The Marketing of Phonograph Records in the United States: An Industry Study" (Ph.D. dissertation, Ohio State University, School of Business Administration, 1966), p. 172.

44. Leo Sacks, "Labels: Video Won't Kill Radio," *Billboard*, 4 August 1984, p. 61.

45. "Bill Drake Interview: His Early Experience and Radio's Future," *Billboard*, 3 June 1972, p. 18.

46. Richard Robinson, "The Record Company," *Crawdaddy*, August 1972, p. 28.

47. Quoted in Paul Hirsch, "*The Structure of the Popular Music Industry*," (Ann Arbor: University of Michigan, Institute for Social Research, Survey Research Center, 1970, mimeographed), p. 58.

48. Quoted in George S. Trow, "Money Music," *New Yorker*, 23 December 1972, p. 43.

49. See Doug Hall, "Promo Folk Go Social at WXLX Audition," *Billboard*, 21 June 1980, pp. 30-31.

50. Quoted in Steve Reiner, "Would You Buy a Used Tip Sheet from This Man?" *Rock*, 7 June 1972, p. 2.

51. Ibid., p. 21.

52. Quoted, ibid.

53. Quoted in Claude Hill, "The Double Whammy Promo Team," *Billboard*, 7 May 1977, pp. 28-31.

54. Quotations from Henry Edwards, "Who Cares About Rock Critics?" *New York Times*, 15 February 1976, p. D-20; Marsh, *Born to Run*, pp. 116-17. Also, Greene, "The Real Thing Is the Hype, Brother."

55. Quoted in Dick Nusser "Labels' Public Relations Efforts Assuming New Import," *Billboard*, 3 February 1979, pp. 3, 10, 73. Ironically, press relations were badly tainted when the labels' economy cuts struck in the latter half of the year.

56. See Harvey Rachlin, *The Encyclopedia of the Music Business* (New York: Harper & Row, 1981), pp. 324-26.
57. "Individual Approach to Market Counts," *Billboard*, 23 May 1970, p. 20.
58. Quotes in Cecelia Lentini, "Expanding Markets Challenge Retail Grip," *Billboard*, 5 September 1981, p. 5m-3.
59. Jack Gelding, "Survival Tools for the 70's," *Billboard*, 23 May 1970, p. 21.
60. Sidney Shemel and M. William Krasilovsky, *This Business of Music*, rev. ed. (New York: Billboard Publications, 1971), p. 103.
61. Quoted from Paul Ackerman, "RCA's Dual Distribution Draws Uptight Responses," *Billboard*, 6 September 1969, pp. 1, 112.
62. Quoted in Paul Ackerman, "Key 'Indie' Record Firms Split on Dual Distribution," *Billboard*, 13 September 1969, p. 1.
63. Ibid., p. 8.
64. Quoted in "$2 Billion Worth of Noise," *Forbes*, 15 July 1968, p. 24.
65. "Mainline: Indie Faces Oblivion," *Billboard*, 13 September 1969, p. 1.
66. "Dual Distribution Posing Promotional Puzzler: Sachs," *Billboard*, 11 October 1969, p. 1.
67. Claude Hall, "Chaos Hits Radio on Disc Service," *Billboard*, 1 August 1970, pp. 1, 34.
68. Quoted in Eliot Tiegel, "Small Label Co-op Urged to Fight Distribution Danger," *Billboard*, 29 August 1970, p. 1.
69. All executive quotations from Lee Zhito, "Execs High on Rest of '70—Distribution Top Problem," *Billboard*, 5 September 1970, pp. 1, 12.
70. "The Transmogrification of Joel Melvin Friedman," *Circular*, 12 July 1971, p. 2.
71. Marc Kirkeby, "Changing Face of Record Distribution," *New York Times*, 18 February 1979, p. F-7.
72. "Jukebox Blues," *Time*, 1 February 1982, p. 61.
73. John Sippel, "Pickwick Distribution Dumped," *Billboard*, 23 April 1983.
74. Gelding, "Survival Tools for the 70's," p. 21.
75. Quoted in "Challenge Thrown to Racks Expose More 'Now' Acts," *Billboard*, 15 March 1969, p. 2.
76. Quoted in Mike Gross, "ABC's $100 Million Rack Jobbing Wing," *Billboard*, 10 May 1969, p. 1.
77. Quoted in "$2 Billion Worth of Noise," p. 26.
78. Quoted in Earl Raige, "Retailer Defends Cut Out as Halt to Bootlegging," *Billboard*, 16 September 1972, p. 55.
79. Lenny Goldberg, "Inside Record Distribution," *Rock*, 1 March 1971, p. 21.
80. "96 on Death Row," *Circular*, 22 March 1971, p. 2.
81. Quoted in Claude Hall, "MCA Brass Sally to Halt Cutouts," *Billboard*, 28 October 1972, p. 15.
82. Quoted in Robert Sobel, "Pickwick's Ira Moss Hits Manufacturers on Cutout Dumping," *Billboard*, 9 September 1972, p. 1.
83. Dwayne Witten, "Breaking the Dump Cycle," *Billboard*, 22 September 1979, p. 15.

# 5

# "And the Hits Keep Coming"? Radio

*Radio what's new?*
*Radio someone still loves you!*

—©1984 Queen Music, Ltd. (BMI)

*Oh I'm a teenager just like you*
*Please won't you help me, here's*
*what to do. Write to your*
*Deejay, send a request. Say*
*that my record is the one you*
*like the best.*

—©1958 Monument Music, Inc.

The "cultural gatekeeper" determines what information is transmitted. Social scientists have come to look for gatekeepers in the media and its reporting of the news, and to a lesser extent in the dissemination of cultural artifacts.[1] David Manning White, for one, found a midwestern newspaper editor who did not use 90 percent of the stories on the national wire service because he felt they were unsuitable for his community. Investigations of radio and television news broadcasts have reported similar censorship. Gatekeepers have been troublesome for many, in light of the credo in the United States of "an informed electorate." But those who determine what the electorate shall know are not confined to the newsrooms; they are also prominent in drama, literature, film, and music. Negative reviews in the *New York Times* and its competitors have closed many a Broadway production after one night. In the area of literature and music the gatekeeper's power is less manifest, in that here the question is one of entry rather than disapproval; for example, the *Times* reviews less than 10 percent of the books published each year. In popular music there exist three gatekeepers: radio programmers, music video outlets, and to a much lesser extent the music press.

Martin Block, considered by many to be the prototype disk jockey, as early as 1942 expressed the notion that the standard of musical excellence was being "left to the good judgment of the man who plays the records."[2] That person's aesthetic judgment in time has become all-important. Few in the music industry would openly challenge the opinion of a Florida record-store owner. "We can get in a pretty good record, but if it isn't played on the radio, it won't sell."[3] Sociologist Howard Jolly, a quarter of a century after Block's remark, commented, "Disk jockeys, above all others, have the almost unique characteristic of participating in promotion and the 'sifting' process through which all records go." He continued to argue that the radio audience is "an electorate, *in its own way*, which is to say that it is in the limited way that a disk jockey is a gatekeeper."[4] Professor Paul Hirsch points to deejays as "institutional regulators" of hit records because "record companies are dependent on radio air play as the only effective vehicle of exposure for new pop records."[5] That was the case prior to MTV.

Hirsch's observation was correct before the advent of music videos, but after their appearance Les Garland of MTV rhetorically remarked, "They [the labels] . . . started asking themselves, 'How in the hell did we sell 7,000 Stray Cats albums in Seattle?' We don't have one radio station up there playing it."[6] Retailers in Top 40 AM ghettos reported a surge in sales of acts without a hit single after MTV was introduced into their market. In the 1980s "Video Killed the Radio Star" was an empirical reality. MTV surpassed radio 68 percent to 63 percent as the prime exposure vehicle for album purchases in 1983, according to A. J. Nielsen.

Whether music video can successfully continue to challenge *the* historical medium of "primary" exposure is an open question. However, radio has weaved a demographic and stylistic web on a very shaky foundation. The audience fed by MTV is younger, while radio advertisers look to a 25-year-old-plus market share. This *may* change with VH-1 and the expansion of cable outlets.

The rock press is the last medium of exposure. It is significant. The press compliments the electronic media. The printed page can bring public attention to the records rejected by the formats of AOR and MTV and to FCC regulations, and can meet the desires of advertisers to reach as large a targeted audience as possible. The printed page can facilitate much greater and wider coverage than the broadcast media. Turning McLuhan, *camera obscura*, on his head, the printed page can accomplish in a few short minutes of reading time what three-quarters of an hour of air play may fail to do. Writers for *Rolling Stone* and the other rock publications do not have to contend with government and commercial restraints imposed upon the public use of airways. *Rolling Stone* could with impunity publish the lyrics of John Lennon's "Working Class Hero" with "the word" and all, even as the most open-minded FM stations were forced to blip out the "offensive" Anglo-Saxonism. The print medium introduced the Sex Pistols and other "disreputable" bands to U.S. audiences. Radio programmers generally ignored the "punk" phenomenon.

Gatekeepers in the music industry are the Berlin Wall between manufacturer and audience. The foundations of this barrier are multiplex in that each medium has its own set of value systems that color the perception of the gatekeeper. The projected demands and responses of an audience or taste cluture, as well as fear of possible failures, all contribute to the makeup of the wall. Program directors know better than to offend their youthful listeners with Amy Grant records, yet they must avoid the FCC. Radio is at a distinct disadvantage compared with its competitors. Cable broadcasters and editors are free of governmental regulatory restraints; their formats dictate content. Although the actual power of cultural gatekeepers in popular music has been brought into question, their control over product and its exposure is undeniable. Block's statement that "programs help popularize tunes" is a commandment engraved in concrete in the music business. "Music critics" may not possess equal power, but in the rags-to-riches world of popular music it is believed foolish to ignore any avenue that may lead to the gold record or stardom.

### The Disk Jockey: Individual versus Collective Gatekeeping

The American Federation of Television and Radio Artists (AFTRA) says the number of disk jockeys can be estimated by "multiplying the number of AM and FM stations by an average of four." According to this formula, at least 32,864 persons were employed as "commercial" announcers in 1983, a figure that excludes employees of the 1,104 "noncommercial" FM outlets. The number of record spinners has grown over the decades, and the role of the disk jockey has changed as well.

The term *disk jockey* is believed to have evolved from a *Variety* cover story by Jack Kapp, in which the pioneer Decca executive coined the term *record jockey*. As Arnold Passman was later to observe, the label came to connote "jockeying or riding a record toward success."[7] A more typical definition is the art of announcing records on a program featuring only phonograph records.

Conflicting notions notwithstanding, the evolution of the disk jockey can be traced to the inception of radio broadcasting, where announcers played shellac records and chatted informally with their unseen audience. The practice of broadcasting records was attractive, especially to smaller stations, considering the minimal investment necessary to fill air time. The opposition of sheet-music publishers and a number of performers such as

Fred Waring and Bing Crosby at the outset hampered the broadcasting of phonograph records but did not end it. As Judge Learned Hand was to rule, copyright control ended with the sale of the record, and radio stations therefore "could not be restrained from using records in broadcasts." This interpretation of the 1909 copyright law, coupled with the publishers' realization that radio could provide a forum for their songs, raised the status of radio as the central avenue for public recognition of the songwriter's product. The bandleaders of the swing era were quick to recognize the value of having their songs on the air.

The radio announcer, prior to the work of Al Jarvis at KFWB in Los Angeles, was aptly described as "the same staff spieler who read poetry [and] announced each disk solemnly, impersonally, and formally enough to qualify as an adept funeral director." Jarvis personalized the announcer's role with the addition of a conversational and friendly microphone style. The approach, perfected by Arthur Godfrey on the East Coast, elevated the announcer from a mere stylized reciter of poetry, ads, and record introductions into a "personality" who commanded the attention of listeners and adopted an equal, if not superior, status to the music he played.

Jarvis also pioneered a format within which his "liberated" radio personality could function with success: "The Make Believe Ballroom." The program format was simply to play dance tunes and simulate an atmosphere of a marathon ballroom with real or contrived conversation with the performers and dancers. Martin Block, a library assistant at KFWB, seeing the success of the format, moved it to WNEW in New York. Block, a former pitchman, parlayed it into a medium-wide phenomenon that in time would spawn "Your Hit Parade" and "Lucky Lager Dance Time," programmed by Bill Gavin, who later became the publisher of an influential record tip sheet.

Arthur Godfrey's approach to his audience was similar to Block's but confined to the early morning hours. He used "earthiness, independence, enthusiasm," and irreverence to announce disks, and a growing list of profit-hungry but masochistic sponsors awaited his barbs. By the late 1930s, it was clear that the record-playing radio personality was a force to be reckoned with. Benny Goodman, in anticipation of things to come, reportedly paid Al Jarvis $500 in 1937 to play his latest recordings. "Ballroom" listeners increasingly came to insist that bandleaders' public appearances be exactly as on records. For the road band, this meant playing the same trademark arrangements identically night after night. Swing historian George Simon described the role of the disk jockey in the big band era: "Some [bandleaders] romanced disk jockeys with intense and sometimes nauseating ardor. Some jocks reacted in kind . . . many disk jockeys actually sought out records by new, upcoming bands and promoting . . .

such discovering remained a labor of love for many a big band disk jockey."[8]

The success of the Jarvis-Block format induced the American Tobacco Company to sponsor "The Lucky Strike Hit Parade" nationally, adding the dimension of ranking records as to popularity. In the early 1940s, Martin Block wrote, "If the platter is a good one, the most effective type of direct marketing has taken place. And sales are sure to reflect the airing of the disk."[9] After nearly 50 years of sporadic attempts to contravene radio, few singers, musicians, record companies, or sheet-music publishers would dispute the merit of this claim.

In the early "Ballroom" days, Jarvis and Block were forced to purchase the records they aired, but the wartime rationing of shellac, as well as the growing recognition of radio impact upon music taste, led to programmers being given personalized sample records. Glenn E. Wallichs, a cofounder of Capitol Records, recalled: "We typed special labels with their [top 50 deejays] names on both sides, pressed them on expensive lightweight, unbreakable vinylite compound and then had our limited employee force drive around and distribute each sample personally. It was a service that created a sensation. *We made the jock a Big Man*, an Important Guy, VIP in the industry."[10] Capitol not only formally recognized the importance of the deejays but also introduced the freebie "exclusive record," a precursor of the payola of the 1950s. The "exclusive" was a form of reward to important deejays in the industry. As Norman Prescott noted in his congressional testimony:

> It was more important for a jockey at that time to get an exclusive record and be able to shout, "I have got it," where nobody else had it on the one or two other stations, than money. . . . As the disk jockey grew into a businessman, he realized his power. At that time, he did not know what his image was, because he was just starting in a relatively new business. So he went into the areas of personnel management, publishing, putting his name on songs, and whatever it is.[11]

The advent of the "exclusive" and the "promo" underlined the industry's recognition that a new institution, with power, had been created. A cultural gatekeeper stood in the path of a record's success. The Blocks, Jarvises, and Godfreys were not mere announcers who filled airtime with the hardiest record around. "Exclusives" and the sponsoring of records by bandleaders and were the opening scenes of what was to become the cost of doing business.

The importance of the disk jockey was even further enhanced by the diversification and proliferation of the record and sheet-music industries. The ability of Broadcast Music, Inc. (BMI), to challenge successfully the all-powerful American Society of Composers, Authors and Publishers (AS-CAP), and the ensuant emergence of independent record companies, or "indies," made airtime, or exposure, all the more precious and difficult to obtain. The disk jockey reigned over airtime and became the arbiter of the economic success of recording companies and songwriters. A *Newsweek* correspondent in 1947 cynically chided deejays: "With all the power in their programs, and no directors to ride herd on them, some are unrestrained in swiping ideas from anyone. They mercilessly play the records that will do *them the most good.*"[12] Dexter attributes even greater influence to the triumphant jock: "His ever-rising power turned the jukes from hit makers to meet little machines that . . . only the music the local jockey ordains. Not even television . . . can affect the nation's music tastes." Dexter's view was echoed in 1979 by Warshaw and Vasapoli: "The record industry would readily concede that the exposure given recorded music by broadcast stations is perhaps the single most important element in the promotion of records."[13] Perhaps until the early 1980s.

Radio's preeminence has been battered by technology. "Drive-time" dominance is indisputable. There are over a million audio receivers in automobiles, and at least half that number of vehicles have a cassette capability; obviously, the two are not played simultaneously. Music video's significance cannot be underestimated, but audio appears the situationally important medium.[14] One owner of a record store exclaimed, "If they don't know about a record, they sure as hell are not going to buy it."

Prior to video, the music industry was reactive. Retailers stocked familiar material and broadcasters aired it. "They're playing a safety game," said country star Waylon Jennings. A program director adds, "People don't know what they like, they like what they know." This was especially relevant in regard to the choices of "name" disk jockeys in key market areas of the country because these market areas greatly determined which songs placed upon the *Billboard* "Hot 100." Other stations then followed. Consequently, only a handful of jocks in key market cities could determine the fate of a record. The concentration of power in the 1950s made payola even more attractive to the donor (especially smaller or independent companies) because it could assure airplay. *Payola* became a trade euphemism for an honorarium for special consideration, or what *Billboard* termed "play for pay."

The significance of the payola scandals of the late 1950s does not lie in the morality of the practice nor in the feet-of-clay posture of Dick Clark and Alan Freed. Rather, payola was the industry's abortive attempt to control its market in a manner similar to its nonentertainment counterparts listed on the stock exchanges.

## Payola: Gatekeeepers for Sale

Payola, despite the outcries of ASCAP and conservative congressmen, is a practice engaged in long before the 1950s. Gilbert and Sullivan reportedly paid vast sums of money in the 1880s to singers to perform their compositions. Abel Green claimed that *Variety* during World War I had objected that some "400,000 was being paid to singers" every year for the same purpose.[15] Paul Ackerman, the music editor of *Billboard*, told a congressional committee that music publishers "embraced payola; payola prior to the age of the disk-jockey and prior to the great expansion of the record business."[16]

Norman Prescott, the opening witness before Congressman Oren Harris's subcommittee investigating "deceptive practices in the broadcasting field" in 1960, aptly described the reason and function of payola:

> The tremendous output of records, and the fierce competition that exists within the industry, it is a matter of who can play what, when there is limited amount of play on the air. . . . Payola has become the prime function of this business to get the record on the air at any cost and dispose of it, because if you do not . . . you cannot get individual income [profit].[17]

Prescott, a former deejay in a top market area, elaborated on this statement, observing that his four-hour popular music show aired 50 to 52 records a day, many of which remained on playlists for four to six weeks. Meanwhile, the industry overproduced some 200 new singles per week, all in the hope of breaking into the magic circle of the *Billboard's* chart. To further compound the situation, deejays in cities such as New York, Boston, Cleveland, Detroit, or Los Angeles were aware of their power. The pressure, as Prescott indicated, was tremendous. Payola was supposed to buy the manufacturer control over the product, making access to the folks in "radioland" a bit more promising.

Payola, as it existed prior to the 1959 scandal, evidenced two dominant forms: "play for pay" and "consulting." "Play for pay" was simply "how many dead presidents [$20 bills] are there for me?" This mode of payola was direct payment from the industry to the gatekeeper for airtime. The most spectacular practitioner was "American Bandstand" host Dick Clark. The "breaking" or introduction of "Get a Job" and "All American Boy" aptly illustrates how "play for pay" worked on the Clark program. The Silhouettes' "Get a Job" was produced originally by Philadelphia disk jockey Kay Williams on his Junior label and then it was purchased by Ember Records. During the transition, the song copyright was transferred to the Wildcat Music Company, which was controlled by "Bandstand" producer Tony Mammerella. Then the national television show "broke" the record. "All American Boy," written by Orville Lunsford, was a talking-blues number about the rise to fame of Elvis Presley. Lunsford took his song to Fraternity Records and was encouraged by Dick Clark. As soon as 50,000 disks were ordered, the song received extensive air play on "Bandstand."Although the song was actually recorded by Bobby Bare, the non-singing Bill Parsons was provided with appearances on the Clark show to promote the record. The money Parsons was paid was charged against his royalties at Fraternity as "promotional expenses."[18] Overall, 50.4 percent of the records available through the companies in which Clark had an interest were played on "Bandstand"; of these, 65.4 percent were played before they had appeared on a *Billboard* chart listing. Quite simply, Clark "broke" records on his network dance show for personal gain, banking on the show's exposure power.

"When I recorded 'Venus,'" Frankie Avalon observed, "Dick got behind it and it sold 1.5 million copies. He's the greatest." Many congressmen disagreed. In the concluding moments of Clark's testimony at the subcommittee hearing, Chairman Harris told the beleaguered television personality, "You are a product of that system, not responsible for it. You took advantage of a unique opportunity to control too many elements . . . in the popular music field, through exposure of records to a vast teenage audience."[19] This overt type of payola was unique in that few disk jockeys commanded the kind of power possessed by Clark or Alan Freed. "Play for pay" was generally found in large market areas and was not widespread. More common was the subtle and covert practice of consulting.

William B. Williams told *Life*, "If a disk jockey had to listen to all these records, he'd go to the kookie house." A fellow jock added, "No broadcasting company expects its men to listen to each and every record. It is just a physical impossibility."[20] The problem, as Paul Ackerman, music editor of *Billboard* at the time of the congressional hearings, correctly observed, was "the abundance of product." Too many records were being released each week. "Competition for exposure is extreme, for without wide public exposure, the potential buyer would never hear most of these records. This is true not only at the broadcast level, where payola enters into play, but also at the retail level."[21]

To circumvent the multitude of releases, the music industry through its local distributors hired "name" deejays to listen to the product; each was listed in ledger sheets as a "consultant." A 1959 sample of 23 major cities found that a total of $263,244 was paid to deejays for consulting and other services. Some distributors and recipients of these fees interpreted them as bribes and acted accordingly; however, many viewed them as earnings for reviewing records on "one's own time." "Consultant" Charles Young said, "One of their problems was on labeled records by unknown artists . . . he [distributor] would send these records to my house, and he would call me and ask me what I thought of these records. . . . It did not influence me in one way or another."[22] The distributor's perception of the transaction was similar. Donald Dumant explained that consultant fees were partially for "equal consideration in listening to my new releases." Another distributor said, "We made payments . . . for these people who gave us their time and attention in listening and helping us evaluate our new releases."[23] "Play for pay" predicted an outcome; consulting provided preferential treatment. Obviously a record familiar to a jock had a better chance than one he had not heard, especially where new artists were concerned.

After nearly a year of investigation and consideration, Congress passed a bill making payola a crime punishable by a fine up to $10,000. Industry and disk jockey were somewhat dismayed by the entire episode. An "indie" record manufacturer told *Billboard*, "Today, it's more difficult to tell if you're actually getting anything for your money. There's absolutely no guarantee your record will be played." A disk jockey reacted. "There are still too many records. . . . Payola still flourishes. . . . Payola is practiced in practically every business I know of. The biggest example and most glaring example I can think of is 'lobbying' in Washington."[24] Payola has continued but in an altered form, as has the perceived autonomy of the individual deejay.

The payola scandals provided an important glimpse into the mechanics of music marketing and the function of gatekeepers. To reach the public, the manufacturer has to go through the radio station, the central vehicle for product exposure. In the case of "play for pay," nearly all risk was removed by purchasing exposure time, in effect circumventing the gatekeeper. Consulting—being paid to listen to records—provided less risk in the quest for precious airtime but it did not insure getting it. The disk jockey in this instance maintained his discretionary powers as gatekeeper. The payola hearings greatly curtailed "play for pay," shifting the gatekeeper role from the individual to the collective of station management. It did not stop the practice.

With the diminution of direct payola, the industry representative or promo man was returned to a position of importance. His task was to gain exposure for his acts. In part, this restored the majors' competitive advantage over the independents because many of the smaller companies, having relied heavily upon payola, did not have a promotional apparatus of any magnitude nor could they afford to develop one.[25] The scandals also indirectly hastened job standardization, particularly in the major market areas. The freedom of the jock had already been severely limited in the midwestern and southern states by the injection of Top 40 radio in the mid-1950s.

In 1955 Todd Storz introduced the concept of Top 40 radio at WTIX, New Orleans, and applied it throughout an entire chain operated by a southern pharmaceutical company. It was based on the formula traditionally employed by jukebox operators: demand determines staying power. Using local record-store sales to ascertain popularity, Storz discovered that the average number of singles that sold well was 40. His fascination with this figure was reinforced by the fact that most jukeboxes at the time had 40 plays. These "top" 40 records were repeatedly aired on the Storz station. The repetitive pattern, radio lore has it, was based on Storz's experience in an Omaha bar where patrons had played certain songs over and over. The *Billboard* chart later, took over the primary function of determining material for popular-music stations. Interspersed with the playing of the hits were jingles and patter in what can best be described as a carnival or medicine-show atmosphere. The philosophy underlying the concept was that the airing of material from the *Billboard* chart, then containing a mix of country-and-western and rhythm-and-blues material, would attract the largest audience, which at that time was the index of success in radio.

For Storz and his imitators, the formula worked. In the beginning deejays in the Storz chain were controlled not by policy but by the mechanics of the format. As one former Storz employee noted, "An announcer was required to cue six turntables with ETs [transcribed commercials and newscasts], records, give time and temperature." He had time to do little else. Later, what he said was monitored by the home office. One executive order was to avoid "excessive talking," thus the rapidity of delivery. Comedian George Carlin, once a jock, recalled that the policy was "shut up and play the music."

The home office of the Storz chain automatically built the playlist behind the established charts, and thus Storz's personnel missed out on the payola given their big-city counterparts. Bribing a Storz jock would be a waste of money because he had no control over the songs he played. The payola scandals introduced similar controls into the cities such as Cleveland, Boston, New York, and Detroit, where the practice of payola had been rampant. Bill Drake streamlined many of Storz's gimmicks into a rigid format—the ultimate in playlist control. The introduction of demographics in polling further tightened up what the jock could play or say because he had to be concerned not with large numbers of listeners but with a specific limited and affluent segment of the audience.

Stations other than those in the Storz chain merely shifted the responsibility of compiling a playlist to support personnel, such as the program director or the music director. In most cases, the result was the same: the era of free-willed deejays was rapidly drawing to a close. The idiosyncratic mike styles of the Niagras, Millers, Carneys, Hancocks, Biondis, and Russ Knights would be synthesized onto one: the boss jock. The "wild and screaming" jock now "does nothing but announce the records, he does this in a hysterical style with fast talk and pitched sell.[26]

The wide acceptance of the Storz "50,000-watt jukebox of the air" had a profound impact upon both the record and broadcasting industries. The highly individualized personality jock had little place within the framework of Top 40 radio. Jocks were merely the arm and voice of the prearranged list. As Top 40 became more refined, Storz expanded his operation into many other cities but ran it from a home office. It was not a network operation or even syndication but simply a formula that was adapted in various southern and midwestern cities. In time Gordon McLendon, Bill Drake, the Bartlett chain, ABC radio, and Metromedia developed similar formats and imposed them on their stations, which made the deejay almost wholly an interchangeable part of a large machine. This seemingly dehumanizing trend prevailed for the simple reason that the Top 40 formula *worked.* Top 40 stations consistently beat their competitors in the Hooper and ARB rating battles; at WINS in New York Alan Freed consistently topped Martin Block's WABC ratings. Indeed, not until "Cousin Brucie" Morrow took over at WABC in the early 1960s did the station become a popular-music power. "Cousin Brucie" was a Top 40 prototype. A competitor said, "There was no personality because you never know what kind of a guy Bruce Morrow is. You don't know whether the guy's got a family, if he went to the ball game. He never says anything. I don't think there is a Cousin Brucie."[27]

Top 40 radio was largely responsible for pushing so-called urban contemporary stations back to servicing the black ghetto. Alan Freed in Cleveland began enticing white youngsters into listening to "race" music, and the feat was repeated in countless large cities. Small rhythm and blues stations found themselves playing Muddy Waters, Ruth Brown, the Clovers, the Drifters, and a legion of other artists for an entirely new and highly appreciative audience. But Top 40 radio stole the economic heart out of those stations. The rhythm and blues hits were originally covered by white artists, but when that failed the original records were incorporated into Top 40 playlists. This action brought many record fans who were young and white to the Storz chain.

Rock historians and nostalgia buffs rarely remind us that the appreciation of black music in the 1950s was highly selective; Fats Domino, Little Richard, Chuck Berry, and a legion of a cappela quartets gained white popularity but the majority of black artists did not. "Down home" music did not fit the *zeitgeist* of the Eisenhower era, so rhythm and blues stations, the birthplaces of rock music, were permitted to evolve on their own. Their evolution, as we shall see, has come to fascinate and perplex the entire pop-music indistry.

### Collectivized Gatekeeping: Boss Radio vs. the Underground

Al Jarvis and Martin Block originated formula radio with their "Make Believe Ballroom" shows. "Your Hit Parade," sponsored by a cigarette company, added the next ingredient, ranking songs as to popularity. Top 40 and boss-sound radio were the end products of a synthesis of record ranking, microphone technique developed by Block, and structured time use perfected into an art by Bill Drake and Ron Jacobs at KHJ in Los Angeles. Boss radio was a highly slick structure into which all of these pieces fit. Nothing was left to chance. Deejays, songs, and even commercials and news ("20-20 News Time") were designed to fit the rigid mold; if they did not, they were not aired.

*Boss, Boss, Boss . . .*

Boss radio first appeared in the Los Angeles area two weeks prior to the opening scheduled by Bill Drake and Ron Jacobs. The catalyst for this unanticipated event was a dejected KHJ newsman. Dick Spangler, in search of another position, had approached competitor KFWB and told its management, "I know what they're going to be doing at KHJ." On the morning of 5 May 1965 KHJ deejay Robert W. Morgan hurried up to KHJ program director Jacobs, saying, "Turn on KFWB! They're calling themselves Boss Radio, they have 20-20 News, and the disk jockeys are called the Boss Jocks." To save the emerging KHJ identity, Don Steele previewed the new format the same afternoon. KFWB retreated, leaving the boss sound to the Drake station.

The unexpected introduction of the boss sound was symbolic of what came before. One of its founders, Jacobs, indicates, "Most of that stuff was ad lib or created out of necessity." It was not, as some would have it, a cool, calculated, and restricted format—at least in the beginning. The generic title itself was adopted as a convenience. KHJ's original slogan in the 1920s, "Kindness, Happiness, and Joy," gave way in its unsuccessful attempt to program rock during the early 1960s, which was overshadowed by "Color Radio" at KFWB. To differentiate the KHJ of the mid-1960s from its predecessor, the management searched for a new slogan; one suggestion was "Boss Radio KHJ." *Boss* at that time was considered an old-fashioned term, but was used on billboards and in newspapers and trade ads, although not on the air. Several hours after KHJ was upped by KFWB, it aired an identification jingle followed by the deejay's name and the time. Jacobs recalls, "So we had the jingle, 'KHJ, Los Angeles' and the guy comes in and says, 'It's 6:30 in Los Angeles.' I was standing there in the booth and said 'That's redundant. We just said Los Angeles,' so I said, 'Try saying "Boss Angeles"' So he did it the next time. Thereafter, we did it every half hour, 168 hours a week, forever."

KHJ brought in other refinements by this fortuitous manner. The first year's playlist was borrowed from a rival station. The famous format was drawn up on a cocktail napkin in a bar by Drake, Jacobs, Gary Mack, and Les Turpin. It consisted of airing 33 current records taken from established charts. The KRLA chart was the source for the first year; then the *Billboard* "Hot 100" and local store reports. Three singles were picked by the program director as "hit bounds." Intermixed with these records were approximately 400 oldies, "goldens." On weekends, especially during rating sampling periods, or "sweeps," "goldens" predominated. Each hour operated on what has come to be called the "Drake clock." The first single was aired at the top of the hour; three minutes later, a commercial or air check; seven minutes after the hour, something else; and then another slot until the 20-20 news. The numerical sequence for spots was "3-7-11-16-20 . . . 30-33-37. . . ." The deejay patter was highly stylized and in time predictable: "Boss Radio . . . handing you the heavy hits, around the clock . . . where the hits always happen first . . . the hits just keep on coming!" With the exception of the rapid-fire and structured deejay delivery, boss radio was an extension of the Top 40 format developed in the 1950s, as Jacobs observes:

> KHJ was just a refinement. If it had the appearance of going faster . . . it was because we were just starting out like crazy with less of the extraneous stuff. . . . There had been a tendency with people like McClendon and Storz, when they got successful, not to protect the amount of music they could play. They would get successful and if somebody could sell another spot to a used car dealer, they would put on another spot.

KHJ kept its limit on commercials, about twelve minutes an hour. It also strictly enforced its policy of minimizing chatter by its disk jockeys. Jocks were told, "Brian Wilson has just spent nine months of his life wrestling with this thing that takes two minutes and forty seconds. So, unless you've got something really terrific to say for your eight seconds, shut up." Its better deejays, like "Humble Harv" Miller, the "Real" Don Steele, and Robert W. Morgan complemented the format. Steele, for example, possessed the ability to provide continuity within the contrasts in the Drake format. According to Jacobs, "He was very loud, and he can rise above all the production things that are engineered, the elements that surround him.

That's quality. . . . [He] really understands this parade of sounds, and that it is a contextual series of contrasts." However, Miller, Steele, and Morgan were exceptional personalities within the format; others were merely imitators captive in a formula that dominated the AM music idiom. KHJ never resorted to buzzers after eight seconds, but other stations may have, thus generating the belief that in boss radio a jock is little more than an appendage to a Top 40 chart. Programming power at KHJ was in the hands of the program director and music librarian Betty Brenemann, who assisted him.

A majority of songs aired at KHJ were charted, that is, were currently on the *Billboard* list or had been, as with the "goldens." The opportunity to break a new record at the station was statistically very small. Open programming slots in a given week ranged from one to five. At least 50 or more singles competed for these slots. Songs were picked on the basis of "pacing, the tempo of the record, the category of the record as to musical configuration, emotional mood at the time, what people are going for, who's happening in television . . . the criteria is what the hell sounds good." In other words, a song was chosen if it possessed a number of qualities and met several conditions, one of which transcended the intrinsic quality of the "in-the-grooves" doctrine so widely quoted in the record industry.

Drake and Jacobs considered "momentum" the key. Momentum meant that an act or record was visibly on the ascent or was, in industry argot, "hot." Sonny and Cher, the Supremes, and the Beatles in the mid-1960s all possessed momentum. A song by an established performer following a previous success more often than not was made a "hit bound" on KHJ. The value of exposure for a proven group was really quite minimal. Jacobs, the recipient of numerous golden records thanking him for making a record a hit, considers many of these awards superfluous because "some of them would have been a hit regardless because the group was so big."

Even momentum, however, did not guarantee KHJ airplay. Timing, or pacing, was equally important. Two records of similar style, volume, sex of singer, and so on would not be played sequentially. As a result the injection of a new record into the field of 33 changed the entire complexion of the playlist. Jacobs would not put three rhythm and blues songs on his playlist in a given week regardless of the quality of record or the momentum of performer. He recalls, "There would never be a week that we would put on Wilson Pickett and the Temptations and Otis Redding, no matter if all three had made their greatest record." In this sense a group with a sound similar to another's with a chart item was doomed to failure. Why play Zager and Evans when Simon and Garfunkel have something going? Only in rare instances does limitation or similarity help a new performer. America's "A Horse with No Name" in 1972 was an instantaneous hit in part because the trio's music was identical to that of the supergroup Crosby,

Stills, Nash and Young, which had not made a record in over a year. It is widely believed that had "Horse" been released at the same time as a Crosby, Stills, Nash and Young record, America would have remained obscure. Timing, therefore, is an important variable in a record's ability to break into a boss sound playlist.

Although timing can help a group, the clock frequently works against it as well. The program director at KHJ, who screened records, had many demands upon his time and must use it to greatest advantage. Jacobs was able to review up to 100 singles in a half-hour simply by listening to the first bar or opening four seconds. If he found the opening not infectious or that a record did not meet the immediate needs of the format, he rejected it. "I can afford to disqualify anything that's going on my station if it doesn't make it in context. If it makes it in context, it has to come on strong in the beginning." Many record producers, being aware of this review policy, would stress strong bass runs for an opening, as in "Smoke on the Water," "Green Onions," "Sunshine of Your Love," or "You Really Got Me," thus providing the "hook" or attention-getting sound. Jacobs's rather cavalier technique was an outcome of the excessive volume of product that the program director was faced with. Citing the statistic that a new album appeared every 90 minutes, he explained that he did not "have the real time capability to listen to all the songs."

The importance of KHJ goes considerably beyond its immediate market area because the *Billboard* chart, the *Gavin Report*, and Kal Rudman's *Friday Morning Quarterback* tip sheets are based partially upon the airplay afforded records in major market areas, of which Los Angeles was foremost. Songs not introduced in these areas rarely are played in the so-called secondary markets, whose playlists draw upon what is popular in the major markets. The catch-22 aspect of the situation distresses promotional people, who have devised numerous ways to get around program directors. Even as he acknowledged the power of a gatekeeper at KHJ, Jacobs mildly dissented from the importance of getting a record played on boss radio: "I'm sure I could give you an example of ten incredible records that were played routinely as hit bounds for two, three, four weeks—nothing happened to them, absolutely nothing." In fact, he did not cite any, and added, "There are *very few* that were totally unknown that we stuck our neck out on just because we liked them. I think *those probably constitute the ones that we got burned on.*" In other words, KHJ basically programmed records with momentum, that is, those by name artists. It utilized its smaller sister stations in the RKO chain to air-test singles that were believed to have potential, thus eliminating the risk factor in the major market area. Still, getting a record on the KHJ playlist was a crowning achievement for any promotion man.

Jay Lasker erected a large oriental-style gong in the executive hallway to be rung by promotional personnel when one of their acts broke on a major market AM station; a dull buzz announced secondary breakouts. WABC-AM in New York must have sounded like London's Big Ben. Lasker, now a MoTown executive, would jump for joy upon breaking into the ultraconservative playlist of the top-rated station in the number-one-market. In his self-serving book *Rocking America*, Rick Sklar outlined the "formula." The PD used 550 retailers and the charts to determine songs "most popular with the most people." The merchandisers were rotated to avoid "label stocking" or influence. WABC was strictly "hot" rotation, playing hits over and over again. Sklar: "Once a song *did* meet our highly selective criteria it would be played with increasing or decreasing frequency as its popularity changed from week to week. . . . Each of the most important songs had its own countdown clock, timing the minutes to its next airplay."[28] The formula worked for decades until FM and cable television eroded its estimated 22 million listeners.

*Free-Form Radio*

Underground, progressive, or free-form radio was born in the still of the San Francisco night. Russ "The Moose" Syracuse, who held forth on the number-one Top 40 station, KYA, during the midnight-to-dawn shift, played material not aired during the daytime "ratings" hours. "All Night Flight" was a staged space voyage with music, exotic characters, and satire. In conducting this simulated air trip, the deejay tapped a reservoir of musical material ignored by the formula stations: the long-playing album. Devotees of the *Billboard* "Hot 100" and other charts in 1965 were oblivious to Bob Dylan, Joan Baez, and the many other artists who had never had a hit single. In San Francisco especially, many local favorites had not yet signed a recording contract. During the daytime hours there was little incentive to change the KYA format; Tom "Big Daddy" Donahue and the other boss jocks were leading Drake-managed KFRC in the ratings race.

In the wee hours of the night Syracuse violated nearly all the canons of boss radio. He did not "shut up and play the music." Much of the music he did air was generally not found on any chart. He played tapes of the Grateful Dead, the Great Society, Wildflower, Big Brother, and the Jefferson Airplane. Because of his time slot, "The Moose" could avoid most management interference. He was able to demonstrate that albums were no longer just one-hit singles with 11 fillers. Donahue explained Syracuse's disaffection with the AM format as partially attributable to the fact that "the Byrds' LP or the new Bob Dylan album were outselling the single records on their playlists, in most cases Top 40 programmers chose to ignore them rather than attempting to determine cuts." In 1966 few Top 40 program directors, deluged with 7,086 singles, had the time or inclination to plow through some 3,752 albums containing 12 cuts each; Syracuse could and did review such material during his six-hour stint; literally "bombing" those he did not like. The new format worked with college students and street people, indicating that a youth audience existed that preferred musical fare other than the normal AM material, something not lost upon advertisers increasingly concerned with demographics.

Demographics became important in radio industry in the early 1960s when some radio stations, either unable or unwilling to compete with Top 40, left "numbers" to such stations as KHJ and KYA. The Top 40 philosophy was "If we had the kids listening, we figured we could be number one because the stations in L.A. before us had gotten to be number one by making the kids listen. . . . Demographics are absolutely silly for programmers to consider." But as the demographic profiles indicate, the major consumers of singles and Top 40 radio in the mid-1960s were in the lower age brackets, ranging from 9 to 18, with an emphasis on bubble-gummers and teenyboppers. Although they were avid consumers of blemish cream and American International films, they did not purchase many products bought by their older brothers and sisters, the major consumers of albums. Top 40 radio centered upon the 9-to-18 audience, and so-called middle-of-the-road (MOR) stations concentrated upon those 25 to 49, which left the highest-consumption demographic—18 to 24—unattended. This economic fact alone lent indirect legitimacy to the Syracuse approach.

A large specialty audience is not to be ignored, especially when that audience buys most of the autos, appliances, and stereos. Its identification gave considerable impetus to formats other than Top 40, as did a contemporaneous choice by *Time* of the "under-25 youth" as "man of the year." As if to underline the existence of an audience with an alternative taste, the Federal Communications Commission in 1966 ruled that AM and FM stations under common ownership must separate their programming formats as of 1 January 1967. The rise of the LP, more sophisticated sampling techniques, and industry awareness of a youth culture, all provided the soil in which underground radio was to flourish.

KMPX-FM in San Francisco was a foreign-language specialty station on the verge of bankruptcy. The station listed "vanity" ethnic shows of which the announcer was also the sponsor. For a time it held an "announcing school," and part of the training was conducted on the air. Of its programs, only Roy Trumbull's folk-music show featuring Bob Dylan, Tom Paxton, Phil Ochs, Joan Baez, and others had any youth appeal. Trumbull, who also broadcast on the Pacifica station KPFA, chatted informally and played requests, usually from university students. This was KMPX's first exposure to the emerging "new community" in the city.

A Detroit deejay, Larry Miller, came to KMPX-FM to do an all-night rock program, the only rock program on the station, that became the style setter of the underground radio format. The management knew nothing about rock music—its forte was the "Portuguese Hour" or "Italian Hour"—and Miller was given considerable leeway. He chose records, asked for requests, introduced songs with the precision of a jazz announcer detailing group personnel. The jargon was "street rap" without any of the verbal acrobatics of boss jocks, in part because of the lateness of the hour. Students crammed for exams with KMPX in the background; others smoked dope. The playlist was huge in comparison to boss radio's 33 selections. Miller used 200 to 300 records by area bands, bluesmen, folksingers and poets, and whatever else seemed appropriate. The show was a success.

A year after the initiation of the Miller show, Tom Donahue joined KMPX as the program director of the first FM free-form station. The programming format embraced rock and roll, traditional folk and city blues, reggae, electronic music, and some jazz and even classical selections. "I believe music should not be treated as a group of objects to be sorted out like eggs with each category kept apart from the others, and it is exciting to discover that there is a large audience that shares that premise."[29] Donahue hired a number of his former KYA people, who compiled their own playlists. An engineering staff of women was employed. Advertising revenues rose from $3,000 a month to $25,000. In the late 1960s Donahue's evening show became the top-rated program in the Bay Area, appealing to the magic demographic 18-to-34 group. An FM show had done the impossible: getting bigger "numbers" than its AM counterparts.

The success of KMPX spawned a vast number of so-called progressive stations. In the 1970s there were an estimated 400 nationwide. One of these was KPRI-FM in San Diego, which employed Mike Harrison. Harrison called his *version* of progressivism "Album-Oriented-Rock," thus coining the acronymic term *AOR*.

For the record industry, the success of underground radio was like a breath of fresh air. An entirely new avenue for the exposure and marketing of product had been opened up. A hit single, while still the most effective catalyst for fame, was no longer the *only* way to break an act. The success of Warner/Reprise in the late 1960s is attributed by many of its executives as being directly connected to the rise of free-form radio. Warner/Reprise originally was an easy-listening album label with nearly 80 percent of its catalog represented by Dean Martin, Frank Sinatra, Petula Clark, Trini Lopez, and Peter, Paul and Mary. These artists rarely broke into the exalted *Billboard* winners' circle. When Warner/Reprise moved into youth music, its reliance on albums did not change. Singles were taken from albums rather than the other way around. Consequently, as an album label the company greatly benefited from free-form radio, which stressed the specialty album as opposed to the Top 40 single. Indeed, the alternative medium established Warner/Reprise as the company with the "hot hand" in the late 1960s. Other companies were equally delighted with the shift away from the dominant-singles emphasis of AM radio. A Columbia Records executive said:

> Thank God for underground FM stations because that's given an outlet for the artist who wouldn't be played on Top 40 or might not get broken on Top 40. One saving light on the horizon. But again, the Top 40 stations are in the position the buyer is in. If they've got, in the case of KHJ, 300 singles to choose from in one week, obviously if they're only going to be able to add 3-4 singles to their playlist that week, and if there's a new Santana or a new Bob Dylan or new Chicago, those are the ones that are going to be the first shot.

Although underground radio had in fact liberalized and opened up playlists and allowed deejays to get away from the "Drake clock," the freedom of this idiom has been an issue since the advent of KMPX.

In March 1968 Tom Donahue and Milan Melvin resigned from KMPX, beginning a long strike and facilitating the emergence of KSAN as a major free-form station. Besides money, a major issue was artistic freedom. The strikers accused the Crosby-Pacific Broadcasting Corporation, which had taken over ownership of the station, of interference. Melvin claimed he had been asked to cut his shoulder-length hair if he wished to be station manager. He chose to strike. A deejay was told not to play classical cuts longer than five minutes so as to maintain program balance. Other complaints centered upon the banning of some songs from airplay, such as "The Pusher" by Steppenwolf and "Parchment Farm" by Blue Cheer.

Meanwhile, in New York Murray "The K" was fired from his free-form show on WOR-FM. The reason was the takeover of the station by the Drake Syndicate. Murray asserted, "The music's back in the hands of the people who don't care. There's no personality on the air and the station is developing a routine and a format."[30] The Drake takeover did, indeed, raise WOR ratings, a fact many Top 40 program directors cite any time liberalization of playlists is hinted at. The assertion that the progressive format has taken on the rigidity of boss radio has considerable merit. Some FM stations have replicated to the last decibel the original KMPX and KSAN sound. After purchase of KSAN by Metromedia, a large conglomerate and communications network, its philosophy was employed in Philadelphia, New York, and other major cities.

A 1972 *New York Times* survey indicated that a considerable standardization of the progressive format had taken place. In some cases the stations had reverted to boss radio. The major catalysts for the decline of free form was the so called Love network on the ABC-FM chain. Love stations were supplied with tapes and radio spots produced in New York. The show for the affiliates was anchored by Brother John, who read poetry and introduced records, certified by trade magazines, over a 24-hour period. All seven FM affiliates instituted this policy and program directors dictated the playlists and the time that certain records were to be played. A network vice-president commented, "We feel that in the last year [1971] there has been a major shift among young people away from radicalism and esotericism."[31] A record-company executive sadly noted, "The free-form stations are nonexistent with the exception of two or three: KMET here [Los Angeles], WBCN in Boston. There are not very many others that I can think of that are either profitable or visible. So it isn't going to change." Pete Fornatale, an FM jock in New York, wrote: "Progressive commercial radio in the United States is a myth. As long as broadcasting remains wed to financial concerns, the idea of a totally committed radio . . . is absurd."[32] The free-form policies of the latter half of the 1960s were rapidly disappearing, other than on college stations.

Allen Shaw, then president of ABC-FM, after a brief fling at free form, introduced his version of the "Drake clock." The Shaw formula was to create a playlist of preselected songs taken from charts, oldies, and cuts from successful albums, which are then inserted into a timetable like the "Drake clock." The deejays are tightly controlled and monitored. They are told to say, "Hi, this is. . . ." Shaw explained, "It's good radio principles: little DJ talk, careful spot placement, call-letter frequency, weather. . . . The jingles are not a limitation." The selection of the playlist of ABC-FM is done in a way quite similar to the boss radio formula:

> We operate on two premises: certain recording artists are more popular than others. Two, a station can choose to present the new, less popular music to a segment of an audience or present only the more popular—without reproducing Top 40. We've been accused of turning into an FM Top 40. What's wrong with it? If that's what people want, then there should be one station in town to do that.[33]

This formula was described as the "Chinese menu," that is, one song comes from an album, another from the *Billboard* chart, another from the oldies list. Obviously AM programmers had gotten the progressive message, but were not willing to go the "prog-rock" route. Album cuts without proven "Hot-100" appeal remained the purview of their FM counterparts.

AM radio was affected by the rise of the progressive stations and by the move away from the free form. A rather typical reaction by AM programmers has been to dismiss the progressive format, as did George Wilson of the Bartell broadcasting chain, which had number-one rated stations in Milwaukee and San Diego until Ron Jacobs came to town. Wilson refused to play album cuts on his Top 40 stations, arguing that LP cuts "lose ratings for you." "People who're into album cuts . . . aren't into Top 40 radio," which he believes commands a greater market.[34] He cited the statistic that only the 18-to-24 age group listens to progressive.

Probably a vast majority of AM popular-music program directors concur with Wilson's sentiments. Don Armstrong, a veteran broadcaster, wholly agrees. Having worked in the southern, midwestern, and Canadian markets, Armstrong believes the audience is "unhip" and desires familiar material. "You can't keep an audience with new material unless they're locked in a building. People don't know what they like, they like what they know. They know those songs that you can hum, sing, whistle, tap your foot to, preferably all four.

### Jacobs Again

To cope with the advent of FM programming, many stations in major markets have begun to play a limited number of cuts from successful albums. The degree of album infiltration into playlists varies and is difficult to ascertain. Even Bill Drake has incorporated some LP material if it has been successful on other stations. The most elaborate attempt was under way at KGB-AM and FM in San Diego, where Ron Jacobs was program director in 1972.

Unlike George Wilson, Jacobs contended that Top 40 stations were getting an increasingly smaller share of the radio audience. To verify his contention he commissioned interviews with over 3,000 local residents regarding musical tastes, radio listening hours, and station preference. Jacobs and the KGB staff used the findings to devise a system in which records circulate around a sequence. To illustrate, "Bridge over Troubled Water" is accorded equal acceptance at any time because it appeals to all listeners, and other songs belong to categories that are played only at specific times of the day. Tempo, length of record, age of song, all are correlated with a projected audience. A track of down-tempo rock by Black Sabbath six minutes or longer, for example, can be programmed in the late-night hours when the dominant listeners are high school and college students.

KGB started playing 1,400 titles on the criteria of a time-style-audience correlation, and in December 1972 was up to approximately 3,000. The mathematical possibilities are immense, compared to the 33 songs that originally were the foundation of the Drake playlist at KHJ. Jacobs observed, "In May 1972 we've put 300 [songs] on since we started and I don't know where we're going to end up. All I know is we have the capacity for

10,000 titles in there." In 1974, when it was playing all of the shortest cuts—2.5 to 3 minutes—KGB broadcast 2,700 songs a week. Jacobs adds, the station was as "free form as a roulette wheel." The formula basically consisted of the organization of time and music.

Jacobs made two major alterations after several months of broadcasting, again departing from tradition. After evaluating listener feedback, he decided that "fifties rock singles" in many instances could not be handled compatibly with more contemporary material. Disregarding the sanctity of golden oldies, KGB eliminated a large portion of the oldies from the playlists so as to focus on "progressive oldies." The sacred repetition of current favorites also was changed, limiting the frequency of airplay for Top 40 material. The belt shifted to older familiar album cuts mixed with current fare; the playlist retained the 2,000 plus items.

Jacobs's belt was a new concept that fed upon, as well as violated, established broadcasting edicts. The all-pervasive "they like what they know" was scientifically documented in a computer storage bank. All tastes could be accommodated, while appealing to the most desirable groups. In fact, the demographic conveyor belt was a sophisticated extrapolation of the Top 40 system *minus* many of the shortcomings of laid-back FM or relaxed FM programming. The rich panorama of the system, encompassing the 18-through-34 age brackets and older brackets, did increase the quantity and quality of the playlist. Hypothetically, the audience could be increased by expanding the time parameters. The cutoff point was measured by the early 1950s when rock and roll was born.

The potentialities of the Jacobs belt for radio programming were revolutionary, but record-company promotion directors, who disliked Jacobs for his tight playlist at KHJ, viewed this innovation with mixed emotions. The opening up of any AM playlist would appear to be a welcome development; however, Jacobs really successfully pushed categories into the background. He plays music, not charted singles. The acceptance of this blueprint, in an industry oriented toward trends, as is radio broadcasting, could have challenged the sacrosanct notions of chart security as well as the future of the single. The elimination of the single could shatter the "singles-make-stars" dictum, one of the few cardinal tenets of faith in the industry. On 13 December 1972 the first ARB figures since the conveyor belt began to roll appeared. Jacobs won the ratings battle over Wilson's Top 40 singles approach. In radio, being number one is the name of the game. Jacobs wrote: "KGB really scored in the exact areas we've been shooting for! So right on it's scary! . . . Ten months of doing something 'weird' that nobody outside our trip believed." The impact of KGB's ratings climb was impressive in light of the competing stations.

Jacobs format was too sophisticated for most AM programmers, and Wilson's views prevailed despite the numbers in the San Diego market. AM would continue the Top 40 journey, with even more conservative "power" rotations of 14 to 18 songs.

Jacobs returned to Honolulu and after several ventures became the morning man on KKUA-AM. He said, "I'm now in the best place I've ever been. I enjoy what I'm doing more than I ever have."[35] FMers were not quite so indifferent. Perhaps it was no coincidence a San Diego competitor would coin the term *AOR* to describe a mode of operation that took on many of the characteristics of the "conveyor" belt.

### Album-Oriented Rock (AOR) and Contemporary Hits Radio (CHR)

The genesis of album-oriented rock (AOR) is not difficult to trace because most radio historians appear to agree on its roots: free-form or progressive FM. *The Radio Format Conundrum* states: "The term 'prog-rock' . . . [made] way for the term 'Album Oriented Rock' (AOR). The style of the plan didn't change basically, but the demographic base was broadened due mainly to 'mass audience' stations picking up on the popularizing some of the artists and groups previously aired only by the prog-rock stations."[36] In simpler language, the authors were generously crediting the free-form or progressive format with (AOR). Jack McDonough is more direct:

> All formats known collectively today as "AOR" are descendents of the experimental programming done in 1967 and 1968 at stations KMPX-FM and KSAN-FM by the "Father Of FM Radio," Tom Donahue, . . . who proved conclusively that there was a new young audience thirsting for a style of radio that would dispense with routine and that would stack together music from the most widely varied sources.[37]

Mike Harrison, then of KPRI-FM (San Diego) is generally credited with coining the term *AOR* in the early 1970s. Harrison is not specific as to the original meaning of *AOR*:

> Album Oriented Rock was neutral, objective and semantically open-ended. . . . Perhaps the most significant common denominator that existed between the diverse factions of AOR during those initial growth years was their unanimous aversion to being perceived as top Forty. . . . [When] AOR first popped up on the scene, it represented a coalition of programming directing and not any one "format" per se.

The nonsingles, heavy rotation approach exhibited two basic formats that Harrison calls "loose" and "tight." "Loose" no doubt refers to the offering of stations such a Donahue's KSAN (San Francisco) as opposed to the tighter structure of Burkhart/Abrams "superstars" programmed by some FMers across the country. Unfortunately Harrison's exposition lacks the clarity or specificity of Storz's or Drake's broadcasting philosophies. (This may explain the nearly useless definitions found in numerous books dealing with broadcasting.)

Since Donahue, Harrison, and others, a myriad of AOR variations have emerged. Harrison writes, "The term 'AOR radio' which has been a commonly used umbrella term in industry jargon since the early '70s, represents an extremely wide diversity of format and philosophical approaches."[38] "Album-oriented" broadcasting is characterized as stressing "group sounds, although some vocalists qualify."[39] This simplistic definition misses the freedom, however limited, in AOR, the "pie chart" that allows for "all" things *if they* fit the demographic.

Morning drive time involves the Doors, Beatles, Prince, and of course Michael Jackson. The traditional "cookie cutting" segment ten to two o'clock stresses softer cuts, especially "Stairway to Heaven"; three to six o'clock is heavy metal time, when deejays are permitted a certain degree of freedom selecting which Quiet Riot or Ratt cut they will play. Some pie charts have more rigidity, again restricting the discretion of the programmer. Consultants frequently will disallow a record even if it is popular in an adjunctive market. One exasperated deejay said, "'X' is hot but Burkhart/Abrams won't let us play it."

A premier illustration of the utilization of the "pie chart" was New York's legendary WPLJ-FM during the latter half of the 1970s. WPLJ in 1978 enjoyed a weekly cumulative of some 1.7 million listeners in the nation's most competitive market. It originally gained its reputation as a free-form giant rivaling Donahue's KSAN, but in 1971 it was structured. The approach worked. The mix was oldies wedded to 30 to.40 cuts from highly charted albums. The WPLJ jocks had some 1,000 titles to choose from; "Stairway to Heaven" was the most requested. Program director Larry Berger explained:

> The DJ knows he has to play a certain number of this and a certain number of that, and that there are certain ingredients which go into the mix, but he doesn't have it all decided for him. There is no way to get the music mix to sound right if it isn't done that way. It isn't all done by computer, and it's mathematical only to a point. But the jock is the extra ingredient that makes it all fit.[40]

When Berger discusses the proper mix he is discussing certain sounds at certain times. This is the essence of a pie chart. Pie charts vary as much as

AOR formats. There are color codes, numerical systems, and alphabetical designations. They all involve some type of rotation with varying degrees of freedom for the deejay.

One of the most successful approaches was the Burkhart and Abrams "Superstars" format. "One of our first big hits was with the superstars on WYSP-FM [Philadelphia]. It was an instant smash there," says Burkhart. He defined the format as "taking superstars like Fleetwood Mac and the Eagles and playing them over and over. There is little repetition because it is the artist being programmed rather than a particular record and we can go back and pick out a lot of their older material."[41]

AOR in the eighties has reflected the political mood of the country: increased conservatism. "It's switching to the right," says Lee Abrams, "and I would say that from a musical standpoint, the fanaticism as far as the instrumental characteristics is dying down. Several years ago people were much more conscious of different bass players and great guitar licks and all that, and now people tend to be more into songs and not techniques."[42] The result of the conservative tide has been the rise of several variations that harken back to the days of Top 40, which is experiencing a rebirth on AM radio. Its FM counterpart is contemporary hits radio (CHR), and Burkhart and Abrams have brought out "Superstars II."

There are factors transcending political conservatism fueling the formats of the 1980s. The population is growing older and music videos have captured a large portion of the teen base. The correlation between the factors and CHR, and even AOR and MTV is striking.

John Leader, a columnist for *Radio and Records* popularized the acronym *CHR.* In a column titled "It's Contemporary Hit Radio" he declared

> Top 40 radio has grown into something more. The format is the best defined as radio that reflects the life-style of a youth-oriented society. . . . We have made the decision, with your input, to change the name of this particular section of *R&R* from Top Forty to Contemporary Hit Radio. If you want to call it CHR, that's up to you . . . [CHR] is simply a broader umbrella under which all of us can come together.

Billy Mitchell, then a CHR music director, said, "CHR is a euphemism for Top 40." It was a term scaring away advertisers, for Top 40 was viewed as targeting only the 12-plus audience. Mitchell used a Top 40 format, adding six to eight "new and upcoming hits that soon will be on the Top 40." It employed what in radio jargon is called a "power rotation"; The higher a song's chart number, the heavier or more frequent the repetition.

Tipster Bill Gavin rejected the term *CHR,* preferring to stick with the older term, *Top 40.* A number of broadcasters object to the Storz designation, suggesting that many so-called Top 40 outlets feature playlists with fewer than twenty titles. Several others indicate that the late Gavin's stance was tied to the reported "father of 'Hot Hits,'" consultant Mike Joseph in Westport, Connecticut. (Some believe that Gavin's unhappiness stemmed from Joseph's claim that "The 'big 30' was played on KPOA, . . . which featured a countdown of the top tunes 7-10 p.m. nightly, just *before* Bill Gavin's 'Lucky Lager Dance Time.'" "Dance Time" helped establish Gavin's reputation and facilitated his influential tipsheet, *The Report*.[43] Gavin died in February 1985 after a long illiness.)

In a rare interview the reclusive Joseph told a reporter, "I spent six months planning, than tendered my resignation [from KPOA, Honolulu] . . . to become a 'program consultant,' which was a term I invented."[44] Joseph was rated as the fifth-most-widely-used consultant in the nation as of the 1982 *Radio Only* report.[45] The 1984 *Radio and Records* "Consultants Report Card" found Joseph dropping out of the top-ten listing. Veteran broadcasting observer Claude B. Hall partially explains Joseph's controversial persona: "He may have done many original things in radio, [but] oddly enough his influence on other program directors has only been slight, perhaps because he was never eager to talk about his philosophies."[46] He generally refuses to be photographed or to speak to most members of the press; however when he does grant an interview, feathers get quickly ruffled.

CHR is one of the most utilized formats of the 1980s, although AOR still grips the FM rock music ratings in most major markets. Radio doctor Dwight Douglas of the Burkhart/Abrams consortium noted that although "CHR is the oldest contemporary format . . . it's still very hot." Moreover, "CHR is a viable alternative to a Beautiful Music format. It's an excellent way to get the station back on the map, and put the bottom line in better shape. You can look toward a 'soft hits' or 'Magic' format approach if you wish, but if you aren't considering CHR then you're being rather short-sighted." WRQN-FM (Toledo) proved Douglas's point. Adopting the CHR format in August 1983, the station moved within an audience share point of the top-ranked AOR outlet in Toledo, WIOT. Ironically, WIOT is a Burkhart/Abrams client. A WRON spokesperson said: "We're at the point now where we're ready to run for that number-one spot. I am confident. The staff is confident. The owners are confident that we are going to make a good mark for the number one position. We were eighth . . . today we're second." WRON has little disagreement with Douglas's view that "the hottest format on the streets today is the Hot Hits concept."[47] (WRON's success was short-lived; the 1984 fall sweeps found it losing a significant audience share in the northwest Ohio market.)

Although exhibiting some of the basic characteristics of the Storz/McLendon Top 40 motif of the mid-1950s, CHR does feature some adaptations. The target audience is the magic 18-to-34 age group, not totally 12-plus. The CHR frequently begins with a teen base, usually derived from MTV viewers. "Then," as one programmer stated, "mom and dad start listening to it, or brother and older sister, and then it gradually goes up." One observer suggested, "The success of CHR seems to be tied to the music of the 1980s. Soundtracks such as *Footloose, Flashdance,* and *Eddie and the Cruisers* have scored big, not to mention Michael Jackson, Prince, and also Lionel Richie. Adults as well as adolescents can appreciate the music. Now if CHR were to go XTC or some of the heavier stuff, that would be a totally different story." Billy Mitchell: "The *Footloose* soundtrack—that movie was a monster. The album had five or six huge singles on it." Prince's *Purple Rain* film score is enjoying a similar fate. The role of soundtracks and their significance to CHR is not dissimilar to that of *Grease* or *Saturday Night Fever* in the late 1970s. The question for broadcasters and the record labels is, will these diverse soundtracks have greater durability than the Stigwood offerings?

CHR's success appears partially tied to trends in music video and cable. Jeffrey Lyons of PBS's "Sneak Previews" indicated vidclips sold movies and the soundtracks. Norman Hunter, of the 152-store Record Bar chain, said, "Cable exposure of movies has the potential to sell more soundtracks than theatre exposure. It presents an easy opportunity for more people to see a film in a month than see it in a year in theatres." *Eddie and the Cruisers,* a box-office disaster, when aired on the pay cable networks jumped in sales from 12 units at Record Bar to over 4,500 within a month.[48] Other sources credit cable with the tremendous success of *Flashdance* and *Footloose.* One cynic stated, "*The Footloose* video clip was better than the entire movie." The music video battle between MTV and its competitors on "exclusives" could impact on CHR by fragmenting the radio audience, as has occurred with AOR.

As Stigwoood, Col. Parker, MCA, and some others have discovered, relying on film scores to promote record sales can be risky business. Conversely, in 1985 it would be foolish to attempt to predict exactly what the impact of cable music video will be on radio formats and record sales.

In the fall of 1982, Lee Abrams reintroduced "Superstars II" or "Timeless Rock" on KFOG-FM (San Francisco), formerly a beautiful music broadcaster. Unlike the AOR outlets of the past decade, Abrams was going directly after the 25-through-34 target audience. The format, again classic cuts from the 1960s complemented by some current material, such as the Stray Cats' "Rock This Town." Burkhart calls this direction "Repetitive refrains, over and over. Instead of having to work to listen to it, you can move into it really quickly, you feel comfortable with it."[49] This fits into his view of the overt sociocultural conservatism of the radio audience.

Harrison's ambiguity in defining AOR in the 1980s has considerable validity. "Remember," he asks "when there were AOR stations and top 40 stations? Today, even the top 40s have become AORish"[50] A glance at the *Radio and Records* chart finds little differentiation between most of the rock formats. Deejay Billy Mitchell says, "The top ten AOR songs [in *Radio and Records*] were . . . also the top ten CHR songs."

AOR programmers are increasingly picking album cuts that are simultaneously hit singles. Probably the major cleavage between AOR and CHR is historicism: AOR will go back several decades for airable material; one CHR music director flatly stated no record older than a year will be aired on his station. Another difference, according to Mitchell:

> Now when the album gets in, we're not going to touch it until there's another hit off it. Whereas an AOR station, they are going to go through, they are going to select the tracks that are simply rockers, and they are going to play those. We could play those tracks very easily, but that gets away from the format of hits. Now AOR radio plays a lot of hits. They also play a lot of obscure album tracks that have never been hits and never will be. That's the difference between the two formats.

Rock radio appears to have come almost full circle from the days of Storz and McLendon with their rotations and familiar oldies. Even the scientifically oriented Burkhart/Abrams advertised, "We were there with Todd and Gordon in the beginning. We were there last book . . . and we'll be there next book . . . 30 years, 3 generations . . . whatever you call it . . . we've been doing it. Proven."

A *Billboard* survey of eleven major markets in the fall of 1983 found CHR or variations on Top 40 leading in ARBs in nearly 40 percent of the regions sampled. "Top 40 has returned—in a big way," wrote Rollye Bornstein.[51] Los Angeles, Cleveland, Boston, and Houston were dominated by the old format. "AOR looked so good for so long because Top 40 sounded so bad. Now the pendulum has swung the other way, but don't write us off," said Mike Harrison, now at KMET-FM (Los Angeles). "AOR built its numbers by playing mass appeal rock," said Milwaukee's Lee Arnold, "but management seems to have forgotten that. Our listeners certainly know what they like—mainstream rock with a metal edge, not Culture Club. We just have to stick to our guns." Larry Berger of WPLJ went CHR, in turn explaining, "Everybody liked Led Zeppelin ten years ago. Today there are so many combinations of who people like and who they don't that it was obvious we couldn't make money programming to just one subdivision." Even Lee Abrams began to tinker with the "Superstars II" format, urging more "horizontal" records. "They've been afraid to play the hits, and we can't shut them out anymore," he said. Vertical cuts are from albums and are the foundation of "Superstars." "Familiarity means the sound of an artist is more important than the specific song."[52]

Going into 1984, CHR and AOR programmers were optimistic. Scott Shannon, a CHRer, noted, "The acts that will probably gain momentum are those with the potential to cross formats, such as Hall & Oates and Prince, and those that maintain a major presence on MTV."[53] AORers saw a cross-fertilization of the two formats. "There's been a snobbery on the part of a lot of AOR programmers toward pop material," observed WNEW-FM's Charlie Kendell, "and I think it's put a lot of them in the position they're in today. Some AOR stations have always played a lot of hits and as a result haven't suffered greatly in the ratings." Mike Harrison: "I see a coming together in '84 and '85 of those tracks that went off in different directions in the late '70s."[54] The differences between the formats exist. Some observers, like Harrison, feel the CHR model may become as oversaturated as AOR once was. However, in the middle 1980s the cleavage is much less marked. In 1985 AOR appears to be making a strong comeback, as Harrison and others predicted.

### The Radio Doctors; The Consultants

The *Wall Street Journal* defines radio doctors as consultants "who try to fix formats to draw more listeners and advertisers." Kent Burkhart is succinct: "We make sick stations well." "The consultant is like a doctor. He writes a prescription and leaves. His station may or may not follow his suggestions as closely as they should, and if the ratings fall the consultant gets the blame," commented Wayne Cornils, radio vice-president of the National Association of Broadcasters (NAB).[55]

The radio doctor may cure the maladies of a station, and may also provide a security blanket. Programmers can blame the consultant for low ratings or tell a record label, "My consultant won't let me play this!" In light of the structural problems of the late 1970s and early 1980s, it is not surprising that radio doctors, regardlesss of cost, have become the "in" thing.

Mike Joseph has repeatedly asserted he "invented the business of radio program consulting" in January of 1958 when his first station WMAX (Grand Rapids) rose from sixth in market share to the top-rated position with the introduction of a Top 40 format. "I do a tailored job and go into low-rated, sick facilities with good potential—and solve the problems on the scene," he told a reporter.[56] Then Joseph treated some outlets of Capitol Cities, a relatively small chain in the Northeast. In 1960 he worked on WABC in New York, where he opted for a long playlist based on the 770 dial position. According to Russ Sklar, "There were seventy records, seven

hit albums, seven soaring singles, seven sure-shot albums, and a sleeper."
He also shook up the staff, hiring "Cousin Bruce" Morrow and Big Dan
Ingram among others. "The station began to develop a distinctive sound,"
writes Sklar. Since that time Joseph had doctored at least 60 more stations.[57] (WABC was one of the most important Top 40 stations in the latter
part of the 1960s and early 1970s. In March 1982 the AM giant adopted an
"all-talk" format.) Joseph, as noted, rarely has received the historical credit
he appears to deserve, although some observers suggest the wound is self-
inflicted.

Bill Drake was *the* consultant of the 1960s, guiding the RKO radio network and its affiliates including KHJ-AM (Los Angeles) when Jacobs created the boss sound. Ironically, Drake and Joseph claim credit for
innovating the "Top 30" playlist used by the station. Every success has
many parents, as someone observed, failures are orphans.

Drake and his partner Gene Chenault stressed "top DJ's, more music
and less clutter." The "shut-up-and-play-the-music" approach became the
so-called Drake syndrome. Time, temperature, and the song titles were the
responsibility of the DJ. Drake-Chenault did the station promotions. Based
on the KHJ experience, the pair went into syndication. By the 1980s they
serviced over 250 stations nationwide, and they continue to consult. In
1982 *Radio Only* listed their firm as the sixth in the top 10 national radio-
program consultants. Despite their numbers, consultants' success rate is
mixed. "There just aren't that many great programmers in the country, the
real turn-around programmers. There are maybe 19 really good ones" said
a leading consultant.

Joseph was probably the first cruncher of market numbers in the consulting business. The philosophy was to match the format to the demographics of the market: "You can't be original with music, but you can with
everything else—sound, techniques, promotion and news."[58] Kent Burkhart and Lee Abrams took the formula to a hi-tech level and in the process
established themselves as the nation's leading consulting firm. Both began
their careers in the music industry at an early age. Burkhart had a 15-
minute radio show in Texas when he was ten years old. In Chicago Abrams
"managed" rock bands prior to entering his teens.

Burkhart worked radio stations while he was in college, and upon gradu-
ation decided to create a "mini-empire of stations." His first acquisition
was KTXL (San Angelo, Texas), which he sold after a year. Moving to
Atlanta, Burkhart became PD at WQXI-AM. The station was acquired by
Pacific & Southern Broadcasting, and he became its radio division president. He was removed from the post in 1972, and was hired by now-cable-
mogul Ted Turner to consult for WGOW-AM (Chattanooga). His client list
rapidly expanded to 20, and in 1973 Lee Abrams became his partner.

The Abrams biography is not dissimilar. During his school days he was a part-time programming assistant at WQAM-AM (Miami). Hal Neal of the ABC network appointed him program director at WRIF-FM (Detroit), an AOR station in a highly competitive market. While at the AOR outlet he consulted at WQDR, a Raleigh, North Carolina, station. Rumor has it the Detroit station objected to Abrams's outside activities and he was discharged. WQDR was a success and reportedly put Abrams on the road to radio doctoring.

Burkhart and Abrams evolved the "Superstar" format for AOR, which put their Atlanta-based firm on the broadcasting map. "The basic Superstar format," according to Burkhart/Abrams vice-president Jon B. Sinton, "targeted the male 16-34 market. Females were tied to Adult Contemporary [A/C] or 'soft rock' stations." Psychographically, the "Superstar" format was for "individuals for whom Top 40 is too Teen/Juvenile—repetitive; A/C is too soft for them." He continued, "The 25-34 group is the core. They are the *Big Chill* generation. They got into radio during Top 40's mid-60's hey-day. . . . They longed for a station that played the Byrds, Stones, Beatles, Who, and Led Zeppelin *without* the Carpenters, Bobby Sherman." The format was a blend of the old with the new. It worked. "In the beginning we had to go out and knock on some doors, but now we don't do that. We let the business pretty much come to us," says Abrams.[59]

In the summer of 1978 Burkhart altered WKTU-FM (New York) from an adult-contemporary, or "soft"-rock, station to "Disco 92." Compiling a list of 150 "all-time" disco hits, the consultant created a top-rated station in the market. "We wanted the listener to feel as if he or she'd just walked into a disco club," he told a reporter. "It is all dance music. We don't include any slower cuts at all. We didn't program 'Three Times A Lady.'"

In the next ARB book WKTU-FM enjoyed the highest ratings or numbers in Gotham.[60] Nationally a myriad of stations stampeded to copy the format. "When WKTU got a 14 share, there was a lemming reaction to the disco format. That lasted a year or less. You have to be discriminating," said Alan Burns of QIOT in Washington, D.C.[61] Many would live to regret the precipitous format change. The demographics of the nation's largest metropolitan area were quite different from, say, Toledo or Dayton, Ohio. Toledo's WMHE-FM is only now recovering its market share.

Burkhart programs "just about everything except all-polka, including Top 40, country, MOR, contemporary 40 (aimed at an audience older than for Top 40) [CHR], some Spanish stations and AOR." His research techniques include a survey in which record-store customers fill out a card stating which record they bought and their name and phone number. "We call them about a week later and ask them how they like the album and which cuts they like best. We'll call about 5,000 a week." The Atlanta firm also has panels consisting of 500 people in three cities, Madison, Columbus, and Baton Rouge, who grade records. Burkhart claims a prediction ratio of nearly 95 percent.[62] Abrams elaborates:

> We have done several different forms of research over the years. One is the call back card—that's amazingly valuable. At about 700 or 800 record stores every week, you distribute these little cards, and whenever anybody buys a record, they fill out their name, age, phone number, the record they bought and put it in the box. And at the end of the week, the music director in that market would select a box filled with cards and send them back to us. We would then have a record of thousands of people who bought any given album. Let's say a Fleetwood Mac album comes out on January 1; by January 7, we have called back thousands of people who bought the album to find out the demographic spectrum of the record, the favorite song, what they don't like about it.
>
> We'd find amazing things. We'd find exactly which cuts sold the album, exactly the right one or two songs to play, and we'd also find that although an album might sell, all people were really interested in was the stereo version of the single.
>
> As this record recession continued, that study is actually more important. People may buy only one record, but we can call back and ask them.
>
> "O.K., if you had the money, what are three or four other records you might want?" So we can find out popular music that may not be selling because of the economic conditions or whatever.
>
> We also do massive distributions of questionnaires. One in particular is distributed year after year—about a million of them every year, all around the country—asks such simple, straightforward questions as: What are your favorite groups. What are your favorite songs? Every year we do a tabulated response sheet and put together a graph for any song or artist. Take the group, Chicago. We look back at the graph and we see that in 1970 they had 85,000 responses as the favorite group. By 1974 it went down to about 30,000. By 1978 to 6,000. And now it's 2,000 and so forth. So if you want to know, right now, where Chicago stands, you pull out the graph and the results are all there, including demographics, by city.
>
> That information continues to multiple. We find out which artists are trending up, which are trending down, so we can get a good handle on exactly what music styles are happening. For example, in the last four or five years we've seen a dramatic decline in singer/song-writers in popularity. So now we have a pretty good idea that that style of music really isn't happening much any more. About three years ago we saw a real boom in orchestral rock—groups like Styx, Kansas and those kinds of groups started trending way up.
>
> And then we do a lot of promotional surveys to find out exactly where people are at, particularly with the superstars format. It's very important to know about the 18-24 age group, for example. The older we get, the more difficult it is to get a handle on how that group thinks.[63]

Burkhart/Abrams services some 150 stations. The clients are charged from $1,000 to $6,000 a month on the basis of market size. Major markets such as New York and Cleveland pay the largest amount. Burkhart justified the cost, saying, "We walked into a station in New York that lost $2 million a year for 10 years. We changed the station, changed its call letters, put a whole new front on it, and the station went to a $2 million operating profit. Was that worth $5,000 a month? The answer has to be yes."[64] The formula appears to be working because in 1981 six of the top-rated AOR stations nationally were Burkhart/Abrams clients. Burkhart/Abrams is not without critics. Larry Berger of WPLJ charged Abrams with "stealing the ABC format and selling it to other stations. . . . He's picked everything out of the air. It's all nonsense that 2,000 songs are researched."[65] One observer suggested that this was a "case of sour grapes" in that AOR formats tended to be fairly similar.

Some programmers believe that consultants in general are too conservative and are losing the feel for the music. Abrams once admitted to being "almost a year late" on Duran Duran, Stray Cats, and MTV star Billy Idol. One of the most severe attacks came from the pen of Mike Harrison:

> A majority of these radio doctors are the industry's prime peddlers of research . . . most of which invariably proves to the client station that he needs precisely the kind of programming that the consultant specializes in. Seems these consultants have made both an art and big business of the old game of selling gut level decisions to management via research. As a result of all this, many of today's younger programmers actually believe that research is a magic substitute for their own cultural ignorance and artistic impotence. It can never be a substitute for individual human experience, intuition and most important, taste.[66]

The reintroduction of Abrams's "Superstars II" or "Timeless Rock" (Jon Sinton: "this format is for the *Big Chill* generation as well. . . . It is pure . . . it does not pander to the fads; it does not promote particularly heavily; it does not run contests. . . . Females are as likely to appreciate its uncommercial feel as much as males."), and advertisers' demographic demands caused one prominent PD, Rick Caroll of KROQ-FM (Los Angeles) to defend the 12-plus audience that is demographically discounted by consultants and advertisers: "Those are the people who go to concerts, buy the records and actively participate in the radio station. If you neglect them, how can you have future growth?"[67] Some call it "franchised radio." Burkhart responds, "Well, McDonald's sells a lot of hamburgers so I'll accept them."[68]

### Tip Sheets

Charted material gets airplay because it is on the charts. If this sounds like catch 22, it is. Many record programmers will "get behind a record" only on material that has already proved itself successful. A midwestern program director proudly announced that his station had *never* broken or introduced a new record to his audience. He played only songs listed in the Top 30 slots on the *Billboard* charts. Others augment the safety of trade charts with the "bibles" or tip sheets.

The two most widely read and used tip sheets are the *Gavin Report* and Kal Rudman's *Friday Morning Quarterback.* Subscribers pay $200 and more annually for the multicolored mimeographed twenty-one pages of selections by Rudman's knowledgeable gentlemen. Four hundred stations pay $245 for the *Gavin Report* and in turn receive a slick 41-page magazine containing a "smash of the week" and other songs labeled as "hot shots" or "sleepers to watch," as well as a recommended playlist. *Report* also provides a list of Gavin's top 20 and an equal number of "hit bounds" compiled from 200 national correspondents who are mostly record people. *Gavin Report* is *the* sheet by tradition, due to the former editor's reputation for honesty. *Friday Morning Quarterback* rivals *Report* for dominance in the tip-sheet market. It includes on its front page a list of hit picks similar to the others. Many programmers, although subscribers, have some doubts about Rudman's dual role of chart picker and record promoter. There are obvious conflicts of interest. Rudman accepts paid promotional material for *Quarterback,* Gavin did not. In 1984 *Report* included industry advertising; one business agent told a reporter, "It puts some people off."[69] Rudman is perhaps no less honest than others, but his credibility is somewhat tarnished in some quarters. An anonymous record-company executive told *Rock* magazine, "Rudman can be bought."[70] In a business where jobs depend on being first, this sentiment explains why many PDs prefer Rudman's "money-music" style.[71] To the record companies, the PD clutching a *Billboard* chart in one hand and a tip sheet in the other is nearly a lost cause, but they must continue to court him, for the trades and tip sheets rarely do justice to their voluminous output of product.

Tipsters are informal and inexpensive format consultants, and their two weekly newsletters parallel those of stock market analysts, such as Joseph Ganville. Both tip sheets are frequently as incorrect as are stock selections. Still, both provide informaton and a sense of security, sometimes shaky, for the broadcaster. As one does with consultants, one finds it is easy to blame Gavin or Rudman for "pick" failures.

There is a less legitimate methodology at work in the shaping of playlists, particularly "picks": the age-old practice of payola and drugola.

### Drugola?

Paul Ackerman, testifying before the Harris subcommittee, attributed payola to "the abundance of product." By 1972 product had nearly tripled.

Competition was intense. Giant conglomerates were pitted against one another in the mighty battle for a "pick" slot on a major market station. Getting "next to" the program director became increasingly difficult. Joe Smith told a 1973 *Billboard* forum, "If there have been excesses [in the promotion of records], it is because this is the only way to get records played today." And in 1972 the specter of another payola scandal cast its shadow.

In 1971 Roger Karshner, a former Capitol Records vice-president, published *The Music Machine,* a book that purported to tell what "really goes on" in the record industry but that received little attention. People at Capitol dismissed Karshner's portrait of the "world of payola, loyola, flyola, hype, phony charts, phony billings, and phonies" as merely a slap at the company that fired him. Other readers thought Karshner took unusual seamy events and presented them as the norm. A year later many of his charges reached a wider audience.

In his column of 31 March 1972, syndicated journalist Jack Anderson announced, "Payola Returns to Record Industry." He charged, "We have uncovered evidence of a new payola scandal in the billion-dollar record industry. Disk jockeys and program directors across the country are provided with free vacations, prostitutes, cash, and cars as payoffs for song plugging."[72] He did not provide specific details, except to point to the soul-music market as the prime example. Record-company executives shrugged off the article.

It was an open secret that soul-market conditions were identical to those of AM popular music broadcasting in the late 1950s. Small companies were pitted against the majors for air play, and "play for pay" was not unheard of. The payoffs were now distributed in product rather than cash. Unmarked LPs were very easy to convert to cash; almost any record store was happy to pay $2.00 for a top-selling album, which wholesaled at that time for $3.40. Some black deejays eliminated the middleman and ran their own retail outlets, all in return for airplay.

Several weeks later Anderson renewed his charge. He claimed promotion men were "buying" airplay with $20-lots of marijuana. Artists were passing on pills to rock writers in return for good reviews. He concluded, "We have learned that drug-for-play promotion men buy dope in broker's lots, charging off the cost to 'routine promotion expenses.' They deal mainly in marijuana although insiders have repeatedly told us cocaine is the 'with it' drug this year in show biz."[73]

The drugola charges were not taken very seriously by industry people. One executive quipped, "We sell dope not records here." He was only half-joking. The record industry does have a tradition of drug use and abuse. Country and western singers who traveled from town to hamlet in the rural

South found that pep pills made their arduous schedules more bearable. Touring swing bands reached a similar conclusion. Heroin made its way into the industry through jazz and later rhythm and blues. Although not encouraged, drug use was tolerated as long as business was not affected. A burned-out artist was considered stupid, not morally weak.

The industry's identification with the youth movement of the 1960s made marijuana as common as booze. Many an executive could be found partaking of his rock band's "lid." Pot, and later other drugs, became very much a part of the industry life-style. Pot, in particular, was as popular with record-company people as alcohol is at General Motors. Some underground radio programmers shared this outlook, and not uncommonly a promotion man in search of airplay might offer a PD a joint or a bag. If a progressive jock was "short," a company rep might give or sell him some "dope." A minority of people in the record industry have expanded the sociability aspect of dope sharing into an avocation. Some rock bands in Los Angeles, during a layover, may moonlight by dealing.

Anderson broke the drugola story but his attention was distracted by charges of corruption in the Nixon administration and the Thomas Eagleton affair during the 1972 presidential election. On the heels of Anderson's revelations the Federal Communications Commission began an investigation of drugola. The Federal Bureau of Investigation and the Bureau of Narcotics were also called into the matter. The FCC, bitten by the "drug-lyrics" controversy was more than anxious to prove that drug use was a broadcast-industry problem. Then in the spring of 1973 the Watergate break-in and subsequent events began to dominate the news media. Headlines and televised hearings daily revealed new misdeeds in the executive branch. The *Washington Post, New York Times,* and "CBS News" took the lead in exposing aspects of the scandal, and Anderson's drugola charges were all but forgotten, or so it seemed.

The last week of May 1973 brought stories on the industry grapevine about the firing of CBS Records President Clive Davis, and his being behind bars for "dope dealing." On 30 May a *New York Times* article confirmed the dismissal; there was no mention of drug involvement, but CBS Records reportedly was charging Davis with having spent $94,000 in CBS funds for personal use and had filed suit against him.[74] The story was industry-wide disbelief. One executive told *Newsweek,* "CBS doesn't sue a Clive Davis just for $90,000. They're trying to get out of something fast."[75] Similar statements abounded. A Warner Bros. spokesman said, "A company like CBS is idiotic to bust a president of one of the major profit-making divisions for a mere hundred G. They're affecting their stock, and the entire record business."[76] In *Billboard,* the newly appointed Columbia president, Goddard Lieberson, denied the firing had anything to do with a drug scandal. Investigative reporters and industry insiders were not convinced.

David Wynshaw, CBS Records vice-president for artist relations, was fired before Davis. Wynshaw was responsible for "getting close to people"; some called him "Dr. Feelgood." Summoned before the Federal Strike Force against Organized Crime, Wynshaw reportedly told investigators of various payoffs to radio stations. He indicated CBS had become involved in payola about the time it entered the soul market two years previously with Philadelphia International Records. He also implicated Kal Rudman before the body, alleging the tipster accepted cash for reviews in his weekly tip sheet.[77]

The New York Times, Newsweek, and New York magazine, all highly regarded "investigatory" publications, carried running accounts of the unfolding scandal. Rona Barrett, the televised Hollywood gossip columnist, nightly made sensational charges without much substance. Nearly all of the material was based on the unproved notion that CBS fired Davis for payola and for supplying artists and broadcasters with drugs. Billboard editorialized that "care" be taken, for "it is still too early to ascertain how seriously the current charges of payola and other evils impugn the total industry."[78]

As during previous scandals, many record-company people, usually anonymously, took advantage of the situation to point a finger. David Clayton-Thomas, who had left Columbia after a contract dispute, repeated the charge that Davis was a sovereign over the company. He complained to the Times, "If the word went out from his office that you're on the blacklist, suddenly no one answers your phone calls. It affects your concerts, which the record company is responsible for promoting; you find yourself playing to empty houses. My royalty checks stopped coming in."[79] Others gave Davis mixed praise. He was "egocentric" but fair; he carried the company around in his back pocket. Rolling Stone said, "Columbia was his label more than he was its president." Nat Weiss, manager of a Columbia group, summed it up: "Clive had created a one-man company with press releases being written about him, and I don't think that was the best situation. But listen: We're all saddened when this kind of thing happens to any human being."[80]

The RIAA formed a committee to investigate the situation. Stories about industry links to mobsters, and more payoffs appeared in print. Still, the main question remained unresolved: Why was Davis really fired? A popular interpretation was that the record industry was a pawn in a political game. Corporate corruption could be used to draw attention away from the Watergate hearings. CBS was especially vulnerable because its television network and record division were under the same conglomerate logo.

"CBS was very concerned about being involved in a scandal," said one employee.[81] It would not do to have a network that was instrumental in exposing the "White House horrors," as former Attorney General John Mitchell called them, linked with a drug or payola scandal. Hence, the firing of Davis. In light of the original comments and Davis's success, this view possessed considerable appeal. It was reinforced in a column by Nixon partisan William Safire:

> I'd like to hear Dan Rather cross examine an official of the Bureau of Narcotics and Dangerous Drugs about what is known so far, and to watch Dan Schorr on the steps of the courthouse in Newark reporting the latest leaks from the grand jury room on the penetration of the record industry by Mafia drug peddlers.
>
> Let the journalists of CBS News cover the story of the CBS Records in depth, Mr. Paley—and after they have finished you can take a few minutes of your own for "instant analysis."[82]

The references were to reporters who were considered hostile to the White House. The following day the Justice Department intensified its probe of CBS Records. CBS News announced its own investigation of the drugola story. Senator James Buckley from New York also charged that CBS may be involved in a "massive cover-up." Senator John McClellan announced a probe into payola by the staff of the Senate Copyrights Subcommittee.[83]

Some six months after the firing of Davis and the excessive media coverage of drugola, the issue subsided somewhat. Senator Buckley read into the *Congressional Record* a paper titled "The Record Industry and the Drug Epidemic," which restated many old right-wing charges concerning drug songs. He charged that record companies were not meeting their public responsibilities by releasing such songs and allowing their artists to use drugs.

The McClellan probe did not uncover any evidence of widespread drugola or payola.[84] Its findings, however, are not the most reassuring. The conclusions of the Senate Copyrights Subcommittee were reached on the basis of a questionnaire sent out to 300 record companies. Nonetheless, the drugola and payola scandal of 1973 did not blossom into the epic proportions of 1959. The result certainly adds credibility to the arguments that Watergate may have inspired the federal investigation into CBS Records.

The drugola case dragged on in the wake of Watergate. The *New York Times* for 25 June 1975 headlined, "19 Are Indicted in Payola Cases." Six corporations were singled out; no deejays were implicated. The prosecutor claimed they had been "very co-operative." Davis, Ken Gamble, president of Arista, and Nat Tarnopol, president of Brunswick Records, were the "star" defendants. Davis was charged with $45,000 income tax evasion. Gamble was accused of meeting with company executives to arrange payments "in excess of $25,000 . . . to disc jockeys, music directors, program directors, and other radio station employees."[85] In the same issue a "think" piece appeared, "Payola Threatens Recording Profits," by Robert Lindsey.

A New Jersey jury convicted four Brunswick executives, including Tarnopol, for under-the-table payments of $350,000 in cash and albums. The story was buried on page 55 in the *Times* of 27 February 1976. Davis, the kingfish of the scandal, pleaded guilty of a failure to report $8,800 in income; the $90,000 tax evasion charge was dismissed. Gamble was fined $10,000 and continues as a major force in the record industry. A friend of Alan Freed, disgusted, asked, "Remember Alan Freed?"

Payola, drugola, or cocainola continues. It lacks the blatancy of the 1950s days of "presidents" or home appliances. Indeed, major market program directors or name "jocks" would be idiotic to jeopardize a six-figure salary for a "rock" or a hooker. "You don't think a one-night stand is going to get me fired. Do I look *that* dumb?"—to clean up the language of several nationally prominent program directors. Yet, with increasingly tight playlists and a shrinking market, rumors of payola keep bubbling up.

### Payola Revisited

In the 1980s innuendos and rumors of a resurgence of payola resurfaced. M. William Krasilovsky, a music lawyer and author of *This Business of Music*, presented an industry-wide glossary of "misbehavior." Of the twelve definitions listed, one was payola. He provided little in the way of specifics, as Stan Gortikov, the RIAA apologist, was quick to note: "If Mr. Krasilovsky wishes to halt the nefarious offenses, then let him report and identify the perpetrators."[86] Influential *Village Voice* critic Robert Christgau observed:

> Names are so hard to pin down legally that I have to keep my generalizations vague. But it seems clear that in the wake of the Great Disco Disaster of 1979 the always common-enough practice of play-for-pay—giving radio personnel money and other emoluments to put records on the air and list them in trade magazine rundowns—has mushroomed into standard operating procedure in singles promotion. The figure that's mentioned most of is $3,000 per record, although some say that's low.

*Rock and Roll Confidential*, a music journalism tip sheet, echoes the *Voice* piece. "What many suspect is happening is that record companies, or managers, are paying fees in the neighborhood of $100,000 to promo men or groups of them. The fees are then fanned out, to subordinates and programmers on the take, though no one seems to know much about how much changes hands." The unsigned article called for an investigation, "right after Santa finishes his milk and cookies."[87]

The two pieces are as close as any investigative reporters have gone public with payola charges. One Sun Belt PD summed up the situation: "You hear it's around. I haven't seen it. Everybody worried about being accused of it. I think the big stations are smart enough not to get involved at all: they don't want to get caught in it, like Watergate."[88]

Major market broadcasters are relatively well paid. In the secondary "windows" PDs annually average $24,000 to $35,000. Their positions, however, are linked to the almighty ratings. Playing a "stiff," even for $3,000, does not make economic sense. More product, rigid playlists, and consultants militate against the widely publicized practices of the late 1950s.

Rick Sklar pointed to "independent promoters" as functioning as "money conduits" in medium-sized markets. They are hired by major labels to supplement the legion of staff people discharged during the "crash of 1979." According to several accounts, they are in command of a tremendous amount of money to push a given record or artist. However, as *Rolling Stone* suggested, "Whoever is doing the paying, though—whether an independent or a label staff—it's almost certain that he's more subtle about it than his predecessors were and therefore much harder to detect."[89] Record company executives refuse to comment on the situation. One asked, "What are they doing with my money?" There are plenty of rumors that "something's happening," but no one yet has found the smoking gun.

Payola in the mid-1980s is not as widespread or lucrative as it appeared prior to the Harris subcommittee hearings. Expensive appliances and television sets in exchange for airtime are history. Still, as one broadcaster said, "It is rampant in the secondary" markets where salaries are low and FCC monitoring is almost nonexistent. (The material included in this section was obtained through interviews conducted for the author's newspaper column. The catch was that all of the information was on an "off-the-record" or even "deep-background" basis. It was agreed that no names be used; in some instances there were other restrictions. All of the material in the above was verified by more than one source.)

One radio person noted,

> In the bigger ones they have to watch their step a lot more closer than in the secondary markets. . . . In the bigger markets the broadcasting corporations are much more tightly knit. I don't think it goes on quite as much in the big ones as it does the secondary ones. I know a lot of people in the secondary ones, and they are getting the same stuff and not from the same people.

"It's very big, alive, and well," said a programmer in 1984. "Drugs, lots of drugs. . . . Girls are always big. That goes over good." Money rarely changes hands. "I was offered money once," said another broadcaster. "It wasn't a whole lot—just $50.00—but, you know, money is money." According to the respondents, payola is widespread outside the major markets.

"It surprised me because before I came into this size market, I had heard about payola and stuff like that . . . I didn't know that stuff goes on. But sure enough, first two weeks . . . I got offered anything from pot to speed to coke. They'll say, 'What is your favorite alcohol?'—beer, all kinds of stuff." This was not merely social, he went on, it was a quid pro quo. "They'll say, 'Add this record, . . . I'll give you an ounce of weed. Give me a number [playlist position] of the next week, and I'll give you a couple of grams of coke or something."

The respondents saw the independents as "real business-like. . . . The independents are even close to what the label people do, and where they get the money to buy this stuff or who they are getting it from I have no idea. All I know is that it is offered an awful lot." Independents work albums by big stars; therefore, the consensus appears to be "they don't need to" engage in drugola or offer other gratuities.

There is little if any fear of FCC sanctions by those engaging in the illegal practice, but they are nonetheless cautious. "A lot of them that offer me this stuff time and time again. I wouldn't trust them with my life. . . . It just depends on who the sources are."

Ratings, believed by many to be the ultimate deterrent to payola and drugola, do not seem to affect the practice because some view it as a game. A "brought" title is added to the official playlist, "but it's buried and played only like between midnight and 5:00 A.M., never during the morning, midday, afternoon . . . it's always overnight. Now if they ask me, lot of times, 'Hey, you playing the record?' I'll say, 'Yeah.' It's on from like 6:00 P.M. until 5:00 A.M. They have no idea it's played between midnight and five. Maybe on a Sunday morning or something like that." Some recipients view the practice as superior to working disco or dance clubs. It is impossible to ascertain how widespread the illegal activity is. However, as one promotion man commented on the general state of radio, "The days of ears and guts are over. It's a business." "Business" has many facets over and under the table.

## FCC, the Amorphous Presence

To place its sound before the public the record industry must contend with many overt barriers. The Federal Communications Commission (FCC) is a gray eminence lurking in the background. The regulatory agency exercises no immediate control over the record companies, but it does have significant authority over and influence upon broadcasters, the gatekeepers of pop, who depend upon the agency for their operating licenses—although FCC power has lessened over time.

The commission, established in 1934, regulates interstate and foreign commerce in communication by wire and radio. It is prohibited by law from engaging in prior censorship of broadcast material, yet FCC's guidelines state that "no application for a broadcasting license will be granted unless the Commission finds that the *public interest, convenience,* and *necessity* will be served by such a grant." The right to interpret the "public interest and convenience" accounts for the considerable presence of the commission among the broadcast media. It expects radio and television to address "the problems, needs and interests" of the community that is serviced. Beyond these general boundaries there exist few objective guidelines as to the proprieties and etiquette of programming. The very amorphousness and uncertainty of its policy provide the commission's social control over radio and network television. Not exercising prior censorship, it acts only after it has received a complaint or discovered some wrongdoing. The ambiguity of the situation has forced many station managers into a highly defensive posture in all areas not clearly outlined by the commission. Popular-music programming has historically been one of these anomic spheres.

Prior to the turbulent 1960s, FCC commissioners were not confronted with material that might be labeled offensive to community mores or standards. The lyrics of the swing and postwar crooner periods were innocent by any but the most austere standards. The not-so-subtle rhythm and blues songs of the early 1950s, such as "Baby Let Me Bang Your Box" or "Work with Me, Annie," addressed to urban Blacks, were ignored by the commission. Double-entendre rock lyrics on Top 40 stations also escaped scrutiny. The inaction of the commission prior to 1971 is partially attributable to the "June, spoon, moon" nature of AM programming. Pop was mainly "our song." Radio stations just did not air controversial material on entertainment shows, and pop music was clearly identified as being in the entertainment-show category. The Noebels, Aranzas, and Larsons had not yet proved "pop" artists as the termites of society.

During the 1960s, the FCC affected and adjusted the relationships between the radio programmer and the record company. It was a prominent and vital catalyst in investigating and catapulting into headlines disk-jockey "consultantships" and Clarkola. The disclosures did alter the "play-for-pay" method of breaking acts, and commission actions and rulings also have altered competitive relations between stations in some markets. In July 1962 the commissioners denied sportsman Jack Kent Cooke's petition to continue operation of KRLA (Pasadena) due to deceptions in broadcasting practices, especially promotional contests. The decision created an imbalance in the Top 40 market in the Los Angeles area and ultimately figured in the RKO purchase of KHJ (Los Angeles) and the birth of boss radio. Four years later the commission disciplined KYA (San Francisco) for "inadequate policies and practices for control of program material"; the implication of allowing the station's license to be renewed for only one year was that payola or "plugola" was being practiced. The action prompted some station personnel to begin thinking about alternatives transcending the confines of boss radio. Several months after its first ruling the FCC granted the offending station the usual three-year extension. The exoneration of KYA did not affect further experimentation in the San Francisco radio scene, allowing it to continue at least on the all-night Russ Syracuse show.

These minor housekeeping decisions were dwarfed by the historical simulcast decision that drastically altered FM programming fare. In October 1965 the FCC ordered that licensees of FM stations in the cities of over 100,000 population cease devoting more than 50 percent of the FM broadcast week to programs duplicated on AM stations in the area. Owned by the same licensees. Nearly 200 of 551 commercial outlets operating in urban communities were affected, but their opposition was unavailing. On New Year's Day 1967 the unpopular order went into effect and the result was an increase in specialty broadcasting on the FM channels. The principal casualty was symphonic material, a prominent feature of the simulcast. Classical and country and western music received greater exposure, but rock and roll was the major beneficiary. Following the decree Pop music accounted for 29 percent of FM broadcast format in the 50 largest cities, and other areas as well. The FCC order had opened up large segments of valuable airtime in which record companies could expose product. The release from the all-pervasive clock allowed broadcasters, who could no longer rely upon the usual 2:37-minute Top 40 fare appearing on the AM outlet, to experiment with longer LP selections to fill their new playlists. This paved the way for the emergence of free-form broadcasting on major FM stations.

Opinion manipulators have discounted the political value of radio, in part due to the demographics associated with the medium. Television traditionally has reached large numbers of older viewers eligible to vote. David Monroe Miller, president of Contemporary Communications, an advertising agency specializing in "opinion ads," notes, "Radio audiences are not composed of the kinds of persons you want to reach."[90] Supportive of Miller's observation is the answer of a junior college student when queried about the "Eve of Destruction": "Protest songs show no class.

Songs should be written for *entertainment*." Sociological studies have re-peatedly noted the universality of this sentiment. A large number of Top 40 listeners do not want "their" music to be concerned with social issues. Prior to the enfranchisement of 18-year-olds, most opinion advertisers considered music spots via audio and video a waste of campaign funds.

The "Eve of Destruction," the pioneer statement of protest to climb the *Billboard* charts, altered the apolitical nature of air fare. Several right-wing organizations in California petitioned the FCC, arguing that "Eve" had violated the "fairness doctrine." This doctrine urges that a station that has "presented one side of a controversial issue of public importance make reasonable efforts to present opposing sides of the issue in its overall pro-gramming." The FCC did not impose the fairness doctrine in regard to popular music in response to petitioning. One explanation may be that most stations conform to the vague stipulation that "opposing views need not be presented on the same program or even in the same series of pro-grams, so long as an effort is made in good faith to present contrasting views in the station's *overall programming*." This means that one 30-min-ute conservative speech could offset ten air plays of "Eve" or "Ohio." Obviously, popular music was best left outside the umbrella of the nebulous "fairness doctrine."

The rise of the counterculture as manifest in rock music and free-form radio found segments of the broadcasting medium attempting to challenge community mores and conventional wisdoms. In time, some popular An-glo-Saxonisms would be voiced on FM radio. Sex, drugs, and other pre-viously taboo subjects would receive attention. The question for the government became, as in pornography cases, "What constitutes com-munity standards?" It is a question that the FCC has never adequately interpreted, much to the discomfiture of programmers, who keep in mind that "no license will be granted or renewed unless the Commission finds that the public interest, convenience, and necessity will be served." Consti-tutionally vague as it may be, the regulatory power is a fact of life for the broadcaster. The commission did fine one FM station that broadcast Jerry Garcia's use of a "taboo" word during an interview; the statement of cen-sure indicated that the commission welcomed court adjudication of its action, but the defendant station chose to pay the fine, leaving the matter of content review untested. During the drug-lyric controversy, several lawyers offered to represent any radio station willing to contest the FCC's au-thority; none of the major commercial stations accepted. One of the attor-neys told *Rolling Stone*, "We also need a plaintiff station, but most stations want to stay out of trouble and make money."[91]

## "FCC Discovers Dope Does Darnedest Thing"

Six months after the 1970 speech of Vice-president Spiro Agnew about drug lyrics, the FCC issued a public notice, in April 1971, "Licensee Responsibility to Review Records Before Their Broadcast." The announcement cautioned broadcasters that whether

> a particular record depicts the danger of drug abuse, or, to the contrary, promotes such illegal drug usage is a question for the judgment of the licensee. The thrust of this *Notice* is simply that the licensee must make that judgment and cannot properly follow a policy of playing records without someone in a responsible position . . . knowing the content of the lyrics.

The document warned programmers that failure to exercise adequate control over broadcast material would raise "serious questions as to whether continued operation of the station is in the public interest." Many radio stations interpreted the notice as repressive. Former Commissioner Nicholas Johnson validated this belief, objecting that the notice "strikes out blindly at a form of music which is symbolic of a culture which the majority [of FCC commissioners] apparently fears—in part concerned about drug abuse, it surely would not choose to ignore song lyrics 'strongly suggestive of, and tending to glorify' the use of alcohol, which is the number one drug abuse problem in this country." Dick Starr, program director at Top 40 station KYA (San Francisco), concurred, "It smacks of censorship, and it'll create a lot of busy work. I'll have to ask for lyric sheets if it goes that far."[92]

The FCC denied that its notice regarding lyrics was restrictive. Instead, Commissioner Robert E. Lee claimed, all that was being asked was that "the Broadcast Industry meet its responsibility of reviewing records before they are played." Tracy Weston, an attorney specializing in civil liberties in the broadcast media, contended the reminder was ambiguous "because the FCC has not had the guts to come out and say what they really mean. They are trying to scare private stations into doing the censorship themselves and avoid the trap." Weston's reasoning had some merit; FCC Notice 71-205 did imply that failure to screen lyrics correctly could affect the "continued operation of the station."[93]

Radio stations licensed by the FCC were placed in the position of making sociopolitical judgments above and beyond their usual aesthetic ones. Numerous people in the record industry, as opposed to those in radio, objected. Sergio Mendes, leader of Brazil '77, stated, "Drug-oriented lyrics many times are a matter of interpretation. Who is going to translate the lyrics?"[94] Max Leon, owner of two radio stations, added, "It is impossible to crawl into any writer's head to find out exactly what they mean."[95] The broadcasters generally acceded to the FCC notice. The Storz chain demanded printed lyrics to singles submitted for its playlists; other chains and stations followed suit. George Williams, with stations in North Carolina and Alabama, told *Billboard* he would even "call someone connected with the record" to get the correct interpretation.[96] The industry complied with such requests: most albums contain the printed lyrics to the songs on the record; more controversial fare usually contains a reminder to program directors to screen a particular cut before providing it airplay. For most PDs such a warning is entirely unnecessary.

Printed lyrics do not solve the problem, as English rock singer Spencer Davis observed, "Lyric sheets will not help. A lot of people read things into lyrics. Look at the stir during the Charles Manson trial about the words to certain Beatles tunes like 'Helter Skelter' and 'Sexy Sadie.'"[97] Davis could easily have added "Lucy in the Sky with Diamonds" to his list of examples of difficult-to-interpret songs. Critics have all pointed to the acronymic "LSD" in the title. Lennon and McCartney denied that the song is about acid, while admitting that a few of their other compositions have drug-oriented themes. There is little reason to disbelieve them about "Lucy." The problem of interpretation of lyrics made stations more cautious in the construction of their playlists. WDAS (Philadelphia), reacting to the order, removed "Let It Bleed," "Comin' into Los Angeles," "Small Circle of Friends," "Needle and Spoon," and "I Am the Walrus" from its record library. WKBW (Buffalo) blacklisted "White Rabbit," "D.O.A." (an anti-drug song), "Monkey Man," and "Eight Miles High." KADI-FM (St. Louis) pulled three songs off its playlist. The major casualty of the FCC notice was Brewer and Shipley's charted song "One Toke over the Line," which they admitted was a "cannabis spiritual." [98] Top 40 stations refused to air the record when they discovered "toke" meant a puff on a marijuana cigarette. Major AM outlets in New York, Chicago, and Dallas removed the song from their playlists, despite its high position in local and national ratings.

The FCC's claim that it did not censor material of the music industry was a hollow statement. A handful of broadcasters resented the interference of the FCC in their programming policies but precious few challenged the notice; in fact, numerous program directors welcomed the guidelines, WNBC's program director, after removing "Toke" from his playlist, explained, "The FCC only makes clear what I've always done anyway."[99] This assertion had considerable merit, for many AM stations were in fact refusing songs with any type of irritation factor, esthetic or sociological. The FCC order was primarily directed at the "more free-form" stations that did air controversial material. AM stations rarely ventured into "irritation" zones.

The record companies were "odd man out" in the drug-lyric fracas. Neil Bogart, then president of Buddah Records, which catalogued "One Toke over the Line," could protest, "The airways fully belong to the people. How do you justify pulling a record that's so heavily requested by the people?" But, there was nothing else he could do. No radio-station owner would jeopardize a station license or engage in an expensive lawsuit to increase Buddah's profits. Indeed, as one program director put it, "I think the FCC is going after record companies, and they can't get at them so they're going through us." This reply aptly reflects radio's view of record companies: "Why should we take a risk merely to fill the corporate coffers of CBS or the WCI?" *Billboard* captured the broadcasters' attitude in announcing the FCC notice:

> Many major broadcasters, who prefer to keep anonymous, say that the FCC has no right to impose this type of censorship upon radio stations—that it's a violation of the first amendment. But most broadcasters are reluctant to march against the FCC *because they are afraid to imperil their frequencies.*
>
> There is considerable speculation that some station will eventually challenge the FCC on its new dictum. But high legal costs may be a deterrent. The general feeling, too, is that most stations will go along with the new demands.[100]

One radio station, WBAI ((New York), a member of the controversial Pacifica network, filed a petition with the FCC protesting the notice. Station manager Edwin Goodman explained: "We have no intention of changing our programming in any way and will continue to broadcast songs which might be construed by someone as advocating the use of drugs. After all, someone might construe the lyrics of 'Tea for Two' as advocating drugs."[101] WBAI was joined by several networks and finally the Record Industry Association of America (RIAA) in disputing the FCC action. The *New York Times* and several trade publications reprinted former Commissioner Johnson's forceful dissent from the notice. The notice also generated a considerable amount of protest mail. On 16 April 1971, some five weeks after the licensee responsibility notice, the commission issued a clarification: "Any attempt to review or condemn a licensee's judgment to play a particular record is . . . beyond the scope of federal regulatory authority with perhaps the exception of the so-called 'clear and present danger' test." It was, as Johnson noted, a "significant retreat"; however, the broadcaster still remains liable for the material that is aired by his station. Leonard

Weinless, the FCC's chief information officer, wrote, "The FCC takes no position on lyrics. No action has been taken against stations on the basis of song lyrics." This does not guarantee that the commission will not take action at some future date.

Nearly 18 months after the FCC notice Yale Broadcasting (WYBC-FM) and the National Coordinating Council on Drug Abuse, with Tracy Weston as their attorney, petitioned the U.S. Appeals Court for a clarification. Weston told the three judges that broadcasters were having to review lyrics to ferret out, from frequently ambiguous terminology, whether songs "promote or glorify" the use of drugs as well as to establish if the song is in the public interest. He presented 150 pages of affidavits outlining the disruptions in the broadcasting industry due to the notice, and urged that the FCC's refusal to outline its standards as "an invitation to take the risk." Presiding Judge Spotswood Robinson appeared to support Weston's position, telling him, "I don't want the FCC to speculate—but to be definite."[102] FCC Counsel Marino replied, the broadcaster "must have some expertise" and that the commission did not want to second-guess the licensee but must, however, act on listener complaints. Marino believed the notice was superior to the FCC's publishing a list of unacceptable songs. Judge Richard Wilkey cautioned Marino, "I didn't mean anything like a listing of recordings, but more precise guidelines for the broadcaster." Judge Robinson concluded the hearing with the observation that the vagueness of FCC rules may be "an impairment of civil rights." The seemingly sympathetic comments of the judges were misleading; in January 1973 the panel upheld the FCC: the commission had not revoked any license for violation of its notice. Ironically, the court freed the broadcaster of some of the prescreening responsibility because of the nature of popular music:

> Some lyrics of songs are virtually unintelligible. To the extent that they are completely meaningless gibberish . . . they, of course, do not communicate with respect to drugs or anything else and are not within the ambit of the Commission's Order. [Nonetheless], at some point along the scale of human intelligibility, the sounds produced may slide over from characteristics of free speech, which should be protected, to those of noise pollution, which the Commission has ample authority to abate.

The noise pollution is the gist of what the FCC was opposed to. As the court restated, "The main thrust of the Commission's Order is that whether a song presents the banal observations of a moon-struck adolescent, resembles two enraged alley cats fighting in a garbage can, or contains the subtle reflections of a master poet, a licensee may not broadcast ignorant of the content of his programming."[103] Several months later Appeals Court Chief Judge David L. Bazelon, a noted civil libertarian, objected to the decision:

"This case is ripe for judicial review." The case went to the Supreme Court, which refused to review the FCC's 1971 notice. By inaction, the Court let stand the commission's power to determine content. William O. Douglas, one of the two dissenting justices, wrote, "Under our system, the government is not to decide what messages, spoken or in music, are of the proper 'social value' to reach the people."[104]

For the broadcaster, the FCC is the sword of Damocles over his microphone and license. It is the very unclear posture of the commission that in fact excludes much material from the airways. The commission took no formal action against several stations that aired John Lennon's "Working Class Hero" or against NET for telecasting "San Francisco Rock: Go Ride the Music," which featured the Jefferson Airplane's "Volunteers" with the complete text. Despite the inaction most program directors adopted KMET's Warren Duffy's position: "We're not willing to risk a license and all the other things we're trying to do for one word."[105] This unstructured relationship between radio and the FCC exaggerates the delicate balance between artistic freedom and the practicalities of breaking a record. Lou Reed, then with the "suspect" Velvet Underground, commented, "All we need is a hit single, but nobody will play our songs." In this manner the amorphous presence of the Federal Communications Commission is a shadowy gatekeeper of material transcending ordinary Top 40 fare. Record companies, as Stan Cornyn suggests, are "ticket sellers" in search of customers, and consumers do not purchase what they do not hear. There are esoteric taste cultures that support performers of avant-garde material, such as the New York Dolls, Mothers of Invention, or the Bonzo Dog Band. These are specialty acts and are not expected to be "hit bounds." The real difficulty lies in the gray area of double meaning.

A program director, knowing a regulatory agency will evaluate his judgment, can adopt a conservation stance in regard to songs open to various interpretation. "Lucy in the Sky With Diamonds," "Eight Miles High," and "Mr. Tambourine Man" have all been cited as drug songs despite the denials of their creators. Moral entrepreneurs may see an innocent song in the same light as the Illinois Crime Commission. "Yellow Submarine" by the Beatles may mean "street jargon for yellow, barbiturate capsules" or "Puff the Magic Dragon" by the folksinging group Peter, Paul and Mary may be interpreted to mean "smoking marijuana and hashish." Considering the diverse interpretations, some broadcasters no doubt take the safest course and do not play these innocuous ditties. One midwestern program director observed, "Why play a song likely to turn off a listener, when I can air something else?"

The presence of the FCC creates another barrier for the record industry added to that of the formal gatekeeper. The government agency becomes yet one more dam the recording company must cope with. This powerful agency, unhappily for the record makers, is at odds with some taste publics the industry wishes to service.

*Rolling Stone,* a magazine believed attuned to the non-Top 40 youth market, strongly attacked the timidity of broadcasters. Its basic premise was aptly articulated in the second issue by disk jockey Tom Donohue: "The music has matured, the audience has matured, but radio has apparently proven to be a retarded child."[106] It is in this spirit that the editorial of 21 January 1971 was addressed to program directors and station managers:

> Where are the courageous and responsible men who have become rich broadcasting the music of the young in the past decade and who now advertise so expensively how "committed" to the music and ideals of a new generation they are? We address ourselves to the program directors, station managers and disc jockeys and to the men in New York City who direct the corporate activities of either the Metromedia Radio Network or the ABC-FM network, both of them owners of chains of at least five commercial "underground" rock stations in the major cities of the United States.
>
> Surely these two companies—and any owners of smaller broadcasting corporations who might also join in—can easily afford the relatively small legal fees necessary to play "Working Class Hero" and defend it in front of the Federal Communications Commission and, if necessary, in the Federal Courts, where certainly that ban would be overturned. And once and for all end the nonsense of the great popular art of our time being censored from public broadcast—when it refers to drugs or uses common language—because it deals in honesty and reality.

Record-company executives, perhaps sharing many of the *Rolling Stone* sentiments, have been extremely cautious in dealing with the relationship of the FCC to their product. Mike Maitland, then with MCA, in the best of political rhetoric said in 1970, "If I am totally aware that something harmful was being put into a lyric, I'd try to stop it. Most of the time we don't know when we are being *put on* and that can go for the hippest label."[107] Joe Smith, then with Warner Bros. Records, observed, "The shakers and movers in this business don't sit around dreaming up campaigns to see cocaine, nor do writers think of clever ways to refer to drugs in their songs." A more candid reply came from Al Bennett, former Liberty-UA president: it would have to be "a business judgment." Irwin H. Sternberg, at Mercury, echoed this approach: "I don't think we [record companies] have the right to decide what is moral. The public should decide what is good and bad." Although civil libertarians would no doubt applaud this statement, radio-station directors, who have one eye on the frequency license, are not so courageous.

The record company's task, then, is somehow to persuade station managers that controversial material is not offensive to their listeners *regardless* of the FCC. One interesting example of this process was to be found in the controversy over Bloodrock's "D.O.A.," the musical account of a drug overdose. Toward the end of the song a sirenlike sound was produced. Many radio stations were hesitant about airing the song because of an FCC notice (70-930) that banned simulated sirens in broadcasts because the sound might cause automobile accidents and public hazards. Capitol Records and Bloodrock producer Terry Knight attempted to persuade PDs to broadcast the record on the basis of its alleged popularity, the notice notwithstanding. Bill Gavin's tip sheet reported: "Phenomenal phone response wherever played plus big sales. Gruesome content has blocked most major station air play, but KINT-El Paso programs it as a public service and reports good reaction from several drivers who said they drove more carefully after hearing it on their car radios." Capitol reproduced this statement in a mailing to radio stations. Knight, then riding the crest of his industry influence as the producer of Grand Funk Railroad, told broadcasters, "To question whether this record should or should not be aired on the basis of a sound effect is both ludicrous and irresponsible. The fact of the matter is clearly that the song 'D.O.A.' is high on all of the national singles charts." Having cited the "get behind the record" ethos, he continued:

> It should now be clear that the song has established its popularity and status from legitimate consumer response. At this point, for a programmer to consider not giving airplay to this song on the basis of his personal opinion of a sound effect which is an integral part of the song is to establish himself as sole judge and censor of his audience. We must not allow ourselves or our programmers to misuse the power with which they have been entrusted by telling the public what it may or may not hear after that public has legitimately substantiated and voiced its majoritive approval. Putting it quite simply, the record is established as a hit and deserves to be aired by programmers with an obligation to program "hit" material. Capitol will continue to support both the single and album to the fullest extent.

Although a considerable amount of Columbia's appeal was industry hype, it makes clear the basic dilemma of the record company: for a song to be popular, it must receive airplay. A possible FCC citation is generally threat enough to keep a record off the air. Consequently, the record companies, once again, must exhibit proof of public support for their product to motivate timid PDs to put the needle on the record.

Another ploy utilized by Capitol to publicize the controversial record further was a series of antidrug spots by Bloodrock. The spots decried drug abuse but also generated exposure. On 8 March 1972, three days after the public notice on "licensee responsibility," Knight announced that another of his acts had taped a series of ten-second spots like "Hi, this is Mark Farner of Grand Funk with a word to my Brothers and Sisters. A clean world begins with a clean body . . . don't pollute yours with hard drugs." The residual purpose of the Grand Funk spots was to introduce Grand Funk to an audience unaware of it; Grand Funk had not yet enjoyed a Top 40 hit. The action also provided stations with visible material that they were "fighting the drug menace."

The industry's insistence that radio listeners are more attuned to their product than are program directors is difficult to substantiate to broadcasters. The sentiment that "most people are unhip" pervades the radio medium. The FCC's presence only makes this feeling more of a reality.

The problem is what to do about the "hip" segments of the audience. Some portions of pop, much of it not aired on Top 40 radio, does reflect segments of the youth market that are in the AOR category. As ticket sellers, the record companies are anxious to serve the older college and alternative-culture people, but it is precisely this group at which, as former Commissioner Johnson suggests, the FCC's drug-lyrics notice was directed. As one observer noted, "Freaks buy records too." Dr. David Smith, director of the controversial Haight-Ashbury Medical Clinic, told the *Billboard* Radio Programming Forum in 1970: "Music—particularly pop music—tends to be a reflection of the times. It is very questionable what comes first: Does rock music influence drug taking, or do people who are participating in drug use like to listen to music?"[108] The exact number of people under 30 using drugs is almost impossible to ascertain. Figures run from 20 to 50 percent for marijuana use. One study reported that 45 pecent of the high school students in New York City occasionally toyed with "psychoactive" drugs. Some observers believe that more college students smoke dope than do not. Few people would deny that drug use, especially marijuana smoking, is prevalent among the young. There is a relationship between this cohort and pop music. Sociologist Erich Goode reports that 90 percent of the pot smokers he studied said listening to music was a richer and more rewarding experience when high. Some unpublished materials seem to hint at some correlation between "drug use and the appreciation of more progressive air fare." No causality is implied, that is, drug lyrics have not been found to cause drug use. The dilemma of the record companies here is clear: Dope smokers, coke heads, and pill poppers buy records, and the companies are quite happy to sell them product, whatever its content. The FCC, with its power over broadcasters, interdicts the traditional buyer-seller relationship. Records, as Terry Knight has proved, can be sold by word of mouth rather than by radio or press exposure; however, only rare acts find this mode of communication effective. The FCC has handed the PD yet another copout that the road promo man must now cope with: "I can't play *that*. I could lose my license."

On 12 February 1975 the FCC issued the following statement: "indecent language . . . describes, in terms patently offensive as measured by *contemporary community* standard for the broadcast medium, sexual or excretory activities and organs." The "community-standard" concept was reapplied. The commission, in keeping with the WBAI-FM ruling, warned that "indecent" material should not be aired during hours in which children—age not defined—might be tuned in.[109] The two justices in that case warned that the regulatory agency should be careful to protect the listening rights of adults, which are protected by the First Amendment. Justice Potter Stewart had dissented more strongly than Justice Douglas. He had contended that the WBAI decision went too far, that radio listenership was voluntary and the audience enjoyed the right to "tune out." Steve Harris, PD at KRLY-FM (Houston) concurred: "Radio is like television: It can't be a baby sitter. A parent has to address his responsibility to his child. . . . If it sounds like its going to be trouble, I try to stay away from it."[110]

Most broadcasters are still playing it safe. During the controversy over "She's Got Papers on Me" by Dimples Fields and Betty Wright, KSOL (San Francisco) pulled the record despite its popularity. "The image of the black woman with the rolling pin ready to attack her man as soon as he walks in was just something we didn't want to exploit," explained PD Marvin Robinson. Olivia Newton-John's "Physical," several months later in 1981, received similar treatment. It was dropped by some stations for "suggestive" lyrics. KFMY-FM added the "exercise" tune to the playlist, but dropped it because of "call ins" from irate citizens.

Some programmers feel themselves to be in a dilemma. Charles Warfield, with an urban contemporary chain servicing New York, Detroit, and Los Angeles, refused to play "Ya Mama" because "it was turning off . . . our audience. The problem of course is that when there is a demand for a piece of product, you play it."[111] The FCC's stance has been "tolerance," but the potential for action is always present. James C. McKinney, chief of the Mass Media Bureau in 1984, noted "the Commission has made no determinations regarding rock lyrics."

The FCC has done little of consequence since the warning to broadcasters in 1971 and the WBAI case. This may reflect changes in administrations. The disappearance of an overt counterculture may be another factor. The lobbying of the New Christian Right may reverse this hands-off policy, but at present the FCC apears to have backed off the drug lyric issue. There are few overtly mind-altering songs on the air, although the commission has created considerable mischief in the arena of AM-stereo. After years of negotiating the FCC finally approved such a move believed to aid this radio band. As of 1985 the issue of the mode of transmission system has not been resolved.

All things change and remain the same. It has been over thirty years since Todd Storz sat in the cocktail lounge and witnessed the human rotation at the jukebox. Top 40 radio in the mid-eighties is back. AOR with its *Bill Chill* audience continues to hold its own, although many add-ons can be heard on CHR formats. Just as the campuses have regressed into the mold of the Eisenhower years, so has radio.

Record companies find AOR and CHR difficult formats to crack. Advertising targets and psychographics have narrowed the degrees of freedom available to broadcasters. Consultants have become predominant players in many markets. Broadcasting content also is haunted by the ever-present but frequently inactive FCC. However, the specter of PTA ratings systems for FMers may move the commission to return to the days of the drug-lyric menace. Consequently, record companies have to look once again at other forms of exposure: the print and video media.

## Notes

1. See R.M. Brown, "The Gate Keeper Reassessed: A Return to Lewin," *Journalism Quarterly* 56 (1979).
2. Martin Block, "The Case for the Disk Jockey," *Billboard Band Year Book,* 26 September 1942, p. 46.
3. Quoted in George Allen Booker, "The Disk Jockey and His Impact on Teenage Musical Taste as Reflected Through a Study in Three North Florida Cities" (Ph.D. dissertation, Florida State University, 1968), p. 48.
4. Howard Jolly, "Popular Music: A Study in Collective Behavior" (Ph.D. dissertation, Stanford University, 1967), pp. 11, 25.
5. Paul M. Hirsch, "Processing Fads and Fashions: An Organization Set Analysis of Cultural Industry Systems," *American Journal of Sociology* 77 (January 1972): 656.
6. Robert Hilburn, "MTV: The Birth of a Rock Sensation," *Los Angeles Times* 21 August 1983, p. 82.
7. Arnold Passman, *The Deejays* (New York: Macmillan, 1971), p. 64.
8. George Simon, *The Big Bands* (New York: Macmillan, 1967), p. 56.
9. Block, "The Case for the Disk Jockey," p. 45.
10. Wallichs quoted in David Dexter, "1930-1945, Disk Jockey: Origin of the Species," *Billboard Annual Supplement,* 27 December 1969, p. 58.
11. Testimony of Norman Prescott, *Responsibilities of Broadcasting Licenses and Station Personnel,* part I. House of Representatives, 86th Congress, 1960, p. 39.
12. "A Jockey's Life," *Newsweek,* 16 December 1946, p. 72.
13. Dexter's position, although generally valid, does ignore a spate of songs popularized through the medium of television. The most noteworthy is Joan Weber's "Let Me Go Lover," featured on a "Studio One" play. Themes from

several shows also reached the number-one spot on the "Hot 100" such as "Davy Crockett." Howard Warshaw and Joe Vasapoli, "The Pay-For-Play Hustle," *Billboard,* 14 July 1979, p. 12.

14. Nearly all of the press reports before and after the payola hearings stress the "mirror" thesis. Howard Miller told *Time,* "I play the things they want to hear. Unless I do, I don't have an audience, and, therefore, I have denied my station, my second integrity, an audience. And the station loses the account of my advertiser, my third integrity." "What Makes Howard Spin," *Time,* 29 April 1957, p. 50.

15. Quoted in Russell Sanjek, "The War on Rock," paper presented at the New School for Social Research, 17 February 1971, p. 17.

16. Ackerman, pp. 900-901.

17. Prescott, *Responsibilities,* p. 39.

18. Testimony of Billy Parsons, part II, *Responsibilities,* pp. 1083-95.

19. Quoted in Mildred Hall, "Clark Winds Up Testimony with Stout Payola Denials," *Billboard,* 9 May 1960, p. 3.

20. "Gimme, Gimme on the Old PAYOLA," *Life,* 23 November 1959, p. 45; and testimony of Joseph Finan, part I, p. 145.

21. Testimony of Paul Ackerman, part II, *Responsibilities,* p. 904.

22. Testimony of Charles Young, part I, *Responsibilities,* pp. 203, 205.

23. Testimony of Donald Dumont, part I, *Responsibilities,* p. 532; and testimony of Harold Dinesten, *Responsibilities,* pp. 355-56.

24. June Bundy, "Payola NOT Dead, Now Underground," *Billboard,* 29 August 1960, p. 1; "Deejays Taboo Payola Probe as Bootless Political Football," *Billboard,* 19 December 1960, pp. 1, 4.

25. Bob Rolontz, "Promotion Man Back in Saddle as Payola Tide Ebbs," *Billboard,* 8 August 1960, pp. 1, 33.

26. A. Bester, "New Age of Radio," *Holiday* 33 (June 1963): 56.

27. Quoted in George S. Trow, "Money Music," *New Yorker,* 23 December 1972, p. 43.

28. Rick Sklar, *Rocking America: How the All-Hit Radio Stations Took Over* (New York: St. Martin's Press, 1984) p. 93.

29. Tom Donahue, "A Rotting Corpse, Stinking Up the Airways," *Rolling Stone,* 23 November 1967, p. 15.

30. Bob McClay, "Murray the K on WOR-FM (They Screwed It Up)," *Rolling Stone,* 9 November 1967, p. 10.

31. "New Trends Alter Underground Radio," *New York Times,* 10 January 1972, p. 46.

32. Pete Fornatale, "Radio and Mediacy: A DJ Spells It Out!" *Rock,* 28 August 1972, p. 25.

33. Shaw quoted in Ben Fong-Torres, "Radio: Ups and Down in the FM Ozone," *Rolling Stone,* 6 July 1972, pp. 22, 24.

34. "George Wilson Propounds His Potent Programming Technique," *Billboard* 12 August 1972, p. 20.

35. Quoted in Don Weller, "Jacobs on an Upbeat at Honolulu KKUA-AM," *Billboard,* 24 June 1978, p. 46.

36. Edd Routt, James B. McGrath, and Frederic A. Weiss, *The Radio Format Condundrum* (New York: Hastings House, 1978), p. 86.

37. Jack McDonough, "'Free-Form' Still Reigns in S.F.," *Billboard* 2 December 1978, p. 58.

38. Mike Harrison, "AOR: Fading Memory of a Simpler Industry," *Billboard* 24 January 1981, p. 31.
39. Philip K. Eberly, *Music in the Air: America's Changing Tastes in Popular Music, 1920-1980* (New York: Hastings House, 1982), p. 243.
40. Quoted in Roman Kozak, "Best Cuts from Hottest Albums at WPLJ," *Billboard,* 25 February 1978, p. 20.
41. Quoted in "Staying in Tune with the Times," *Broadcasting,* 25 August 1980, p. 54; Bill King, "Burkhart Opens Doors to Suite and Format Secrets," *Billboard,* 23 September 1978, p. 22.
42. "Staying in Tune with the Times."
43. See "Consultants Report Card," *Radio & Records,* 24 August 1984; Claude Hall and Barbara Hall, *This Business of Radio Programming* (New York: Billboard Books, 1977), p. 17.
44. Quoted in Mike Adaskaveg, "Mike Joseph & How He Evolved into a Top Programming Figure," *Billboard,* 3 September 1977, p. 30.
45. "Top Consultants and Researchers," *Radio Only,* May 1982, p. 14.
46. Hall and Hall, *This Business of Radio Programming.*
47. Quoted in Joel Denver, "CHR: The Consultants' Eye View," *Radio & Records,* 12 November 1982.
48. "Pay Cable Films Boost Track Albums," *Billboard,* 1 September 1984, p. 1.
49. Quoted in Ben Fong Torres, "Rock Radio's New Twist 'n' Shout," *GQ,* July 1984, p. 32.
50. Harrison, "AOR."
51. Rollye Bornstein, "Top 40 Dominates Four Major Markets," *Billboard* 15 October 1983, pp. 1, 15. Also, Leo Sacks, "Top 40 Sound Returns to Radio," *Billboard,* 3 September 1983, pp. 1, 16.
52. Quoted in Leo Sacks, "AOR Stations at Crossroads," *Billboard,* 5 November 1983, pp. 1, 16.
53. Quoted in Paul Grein, "Top 40 PDs See an Uptempo '84," *Billboard* 7 January 1984, p. 1. Also, Rollye Bornstein, "Arbitrons: Hits Still Hot," *Billboard,* 13 October 1984, pp. 1, 71.
54. Quotations in Paul Grein, "AOR Programmers Plan More Variety," *Billboard* 14 January 1984, pp. 1, 66.
55. Laura Leff, "Radio Stations Hire 'Doctors' To Fix Formats," *Wall Street Journal,* 7 January 1981, p. 1; Mitchell J. Shields, "Got a Sick Station? Dial a Radio Guru," *Advertising Age,* 11 July 1983, p. 1.
56. Ray Herbeck, Jr., "Joseph Reprograms San Juans' WKAQ to Repeat Top Ratings," *Billboard,* 2 September 1978, p. 21.
57. Sklar, *Rocking America,* p. 77.
58. Adaskaveg, "Mike Joseph and How He Evolved into a Top Programming Figure," p. 30.
59. Shields, "Got a Sick Station?"
60. "WKTU Flies Burkhart Disco Flag," *Billboard,* 26 August 1978, p. 50. Also King, "Burkhart Opens Doors."
61. Quoted in Joanne Ostrow, "Radio Consultants Tell Stations What's Music to Listeners' Ears," *Washington Post,* 6 July 1981, p. 18.
62. King, "Burkhart Opens Doors."
63. "Quoted in "Staying in Tune with the Times," pp. 54-55.
64. Shields, "Got a Sick Station?"
65. Doug Hall, "WPLJ's P.D. Says Format Stolen, Sold," *Billboard* 1 April 1978, p. 46.

66. Mike Harrison, "Research Is No Substitute for Taste," *Billboard* 27 February 1982, p. 17.
67. Doug Hall, "AOR Nears Crucial Crossroads," *Billboard,* 22 May 1982, pp. 1, 65.
68. Ostrow, "Radio Consultants Tell Stations," p. 17.
69. Trow, "Money Music," p. 32.
70. Quoted in Steve Reiner, "Would You Buy a Used Tip-Sheet from This Man?" *Rock,* 7 June 1972, p. 21.
71. Quoted in Ben Fong-Torres, "Bill Gavin on Top of the Pops," *Rolling Stone,* 7 December 1972, p. 16. Several PDs are especially critical of conferences "to better the industry"; they believe all they are doing is giving away their "own broadcasting secrets to those who may one day be their competitors."
72. Jack Anderson, "Payola Returns to Record Industry," *New York Post,* 31 March 1972.
73. Jack Anderson, "Spinning Out a Scandal," *New York Post,* 21 April 1972.
74. Fred Ferretti, "C.B.S. Ousts an Executive and Sues Him for $94,000," *New York Times,* 30 May 1973, p. 62.
75. "The Specter of Payola '73," *Newsweek,* 11 June 1973, p. 79.
76. Quoted in Ben Fong-Torres, "Clive Davis Ousted; Payola Coverup Charged," *Rolling Stone,* 5 July 1973, p. 32
77. Grace Lichtenstein, "Mob-Linked Conducts Get Subpoenas in Payola Case," *New York Times,* 8 June 1973, p. 23.
78. "Editorial: Care and Action," *Billboard,* 16 June 1973.
79. Quoted in Grace Lichtenstein, "Pop-Music Scandal Laid to Pursuit of Fast Money," *New York Times,* 11 June 1973, p. 63.
80. Quoted in Fong-Torres, "Bill Gavin on Top of the Pops," p. 34.
81. Ibid.
82. William Safire, "The Drugola Scandal," *New York Times,* 21 June 1973, p. 39.
83. Fred Ferretti, "Buckley Wants Record Industry Investigated by Four U.S. Agencies," *New York Times,* 26 June 1973, pp. 1, 13.
84. Mildred Hall, "Record Cos. Deny Payola in McClellan Promotion Quiz," *Billboard,* 3 November 1973, pp. 1, 10; Mildred Hall, "Payola Replies Show Promo $ Hike," *Billboard,* 10 November 1973, pp. 3, 14.
85. Murray Schumach, "19 Are Indicted in Payola Cases," *New York Times* 25 June 1975, pp. 1, 46.
86. "Commentary," *Billboard,* 2 May 1981, and 9 May 1981.
87. Quotations in Robert Christgau "Rock 'n' Roller Coaster." *Village Voice* 7 February 1984, p. 44; "The Great Payola Follies of '84," *Rock and Roll Confidential,* February 1984, p. 1. Also see Sklar, *Rocking America,* pp. 148-49.
88. Quoted in Robert Lindsey, "Payola Threatens Recording Profits," *New York Times,* 23 July 1975, p. 20.
89. Mark Kirkeby, "Record Business in Uproar over Independent Promotion," *Rolling Stone,* 11 December 1980. Also see "Payola Returns to the Airwaves," *Sentinel Tribune,* 7 March 1985, p. 5; William Knoedelseder, Jr., and Ellen Farley, "Record Firms Don't Always Get the Radio Play They Pay for," *Los Angeles Times,* 18 March 1984, sec. 5, pp. 1, 8.
90. Quoted in Robert J. Gwyn, "Opinion Advertising and the Free Market of Ideas," *Public Opinion Quarterly* 34 (Summer 1970): 249. Also Daniel L. Brenner and William L. Rivers, Ames, Iowa: Iowa State University Press, 1982.

91. Quoted in Ben Fong-Torres, "Radio: One Toke Behind the Line," *Rolling Stone,* 15 April 1971, p. 10.
92. Quoted in Ben Fong-Torres, "FCC Discovers Dope, Does Darnedest Thing," *Rolling Stone,* 1 April 1971, p. 6.
93. Quoted in Fong-Torres, "Radio," p. 10.
94. Quoted in George Denemeyer, "FCC Lyrics Notice Blasted by Artists," *Billboard,* 1 May 1971, p. 8.
95. Quoted in Bob Glassenberg, "Lyric Rule Poses Stiff Question," *Billboard,* 20 March 1971, p. 29.
96. Claude Hall, "Storz Follows FCC Rule—Demands Lyric with Disk," *Billboard,* 3 April 1971, p. 8.
97. Quoted in Denemeyer, "FCC Lyrics Notice," p. 8.
98. Quoted in Fong-Torres, "Radio," p. 10.
99. "WNBC Bars Lyrics as 'Drug-Oriented,'" *New York Times,* 27 March 1971, p. 45.
100. Glassenberg, "Lyric Rule Poses Stiff Question," p. 1.
101. "WBAI Criticized Ban on Drug Songs," *New York Times*, 6 April 1971, p. 65.
102. Quoted in "Appeals Court Argues Drug Lyrics Policy," *Billboard*, 4 November 1972, pp. 3, 86.
103. Court opinion quoted in Mildred Hall, "Court Decision on Drug Lyrics," *Billboard*, 20 January 1973, p. 66.
104. Quoted in "Drug Lyrics Appeal Fails," 27 October 1973, p. 6.
105. Quoted in Ben Fong-Torres, "Lennon's Song: The Man Can't F**k Our Music," *Rolling Stone,* 18 February 1971, p. 6.
106. Tom Donohue, "A Rotting Corpse Stinking up the Airways," *Rolling Stone,* 23 November 1967, p. 14.
107. Eliot Tiegel, "Curb Stirs Meat—Morals on $$?" *Billboard,* 14 November 1970, p. 10.
108. Lee Zhito, "Music Trips Up Drug Culture," *Billboard,* 6 November 1970, p. 70.
109. "FCC Asks Congress Curb Radio-TV Obscenities," *Billboard* 26 June 1976, pp. 3, 20.
110. Mildred Hall, "Supreme Court Nixes 'Patently Indecent' Air Language," *Billboard,* 8 July 1978, pp. 3, 14; Leo Sacks, "Urban Programmers Hit 'Suggestive' Song Lyrics," *Billboard,* 5 March 1983, p. 14.
111. Ed Harrison, "Station Banning Olivia's 'Physical,'" *Billboard* 7 November 1981, p. 10; Eric Gelman, "A Flap over a Rap," *Newsweek,* 31 July 1981, p. 65. For the latest attack on rock see David Zucchin, "Big Brother Meets Twisted Sister" *Rolling Stone*, 7 November 1985, pp. 9 ff.

# 6

# Print: A Necessary Evil?

*Wanna see my smiling face*
*on the cover of the* Rolling Stone

—©Eve Music, Inc.

Radio and music video sell records. Print is an alternative, added support vehicle of album and artist exposure. The value of the printed page, however, is difficult to ascertain. Many important label executives and, surprisingly, public relations people firmly believe "publicity doesn't sell records."

There is little statistically valid evidence to support the value of the press media. Mike Shallet, claiming a sample as representative as that of Gallup or Roper, reported only 7.4 percent individuals found out about new albums via the press. The "On Target" survey deals only with exposure, not reaction or momentum, and on the basis of these 1984 data, the role of the press remains murky. A sales slump generally finds envelopes with pink slips going to the publicity offices. Still, "bizzers" acknowledge that the rigidity of broadcast formats requires an end-run strategy.

"Getting to radio through the back door," was the way Warner's Bob Regehr described it. Another Burbank executive called it "insurance" because "anything and everything to *expose* our product is of value." Kenny Rogers: "Press is important in the long-term sense because it builds *careers,* not just oneshot hits. It makes you credible, valid, and established, and it deepens people's sense of you as an artist and personality." A *Rock* magazine contributor said, "Record reviews are as important as film reviews in influencing the sale of a particular record."[1]

Some public relations people and journalists are skeptical, as witness a former writer-turned-publicist: "The so-called working rock press is invalid unless it has a lot of other things going along with it. . . . Nobody reads rock critics anymore except industry people, and . . .industry people don't buy records." Mike Ochs observed, "People don't buy records on the basis of a

*Rolling Stone* review," "they're not going to buy it blind, which is what a review is." A veteran critic privately commented, "Realistically, a good review doesn't sell an album, but it does *reinforce* the consumers' tastes. Praise an artist or album. . .everybody is happy. Send in the tear-sheet and the record company is delighted. They turn to their boss and the artist and say, 'Look what a great job we're doing.' It shows the label cares."

In search of record-company advertising, *Rock* in its second reincarnation provided the following subscriber demographics in a full-page, color ad in *Billboard,* 21 July 1984:

> *Rock* magazine is the only music publication serving primarily young adult women. Our average reader is 21 years old.* Our readers buy an average of 4.5 records per month: 93 buying at least one record each month.
>
> ――――――――――――
> * ROCK Magazine has been published for 3 years and is monthly. It is distributed in all 50 states plus 35 foreign countries.
>
> [Reader survey data supplied by Facts Consididated, Inc. Readership includes verified passalong. ABC auditing second half 1984. July 21, 1984, p. 65.]

The advertising departments of music publications have slick promotional pamphlets that describe their readers as "heavy record buyers." The readers probably are—otherwise they would not be looking at the magazines—but the advertised figures do *not* establish a causal link between coverage and record purchases.

Bad record or concert reviews rarely parallel the impact of the devasting reviews of New York Broadway drama critics. Film and television writers enjoying the benefit of prescreenings can affect audience size, as was the case with *Heaven's Gate.* Only the most arrogant or inexperienced record or concert critic believes that he or she possesses such power. Most record reviews appear after the fact, akin to Monday mornings' football scores, and concert reviews are reactive. The show's over and the entourage has left town, but readers like to be told what a good time had. Positive reviews are normative. Negative assessments usually are aimed at superstars, who rarely care, although a few reviews get abusive and their fans write indignant letters, for example:

> As soon as Adam graced us with himself on stage I don't think the wild screams ceased from that point. . . . I really find it difficult to believe at all that you even went to the concert (I, of course, was there).
>
> Sign me
> "An Antmusic Fan"

Whatever else, the coverage is important. "Big Mo," or momentum, is reinforced by the media. As Kenny Rogers indicated, the press does play an important role in keeping an artist in limos and gold records. Even negative coverage suggests an artist is newsworthy. The Jacksons' 1984 "Victory tour" was a PR person's nightmare. When the national television networks, news magazines, and thousands of dailies focus on a subject, it is a "happening." Press attention, positive or negative, is an asset. Horror stories about the Sex Pistols provided the ill-fated band with a million dollars, worth of free publicity. Ozzy Osbourne, Black Sabbath, Dio and other heavy metal bands have benefited from the devil-worship backmasking controversy. The demand for Led Zeppelin's untitled fourth album soared when Congressman Dornan used "Stairway to Heaven" as an example of crowlenization, that is, "satanic messages." The old publicity adage "I don't care what you say, just spell my name right" is true. Most record companies but not all artists realize this media truism. (There are some thin-skinned performers. Chet Flippo was kicked off a Rolling Stones tour while covering the cross-country extravaganza for the *Stone*; he was reinstated.)

Garnering press exposure, except in *Rolling Stone*, is easier than bucking Bob Pittman's MTV rotations or Lee Abrams's AOR playlists. Free-lancers and columnists have a fair amount of discretion in regard to coverage. Nationally distributed music magazines run the gambit of format and space restrictions. *Creem* has a distinct psychographic blue-collar orientation, while *Circus* "will jump on anyone's bandwagon."[2]

The relationship between the record industry and the press continues to be mercurial. The creative tensions found in standard reportorial interactions are frequently absent because of excesses on the part of both parties.

Music is a time-honored journalistic subject. Writers in dailies and specialty magazines addressed to the arts or to specific musical tastes such as jazz, classical, folk, or polka have always held forth on the relative merits of performances, festivals, and records. During the first ten years of its existence, rock music lacked the intellectual respectability afforded these other genres. Other than lengthy analyses of the sociocultural implications of rhythm and blues groups and rockabilly, most reportage was negative or appeared in fan-idol teen publications.

Rock and roll's early newspaper treatment mirrored parental opposition to the new sound. The *New York Daily News* in 1956 informed readers there was a "gathering public disgust at a barrage of primitive, jungle beat rhythms, which when set to lyrics at all, quite frequently sound off with double-meaning lyrics few adults would care to hear." *The Journal-American,* now defunct, was equally anxious to write the obituary of the offensive musical genre in "After Rock 'n' Roll, What?" The generally objective *New York Times,* ran a piece entitled "Experts Propose Study of Craze."

One authority compared rock to St. Vitus's dance, "beyone all accepted versions of human dancing." It appears that only the *Post's* Charles Gruenberg was willing to give the infant musical formula a chance; he wrote a 12-part series attempting to explain the phenomenon.[3]

Teen magazines, not surprisingly, were the first to feature rockers in movie-book fashion. Presley was a sure-fire seller, followed by the Beatles, who were big in the "one-shot" market—picture/poster single-issue magazines devoted to one artist. Publications addressed to the adolescent female audience proliferated: *Seventeen, Teen*, and *16*, followed by such muscially oriented pulps as *Flip, Tiger Beat*, and *Fave*. In 1966 *Hullabaloo*, aimed at 16- to 22- year-old males, appeared; the name was derived from the short-lived television show. Three years later the name was changed to *Circus*.

Serious rock journalism began in fanzines or Chet Flippo's "peer group writing."[4] Rock criticism, or what Patricia Kennedy of *Jazz and Pop* termed "musical cum-politico/socio/cultural commentary," was born in the Ivy League grid of Massachusetts in 1964, largely through the efforts of an 18-year-old Swarthmore College student, Paul Williams, who founded *Crawdaddy: The Magazine of Rock*. It was the first fanzine. A fanzine, according to Greg Shaw, is "usually the product of one person, published at this own expense and in his own house, for little or no reward above the pleasure of self-expression and writing about something he loves that is ignored in the larger press. They are read by people with the same interest."[5]

The first four issues of *Crawdaddy* were crudely stapled, mimeographed, multicolored pages distributed in the Cambridge area. Within two years *Crawdaddy* had become a nationally distributed, color slick selling 20,000 copies per issue, most of these were over-the-counter and newsstand sales along the East Coast college circuit. The magazine boasted a modest 2,000 mail subscriptions. Record criticism in the journal was typified by a flowing, literary, experiential stream of consciousness. *Crawdaddy* was, as Williams once wrote, "our letter to you." The editor's reviewing style ranged from Joyce-like prose to historical reporting:

> Earth Opera/Joni Mitchell are an aspect of experience, as well as the product of same; what we are today and soon is shaped by what we hear of them. And we are you and me. Our understanding of the world is daily added to, crossed out, erased, struck over, pasted together by various cyclones and breezes that blow through.[6]

Contributor R. Meltzer adoped a quasi-academic style, using song titles and lyrics as footnotes in a Teutonic effort to find philosophical import in the most banal subjects:

The unit of rock significance is the whole of rock-'n'-roll, and this is not merely the result of the failure of reduction, as Hegel's unit of historical significance as all of history seems to be. Just as permissible, anyway, is Jamies' position in 'Summertime, Summertime,' which resembles Hegel's end of history. 'No studying' history.[7]

Jon Landau and Robert Somma employed more conventional journalistic and analytic techniques, which have predominated in record-review sections since the 1970s. Landau and Somma placed albums and performers into historical niches reminiscent of the *auteur* school of film criticism. A review would usually begin by placing the performer into some tradition, with a mention of the higher points and performers in that genre. The record under consideration would then be compared to the entire field and rated accordingly. Somma especially labeled some performers as indicative of social trends in the United States, thus allying himself in part with the *verte* material of Richard Goldstein.

After 19 issues the magazine was sold to Chester Anderson, formerly an editor of the San Francisco *Oracle*. It ceased to be a rock journal, and its name became *Crawdaddy: A Magazine of Roll*. Unlike the French *auteur* school of film criticism or the socialist *Masses* of the 1910s, *Crawdaddy* did not develop a standard technique; instead, it set a precedent and provided a model but not a direction for other publications.

On the West Coast a "new" community in San Francisco was slowly beginning to develop a critical awareness of its music. In 1966 Greg Shaw and David Harris founded *Mojo Navigator Rock and Roll News*, the second fanzine. The first 12 issues were mimeographed and generally confined to the Bay Area. The magazine, with a top circulation of 1,000, ran feature articles and reviews during its two-year span. Landau would call this "cultism," in which passion and emotional involvement are the basic motivation for reviewing or publishing.

Other fanzines are devoted to the esoterica of rock and roll, such as the history or discography of countless one-hit groups. There have been literally dozens of them, appearing such exotic names as *King Harvest Review, Zoot, Flash, Tuesday After Lunch, IFF, Who Put the Bomp, Rockpile, Let's Rock and Roll, Stormy Weather*, and *Blue Flame*. The structure of *Blue Flame*, a Chicago-based magazine, was fairly typical:

BLUE FLAME is published by students, ages 14 through 21. That's quite a range, but we've managed to put out seventeen big issues. We find, now, however, that time is becoming scarcer, prices for printing and supplies are rising, and that we're really becoming TOO big. Letters pile in each day, and we have so little time to answer them all. We've been breaking our original promise of keeping in touch with all of our readers. Every spare moment, however, is spent behind this typewriter, or at the Chicago, Wilmette, or

Evanston post offices weighing, paying, and filling out bullshit forms. Also, there's zero space left for more issues in our spacious ½-of-a-bedroom office at 2701 Birchwood Avenue. We're bursting at the seems.[8]

Greg Shaw's *Who Put the Bomp*, a follow-up of *Mojo*, started with 50 copies and lasted for ten years. Some of rock's best writing and writers appeared in its cultist pages. *Bomp* did have industry support and was able to attract a circulation of 30,000. It folded in 1979 when Shaw shifted his attention to Bomp Records.

*Blues Unlimited*, an English publication, also carried industry advertising because of its large subscription list. Most fanzines, however, subsist on only their meager subscription lists and the economic resources of the publisher. *Blue Flame* folded after 17 issues. Editor Gary Baker explained: "I made this decision after losing quite a bit of money and after two years of being tied down to a typewriter and a post office." Tom Bingham of the New York-based *IFF* wrote a similar postmortem:

"IFF died early this week. I'd put months and months of hard work into it, before I decided I was killing myself, both financially and physically, over the whole thing, and I finally convinced myself that it just wasn't worth it. My health hasn't been good for quite some time, but it's not any wonder, working on an MA (in math no less), teaching as a grad assistant, writing reviews and articles for close to a dozen magazines . . . and trying to put out a 50 page fanzine. Something had to go, and not wanting to put out a zine at all if it couldn't be the zine I wanted it to be, well it was either IFF or me I really feel miserable about it, it was pretty much my life.

Bingham's remarks aptly capture the love for the music nearly all fanzine writers express.

Bingham returned to the fanzine world with the *WIUS Tipsheet* in the summer of 1974. WIUS AM-FM is the Indianapolis radio outlet that distributed the mimeographed four-page handout. In the first number the lead story by "Mr. Bear" was "Fanzines," which listed eight publications, among them *Bomp*. Unlike the original fanzines, the mid-1970s crop was regionally and musically specialized, a reaction to the prozines. "Some concentrate on particular artists or types of music," wrote "Mr. Bear." The fanzines reportedly fill a void, as *Goldmine's* David Ginsburg indicates: "Their music just isn't covered in the commercial publications, so if it's going to be done, the fans have to do it themselves."[9]

The staying power of a fanzine is closely tied to the tides of a musical scene or style. *Hype* appeared and faded as "glitter/decadence" gave way to punk. *Slade Parader* went with the misfortunes of the English band. *Good Day Shineshine* and *Mother People* focus on rock legends whose glory days are past. The Beatles plus rock genuis Frank Zappa, new wave and especially punk revitalized the fanzine world. *Rolling Stone*'s Michael Goldberg estimated in 1984 that some 500 peak-group publications may exist. *Flipside* plus *Trouser Press* came to prominence because of the punk cult.

*Flipside* began in Los Angeles in 1977 and has entered its seventh year with a sale of 6,000 copies per issue. The publishers explain their commitment is generated by freebies and access to groups. "You get in free to all the shows. And free records," said a staffer. Southern California is one of the last bastions of punkitude in the United States.

Ira Robbins and a few associates started *Transoceanic Trouser Press*, named after a Bonzo Dog Band tune, in 1974 with sixty dollars. Early hand-stapled, mimeographed pages were sold for a quarter following Manhattan rock concerts. *Trouser Press* (as it was later called) concentrated on British acts such as Queen and ELO. The turning point was 1977, when it became a newsstand slick in appearance and featured the Sex Pistols. Robbins was in the vanguard: "All it took was to hear 'Anarchy in the U.K.' or 'God Save the Queen' and it was rock 'n' roll love at first sight." For almost two years the unorthodox magazine flourished. Its increasing success was to be its downfall, following in the fatal footsteps of the Sex Pistols and other punk bands. "It's like building a statue in sand," Robbins said, "and then watching the tide come up." The tide was MTV and the ensuing changing of the musical guard. Robbins was not willing to "lunge for the commercial jugular" by stressing Boy George, Duran Duran, or other video fixtures.[10] On its obituary page *Rolling Stone* led "'Trouser Press' magazine, March 1974 - April 1984."

Only three U.S. fanzines achieved a major place in rock journalism; *Crawdaddy, Bomp,* and *Trouser Press* played a significant role, although overshadowed by the *Rolling Stone* and in a limited way *Creem.* As Robbins and Shaw illustrate, fanzines possess the spark, dedication, and enthusiasm of writers whose commitment to music prompts endless analyses and reams of prose. Fanzines also had a less positive imprint on the whole of rock journalism.

The labor of love with its inherent informality and emotionalism violated many of the foundations of professional journalism. Fanzine writers frequently were ignorant of the sacred "5 W's" lead paragraphs and even the need for reportorial objectivity. In this fogged milieu of idealism some brilliant writing materialized, sidebarred by mushy accolades from the maven of the latest rising star or cult artist. Like the scripts of old movies, fanzine writing could be stimulating, but most of the time it was amateurish.

One fanzine survivor termed his experience as "on-the-job training," making all "your mistakes in print." In the underground press tradition, fanzines were a training ground, like university newspapers, for music journalists. Some graduated to the big leagues through the ranks of the prozines when columnists were required to fill space in the entertainment sections of dailies and newsmagazines. The graduates, however, carried some unfortunate baggage. Many publishers viewed music critics as second-class journalistic citizens. The late Connie Hechtor, publisher of *Insider* in Minneapolis, told a group of rock critics, "You sit on your ass and listen to an album and then write a review. What makes that worth five dollars an hour? Huh?" Most music critics were employed as stringers, paid on a per-item basis. Neophyte staff writers frequently were assigned concert reviews on the assumption that "anybody can write about music."

Fanzines rarely could afford salaries, and the writers did not seem to mind. But this economic reality based on hardship was incorporated into the more affluent structure of prozines, creating an unhealthy journalistic environment.

Because few writers can live on an income derived from writing, they are in a dependency role vis-à-vis the music industry. Former publicist Lew Segal tells of a Los Angeles music writer who earned $800 in one year during the early 1970s, the golden age of the rock press. The rest of his income was provided by record company perks. Chet Flippo, who was once with *Rolling Stone,* recalls several of his colleagues who managed on $1,200. Mike Ochs described the Los Angeles writer's life-style:

> With the fringe benefits, like for all the press parties you get free food, you get free records, and so you get like 500 records in the mail. Say you're going to sell 450 of them, so you've got money coming in. There's just a lot of freebies that keep you going. The average mediocre writer just cannot make it. There's no way you can make a living off of it, because the papers don't pay that much.

The cost of servicing the rock press has been a bone of contention with record-company executives. One said, "It's not the record companies' responsibility to support free-lance writers any more than it is the freelance writer's obligation to return a good review for a free drink." Furthermore, "A lot of kids who turn four reviews for the [L.A.] *Free Press* suddenly feel that it is the obligation of the record industry to indulge them and entertain them. I look at it as investment and return." Bob Garcia: "I will honor a request from a kid that can't by a Humble Pie album in Cleveland, Ohio, before I will for a second-string writer. . . because I know the kid's going to get more fun out of that record than that critic. And the critic isn't going to do the record any good anyway." Prior to the "crash of '79" many labels did service a large number of writers with everything from free meals to press parties, especially in Los Angeles and New York. "If you're gonna live off the industry, L.A.'s the place to do it," the author was told.

The "crash of '79" changed much. Promotion budgets were trimmed, sometimes axed. Press parties were special occasions. Guest lists become more selective. Free T-shirts disappeared. "Street" writers in the *L.A. Free Press* tradition dwindled in number. All this left a handful of cultists and avocationists as the outside watchdogs.

Jon Landau believes that cultists become careerists because of the freebies:

> The music critic is oppressed by records. He is surrounded by them. In fact, he may be receiving as many as a hundred in a week, all free, and all crying out for his time, energy, and interest. Whether he realizes it or not they become merchandise . . . he searches through stacks looking for something interesting, something he can love, something he can hate, something he can respond to. Because of the limited time and the unlimited volume of what lies before him, three plays of an album is a lot.

Another critic echoes this statement:

> Say you hear a thousand records in a year, the odds are you aren't going to like very many of them because you get to know what is derivative and what isn't. The kid on the street gets off on Grand Funk. The writer just passes, saying there isn't one original lick there . . . the kid gets off on it. He doesn't care.

Both points are well taken. Reviewers were inundated with records and free concerts, thus minimizing their emotional involvement. In this manner cultists become careerists. Economic realities impinge on careerists, whose journalistic tenures are relatively short-lived. Rock writers, a friend observed, "either become publicists, professionals, or simply disappear." In the early days prozines advertised for cultists willing to work for fanzine "wages" in the journalist big leagues.

## The Prozines

Richard Goldstein was the first of the prozine writers. His *Village Voice* column, "Popeye," treated many artists and concerts in a descriptive *verte* fashion, but Goldstein was really a chronicler of the music scene as it existed in New York.

*Cheetah,* a monthly and a well-produced slick, was written for young people rather than by them. Articles like Tom Nolan's "Groupies: A Story of Our Time" and Harry Shearer's "Captain Pimple Creems Fiendish Plot" dotted its pages. They addressed the more bizarre and sensational aspects of rock, leading one *Crawdaddy* partisan to write, "Everything reads very well, but you never remember anthing when you finished reading it."[11]

Following the lead of the *Voice,* other underground papers included pop-music criticism and articles in their back pages. The first issue of the *Oracle,* then titled *P.O. Frisco,* contained a review of the Beatles' *Revolver* and the Jefferson Airplane's maiden album, *Takes Off.* The unsigned reviewer praised both albums but chided Ralph J. Gleason's handling of the Airplane's liner notes as "unfortunately little more than a Madison Avenue toothpaste commerical." After an editorial change to a totally psychedelic format, the *Oracle* carried record reviews only when it recommended some albums as proper for "inner space flights," and that was rarely.

The *Los Angeles Free Press* and *Open City* ran occasional record reviews by writers such as Liza Williams, Bob Garcia, Clair Brush, Pete Senoff, and Michael Ochs. All of these critics went on to publicity departments of major record companies. Only the *Free Press's* spirited John Carpenter, now dead, did not retire into the industry scene.

The *Berkeley Barb* featured a weekly column by Ed Denson, former manager of Takoma Records and later Country Joe McDonald's road manager, dealing with happenings at the Fillmore and the Jabberwock, a folk-music club. Denson, a folkie by heritage, devoted much of his column to this genre. While with Country Joe, Denson wrote a chronology of their tours and encounters with fans, other bands, and the police.

For the Bay Area music buff, Ralph J. Gleason was the only aboveground, regularly printed critic. His musical credentials were rooted in the world of jazz, where he spent many years as a critic for *Downbeat* as well as a San Francisco daily. The increasing fragmentation of jazz into esoteric subgenres, the closing of the Blackhawk night club, and the decline of the big bands left Gleason with only the folk-music revival to fill his "On the Town" columns in the *Chronicle.* He began covering nightclub appearances of pop and folk singers at the Hungry i and the Purple Onion, with occasional treatments of "Fatha" Hines and visiting jazzmen.

The pro-civil rights thrust in folk music in 1963 and 1964 found a natural ally in the former jazz critic. Gleason devoted a number of his columns and Sunday features to the Weavers, Joan Baez, and especially Bob Dylan. Dylan's, first West Coast appearance at the Monterey Folk Festival converted Gleason. Glowing headlines such as "Dylan Places Poetry in the Hands of Youth," "The Voice of the New Generation," and "Bob Dylan, Poet of the '60s" typified Gleason's approach to the singer. When Dylan fled the folk genre he took many followers into the rock scene, Gleason among them. Unlike the East Coast Greenwich Village setting where white blues interpreters reigned supreme, San Francisco provided the writer with an endemic rock milieu composed in part of people who had made a similar musical transformation. The Jefferson Airplane gleaned its name from bluesman Blind Lemon Jefferson. Many local groups such as Wildflower,

Quicksilver Messenger Service, Big Brother and the Holding Co., and the Warlocks, later called the Grateful Dead, specialized in folk-rock and blues. Gleason became friend, counselor, promoter, and critic of the entire commerical San Francisco rock scene. In the "This World" section of the *Chronicle,* Gleason frequently did album reviews in a style reminiscent of his *Down Beat* days, pointing to the brilliant guitar work of Jerry Garcia or the improved bass playing of Phil Lesh.

By 1967 certain clear paths of popular music journalism were on the horizon. *Cheetah* and *Eye* were prozines. They were profit oriented, and some of their material consisted of play-by-play descriptive coverage. They directed the reader's attention but did not excite. Jon Landau labeled writers for these publications as "careerists" who lacked imagination and passion for their subject matter. Indeed, he claims the cultists in time became careerists: "Growing professionalism begins to contain their emotional involvement with the subject, ultimately bleeding it dry. Their inspiration recedes, the ambition expands, and we are left with another critic whose career outlasts his commitment."[12]

*Crawdaddy* appeared as a labor of love, flouting convention, missing publications dates, skipping issues; it was in fact an informal "open letter." Most of its early contributors were students and music freaks long before the term *freak* was popularized. Only the most dedicated fan could read through its free associational prose and science fiction without a sense of bewilderment. Neither *Crawdaddy* nor *Cheetah* fulfilled their own goals, but the posture exemplified in the two journals became recurrent themes. Terms such as *fanzine* and *cultist* would be applied to *Crawdaddy*-like critics and magazines, while *prozine* and *careerist* would be indicative of the *Cheetah* approach. Somewhere between these two approaches lay the ideal emotionally motivated, technically good music criticism.

### *Rolling Stone*: Prozine and Fanzine?

*Rolling Stone* attempted to merge the excitement of a fanzine with good professional writing. The idea originated with Jann Wenner, a former University of California student who had written a rock-music column for the *Daily Californian* and then gone on to a brief stint as entertainment editor for *Sunday Ramparts.* In the summer of 1967 the unemployed journalist approached *Ramparts* colleague Ralph Gleason with his plan for a rock paper. Wenner recalled, "I knew we could do it right. We'd have something that was clearly needed and nobody else was doing."[13] With an investment of $7,500 and a part-time volunteer staff, *Rolling Stone* appeared in November 1967 as a 16-page magazine. The first run of 45,000 copies earned $1,000 from four pages of records ads, and sold 6,000. The paper introduced itself to a few curious readers saying:

> You're probably wondering what we are trying to do. It's hard to say: sort of a magazine and sort of a newspaper. The name of it is ROLLING STONE, which comes from an old saying: "A rolling stone gathers no moss." Muddy Waters used the name for a song he wrote: The Rolling Stones took their name from Muddy's songs, and 'Like A Rolling Stone' was the title of Bob Dylan's first rock and roll record.
>
> We have begun a new publication reflecting what we see are the changes in rock and roll and the changes related to rock and roll. Because the trade papers have become so inaccurate and irrelevant, and because fan magazines are an anachronism, fashioned in the mold of myth and nonsense, we hope that we have something here for the artists and the industry, and every person who "believes in the magic that can set you free."
>
> ROLLING STONE is not just about music, but also about the things and attitudes that the music embraces. We've been working quite hard on it and we hope you will dig it. To describe it any further would be difficult without sounding like bullshit, and bullshit is like gathering moss.

The paper was an unusual mix of the *London Times* Roman typeset and the underground press format. The opening section included news stories; feature articles on music, drugs, and politics; an interview section; and finally book and record reviews. Early issues urged readers to submit articles and reviews. The *Stone,* as Wenner is quick to point out, was not an underground newspaper. It was instead, a hybrid encompassing some of the fervor of fanzines, for some of the early contributors did come from this tradition, but with a distinct leaning toward the professional journalism absent in some fanzines and segments of the underground press. *Rolling Stone* did not adhere strictly to rock music; it also focused on segments of the "new culture."

Articles appeared on custom cars, the roller derby, political gatherings, and films, prompting *Newsweek* to characterize its fare as "executed with news sense, style, intelligence and fervor by a young staff for whom rock is a way of life." Wenner's business tactics and philosophy that "capitalism is what allows us the incredible indulgence of this music" evoked considerable criticism.[14] Abbie Hoffman, for one, in a letter to *Rolling Stone* (28 October 1971) accused the paper of being controlled by the Xerox Corporation. Wenner's placement of an expensive full-page ad in the *New York Times* that concluded, "If you are a corporated executive trying to understand what is happening to youth today, you cannot be without *Rolling Stone*" and various promotional gimmicks such as free books and records with subscriptions all raised eyebrows in the "new community."

The *Stone's* relationship to the music industry and politics inspired polemics. Mike Lydon, a free-lance writer and vociferous critic of the music industry, charged in a *Newsweek* interview that *Rolling Stone* had "lost the battle to be a newspaper independent . . . of the industry. They're still a trade magazine."[15] This description was not without some merit in the early years when much of the publication's income was derived from music-industry advertising. By late 1970 the dependence was considerably reduced when newsstand sales, estimated at around $60,000 a month, matched the advertising revenue of the paper. Subscriptions were an added plus for the paper. With a circulation of 400,000 and an operation with a "book value" of $7.5 million, Wenner is proud of himself: "We've never missed a payroll; that is just being a smart businessman." The fact that Wenner is a self-admitted high-salaried executive did not endear him or the paper to segments of the counterculture.

Wenner and *Rolling Stone* have been frequently attacked for lack of political commitment. Frank Kofsky, writer for *Jazz & Pop,* asserted, "*Rolling Stone* is the ideal vehicle for corporate-liberal ideology . . . because it is striving manfully to reduce the revolution in youth consciousness to nothing more than a handful of novel consumer tastes."[16] Closer to home, Greil Marcus, former record-review editor for the *Stone,* told one journalist the paper had neglected the significant issue of the times, such as the shootings of college protesters and Black Panthers. He said, "I didn't find that Jann was really interested." Wenner denies the allegation, pointing to numerous stories dealing with street and campus confrontations. Former editor John Burks was more cautious: "Kent State and Cambodia have concerned more of us. . . than the latest news on Paul McCartney." This, he continued, was "the trivialization of *Rolling Stone.*" To these charges Alan Rinzler, the head of *Rolling Stone's* Straight Arrow book publishing line, replied, "There's no rhetoric in *Rolling Stone,* no doctrinaire position. I know a lot of people have accused the paper of making millions off the movement, but that's just nonsense because. . . it's never made a dime. It's just out there, and it isn't exploiting anyone."[17]

For music-industry executives, *Rolling Stone* was "out there" as a barometer. Record makers in mod clothing read it as closely as *Billboard, Cashbox,* or the *Wall Street Journal.* Texas blues guitarist Johnny Winter reportedly received a $300,000 contract from Columbia Records on the basis of an audition made possible by a story in *Rolling Stone.* A Columbia executive claims it was the curiosity factor—"Who's worth that much?"—and not the praise that resulted in the signing. Quotations from laudatory reviews frequently are used in record ads. Indeed, many industry people believe that good reviews are valid only for future advertisements. Ruthann Ponnech, a former Epic Records publicist, recalled, "Their main function is to clip out for advertising. And it's through advertising and getting a record played on the radio that you really get it sold."[18]

This was especially true after the spring of 1972 when *Rolling Stone* began to withdraw from the rock music as its major staple. The presidential campaign of George McGovern further reduced an already skimpy record-review section. Wenner decided that the publication should become "the *Time* magazine of youth." *Rolling Stone* began to stress the abortive McGovern run, the California marijuana initiative, the activities of narcotics-control agencies, Jane Fonda, and some "news briefs." "It doesn't take me *as* long to read it" was a frequent comment from subscribers. The magazine carried more material, but it was material not geared primarily to the music fan. *Creem* began to advertise itself as "America's only rock 'n' roll magazine." The *Stone's* Los Angeles editor, Bob Chorush, resigned in protest and was replaced by Judy Sims, a Warner Bros. publicist. The music stories began to shift to the more bizarre or to artists like David Cassidy and Grand Funk, previously considered beneath the tastes of *Rolling Stone* readers. David Bowie, Alice Cooper, and Black Sabbath received extensive coverage. In August 1972 Jon Landau mailed out his first impersonal duplicated letter to reviewers announcing his move to New York. Stephen Davis, a friend from Cambridge and a virtual unknown to most West Coast critics, took over as review editor. Davis maintained the writers of the Landau regime. In the issue of 3 August 1972 the review format changed: longer, more in-depth reviews of established artists. Only 22.5 percent of the 151 reviews printed in 1972 under Davis's editorship were of new artists; many were either on blues reissues series or on jazz artists generally foreign to rock music fans. More than three-quarters of the reviews treated known performers; even some "greatest-hits" albums got space. In 1973 Landau temporarily returned to the record review section.

Following the Nixon landslide victory, subscribers to *Rolling Stone* received a letter announcing, "Evil, mysterious elements of our society are trying to put us out of business. Our costs have skyrocketed because of these friends." The "friends" turned out to be the forces of inflation plaguing the entire U.S. press. "They charged us more for paper, for printing, for postage. Yes, postage too. To continue putting out 26 great issues a year and deliver them to your eager fingertips is costing us an arm, a leg, and possibly a few other vital organs." Readers were asked to renew prior to the expiration of their subscriptions. *Life* magazine announced its dissolution, but *Rolling Stone* was not destined to a similar fate. It is no longer predominantly a music magazine, however, Ben Fong-Torres, one of the few original staffmen with the paper, then said, "Many of us turning 30 are less enthralled with the teenybopper approach to music and are therefore more interested in other cultural events."[19]

By the mid-1970s, *Rolling Stone*'s claim to being a music magazine was questionable. Record-industry people grumbled to one another about the changeover. One publicist said, "Jon Landau's doing a good job with the review section, but the rest of it". . . A *Stone* staffman said privately that even the music covered is now totally conservative and tied to the *Billboard* charts. One artist confessed, "I got covered in the *Stone* because I told them an album was coming out!" Unsigned artists were no longer welcome in the pages of the paper.

Wenner geographically emphasized the new approach by transferring to headquarters in New York, the nation's media center. The move to the world of Madison Avenue and Wall Street dispelled any lingering doubts about the magazine's upward mobility.

The internecine warfare at the *Stone* and its success launched and kept alive a legion of fledgling quasi-prozines. The internal disputes created a legion of unemployed writers and reviewers anxious to continue *the* lifestyle.

### "The Others"

The unprecedented success of *Rolling Stone* spawned a large number of other rock magazines, many of which received industry encouragement if not actual economic support. *Crawdaddy,* under new ownership, was revived in tabloid form. Many other papers, such as *Circus, Rag, Rock, Creem, Phonograph Record,* and *Zoo World,* appeared on the scene. Nearly all fall somewhere on the continuum between the fanzine and the overt professionalism of *Rolling Stone.*

*Creem* was unique because it began as a platform, for Detroit John Sinclair's punkrock. This school saw rock music as a revolutionary force; rock generated "engery," which was then transformed into sociopolitical action. Groups like the MC-5 were presented as "killer bands" that produced loud music with exaggerated stage performances. Subtle, longlauded "in" folkrock and Beatles material was considered too intellectual and bourgeois. Some of the assumptions of the Sinclair school would in time reemerge in the reviewers' debate over the esthetic quality of Grand Funk Railroad, a group from the Ann Arbor-Detroit grid.

*Phonograph Record* magazine was originally owned by United Artists Records and used name reviewers. It was a successor to the *Liberty Record,* a promotional magazine circulated during the early 1960s that was described as being "published in the interest of Liberty loving people"— which it was, featuring ads, many in-house communications regarding sales figures and gold-record presentations, and a great deal of hype. Norman Winter, who later made Elton John into a star, was the editor of

*Liberty Record. Phonograph Record* was staffed by many *Rolling Stone* and *Creem* reviewers, and had a circulation of over 100,000 via distribution through radio stations in major markets such as Cleveland, St. Louis, Detroit, Los Angeles, and Chicago. Editor Martin Cerf claimed, "It is not a UA hype sheet. The way it helps United Artist is that we have advertising in there—exclusive advertising except for usually half a page we give to a record company we editorially feel needs exploitation and isn't getting that chance to have their product where it's seen." The only United Artists acts that received exposure in *Phonograph Record,* according to Cerf, were those discussed in other publications: "We get percentage of product covered in our publication that would get into any publication because when it comes time for us to have something meaningful in there then people believe it." Cerf readily admitted that *Phonograph Record* was designed to get around the usual gatekeeper; with it United Artists was in a position to reach both media and customer. United Artists considered it a good investment until mid-1973, when Cerf departed. *Phonograph Record* solicited ads from all record companies,[20]and temporarily it did quite well but folded in 1979.

Music magazines in the mid-1970s were in trouble. Wenner's strategy was correct. More important, he had the resources to hire feature writers in politics and film. The competition was tied to similar cover stories, tours, concerts, and record reviews. Style of presentation and quality of writing varied from magazine to magazine but content remained remarkably similar in all. Only *Creem,* having hooked onto the Kiss phenomenon, maintained its readership; in 1976, it claimed 800,000, or 6.1 persons per issue. Almost two-thirds of its audience was under 24 years of age. *Creem's* "narrowcast" demographic formula worked while other publications fell like autumn leaves. The 1960s generation was outgrowing the rock culture, and only specialty magazines like *Creem* or young-adult, general-interest publication like the *Stone* survived.

### The Cultural Commentators: The Reviewers

The precise role of the record reviewer in regard to the industry and readership is unclear. Robert Christgau, a *Village Voice* and *Creem* writer, sees reviewing as a "consumer convenience." An anonymous introduction to a collection of *Rolling Stone* reviews defines the reviewer as standing "between the listeners and the incredible mass of phonograph records cast forth by the music industry every month. Compared to the burdens and responsibilities of the reviewer, the work of Nader's Raiders is mere child's play."[21] A record once purchased remains with the consumer, at least when the defects are aesthetic rather than mechanical. This is a highly romanticized view of the reviewer.

As the prolific late Lester Bangs noted, "Rock writers are absolutely expendable, unnecessary slots filled for reasons of tradition and capitalist publishing ventures." Another critic hazarded that a review in *Fusion* or *Changes* might possibly yield "37 album purchases in either a direct or indirect manner."[22] Bangs declared that many industry people believe that reviewers "know something industry people don't"—a highly dubious proposition because a large number of "name" reviewers are in fact employed by recording companies in their publicity departments. The critic-publicist route is a well-traveled one. Geoffrey Stokes of the *Voice*: "Record companies hire rock writers as publicists; the same writers then publish favorable articles about their clients."[23] Chet Flippo of *People*: "Some of them also—sometimes under pseudonyms—write reviews for various rock magazines. Often the reviews are of groups that they represent."[24] Such covert activity is difficult to justify. One publicist/writer cynically commented on the practice, "It's only a record review!"

Sub-rosa writing is generally unnecessary because review editors frequently assign albums to free-lancers knowledgeable about and partial to particular styles and artists. In such cases the odds of a favorable review are enhanced. The ploy does not always work because there is no fury like that of a music cultist angered by a flawed or out-of-character performance by a favorite artist. Stylistic changes by the Rolling Stones and Bob Dylan generated a negative outcry from coast to coast.

The main function of record reviewers for both the industry and the audience is to expose. A review by Jon Landau motivated one reader to write: "I'd heard some of those LPs he recommended before, ran out and got all the ones he cited that I hadn't heard, and he was fucking right. They are all excellent." With a few well-chosen paragraphs a reviewer can convey, at least in part, a message that would take at least 45 minutes of airplay. Moreover, a review section can accommodate 10 to 20 reviews, depending on space. The defunct *Trouser Press* ran 150 in one issue. *Rockin' Chair,* also defunct, contained minireviews cover to cover.

Time and space are finite. The electronic media is governed by the almighty clock; space is supreme in print. The mechanics of allotting space are a nightmare, especially for record reviews. *Rolling Stone* recently has presented a five-column layout, which works out to 30 to 40 columns, depending on 6 to 8 pages set aside for reviews and the amount of advertising. In the issue for 18 March 1982 the record editor had eight pages that yielded 20 full- or half-page columns to work with. Simon and Garfunkel's *Concert in Central Park* led the section with three columns of copy and four columns devoted to a Blair Drawson illustration, leaving 13 columns and half-columns for 17 other reviews. Two and a half years later the Jacksons' *Victory* album took 9 columns—4 devoted to a graphic—from a total of 16; the remaining 7 columns went to a similar number of artists. In both instances the front review dominated, consuming approximately half the space allocation. Such editorial decisions leave little room for lesser-known artists and established acts should they have the misfortune to release simultaneously with star product.

Space limitations are as constraining as CHR playlists. A record editor for a defunct paper said: "If a superstar released a record, especially one hot in this market, there goes most of the space not to mention five or six albums." And: "One issue, Elektra had Carly Simon, Bob Dylan, and Joni Mitchell. That was it. A lot of copy went into that garbage." When writers get paid by the item this is unpleasant. Staffers normally write the superstar reviews. Readers appear more concerned with aesthetically poor efforts by familiar names than "exciting" new bands or artists.

One editor has a system whereby albums are stacked on the basis of name recognition, style, and unsuitables, and records are assigned for review in that order. It is only by chance and luck that any of the "unknowns" get a listen: "The last time was Dire Straits and that was because a friend raved about them."

*Popular Music and Society,* a 14-year-old quarterly, had an abundance of space for record reviews, but recently, with an increase in music books and a video section, coverage became a problem. The journal is considered a secondary source and most of the best-selling albums take a back seat to lesser-known artists unless the album is especially newsworthy. *PMS,* however, has a different philosophy and orientation than mass-marketed publications.

Rock journalism in dailies is dictated by several factors. What is "newsworthy" translates into "of local interest" and the writer's proclivities. In light of space considerations, local-interest items have top priority. "When a band comes to town," said one columnist, "they almost automatically get a feature story and a concert review." The assassination of a music star might alter the pattern but it is unlikely because critics depend on promoters for tickets and backstage passes. Slack time does allow for some discretionary writing. A writer's interest may see the light of day, assuming the wire services and the editor permit. "I researched a piece for a week and the Grammy nominees were announced. There went the story," said a journalist.

With the demands of profit versus loss, advertising takes precedence over copy. Adding more pages and columns is expensive. The result is that content suffers but the owners are happy.

For the industry exposure is properly another avenue by which the potential consumer can be reached. As Mike Gormley of A & M once noted, "Once they hear him, all is well." To accomplish this end, record companies employ a number of gimmicks ranging from a myriad of press releases to West Coast junkets with all expenses paid. Before 1979 some writers did well. Loraine Alterman, once a contributor to *Rolling Stone,* estimated that in a three-week period she received 65 pieces of mail from 22 record companies and assorted flacks—"That makes a three-inch pile." Many reviewers were mailed anywhere from 25 to 30 albums a week, freebies that appeared to attract many writers into reviewing. Marty Cerf said he was in the business "to get records." Mike Ochs hosted a late-night jazz show while he was at Ohio State so as to secure free records. Another writer, who preferred anonymity: "The promo stuff corrupted me in college. I have to keep writing to receive the ever-increasing number of LPs. I would go broke buying them." Some prominent critics, like Greg Shaw, Chet Flippo, and Ochs are avid collectors.

In addition to albums, critics were given posters and a variety of knick-knacks. Stan Staaph of *Rock* magazine received a Joe Cocker watch, harmonicas, maracas, a Jeremy Steig flute, and many T-shirts. Reaction to these goodies varies from recipient to recipient. Loraine Alterman considerd much of her mail to be "garbage." Others seemed delighted to be recipients. One critic stated, "One of the nicest aspects of doing this was that it was Christmas every weekday morning. You never know what goodies the mailman may bring." Established "name" reviewers were occasionally flown out to the West Coast for a weekend convention by some company or for a gala evening being given by an act.

Record companies serviced a large number of writers who had bylines; they were given everything from junkets to free food to well-stocked press parties. Chet Flippo provides an illustration of *la dolce vita* in the mid-seventies:

> An acquaintance of the author has recently traveled to the Caribbean, New York City, Los Angeles, Chicago, Denver, and San Francisco and is now on the waiting lists for Tokyo and London. Last year, his income from writing was approximately $1,300; but his expenses, aside from rent, are negligible. When he's not on a junket, there are always record company publicists who will take him to lunch. Then there are press parties for touring rock groups: free caviar, quiche lorraine, and the best liquor. His outfit consists of two pairs of jeans and a dozen free record company teeshirts. For beer money, he sells about $25 worth of free promotional records each week. If he needs money for a new turntable, he can call a friend at a record company and earn $100 for writing a quick press release or short "artist biography." He maintains that he is under no obligation to the companies that are paying his way but he also

realizes that the writers who get the junkets are those who can be depended upon to turn out "favorable" or "positive" articles.[25]

The effectiveness of press agentry and openhandedness is difficult to assess. Nearly all of the larger record companies participate in the ritual, negating any advantage one company might derive over another. One industry executive indicated that some reviewers will accept gratuities in exchange for a good review. This may be true, but there is precious little reported evidence. (In the author's 20 years of music writing and reviewing he has yet to see or hear about the exchange of cash for a review.) Other corrupting influences may be more significant. The personal contact between writer and artist may in some cases influence a review. Bruce Harris of *Cashbox*: "As soon as you hear a rock critic say he hangs out a lot with so-and-so, run. They guy is not to be trusted."[26]

Harris's remark is idealist. Interaction between writers and acts are occupational. A onetime road manager of Waylon Jennings said, "It's just friends. It's all on the basis of friendship." Only the most naive neophyte would accept that statement. Artists want *good* press. Writers desire a *good* story. The two are not the same. A publicist told a journalist, "That was a great interview with [so-and-so]; he really opened up. *But* don't do that to any of my people." The relationship between a journalist and an artist is utilitarian. "Using" is the name of the game. Relationships between label publicists and writers are considerably more difficult.

Many publicists are journalists. Friendships do exist or develop, and appear to have considerable influence in getting a reviewer's attention. Attention does not always insure a positive review of the publicist's act; several people take the position that in many cases it is kindness not to write about an album. *Rolling Stone* avoids running critical reviews, especially of a new act: "It's better simply to ignore a record like that," says Tim Ferris.[27] Friendships do work in a publicist's favor when the publicist is aware of the tastes of various writers. "Knowing that a critic is really into an act is a great help," said one publicist. A former RCA executive observed that friendships affect what appears in print: "Critics write for each other, a kind of Freudian-Skinnerian reinforcement or whatever." In all, the bias in record reviewing appears to be more structural than consciously induced, at least when publicity people are not writing the reviews.

Publicists appeal to the preferences of contributors. For example, a writer known to be a strong supporter of a particular act is given an advance copy of a record. The odds of a bad or mechanical review in such a case are negated. "Off the record," said one nationally known writer, "X knows I'm into a performer. So he assigns me his new album. Ain't *no* way the review will be a turkey." This practice eliminates much of the careerist aspect of journalism. Although certainly not as objective form of journalism, such an assignment procedure does provide generally well-written and researched reviews. Record companies resort to other techniques to reach the music writer.

MCA Records sent out a press release with albums bearing the admonition "Damn it, this is important, read it." MCA released albums in staggering amounts. One press release informed the critic:

> In keeping with our policy, unofficially known as DOTP (Don't Overload the Press), PART ONE of our "FUNKY FALL" release consists of a mere hot half dozen new albums offered for your delight and delectation. PART TWO will include some equally exciting releases and you should be receiving them within a few weeks. In the meantime, it is hoped you'll *set aside a few quiet hours to allow yourself* a chance to get into the goodies [constituting] PART ONE.

The request would not be unreasonable under normal conditions. However, when one multiplies the number of competing companies making less-polite requests for time, the result is predictable. Many labels have resorted to a "by-request" system for album service. To illustrate, RCA sends out a monthly release list, on which the recipient checks off the desired product. This works efficiently but there is the problem of turn-around time—some product arrives after the publishing deadline.

In the glory days of rock journalism, excessive product volume was a problem. Many writers used Ron Jacobs's yardstick: if the opening cut on side one does not have a "hook," forget it. The result is that most new acts find their records, one week after release, in Sam Goody's or Emmanuel Aaron's used-record bins where they are traded or sold for "known winners." As one critic put it. "You're not gonna wanna *keep* every album by the Putnam Sisters, are you? Or even play all the cuts." Martin Cerf, when announcing the release of *American Pie,* wrote, "So before you put it in your Goody's or Aaron's Record Store pile, I suggest if you don't have an opportunity to hear it, you at least hold on to it." Cerf's advice in this instance was valid; *American Pie* was one of the most aesthetically successful albums of that year. A year later Capitol Records attempted a similar maneuver, sending reviewers one Bloodrock album for trading and the other (minus the jacket) for listening. Copies without the jackets were still sent on to Aaron's, and Bloodrock did not receive the critical acclaim the company desired. The explanation for this may be simply that *American Pie* would have sold regardless of the Cerf letter; however, as one United Artists commented, "But then it may not have. You never know." The number of "good" acts that escape recognition is almost impossible to estimate, considering the relativity of critical judgment. Many outstanding albums did and do go through the reviewing cracks.

During the mid-1970s the wave of promotional gadgets and T-shirts subsided. T-shirts were becoming a highly profitable merchandise item at concerts, and licensing agreements occasionally barred labels from using the flimsy shirts as promotional tools. Review albums also became less attractive as saleable items. Writers Segel and Flippo claimed "to make more money selling their promo albums than they make writing about them—$1,000 a year is not an exaggeration"[28] Rather than drilling or clipping album corners, companies embossed "Not For Sale" or "Ownership Reserved/Sale is Unlawful" prominently on covers. This practice did not stop sales to retail outlets but did lower the black-market value of the goods. Merchandisers carrying "promo" material still received cartons of new products from other industry sources (see the section on payola in chapter 5). Labels could not take on major radio stations or control their field personnel, who received the bulk of promotional recordings. Following the "crash of '79" review service lists were chopped. Experienced publicists were terminated (see chapter 3). *Popular Music and Society's* record service, for example, was cut by 60 percent and has not recovered. Journalists in secondary markets were equally affected, and scarcity of reviewable product became a concern; a media person bitterly wrote, "It's not who you are. It's *where* you are." Junketing became rare especially when the so-called opinion makers worked for news organizations that prohibited such trips. The "fat farm" days apparently were history.

The numerical decline of prozines and lack of industry goodies altered the nature of rock journalism. "Avocationists" became significant factors in rock journalism. They are older, a synthesis of Landau's dichotomy: postcultists/careerists choosing to dabble in the business while also pursuing more lucrative means of support.

Free-lancing and "stringing" is difficult. The pay is minimal and irregular. The market has dwindled considerably since the 1970s. Some experienced writers feel uncomfortable with newer styles and music video publications geared toward a teenage market. "I didn't like *Creem* a decade ago. *Rock Video's* not much better," said a free-lancer. "The remaining magazines that are halfway literate use staffers. They don't pay worth a damn in contrast to some of the skin or adventure men's magazines." A few avocationists are strictly in the business for the music. "I like to keep up. . . there's still some good stuff being released that you'll never hear unless you're a jock or a critic."

Old critics never die, the adage goes, they just become public relations types, academics, or legitimate writers. A number are professors, usually in the humanities or social sciences. Four are sociologists who teach or have taught courses treating the music business. One believes hands-on experience is essential. Teaching university classes dealing with the industry evokes little if any assistance from the labels. Without a press card and a byline, it is very difficult to stay abreast of the dynamics of the industry. One academic-writer rarely mentions the professorial role. A Capitol publicist used the phrase "closet academics." *Newsweek*'s Jim Miller is a member of the ivy-tower crowd. Authors supplement their semiannual royalty checks with features and reviews. In light of the Author's Guild report that their average bookish member earns a little over $4,000 a year, the economic motivation is clearly evident.

The avocationists, no matter how well trained, can be generationally biased. A letter to the editor of the *Honolulu Star-Bulletin* underscores the situation: "I am 14 years old and maybe age has something to do with our difference of opinion." With the exception of the ageless Dave Marsh, a host of still-active writers are uncomfortable with, or frequently avoid, contemporary pop music artists. Some have transferred their allegiance to country music. Others write *auteur* reviews of older acts with considerable fervor. Applying the criteria of the 1960s and 1970s to current favorites does create a generational gap even if criticism is well reasoned. Asked by Ted Koppel, moderator on ABC's *Nightline* if the Jacksons, "Victory Tour" at "thirty dollars a crack" was worth it, Griel Marcus, the authoritative writer, answered, "No, because it was a standard show; because there were other shows that offered as much or more for far less." A majority of seasoned reporters covering the opening of the controversial "Victory Tour" agreed; the white middle-class MTV fans who could afford the concert disagreed. Indeed, coverage of music video (MV) especially MTV has been lukewarm at best.

MTV's debut was virtually ignored by music media other than trade magazines (see chapter 7). (The definitive article on the origins of video clips was written by Terry Atkinson and appeared in the 26 July 1979 issue of *Rolling Stone*.) Robert Hilburn, a syndicated *Los Angeles Times* writer, was a minority of one in his 4 August 1981 column.[29] Music journalists generally left the new cable network to the television critics. By 1983 MTV, like a noise in the dark of night, could not be overlooked. Articles headed by Steven Levy's "Ad Nauseam" in *Rolling Stone* led the assault. *Rock and Roll Confidential*, a music writers' peer-group trade paper, applauded and religiously hurled charges of racism at "Monopoly Television." Some of the criticisms leveled at Bob Pittman's brainchild have merit. Unfortunately, few writers objectively presented what MTV is doing; rather, most stressed what it should be doing. A *Guardian* writer labeled the channel "EMP-TYV"; Rob Baker of the *New York Daily News* called music video "moron TV." This all harkens back to the critical dichotomy that began with the advent of groups like Led Zeppelin and Grand Funk Railroad.

Early rock writing and reviewing was directed at a small peer group of music lovers whose tastes were relatively similar. Most listened to the Beatles, the Rolling Stones, the Zombies, and the Byrds. By 1967 bands had proliferated, and many different hyphen-rock bands existed. Critics no longer spoke for a monolithic body of fans, as they had during the days of Beatlemania. Monkees fans outnumbered the older rock-music buyers, but rock critics ignored so-called teenybop bands like Blue Cheer and the Strawberry Alarm Clock. Any comparison of a band reviewed in *Rolling Stone* to the Monkees was a distinct put down. Led Zeppelin, a spin-off band from the Yardbirds, muddled the distinction between the teenyboppers and the more avid Cream fans. Led Zeppelin was loud, flashy, and raunchy in the eyes of most critics, "heavy" in the most negative respect possible. Critical judgment notwithstanding, Zeppelin was an enormous commercial success. *Rolling Stone* readers attacked John Mendelsohn's reviews of the group. One called the analysis "a 100% lie. Pure bullshit." A Boston broadcaster complained, "If I used your record reviews as a guide to my personal record purchases, I would have the worst pile of garbage in the history of record collecting." The band itself, while in Los Angeles, tried to find Mendelsohn. Led Zeppelin more than any other group introduced the distinction between popularity and traditionalism. Other performers and fans, seeing their favorite acts ignored or panned, joined in : "What do we need critics for?" At first much of the dissent was labeled sour grapes and ignored. The continuing fragmentation of the rock-music scene in the late 1960s and the disbanding of many of the "quality" bands revived the issue of popular (prozine, careerist) versus aesthetic (fanzine, cultist) as the criterion of quality.

Terry Knight made Grand Funk the principal pawn in the controversy. Prominently displayed on a Grand Funk poster is a clipping of a review in *Rolling Stone*:

> *On Time*, Grand Funk Railroad (Capitol ST-307). One of the most simplistic, talentless, one-dimensional unmusical groups of the year. The drumming guaranteed to send you up the wall. Absolutely unbelievable.

Another, from Mike Jahn, formerly of the *New York Times*, termed the group "hideous." Also included on the poster were fan letters printed in crayon. The letters and the negative reviews clearly pointed up the adolescent public to which Grand Funk appealed. Most of the rock press, until the summer of 1971, ignored the trio as best it could. Private conversations at times raised the issue of Grand Funk's popularity and the taste of the record-buying public. Jahn's comment that "Mussolini was popular, too" found a sympathetic hearing, but Knight's success was not to be denied. After the Beatles' dissolution, Grand Funk became Capitol Records' major property, selling upwards of 10 million records. Knight's explanation was "noise. Pure undiluted, earsplitting, brain-numbing noise." He added,

"The reviews just don't matter. Take *Rolling Stone*, for instance. Its importance is a myth. Word of mouth travels faster than their presses. . . . *Rolling Stone* means nothing to the success or failure of a record or a concert." [30]

The only prozine to follow Knight's lead and raise the touchy cultist/careerist dichotomy was *Creem*, no stranger to loud bands. Detroit, after all, was the birthplace of shock-rock. Knight and his proteges were products of the area. In the June 1971 issue of *Creem*, Greil Marcus, a former *Rolling Stone* review editor, presented a lengthy analysis of rock writing and ideology. Music is the possession of teenagers who want something of their own, he wrote. "The fact that what they've got is scorned by critics and the people they speak for can do nothing but heighten the sense of delight in being separate and self-contained, bound together by a sense of common and exclusive experience." [31] Marcus singled out Grand Funk Railroad, echoing Knight's charge, "only *the* people like the group." The act, he continued, was the "biggest group in the world" despite the fact that their material was not aired on FM or AM radio, their records were panned or ignored by the rock press, and many older rock fans were either unaware or contemptuous of them. Marcus went on to challenge the sociopolitical assumptions of rock, arguing that the music essentially is "noise, fun and sound." Much of the article was a repeat of Knight's charges, but the speaker was a highly respected member of the rock fraternity and could not be easily ignored, especially because his departure had left *Rolling Stone* with numerous internal conflicts, personnel changes, and "commercial excesses," In *Creem* Marcus found a sympathetic audience that saw *Rolling Stone* as establishmentarian and Detroit as more "energized" and grass roots than other cities. One *Creem* reviewer, Richard Pinkston IV, looked upon Marcus's piece as vindication: "How come when I said all the things that Greil Marcus said . . . everybody laughed and called me a punk kid?"[32]

Donny Osmond of the Osmond Brothers, a bubble-gum group, entered the fray in a letter to the *Village Voice*. He contended that the time had come "for old rock critics to quit knocking the music people my age [14] like." In a defense of Black Sabbath, a group compared to Grand Funk Railroad, Osmond asserted that critic Bob Christgau was of another generation and did not understand the new sounds:

> Your column probably started long before I was ever a teenager. The Kennedys, the Movement, hippies, San Francisco, and so on—a lot of hopeful myths turned sour were all dismal failures by the time I was old enough to get stoned and buy records. . . . Watch out, Bob, admit you don't understand our music and concentrate on yours. Otherwise you'll sound like those old '50s jazz writers who used to try to analyze the Beatles.[33]

*Creem*, unlike the *Stone*, still requested submissions and reviews from readers, urging, "Nobody who writes for this rag's got anything you ain't got." David Marsh, then the editor of *Creem*, suggested that the magazine had ignored "people who are really significant" because there was a "whole new audience and the rock 'n' roll writer suddenly finds that he's the one freezin.'" Furthermore, "TEENAGE would seem to me to be one definition of rock 'n' roll, in the first place."[34] His essay outlined the position taken by Woody Guthrie, "You can't write about a whorehouse unless you been in one."

Patricia Kennedy lamented this trend in *Rock* magazine. "The Decline and Fall of Intelligent Rock Journalism" took note of the esthetic debate: "The criticism fell off to the point where . . . rock writers (there are probably no real critics anymore) find themselves justifying a horror like Grand Funk Railroad for the sole reason that if so many kids like Grand Funk there must be something there. Pigswill."[35] Several months later Jon Landau acknowledged that the critic was being polluted by his role because he doesn't "live with the record; he only plays it." The role of critic has built-in elements of careerism. Landau contended that such conditions can be overcome if the writer is committed to music: Commitment is the prerequisite of all valuable criticism."

*Billboard* writer Don Weller took issue, in part, with the Landau formulation of the rock reviewer as careerist:

> Critics of course cannot do their job and remain a "cultist." That's because whether they realize it (or desire it) or not, they are by occupational definition, an elite. The critic is a neurotic antenna, not an enthusiastic fan. He discriminates more than the fan. He thinks more. He knows more. He feels differently about music. And, there is nothing wrong about that, nothing to put the critic down for. Because the critic, as a member of a special elite, has special functions attached to his job.

Weller's point is not without support. Many critics do in fact believe, as does much of the press, that their knowledge is objectively superior to that of the everyday music fan. However, there is a good deal of dissent as to whether this accumulated expertise is careerism or transcendental vision.

The fan/writer cleavage is very real. By the mere act of buying a record or a concert ticket the fan has expressed a positive opinion. Concertgoers are in the venue by choice and preference. Critics generally attend for tomorrow's paper. "My schedule is determined by questions like who's in town tonight? Because obviously if I'm going to write about rock, I *ought* to go see [any act] . . . I owe that not only to the people who read this column, but to myself if I'm going to feel competent to write it," declared Geoffrey Stokes of the *Village Voice*.[36] There is a difference, as Bob Christgau suggests, between a paid fan and a paying fan. Albums can be a chore for a reviewer; a fan, at least momentarily, welcomes the experience. Occasionally there is a meeting of the minds, but more often they each look and listen for different things.

Critics have no psychic or economic commitment to an artist. Ticket and record buyers do. Writers observe, listen and, analyze. Fans have a good time, and in many cases know the material. The critic does not. Note the number of complaints in concert reviews that so-and-so "doesn't introduce songs." An experienced critic in a concert situation usually uses the crowd as the arbiter of the performance. Tom Basham of the *Baltimore Sun*: "I thought the Doobie Brothers were awful. The other 21,000 people in attendance seemed to love them."[37]

Lighters held aloft, screams, and applause do influence a review, especially when the writer is unfamiliar with the act, which is occasionally the case. This is a factor in the short shrift given to warm-up acts, especially those without a record company to provide a bio or an album. A well-stocked record library or a shelf of rock reference books are useless in dealing with an unknown group. This is an opportunity many labels and artists' management companies seem to miss. They assume the promoter staging the concert will publicize the opening act, something rarely done. The vast majority of press releases announcing a concert focus on the headliner.

Records and video cassettes pose a different set of criteria. An album like *Purple Rain* shipping platinum is not easily dismissed. Especially when it climbs to the *Billboard* top-twenty albums in a week. Other product is much less easily judged and the expertise of the writer comes into play. It is deemed good or bad based on his or her standards, standards shaped by months or years of musical exposure do color the end result. A factor explaining the "pans" received by "new music" groups is that for many writers the music is far from new. Writers commenting on the 1980s heavy metal always invoke the Velvet Underground, Deep Purple, and Led Zeppelin as pillars of comparison and find most new acts paling in contrast. Some fans are aware of Led Zeppelin, but the Velvets, who disbanded in 1970? (In 1985 the Velvets' old Verve material was reissued.)

The tone of this discussion underlines the nebulous nature of the role of record reviewers. They are expected to be a cultist representative of a specific taste public, yet Terry Knight accuses all of them of being insensitive to his acts. In one interview Knight acknowledged that his complaints regarding critics were publicity-getting devices: "We've baited the press, and I'll be the first to admit it." After that his group had reached the stardom, he added, "We don't need the press today to make Grand Funk more popular."

The assumption that one group popular with adolescents personified all of pop in a given genre in the 1970s is difficult to accept, considering the varieties of hyphen-rock available. What Knight had to say, however, does have merit, a point Landau by implication concedes. Grand Funk was a totally experimental unit a few, if any, pretensions. Minus its symbolism as targets of an establishment elitist press, Grand Funk probably would not have surpassed Knight's first group, the Pack, which failed dismally. About the followeres of Grank Funk, Knight admitted that *Rolling Stone*'s antipathy "made them rebels. If Grand Funk could overcome it all, they could, too. It offered the kids a hope and an escape." The difficulty lies in the fact that most critics are no longer 14-year-olds in need of escape and rebellion. Reviewing practices are greatly influenced by the taste preferences of reviewers. Music columnists, writes Tom Basham, "actually tell you more about the reviewer than they do about the review."

### Can't Buy Me Love?

An overt dependence on the record labels was born in the early days of rock journalism. Individual writers were especially vulnerable. Sam Maddox wrote, "None of the pack wants to be the one to test the corporate power structure's mettle."[38] The relationship between the industry and music publications is murky. "Especially with the smaller magazines, the record industry does exert a great deal of influence and can—and often does—decide that "it's time" a certain performer or group got a feature article. Editors do not like industry pressure but they don't talk about it."[39] A former *Rolling Stone* advertising director said, "Record companies can be awfully emotional about buying ads, which isn't true of other advertisers."[40]

Labels do become exercised about the nature of exposure they receive, bringing out the ultimate weapon, advertising, which is secretly done on rare occasions. The extent of this economic pressure occasionally surfaces.

A writer for the small, regional Cleveland-based *Exit* was told that a label would buy a full-page ad if a feature story on the artist could be arranged. Two weeks prior to the phone call the act had been interviewed but the editor had accidentally erased the tape, which meant the advertising revenue was lost. On another occasion the branch people of a major label threatened to curtail its advertising because it had published a negative quotation from one of its artists. Regional promotion offices, especially of a dominant label, can be *very* insistent.

During the bootleg phenomenon of the late 1960s a number of record labels became incensed over the practice and the antibusiness attitude of the rock press. *Rolling Stone* began to treat Rubber Dubber's bootleg records as legitimate releases. At the time the *Stone* was heavily dependent on industry advertising. Joe Smith, then with Warner Bros. Records, called

Jann Wenner to express considerable displeasure with the attitudes of the rock press concerning the bootlegs: "I cannot understand how you could even talk about those things."

> What disturbed me most was this great cavalier attitude the press took about that, and the rock community. . . . Wow, here's this Robin Hood coming along. Ain't that good, look what he's doing. Bullshit, they're not paying anybody. . . . I really was incensed with this rob from the rich and give to the poor attitude. Because they were robbing from the rich and weren't giving to anybody. They were getting rich from robbing from the rich.

In the following issue Ralph J. Gleason warned that counterfeiters such as Rubber Dubber and bootleggers were "simply thieves." Gleason went on to accuse the music industry—artists and companies—of being responsible for the bootleggers because they charged "inflated prices." This rip-off of the counterculture produced a spate of "quack Robin Hoods" who posed as public benefactors, "giving the public a chance to get some more of what they wanted when the artists themselves (and companies) were unable or unwilling to supply the demand." He reiterated Greil's argument that most of the Dylan bootlegs could have been curtailed if Columbia had released the "basement tape." Gleason went on to list who were being harmed by bootleggers: composers, band members, the public, and record companies. Regarding the companies, "It is fashionable these days not to worry about corporate entities in this way, a dangerous fad as time will show." Gleason compared the claimed "public service" aspect of bootlegging, to procuring or pimping, and closed on a new note for the rock and underground press:

> The artist has a true right to work at his art and to make it come as close as possible to what he envisions for it. In the instance of making phonograph records, this includes the right to reject performances in favor of other performances and he should not have to suffer the indignity of hearing his rejects on some underground radio station just because the public is insatiable in its lust for him.

One staffer reacted: "RJG has tons of jazz bootleggs . . . what the hell's he bitching about."

Writing in 1974, Chet Flippo noted: "None of the rock magazines has ever delved into the economics of rock in any serious manner, primarily because of dependence on the record companies for advertising revenue."[41] *Rolling Stone,* following in the footsteps of national news magazines, after 1979 began to look at music industry practices and actually opposed the "Save America's Music" anti-home-taping campaign. The explanation might be that the magazine's advertising base had expanded dramatically since the San Francisco period. In 1983 Dave Marsh was informed his "American Grandstand" piece on corporate tour sponsorship would put *Record* "out of business for lack of advertisers." He wrote, "I withdrew the column. Ironically, the *New York Times* ran a lengthy piece on the subject.[42]

The "Bible of the industry," *Billboard,* and the influential *Los Angeles Times* were not immune from economic reprisal. Two record labels put their pressing plants into twenty-four-hour production schedules following John Lennon's murder, which generated a spate of tributes and stories in all of the media. *Billboard* sidebarred the story on its front page, as opposed to *Record World* and *Cashbox* memorial covers. The leading trade did, however, run many Lennon items, including "Lennon's Ego and Intransigence Irritated Those Who Knew Him: Nobody's Perfect" by David Dexter, Jr. The former Capitol Records executive recalled several unflattering episodes involving the slain singer, concluding the balanced article in this way: "But for all the difficulties those who were associated with him experienced, Lennon will be remembered well for his musical contributions. Unlike himelf, there was nothing eccentric or unlikeable about John's artistry. And that's what all of us will remember."[43] Not so. Dexter's piece violated the industry's view of a trade paper. A trade paper, according to Joe Smith, "is working for that industry; it can't obviously reflect what's going on."[44]

As numerous biographers have suggested, Dexter's characterization of Lennon's interpersonal relationships was quite accurate. A number of influentials remembered the "Nobody's Perfect" article. Calls and letters bombarded *Billboard.* A sampling of the negative responses included some very "heavy hitters' in the business. Sal Licata: "It is an understatement to say that this tasteless, poorly timed article has outraged me as well as the entire industry. Therefore, I am asking for a formal apology from *Billboard* to the Lennon family and the industry." The late Neil Bogart: "I'd hoped that your magazine would have given eloquent expression to our feelings of loss. Instead, by allowing this bitter, self-serving commentary to masquerade as reportage, you've only added to our pain. It is cause for shame." Added Allan Steckler of ABKCO Industries, "Most disturbing is *Billboard's* lack of discretion in allowing this singularly negative and tasteless article to grace its pages."[45] Obviously taken aback by the hostile reactions, *Billboard* editorially retreated:

> A number of *Billboard* readers have protested the content of the Dexter article. This publication and Dave Dexter Jr. had no intention of offending anyone. It was our desire to provide as complete and well-rounded a report as possible, and to take advantage of a staff member who had known and worked with a great artist whom we join the world in mourning.

We profoundly regret that some readers found it objectionable. We had no such intent and we apologize to those who were offended.

Nobody's perfect—not even *Billboard.*[46]

Unmollified, David Geffen mobilized an industry-wide, month-long advertising boycott of the trade paper. "I would feel the same way if it were any other artist. That kind of insensitivity cannot be ignored" he said. "To allow it to go unnoticed would be to say that nobody gives a shit. I do give a shit."[47] Lennon and Yoko Ono's *Double Fantasy* was a recent Geffen Records release.

The exact effect of Geffen's proclaimed embargo is unmeasurable. "Certainly many people were displeased with the coverage, and certain executives voiced righteous indignation, but in no way did that affect their advertising policies." *Rolling Stone* estimated a possible $50,000 loss in revenue.[48] The exact impact is secreted away in *Billboard's* accounting department. *Billboard,* properly chastened, returned to business as usual. Although its reportorial coverage was evenhanded during the anti-home-taping controversy, the trade paper editorially sided with the labels.

Emboldened, perhaps, by its victory over MTV's impregnable format, CBS suspended advertising in the *Los Angeles Times* in late May of 1984. Reportedly, Walter Yetnikoff was angered by articles by investigative reporter William Knoedelseder that dealt with the RIAA and antipiracy laws. CBS was not mentioned in the two-part series.

"Record Piracy: A Controversy over Pricing" was the first piece; its offensive passages appear to have dealt with FBI raids on pirates and RIAA's estimates of the problem.

> Victims of such raids say the RIAA grossly exaggerates the figures in piracy cases and thereby overstates the seriousness of the problem. They allege that the trade group has used federal agencies—the FBI and the Justice Department—in an effort aimed primarily at protecting record company profits, enforcing those companies' pricing policies and eliminating other competition. While the RIAA has had major successes against big-time counterfeiters in the past, a majority of the most recent raids have been against inconsequential, "mom-and-pop" operations.

The article went on to document a series of raids that on the surface were inconsequential. One copyright lawyer told the *Times:* "Their thinking is that anyone who undersells the major companies *has* to be doing something illegal and therefore is a fair target for investigation." The piece further suggested that a number of raids were instigated by the RIAA rather than governmental agencies.

The second article presented a debate between respected copyright lawyer Melville Nimmer of UCLA and consumer-right advocate Thomas Grumuglia of Massens. Gramuglia made the most critical statement: "Because of present industry trade practices, the copyright laws take a man's creation after publication and give it to the large copyright conglomerations." This statement was only partially correct because royalties accrued by the largest publishing and record companies were shared with the artists *most of the time*. Suits by the Bee Gees and Eagles, however, have suggested otherwise.[49] Stan Gortikov asserted that the series sided "with criminals rather than the victims . . . . The importance of copyrighted works to this nation can justify more FBI priority, not less." The Knoedelseder articles raised civil liberties questions; Gortikov and CBS magnified them.[50]

The *Times* boycott going into July brought a chorus of indignant responses from merchandisers and *Rock and Roll Confidential* (RRC). *Rolling Stone* and other music magazines were conspicuously silent on the matter. Music Plus's Mitch Perlin complained, "In Los Angeles there's no second newspaper [with the *Times*'s circulation] . . . and while I could buy in the *Santa Monica Evening Outlook*, the *Daily News* or other regional papers, I still won't get the same penetration I could have." "It definitely puts a crimp in our exposure of product," said a Tower Records merchandiser. Some retailers questioned the embargo at a time when the Springsteen album and Jacksons' album were newly released. "We're spending more money on radio," summed up Perlin, "and probably getting fewer sales which is hurting both us *and* CBS."[51]

Entering the lucrative fall season the CBS boycott was still in force and southern California merchandisers were vocally displeased. The general reaction, according to *Billboard*, was "It's gone too long" or "It's pointless." A Tower spokesman said, "Right now, the CBS ban is influencing my running a *Footloose* ad. I want to combine a prerecorded videocassette with the Columbia album, and I can't do it because I can't get the CBS ad allowance for the album."[52] *RRC* asked, "To what was Yetnikoff over-reacting? And why was he allowed to risk tarnishing the treasured liberal halo of CBS Inc. by attempting to muscle a major press institution?"[53] One newsperson sadly observed, "If they can buck the *L.A. Times*, we're all in trouble."

CBS's publicity department was silent. An upset retailer observed, "They were mum with me on why the hold was put on." The economic intimidation, First Amendment issues, and the overall posture of a corporation that presents "60 Minutes" on television are puzzling. They do, however, send a very ominous message to the print media as a whole; the boycott is nearest link in the gatekeeping structure. By the Christmas season the CBS Group terminated the boycott.

In his long-running "American Grandstand" column Dave Marsh wrote "an open letter to Michael Jackson." Two months prior to the "Victory tour" he warned of many of its pitfalls: "If you do this tour as presently planned, it's the biggest setup in showbiz history. You'll take a fall, with almost nothing to win (unless, of course, you need the money) and a world of credibility and affection to lose."[54] Media response to the tour proved Marsh correct. After the appearance of the "letter," according to Marsh, "Jann Wanner informed David McGee, *Record*'s editor, that the column must be dropped. Wenner said the purpose of his publications was 'not to lecture rock stars on their responsibilities.' Shortly afterward, my name was stricken from the masthead of both *Record* and *Rolling Stone*, thereby ending a ten year relationship that had become embarrassing anyway."[55] Wenner's firings are legendary, but on the heels of the MTV and *Los Angeles Times* actions it is difficult to dismiss the fact Michael Jackson is a CBS Group artist whose *Thriller* has sold 35 million units.

Print, while lacking the power of its electronic counterparts, can present problems. *Rolling Stone*'s pro-home-taping stance more than merely upset the RIAA. Frequently the significance of rock journalism is not in what is said but lack of coverage. A factor, certainly not an overriding one, in the sluggish video music market has been the general antipathy of the press.

Within a week of each other the *New York Times* announced, "Music Video Uncertain Payoff," and *Newsweek*'s cover story was "The Video Revolution: How the VCR Is Changing What You Watch." The latter national magazine optimistically noted 10 million American homes have VCRs and an estimated 5 million more would be bought by the end of 1984. With all that hardware and the popularity of MTV, music video (MV) should be selling; it is still unprofitable. Only *The Making of Michael Jackson's Thriller*—750,000 cassettes sold—has generated huge profits, and observers consider it an "aberration."

There are myriad factors accounting for the uncertainty of the MV market. One is press treatment. *Rolling Stone*, which did the pioneer vid-clip story in 1979, has generally toyed with the phenomenon in the 1980s. *Record*, a *Rolling Stone* spin-off, did eventually introduce a MV section while Dave Marsh sniped at MTV in his "American Grandstand" column. Several MV magazines surfaced using the *Tiger Beat* and *16* motif with wall-sized color centerfolds.

The appearance of videodisks and cassettes generated little excitement in the established rock media. The hardware was expensive; the software limited. Moreover, the pioneer MV situation violated a number of ingrained journalistic norms. This may explain the compatibility of film and TV critics with music video as opposed to the rock press.

Film critics are accustomed to free film screenings and press packages. Music writers traditionally added records to their libraries or disposed of the product in sub rosa fashion. Producers of video cassettes provided a new wrinkle to the standard music reviewing procedures. Publicity departments at music video companies are cooperative and responsive; however, many operate lending libraries to service journalists expressing an interest in previewing their releases. Cover notes accompanying the cassettes state, "Please note that the cassette is a library review copy and should be returned in a week," or "Our lending library is small, so please return the video cassettes when you are finished with them," and also "Return the tapes to me at your earliest convenience." The practice is not popular with reviewers, especially those receiving the standard $20 fee per item. One old-timer exclaimed, "They've carried this loaner bit too far. They really mean it." Promotional records are stamped "Lent for Promotional Use Only. Sale or Unauthorized Transfer Is Prohibited and Void Subject to Return Upon Demand by Owner. Acceptance of the Record Constitutes Agreement to the Above." This warning is frequently ignored. Media people see records as an occupational perk *or* right.

Writers are very much aware that print advertising is expensive. "An ad in my alloted space would cost the labels a helluva lot more than a free album or even a video cassette. Plus a review is more believable than Madison Avenue copy," grumbled a journalist. The idea of having to return video cassettes to the manufacturer caused an uproar. Reviewing cassettes became the journalistic equivalent of military KP, except when the writer possessed a dubbing capability, and few did.

MVs were also time consuming. Concert-reviewing techniques were more applicable than the hurried scans of albums. Unless assigned a specific title, many a writer will sample several cuts per LP by unknown artists before choosing a subject.

MV labels avoided the used-promo problem, but at a price. A host of experienced writers familiar with groups such as the Beatles, Kinks, Everly Brothers, and other historic superstars did not want to deal with the new idiom or technology. (In the author's experience many qualified reviewers do not own VCRs and/or found the specified procedures distasteful.)

Concept videos created a new host of problems. Writers with the best discographical minds were frequently ignorant of Andrew Sarris or *auteur*. Music was one genre, film quite another.

A good deal of music journalistic antipathy to MTV can be attributed to the requirement of dealing with Steve Barron or John Landis on *Thriller*. A picture may be worth a thousand words, except in McLuhan's world of media.

The idiom causes problems for some. Filmed ninety-minute concerts are a bore, according to several writers. A common sentiment is that they lack the excitement of the milieu. Others object to the cinematography, and especially the editing. Only Sony's Video 45's—which are not loaners—seem to receive high marks. "I never like Duran Duran," explained a critic, "until the vidclip. In ten minutes or so they were better than an hour of concert footage." Sony may have the answer to a sticky problem.

John Diaz, of Picture Music in New York, told the *Times*, "The music video market, despite escalating demand for its products has not yet become profitable for its producers.[56] Reaching a mutually satisfactory accommodation with segments of the established music press may help. One-shot picture tabloids reminiscent of the 1950s and teen-oriented rock video publications do more to promote MTV than Vestron, MGM/UA, or RCA/CBS. The rock press's import is an open question; however, trade magazines like *Billboard* appeared impregnable.

### . . . With a Bullet: The Trades

The trades (Arnold Shaw's *Dictionary of American Pop/Rock*: "Short for 'trade papers.'") in deejay's Rich Frank's view are "the vital thread in the music business." Yet, despite this import, industry publications are somewhat mysterious.

Trades—mainly *Cashbox*, *Radio and Records*, and the "Bible of the industry," *Billboard*—are a *service* to the industry they service. *Billboard*, founded as a "carny" newsletter in 1894, tells subscribers, "BILLBOARD provides news, ideas, facts, figures, charts, merchandising aids and a lot more. All ready to work for you the moment they arrive each week." Moreover, "*Every* issue is written, edited, and published with *your needs* and interests in mind. . . . For you . . . whose livelihood depends on getting and using the last and best information available" (emphasis added). *Billboard* serves the "needs" of merchandisers, distributors, record labels, artists, talent agents, music publishers, and media, especially radio—although some CHR programmers dispute its contribution. The most-examined section of both *Billboard* and *Cashbox* are the almighty charts, the weekly lists that track the rise and fall of records in popularity, sales, and airplay.[57]

*Billboard* began its chart 27 July 1940 with the "National and Regional List of Best Selling Retail Records." Tommy Dorsey's "I'll Never Smile Again" was in the number one-slot of ten titles. The chart and its significance have evolved considerably since that small beginning.

The trade weeklies, wrote Arista's Clive Davis, "have the industry's most sought-after information, the charts."[58] The charts provide the vital threat in that precious airplay and sales are heavily influenced by the weekly rankings. The "Hot 100" is based upon airplay, shipments to distributors, and sales from a "selected" sample. After a title goes beyond the midpoint on the chart, sales are increasingly factored into the positioning of the record. Otherwise, it is quite possible for a novelty song to become a "chart hit." Broadcasters and retailers act in accordance with the progress of a recording. *Billboard* charts printed in daily newspapers appear to have an immeasurable affect.

There are problems with these ratings because airplay and sales do not always correspond.[59] Chart inaccuracies are a universal concern. Despite some problems *Billboard* generally receives high marks for its rankings. It is viewed by some as "conservative," and program directors appreciate such a designation. Joe Smith philosophically told *Rolling Stone*:

> None of them truly reflects what's going on. We have such inequities—we have a couple of albums on the charts, one ahead of another. One sells 85,000 and that's number 38, and the one that's 39 has sold 220,000. You learn after a while that you win a few, you lose a few and you get a few ties with the charts.[60]

The charts and features in the trades "synthesize, and distribute data from a large number of geographically dispersed sources."[61] This allows labels, through their branch operations, to plot marketing strategies.

Programmers identify markets demographically paralleling theirs, and frequently "copy" break-outs or prime movers on the air. This creates the appearance of momentum. One vice-president in charge of promotion said, "It feeds on itself. I don't care what they claim . . . without those bloody charts they'd be lost." Charts may be a security blanket for some program directors, but they are a source of vexation for company executives plus artists. Still, the charts and now MTV's rotation order are industry imperatives.

News coverage in the trades can be myopic. When Vietnam fell, one trade weekly lamented the loss of Saigon as a record market. Coverage of industry events is reportorially upbeat. Surveys of sales during the dismal slump of the early 1980s were bullish. The "sky-is-falling" observations of retailers such as Cleveland's John Cohen tended to close the piece. The home taping argument between the labels and hardware manufacturers was fairly evenhanded, although *Billboard* finally sided with the *RIAA* (see chapter 3). The hard reality is record companies provide *Billboard* with most of its advertising revenues.

Lee Zhito and associates do resist most industry pressure, but there is a lingering and widespread belief that full-page color ads help a single or an album become a "pick" or the "recommended" record of the week. *Billboard* vehemently denies the allegation. Its chart credibility, however perplexing, is generally high. Consultant Bill Drake: "The information on the *Billboard* "Hot 100 Chart' is really incredible when you compare it with others, it's a very complete type of chart."[62]

Some programmers, especially in the fast-moving world of contemporary hits radio (CHR), have reservations about *Billboard*'s singles charts. Bill Mitchell is one of the most articulate of the dissenters. He admits the trade has "very good credibility" but adds, "The songs on *Billboard* move so much slower than the action is paced today. . . . It's really hard to base the songs you're going to play on the 'Top 100.'" Pausing, "I don't think their record charts keep up with what's going on in today's music. They seem to hang on to records much longer than they should. . . ." Concluding with a common perception, he says, "*Billboard* is based on volume shipped. Volume doesn't mean a thing." He, like others, points to the returns situation. Other programmers claim to "look" at *Billboard*, while expressing a preference for *Radio and Records* and several tip sheets (see chapter 5 on tip sheets).

Trades differ from the "zines" because they are designed to appeal internally to the industry. Ratings-conscious programmers are not moved by slick color ads or feature stories promising the reincarnation of the Beatles or a new trend; in fact, too much hype with supporting evidence can be counterproductive. They are, however, impressed by the demonstration of a record company's support for the product and act. Artists and managers share this view. Consequently, trade hype aids the company's image. Stan Cornyn, Warner vice-president, has been a master at projecting the label's image through the trades.

The print medium in the music business lacks the importance of the *New York Times* or *Washington Post*. It provides exposure but lacks the immediacy of electronic media. *Rolling Stone*, despite the drastic reduction of music coverage, remains the mass-market rock magazine. The status of the "dailies" columnists, surprisingly, is increasing while fanzines, prozines, and even *Record World* cease publication.

Overall, the impact of the music press is inside the industry rather than external to it. "As long as the tearsheets keep coming," things are on course. The industry, however, has found a new vastly more powerful vehicle of exposure: music video.

### Notes

1. Quotes in Kenny Rogers and Len Epand, *Making It with Music* (New York: Harper & Row, 1978), p. 163; Dick Nusser, "Labels Public Relations Efforts

Assuming New Import," *Billboard*, 3 February 1979, p. 10; Tom Seligson, "The Media: From Groups to Groupies," *Crawdaddy*, August 1972, p. 38.

2. *The Rock Yearbook 1982* (New York: St. Martin's Press, 1981), p. 252.

3. Jesse Stearns, "Rock 'n' Rolls Runs into Trouble," *New York Daily News*; William A. Coleman, "After Rock What?" *New York Journal American*, 8 July 1956. Milton Bracker, "Experts Propose Study of Craze," *New York Times*, 23 February 1957, p. 12; "The Rock and Roll Story," *New York Post*, 1-14 October 1956; Rand Hoffman, "The Response of the Printed Media to the Beginnings of Rock and Roll" (unpublished paper, 1974).

4. Chet Flippo, "Rock Journalism and *Rolling Stone*" (M.A. thesis, University of Texas at Austin, 1974), p. vii.

5. Greg Shaw, "The Real Rock 'n' Roll Underground—Fanzines," *Creem* 3 (June 1971): 24.

6. Paul Williams, "The Way We Are Today: Earth Opera and Joni Mitchell," *Crawdaddy*, 17 August 1968, p. 26.

7. Richard Meltzer, "Aesthetics of Rock," in *Age of Rock*, vol. 1, edited by J. Eisen (New York: Vintage Press, 1969), pp. 224-53.

8. "Deflamation," *Blue Flame* 17-18, p. 4.

9. Quotations in "Fanzines," *WIUS Tipsheet* (1974), p. 1; Michael Goldberg, "Rock 'n' Roll Fanzines: A New Underground Press Flourishes," *Rolling Stone*, 29 March 1984, p. 57.

10. Quotations in Parke Puterbaugh "Voice of Pop-Rock Underground Folds After Ten Fan-Filled Years," *Rolling Stone*, 24 May 1984, p. 68.

11. Jon Landau, "Rock and Roll Music," *Rolling Stone*, 4 March 1971, p. 50.

12. Jon Landau, "Performance," *Rolling Stone*, 28 October, p. 56.

13. Quoted in "Rocking the News," *Newsweek*, 28 April 1969, p. 90.

14. Quoted in "Rolling Stones Rock World," *Time*, 25 April 1969, p. 78.

15. Quoted in "Rocking the News" p. 90.

16. Frank Kofsky, "The Scene," *Jazz and Pop* 8 (June 1969): 31.

17. Quoted from Jane Wilson, "Communicating Via Arrow," *Los Angeles Times West*, 22 November 1970, pp. 37-45 (magazine section).

18. Quoted in Seligson, "The Media," p. 38.

19. Quoted in "Gathering No Moss," *Newsweek*, 18 March 1974, p. 68.

20. Flippo, "Rock Journalism and *Rolling Stone*.

21. *Rolling Stone Record Reviews* (New York: Pocket Books, 1971), pp. 3-4.

22. "Sam Swanson" [pseud.], "A Sam Goody's Discography," *Who Put the Bomp* 7 (Summer 1971): 23-26. Also see Lester Bangs, "Free Form Music in San Francisco," *Phonograph Record*, November 1971.

23. Geoffrey Stokes, "Nothing but the Nice Truth," *Village Voice* 24 January 1974, p. 67.

24. Flippo, "Rock Journalism and *Rolling Stone*," pp. 146-47.

25. *Ibid.*

26. Quoted in Patricia Kennedy, "The Decline and Fall of Intelligent Rock Journalism," *Rock*, 20 December 1971, p. 28.

27. Quoted in Seligson, "The Media," p. 38.

28. Sam Maddox, "Fear and Lust in Promo Land," *Third Rail* (RCA publicity mailing; n.p., n.d.).

29. Robert Hilburn, "MTV: The Birth of a Rock Sensation," *Los Angeles Times Calendar*, 4 August 1981, pp. 1, 3.

30. W. Steward Pinkerton, Jr., "Grand Funk Railroads Is No Penn Central: It Makes Noise, Money," *Wall Street Journal*, 15 June 1971, p. 1; Robert Hil-

burn, "Grand Funk, Rock's Newest Phenomenon," *Los Angeles Times Calendar*, 21 February 1971, p. 1.
31. Greil Marcus, "Rock A-Hula Clarified," *Creem* 3 (June 1971): 42.
32. Richard Pinkston IV, "Mail," *Creem* 3 (September 1971): 4.
33. Donald Osmond, "Letter to the Editor," *Village Voice*, 14 December 1971, p. 22.
34. David Marsh, "Looney Tunes," *Creem* 3 (October 1971): 24-25.
35. Kennedy, "The Decline and Fall of Intelligent Rock Journalism," p. 13; "Who Are These Guys: 36 Rock Critics Tell All," *Coast* 14 (April 1973): 58-72.
36. Geoffrey Stokes, "Trading Innocence for Expertise," *Village Voice*, 18 July 1974, p. 50.
37. "Reviews of the Who's Latest: What's the Score?" *Baltimore Sun*, 29 May 1981, p. B-7.
38. Maddox, "Fear and Lust in Promo Land."
39. Flippo, "Rock Journalism and *Rolling Stone*," p. 166.
40. Gregg Kilday, "Things Are Falling into Place at Rolling Stone," *Los Angeles Times*, 2 January 1972, p. 12.
41. Flippo, "Rock Journalism and *Rolling Stone*," p. 42.
42. *RRC*, October 1983, p. 1.
43. *Billboard*, 20 December 1980, p. 30.
44. Jann Wenner, "The Record Company Executive Thing," *Rolling Stone* 8 July 1971, p. 33.
45. "Letters to the Editor," *Billboard*, 27 December 1980 and 17 January 1981.
46. *Billboard*, 27 December 1980, p. 12.
47. Quoted in Steven Pond, "Geffen Boycotts 'Billboard,'" *Rolling Stone*, 5 March 1981, p. 16.
48. Ibid.
49. *Los Angeles Times Calendar*, 20, 21 May 1984.
50. "Times Blasted by Gortikov," *Billboard*, 2 June 1984, p. 3.
51. Sam Sutherland, "CBS Ad Boycott of L.A. Times Causing Concern Among Chains," *Billboard*, 14 July 1984, p. 3.
52. Earl Paige, "CBS Times Ban Cast Yule Pall," *Billboard* 25 August 1984, p. 3.
53. *RRC*, August 1984, p. 7.
54. *Record*, June 1984, p. 64.
55. Quoted in *RRC*, September 1984, p. 8.
56. Quoted in Peter Kerr, "Music Video Uncertain Pay Off," *New York Times* 29 July 1984, p. F-4.
57. See Joe Csida and June Bundy Csida, "Charting the Hit Songs, Artists and Records," *Billboard*, 4 July 1976, pp. MR-10, 30, 78. Also George H. Lewis, "Dimensions of the Popularity: A Comparison of *Billboard* and the Gavin Report Singles Charts, 1970-1979," *Popular Music and Society* (1983) pp. 54-60.
58. Davis, p. 200.
59. For complications of charts, see Peter Hesbacher, "Some Proposals Concerning the Methods and Procedures for Compiling Billboard Charts (unpublished *Billboard* report, 1973); Peter Hesbacher, "Sound Exposure in Radio: The Misleading Nature of the Station Playlist," *Popular Music and Society* 3 (1974): 189-201; Peter Hesbacher, Robert Downing, and David G. Berger, "Sound Recording Popularity Charts: A Useful Tool for Music Research, II. Some Recommendations for Change," *Popular Music and Society* 4 (1975): 86-99;

and Peter Hesbacher, Robert Downing, and David G. Berger, "Record Roulette: What Makes It Spin?" *Journal of Communication* 25, no. 3 (1975): 75-85.

60. Wenner, "The Record Company Executive Thing," p. 33.
61. Richard Frank, "The Vital Threat: Music Industry Trade Publications," (unpublished paper, November 1983), pp. 1-2.
62. Quoted in Claude Hall and Barbara Hall, *This Business of Radio Programming* (New York: Billboard Publications, 1977), p. 256.

# 7

# Video Killed the Radio Star?

*Oh wouldn't you be in great shape if your life was on video tape.*

—©1984 Big Ears Music Red Pajamas Music (ASCAP).

*Pictures came and broke your heart . . . video killed the Radio Star*

©1979 Carbert Music Inc. (BMI).

"We really integrated the most powerful forces in our two decades," said MTV Vice-president John Sykes, "TV and rock 'n' roll."[1] The wedding was prefaced by a very stormy courtship period exhibiting all of the mood swings of a popular soap opera.

### "Talkies and Soundies"

On 6 October 1927 the *Jazz Singer*, starring vaudevillian Al Jolson, introduced the talking motion picture. Critics were skeptical. The *New York Times* described the film's story "one of the few subjects that would lend itself to the use of the vitaphone [sound]." The *Herald Tribune* noted, "This is not essentially a motion picture, but rather a chance to capture, for comparative immortality, the *sight and sound* of a great performer" [emphasis added]. Warner, in planning the film, shared these sentiments. Harry Warner was quoted as saying, "Who the hell wants to hear actors talk. The *music*—that's the big plus about this."[2] Whatever the initial response to the *Jazz Singer*, audio and film were merged into a major genre leading to the Busby Berkeley musical extravaganzas, singing cowboys, "soundies," and the jukebox movies of the 1950s.

Busby Berkeley's productions were a platform for his dynamic musical numbers, a motif derived from the *Jazz Singer*. The characters "had a logical reason to participate in the song and dance numbers as rehearsals, backers' auditions, and out-of-town tryouts provided the rationale for the musical numbers."[3] Cowboy films equally fashioned stock plots with appropriate moments for harmonizing around the campfire or at a square dance. The old Monogram and Republic second features were vehicles for Gene Autry, Tex Ritter, Roy Rogers, and a host of other balladeers who could ride and shoot. Any of the cowboy stars could have said, "Them bandits have beaten mah mother, ravished mah girl, burned down mah house. . . . Ah'm agonna get 'em if'n it's the last thing ah - do - but first, folks, ah'm agonna sing ya a little song."[4] The low-budget Grade-B western legitimized country music outside the then predominantly rural market.

"Shorts" or three-to-five-minute film clips were employed to highlight the talents of musical performers from vaudeville and radio. Jimmie Rodgers, the "Singing Brakeman," starred in a short prior to his untimely death.

"Soundies" surfaced in the 1940s. They were an ambitious attempt to merge the jukebox concept with three-minute film clips—this preceded MTV by forty years. Soundies originated at the Mills Novelty Company, a Chicago-based firm that specialized in chromium-plated cigarette machines and jukeboxes. In 1941 Mills began the manufacture of Panorams (viewing and listening machines), and Soundies Distributing Corporation of America was the sales arm of the operation. James Roosevelt, son of the president of the United States, was a vice-president of the affiliate. Marketing and distribution of Panorams were patterned after the jukebox model. Mills expected soundies to banish the Wurlitzers to the dustheap of history.

For a dime inserted in a Panoram the patron could see a three-minute film clip projected on a 17-by-22½-inch plastic screen by means of special lenses and combinations of mirrors. A closed-loop projection system allowed for the housing of eight or ten segments, which the distributor changed twice a month.

A deluge of clips appeared; some 2,000 subjects were released by Minoco, R.C.M., Film Craft, and others. At the peak of this phenomenon a legion of artists performed in them. Established bandleaders like Duke Ellington, Louis Armstrong, Cab Calloway, and Les Brown were featured. Billy Eckstine, Nat "King" Cole, and Louis Jordan used soundies to advance their careers. Country fare included Merle Travis, Tex Ritter, Spade Cooley, and Denver Darling, who were cataloged as "hillbilly" or "western" subjects.

As with record distribution, a definite racial differentiation was created by producers and merchandisers. The catalogs were divided into "white" and "negro" sections. The eight-subject reels were generally made up for distribution along color lines, and the result was narrowcasting in its worst form. A "hillbilly" or big-band reel would automatically exclude Fats Waller or the Mills Brothers—a precursor of the Rick James-MTV controversy of the 1980s.

Soundies evolved a specific format. Screen size precluded elaborate vista-like shots; close-ups were the rule. Facial and instrumental frames were overdone. Lip syncing was erratic. Ironically, similar dilemmas plagued network television's early presentation of music.

Structural problems led to the genre's demise. The production of subjects could not keep pace with record releases. Machine operators could not rotate films often enough to maintain a sense of immediacy. Soundies exhibitors found reels outdated in a matter of days. And there were technical difficulties as well. Panorams suffered from a built-in obsolescence. Customers were forced to pay into the devices, as they did into slot machines. They could choose a reel but not the actual clip; the reel dictated the upcoming selection. Choice was severely limited. In some instances a dime was inserted into a device with no selection buttons.

The visual jukebox was not in line with the musical life-style of the swing period. People preferred jitterbugging or fox-trotting to screen images, and a nickel in the jukebox meant they could dance. Soundies simultaneously died with the big-band era.

The motion picture was an effective medium for singer-actors like Bing Crosby and Gene Autry who used the big screen to introduce songs. "White Christmas" by Irving Berlin came from *Holiday Inn*; some people considered it an "ideal" wartime song. "Back in the Saddle" was the title song of an Autry action flick.

The big-band era popularized the "showcase" film that served merely to display "name" swing performers. Plots were almost identical: rags-to-riches stories that provided recording artists the opportunity to exhibit their musical material. Benny Goodman did *Hollywood Hotel*; Tommy Dorsey, *Las Vegas Nights*; and Artie Shaw, *Dancing Co-Ed*. With the exception of Glenn Miller's *Sun Valley Serenade*, critic George Simon described the swing band films as "everyone of them forgettable."[5] Similar statements echoed in the 1950s for the visual.

The story lines of rock vehicles like *Don't Knock the Rock, Rock Around the Clock, Mister Rock 'n' Roll*, and Presley's *Loving You* had no purpose other than to set up musical numbers. *The Girl Can't Help It*, starring Jayne Mansfield and a cast of singing stars worked as a total picture. Films such as *A Hard Day's Night* and Presley's *King Creole*, based on *A Stone for*

*Danny Fisher* by Harold Robbins, had dramatic value. Of the approximately seventy films with rock music made prior to 1964, only a handful received any critical acclaim or were distributed outside the drive-in circuit. General sound tracks occasionally proved sales spectaculars.

Peter Goldmark's main motivation in developing the long-playing (33⅓ rpm) record was to make possible uninterrupted symphonic music. CBS's earliest LP releases were in that genre. Jazz, mood music, and Broadway shows were added to the catalog to appeal to an older, wider, affluent audience. Single 45s were addressed to a teen market. Sound tracks became top sellers due to their universality. They attracted people who rarely brought records. *Mary Poppins* and *Sound of Music* did particularly well. *Sound of Music* reigned for over a decade as *the* top seller in the *Guinness Book of World Records*, to be replaced by another film score, *Saturday Night Fever*. *Thriller* ended the dominance of sound tracks in dollar sales. After the successes of *Grease* and *Saturday Night Fever* some films were actually made to sell records; box-office receipts were incidental. In the 1980s *Flashdance* and *Footloose* repeated the successes.

In 1939 at the New York World's Fair the Radio Corporation of America (RCA) demonstrated a "new" invention, a radio with pictures. By 1952 one-third of American families had television sets. In the 1980s 98 percent of households have a minimum of one set—more than enjoy indoor plumbing.

Television with its insatiable appetite for programming picked up many popular network radio shows. "Jack Benny," "Amos 'n' Andy," "Your Hit Parade," and others were transposed to video prime time. "Your Hit Parade" was originally simulcast on NBC radio and television (1950-53). As millions of antennas filled urban skylines, radio and film became "second-class citizens" in the quest for entertainment dollars. The film industry resorted to spectaculars and big-screen gimmickry, and broadcasters dusted off records in their music libraries. In time the vacuum would provide fertile ground for the seeds of rock and roll.

"Your Hit Parade," featuring four former band singers, followed the radio format developed in the late 1930s: the top seven songs of the week were presented in reverse order. (The songs did not come from an accepted chart but were chosen by Lucky Strike's ad agency.) The demands of the visual medium dictated that skits be added to the music. "How Much Is That Doggie in the Window," "Melody of Love," "Hey There," and other tunes were presented in a sometimes ludicrous fashion. A rule of thumb was that the longer a song remained on the show, the more ridiculous and farfetched the skits. Producer Bob Forman described the progression:

> After a dozen weeks on the boat ["Shrimp Boats"] ("their sails are in sight"), at the quay ("there's dancing tonight"), and in a shrimp market, we had to

resort to things like Dorothy [Collins] singing it lullaby-fashion to a bundle of swaddling clothes. Or Snooky [Lanson] in the bath tub. . . . The Hit Parade Dancers didn't look much like the women who wait for the shrimp-fishermen.[6]

The advent of rock music further undermined the presentations. "Tutti-Frutti" and "Hound Dog" transcended any story line the writers on "Your Hit Parade" could conceive. In 1959 the show was mercifully cancelled by NBC. "Your Hit Parade," despite its aesthetic shortcomings, would serve as a prototype for Top 40 radio and, some three decades later, "Solid Gold."

Although few demographic data are availablle, "Your Hit Parade" was billed as "family programming." It appeared to cut across generational lines, at least in the early years when homogenized crooners and singing quartets dominated the charts. None of its stars was in the "teen-scream" mold of a Frank Sinatra and other bobby-soxer idols during the 1930s. Sinatra was a regular on the original radio version of the "Hit Parade" broadcast.

### Teen Video Idols

The link between musical teenage heartthrobs and television began with Eddie Fisher. Fisher was a child of the video revolution, winning an Arthur Godfrey "Talent Scout" contest. After a string of RCA hit records, he headlined "Coke Time," which was carried by 700 NBC affiliate stations, and became the first postwar bubble-gum attraction via television. Fisher enjoyed his status for a brief period and then was replaced by a diametrical opposite from the Old Confederacy, Elvis Aaron Presley, the "Hillbilly Cat".

Presley appeared on "Stage Show," hosted by swing greats Tommy and Jimmy Dorsey. The program's producer, Jack Philbin, chose Presley on the basis of his appearance: "He's a guitar-playing Marlon Brando."[7] Philbin did not especially appreciate rockabilly. Presley's appearance vaulted him into national prominance, or perhaps infamy. Numerous variety shows hosted by the likes of Steve Allen, Milton "Uncle Miltie" Berle, and Ed Sullivan featured the controversial singer. The grim-faced Sullivan insisted that Presley be shown only from the waist up. Following this ratings success Sullivan did provide visual opportunities for rock artists, with his usual, "And-now-for-the-youngsters" seque.

Television in the latter half of the decade catapulted a number of young actors onto the charts. Tab Hunter, Edd "Kookie" Byrnes, and Ricky Nelson enjoyed hit records. Only the youngest child of the "Ozzie and Harriet" family exhibited any lasting musical ability. The accent-on-youth formula did not escape the notice of an enterprising Philadelphia deejay about to assume the reins of a televised afternoon dance party.

Dick Clark's "American Bandstand" was targeted at teenagers. It consciously encouraged and presented a legion of attractive but innocent adolescent male singers such as Fabian, Frankie Avalon, Bobby Vee, and Bobby Rydell. By the early 1960s television had become an important tool in providing exposure for artists and their lipsynced songs. In many cases vocal ability was secondary to the *person* on the blue-lined screen. Clark was packaging teen idols, but they all lacked the innate dynamism of Presley, who had been drafted into the army.

Many rock historians date the "British invasion" to the "Sullivan Show" of 9 February 1964, when the Beatles captured the hearts and minds of bubble-gummers in the United States. Anthropologist Lionel Tiger described the phenomenon:

> By Monday afternoon, the day after the Beatles' first Sullivan show, every girl had chosen a favorite, and he was symbolically taken home to meet mom and dad, or at least discussed forcefully with Sue and Jill. . . . The reaction of these female adolescents was sweeping because there were millions of them.[8]

Millions there were, and their purchasing power was quickly recognized. The merchandising of the "mop-tops" began in earnest. The Beatles were as much a visual as a musical phenomenon. Some of their earliest material was pure "puppy love." The Sullivan appearances, and two Richard Lester films propelled them into a stratosphere enjoyed by only one other, the reclusive "King" in his Memphis mansion, Graceland.

The Beatles and successive British musical cohorts revolutionized segments of the music industry. The ascendancy of the "British invasion" could best be measured in the pound sterling not dollars, but other than Capitol Records few of the majors were directly profiting.

In the midst of Beatlemania and the discotheque à go-go craze, the American Broadcasting Company unveiled a prime-time "rock" variety show. The rationale for the television show was the success of Sullivan's "And-now-for-the-youngsters" segment spotlighting British bands. "Shindig" was masterminded by English producer Jack Good, a legend in London broadcasting circles.

During the mid-1950s Good had introduced "6.5 Special" on the BBC, which had pioneered audience participation with a hip host. His innovations were similar in the use of infant cinematic techniques. Jenkinson and Warner credit him with "link[ing] the sound with the visual experience, and it is certain that his influence on this ["6.5 Special"], and other shows (Oh Boy and Boy Meets Girl), carried clear through to the truly filmic rock."[9] Good, before leaving for the U.S. market, was described as "the D.W. Griffith of the pop style."

"Shindig" fit the "6.5" format, minus some of the excesses of the original BBC production. Jimmy O'Neill announced the show with a background of the required modishly choreographed dancers. The telecast relied heavily on U.S. acts and celebrity guest hosts, many having no connection to the music scene. The show premiered on 16 September 1964 with Sam Cooke, the Righteous Brothers, the Everly Brothers, and unknown teen singer Bobby Sherman. Other than the Righteous Brothers, Glen Campbell, and Sonny and Cher, the regular guests were fading stars. Good also used London-made videotapes of established and promising artists.

Good, by way of his English connections, was able to obtain an impressive number of taped performances from Rediffusion's "Ready, Steady, Go" and the BBC's "Top of the Pops." Some of the artists were unfamiliar to U.S. audiences. Tapes of the Beatles, the Rolling Stones, the Kinks, the Dave Clark Five, the Who, Gerry and the Pacemakers, and others were aired. "Shindig," however, lacked continuity, and the clips were awkwardly fitted into the format that increasingly relied on Hollywood personalities. The show on 23 September 1965 featured the Yardbirds, Pretty Things, and Jerry Lee Lewis, and was *hosted* by actress Raquel Welch.

Four months after the appearance of "Shindig," NBC aired "Hullabaloo." The format was similar, stressing miniskirted dancers and "the girl in the cage." Lada Edmund was termed "TV's high priestess of pop terpsichore." Producer Gary Smith called Lada "the show's image."[10] Fraternities reportedly watched the show with the sound off. A guest host was rotated each week. A majority, such as Jerry Lewis, Dean Jones, and Skitch Henderson, had little to do with the rock scene. Ballroom pianist Peter Nero and operatic soprano Judi Rolin appeared. The high brow material no doubt contributed to the turning of volume buttons. A brief spate of creativity was a short-lived segment introduced by the Beatles' manager, Brian Epstein. He was able to highlight some of the invasion's bigger guns, except for his "Fab Four" clients. The London portion of the show lasted for only three months.

By mid-1965 both "Shindig" and "Hullabaloo" were on the wane. "Shindig" resorted to a familiar variety-show motif with nonrock personalities like Zsa Zsa Gabor and comedian Ed Wynn. Its last telecast was the opening week of the 1966 season; it had had a nineteen-month run. The same week "Hullabaloo" showcased a clip of the Beatles. "Hullabaloo," too, was not renewed.

The music programs died from low ratings that were caused by a lack of contemporary star performers. The artists existed but network censors were not ready for hard, folk, or acid rock. The artists' British counterparts, some denied work permits, were generally unavailable. Ironically, the Stones with the legendary Chuck Berry, did appear on "Hollywood A-Go-

Go." Despite the overall constraints on these teen-oriented shows, many big-name groups did appear on them, but too infrequently and normatively on imported tapes. As the "Smothers Brothers Comedy Hour" aptly demonstrated, the "big three" networks were unprepared for the rock revolution or the subculture leading it. One critic observed, "All those shows produced were foxy ladies and Bobby Sherman." Most historical accounts of rock and roll in the United States ignore these variety telecasts. (Biographies of British acts frequently make mention of "Shindig" and "Hullabaloo" as early video exposure in the U.S. market.)

The rise of the domestic hyphenated-rock groups, despite "Shindig," did not create "teen-scream" idols even remotely approaching the Beatles. They lacked the required innocence and were too "far out" to qualify. Teen idols must possess a specific set of personal and musical qualities to play their fleeting role.

The United States has no initiation rite to guide the individual from childhood to adult status. No ceremonies exist to celebrate passage of the person from the innocence of toys, trucks, and dolls to puberty, dating, and marriage. Popular music, especially for young girls, serves as a rite of passage from Raggedy Ann to boys. Girls between the ages of 8 and 12—an age bracket rapidly expanding to include 6-year-olds—purchase the lion's share of singles. Teenagers as a whole, it is estimated, buy at least 60 percent of the singles sold. The type of record purchased by 9-to-12-year-old girls customarily falls into the "teen-idol" category. As one crop of teenyboppers graduates to actual dating, another crop takes its place. A new idol ascends as the object of teen-scream, and the old one is discarded along with other "kid stuff," fan magazines, and wall posters. After the age of 12 or 13, adolescent tastes tend to reflect FM programming. AOR becomes an integral part of their waking hours.

Fans heap their hopes, wishes, and desires upon their idols. Idols are symbols, suitors, and rebels for bubble-gummers—the 9-to-12-year-old cohort called teenyboppers (prepuberty) by the industry—who use the idols to fulfill their emerging curiosity about boys. Idols are "paramours in absentia."[11] A *TV Guide* writer presented the idol as one appealing "to that twilight zone between childhood and maturity when girls from 6 to 16 start to become interested in boys but don't know why. His youthful idolators are reaching out for a shy, good-looking boy who sings about puppy love and acceptance, who gyrates in a manner that looks 'groovy' but is not overtly sexy." Michael Jackson is "the prototype rock teen idol, he's cute wholesome and pious." Bobby Sherman, when the object of bubble-gummers' affection, said, "I'm part of the process of becoming mature for these girls."[12] Teen idols in the record industry are unique in that they are total personality packages who incidentally sing, as opposed to the regular pop act that concentrated upon making music. Not infrequently teen idols become singers *after* becoming national heartthrobs.

The essential ingredient of the idol is a role as fantasy object. "However much," writes George Melly, "they scream outside stage doors or besiege hotels and airports, they need to believe in the non-reality of their idols, and give the impression of being secretly relieved to be held back as this allows them to avoid putting their faith to the test."[13] Fantasies must not be compared to reality, otherwise they are shattered.

The idol is remote, and in distance there is safety. Psychiatrist Stanley E. Willis observed, "A critical factor in a celebrity fantasy is the total un-availability of that celebrity. It is the unavailability which keeps the illusion safe from the chilling discovery that the idealized image is, in fact, not ideal and experience less than its fantasy form."[14] The barrier between the celebrity and audience is a dominant feature of his career. Elaborate security precautions are utilized to protect the performer from the milling, scream-ing, and nearly hysterical fans. Security precautions for Michael Jackson, rivaled those for the president of the United States. One road manager printed up a set of guidelines for concert promoters blueprinting plans for his protege's escape. Presley was out of the venue before the last note of the closing song was struck. David Cassidy was whisked away in a nondescript Volkswagen while hiding under a blanket; a conspicuous $250-a-day lim-ousine diverted his fans' attention. Brother Shaun: "I've snuck by crowds by disguising myself as the chauffeur."[15] In the 1980s Duran Duran faced the same frenzy and adulation from screaming teenage girls; Simon LeBon and band entered the crowd. Capitol wanted "Duran Fever" publicized in *Rolling Stone.* Generally the motto is "Look, buy, but don't touch." All these precautions remove the possibility of the fantasy's being ruined by the cold reality of flesh and blood. Not to mention the physical security of the million-dollar human commodity.

"Bigger than life" is the description frequently bestowed on motion pic-tures and television. Most major teen idols in popular music were brought to public attention through these two visual media. These media are essen-tial ingredients in the creation of the teen idol.

### Monkees Not Beatles: Day Dream Believers

"The Beatles had become too removed from people, . . ." explained Don Kirshner, "yet there was a whole new group of kids there who needed somebody to sing to them. They needed a group to say: "I saw your face and now I'm a believer."" There was no such act; one was "manufactured."[16]

To capitalize on the success of the Beatles, Bert Schneider, Robert Rafelson, and James Frawley of Screen Gems plotted a television series based upon the film *A Hard Day's Night.* Four young men were recruited to romp or improvise through a television series. The Hollywood trade papers ran an ad calling for "four insane boys, 17-21, with courage to work." The name of the group could well have come from the proverb "Monkey see, monkey do." Even the overnight act's name "Monkees" was a parody of the mispelling *Beatles* (as opposed to beetles). Davy Jones, Mickey Dolenz, Peter Tork, and Mike Nesmith signed for the group, were paid $500 a week despite the awkward fact that they were not rock musicians. Their original records were performed by studio musicians, yet these curious conditions did not prevent the unit from selling 6 million singles and 8 million albums in a four-month period after the airing of their weekly television series. The Monkees received 20,000 fan letters a week. Surrounding the television act was an entire industry geared to the bubble-gummers "With 30,000,000 people watching them regularly Monday night they should be bigger than the Beatles," said a Screen Gems official. They even published an instruction book, *Learn to Play like the Monkees Play.*

Chuck Laufer, the publisher of *Tiger Beat,* a fan magazine, recalls: "When the Monkees came along in 1966, I began to see the direct connection between magazines and TV. I worked out a deal with Screen Gems. We began to sell a lot of books and photographs and posters."[17] The Monkees proved that a properly manufactured band could be very profitable. A regular television series was considered requisite for the creation of a "teenybopper group." Performers were cast for the purpose.

At Screen Gems, Ward Sylvester, a graduate of the Harvard Business School, discovered Bobby Sherman, a "Shindig" veteran, making a guest appearance on the then-sinking Monkees show. Sherman became the first in a series of packaged solo artists whose prime base of operation was a television series. "Getting Together" and "The Bobby Sherman Show" were built-in commercials for the "Bobby industry," as it was called.

David Cassidy came to public attention through a bit part of the "Marcus Welby, M.D." series. However, as Wes Farrell indicated, "Nobody had asked him if he could sing."[18]

With the exception of Presley and the Beatles, both unique talents, teenage idols have been more an artifact of television than of records. Presley, of course, became a motion picture star. The Beatles were featured in an animated television series, as were many of their bubble-gum successors like the Jackson Five. Records are but one aspect in the midst of love kits, posters, photos, magazines, and other mementos. Bobby Sherman's record sales grossed $20 million, but the entire "Bobby industry" earned $35 million. Records accounted for only 20 to 30 percent of David Cassidy's annual $250,000 salary. Unlike performers who address themselves to older audiences and whose music is primary, the idol is a total product that

| Teen Scream Cycle: Rock and Roll Artists and Television, 1952-1984 | | |
|---|---|---|
| 1952 | Eddie Fisher | "Coke Time" |
| 1956 | Elvis Presley | Introduced on "Dorsey Bros. Stage Show" |
| 1956 | Ricky Nelson | "Ozzie and Harriet" |
| 1961 | Fabian, Avalon, Anka, etc. | "American Bandstand" |
| 1964 | Beatles | Introduced on "Ed Sullivan Show" |
| 1967 | Monkees (Davy Jones) | "The Monkees" |
| 1969 | Bobby Sherman | "Shindig," "Bobby Sherman Show," "Getting Together," "Here Come the Brides" |
| 1971 | David Cassidy | "Partridge Family" |
| 1972 | Donny Osmond | Regular on "Andy Williams Show" and "Donny and Marie" |
| 1975 | Shaun Cassidy | "Hardy Boys" |
| 1979 | Rex Smith | "Soon or Later" TV movie |
| 1979 | John Schnieder | "Dukes of Hazzard" |
| 1981 | Duran Duran | MTV clips |
| 1982 | Rick Springfield | "General Hospital" |
| 1982- | Michael Jackson | MTV clips, "Billie Jean," "Beat It" |

is packaged, and television makes promotion possible. It allows the performer to forgo many of the arduous paths confronting the less glamorous act. He does not have to contend with the usual gatekeepers who have little interest in attracting bubble-gummers to their FM stations that feature an AOR (album-oriented radio) format.

The Bobby-David-Donny-Shaun phenomena were parallel to the string of fleeting idols who lipsynced their way to fame on the "American Bandstand" program shortly after Presley's departure for two years in the army. Even though they were older, Sherman and the Cassidys looked 15 or 16. They were slight of build and medium in height, and both possessed a quality imperative for teen-idol status: role ambiguity. The liner notes of the Shadows of the Knight first album outline this contradiction: "If you invited them over for dinner, your parents would, at first, have you examined or call the police or run screaming to the neighbors. If your parents stayed around, they would find that the Shadows are polite, quiet, considerate and that they might even grow to like them." Presley and all of the other real or aspiring teen idols have this confused image, which provides the illusion of revolt against parental values. Parents see the flirtation of their young daughters as a passing phase. One mother wrote: "Look how well Sarah's affections for Duran Duran have worked for her and for us. Without them she might be out chasing boys."[19]

In their remarks about pop music, parents may convince the idol worshipper that she is actually rebelling. Megan Rosenfeld of the *Washington*

*Post* observed that this image combined "respect for parents and a happy family with a smattering of rebellion (long hair . . . ). They get into scrapes, but everything turns out happily because they are basically good honest and cute. The idols are expected to be as untouchable in real life as they are on TV."[20] Presley, although the Hell's Angel on stage, was characterized in fan magazines as a churchgoing young man who was a devoted son, a patriot, and a frequent contributor to charity. The Beatles were similarly pictured as playing dual roles. Sociologist Renée C. Fox described them: "They appear to be good boys [yet] nevertheless dress and pose as bad ones—London's Teddy Boys. And their fancy, Edwardian-style clothes [Elektra's Sally Stevens states the "rags were Pierre Cardin"] suggest a sort of sophistication which contrasts with their 'home-spun' commoner style of performance."[21] The Monkees, in a similar vein, were zany but decent rogues. Bobby Sherman says, "My songs never have any hidden references to drugs or sex. When I sing 'I Love You, Baby,' or 'Will You Be Mine' the connotation is always strictly romantic."[22] David Cassidy's "I Think I Love You," Shaun Cassidy's "Morning Girl," and Donny Osmond's "Go Away Little Girl" are equally innocent. Both depict an uncertain teenager trying to cope with the emotion of love. These songs mirror great "first-kiss" debates found in fan magazines specializing in the bubble-gum market. Although the teenage idol is certainly not a threat to cherished American institutions, he is not a part of the immediate world either. Idols, clothed in fantasy and glamor, are highly mercurial commodities.

The relationship of the teenybopper is taken directly from romantic-love novels, the poems of Elizabeth Barrett Browning, or Erich Segal's *Love Story*. The familiar elements of "June, spoon, moon" are all present. "She has posters of him all over her room and kisses them every night," said a mother of a 7-year-old girl. Teen idols receive a tremendous amount of fan letters proclaiming devotion. David Cassidy received, at the height of his popularity, approximately 3,000 pieces of mail weekly. One letter to him said, "I'v always dreamed I was going steady with you, but now I blush whenever I think about it. I heard you are 20 years old." The late Gloria Stavers of *16* magazine explained these feelings: "It's an oral age for the girls. Their idea of sex is malts and hamburgers, a kiss. It's a romantic thing, not physical or orgiastic. They think of their idol as a teddy bear, a blanket, a cuddly thing."[23] More typical responses to bubble-gum music stars involve the word *like* instead of *love*!

Fantasies have a way of becoming realities. This is the bane of "nubie" idols. The idol introduces the preadolescent female to a "love" object; as with Barbie dolls, roles are learned along with many half-truths. But, as *Flip* editorial director Valerie Gerger stated, "These little girls have a lot to give and they must channel it somewhere."[24] Time and maturation impact upon the bubble-gummer, and few idols remain in that position for any length of time.

The teen-scream cycle is unstable. Davy Jones in 1967 told an airport news conference:

> The Monkees are getting the same enthusiasm and fan fever that greeted the Beatles. I think the Beatles are tired out now and the Rolling Stones sing questionable songs. The British scene in America is dead as a dodo and it'll be a new year for single singing stars. The Monkees hit it big because the Beatles are on the way out, not everyone wants to go on listening to the Hermits singing about Mrs. Brown or the Stones singing rude songs. We came along at the right time and hit lucky. But we'll be one of the last groups to hit it big in America.

The successs of the imitation Beatles blinded them and their merchandisers to the transitory nature of top-idol status. *Flip* magazine, for one, neglected the decline in Monkees fan mail and lost $50,000 because of its continuing support of the foursome while Bobby Sherman was ascending the bubble-gum charts. Now fan magazines monitor television shows in search of new potential stars. Sherman's reign was tied to his weekly show, and its cancellation was followed by a sharp drop in fan interest. In May 1972 Gloria Stavers predicted to *Rolling Stone,* "David's passed his peak already. But his effect will last until the end of the year." In September of the same year the Record Industry Association of America (RIAA) announced that the Osmonds had earned ten gold records in one year, breaking the Beatles' mark of nine. A new teen idol, Donny Osmond, displaced "The Partridge Family" act. The ever-changing cycle is perhaps a partial reflection of the fickleness of 12- and 13-year-old girls, who outgrow their idols. A fan wrote *Tiger Beat:* "For a long time Bobby Sherman has been my special fave, but then David Cassidy came along and my heart was torn between the two. But everything worked out fine, because one half of my heart is for Bobby and the other is for David."

The fantasy is replaced by the reality of dating. "By the time they're 16," says Chuck Laufer, "they're having dates, and they don't need them anymore." One sophisticated teenager concurred: "When you're 13 and have had a real date, you don't go in for crushes anymore." Another teenager disclaimed David Cassidy: "It's the thing to say you can't stand him."[25] Reality and the pressure to conform find idols being discarded with growing rapidity.

In the bubble-gum world of popular music, taste generations are not 15 or even seven years in duration but, on average, less than three years. David Cassidy acknowledged, "There are just a couple of years of this sort of thing."[26] Preteens reject the idols of their older sisters and adopt their own.

Following in his half-brother's footsteps, Shaun Cassidy was the last consistent teen idol of the 1970s. His "Hardy Boys" series survived a three-year television run. Cassidy was replaced by a succession of fleeting heartthrobs as the tube momentrily gave way to the big screen and *Saturday Night Fever.* Gold-plated idols would await MTV.

### Rock TV Tries Again

During the 1970s a number of late-night rock music shows were aired. "In Concert" opened in November of 1972 with good ratings, especially in the wake of the Alice Cooper controversy. The numbers sagged after the curiosity was gone. An ABC exective said, "It was pulling down the overall ratings of Friday night." Bob Shanks, ABC's late-night programmer, declared it "probably will be cancelled," but it took until the summer of 1975 for the network axe to fall.

NBC aired "Midnight Special" Friday nights at 1:00 A.M. Producer Burt Sugarman explained the hour: "The kids who watch shows . . . come home around 12:30 or 1:30, so we pick them up."[27] "Special," which lipsynced performers in "Bandstand" fashion, was popular with record companies, which frequently packed tapings with employees to generate excitement. Record labels, claimed Sugarman, "could feel the impact of [the show] . . . on sales." Like "In Concert," Sugarman's show ran into ratings difficulties and expanded into an adult contemporary format hosted by Helen Reddy. Sugarman explained, "There aren't enough rock fans. The music's changed. Now it's discos and MOR. There's maybe five big rock acts, that's all." These acts and others disassociated themselves from the show, claiming it would damage their images.

"Rock Concert," the program of Don Kirshner, the musical Svengeli behind the Monkees, was also having difficulties. Being syndicated, it lacked immediacy because there was a considerable gap between taping and airing. The time-lag hurt the telecast because artists reluctantly appeared to get exposure and sell product. A dusty video tape did not fit into many marketing strategies. "Rock Concert" aired in fewer than a hundred markets. None of the rock showcases survived the mid-1970s.

Time slots, ratings, technology, economics, and artists' attitudes contributed to the combative atmosphere between rock musicians and television. Two personal managers of "name" rock acts complained that "TV is a pretty inhospitable environment for musicians . . . not much of the money goes to musicians . . . around TV musicians aren't much more than lackeys."

Money was a factor in television's inability to attract top-notch performers. Even shows that paid above scale—$320—could not match concert grosses. Rock stars viewed video opportunities with the same scorn country performers reserved for Saturday night appearances at Grand Ole Opry; Tanya Tucker explained she could gross $25,000 on the road while the Opry paid scale. Rock artists applied to some logic to prime time-television. Kenny Loggins's manager told *Rolling Stone* that television is good exposure for a new artist, "but after a group's become a headliner, giving away the act is detrimental."[28]

The detrimental aspect was the television medium. Sound quality on the tube was primitive, akin to a very cheap transistor radio. "TV people are used to mixing *I Love Lucy* and don't know shit from beans about mixing rock," said Butch Stone, manager of Black Oak Arkansas. Moreover, flubbing in front of millions of viewers can "embarrass yourself badly."

Censorship by television executives turned off many artists. The banning of Bob Dylan and Pete Seeger songs was legendary. Sullivan's demand that "Let's Spend the Night Together" by the Rolling Stones be changed was another illustration of the wasteland mentality. An ABC executive admitted, "A lot of rock music is simply too sexy for TV . . . the . . . audience is not ready for any but the more lame breeds of rock."[29] The Captain and Tennille may have passed network inspection, but rock fans tuned them off. Wimpy rock targeted at a mass Nielsen audience almost guaranteed low ratings. Rock was not ready for network prime time. *Billboard*'s observation that "somebody up there in the ivory tower of TV doesn't like music" was correct. *Like* may have been the wrong verb; *understand* or *grasp* might have been more appropriate.

Syndication, as the success of "Hee-Haw" demonstrated, is a risky but potentially rewarding alternative to the conservative caprices of network television. Through its Operation Prime Time, Paramount Television debuted "Solid Gold" as a two-hour special headlining Glen Campbell and Dionne Warwick. The format was "Your Hit Parade" revisited: a reverse chart countdown was used. Artists generally performed their own hits. "Nothing's new," said Paramount Vice-president John Goldhammer, "but, in brute testimony to how the music itself has changed, you don't succeed today by having other people singing all the songs."[30] The formula worked; sponsoring stations demanded a weekly series. Warwick became the regular hostess but personality problems forced her exit, and Andy Gibb and the Fifth Dimension's Marilyn McCoo took over. Gibb, because of personal problems, was displaced by Rex Smith. "Solid Gold" was a success. Ratings showed that it was topping competing syndicated, network programming with an increasing number of viewing households, a comfortable 10.5 to 15 million. One of the program's draws was its scantily clad dancers, not the usual everyday network fare. "Solid Gold" has been aired for half a decade. Its acceptance demonstrated that pop/rock music was a viable product on television.

### Enter If You Dare! MTV

Every brainchild has a legion of progenitors. The emergence of MTV can be credited to four men at Warner Amex Satellite Entertainment Company (WASEC), a WCI and American Express joint venture. WASEC was planning a third cable operation—*Nickelodeon* and *The Movie Channel* were already in place—and John A. Schneider, president and chief executive officer of Warner Amex; John Lack, executive vice-president, John Sykes, and Robert Pittman, another vice-president and the music channel's operationalizer, were the chief architects.

Schneider is generally credited with overseeing the making of a video music network. "We had to do something different," he recalled, "to reach an untapped 12-to-34-year-old audience." The segment of that demographic that in Schneider's view was not being served by electronic media was 12-to-24. "There is a body of young people who are being ignored"[31] Demographically, the targeted group fit between the offerings of Nickelodeon and The Movie Channel.

Lack, a rock-music maven since his teens, was the conceptualizer, having approved "Pop Clips" and QUBE's "Sight on Sound" in Columbus. In October of 1979, he hired Pittman, who implemented the blue-sky notion. As a sociology major, Pittman was more than aware of the usefulness of number crunching.[32] Pittman was a broadcasting *Wunderkind*. Coming to prominence as a research director at WDRQ-FM (Detroit), he moved up to progam director at WPEZ-FM (Pittsburgh), where his ratings—"numbers"—were impressive. Chicago was the next stop, first at a country station, WMAQ, then WKQX, an AOR-FMer; using a highly researched format, he surpassed the ABC affiliate. Pittman then took over WNBC-AM in New York, facing the Top 40 flagship, WABC. Minus jingles and with fewer commercials and three-minute-plus songs, WNBC successfully challenged the Top 40 giant. But Pittman was becoming increasingly disillusioned with formatted radio; he viewed it as excessively conservative and a major ingredient in the ongoing lethargy of the music industry. Reportedly the highest paid PD in the nation, Pittman received an "offer he could not refuse" from Warner Amex. As he moved his way up the major market ladder, psychographics became an important survey addition to basic demographic data.

Psychographics, according to radio consultant Rob Balon, consists of "categorizing people by stated attitudes, observable social behavior of life styles, and psychological traits." Psychographics attempts to identify the variables that influence the media participation of individuals and groups. Balon cautions, "Stop thinking in terms of age. Start thinking in terms of predisposition to behave (another way of describing attitudes) because that's where . . . it's going to be at."[33] Psychographically, a male 30-year-old executive can be an AOR listener based on his preference for heavy-metal music. The Clash, with its socially conscious lyrics, can appeal to an activist lawyer as well as a high school sophmore; the Clash was an AOR mainstay. The rock culture is a taste public and a psychographic category to be targeted.

Pittman explained his appreciation of the psychographics marketing strategy: "When you're dealing with a music culture—say, people aged 12 to 30—music serves as something beyond entertainment. It's really a peg they use to identify themselves. It's representative of their values and their culture." The trick was to reach the "rock nation" with programming that fit its life-style.

From the beginning MTV was blatantly narrowcast to a very specific demographic. Pittman told numerous reporters, "Our core audience is the television babies who grew up on TV and rock 'n' roll."[34] Having selected a specific audience segment, WASEC began a research campaign. Four telephone surveys of 600 randomly selected persons between the ages of 12 and 34 ascertained information about such matters as musical preference, audio equipment, and the like. The key item asked whether respondents would view a video 24-hour-a-day rock music channel; 85 percent replied affirmatively. An interesting follow-up question might have concerned interviewees' perception of rock video. Unlike viewers in the United Kingdom, Americans had only vague notions about what the concept involved.

Having established the feasibility of music video outlet, Marshall Cohen devised a market-segmentation study. A shopping list of 150 artists was assembled in light of their attractiveness and desirability. Life-styles were examined by means of program content. Cohen tried to discover "the way the channel should feel, the image, the style, what veejays should wear— should they wear suits or punk clothes?" The overtly young, white, middle-class sample disapproved of bearded video jocks but did allow for one black VJ. J.J. Jackson would be chosen to fill that slot. "We believe [MTV] was the most researched channel in history," claims Cohen."[35]

With part of the psychographic puzzle apparently solved, Pittman was faced with piecing together a format with the proper mood-evoking programming. "The strongest appeal you can make is emotional. If you can get their emotions going, forget their logic, you've got them. . . . MTV fits in with all of this because music deals with mood, not continuity or plot."[36] Pittman and associates had the marketing data and a game plan, but in the early 1980s American videos in the rock genre were scarce.

Preservation of the audio and visual history of U.S. rock music has been sadly lacking. As collectors are quick to note, thousands of significant records are cutouts. Television kinescopes have deteriorated or been discarded. Presley's early television material is unavailable. *Video*'s John Walker comments, "Most of the more collector-oriented material is apparently lost to the ozone until the next wave of desire and/or permission descends and some one sees fit to re-release it."[37] Dick Clark's "American Bandstand" library, a treasure chest of golden oldies, was dated and, more important, unavailable. This left a handful of concert clips and movies. Concert videos, as experience had shown, translated badly onto the 25-inch screen.

The technological limitations of "In Concert" remained. Significant acts, according to Joe Jackson and others, seemed ill-suited to the demands of television. "Many artists lose their credibility and/or self respect by coming across as bad actors rather than as good musicians." Hall and Oates declared: "We're musicians, we're not half-assed movie actors, you know, and I think as soon as you try to do [television] then you lose what the musician has to offer." The Tubes' Mike Cotton says, "Some don't have much to say musically let alone visually."[38] These reservations had merit. As concert reviewers often note, great lyricists and musicians can be visual disappointments. This problem would be compensated for with the visual "concept" or mini-film clip, on which professional actors are used to illustrate the story line. Timid musicians can remain in the sanctuary of the recording studio. There is a drawback to concept clips: they are vastly more expensive to produce than taped concert appearances.

A handful of artists foresaw the potential of video. Former Monkee Michael Nesmith, no stranger to television, was in the vanguard. "I became more and more convinced that audio-only recording was becoming obsolete," he said. "What's happening in the video business is not the death of the record business, but the beginning of a new era. I'm not kidding when I say it's the most important event in the history of rock 'n' roll."[39] Directed by Bill Dear, Nesmith produced "Elephant Parts," a visual album. It received a Grammy in 1981 for innovation. Todd Rundgren, fortified in his Woodstock studio, began Utopia Videos. He and Woody Wilson provided the U.S.A. Network's "Night Flight" with a number of experimental concept clips stressing arcade-game technology. Ray Davies of the Kinks spliced together a video album that sold 5,000 copies even without an elaborate promotional campaign. Marty Balin recorded a vignette titled "Rock Justice." The plot, according to *Panorama,* was a satire about a singer who falls asleep during a recording session and dreams of being put on trial for a crime of making a "stiff" for a record. Some 15 musical interludes occur in the opus. The effort was a financial and critical flop. A *Billboard* review called it a "failed experiment. One hopes that he'll think over his next ideas more carefully or one day Balin may find himself on trial for failing to produce a hit video."[40]

The inventory of available rock videos meeting MTV's broadcasting standards was quantitatively and qualitatively in short domestic supply.

### The second "British Invasion"

Rick Sklar has repeatedly called music video "The second [major] British Invasion." Sklar's characterization, although influenced by his "hits-only" philosophy, is historically valid, for Britain's contributions to U.S. television transcend "Masterpiece Theater" and other highbrow PBS specials. The English pioneered the rock video clip, the lifeblood of music television.

The United Kingdom and Continental countries have highly concentrated state-run broadcasting monopolies. "We have only one or two radio programs in England," says Peter Frampton. "There is a certain amount of media missing in England, I mean in the days of 'Ready! Steady! Go!' and 'Thank Your Lucky Stars' it was great. . . . But, now we haven't got a station that you can listen to albums all day long, you can here."

English television in the 1960s and 1970s had two networks, the BBC and ITV, a commerical outlet. ITV pioneered the vanguard pop music shows "Ready! Steady! Go!" ("RSG"), "Beat Room," "Thank Your Lucky Stars," and "That's for Me." "RSG" was the "in" 1960s version of free-form television. It was described as having a wide and progressive playlist, not confining "itself to the safe favorites."[41] "We'd stick to a very rigid booking formula of only using artists we liked. Now that I think about it, this was incredibly pretentious of us—but it worked," recalled producer Vicki Wickham.[42]

Cathy McGowan was *the* veejay. British critic Nik Cohn portrayed her as an uncomfortable amateur stumbling on lines "like some fan. She wasn't some fat middle-aged DJ with a toupee and plastic smile; she was almost a teeny bopper herself, and she was genuinely thrilled because she met pop stars."[43] Influential fashion writer George Melly commented, Cathy "*was* RSG. The bridge between pop and its audience."[44] "The audience can identify with us. They can certainly identify with me more than they can with Pat Benatar. I'm one of them," said MTV veejay Martha Quinn in 1983, nearly twenty years after Cathy McGowan.

"RSG" has been perceived as the revolutionary program of its time—a television version of San Francisco's KMPX-FM. Some of its boldness was of necessity, not innovation. The powerful British Musicians Union put a stop to lipsyncing on "RSG," something the AFM could not accomplish with "American Bandstand." The ban forced "RSG" to go live, launching the fledgling Rolling Stones, the Who, the Kinks, the Animals, and future rock celebrities. To fill airtime further, experimental film clips were used, frequently put to music. These "far-out shorties" have been called the primitive prototypes of contemporary video clips.

"RSG" had a style—Pittman's "mood."

> For anyone who finds live musical performances as exciting to watch as they are to listen to—it is a visual goldmine: Cameras swooping back and forth like robot jivers, tangled black leads from the guitars, and Pop Art decor, . . . all of these serve to exaggerate the excitement of the music. . . . It is one of the few channels through which knowledge of the latest fashions can be obtained.[45]

A description of MTV? No, "RSG" (c. 1964). Melly's view of the Rediffusion program equally fit Pittman's psychographic model: "It plugged in direct to the center of the scene and only a week later transmitted information as to clothes, dances, gestures, even slang to the whole British teenage Isles."[46] Wickham and associates had stumbled into what Peter Townshend called "rock television at its best." They rarely mentioned the reasons for format changes caused by powerful labor unions behind the scenes. Pittman's foray was computer calculated to achieve similar results.

"RSG" lacked the staying power or the exposure of its BBC-TV imitation, "Top of the Pops," a visual transposition of BBC radio. MTV denies any influence by "RSG." "Top" paralleled many of the excesses of "Your Hit Parade." It was a "dated weekly essay in nubility and careless superlatives." The show also sold artists and their current releases. A last-minute apppearance by the "new" group, the Who, propelled "I Can't Explain" to the number-eight position on the BBC charts broadcast on the televsion show. Many English musicians detested "Top" for its musical conservatism and its power. Peter Frampton commented on BBC videos: "English people, that's all they get rammed down their throats everyday, and on 'Top of the Pops' every week. You know, Gary Glitter's new record [c. 1975] 'Hump me, hump me, darling, . . . while I tie your legs down,' I mean really, well, crude and I don't dig it at all to see a 42-year-old man dressed in sparkle glitter dust." By the mid-1970s video clips were almost a staple on the program because a live appearance frequently conflicted with tours. Film also transcended the constraints of a sound stage.

Director Bruce Gowers used "Top" to showcase a concept video of the post-Wagnerian "Bohemian Rhapsody" from Queen's *A Night at the Opera* album. Composer Freddie Mercury called it a misunderstood "operatic six minute epic" while on a sold-out countryside tour. "Rhapsody' stayed on the BBC charts for nine weeks. "Top" video clips exported to Europe substantially increased record sales there. "We made a big splash with video early on in England when nobody was really doing it," recalls Queen's Brian May. "It was a reaction to having to go on the normal programs and do the normal mime, so we told our story with 'Bohemian Rhapsody.'"'

U.S. record labels with international branches, such as WEA and EMI, entered the video clip arena to promote acts on the Continent. "Radio was too limited in Europe," says Sklar. A majority of the promo clips were made in England; the experience of British artists and producers with video placed them in a highly advantageous position when the idiom was being considered for U.S. audiences. Greg Geller, RCA Records vice-president, said, "The network [MTV] . . . had a crying need for groups that were worth looking at. It was a great opportunity for the English."[47] There were English groups worth a look who could not break into the AOR market. Human League, Flock of Seagulls, and especially video specialists Duran Duran were prime candidates for MTV exposure. American artists were still reeling from the "crash of '79." If the rock press was correct, the "new music" would be English.

Video clips were expensive promotional tools when compared to audios, and the issue of payment arose. Pittman, a radio veteran, instinctively looked to the record companies. Radio since World War II had been the dominant promotional vehicle in exposing records. Labels serviced broadcasters with free product—why not video clips? The socioeconomic conditions that gave birth to music video across the Atlantic were relevant to the United States in the 1980s.

Label access to U.K. and European radio formats was severely hampered because of singles domination. The few available venues were highly fragmented. "There are as many small clubs as styles and fads in London," wrote one American visitor. Video clips fit formats emphasizing one song or "individual hit." In England and the Continent this is important. A former member of Yes explained, "When they buy records, they have to sorta like buy one a month." A well-done intriguing video could bring attention to a specific album cut for a cost-conscious music fan. A spot on BBC-TV's "Top of the Pops" could double or triple a song's sales within twenty-four hours.

John Lack launched his promotional campaign in late in 1979. A year later as the Warner Amex representative to the *Billboard* Video Music Conference, Pittman told the Broadcast Video Music Panel that "radio stations' objectives are not the same as record companies' objectives," continuing to blame the AOR format for the sales slump bedeviling the labels. He contended that cable television, with its narrowcasting, could zero in on potential record buyers abandoned by radio stations.[48] This authoritative argument was repeated frequently. Pittman made his pitch in a major *Billboard* interview. The proposed music channel would be as "important as radio." He explained:

> We will be putting more of an emphasis on new music than radio does. We will take extra pains, in fact, to sell new music. We will also explain who the new artist is.
>
> Radio is going through a big problem now because nobody wants to take a shot with new music. But they are all complaining that there is no new good music out there, just the same old artists and the excitement of music is dying down. What we will do is expose a whole new genre of artists and we will give them familiarity and break them. Radio will then have new artists to draw from. A music radio station will benefit from having this service in their market. The end result also is that record labels will now have two very strong promotional weapons for product.[49]

Pittman pushed all of the proper attitudinal buttons. The new-music promise fit the "Third-Coming" model. Part of this thesis would be picked up by the established U.S.A. Cable Network. On 5 June 1981 "Night Flight" was launched with a feature film format.[50]

The narrowcasting concept from its inception created problems for the proposed music channel. Audience size was limited to the number of households wired into cable systems; in 1981 an estimated 30 million households were on line. MTV was dependent on cable operators for exposure and the size of their individual markets. Many large metropolitan areas (SMSAs) were without cable because of franchise wars. The finite audience was further divided by Lack, Schneider, and Pittman's narrowcasting to the 12-to-34 demographic. Originally dependent on advertising spots for revenue, Warner Amex was in the shaky position of selling a potential audience within a narrowcast model. The same demographics that spawned the concept simultaneously scared off some record labels and especially ad agencies. Madison Avenue is skeptical about and uncomfortable with new and therefore unproved enterprises. Advertisers, said Jay James of Doyle Dane Bernbach, "are too conservative to look for the newest way to spend money." Cable was too new. "Out of fear, if they don't understand it, they won't commit dollars to it."[51]

MTV did have a persuasive weapon in its arsenal. Much of commercial cable was narrowcast: ESPN (sports), CNN (news), and Nickelodeon. Giants like Home Box Office refused advertising because the claim "commercial-free, uninterrupted movies" was a key to their preeminence. Soft-drink companies, like auto manufacturers, went to extremes to break into the HBO, Showtime, and Movie Channel world by negotiating agreements with movie studios to include their products in films. News plus sports are highly desirable merchandising tools by standard Nielsen surveys. The bottom line on rock music shows proved mixed although the syndicated "Solid Gold" did have "good numbers."

"The concept [MTV] is excellent and there already is a lot of music programming on the air. But the execution will determine how well it is received," cautioned Arnie Semsky of Batten, Barton Durstine and Osborne, the ad agency that some thirty years earlier had secretly compiled the "Your Hit Parade" selections.[52] At the time the format was still vague; the blueprint consisted of 80 percent videoclips, with a veejay interrupting two or three times an hour with music news and tour dates. Eight minutes each hour were allotted for advertising, and two minutes allocated to cable operators. There were to be rock movies, documentaries, and a live simulcast on Saturday nights. Execution or the essential mood atmosphere was essential. Few details, from the unique logo and set design to the five key veejays, were missed.

Fred Seibert and Alan Goodman working with Manhattan design approved the logo. Seibert, formerly an independent producer and director of creative services for WHN (New York) had a very specific concept:

> The animation that initially ran on MTV people would say was stuff my 11-year old brother could do. Every audience wants a piece of communication to communicate with them. MTV is most different . . . because in the areas of least interference with communicating with that audience nobody knew the answers. Nobody knew what technique would connect. We tried to keep it simple and we fought like hell to keep it that way."

The result was a mobile logo, "something like Gumby" A large dominant M and lower-case tv were in constant movement. A *Village Voice* reviewer wrote, "It is anything from the MTV being constructed out of french fries and ketchup to a clay elephant walking through a jungle."[53] Despite opposition, the moving logo was accepted. It would be nominated for the prestigious New York Art Director's Club prize and the Clio Award. More significantly, the cartoonish logo fit the "mood."

The studio set was another atmospheric or mood-sustaining device. It had to be reflective of Pittman's view of rock culture as psychographically defined. Originally it was to be a fantasy environment for adolescents, with all the status symbols of the generation. Posters, albums, stereo equipment, and other middle-class teen toys were prominant. The veejay would be surrounded by this high-tech wonderland. When the television version of teenage heaven premiered, it lacked vitality according to some insiders; it was akin to a rock version of "Masterpiece Theater." Normal television lighting and teleprompters disappeared. Veejays were instructed to ad-lib. Mistakes in the best "RSG" tradition related to the audience. *Rolling Stone* described the final look: "something casually thrown together, scripted patter that sounded like it was made up on the spot, an ironclad format that proceeded like a random chain of events, well trained actors who came on like folks you'd meet at a campus mixer, and a generally perfectionist attitude in bringing about a what-the-hell-let's boogie mood."[54]

The aura of calculated "laidbackness" was exactly what Pittman wanted. "Any young person with the resources of Warner Amex could do it." This was a page torn from radio's co-optation of the KMPX-KSAN-FM free-form underground sound formatted into AOR with a thinly disguised sense of informality.

The actual MTV format was the "clock" pioneered by broadcasting legends Storz, McLendon, Drake, and others (see chapter 5). The MTV clock minus the "20-20" news breaks, public-service announcements, and weather was fairly standard. Extrapolated to a twenty-four-hour day, a weighted order of exposure was devised. Five to eight telephone interviewers called viewers in areas in which MTV was available. If the person called agreed to listen, songs from clips were played and reactions were coded on a high-to-low scale. Underplayed was a high; overexposed, low; and so on. The reactions were then fitted into four categories: heavy (four plays per day), medium (three plays), light (two plays), and the add-ons, which would either break into the rotation or be discarded.

With the structure seemingly in place, five environmentally compatible veejays were needed. They would underscore and continue the "magic" the format provided. Rick Sklar, commenting on the voices of WABC at its peak, gave the ideal job description: "No matter which one was on the air, the station's own personality always came through and was instantly identifiable."[55] Pittman wanted "human faces you could relate to" or someone who mirrored the projected audience. He held a "cattle call" of sorts, requesting tapes, and then held interviews and auditions.

Five veejays were chosen. Nina Blackwood, an actress and model with some broadcast experience headed the list. She was the network's answer to "the girl in the cage" on "Hullabaloo." Mark Goodman, a teen-idolish deejay from the New York and Philadelphia markets, was Blackwood's male counterpart. J. J. "Triple J" Jackson was the lone black video jock with television and radio experience in Los Angeles and Boston. Martha Quinn, "the Cathy McGowan of MTV," had been the assistant music director of WNBC (New York), Pittman's one-time employer. Quinn had done extensive radio and television advertising work. The last to be chosen was unemployed actor Alan Hunter. A television critic described him as "a sophomore on his way to class." Hunter claimed little knowledge of the music; he was just a "a classic case of being at the right place at the right time," that is, bartending a party that Pittman had attended. A month later he was called for an audition. Hunter recalls, "I was pretty horrible. I was confused about what the show was, so I didn't know what to do. As it turned out, that was okay because no one knew exactly what it was. Every time I was called back. I got another explanation." Within Pittman's format and in the studio decorated by Sue Steinberg and Bob Morten, the five deejays would "maintain the continuity of the channel."[56]

MTV was launched 1 August 1981 at 12:01 A.M. (EST) with the Buggles' 1979 British hit "Video Killed the Radio Star." "Pictures came and broke your heart," trailed the lyric. Two hundred twenty-five cable systems with approximately 2.1 million homes were on the line. By month's end 2.5 million homes were receiving the new outlet and its handful of advertisers: MTV had sold 30 percent of its designated airtime. According to Larry Divney, then vice-president of advertising sales, MTV was selling sixteen to twenty products on the air. Its first commercial was for school binders, a time purchase by Majestic Industries. *Cablevision* estimated a 30-second spot on the channel cost between $350 and $650. The other early advertisers were big players in the youth market: Gap Stores, Dolby Laboratories, Pepsi-Cola, Mountain Dew, 7Up, Warner-Lambert's chewing gum products, Listermint, Jovan, Warner's Atari, and the U.S. Navy. The dominant advertisers were moviemakers: Warner Bros., Universal Pictures, United Artists, Avco-Embassy, and Filmways hyped their latest repeat youth-oriented releases to their favorite constituents, the under-25 viewers.

*Advertising Age* optimistically estimated that at $1,200 per 30-second spot, and eight advertising minutes per hour, the maximum MTV could gross in 24 hours was $460,800; 30 percent of that figure is $153,600. The 6-minute national slots would gross $115,200. Neither of these accounting dreams was fulfilled. Rate cards are normatively revised downward for major time-block purchases. Actual revenue figures for the last five months of 1981 are available. (WASEC combined MTV and Nickelodeon revenues in its public reports, thus making it almost impossible to determine MTV's earnings without insider information.) The year ended in red ink, as was expected. Several executives inside and outside MTV believed the project would be fortunate to see a profit by 1984. However, advertising as well as music industry trade publications were generally supportive. A cable systems analyst told a reporter: "Outside of the news- and sports-oriented, ad-supported cable programming services, MTV is the only one that I see having any possibility of making significant money in the next few years."[57]

Record companies expressed reservations focusing on the narrowcasting premise. PolyGram and MCA refused to provide clips. Pittman dismissed the two labels as being short-sighted: "We can't expect every record company to have vision. PolyGram doesn't really have any acts that we want, and as for MCA, we have Tom Petty through his manager. The doors are still open. . . . If we play a hit 500 times a year, on our rate card that is $1.5 million worth of free advertising."[58] Others privately questioned MTV's ability to sell records with its "limited cable audience," but with the prevailing mood of open desperation most labels were willing to try any innovation to increase unit sales.

Most of the majors were international and already in the Common Market vidclip business. Providing MTV with duplicates did not, on the surface, appear unreasonable. Dave Robinson, president of Stiff Records, saw MTV as a catalyst for new horizons in music. "I am looking forward to Warner Amex," he said, "which will amaze people."

MTV's content was based on the largest record labels. From the beginning Lack, Pittman, and other Warner Amex officials stressed the promotional aspect of the music channel. The thesis was buttressed by the industries' exasperation with AOR programming and the diminishing returns of touring (see chapters 3, 5). A strong selling point was that a national tour of several months duration might touch only several hundred thousand potential record buyers in major and secondary markets. A video clip on MTV could extend to millions of viewers in communities of every size. This meant reaching people hundreds of miles away from the customary concert routes. Videoclips averaged only $6,000 to $20,000 to produce, at least in the early days.

Television had a history as a medium for breaking musical material. It had proved effective with the *Tiger Beat* and *Fave* set. Television themes occasionally were charted, like their soundtrack counterparts. Few did as well as "Chariots of Fire," "Tammy," and "Saturday Night Fever." Joan Weber's "Let Me Go Lover" from a CBS "Studio One" segment was a major hit, reaching the number-one position in five days and staying on the chart for sixteen weeks. But that was in November of 1954, just prior to pop's rock-inspired generational fragmentation. It was obviously incumbent on Pittman, Lack, and Sykes to demonstrate a causal link between MTV and record sales.

*Billboard* for 10 October 1981 applauded MTV's ability to promote new and established artists ("MTV Cable Spurs Disc Sales of Artists Aired"). In a spot check of merchandisers located in markets penetrated by the music channel—Tulsa, Des Moines, Syracuse, and Wichita—the trade publication found increased sales of albums by performers on the cable network. Retailers, particularly in secondary and tertiary markets, reported climbing sales. A New England retailer said, "We're feeling its impact really big. It's giving older groups new life and new groups a way to promote their albums." "Innovative groups are up 15% to 20% because of MTV," declared a merchandiser in Oklahoma. Similar comments were made in other areas of the country.

A companion story quoted Lack as foreseeing a household increase of at least 4 million units, if not more. He predicted MTV entrance into the massive Los Angeles market in the first quarter of 1982.[59] MTV promised more retail-store promotional material, such as a "Survival Kit" containing the usual buttons, banners, and stickers. It brought a full-page ad to "underline the enthusiasm for MTV's unique format"

Tom Freston, the channel's marketing head, was euphoric. "MTV exposes records and artists. . . . I understand if record companies are still a little unsure about the impact of MTV or LP sales," he said. "We think it will become much more evident in the future and hope to coordinate research with record labels."

The nationally syndicated Knight News Service echoed *Billboard*'s optimism. In part the story indicated MTV was "good news" for labels experiencing "decreased sales and creative malaise." The *Baltimore Sun* headlined, "Bored with Top Forty? There's Music TV" (17 November 1981).

During the 1981 holiday season, record dealers again praised MTV's role in an otherwise lackluster sales period. In a still-slumping industry MTV appeared the only positive light at the hoped-for end of the tunnel.

Retailers, concert promoters, and Warner Amex executives were pointing to MTV "finds." Human League, the Buggles, Squeeze, and Men at Work were originally mentioned as beneficiaries of cable exposure. Men at Work's *Business As Usual* went platinum because of AOR and television exposure. Participants clash as to the import of each medium. "We broke Men at Work," said Les Garland. Al Teller at Black Rock disagrees: "MTV doesn't break an act, but MTV was certainly a contributing factor in bringing the record to the public's attention." More diplomatically, Barbara Cook of CBS explained, "There were radio stations who played it, and the record stood on its own musically. And then the video came on, and it gained in momentum and rotation. . . . [MTV] is very positive."[60] MTV's inadvertent reliance on imported clips made it a champion of "new music" and an important medium of exposure. AOR program directors were becoming as conscious of MTV, as their AM ancestors had been of "American Bandstand" in the early 1960s. "Now everyone's talking about the influence video has on radio, and there are a lot of new acts who owe their livelihood to video," Dick Clark observes with a sense of satisfaction, "but 30 years ago, top 40 stations had secretaries sit down and list all the songs that were played on *Bandstand*."[61]

## MTV in '84: An Orwellian Prediction

The televised 1984 New Year's festivities on MTV could have been held in the executive offices. Putting the red ink aside temporarily, the channel had in less than two and a half years become a giant in the music industry. From the newfound position of apparent strength, MTV's status had to be solidified. Getting to the top is easier than staying there. Economics was a compelling concern. The losses had to be reversed, for the accountants' ledgers were quite different from MTV's media coverage. Rumors were rampant regarding the parent management's displeasure with the music channel's operating budget and the slowness of revenues. The "if-we're-so-good-why-aren't-we-rich?" mentality was creeping into the picture. The ragged-but-right notion worked in the beginning but was wearing thin in the midst of ego-inflating trade and popular-press coverage. *Billboard* reported telephone surveys showing MTV's stimulative role in record sales. Ironically, *Thriller* was leading the pack, and credit for breaking *Thriller* has been subject to polemics.

The 1983 A.C. Nielsen data were sacrosanct ("The Nielsen's" have been roundly criticized by statisticians and pollsters for years, and Arbitron is not without its detractors. Both ratings services are used by Madison Avenue for time buys. They may be flawed but are *very* valid.) A whopping 68 percent of the 2,000 MTV viewers surveyed said they had bought an album after seeing an artist's video clip; 81 percent claimed their initial exposure to a "new" act was on the music network. The central point was, which medium stimulated an album purchase. Radio received a standard 63 percent; MTV, 68 percent. Radio historically had been *the* key medium of exposure and purchase motivation.

AOR programmers saw the channel as a broadcasting threat to their ratings. Record labels were thinking video when signing artists. This was all to the good, but nonetheless Warner Amex needed capital. The momentum of 1983 coupled with a projected profit breakthrough made insiders believe this was the time to fortify. Pittman had very quietly adopted several corporate strategies that would raise a major storm by midyear. This was a major accomplishment by itself in an industry with as many news leaks as the nation's capital.

*Billboard* in January of 1983 unveiled its "Video Programming" chart that reported MTV weekly rotations with add-ons. Weekend specials and the guests on "Liner Note" were featured. The trade announced the new chart, praising the Satcom-3 network: "Its acknowledged success in exposing and helping to establish new and developing acts has led to increased attention to the entire video music field from industryites at labels and in radio and retail, as well as artist managers and artists, venue operators, producers and others." The trade had legitimized MTV's significance as an industry force. The action drew tangible results. One executive noted, "There are some accounts who order an additional 700 to 1,000 pieces of product simply on the basis of there being a video on MTV." Merchandisers could now scan the new chart along with the "Top LP's" and "Hot 100."

Trend analyses formal and informal, strengthened MTV's leverage. Viewers had increased a spectacular 74 percent in one year; MTV was in 18.2 million homes. Its Nielsen figure was impressive for cable: 1.2 total daily share without a *TV Guide* listing.

Only *two* of the top 20 songs on the *Billboard* chart in the autumn of 1983 did not have an MTV clip. One absent artist was Michael Jackson. Forty-seven of the best-selling fifty charted albums had accompanying video clips. An AOR radio personality in Boston said grudgingly, "MTV is fast becoming the main outlet for exposing new acts . . . the possibility that MTV can cut into radio revenues down the line is very real." AOR guru Lee Abrams agreed, adding a qualifier, "Some programmers regard MTV as 'the enemy,' but it's helped radio to open its eyes. . . . More than ever, our stations are taking a hard look at what MTV is playing. We were almost a year late on Duran Duran, Billy Idol and the Stray Cats, and I don't ever want that to happen again."[62]

Labels were fully aware of the situation. Randy Edwards at Elektra said, "Last year we did very few videos, and only because of artist pressure, today, nobody looks at video as a luxury anymore, it's a necessity." Artists were being signed as "great film performers." Artist contracts began to include video production clauses. Costs were to be deducted from future record royalties: "Throughout the industry, labels are requiring and receiving financial assistance in a number of ways from artists toward the production of video: direct sharing of costs, charges against royalties, and so on."[63] Video had become an expensive necessity. Artists' advances in light of their failure rate was only a partial cushion. Getting on MTV or "Night Flight" had changed drastically since 1981. "It makes me wonder if we released Duran Duran today," a Capitol spokesperson speculated, would [Duran Duran] be willing to make the commitment they did a year ago?" Len Epand of PolyGram remarked, "There's so much more video competition now that new acts have trouble getting prominent exposure on MTV."[64] This argument was older than Top 40 Radio. In the 1980s the costs were significantly greater. Steve Burron producer of "Billie Jean" was asking $65,000 for his services; the legendary Russell Mulcahey demanded $85,000.

A sixty-six-page report by the investment firm of F. Eberstadt & Company suggesting that the genre was an indicator of the future buttressed the importance of music video. Few doubted the import of Lack's innovation, but its accessibility was a growing and troubling matter. MTV was needed. Warner Amex required a financial transfusion, and a mutual quid pro quo was evolving.

The record communities in New York, Los Angeles, and particularly Nashville have a twenty-four-hour grapevine. *Billboard's* "Inside Track," the last-page gossip column, carries week-old rumors. During the holidays, industry bar talk and cross-country WATS lines were full of exclusivity deals involving the music channel in conjunction with record labels. Capitol was the partner most frequently mentioned but other majors were cited as well. *Billboard*'s then video editor Laura Foti went public with a front-page story in February. Few of the principals would go "on the record" (no pun intended), but, she wrote, "Labels are seeking a percentage of MTV's advertising revenues in exchange for the video clip programming they now supply free, *once* MTV becomes profitable." She added that "a window of exclusivity" would be part of the deal. MTV's ad revenues amounted to $25 million in 1983, up from $7 million in 1982. Projections had the network in the black in early 1984. An unidentified source suggested MTV may be the major beneficiary in this kind of deal because it would make the channel secure and "protect [its] Madison Avenue investment."[65]

Capitol was the first to admit the mutually beneficial courtship was in progress. Reportedly, MTV offered $1.25 million over a three-year span, free advertising slots, and a "guaranteed rotation" of the label's videos in the "breakout" category. In return MTV would get 35 percent of Capitol/EMI videos a month prior to general distribution to its "competitors." MTV would retain flexibility on "content and format." The "leaked" document was dated 1 December 1983, and signed by Pittman.

Capitol's stake in this would be regular exposure plus income to offset the skyrocketing costs of video production. MTV's video rivals were angry and threatened lawsuits. Articles in the trades plus the *Village Voice* fueled the commotion. Cynthia Friedman of "Night Flight" retorted, "It's an opportunistic move. . . . But I can't believe the record companies are silly enough to cut off their other sources of promotion just to concentrate on one outlet." "To us it smacks of restraint of trade," declared the Video Music Channel's Mike Green, "we've been looking at it for three months." He continued to charge that MTV's policy was to neutralize Ted Turner's "Night Tracks."

Pittman finally went public, explaining that MTV was attempting to avoid the past mistakes of the radio industry. "Record companies," he observed, "have no access to radio—they couldn't count on access." Moreover, the exclusivity deal would help MTV and the labels. The companies would enjoy insured exposure and Pittman's channel would be top dog.

Label accountants liked the proposition. Escalating video and promotional costs would be curbed. A slice of MTV's growing time buys could contribute to company coffers. In fact, MTV's rate card, which opened 1984 with a $2,000 per 30-second charge, would be hiked to $2,400 a half-minute by March.

The marketing or operations executives, as usual, disliked the strictly bottom-line argumentation (see chapter 4). They generally opposed "exclusives," recalling the power of Rick Sklar at WABC-AM (New York City) during its heyday. One promotion person remarked, "The idea of exclusives means you have to rethink the entire idea of promotion." Others grumbled about the MTV format in relation to their rosters.[66] The gossip spread like wildfire, but concrete agreements did not emerge.

The other shoe dropped in June. The two M's dominated the industry. Michael Jackson's "Victory tour" was steeped in public controversy. MTV would supposedly start its own controversy in the pages of *Billboard*. Without identifying the labels, MTV issued a statement indicating an "exclusivity" pact with four majors. CBS, MCA, RCA, and the WEA-distributed Geffen Records were commonly cited as cosigners of the pact. The "gang of four" constituted 35 percent of the video clips aired by the channel. These would be aired exclusively by MTV for a month. In return CBS would receive $8 million over two years, covering its video costs. MCA and RCA would each earn $2 million during a three-year span.

Before Independence Day, WASEC made public a stock offering of 5.12 million shares on the MTV and Nickelodeon transponder channels. Warner Amex hoped to raise $82 million; $75 million would be used for outstanding bank debts plus general corporate costs, including the "exclusivity" deals no doubt.

MTV became a profit-making operation in the opening quarter of 1984 with $10.9 million in advertising sales; an additional $1.7 million was derived from cable operators in licensing fees—ten-cents per new household since 1983. Prospects looked brighter, at least for Pittman, Garland, Sykes, and associates. Segments of the broadcast and record industries objected with a vengeance.

"Let's Talk About It," on *Billboard's* editorial page, outlined some of the issues:

> Video music has excited and energized—some would even say saved—the record industry in the U.S. during the past couple of years. MTV deserves much of the credit for this.
>
> Even as labels move to formalize and institutionalize their relationships with the cable channel, let the debate continue. Many in the industry want their MTV, probably even more so now that payment for clips is forthcoming. Others have reservations. But everyone is served by open, vigorous discussions of the various issues at stake, confidentiality clauses or not.[67]

In the same issue, 30 June 1984, "the industry Bible" ran a piece headed "Music Video Looming Larger Than Ever." *Billboard's* search for a debate was unnecessary; few "bizzers" were going public. The dialogue actually started in mid-June. Elektra's Lou Maglia said of the CBS arrangement, "We want the freedom and flexibility to work [video clips] as we see them." He believed some of his artists, like Motley Crue, transcended the format of MTV. (Elektra would shortly sign with MTV.) Usually eloquent label executives had a brisk "no comment." In "Deep-Throat" fashion one paraphrased Santayana's famous dictum on learning from history. Record companies have been wholly unsuccessful in predicting trends or maintaining them. Warehouses full of returns are a testament to the fleeting nature of public tastes.

Officially launching *Billboard's* discussion, Stephanie Shephard contended that MTV possessed a paticular demographic, and singularly servicing this targetted audience "will limit the number of viewers who will be exposed to the latest videos." Moreover, "little of today's music has lasting value."

MTV's cable competition did not care to take the long-range perspective. Going in, they were at a disadvantage. The MTV contracts would only legalize the status quo or knock them out of the ball park entirely. All things being equal, U.S.A. and WTBS had sufficient subscribers to challenge MTV on weekend nights. ABC plus NBC were independent of cable hookups. Numerically the four could gang up on the all-music channel during the primetime aimed at the youth market. Late-night weekend broadcasting zeros in on the 18- to 34-year-olds, going back to the "In Concert"-"Midnight Special" era.

Alternative programmers still contemplated possible legal remedies. A spokesperson for "Night Tracks" warned again, "We'll take whatever steps are needed to counteract it." His prospects were not good. The producer of NBC's ninety-minute "Friday Night Videos" suggested MTV's format was too limited demographically. Narrowcast was the outlet's original strength, and in 1984 David Benjamin was using it as the Achilles' heel: "People who buy records are not only white and middle class."[68]

A potential storm cloud did loom on the horizon. Prior to the advent of MTV the generational life span of television teen idols was approximately three years. Duran Duran, Culture Club, Men at Work, Adam Ant, and others were approaching the midnight hour. These acts still graced the covers of teenybop magazines in the fall of 1984. Whether the original MTV audience would remain loyal as the younger siblings entered the picture was to be a true test of the psychographic format.

### "It's the Format:" Problems of Narrowcasting

The fantasy electronic teenage rec-room concept of MTV was the most important marketing breakthrough of the 1980s for record labels. The highly researched formula, however, had its drawbacks. Because of its original audience, the rock channel's advertising rate card did not reflect its cable industry position. Few people outside the music video industries were terribly concerned that MTV's 1982 pretax losses were approximately $12 million, but its content stirred considerable attention. Media observers noted the music rotation was "lily-white."

A *New York Times* television critic encapsulated a concern expressed from coast to coast by print and electronic journalists. John J. O'Connor wrote:

> The problem is that MTV seems curiously bent on returning the black musician to the status of invisible man! The problem can be watched for hours at a time without detecting the presence of a single black performer. Critics have wondered if this "oversight" is intentional, a demographic ploy for making MTV more palatable to the suburbs of middle-class white America. MTV executives, for their part, have insisted, not a little arrogantly that their product is focused on rock-and-roll, an area of music that supposedly is not frequented by black performers. . . . The prospect of continuing musical segregation leaves a new venture sadly stained.[69]

O'Connor was correct in his analysis. He may have added that formatted narrowcasting inevitably creates parameters or boundaries creating "ins" and "outs." The format was bordered by AOR offerings and pop-rock. Country, soul, and other so-called specialty areas were outside these boundaries. Because country, and rhythm and blues are the parents of rock and roll, there was some internal debate concerning the rigidity of the format prior to MTV's first broadcast. One insider told *Rolling Stone:* "I voiced my opinion to Bob. . . . He knew what they [WASEC] wanted was an AOR channel. 'The AOR audience is not conducive to black music. Cable's in the suburbs.'"[70] This was before *Thriller.* The playlist equally excluded the old and the futuristic. Buddy Holly, Chuck Berry, Captain Beefheart, and even Presley did not fit into the model. Pittman said, "I don't think our audience is very interested in the past." Beefheart and Laurie Anderson were dismissed as "too avant-garde."[71] The material telecast had to meet the narrowcast specifications, a rigid policy that triggered cries of racism and discrimination. Rick James, a partially successful black crossover artist, explained, "I hate my MTV." Maurice White of Earth, Wind and Fire: "I have trouble getting to play on it. Even though our music has broken all barriers they consider our music [deleted] so they say that they're only playing rock music, which I don't believe." Labels with potential crossover artists were becoming incensed with "the magic format." "It is visual AOR," said one executive contemptuously.

Music journalists bombarded Pittman with questions regarding the segregated playlist. His basic response:

> Rick James is great. . . . But we turned down Rick James because the consumer didn't define him as rock. . . . You'd think some of [AOR's] listeners would accept [him] but they don't.

> We are the art galley and not the artist. We are as broad as we can be and yet have the same audience . . . when you're doing the 12-to-34-year old audience, that's easy. Country has very little appeal. Disco has some. . . . But 85 percent of the target audience likes rock. . . . So it has to do not with race, but with sound.[72]

He complained rhetorically to a *Times*man: "Why doesn't anyone talk about all the music barriers we *have* broken down, like the areas between punk and new wave and mainstream rock?"[73] Pittman was a prisoner of the million dollars' worth of research that created "the magic format," and was not necessarily racist, as the *Thriller* episode illustrated.

CBS submitted "Billie Jean" to MTV. The cut from the hot-selling *Thriller* album was produced by Steve Barron of Limelight Productions. Did it fit the format? The question apparently raised a storm. Few of the principals involved will discuss the decision, but industry sources strongly suggest a CBS ultimatium was the deciding factor; CBS President Walter Yetnikoff, it is alleged, threatened to stop providing video clips. CBS was one of the few labels in a position to play this card because it dominated the charts at the time. On this occasion "friendly persuasion" worked in the executive suites of Warner Amex. "Billie Jean" was placed in the heavy rotation category. Sales soared to a million albums in two weeks. "Beat It" followed, as did Prince, Eddie Grant, and a few others. One economic imperative superseded another. Michael Jackson's record buyers were estimated to be 80 percent white. Prince, considered by some as a reincarnation of Jimi Hendrix, equally enjoys a large Caucasian audience.

The racism charge appeared defused. A black artist saw Jackson's inclusion as "very healthy," but Rick James still was not happy: "It hasn't gotten any better for me and other black acts. Michael Jackson was forced on MTV. . . . I still don't like MTV." The feeling is mutual. In the mid-1980s James, a Motown artist, has little chance of making the MTV rotation. "The two M's—MTV and Michael—are *it*," said a critic. A top chart hit could change the situation.

The racism charge was MTV's most volatile issue, but there were other special interests looking with displeasure at MTV's visual fare. Journalists, artists, and the New Christian Right were watching.

Music journalists can be an ornery lot. They are jaded, spoiled, and yet generally poorly paid, unwitting pawns of labels, concert promoters, and employers. They are journalists, also—critics with a perspective. Few listen to AM radio or praise music films, with the possible exception of "rockumentaries" (an Ehrenstein and Reed term), "The Last Waltz," "Don't Look

Back," or "Woodstock." A majority disliked the Rolling Stone's "Let's Spend the Night Together." Aesthetically, MTV violated preconceived canons of behavior. Heavy rotations, concert clips, and veejays are generally antithetical to a generation of writers weaned on free-form and live concert performances, usually from the front-sections center. The emergence of MTV was met by a long drawn-out silence. The writers, aware of the cable service, assumed it was a visual jukebox or a twenty-four-hour version of "American Bandstand" revisited. Others could not receive it. "A friend sent me a video cassette in the early part of 1982," said one midwest journalist. "I was curious after seeing the *Billboard* coverage and people asking me about Men at Work and some other bands." Television critics provided the majority of the early ink for MTV. The *Baltimore Sun* said, "MTV is to American Bandstand what the space shuttle is to the Wright Brothers' craft." A previous *Sun* review characterized the channel as featuring "dynamic, dramatic and often wildly innovative visualizations of contemporary rock songs." Syndicated television-film writer Vernon Scott called MTV "the hottest gimmick on the tube." The venerated Robert Christgau in a "trend piece" gave the devil his due: "MTV provided a breath of proverbial fresh air for the rock audience and a shot in the proverbial arm for record sales. . . . I'm willing to venture that MTV won't ever be as conservative a cultural force as AOR."[74] Robert Palmer in the *New York Times* credited MTV with affecting record sales. Comments on the negative aspects of the programming came later. Racism was one of the first charges hurled at the company. Repetitiousness and uneven quality of vidclips were also noted. MTV executives quite candidly concurred, pointing to the dominance of the format and their dependence on the visual material produced by record companies, especially by hot artists. Would they air a "poor" clip by a superstar? Yes!

A more telling criticism was raised by journalists mirroring the views of disenchanted artists. Steven Levy of *Rolling Stone* titled his lengthy, outstanding analysis of music video "AD Nauseam: How MTV Sells Out Rock and Roll." He concluded MTV was surrendering the essence of rock "to the proper psychographic." Stephen Holden, of the *New York Times,* specified the argument, indicating music was being written and produced for its visual effects. "These synthesizer-dominated international pop bands write songs that are very terse. . . . They're really like coded telegrams or computer language, and I think that rock videos are in part responsible for pop music moving in that direction."[75]

Video was seen as the final institutionalization of a pattern hatched in the 1970s when touring became *the* alternative to broadcast exposure. Some acts were stage successes with anemic record sales. The Grateful Dead with an army of Dead-heads lived on tour; its album sales rarely exceed 200,000. Genesis, Pink Floyd, Kiss, and even Bruce Springsteen received better concert than album reviews. Kiss, according to Gene Simmons, was a third-rate New Jersey bar band without the visuals. Filmmaking at the hands of Steve Barron, Russel Mulcahey, Simon Milne, Brian Grant, and David Mallet appeared to be overpowering the music. Rod Stewart: "I feel it's got nothing to do with the song whatsoever. . . I mean, you think the guys that are directing videos now are trying to make *Gone with the Wind*." Composer Randy Newman sardonically added, "It doesn't matter, the picture is worth a thousand words." Styx took acting lessons. According to Portrait's Dan Beck, Cyndi Lauper "was signed because she'll be a great film performer; she has the dynamics to create interesting visuals."[76] Musicians did not like the notion of being 1980s Fabians. Duran Duran attempted to distance itself from the medium that brought it U.S. recognition. Simon LeBon: "If we started concentrating more on the video, the songs would suffer."

Duran Duran's first EMI single "Planet Earth" was released 2 February 1981, accompanied by a surrealistic video directed by Russell Mulcahey. In May the group performed several U.S. concerts. The next month *Duran Duran* was released; it stiffed in the States but was number two on the British charts. "We'd broken in a lot of other countries," recalls Nick Rhodes, "but in the U.S. nobody even knew who we were. That's because radio stations had very strict programming [and only played acts like] REO Speedwagon, the Doors and Led Zeppelin."[77] Lead guitarist Andy Taylor complained, "We couldn't have sold eggs in America [at that time]"[78] Duran Duran issued another single, "Girls on Film," with a spicy video by Kevin Godley and Lol Creme. One version of the video was unacceptable for MTV, and was scheduled for "Hot Rocks," a Playboy channel experiment. The clip was described as "being the most blatantly sexist [video] with its parade of half-naked women."[79] Visuals were paramount in marketing the group. Simon Le Bon: "You can gain maximum exposure from a business point of view in, say, Germany, Australia, Japan, and Britain all on the same day." Rhodes adds, "Video to us is like stereo was to Pink Floyd."

In line with its video strategy, the group flew to Sri Lanka to tape three songs in an exotic atmosphere, and Mulcahey directed. One of the songs was "Hungry like the Wolf." Two more videos were taped in Antigua by Mulcahey: "Rio" and "Night Boat." The album *Rio* was released in May of 1982. With one very notable exception, the album skyrocketed up the charts worldwide. *Rio* was dormant in the United States. MTV added "Hungry like the Wolf" into a heavy rotation: four plays per day.

"The ongoing exposure of Duran Duran's videos on MTV last year kept the *Rio* album alive at the retail level and generated some interest on the part of radio," said Walter Lee, Capitol vice-president. MTV exposure pushed "Hungry like the Wolf" onto AOR playlists, and Duran Duran was on its way to stardom in the United States. *Rolling Stone* reported, "The band was a natural for music television. They may be the first rock group to ride in on a video wave."[80] Monkees mavens may disagree. Duran Duran does not like being compared to the Monkees or even the Beatles. Says Le Bon, "We're interested in making our own history, not rewriting anybody else's." Musical comparisons aside, Duran Duran became multimedia stars because MTV, to paraphrase bassist John Taylor, could not get videos of "Stairway to Heaven."

Bruce Springsteen voted with his feet. One day into the filming of his first video, "Dancing in the Dark," the superstar killed the conceptual footage; a "live" concert clip of "Dancing" directed by Brian DePalma would replace the concept visual. Privately other artists grumbled, "I'm a singer not an actor." Pittman is uncomfortable with this entire subject because MTV was hyped inside the industry as a promotional device for the exposure of records. Video cassette sales, despite "The Making of *Thriller*," were cost ineffective. Should this change because of VCR proliferation, the structure of rock music and its makers could be affected. Traditionalists, critics, and artists seem to be waging a rearguard action by appealing to historical norms and values. International Resource Development cautioned: "They appeal to the same fickle, faddish, 12-to-24-year age group and eventually become very boring in their repetitiveness. Besides, they monopolize precious TV screens within the household." An Eberstadt ad executive predicted, "It will be very much like radio. Over time, the audience will start to fragment as cable reaches more homes and as more video clips are produced." Pittman disagrees; he told a panel that his channel and perhaps a twenty-four-hour rock-and-roll format would dominate the music video market. Technology and consumer reaction to it will be the final arbiter. Pockets in U.S. society would like the entire evolution of rock and television to change course or terminate.

## MTV May Be Harmful . . .

As MTV's penetration continued into the U.S. heartland, the antitelevision lobby was rejuvenated. Music video was perceived as combining the two major influences on youth: rock and television. John Sykes saw the combination as a "powerful force" in broadcasting; the "antis," as a societal threat.

In September of 1982 the Institute for Living in Hartford, Connecticut, issued a statement by Dr. Richard M. Bridberg, the director of the private mental institution. In part, he said, "We have observed ill effects on certain of our patients as a result of viewing MTV." The press release created a mild stir. The hospital's public relations officer told a journalist, "These patients are very vulnerable and we have to be very careful with them and we try to monitor what they see. Many of them are hallucinating. And when you have scenes of people regurgitating or decapitations, this kind of thing is detrimental. Some of the rough edges have to be smoothed out for our patients. MTV is too much."[81] This psychological judgment, however reasonable, was treated with some levity in the media. The notion of "MTV is too much" went beyond the confines of a mental-care unit.

Wood TV, located in a university community in Ohio, included MTV in its cable operations even as the channel was being blacked out in Hartford's medical facility. Roger Wise of Wood TV said, "There wasn't any channel, really, that served our music needs as we would have like them served, and MTV was going across the country in great shape. Four hundred people directly accosted me about why wasn't it on our cable system, in light of the fact that we had several what they termed repeat network offerings. Why didn't we have one that was entirely music oriented, and that was the favorite that they suggested." He looked into the matter and after some study that included the *Market/Media* report decided to program the music channel.

The move provoked letters objecting to the loss of one of the three NBC feeds on the system, but the subject of the storm was MTV. Wise commented: "I heard about not only obscenity but . . . the use of instruments in certain fashions, and violent production techniques where it is backlighted and rear projected. Yes, we've had some serious objections."

The objections come from concerned parents, school teachers, and even some university people. A typical letter to the cable company: "MTV is completely disgusting and a waste of our money. If people want to watch it they should pay extra. It is suggestive and offensive for young children." The writer labeled the channel as basically a "negative influence." Other letters and calls were "a little more frank than that." Unfortunately, the more adamant notes and phone objections have been lost, but Wise added, "We've had some really tough letters and phone calls."

Wise, a veteran broadcaster, suggested a difference between the anti-MTV campaign and similar campaigns in the past. With Benny Goodman's New York Paramount Theater concerts and rock radio, parents had little control over the medium or content; they tried, usually in vain, to control their children. Cable is another matter; it is a subscription service. Wise said, "I now have a one-to-one relationship more than we ever did in the broadcast business. It was never as pointed or as vicious as the attack on MTV." He might have added that dissatisfied parents can cancel the service, something not possible in the past. Few people blacklisted Benny

Goodman or threw away their radios. "Deviance," wrote sociologist Howard Becker, "is in the eye of the beholder." This seems to be the case with MTV.

The objections to Wood TV programming were fairly moderate yet typical. Wise reports the letters have abated, although he still receives telephone calls that "X" is watching too much MTV." Cancellation threats have mostly disappeared.

Emporia, Virginia, exhibited more stridency regarding MTV. The summer of 1983 found Pembroke Cablevision broadcasting the music channel into the city of 4,800 people. A furor arose. Robert Wilcher, a youth adviser at the Calvary Baptist Church, said he found it "vulgar and distasteful." He was one of the leaders of a campaign to ban the channel that succeeded only partially. Pembroke Cablevision, by request of the city council, moved MTV to a limited-access or pay channel; it now costs $120 more annually to see the Warner Amex offering. Local teenagers were decidedly displeased with the actions of some of their elders. Some found "life boring without it." A 14-year-old reasoned, "If they don't like it, they don't have to watch it." The Emporia experience appears to be a relatively isolated case. It does illustrate the vulnerability of cable systems and content to pressure groups.

MTV has a standards and practices division that generally considers R- and X-rated vidclips as unacceptable. David Bowie's "China Girl" and the Tubes' "White Punks on Dope" were rejected. After the editing out of a seminude beach scene, the Bowie clip was aired. "Naked women running around or throwing babies out of trucks" was unacceptable to Pittman's format. Commercials for cigarettes, hard liquor, drug paraphernalia, birth control devices, and dating services were rejected as well. Ironically, several observers had suggested that jeans commercials are more erotic than the visuals. The cable transmissions of MTV transcended the disfavor of local moral entrepreneurs.

Feminists objected to the perceived sexist attitudes in some of the vidclips. Elayne Rapping in *The Guardian* observed: "There's nothing subtle or ambiguous about MTV's sexism—indeed, its misogyny. . . . From Hall and Oates' 'Maneater' to the Stray Cats' 'Sexy and Seventeen,' women are depicted in many videos as bitches, teases, castraters and all-around sex-things."[82] Frequently added to the feminists' list are Duran Duran's "Girls on Film" and Billy Idol's "Dancing with Myself," implying bondage with the silhouette of a naked woman tied to a post that flashes momentarily on the screen. The reminder of the clip finds raggedly clothed women crawling toward the leather-clad blond singer. Sue Steinberg, MTV's former set designer and executive producer, noted: "The emphasis on certain images contributes to the illusion of violence and sexism. They seem to see how far they can go. And it's getting worse."[83] That appears to be a matter of opinion. Rock videos, unlike album covers, have escaped the wrath of feminists like the National Organization for Women (NOW). So-called media watchdogs were another matter.

The National Coalition Against Television Violence (NCTV) denounced MTV for "sexually sadistic violence of a very intense nature." To support this charge NCTV claimed half of MTV's fare was overtly or at least covertly violent. Moreover, it claims that in an hour of viewing there is an average of 18 violent acts portrayed on the screen, most of them sexual in content. The organization lists 75 especially violent videos, ranging from Billy Idol to Pat Benatar's "Love Is a Battlefield." Violence, according to the coalition definition is "hostile, verbal or physical expression." In light of the FCC deregulation of cable content, NCTV could voice its concerns only while supplying its evaluations to community action groups.

Canada is different; cable transmissions can be censored there. In January of 1984 the Coalition Against Violent Entertainment (NCTV's branch) called for action by the Radio-Television and Telecommunications Commission, Canada's FCC, a move designed to bar MTV from the airwaves. The ploy worked as much. Music became the maple leaf's version of MTV.

Citing the Canadian fray, U.S. Surgeon General Everett C. J. Koop warned, "Violence and pornography are at a crossroads right now. One place they are crossing is in these rock video cassettes that have become so popular with young people." Speaking at the University of South Carolina's medical school, he continued, "It's hard enough to make adequate relationships with members of the opposite sex." He equated vidclips with tuberculosis and "communicable diseases."[84] Koop's remarks garnered considerable press coverage after they were reported by the two wire services, but they had minimal affect in contrast to Spiro Agnew's "drug-song" admonition in 1970.

The accusations of violence and sexism had little if any influence on MTV officials. Pittman is said to have replied, songs "are unhappy. Some have a dark message. It's the essence of rock." The format remained intact.

The only significant contextual threat came from CBS Records when the corporation forbid the use of its clips on a program sponsored by a blank tape or hardware manufacturer. It also objected to the visual promotion of duplicating tools. This was prior to the Supreme Court's Betamax decision or Warner's judicial argument in the PolyGram merger case that home taping kept record prices competitive.

Tom Ford of the *Toledo Blade* summed up the controversy over rock images, writing, "Those who criticize the violence and sexual suggestion in the videos are committing the first cardinal sin of rock and roll appreciation. They are taking things much too seriously."[85] Such is the essence of MTV's video fantasyland.

## "Footsteps"

"This industry is made up of followers," commented Harvey Leeds, Epic's director of video promotion. MTV was the leader of the pack even though "Night Flight" historically preceded it. The claim "Cable television's original music show" introduces "Night Flight" on Friday and Saturday nights. A good deal of chronological debate could be spared if *national* were specified in the opening. (The first cable music network was "Video Concert Hall," which first appeared in November 1979; it ceased in March 1981.) "Night Flight" appeared on the sports outlet 5 June 1981 with Neil Young's *Rust Never Sleeps*, a film that flopped at the box office. The series produced by ATI-Video promised feature films, such as *Lenny Bruce without Tears, The Alice Cooper Special,* and *Volunteer Jam,* among others, to be followed by "New Wave Theater," a half-hour show featuring "new" acts. Jeff Franklin, executive producer, said, "We want to screen anyone who has any film, of known acts or unknown acts, recorded acts or unrecorded acts. We will give unrecorded acts their first real chance at being seen, in many cases. We are looking for programming and we will pay." Originally, he had only six hours to fill. Franklin was obviously aware of the shortage of video material, especially full-length motion pictures.

The blockbusters distributed by Warner were *Woodstock* and *No Nukes,* signed to pay movie networks. "Night Flight," on the video weekends, was going head-to-head with NBC TV's youth-oriented programming. ATI-Video's series was scheduled to commence while "Saturday Night Live" was involved in a union dispute and off the air. Six minutes of advertising was scheduled per hour at a rate of $1,600 a minute. One minute was allocated for local cable operators. Reaching 7.5 million homes, Franklin was able to attract Miller Beer, Wrangler Jeans, and Pepsi as sponsors. "I think we got something that nobody has ever done before," said Franklin, adding he was not challenging the then-proposed Warner Amex project. In time "Night Flight" expanded to eight hours, plus a repeat of the original broadcast in the wee hours of the night. Each show is listed as highlighting a theme, such as "Take Off to . . . "—topics such as politics, video art, or body language. The body language show was billed as "a look at the many ways in which the human form is exploited in music videos, featuring Queen, Randy Newman, and others." This thematic segment is less than fifty minutes, usually dictated by the availability of video clips and with very sparse introductions. A viewer expecting an in-depth discussion illustrated with vidclips is in for a disappointment. Once the movies were exhausted, "Night Flight" lost its main attraction. The ATI executive producer was accurate in suggesting the ATI enterprise was not competing with MTV in promotion or content. The original industry draw of "Night Flight" was U.S.A.'s cable audience share. By the fall of 1983 cable and commercial networks were getting into the visual music business, even as filler for the movie channels.

In light of Pittman's rigid format and a 20 percent record sales share, a country music outlet was a natural. Two went on line in early March of 1983. The Country Music TV Network (CMTV) opened several days prior to the Nashville Network (TNN). Glenn Daniels of Video World International described CMTV as "sort of loosely based on the MTV-type format. . . . We wanted to pattern it on an easy-listening country music radio style." In time the channel planned a "Top 100." The unpretentious network faced severe competition from highly publicized and financed TNN.

The Nashville Network was a joint venture launched by WSM, Inc., with Group W Satellite Communications. Reportedly with $50 million seed money, it debuted in 6 to 7 million homes transmitted by 725 cable systems. The venture was promoted as the biggest launch "ever" in cable history. MTV had originated with, optimistically, 2 million households on approximately 200 local operations. A broadcasting observer said, "Looks to me like one of the best ideas I've seen in quite a while for advertiser-supported cable." Twenty advertisers including Sears, Ford, and Levis concurred. Dan Ruth of Group W said, "We sold all the time we had"; the rate card was a modest $800 per minute. TNN, a narrowcast with crossover potential was a success, although some viewers prefer CMTV because of their dislike for amateurish "country" sitcoms and game shows. Both of the Music City-based outlets posed a challenge to MTV.[86]

Ted Turner unveiled "Night Tracks" on his super station WTBS on 3 June 1983. At the time "17" enjoyed a commanding 24-million-household lead in the cable industry. A six-figure amount was invested in "Night Tracks." Based on 80 video clips, the show airs late-night weekends. Coproducer Thomas Lynch, formerly of "Don Kirshner's Rock Concert," characterized the package as exhibiting a "Top 40 orientation. And yes, we will play black videos," an obvious reference to MTV's playlist. "Night Track" selections are "determined" on the basis of the most requested country songs of the week as compiled by Burkhart/Abrams client stations. The consulting firm was also retained by MTV. The first weekend promised visuals of superstars Kenny Rogers, Michael Jackson, and a host of rock and soul as well as country performers. This fit the older 18-40 demographic sought: "Any song that's in the top 40 has a built-in-black and white core."[87] The "Night Tracks" philosophy paralleled that of the overground networks: targeting audience coupled with mass-appeal potential.

NBC's "Friday Night Videos," produced by Dick Ebersol of "Saturday Night Live," was a mix of approaches relying on clips with an off-camera announcer. The 13 July 1984 list of clips included Jermaine Jackson, Def Leppard, the Cars, and Womack and Womack. Two of the acts were MTV rotations; Jackson and the Womacks were soul artists beyond the format.

"ABC Rocks" opposed NBC as well as the numerous independent on-air broadcasts of "Solid Gold." Music was overexposed on weekends after 11:00 P.M. There were other programs from Black Entertainment, Nickelodeon, and the Satellite Program Network with "Music Channel," a morning show. Most of the movie channels used musicals as segues, with an occasional concert or special. HBO had "Video Jukebox" with its companion, Cinemax's "Album Flash," a half-hour clip derived from a recent LP. For example, Waylon Jennings's "Never Could Toe the Mark" included four cuts with a supporting cast of Robert Duvall, John R. Cash, and Jessi Colter. The plot was arranged so each song could be edited for individual telecasting, as RCA announced in a full-color trade-paper ad. "As seen on *Album Flash*" appeared on the album skin.

None of the myriad vidclip-dominated shows were real assaults on MTV, for most were bunched in common time frames. Their heterogeneous Top 40 bent was fairly similar. Caesar's admonition of divide and conquer was applicable. Most media observers expected a shakeout because of the expensive spillage occurring.

The alternative broadcasts did present a needed contrast to MTV's format. They provided a flexibility heretical to strict narrowcasting. All of these endeavors caused one industry person to sardonically jest: "If the record company lays me off I can always get a job with a film studio or a network. Disney's buying music rights for old cartoons. . . . Where's it going to end?"

The video storm clouds formed in August of 1984. The Hughes-affiliated Discovery Music Network announced plans for entering the market in December, assuming that cable operators would join in the endeavor. Ted Turner joined the melee with a contractual letter on 7 August to 8,000 cable operators offering a twenty-four-hour music video service. MSOs were given until the middle of the month to agree to a five-year "free" service. The agreement would apply only if 10 million subscribers could be guaranteed to the Atlanta-based mogul. Depending on the response, Turner promised a decision within a matter of weeks. Turner's undisclosed format reportedly would be similar to MTV's; no hard-core country or soul would be aired. The obvious question is whether an already dominated yet limited audience can absorb this amount of competition.

For Ted Turner the answer was not long in coming. In less than five weeks after his 26 October launching, "the mouth of the South" sold out to MTV. At the time CMC had 335,000 households. On New Year's Day, 1985, MTV aimed at the market CMC could not attract with "Video Hits One" (VH-1). The verdict on this project is still out.

Popular music has come light years since the days artists were fill-ins on variety shows and rock music was a novelty. Historians will credit MTV. Only the proud British music press will remember where it actually originated.

There are inponderables. The direction of vidclips and the content is wedded to the technology that created the images. Will the "Mr. Rogers" generation stick with music video or fickly disappear into the over-30 abyss, the dark hole the music industry will increasingly need as the nation grows collectively older.

The 1980s have been dominated by the graphics and visuals of Prince, MTV, and Russell Mulcahy. Prognostication or searches for megatrends seem to reside with the John Lacks and Robert Pittmans of the business.

## Notes

1. Quoted in Jim Sullivan, "Triumph of the 'New,'" *On Campus,* March 1984, p. 24.
2. Quotations in William R. Meyer, *Warner Brothers Directors* (New Rochelle, N.Y.: Arlington House, 1978), pp. 69-70.
3. Allen L. Woll, *The Hollywood Musical Goes to War* (Chicago: Nelson-Hall, 1982), p. 22.
4. Quoted in Robert Shelton and Burt Goldblatt, *The Country Music Story* (New Rochelle, N.Y.: Arlington House, 1966), p. 157.
5. George Simon, *Glenn Miller and His Orchestra* (New York: Thomas Crowell, 1974), p. 253.
6. Bob Foreman, "I Remember Snooky . . . ," *TV Guide,* 22 May 1978, p. 13. Also Philip K. Eberly, *Music in the Air,* (New York: Hastings House, 1982), p. 131.
7. Quoted in Albert Goldman, *Elvis* (New York: McGraw-Hill, 1981), p. 176.
8. Lionel Tiger, "Why, It Was Fun!" *Rolling Stone,* 16 February 1984, p. 28.
9. Philip Jenkinson and Alan Warner, *Celluloid Rock: 20 Years of Movie Rock* (London: Lorrimer Publishing, 1974), p. 35.
10. Robert Higgins, "Kicking Up Her Own Hullabaloo," *TV Guide,* 15 January 1966, p. 23.
11. Bill Doherty and George Uhlman, "Kiddy Rock," *Rock,* 10 April 1972, p. 5.
12. Quotes in Diby Diehl, "Bob-b-e-e-e-e-ee: A Portrait of Bubblegum Charisma," *TV Guide,* 25 December 1971, pp. 18, 19; Jim Miller "The Tour, the Magic, the Money," *Newsweek,* 16 July 1984, p. 65.
13. George Melly, *Revolt into Style: The Pop Arts* (Garden City, N.Y.: Anchor Books, 1971), p. 39.

14. Stanley E. Willis, "Falling in Love with Celebrities," *Sexual Behavior* 2 (August 1972): 3-4.

15. Quoted in Burt Prelutsky, "Once More with Screaming," *TV Guide* 5 November 1977, p. 28.

16. Kirshner quoted in *Rolling Stone,* 7 December 1972, p. 10.

17. Quoted in Dwight Whitney, "It's Practically a Branch of the U.S. Mint," *TV Guide,* 15 July 1972, p. 25.

18. Quoted in "Pop Records: Moguls, Money and Monsters," *Time,* 12 February 1973, p. 65.

19. Sally Vallongo, "Duran Duran: All Things to a Teen-Age Heart," *Toledo Blade,* 25 February 1984, p. P-1.

20. Megan Rosenfeld, "The Selling of the Bubblegum Kings (Oh Donny, Oh Donny, Oh!)," *Toledo Blade Sunday Magazine,* 1 October 1972, p. 12.

21. Quoted in "Inside Beatlemania," *San Francisco Chronicle,* 17 February 1964, p. 9.

22. Quoted in Diehl, "Bob-b-e-e-e-e-ee," p. 19.

23. Quoted in Robin Green, "The Naked Lunchbox: The David Cassidy Story," *Rolling Stone,* 11 May 1972, p. 42.

24. Rosenfeld, "The Selling of the Bubblegum Kings," p. 15.

25. Statements of fans from Angela Taylor, "'David!' They Yelled, and Parents Quietly Paid," *New York Times,* 13 March 1972, p. 44.

26. Quoted in Leslie Raddatz, "Dear David—I Am 9 Years Old," *TV Guide,* 22 May 1971, p. 27.

27. Quoted from Judith Sims, "In Concert Rockin' Out?" *Rolling Stone,* 10 April 1974, p. 16.

28. Quotations from Ben Fong-Torres, "The Decline and Fall Season of Rock on TV," *Rolling Stone,* 9 October 1975, p. 14. Also Max Gunther's two-part *TV Guide* series, 22, 29 July 1978.

29. Gunther, *TV Guide* series.

30. Quoted in Sam Sutherland, "Gold Has Solid Foothold on TV," *Billboard,* 23 July 1983, p. 6.

31. Quoted in Gail Bronson, "Music Video-TV's Newest Wrinkle," *U.S. News and World Report,* 27 February 1984, p. 72. Also John E. Cooney, "Cable TV Will Get All Music Channel Running 24 Hours," *Wall Street Journal*, 4 March 1981, p. 56.

32. R. Serge Denisoff, *I Want My MTV* (New Brunswick, N.J.: Transaction Books, forthcoming.)

33. Rob Balon, "Uses of Psychographics," *Billboard,* 7 November 1982, p. 26.

34. Quotations from Steven Levy, *"Ad Nauseam*: How MTV Sells Out Rock and Roll," *Rolling Stone,* 8 December 1983, p. 33.

35. Ibid.

36. Quotations from Pat Wadsley, "Rock Around the Clock," *Video,* April 1983, p. 51. Also Levy, "Ad Nauseam," p. 33.

37. "Stalking the Vanishing Elvis Tapes," *Video,* March 1984, p. 69.

38. Quotations in "Video Clips: A Personal View," *Billboard,* 16 August 1984, p. 10.

39. "Video Music May 'Date' Records by 1990," *Sentinel Tribune,* 26 December 1981, p. 11.

40. Rick Forrest, "'Rock Justice' a Noble Failure," *Billboard,* 10 January 1981.

41. Richard Mabley, *The Pop Process* (London: Hutchinson Educational, 1969), pp. 105-7.

42. David Marsh, *Before I Get Old* (New York: St. Martin's Press, 1983), p. 153.
43. Nik Cohen, *Rock from the Beginning* (New York: Pocket Books, 1970), p. 168.
44. Melly, *Revolt into Style,* p. 197.
45. Mabley, *The Pop Process,* pp. 106-7.
46. Melly, *Revolt into Style,* p. 187.
47. Quoted in Jim Miller, "Britain Rocks America—Again," *Newsweek,* 23 January 1984, p. 50.
48. George Kopp, "Cable, Pay TV Satellite Distribution Loom Big," *Billboard* 10 January 1981, p. 53. Also "Music Videos—Going the Way of Videogames?" *Cable Communications Magazine,* November 1983, p. 92.
49. Jim McCullaugh, "Cable Channel Seen Helping Record Sales," *Billboard* 14 March 1981, p. 16.
50. Quote in Roman Kozak, "Take Off Nears for 'Night Flight' Films," *Billboard,* 16 May 1981, p. 85.
51. Quoted in Leo Sacks, "Madison Ave Warming to MTV," *Billboard,* 2 July 1983, p. 64.
52. Cooney, "Cable TV Will Get All Music Channel Running 24 Hours," p. 56.
53. Quotations in Mary Beth Durkin, "Fred and Alan: Cable's Newest Wunderkinds," *Village Voice,* 4 November 1983, p. 86.
54. Levy, "*Ad Nauseam,*" p. 16.
55. Rick Sklar, *Rocking America* (New York: St. Martin's Press, 1984), p. 167.
56. Quotations in Bob Wiseman, "MTV: Rock Around the Clock," *Baltimore Sun,* 23 August 1982, p. B-6.
57. Ed Levine, "TV Rocks with Music," *New York Times Magazine,* 8 May 1983, p. 44.
58. Quoted in Roman Kozak, "Warner Amex MTV: Debuting New Music," *Billboard,* 22 August 1981, p. 52.
59. "MTV to Be in 4½-5 Mil Homes: Lack," *Billboard,* 10 October 1981, pp. 68, 82.
60. Quotations in David Handler, "It's Rock 'n' (Bank) Roll," *TV Guide,* 12 March 1983, p. 18. Also Roman Kozak, "How Men at Work Made It," *Billboard,* 6 November 1982, p. 40.
61. Quoted in Ethlie Ann Vare, "Music Video an Oldie to Clark," *Billboard* 27 August 1983, p. 6.
62. Quotations in Leo Sacks, "MTV Seen Aiding AOR Stations," *Billboard,* 28 May 1983, pp. 66.
63. Quotations from Dennis Kneale, "Weirder Is Better in the Red-Hot Land of the Rock Videos," *Wall Street Journal,* 17 October 1983, p. 1; Laura Foti, "New Act Pact Take Vidclip $ from Royalties," *Billboard,* 2 July 1983, p. 58.
64. "Labels Differ on Vidclip Timing," *Billboard,* 3 September 1983, p. 86.
65. Laura Foti, "MTV, Labels Talk Payments," *Billboard,* 11 February 1984, pp. 1, 74.
66. Quotations in Peter Hall, "MTV Wants It All," *Village Voice,* 21 February 1984, p. 48; Tony Seidman, "MTV Plan Shakes Label Exec Suites," *Billboard,* 31 March 1984, pp. 1, 60.
67. *Billboard,* 30 June 1984, p. 8.
68. "Other Clip Outlets Blast MTV Pacts," *Billboard,* 23 June 1984, p. 67.
69. "MTV—A Success Story with a Curious Shortcoming," *New York Times,* 24 July 1983, p. H-23.
70. Levy, "Ad Nauseam," p. 35.

71. Levine, "TV Rocks with Music," p. 45.
72. Wadsley, "Rock Around the Clock," p. 113.
73. Levine, "TV Rocks with Music."
74. "Rock 'n' Roller Coaster," *Village Voice,* 7 February 1984, p. 38.
75. Quoted in Levine, "TV Rocks with Music," pp. 42ff.
76. Quoted in Kneale, "Weirder Is Better in the Red-Hot Land of the Rock Videos," p. 14.
77. "Duran Duran: We're Not Just a Video Band," *Billboard,* 18 February 1984, p. 36.
78. Quoted in James Henke, "Middle Class Heroes," *Rolling Stone,* 2 February 1984, p. 26.
79. Durkin, "Fred and Alan," p. 88.
80. Quotations in Parke Puterbaugh, "Duran Duran: The Little Girls Understand," *Rolling Stone,* 12 May 1983, pp. 64-65.
81. Quotes in Roman Kozak, "Caution, MTV May be Hazardous to Your Mind," *Billboard,* 11 September 1982, pp. 10, 60.
82. Elayne Rapping, "EMPTYV," *The Guardian,* 8 February 1984.
83. "Video: Music's Worst Best New Thing," *Campus Life,* March 1984, p. 61.
84. "Watching Rock Videos Is Hazardous to Your Love Life, Koop Warns," *Sentinel Tribune,* 16 March 1984, p. 1.
85. "Rock Music with Pictures: A New and Disturbing Art," *Toledo Blade,* 3 June 1984, p. G-1; "MTV Sparks Sex, Violence Concern," *Cablevision,* 30 April 1984, p. 48.
86. Quotations in John Ponce, "CMTV Cashing in on Popularity, Style of MTV,"*Satellite TV Weekly,* June 1983, p. 3; Richard Stengel, "Country Comes to Cable," *Time,* 21 March 1983, p. 68; Victor Livingston, "Viewers Keep TNN on the Right Track," *Cablevision,* 2 April 1984, p. 15.
87. Quotations in Leo Sacks, "Turner Vid Clip Show Bowing," *Billboard,* 4 June 1983, pp. 1, 64; Eric Taub, "Purveyors of a Phenomenon," *Cablevision/Plus,* 12 December 1983, pp. 30-37.

# 8

# Backmasking, Bonfires, and the Right

Once a record has surmounted the many hurdles in its path and actually attracted the attention of gatekeepers and distributors, it is still not guaranteed success. In a small number of cases a "hit-bound" record or even a charted song may be subject to the interference of ideological groups and the imposition of social sanctions. Some of these groups see popular music as an evil antithetical to their values. Many adults regard pop music as an aesthetic disaster area, but some impute to it more sinister connotations.

With these mind-sets flying high, campaigns have been launched to suppress the portions of popular music—songs and artists—deemed harmful to Top 40, AOR, and MTV audiences. Petitions have been aimed at broadcasters and their sponsors, urging the removal of "offensive" records from the stations' playlists. Record stores in some communities have been boycotted for stocking "offensive" records. Citizens committees have approached the Federal Communications Commission (FCC) to complain that local broadcasters had not carried out their responsibilities to the "public interest" because they had played certain songs. Several successful artists, Jerry Lee Lewis and Chuck Berry in the late 1950s, were blacklisted from AM radio for alleged "immoral behavior"; Berry was consequently put in a federal penitentiary. The organizations most responsible for these assaults since the early 1950s have been the political plus fundamentalist Right.

## The Radical Right and Popular Music

Surrounded by the splendor of a Las Vegas gambling casino, former Vice-president Spiro Agnew told a crowd of assembled reporters, "We should listen more carefully to popular music, because at its best it is worthy of more serious appreciation, and at its worst it is blatant drug-culture propaganda." Nearly all of the media carried Agnew's statement that some rock music was harmful to the country's young. Pop music had become yet another target Agnew's efforts in congressional campaigns in

1970. For the Radical Right this was absolution. At long last a ranking government official had validated its contention: rock was corrupting youth. For the Radical Right this was no mere Agnewism but the high-water mark of a 20-year struggle to rid popular music of "subversive" elements.

In the public mind the Right is a collection of "little old ladies in tennis shoes" allied with the Moral Majority, obsessed with putting prayers back into classrooms, getting the United States out of the UN, and opposing abortion. Each foray undertaken by the Radical Right is believed by it to be an assault on the machinations of an international communist-human-ist conspiracy. Fluoridation, school-board elections, and Supreme Court decisions all have been pawns in that imagined conspiracy. The Radical Right, however, has a more grandiose worldview. According to sociologist Gary B. Rush, the Radical Right is basically a multitude of groups that maintain as an ideal the principle of "limited individualism," that is, "the opposition of 'collectivism' in government, international relations, to modern social principles, and modern social structure and operation."[1] Put another way, the Radical Right is profoundly concerned about changing social values and styles because it assumes that individual character is by itself weak and corruptible when devoid of traditional values. The late historian Richard Hofstadter termed this outlook the "revolt against mod-ernity." For the record industry the revolt has been manifested in the con-demnation of popular music.

The Right's introduction to popular music came by way of a folk-music group called the Weavers, which became an overnight success just as Mc-Carthyism was blossoming into a potent sociopolitical force. With "Tzena, Tzena," "Good Night Irene," and Woody Guthrie's "So Long, It's Been Good to Know You," the quartet dominated the popular-music charts of 1950. The junior senator from Wisconsin, Joseph McCarthy, held sway over the news. There were Communists in high places in the United States, he charged, including the entertainment media. The senator was preoc-cupied with government bureaus and agencies, so the task of investigating the entertainment world was left to the House Un-American Activities Committee (HUAC). During its investigations into the subversion of American culture, HUAC called professional witness Harvey Matusow, who claimed that the Weavers were Communists. After this "identifica-tion," and a similar charge in *Red Channels*, a guide to the political re-liability of entertainers, the Weavers were blacklisted from the media and finally forced to disband at the peak of their popularity. Other than Matusow's testimony, which later he recanted, and the *Channels* citation, there was no evidence to support the charge. Several members of the group—Pete Seeger and Lee Hays—had on occasion appeared before left-wing audiences, but this did not necessarily make them card-carrying Communist party members. Ironically, the ties that *did* exist between the Weavers and the party were never aired, either before HUAC or in *Red Channels*; in 1950 mere accusation was enough. Having successfully removed the Weavers from the airwaves, the Right turned its attention to more pressing matters: the "betrayal of China" and the persecution of Senator McCarthy by the "Eastern liberal establishment."

In time "communism in high places" took a back seat to the issue of school desegregation. The Supreme Court had ruled in the landmark *Brown* decision that segregated schools were unconstitutional and therefore must be eliminated. Coincidentally, 1954 also witnessed the emergence of something called "rock and roll." Rock was a first cousin to what had been called "race" music. This relationship would later become a central issue with the Radical Right.

### Racism and Rock and Roll

For most adult Americans, rock and roll was a loud new irritant that just might lead their children to juvenile delinquency. Several communities attempted to control it by legislating against "record hops," as they would do against rock festivals some fifteen years later. The prime impetus for the popularity of the music was the medium of film. *Blackboard Jungle* was the story of a middle-class, white, high school teacher laboring in the vineyards of a New York ghetto school. Its theme music was Bill Haley's "Rock Around the Clock." The significance of this film was astronomical. Frank Zappa, years later, recalled: "I didn't care if Bill Haley was white or sincere . . . he was playing the Teenage National Anthem and it was so LOUD I was jumping up and down. *Blackboard Jungle* . . . represented a strange sort of 'endorsement' of the teenage cause: "They have made a movie about us."[2] The impact of "Rock Around the Clock" was such that in a matter of months white "covers" or copies of black rock material all but dominated the "Hit Parade," much to the dismay of traditional crooners. It was artificial but it sold. Elvis Presley was a mixture of all of these elements. His stage dress was from *Blackboard Jungle*. He covered black material, leaving much of the original intent. When he sang "Shake, Rattle and Roll," no one thought he meant dancing. Efforts were made to stop Elvis "The Pelvis" by various parent-teacher groups with some success. Ed Sullivan broadcast only the upper half of the famous torso. In Florida the police insisted he stand still. The Right concurred, but disagreed as to the true meaning of the new popular musical trend.

Asa Carter, executive secretary of the North Alabama White Citizens Council, told the *New York Times* that the National Association for the

Advancement of Colored People (NAACP) was "infiltrating" southern white teenagers with rock and roll. (The NAACP had been instrumental in pressing the *Brown* case to the Supreme Court). Carter proposed that his organization survey jukeboxes and radio stations so as to purge those sources of "immoral" records. He went on to urge that deejays and coin operators who violated his ban be publicly harassed. Lacking the legal support afforded some northern antirock forces, Carter met with considerable opposition from industry people. A local record distributor, Harry Hurrich, retorted, "I consider Carter's proposal an invasion of the freedom of liking what you want to."[3] A programmer at a local radio station replied, "The only dictation in our business is that of our listeners. Carter's statement . . . is absurd." Roy Wilkins of the NAACP, obviously not a rock-music buff, equated it with disease and nuclear radiation, while denying the charge, "Some people in the South are blaming us for everything from measles to atomic fall out."[4] *Billboard* said, "Teenagers are unanimous on two points. They like rock and roll and they don't want it taken off the machines."[5] This rather obvious point did not dissuade rock's southern opponents. The Citizens Council of Greater New Orleans printed a handbill proclaiming:

> The screaming, idiotic words, and savage music of these records are undermining the morals of our white youth in America.
>
> Call the advertisers of the radio stations that play this type of music and complain to them!
>
> Don't Let Your Children Buy, or Listen To, These Records.

But the children did, and the Right's attempt to link rock and roll with the school integration decision failed. Rock itself was defused as a political issue upon its absorption by "American Bandstand." Presley's engineered image change from "hood stud" to churchgoing GI left the Right with nothing to do except concern itself with the reappearance of Pete Seeger, the Weavers, and the folk-music revival.

### Marxist Minstrels

When Seeger was barred from the mass media in the 1950s, many of his "progressive" supporters already had gone underground or fled the political scene because of the invasion of Hungary by the Soviet Union (1956) and the famous Khrushchev "secret speech" that same year at the 22nd Party Congress. All that remained for the charismatic folksinger was the college circuit, where phone calls from the American Legion went unheeded. Going to a Seeger concert became an act of political courage.

Seeger cultivated collegiate interest in the songs of Leadbelly, Woody Guthrie, the Weavers, and traditional folk material. His activities infuriated the Right, especially after folk music became a national trend of several years' duration.

Seeger was a prime mover in the folk-music revival and was accepted by collegians and young people outside the South, regardless of his alleged Communist sympathies and his citation by the House Un-American Activities Committee for contempt of Congress. The Right devoted a considerable amount of press space to the folksinger and his musical descendants, including Bob Dylan. Dylan played a central role as villain; he was the link between folksinger Pete Seeger and the Beatles. Jere Real, writing in the John Birch Society organ *American Opinion*, went through the usual congressional and right-wing citations "proving" that Woody Guthrie and especially Seeger were Kremlin agents. He did not stop with People's Songs, Inc., but also indicted Dylan as a "student of old time Communist Woody Guthrie." He portrayed Dylan's songs as "typical . . . filled with the bitter polemic which characterizes the Communist folksong."[6] The recitation of these charges was not particularly important in itself because displeasure with folksingers has been a traditional rightist position dating back to pre-World War II days. The linkage was dubbed "folk-rock" by *Billboard*'s Aaron Sternfield and came to the fore in 1965, much to the consternation of segments of both the Left and Right. The Left in many cases believed rock an unworthy bearer of political themes. The Right saw it as an unholy alliance of civil rights and communism. This was the year that the John Birch Society and the Billy James Hargis's Christian Crusade "discovered" rock and roll. The events that engendered this attention hinged on the introduction of "protest material" into the previously apolitical Top 40 and the Beatles alleged anti-Christ posture.

On 21 August 1965 a song entitled "Eve of Destruction" climbed to the fifty-eighth position on the *Billboard* "Hot 100" chart. The song was in the folkrock genre, pioneered and developed by the Byrds and Dylan, fundamentally a wedding of contemporary and topical lyrics with a subdued $4/4$ rock progression, maximizing the poetic or political statement. The sentiment of "Eve" was that the world was on the brink of nuclear war and would be destroyed unless humanity came to its collective senses. P.F. Sloan, the song's 19-year-old composer, defined its message as "a call to arms. We're on the eve of destruction and it doesn't have to be that way." He told another interviewer that the song was indicative of "decaying everywhere . . . . Society is so confused. There are triple road-blocks and detours wherever you go, and no one knows which road to travel. The Bomb? It's like a cloud hanging over me all the time."[7] "Eve" provoked immediate controversy. Some broadcasters wondered if "an entertainment medium should be used for propagandistic purposes." Folkniks denounced it as commercialization of protest. For the Right, it was a call to arms. On 9 September "Eve" reached the exalted *Billboard* top ten, which prompted a massive letterwriting campaign to the media. In California the Citizens for Conservative Action and the Young Republicans for a Return to Conservatism petitioned the Federal Communications Commission, contending that the song was in violation of the "fairness doctrine." There was even some talk of the Beach Boys or some other major group recording a reply. None did, although the Spokesmen did release an answer song, "The Dawn of Correction," which in industry jargon was a "stiff." The letter-writing campaign threatening an economic boycott was partially successful. The American Broadcasting Company forbade its affiliates to air the song. Many disk jockeys echoed Bob Eubank's statement: "How do you think the enemy will feel with a tune like that No. 1 in America?" "Eve" generated a number of imitations dealing with high school dress codes and superficial statements about ghetto conditions. After eleven weeks the song dropped off the charts. The Right's indignation was not stilled, primarily due to the efforts of the Reverend David A. Noebel.

Noebel began his career in the Radical Right while a student at the University of Wisconsin, where he taught fundamentalist Bible classes off campus. He was recruited into the Christian Crusade by its founder, Billy James Hargis, and quickly rose in the movement's hierarchy. Lecturing as a bespectacled neighborhood high school coach, he lent his voice to those fighting the popularity of folk music. At first, he exhibited the by now time-tested posture, charging that folk-music books and records used in the schools were corrupting the minds of unsuspecting children. He wrote several tracts charging that Young People's Records—now owned by *Good Housekeeping*—and the publishers of the *Fireside Book of Folk Music* were communist fronts. These accusations had been made on several previous occasions by various right-wing newspapers in southern California and were not terribly original except to those outside the Los Angeles area. Noebel's campaign did establish him as *the* Crusade authority on the impact of music upon youth. With these credentials he attempted to send the Beatles back to Liverpool and Dylan to Hibbing, Minnesota.

In 1965 Noebel produced a pamphlet titled *Communism, Hypnotism and The Beatles: An Analysis of the Communist Use of Music*. In a style that would become his trademark, he presented a manifesto with the air of a behavioral psychologist. The twenty-six-page pamphlet contained ten pages of obscure citations ranging from Pavlov to HUAC publications to a television guide purchased at a Rexall Drug Store. The essence of the tract is captured in his statement that "to understand what rock and roll in general and the Beatles in particular are doing to our teenagers, it is necessary to return to Pavlov's laboratory. The Beatles' ability to make teenagers take off their clothes and riot is laboratory tested and approved. It is scientifically labeled mass hypnosis and artificial neurosis."[8] Noebel further suggested that the Liverpool foursome was acting in the interest of the Soviet Union by weakening the moral fiber of the nation's youth, thus rendering them useless in the fight against communism.

Noebel's attack appears to have been triggered by an offhand remark by Derek Taylor, then the Beatles' press aide, to the effect, "They're completely anti-Christ. I mean, I'm anti-Christ as well, but they're so anti-Christ they shock me." In a radio address from the United Kingdom, Hargis picked up on this remark, saying, "The beatnik crowd, represented by the Beatles, is the Communist crowd." Agents of the anti-Christ were employing a subliminal form of musical brainwashing or propaganda, which Noebel claimed would lead to a massive "teenage mental breakdown." In his book, he warned: "Cybernetic warfare is the ultimate weapon and we can't afford one nerve-jammed child. Throw your Beatle and rock and roll records in the city dump. We have been unashamed of being labeled a Christian nation, let's make sure four mop-headed anti-Christ beatniks don't destroy our children's emotional and mental stability and ultimately our nation." In a follow-up work, *Rhythm, Riots and Revolution*, the Christian Crusader attempted to develop a cohesive explanation and causal relationship wedding the Communist conspiracy, folk music, rock and popular music, and its singers. Folk music and rock, he wrote, had primitive African roots. Rock, particularly, exhibited mindless sensual rhythms, made all the more dangerous by the lyrics of Seeger, Guthrie, Ochs, P. F. Sloane, and Dylan. To support this argument, Noebel presented a seemingly scientific comparison of two small-sized cities: Paducah, Kentucky, and Cape Giradeau, Missouri. In one community rock and roll was a pervasive part of life; the other city was relatively free of its influence. The combined rate of illegitimacy, school dropouts, fatal auto accidents, burglaries, and vandalism in the former was, according to Noebel, "fifty percent higher than it is in the city where good dance music rules."[9]

Political lyrics made rock and roll even more dangerous. "Eve of Destruction," Noebel claimed, was a case in point because it included words that "are obviously aimed at instilling fear in our teenagers as well as a sense of hopelessness. 'Thermonuclear holocaust,' 'the button,' 'the end of the world,' and similar expressions are constantly being used to induce the American public to surrender to atheistic international Community." With these two works and a series of articles in *Christian Crusader*, Noebel established himself as the Right's leading authority and spokesman on musical subversion. Unwittingly, several music-world personalities appear to have added fuel and legitimacy to Noebel's accusations.

John Lennon, in an interview printed in the London tabloid *Evening Standard,* remarked that the Beatles were "now more popular than Jesus." The remark referred to the declining influence of the Church of England. As reported in the U.S. press, the observation revived the Right's antipathy for the group and rock music. The statement was circulated widely throughout the Bible Belt, resulting in several public burnings of records under the aegis of the Ku Klux Klan and the Citizens Councils. Fundamentalist radio stations vowed never again to air Beatle records. The Beatles were burned in effigy in many sections of the rural South. There was some discussion of postponing their U.S. tour; however, promoters, mayors, and local officials argued there would be trouble from irate fans if any concerts were cancelled. The Beatles' overall popularity and the publication of the entire interview greatly mitigated the impact of the remarks, for few could objectively dispute the notion that the Beatles did outdraw and receive more attention than the Church of England, something many English churchmen readily conceded. The incident quickly passed from public memory except in the tracts published by the Right. Noebel, in yet another analysis of the Beatles, returned to the affair some three years later. Besides labeling the quartet the anti-Christs, he also found them in large measure responsible for the rise in drug abuse in the United States.

### Drugs and Popular Music

The passivity and introspection believed to be a consequence of marijuana smoking, coupled with the addictive features of various amphetamines and heroin, fit comfortably into Noebel's schema that the purpose of Dylan, the Beatles, and others was to incapacitate the young. Unlike the "made-in-Moscow" thesis, the association between music and drugs had some basis in fact.

Luria Castell, a founder of San Francisco's Family Dog, called the city an "American Liverpool." She saw the bay city as the only metropolis capable of maintaining a "scene" similar to the one that gave rise to the Beatles and the Mersey sound. While certainly not the only ingredient, the dominant social glue of the Haight-Ashbury scene was the drug culture. Kesey's dictum of "being on the bus" during the Trips Festivals period was primarily derived from dropping LSD. Consequently, a good portion of the music emanating from San Francisco was *drug oriented,* an influence that quickly permeated Los Angeles bands such as the Buffalo Springfield, the Byrds, and the Seeds, who frequently appeared in San Francisco. In most cases the music was *complementary* to the acid or pot itself. The instrumentals were prolonged and improvised, akin to the jazz riffs of the beat days of North Beach. Various devices to emphasize higher octaves and lower basses were employed to highlight the experience.

To those "off the bus" the songs no doubt sounded a bit long and somewhat strange. The material of the Grateful Dead, Sons of Champlin, Quicksilver Messenger Service, or The Jefferson Airplane, mixed with strobe lights and color slides, provided further stimuli to the drug itself. As Donovan would write, "Fly Jefferson Airplane gets you there on time . . . Captain High at your service." Lead guitarist Jerry Garcia of the Dead was aptly nicknamed "Captain Trips." Minus the McLuhanesque affectations, much of the music sounded rather innocent with the overt exception of the Airplane material, especially "White Rabbit," which remains the archetypal drug song. Folk-rock groups outside Haight-Ashbury also toyed with this theme. In Los Angeles groups calling themselves the Seeds and the Doors emerged. The latter group chose its name from the Aldous Huxley book *Doors of Perception,* which chronicled his experiences with peyote and mescalin. There is little doubt that from 1965-67 a number of West Coast groups had some connection to the drug subculture; however, their advocacy of narcotics was another matter.

With increasing awareness of the "hippie phenomenon," Sunday supplement writers, ministers, and "moral entrepreneurs" in 1966 began to associate popular music with drugs. In the beginning, critics ignored the obvious Trips Festivals and concentrated on ambiguous Dylan songs such as "Mr. Tambourine Man" and "Rainy Day Woman #12 and 35," which contained the chorus "everybody must get stoned." The Byrds, who began by covering Dylan songs, including "Mr. Tambourine Man," added "Eight Miles High" to their repertoire to further fan the flames. The defense offered by the Byrds that their song referred to an airplane flight over London was ignored. Their detractors insisted that it was indeed a drug song. Donovan's album *Sunshine Superman,* the Amboy Dukes' *Journey to the Center of the Mind,* the Beatles' *Sgt. Pepper's Lonely Hearts Club Band,* and the Jefferson Airplane's *Surrealistic Pillow* furthered the rock *qua* drug syndrome. The Jefferson Airplane's "White Rabbit," taken from their album, was based on the Lewis Carroll character in *Alice in Wonderland* and advocated the expansion of an individual's awareness state or consciousness:

> *One pill makes you larger*
> *And one pill makes you small*
> *And the ones that mother gives you*
> *Don't do anything at all*
> *Go ask Alice, when she's ten feet tall.*

The song, using a bolero tempo, ends with a crescendo urging the repeated cry of "feed your head." Very few songs played on AM radio made similar statements.

After 1967, and the disintegration of the San Francisco Summer of Love, the drug-song phenomenon subsided. Only "Don't Bogart Me," featured in the film *Easy Rider*, and Brewer and Shipley's "One Toke over the Line" transcended the esoteric underground networks. At yet another level folk-rock artists such as Jamie Brockett ("The Legend of the U.S.S. *Titanic*"), Arlo Guthrie ("Flying into Los Angeles"), Tom Paxton ("Talking Vietnam Pot Luck Blues"), and John Prine ("Illegal Smile") have toyed with the relationship of grass to the law and other social institutions.

In 1969, two years after the peak of the drug-song phenomenon, the Christian Crusade, the John Birch Society, and other extreme-right organizations took up the banner of rock as drug music. Interpretations of "Along Comes Mary" or "Lucy in the Sky with Diamonds" were esoteric, for moral entrepreneurs could easily have confined themselves to Donovan's *Sunshine Superman* album or the Jefferson Airplane's *Surrealistic Pillow*, which they discovered some three years *after* their first appearance. Even Agnew's famous Las Vegas news conference echoing the famous opening lines, "One pill makes you larger/And one pill makes you small," did not take place until 1970. In 1966 and 1967 the Right was still preoccupied with the wayfaring minstrels Pete Seeger, Joan Baez, and the Beatles.

Noebel continued his attack with articles such as "Columbia Records: Home of the Marxist Minstrels," which appeared in *Christian Crusade Weekly*. The Crusade also released several record albums featuring the Reverend Noebel discussing his favorite topic, the Communists' control of popular music. Noebel's thunder was taken up by a young musician, Bob Larson, who was converted to fundamentalism by country singer T. Texas Tyler. David Wilkerson, author of *The Cross and the Swtichblade*, persuaded Larson to enter the ministry. In 1967 Larson published *Rock and Roll: The Devil's Diversion,* in which he portrayed himself as a professional guitarist—prior to his conversion—who now tells all about the sin-ridden genre of rock. In one section Larson talks about how record-company executives demanded he write immoral lyrics to songs, and he observes, "Those songs that I wrote seem tame compared with the morally degenerative lyrics of today's rock songs. . . . Lyricists fancy themselves to be part poets. They're using existential themes of life, death, lonliness, alienation and existence. War, the pill, drugs, and promiscuity are all a part of a music that is a complete expression of its time and its audience."[10] Larson, using his personal experiences, complemented by the usual gaggle of inconsistent footnotes, touches upon most of the major themes found in the White Citizens Councils and in Noebel's work: the subliminal impact of rock, the advocacy of immoral acts, and so on. Even the racial connection is present: "The same coarse bodily motions which lead African dancers into a state of uncontrolled frenzy are present in modern dances. It is only logical, then,

**EXHIBIT 8.1**

| | | Date of | | Weeks on |
|---|---|---|---|---|
| *Name* | *Title* | *appearance* | *Position* | *chart* |
| Amboy Dukes | "Journey to Center of Mind" | 6/29/68 | 16 | 12 |
| Association | "Along Comes Mary" | 6/04/66 | 7 | 11 |
| American Breed | "Bend Me, Shape Me" | 12/20/67 | 5 | 14 |
| American Breed | "Step Out of Your Mind" | 6/03/67 | 24 | 9 |
| Beach Boys | "Good Vibrations" | 10/22/66 | 1 | 14 |
| Beatles | "Strawberry Fields Forever" | 2/25/67 | 8 | 9 |
| Byrds | "8 Miles High" | 4/09/66 | 14 | 9 |
| Byrds | "Mr. Tambourine Man" | 5/05/65 | 1 | 13 |
| Bob Dylan | "Rainy Day Women #12 & 35" | 4/16/66 | 2 | 10 |
| Donovan | "Mellow Yellow" | 11/12/66 | 2 | 12 |
| Donovan | "Sunshine Superman" | 7/30/66 | 1 | 13 |
| Electric Prunes | "Had Too Much to Dream" | 12/10/68 | 24 | 6 |
| Esquires | "Get On Up" | 8/19/67 | 11 | 15 |
| Fifth Dimension | "Up-Up & Away" | 6/03/67 | 7 | 12 |
| Jimi Hendrix | "Purple Haze" | 8/26/67 | 65 | 8 |
| Jefferson Airplane | "White Rabbit" | 6/24/67 | 8 | 10 |
| Lovin' Spoonful | "Full Measure" | 1/07/67 | 87 | 3 |
| Nitty Gritty Dirt Band | "Buy For Me the Rain" | 4/08/67 | 45 | 7 |
| Peter, Paul and Mary | "Puff the Magic Dragon" | 3/16/63 | 2 | 14 |
| Rainy Daze | "That Acapulco Gold" | 3/11/67 | 70 | 4 |
| Raiders | "Kicks" | 3/19/66 | 4 | 14 |
| Rolling Stones | "Get Off My Cloud" | 10/09/65 | 1 | 12 |
| Rolling Stones | "Jumpin' Jack Flash" | 6/08/68 | 3 | 12 |
| Rolling Stones | "Lady Jane" | 7/23/68 | 24 | 6 |
| Rolling Stones | "Mother's Little Helper" | 7/09/66 | 8 | 9 |
| Steppenwolf | "Magic Carpet Ride" | 10/05/68 | 3 | 16 |
| The Who | "I Can See For Miles" | 10/14/67 | 9 | 11 |
| The Who | "Magic Bus" | 8/10/68 | 25 | 9 |
| Ian Whitcomb | "You Turn Me On" | 5/22/65 | 8 | 13 |
| Yardbirds | "Over, Under, Sideways, Down" | 6/25/66 | 23 | 11 |
| Yardbirds | "Shapes of Things" | 3/19/66 | 11 | 11 |
| Yellow Balloon | "Yellow Balloon" | 4/01/67 | 25 | 10 |

Table title: Charted "Drug Songs" Cited by Critics, 1965-1969

that there must also be a correlation in the potentiality of demons gaining possessive control of a person through the medium of the beat." Larson attributes the source of this material to missionaries who have returned from the primitive jungles of Africa. At the end of his book is found the "Anti-Rock Pledge."

## The Anti-Rock Pledge

CONFESSING my faith in Christ and desiring to communicate his love and truth to my generation, and

RECOGNIZING that many of the songs and singers of rock music express and promote a morality and life-style contrary to the highest of Christian principles,

I HEREBY PLEDGE MYSELF TO THE FOLLOWING:

1. I will abstain from voluntarily listening to rock music so that I may adhere to the admonition of the Apostle Paul to "Think upon those things which are pure, honest, just, lovely, and of a good report." (Philippians 4:8)

2. I will destroy all rock records and tapes in my possession as an outward, symbolic act signifying my inner dedication to conscientiously discriminate as to the records I buy and listen to. (I John 5:21)

If after reading this book you can take the above pledge, please fill in the blanks below and send this signed pledge to:

BOB LARSON
BOX 26438
DENVER, COLORADO 80226

---------------------------------------------------

|       age       | name and address |       date       |
| 1. _____ | _____ | _____ |
|                 | _____ |                  |
|                 | _____ |                  |

*Rock and Roll: The Devil's Diversion*, revised several times, has reportedly been quite successful. Larson followed up this book with three more—*Hippies, Hindus and Rock & Roll, Rock and the Church,* and *The Day Music Died*—that outline the role of the music in the growth of the counterculture and its infiltration into Christian worship.

Another former musician and a faculty member at "America's largest fundamental Christian school," Bob Jones University, Frank Garlock published *The Big Beat: A Rock Blast*, echoing the charges Noebel and Larson had popularized: "Rock music is the devil's masterpiece for enslaving his own children. By the grace of God, let's keep him from also using it as a tool to weaken the children of God so that they are powerless to win this generation to Christ."[11]

Two years *after* its residents had declared Haight-Asbury dead, the Radical Right launched its main offensive against rock and roll. In film, record, pamphlet, book, and article the cry went out, "Pot, Rock and Revolution." Constructive Action, Inc., located in Whittier, California, the birthplace of Richard M. Nixon, made available a 30-minute, full-color film entitled

Jann Wenner (Courtesy of Rolling Stone)
MTV Video Jocks (Courtesy of Music Television)

**Aleister Crowley (Courtesy of The Bettman Archive/BBC Hulton)**

Ricky Nelson (Courtesy of United Artists Records)
Fleetwood Mac (Courtesy of Warner Brothers)

Rick James (Courtesy of Mowtown Records)
Black Sabbath (Courtesy of Warner Brothers Records, Inc.)

"The Pied Pipers." Rock groups, according to the film, were the Pied Pipers leading U.S. youth into the narcotization of drug use, and the Beatles were prominently featured. In 1969 Noebel published another book, *The Beatles: A Study in Drugs, Sex and Revolution*, which restated his earlier position; by 1971 it had gone through five printings. The less extreme John Birch Society also joined the battle. Gary Allen's "The Music: There's More To It Than Meets the Ear," placed *American Opinion* foresquare behind Noebel, Larson, and Garlock. "Rock singers are in constant communication with our teenagers, promoting attitudes and ideas which, if they were aware of the message, would blow the minds of most parents."[12] The article, of course, went on to alert parents as to what Allen thought rock music was saying: "Listen to the Beatles' new hit about how great it is to be out of America and 'Back in the USSR.'" Allen continued through the role citations of Dylan's connection with folk music, acid rock, and the subliminal power of music. He did add a new twist to the Right's perception of rock, exclaiming that *National Review*, the conservative magazine, had totally misinterpreted "Revolution" by the Beatles. William F. Buckley's publication had said that "Revolution" was a put-down of violence and radical politics. Not so, claimed Allen; "'Revolution' takes the Moscow line against Trotskyites and the Progressive Labor party."

*National Review* responded with its own authority on youth culture and Trotskyist tactics, Phillip Abbott Luce. Luce was one of the original members of Progressive Labor party who had been expelled from the movement. He later disavowed his previous associates and became an "informed" witness before congressional investigating committees and right-wing rallies. In "Are the Beatles Termites? The Great Rock Conspiracy," Luce accused Allen and the John Birch Society of campaigning against the devil with ridiculous footnotes and of totally misrepresenting the Beatles and rock music. "'Back in the USSR'," he explained, is a "total put-on" that did not laud the Soviet Union. He reaffirmed the validity of *National Review*'s original interpretation of "Revolution," citing a Young Americans for Freedom review that had observed, "Musically and polemically the Beatles urge the generation they helped create to free its mind from revolutionary enticements." Luce cynically added, "Perhaps it would be advisable for Mr. Allen and his 'hip' friends to ignore rock and roll stations."[13]

As the John Birchers and *National Review* were having one of their sporadic internecine ideological spats, a Michigan minister was staging record burnings. Reverend Riblett of Garden City built a seven-foot cross made of rock-and-roll records contributed by his congregation and set it afire. Part of his explanation for this action was, "The Beatles are an immoral bunch and I guess all of 'em have been convicted of marijuana smokin' and heaven only knows what else. I don't think it's the greatest idols for our teenagers to look up to."[14]

Unlike most Radical Right charges the drug-song issue was taken over by a number of more dignified public figures and politicians. The late Congressman James Utt frequently inserted Noebel's charge of Pavlovian brainwashing into the *Congressional Record.* Former California Superintendent of Schools Max Rafferty echoed the same charges. Television entertainer Art Linkletter, following the suicide of his daughter, charged that rock's advocacy of drugs was an important factor in her death. Linkletter told one congressional subcommittee that the Beatles were "a terrible example for youth," a charge he has repeated often on the lecture circuit and in print. President Nixon bestowed a public service award upon the celebrity for his antidrug activities.

Former Vice-president Spiro T. Agnew injected this argument into the 1970 congressional campaign. While denying that the Agnew speech had any influence, the Federal Communications Commission several months later issued a warning to radio broadcasters to the effect that they would be responsible for the lyrics they put on the air.

The Agnew statement and the FCC warning were hollow victories for the Right because the drug-music problem by 1970 was virtually nonexistent, as both *Rolling Stone* reporter Ben Fong-Torres and FCC Commissioner Nicholas Johnson then reminded the public. *Sgt. Pepper, Surrealistic Pillow,* and *Sunshine Superman* were all buried in the symbolic coffin commemorating the death of Haight-Ashbury. The Beatles at that time were on the verge of their famous breakup, and Donovan was an ardent antidrug spokesman. By 1970 the prodrug song was all but a novelty left to folksingers and basically addressed pot smoking rather than "speed" or "smack." Indeed, as Commissioner Johnson observed in a reply to Vice-president Agnew, there were as many antidrug songs in 1970 as there songs were in favor of its usage. Perhaps the most telling criticism the "rock turn-on" thesis is that there is no real evidence to support it. Conversely, the few existing studies on the influence of songs indicate large portions of those sampled denied that popular music had any effect upon their sociopolitical attitudes. In one study of Canadian high school students, 81 percent believed songs had no influence on them; only .031 percent believed the predominant theme in popular music was drugs. In a college survey, 90.3 percent of the respondents reported no change in their attitudes and lifestyle as a result of what rock songs were saying.[15]

A more significant figure perhaps is that the Right's own documentation shows fewer than 30 examples of so-called drug songs. Gary Allen's often-cited number of 28 is considerably less than half of the singles material released in one average week in the record industry, yet his sample is derived from a four-year time span, which renders the figure an infinitesimally small portion of one percentile. Despite these figures the drug-song conspiracy continues to be a popular topic in right-wing circles, with films, records, tapes, and lectures all addressed to this question.

### Sex and Rock and Roll

The advocacy of promiscuous sexual relations is another charge directed at rock music by the Right. Early rhythm and blues songs, as noted, had overtly sexual lyrics. "Roll All Night Long" and "Work with Me, Annie" meant just that. These songs had nothing to do with dancing, as the later "covers" by Pat Boone, Georgia Gibbs, Teresa Brewer, and others tended to imply. Presley's lyrical material in most cases was rather innocent; however, his stage presence did in fact have a strong sexual overtone. His gyrations, word inflections, "Ah wannn . . . t you, Ah nee . . . d you . . ." all conveyed the sexual intentions of a hillbilly stud. On the other hand, Dick Clark's tutelage over the music as well as the Beatles' "I-Want-to-Hold-Your-Hand" image generally presented a most wholesome portrait of rock.

In time, as another Beatle song indicated, "love" became "more than just holding hands." Songs, particularly those in the so-called underground category, began to address the topic of sex in interpersonal relations. Performers such as Mick Jagger, Iggy Stooge, David Bowie, and Jim Morrison combined both the lyrics and the rhythm and blues era with the bump and grind utilized by Presley. Jagger's interpretation of "I'm a King Bee" left little to imagination. Songs such as "(I Can't Get No) Satisfaction," "Light My Fire," and "Good Lovin" were the exception on the *Billboard* charts of 1965 through 1968. As with the overtly drug-oriented songs, pieces such as "Let's Spend the Night Together" or "I'll Be Your Baby Tonight" usually were confined to the underground stations or private home stereo systems.[16] Not even the most liberal radio-station programmers would play the "Fish Cheer" by Country Joe, John Lennon's "Working Class Hero"—with the "word"—or the Fugs' "Wet Dream." The Right's interpretation of sex images in rock did not comment on the de facto radio censorship. Noebel observed, "Rock and roll is a necessary ingredient of the sex revolution." Gary Allen saw it as an open exhortation "to indulge in illicit sex acts [that] . . . are also a factor in the demoralization of youth." To support this connection, the right-wing press frequently cites the now-famous Jim Morrison "indecent exposure" case in Miami Beach.

The late Jim Morrison, lead singer of the Doors, reenacted the role that first brought Presley to public attention. Both on record and on stage he became a purveyor of sensuality. The Doors' first and biggest hit record was "Light My Fire." Wearing tight black leather pants or a snakeskin suit,

Morrison took pleasure in eliciting the same shrieks and screams that had characterized Presley and Rolling Stones appearances.

On 2 March 1969, Morrison, according to his manager Bill Siddons, was putting on "just another dirty Doors show" for a Miami audience. This time he was charged by the local police with "lewd and lascivious behavior in public by exposing his private parts and by simulating masturbation and oral copulation." All of the living members of the band deny it occurred. John Densmore said, "Jim didn't expose himself . . . three days later warrants were issued. It was political." "Jim was drunk out of his mind at that show, but he never did it. I never saw it," recalls Ray Manzarek. Robbie Krieger declares, "He never whipped it out. Nor did he ever simulate oral copulation on the guitar player, which was me,"[17] This was not "just another" performance.

The reaction to the Morrison incident was overwhelming and somewhat unexpected; a local reporter commented, "They'd crucify him if they could, they're so worked up." The *Miami Herald* called Morrison "The King of Orgasmic Rock" and pictured him as being "hypnotically erotic" and as "flaunting the laws of obscenity, indecent exposure and incitement to riot." The Crime Commission of Greater Miami called for an investigation into the concert and why it had been allowed to take place in the area. The State Attorney's Office issued warrants for Morrison's arrest. The mayor of neighboring Jacksonville cancelled a forthcoming Doors concert. Finally, the entire tour was scrapped. Morrison was subsequently tried in Dade Criminal Court and found guilty of drunkennesss and exposure; he was acquitted of all other charges.

This event mobilized what one reporter termed a "decency movement." Mike Levesque, a 19-year-old football player at Miami Spring High, organized the Rally for Decency with the aid of the Catholic hierarchy, which was held on 23 March at the Orange Bowl. There, 30,000 people, half of whom were adults, saw and heard Jackie Gleason, Kate Smith, Anita Bryant, and the Lettermen. "Longhairs and weird dressers" were not allowed to attend. Numerous religious organizations were present. The American Legion distributed 10,000 small U.S. flags as young speakers gave three-minute orations on "behalf of goodness and virtue." "Down With Obscenity" signs dotted the audience. Gleason told the crowd, "I believe this kind of movement will snowball across the states and perhaps the world." President Nixon sent Levesque a letter of support. George Wallace appeared at a "Youths for Decency" rally at Enterprise, Alabama. Several other such affairs took place in Cincinnati and Baltimore. The Baltimore rally attracted 40,000 youths to hear five rock bands characterized by one participant as "second-rate . . . even for Baltimore." The concert ended in a violent race riot. Plans for future "decency" rallies did not materialize.

The short-lived "decency movement" operated at several levels of consciousness. Levesque represented one of these. He told one interviewer, "I like the Doors' *music.* And I like a lotta good groups. I mean, I'm not like a guy who just likes Rickie [*sic*] Nelson or somebody like that. I like all these modern groups."[18] What he objected to was the sentiment offered by some rock performers who had "nothin' constructive to say" about the United States. The more radical rightists found rock to be a more Machiavellian symptom of the moral deterioration of youth. The fact that no rock groups were represented at the original Rally for Decency is illustrative. As the Reverend Riblett explained, "Rock and roll is the devil's diversion. It's been traced back to the jungle drums. That's where it all comes from. The head hunters use the same beat before they go out to hunt heads and all this." Noebel, perhaps, best summarized the relationship of the Right to rock: "Present day rock is having a holiday ridiculing religion and morality while at the same time glorifying drugs, sexual promiscuity, and revolution—and all the time claiming to do so under the guise of art!"[19]

## God-Rock and the Right

By mid-1971 nearly all of the threats perceived by the Radical Right from popular music had disappeared. Dylan was past protesting, acid rock was history, and the Beatles were not "more popular than Jesus." The Beatles no longer existed, and the most popular album in the United States was *Jesus Christ Superstar.* Even Billy Graham had a kind word for rock and roll, which he had rejected some years previously. He told the *Los Angeles Times,* "A lot of rock music is basically religious music . . . we don't realize how serious our young people are."[20] "Jesus People" were beginning to appear, making witness to the glory of the son of God in a manner reminiscent of zealous Jehovah's Witnesses. Many denominations welcomed this more serious interest in Christianity on the part of the young. A Catholic lay leader, observing the "Jesus People," explained to a *Time* reporter, "We are on the threshold of the greatest spiritual revival the U.S. has ever experienced."[21] Even Jesus-rock bands were emerging. Many segments of the Right treated this phenomenon with considerable disbelief and bewilderment, and some groups with a fundamentalist theological bent raised objections to the portrayals of Christ in drama and in song.

Again, Noebel led the charge. *Jesus Christ Superstar,* he claimed, "is blasphemous, sacrilegious, irreverent, profane, desecrating, apostate and anti-Christian."[22] The humanization of Christ, he reasoned, was the work of unbelievers. He concluded a lengthy indictment saying, "Those who thought John Lennon was right were wrong; and those who think Rice and Webber [the producers] are an improvement over Lennon are also wrong. The Great White Throne will someday reveal just how wrong they were." The last allusion was directed toward liberal Christians who applauded *Superstar.* The *Superstar* campaign did not generate the furor that anti-Beatles efforts had. *Christian Crusade Weekly* did publish occasional barbs against Broadway and God-rock but with—for it—considerable restraint.

Some six months after the Noebel charges, a *Christian Crusade Weekly* reader inquired about the Crusade's position on the musical *Godspell.* "Crusader's Action Line" replied that although the play was "blasphemous," it was an accurate but trite portrayal of the life of Christ. Little further mention of God-rock was made until nearly three months later another reader asked about the "Jesus Watch." The reply was negative, attributing the watch to the *Jesus Christ Superstar* crowd; the play was characterized as having brought "Christ down, and it has done very little to exhalt him." This answer was mild in comparison to the follow-up material from Noebel and Hargis, who normally left musical affairs to Noebel. Noebel began the assault by attacking the Broadway stage and its anti-Christian and anti-American material, especially as found in *Hair*, which Noebel believed dealt with "pot, homosexuality, fornication, nudity, astrology, anarchy, anti-patriotism, and playboy-love." During the first week in March 1972, *Jesus Christ Superstar* opened in Tulsa, Oklahoma, the Crusade's home base, to a capacity crowd of over 6,000 people. Hargis was enraged, urging all Christians to leave any church that would sanction a "satanic production" that treated "Judas [as] the hero, Jesus and His Apostles [as] drunkards, Mary [as] the secret lover of the Lord."[23] In the same issue of *Christian Crusade Weekly* readers were urged to join the Seventh Day Adventists in combating the production. Noebel's original barrage was reprinted to add further ammunition to the Hargis denunciation. Again, the campaign did not get off the ground. Noebel planned to revise his magnum opus *Rhythm, Riots, and Revolution,* and to retitle it *The Marxist Minstrels.*

It is tempting to dismiss the Noebels, Larsons, and Allens as right-wing crackpots or opportunists. Gordon Friesen, the editor of *Broadside* (New York City) and a frquent target in Noebel's books, writes: "I have a young relative who knows Noebel personally. He describes him as a cynic who 'was laughing his head off' at the thought of people gullible enough to fall for the crap he was laying down in *Rhythm, Riots, and Revolution.* That's the kind of a cat you are dealing with." To this Noebel might reply, "Oh we laugh at ourselves all the time and we have a lot of fun doing what we are doing, but we still think it's very serious business."[24] University of Texas historian Jerome Rodnitzky offers a more convincing explanation: "Sheltered in places like Tulsa, Oklahoma, and viewing the young from afar, it is perhaps too easy for them to see the new youthful life-styles as aberrations imposed by alien and allegedly hypnotic forces such as the Beatles. Noebel's book, thus, tells far more about the Christian Crusade than it does about the Beatles."[25] Surprisingly, Phillip Luce joined with the professor, accusing Gary Allen of myopia and paranoia: "Some writers at *American Opinion* . . . relate everything they dislike or don't understand to the thrust of the Illuminati (presently referred to as THE INSIDERS). The Illuminati preside over The Conspiracy and The Conspiracy extends even into record stores and radio stations."[26]

Happily for the recording industry, the Radical Right's ability to impose its will is not uniform. Outside its own small constituency, generally confined to rural regions and one or two midwestern or southern cities, it was powerless. An occasional letter to a program director has little effect if the "offensive" record or artist has public appeal. That was correct until the 1980s.

### Old Wine in a New Bottle

The rise of Christopher Lasch's "culture of narcissism" or Tom Wolfe's "Me Generation" in the 1970s altered the focus of moral entrepreneurs. The Right's sting had been blunted by Watergate and the discreditation of the Vietnam adventure strongly supported to the end by supra-anticommunists. Simultaneously, counterculturites had quietly been woven into the social fabric. Feminism and the environment were the key topics on the social agenda. The proponents lacked the visibility or currency of the Woodstock Nation. Phil Ochs's line seemed appropriate: "There are no more songs."

In the wake of Jimmy Carter's surprising presidential victory and several Supreme Court decisions, the "new" Right regrouped. Richard Viguerie, a pollster and strategist, looked to the apolitical evangelicals as a potential base of support. The evangelicals or "born agains" were ripe. Their sensibilities have been battered by perceived social permissiveness, and changing sexual roles and mores. The times they were a-changing. Religion scholar Martin Marty noted, "When people are nervous about their personal lives or unsure about national direction, or when they lose faith . . . [they] become interested in a religion that gives you a very strong personal experience, supported by a very strong sense of authority." A union of political and theological conservatism was arranged. The offspring was the New Christian Right with a shopping list of social issues stressing a return to the traditional family and country. Promiscuity, abortion, and the equal rights amendment (ERA) were assaults on the structure of a Norman Rockwell vision of the nation. Sociologist Milton Yinger observed, "They believe the fundamental values that should govern civil society are endangered." These social issues are "weakening the moral fiber of the nation."[27]

"We're in mortal danger from without and within," said the Reverend Jerry Falwell. The preacher, founder of the Moral Majority, told an interviewer:

> I think that the American tradition. . . is the sanctity of the family . . . unquestionably the cornerstone of this republic. And we need to work towards its preservation, not its destruction. And today the television industry, without any question, is geared towards and directing all of its energies towards the ridicule of that basic institution . . . When we take what is sacred—and sex is sacred, marriage is sacred, the marriage act is sacred—when we take what is sacred and cheapen it by making it something less than God intended it to be, then it becomes pornography.[28]

Minister Don Wildman at the Southhaven First United Church of Mississippi on Falwell's advice founded the National Federation for Decency (NFD). NFD surfaced nationally with the Coalition for Better Television (CBTV), which monitored network programming. Using CBTV's results Wildman compiled a "Top Sponsors of Sex" list. The device was to be used to boycott offensive sponsors. Other television watchdogs were somewhat leary of CBTV's ratings and tactics. Dr. Thomas Radecki, a psychiatrist and chairman of the National Coalition on Television Violence, objected, "In our opinion, the research on the social effects of sexuality on TV is still inadequate. We are also troubled that there is so much disagreement—even within the Christian community—as to what is, and what is not appropriate 'sexual' portrayal." "We don't favor boycotts," noted Everett C. Parker of the United Church of Christ's Office of Communication. CBTV claimed credit for the cancellation of prime ABC-TV offenders "Soap" and "Charlie's Angels," but ABC explained that the cancellations were reflective of the shows' low ratings. "We have a religious mandate," countered a California Moral Majority spokesperson, "We must return to broad principles of Biblical law to restore order to our society."[29]

The sexual revolution of the 1960s frightened and angered many fundamentalists. *Wade* v. *Rowe*, the abortion decision, and ERA were the results of changing sexual interrelations. Rock music was perfect as a villain in this saga.

Since *Blackboard Jungle* conservative churchmen have led the assault on rock and roll. Some of the exploitive American International "jukebox films" cast preachers as narrow-minded censors of the new music. A classic example was Alan Freed's pioneer quickie serial musical *Shake Rattle and*

*Roll* (1956), which pitted SPRACAY (Society for the Prevention of Rock and Roll Corruption of American Youth) against rockers. The film spawned others like *Rock Around the Clock* and *Don't Knock the Rock*. Life imitated art during the reign of the Beatles and the sounds of "flower children." By the mid-1970s the social upheaval seem to have dissipated at least for large segments of the population.

The Christian Crusade lowered its rhetorical guns. Hargis and Noebel were occupied with the newly established American Christian College in Tulsa. Their energies were redirected to fund-raising rather than folksingers or the divided Beatles. The founder of Christian Crusade was partially discredited when he was accused of having sexual relations with his scholastic charges. He explained that "genes and chromosomes" caused the indiscretions. Noebel with some supporters resurfaced when Monty Python's film *Life of Brian* opened in the Oklahoma City. They charged the British comedy teams with "blasphemy and sacrilege." The torch was being passed to the lesser-known crusaders.

The New Right's campaign was essentially a grass-roots phenomenon. Spokespersons did appear on evengical programs like the "PTL" and "The 700 Club." Few of the major occupiers of the electronic pulpits were ardent supporters.

The Communist-conspiracy accusations were absent. Only the most ardent of segregationists clung to the racial motivation behind rock music. The cold-war arguments of *Red Channels* and the Christian Crusade fadded into history. Dylan, the target of Noebel's misguided charges, was now singing born-again ballads like "You Gotta Serve Somebody."

Bob Larson was the heir apparent. He dropped the Kremlin menance characterization of the Beatles. Finding more suitable Biblical guides, he advocated boycotting the disbanded Fab Four's catalog albums: "John, Paul, George, and Ringo taught us to accept pop idols as arbiters of sex, politics, and religion. The Beatles may have been only temporarily 'more popular than Jesus' but it was long enough to alter the music and morals of the Western world."[30]

Larson applied the "profamily" rationale to rock music, cautioning parents, "Encouraging your child to boycott the music of artists who advocate or use drugs is a moral action that would save this generation a lot of misery. It also might save your family." In *Rock* the Colorado minister lists candidates having an "objectionable moral impact," and another updated "don't buy" list of twenty followed. Objectionable artists range from Abba to the Who, and include Boston, Elton John, and the Beach Boys; however, most fall into the heavy metal genre. It's now speculation whether former Interior Secretary James Watt was aware of Larson's black list when he banned the Beach Boys from appearing at a Fourth of July concert in the nation's capital. (Watt admits to knowing very little about rock music, as the Beach Boys furor demonstrated. He is a "born-again" Christian from Colorado, as is Larson. A few conspiracy-minded journalists indicated there might be a connection.)

The "profamily" plank in the Christian Right's platform provided a theological umbrella with which to attack rock performers and the music.

### " . . . Working like the Devil for the Lord"

The New Christian Right's agenda in the 1970s and 1980s was the restoration of the traditional family. The Reverend Jerry Falwell suggested a litany of "stress points" threatening the family, and one was premarital sex. Fundamentalist views regarding premarital sex hardly fit the mores of the counterculture or the "me" generation. The *Playboy* philosophy has not swept the land, but sociological studies agree that attitudes and behavior have changed. Sex in the backseats of cars has escalated considerably since the fumbling and heavy petting of the *"Happy Days"* period. Media, for many, were the culprit. The "music-corrupts-youth" canard resurfaced. (Plato's *Republic* suggests music as a threat to the state; he does *not* specify youth, as is popularly claimed.) As noted, the sexuality in popular musical forms can be traced to preliterate societies. The conspiracy notion appears during xenophobic periods in history. The Communist or "Negro" scares of the 1950s and 1960s are illustrative. A decade later the "multibillion"-dollar record industry was the dispenser of rock and roll induced immorality, or premarital sex.

The director of the American Association of Sex Educators and Counselors (AASEC) planted the intellectual seed in 1970. Speaking to a reporter, Dr. Particia Schiller indicated that a survey of 400 pregnant teenagers and 91 nonpregnant university females between the ages of 12 and 21 showed that the beat and lyrics of rock songs excited the listeners; they then engaged in foreplay and occasionally intercourse. (Paradoxically, the AASEC has been in a state of declared war with fundamentalists over "sex education" courses and content. See "Moral Majority in Court Over Sex Education Film," *ST*, 23 February 1981, p. 12.) Younger girls were especially vulnerable: "The music can be disturbing to 12-and-13-year olds who are just beginning to be aroused and have trouble expressing their feelings," she said. "Most of the singers are men and while the girl is sitting with her boyfriend, the record seems to be saying the things he wants from her but is too shy to request." The sex educator pointed to the Rolling Stones' "Let's Spend the Night Together," along with "I Can't Get No Satisfaction" as prime examples, and also mentioned the songs of Tom Jones and soul singer James Brown. Schiller opposed direct censorship but cautioned radio stations to be more "discriminate." Parents, she added, should "listen, and don't buy something that will explode in the child's face."[31] Her comments were nationally distributed by the *Chicago Daily News* service.

Five years later the rock-music fornication theme again made the news wires and attracted the attention of a nationally known syndicated columnist. The Reverend Charles Boykin, associate pastor and youth director working at the Lakewood Baptist Church in Tallahassee, claimed, "Of 1,000 girls who became pregnant out of wedlock, 984 committed fornication while rock music was being played." He could not remember where these unique statistics originated, but told the *Chicago Daily News*, "This man. He's from West Virginia. Or maybe Virginia. He stopped in our church one day and gave us the statistics . . . . He's an evangelist. He travels all the time." Boykin told another journalist the findings were from a sample of North Florida teenagers. Skeptical journalists pressed the minister. He cited the "syncopated-beat" content on from the big band era. "The low bass tones of the bass drum and the bass guitar make people respond sexually . . . the debauchery began when Benny Goodman introduced swing music. You can trace it, all the way back to the jungle, where the beat was introduced. It is primitive, pulsating, hypnotic." Boykin did object to the Associated Press item: "They didn't all listen to it during the sex act. I was speaking of listening to it as a prelude to fornication, as well as during." Mike Royko mused in his column, "I considered getting a portable radio and blasting rock music at the first 1,000 women I met."[32]

The "syncopated beat" explanation did cause one fundamentalist minister to caution, "Some evangelicals have a real hang-up regarding drums." Larson, an accredited foe of rock, echoed John Wesley's pragmatism that the syncopated beat could "demonstrate the attributes of God."[33]

The evangelicals found unique allies in civil rights spokesman and a future aspirant to the 1984 Democratic presidential nomination, the Reverend Jesse L. Jackson. The Baptist minister cited another "study" indicating that 90 of 100 unwed teenage mothers were impregnated while listening to rock music—but, unfortunately, the study was unavailale. Jackson blamed the media: "People actually believe that because they're making money they have a right to pollute the pond. . . . This has gone too far and we must do something about it." "Mind-polluting" songs like "It's All Right to Make Love on the First Night" and "Shake Your Booty," a disco tune, were subjects of a proposed boycott. Record labels, merchandisers, and especially broadcasters were to be the prime targets.

Radio executives, as in the drug-song stir, pointed to artists and labels. Jerry Boulding of WVON (Chicago) declared, "In order for this boycott to be successful it must start with the record companies." Companies looked toward the artists: "The pop acts who are recording this music now have gotten it from the black artists, maybe not even consciously, but it's an evolutionary process." Retailers joined the "Who,me?" chorus. "There has been an upsurge in records with suggestive lyrics because radio stations are now playing them." Obviously Jackson's threats were taken seriously, as opposed to those of "record burners" like Boykin. Few questioned Jackson's statistical data or the source. Warner Bros. Vice-president Tom Draper raised the censorship issue, but most "bizzers" were strangely silent on the issue. The black demographic constituted 10 percent of unit sales and could not be totally dismissed. The evangelicals had not posed a significant organized threat in early 1977; their vocal and visible burnings of purchased records had had no impact on the industry.[34] Previous boycott attempts had failed. Some veteran executives relished right-wing attacks as stimulating rather than harming sales. The "forbidden-fruit" argument prevailed in *Christianity Today* and in the executive offices in New York and Hollywood. Nashville enjoyed the best of all possible worlds, producing gospel groups and "skin" songs perhaps *more* suggestive than those in the rock-music bins.

The adolescent pregnancy issue faded, Jackson's boycott did not materialize despite 1977 hit titles, such as "Nobody Does It Better," "Do You Wanna Make Love," "Give a Little Bit," or "Hotel California," described by Larson as "diabolical." (Privately, some people indicated that Jackson was engaging in "guerrilla theater." A reporter later said, "Jesse has the attention span of a hummingbird.")

That rock and roll causes unwed teenage mothers was an exercise in preaching to the converted. Only Schiller's dated findings were open to social scientific methods of replication. Had they been published, the Boykin and Jackson "samples" could be dismissed.

During the first Reagan term, the Public Health Service (PHS) offered research grants to study rock music as a "suggested cause of the increase in adolescent pre-marital sexual relations."[35] The grant recipient was to use PHS survey data; the data did *not* contain one item or question dealing with rock music. The proposed research was mission impossible. Several academics commented, "It was a political bone for the fundamentalist Right. They're the only ones who believe that hypothesis." When Jackson was campaigning for the Democratic presidential nomination, he did not mention the rock issue.

Record burnings evoke images from *Fahrenheit 451* or the Nuremberg rallies of the Third Reich. Even some vociferous "born-again" critics of rock music disavow such events. "It's a bad tactic," said a midwest pastor.[36] Record burning is older than rock music, even though records do not actually burn. The rise of rhythm and blues, and rockabilly in the 1950s motivated White Citizens Councils in the Old Confederacy to use fire when boycotts failed. A number of Fab Four pressings were burned in the wake of Lennon's "more popular than Christ" misquotation. The practice appears to have subsided during the early 1970s. The wire services were silent on the subject until 1975.

Boykin heaped over $2,200 worth of vinyl and cardboard onto a blazing fire, his defense being, "Teenagers in the church felt they couldn't give the records away. As one of them put it 'That would be like giving dope away.'"[37] A ninety-minute sermon convinced teenage members of the congregation to surrender their rock records to the flames.

David DeVoss, writing in *Human Behavior*, a popularized social science magazine, opined that the "protest did little good, since one does not have to buy an album to hear sex music. . . . Radio has become an electronic orgasmatron crammed with climactic groans, love grunts and bleats of ecstasy."[38] (Other groans echoed from students of popular music lyrics in the behavioral disciplines.) Most of DeVoss's illustrative titles were confined to esoteric urban discos, yet undiscovered by mavens of *Saturday Night Fever*, or inner-city specialty markets. Top 40 and AOR stations ignored the songs in question because they were outside their rigid formats. Jackson's proposed media boycott had generated more heat than light, and after the splash headlines the drive vanished.

Lester Roloff, a Texas preacher jailed three times on child-abuse charges, told a Proctorville, Ohio, church audience, "Rock 'n' roll is the filth that has poisoned the minds of this generation. If you knew what that music has done to your children's minds, you'd bust every one of their records over their heads."[39] Roloff was one of many fundamentalist churchmen attacking rock in the latter part of the 1970s; however, no central foci had yet emerged.

### "You Gotta Serve Somebody"

Social scientists repeatedly have analyzed theological and political ultra-conservatism as a negative reaction to modernity or rapid societal change. A similar explanation was utilized in explaining belief in the Prince of Darkness. Historian Josef Barton reasoned, "In times of great social unrest and political instability the individual's feelings of impotence tend to elicit a sense of overwhelming evil at work." The devil, he told *Newsweek*," is an ancient way to symbolize the existence of such evil." Another religious historian, Professor Peter Williams, observed, "Belief in Satanic forces is a way of focusing anxiety about a diffuse threat. It's something you can get hold of that explains everything."[40]

Interest in Satan and the occult skyrocketed in the 1970s. Best-selling novels, *The Exorcist*, and films such as *Rosemary's Baby* and *The Omen* vividly described the assault of demonic spirits against helpless humans. Hal Lindsey's apocalyptic *The Late Great Planet Earth* provided a Dooms-day scenario with Satan playing a central, villainous role. The evangelicals professing their "literal" interpretation of scripture readily accepted Lu-cifer as the catalyst of the valuative changes affecting their traditional worldviews. Events could, therefore, be battles in a much larger war be-tween the historically combative forces of good and evil. Atheistic commu-nism, the Supreme Court, X-rated films, and rock music were simply weapons of the devil. Conspiracy theories fit most "isms" experiencing a real or imagined threat.

Rock *qua* satanism fit with the fundamentalists' definition of the social situation. The country was "going to hell in a hand-basket." Satan was carrying the proverbial container. A holy war against the machinations of evil justified some drastic actions.

A Topeka, Kansas, minister justified rock bonfires by quoting the Old Testament. Reading from Deuteronomy 7:25, "Graven images of their gods shall ye burn with fire," he approved the controversial practice. "All occult phenomena come from Satan, who is the enemy of God. Therefore, anyone who avows or advocates participation in such demonic practices has declared himself in opposition to the Lord," the Reverend Bob Larson advised parents, adding, "A good bonfire may be in order."[41]

The demonic description of rock appealed to pockets of evangelicals prior to cable television. Larson appears to have been one of the first actually to link rock to an earthly manifestation of satanism. The evan-gelist accused Led Zeppelin lead guitarist Jimmy Page of being a follower of "the late infamous British spiritualist Aleister Crowley, a man so evil (noted for murders and sexual perversion), he literally renamed himself 'The Beast of 666'" [Revelation].[42] The *Encyclopedia Britannica* lists Crowley as a prominent "modern satanist." Others have labeled the British eccentric "the most evil man ever to have lived." Establishing a connection between the deceased occult ritualist and the most popular heavy metal group of the 1970s was a coup. Larson originally had little inkling of the future significance of this find. The entire "backward-masking" conspiracy would later be traced to Crowley. Larson's discovery was largely overlooked by antirock zealots, who chose to equate rock with the devil's music as a matter of faith, assisted by a few unsubstantiated testimonials. Little Richard witnessed: "I had forgotten all about God. Going from town to town, country to country, not knowing that I was directed and commanded by another power. The power of darkness. The power that you've heard so much about. . . . The power of the Devil."[43]

Two young North St. Paul ministers perfected the lecture "What the Devil's Wrong with Rock Music." Steve and Jim Peters ended some seminars with "a real kegger," a burning. Jim Peters told *Rolling Stone* that rock music is "one of the largest satanic forces in the country. . . . There were a lot of subliminal things going on in rock 'n' roll . . . it becomes obvious that it's not from the Lord." In a year of crusading the ordained brotherteam had encouraged the destruction of records, tapes, and magazines worth an estimated $500,000. Their first antirock rally attracted some 150 teenagers who "keggered" $15,000 worth of recorded sound, $100 in spending money per adolescent.

Jim Peters had a shopping list of offending artists. Kiss was a acronym signifying Kids in Service to Satan. "Hotel California" described the church of Satan, one of Larson's favorite lyrical analyses. The Peterses believed their antirock blazes focused media attention: "We realize that the media is an excellent way to witness to thousands of people you could never meet otherwise."[44] *The Minneapolis/St. Paul Magazine, Rolling Stone,* and electronic media provided the duo considerable local and national attention. Public conflagrations were scheduled for "slow" news days, with pyrotechnic displays suited for the nightly television newscast that precedes adolescent prime-time rock video on "Saturday Night Live."

Antirock demonstrations gathered momentum on the revivalist tent circuit. Alton Garrison held a number of rallies, preaching, "The body is a temple and the Devil must be tossed out. . . . Praise the Lord. . . . We're tired of being receptacles of the devil's trash." In a suburb of Dallas, Garrison was denied a fire permit for the customary bonfire. City officials pointed to the air pollution caused by toxic hydrocarbons generated by burning vinyl. Instead, the promoter, the operator of a gospel music radio station, hauled the heaps of records to his parking lot to "smash them."

The rock eradication program, while grabbing the "man-bites-dog" sections of local newspapers, was generating heightened criticism. "Some mothers complain to me about the burnings. They think they're too severe. Some say it reminds them of the burnings in Nazi Germany. I shouldn't say this, but when we were in high school, we thought Mr. Hitler had some pretty good ideas," said one of the Peters brothers. A participant at the Garrison rally concurred with the "devil's-trash" thesis but objected to the destruction: "It's easy to attack albums."[45] Six months after Garrison's highly publicized event, the Perry Mason surprise introduced a new term into the theological vocabulary: *backward masking.*

Fundamentalists appreciated the power of satellite-fed cable systems (MSO) before much of the secular world. Desiring to escape the low-rated Sunday-morning network ghettos the Christian Broadcasting Network (CBN) Trinity Broadcasting (TBN), and American Christian Television

System (ACTS) came on line. Cable would preach the word. "The communications media are fashioning the mind-set of the country," observed Bill Nichols of ACTS. "We as Baptists, have a serious responsibility to use these tools to reveal truth and help shape, positively, the value system and philosophy of life of our nation's people."[46] The power of cable could be used to transmit the Southern Baptist and Pentecostal (TBN) theologies to a national audience.

The impact of the religious cable systems transcended the limitations of revival-circuit pamphleteering and religious bookstores. The hidden satanic message controversy was a product of the neophyte religious networks. The so-called backmasking issue surfaced on 14 January 1982 on the evangelical "Praise the Lord" (PTL) show hosted by Paul Crouch in a statement by William H. Yarroll of Applied Potentials Institute in Aurora, Colorado. The self-styled "neuroscientist" claimed that rock stars were in league with Anton LeVey's Church of Satan and were placing hidden messages on records in reverse so the subconscious mind could grasp the "secret" or subliminal communications.

A 20-year-old housewife from Lancaster, California, Monika Wilfrey, saw the PTL segment. She rotated rock records backwards with the index finger and heard the demonic utterances. "We threw away a lot of records and tapes and such. It was really frustrating," she told Associated Press. "Some of them were new." Wilfrey reportedly contacted conservative California assemblyman Phil Wyman. Wyman, facing an uphill reelection campaign, jumped on the issue.

Assembly Bill 3741 was introduced in the California legislature as "a consumer protection statute warning of subliminal messages." In a widely publicized press conference, Wyman, holding up copies of ELO's *Face the Music* and Led Zeppelin's untitled album (*IV*), contended rock records "can manipulate our behavior without our knowledge or consent and turn us into disciples of the anti-Christ." A meeting of the Consumer Protection and Toxic Materials Committee heard Yarroll's testimony, and a tape of "Stairway to Heaven" in reverse. Some members of the committee were noncommittal or skeptical;[47] audiologists and psychologists were openly critical. Marcel Kinsbourne, who is affiliated with Harvard University, called the Yarroll thesis "fantasy" and said there was nothing to support the subliminal reception of "hidden messages."[48]

Assemblymen Wyman appeared on the Trinity Broadcasting Network (TBN) "Behind the Scenes" program to promote his antibackmasking bill. One highly interested viewer was the Reverend Rusty Mayfield of Topeka, Kansas. He would soon be making national news with a traditional burn-and-smash rally. Congressman Robert K. Dornan (R-California) issued a statement: "It is especially important that parents and their teenage consumers be alerted that several major selling rock albums contain messages glorifying Satan." The technique for transmitting the messages was "backward-masking." Backmasking (a misnomer) was a recording technique by which "a message can be heard audibly by playing the record in reverse, but the same message is *also* subconsciously registered when the record is played forward. How widespread this practice is, I don't know. But I do know that it is dangerous, deceptive, and consumers should be warned."

Dornan's office offered Styx's Paradise Theatre and "Stairway to Heaven" as prime examples of the practice Dornan deplored. James Young of Styx denied the anticocaine song "Snow Blind" contained the backmasked phrase "Oh Satan, move through our voices." Led Zeppelin's Jimmy Page merely observed, "To me, I thought 'Stairway' crystalized the essence of the band it had everything there and showed the band at its best."[49] "Stairway to Heaven," the most popular rock album cut on FM radio, proved a bullseye. A few conjured visions of a piper calling listeners to "join him"; "sometimes words have two meanings." The closing verse of the ballad was electronically accelerated so as to render the lyric unintelligible. Dornan's office claimed passages such as "Here's to my sweet Satan," "I live for Satan," and "He will give you 666" were subliminally transposed. On 12 May 1982, Dornan introduced in the House of Representatives H.R. 6363, a bill requiring labels on album jackets warning that satanic messages can be dangerous. The conservative California representative was quickly making the rounds of the talk shows, including "Today."

Backward masking or backmasking is not a new phenomenon devised by satanic rock musicians. Audiologists and engineers had been using the technique in perception tests for some time. Audiologist Michael Walker has studied audio transpositions for several years. He rejects the term *masking*; rather, he and Professor Raymond Daniloff assert the phenomenon is a slurring frontward of song lyrics such that when played back they imply "a meaningful message."

The line "There's still time to change" from "Stairway to Heaven" when transposed under proper conditions sounds like "Here's to my sweet Satan." Walker and Daniloff suggest that vocalist "Plant does 'slur' the words of the song to enhance the intelligibility of the backward version. With Plant's style of delivery this is not obvious since he slurs lyrics routinely." This is specific to Led Zeppelin IV. The "live" version of "Stairway" on *The Song Remains the Same* lacks a backward message. The audiologists conclude that "many attempts were made in the studio before singer Robert Plant produced the appropriate utterances which when played backward become audible messages."[50] The researchers in an experiment found that "it is unlikely that anyone could correctly identify normally spoken multi-syllabic words played backward, let alone entire sentences."

During the "Paul McCartney is Dead" hoax of 1969, "turn me on, dead man" was apparently found backmasked on "Revolution #9" by a studio engineer along with "number nine" being repeated approximately fifty times. *Rolling Stone* reported the phrase as audible "when played *backwards.*"[51] Once the rumor was dispelled, backmasking ostensibly returned to the world of audio engineers.

The original source for "crowlenization," as Walker calls hidden messages, stems from the "born-again" media. Yarroll is the most likely candidate for deciphering "Stairway" in reverse. Larson, the fundamentalist antirock theoretician, implanted the Aleister Crowley connection to Led Zeppelin. The molder of the conspiracy deserves the "Stephen King Fiction Award" for witchcraft demonology. A scenario of an obscure, deceased English occult ritualist converting some of the kingdom's leading rock superstars as apostles for some his bizarre theories and practices using some of the most hi-tech electronic weapons available is impressive. The backmasking theory may be as transitory as rumors of McCartney's death. Crowlenizing is a reality, but not in the Phil Wyman, Bob Dornan, or PTL sense. Indeed, Larson in a cryptic press release disavowed the "backmasking" thesis: "It is my personal opinion that such sounds (deliberate or unintentional) are not linguistically definable, therefore, they cannot necessarily be labeled as being satanic in origin."

### 666 fo tsaeB ehT

Dualism came early in Aleister Crowley's developmental years. Born in 1875 to rigid parents belonging to the fanatic fundamentalist sect, the Plymouth Brethren, he fantasized being a champion of the Christian faith, a crusader defending the doctrine. At the age of 11, following the death of his father, a severe attitudinal transformation occcurred: Crowley rebeled. The "quackery" surrounding Edward Crowley's cancerous end engendered adolescent thoughts of violence, torture, and gore. "From the moment of the funeral," wrote Crowley, "the boy's life entered on an entirely new phase. The change was radical." His goal was to be a knight of Satan. Repelled, his mother called Crowley "The Great Beast of 666" from the biblical book of Revelation (13:6): "And he opened his mouth for blasphemies against God."

Emily Crowley became a "brainless bigot" in the boy's eyes. A passionate hatred of Christianity dominated his adolescence. His £ 40,000 inheritance allowed him to act upon the obsession. Biographer John Symonds noted, "What, however, is peculiar in Crowley's case is not that he chose 'evil' but that in his revolt against his parents and God, he set himself up in God's place." The mind-set led to his interest in magic and the occult.[52] It is difficult to ascertain whether Crowley even at this young age was a satanist or merely perceived the Anti-Christ as an allied force. (This is an important distinction as the rock *qua* Satanism backward-masking conspiracy rests on Crowley's perception of the devil.)

Entering Cambridge's Trinity College, Crowley published a book of verse and began toying with the supernatural. Arthur Waite's *Book of Black Magic and of Parts* had a tremendous effect on him. He joined the Hermetic Order of the Golden Dawn, a magic occult secret society. He exhibited an uncanny knack with magic and rose in the order.

In 1899, while searching for a secluded spot for ritual ceremonies, the magician located Boleskine House near Foyers in Scotland. The site had a magnificent view of Loch Ness, and a steep hill rose behind the property, which allowed Crowley to indulge his love of rock climbing.

*The Book of Law* that he believed to have been dictated by Aiwass, the guardian angel or messenger, contained the infamous slogan: "There is no law beyond do what thou wilt." The sentence justified Crowley's view of unrestricted social behavior. The sorcerer had "transcended" nature: "As a God goes I go." To prove his spiritual superiority, he crucified a toad after baptizing it Jesus of Nazareth. He chanted: "Give thou place to me, O Jesus; thine aeon [era] is passed; The Age of Horus is arisen by the Magick of the Master the Great Beast that is Man." The Aeon of Horus, the 2000-year period of force and fire, had dawned in Crowley's 1904 vision. Some credit Crowley's Aeon of Horus as the basis of "The Age of Aquarius" popularized in the rock musical *Hair.* In light of Crowley's awareness of astrology this assertion, like many others, is dubious.

Crowley's mystical trances and visions may have had a chemical rather than a supernatural base. Peter Haining writes: "Unhampered in those years by any social restrictions on the taking of drugs, he made liberal use of heroin and cocaine." In 1909 *Equinox,* a magic journal, appeared in London. Crowley was the owner and principal contributor.

In 1912 a ten-year-old secret society, *Ordo Templi Orientis* (OTO), publicly announced its function: "Our Order possessed the KEY which opens up all Masonic and Hermetic secrets, namely, the teaching of sexual magic, and this teaching explains, without exception, all the secrets of free masonry and all systems of religion." Crowley had been a member for two years prior to the *Oriflamme* magazine proclamation; he appreciated its sexual interpretations. The purpose of intercourse, according to the OCO, was that at the moment of orgasm partners could envision their bodies merging with God "into one," a notion supporting Crowley's concept of self.

In the early 1920s Crowley was headquartered on the Sicilian island of Cefalu. He called the one-story brick building "The Abbey of Thelema."

The largest room was a "temple" with bizarre symbols of sexual-magical practices. Crowley and his communal followers were deported after a judicial inquiry. After this period he introduced writer Aldous Huxley to peyote in Berlin, the 1929 Art Deco capital of the Weimar Republic.[53]

Returning to England, Crowley resumed writing. *Magick in Theory and Practice* was his seminal work. The "K" was added to signify the occult. In the book Crowley initiated the occult magic rationale for "backward" action.

The 436-page treatise was sprinkled with ritual, metaphysics, and astrological and theological self-indulgent, image-filled references that helped explain his concept of the mystic solidarity of opposites.[54] Crowley synthesized the magic rituals of the Golden Dawn, a secret masonic society; his *Book of Law;* and the sexual teachings of the OTO in *Magick.*[55] The work was an attempt to outline his previous writings for "scientific and practical minds, such as I most designed to influence," but failed in this purpose. Buried in the obscurantism of ceremonial occultist magic was the "backward masking" phenomenon to be used as a consciousness-raising exercise. (Crowley *never* used the term *back masking*; it was always *backward*. See *Magick,* p. 417.)

Crowley's usage of *praxis* or dualism was central to the "backward" exercise. To achieve a balance or equilibrium, two opposites *must* exist: "'Truth' is the necessary relationship of any two things; therefore, although it implies duality, it enables us to conceive of two things as being one thing such that it demands to be defined by complementals." Continuing, "If you have anything in the North, you must put something equal and opposite to it in the South." By doing this "a higher harmony" can emerge. For example, "The Cross is both the death of the 'Saviour' and the Phallic symbol of Resurrection" or "All truth is in one sense falsehood" (pp. 60-63). In simpler terms, good cannot exist without evil, as in vice/virtue. This revelation is difficult to understand without repetitious incantation: "Exalting the consciousness . . . is no more extraordinary than *music* of any kind should do." The power of melodic tones is great. Crowley points to the bell and the drum as "the most generally useful." (In medival rite the bell's toll was considered a weapon against demonic spirits.)

Repetition is equally important in the use of verbal symbols: "A word may become *potent* and terrible by virtue of constant repetition." To illustrate: "When a child, was told that he could invoke the devil by repeating the 'Lord's Prayer' backwards. He went into the garden and did so. The Devil appeared, and almost scared him out of his life" (pp. 69, 71).

In the maze of magical imagery, Crowley's credentials as a satanist are not always definitive. His use of Holy Guardian Angel throughout implies he is invoking a disembodied intelligence or the inner self (called Aiwass).

Individual consciousness is divided in a Freudian manner: "The recognition of the Angel as the True Self of his subconscious self, the hidden life of his physical life." To achieve this heightened awareness, Crowley urges that the "Adept" (neophyte and/or student) train to think, write, and walk backward. He insists in the central passage of *Magick,* "Let him constantly watch if convenient, cinematatographic films, and *listen to phonograph records, reversed,* and let him so accustom himself to these that they appear natural and appreciable as a whole" (emphasis added).

Such exercise will in time allow a Freudian flashback into the infantile years of the unprotected "id" or "True Self." The mind, having been allowed "to return for some hundred times to the hour of birth, . . . should be encouraged to endeavor to penetrate beyond that period." Heightened karma requires a grasp of the past. By traveling into the prenatal abyss, the adept equally reaches the world beyond life. (For an elaboration see *Confessions,* p. 675.)

*Magick* was the highpoint of Crowley's occult writings. *The Encyclopedia of Occultism and Parapsychology* described it as "a remarkable work, although full of private jokes and mystifications." Biographer John Symonds wrote: "*Magick* is difficult to understand. It is a city within a city, and the key to the gate of the inner city is not supplied with the book; it can be got only after a study of all Crowley's works, *especially* his unpublished works." A great deal of confusion and misinterpretation has arisen from *Magick.* Crowleyans are still arguing as to the "true" meaning of the volume.

In the 1930s Crowley turned litigious. He sued a small bookshop owner, winning £ 50 for libel. Victorious, the increasingly eccentric wizard filed again. Prominent British sculptress Nina Harmnett was the accused; in *Laughing Torso* she had stated that Crowley practiced black magic. Disclosures at the trial generated considerable notoriety. The magistrate characterized the Crowley as wickedly depraved and loathesome. The *Sunday Express* labeled him "The King of Depravity." He predictably lost the suit, but he enjoyed the publicity. Then creditors descended. The second Mrs. Crowley filed for a divorce. The magician was bankrupt, having squandered his inheritance. He sought, but never found a wealthy "Scarlet Woman," the name for his numerous mistresses. After several publication failures, he withdrew. The last *Equinox* was published in the United States at the close of World War II.

Crowley spent his remaining two years in a rustic boarding house in Hastings. A visitor described the flamboyant ritualist as "shrunken into his clothes and the fleshiness had vanished from his face . . . [he] did look a little wicked, but mostly rather exhausted." His large daily intake of heroin provided some surcease. In the night of 1 December 1947, the 72-year-old ritualist died of myocardial degeneration and severe bronchitis. Even the cremation ceremony at Brighton caused a stir, for a Crowleyan read an ode to Pan, the horned god of pastures who was the model for the medieval image of the devil.

Crowley dabbled in black magic but does not appear to have been a devil worshipper; his lifelong parental rebellion coupled with attention-seeking flamboyance led to this misinterpretation. The repeated invocation of a panorama of esoteric gods from mythology furthered the confusion. Symonds, his literary executor and biographer, insightfully observed, "Christ's enemy was Satan; therefore the Devil is not so bad as he is painted; *together* they will make war upon Christ and with his destruction the real lord of the universe will arise." The legitimate lord would be Crowley.

Appraisals of Crowley ranged from "the archetype of Lucifer, or the Magician" to "sinister or merely absurd." Crowley had achieved his desire of becoming "widely known during his lifetime." He would be remembered, especially in the Age of Aquarius, when his "hippie life style [of] wild fantasy, astral communications and drug revelations" appeared innovative.[56]

Crowley crept unnoticed into the world of rock as a member of the *Sgt. Pepper* crowd-collage cover. George Martin: "They wanted the faces of all the people they had ever admired to be in the photograph . . . with a lot of people they didn't admire at all." The ritualist was included in one of those categories. Karl Marx, Bob Dylan, W. C. Fields, and others. British journalist Philip Norman saw the faces as coming from "the pantheon of Pop Art pseudo-worship."[57] Fearful of lawsuits, EMI originally refused to release the cover, but McCartney purchased an unnecessary insurance policy to protect against potential legal actions. The only apparent reason for the Beatles' inclusion of the Crowley likeness (second from left top row) was the English art world. John Lennon had attended art college in Liverpool with the deceased Stu Sutcliffe, yet this artistic experience hardly constitutes a mystic bond.

The "hidden messsage" on "Revolution #9" has never been properly explained. It is a cacophony of sounds with an incessant engineer's repetition of "Number nine, number nine." One critic characterized it as "a formless length of electronic noise interpersed with vocal gibberish." Lennon recalled: "Just abstract *musique concrete,* kinds of loops and that, people screaming. I thought I was painting in sound a picture of revolution—but I made a mistake, you know."[58] Lennon had composed the lyric during the Rishikesh retreat at the Maharishi's ashram. After repeated listenings any forward message might be plausible. (One aficionado points to George Harrison's collaboration with Eric Clapton on the "white album." Clapton was reportedly Jimmy Page's "roomie" during the Yardbirds' tenure. "Layla," recorded by Clapton is Leila Waddell, a "Scarlet Woman," according to Michael Walker.) George Martin and McCartney attempted to delete "#9" from the "white" album, but Lennon insisted on its inclusion. Most observers credit "#9" with having pioneered rock backwarding. (George Martin used an "amalgam of carousel noises" on "Being for the Benefit of Mr. Kite" in *Sgt. Pepper*.) "Revolution #9" may be the worst Beatle selection put to vinyl but it lacked any satanic overtones. Only Beatle historians and "Paul-is-dead" buffs took any notice of the electronic maze.

Led Zeppelin's "Stairway to Heaven" is the backmasker's *cause célèbre*, heightened by Jimmy Page's interest in Aleister Crowley. Page is vague and secretive about his perceptions of the supernatural. A one-time choir boy, he admits to having studied religion in school, "but I stopped." It is believed Page developed an interest in Crowley while in art school.

Crowleyan theory and practice has a myriad of intellectual stripes. The guitarist appears to have flirted with the ritualist aspects of magic. "I do not worship the devil," he explained, "but magic does intrigue me. Magic of all kinds. Magic is very important if you can go through it . . . I think Crowley's completely relevant to today. We're all still seeking for truth: the search goes on." Led Zeppelin's vocalist Robert Plant concurred; Page was fascinated by Crowley not satanism. "I don't think that Jimmy was particularly interested in the occult, but only in Aleister Crowley, as a great British eccentric. All eccentrics are interesting, but Crowley was a very clever man. Jimmy had an innocent interest in him."[59] Page reportedly called the ritualist "the unrecognized genius of twentieth century." An exercise in Crowley's magic rite was learning "to think backwards. . . . It should then be easy to understand the general object of one's existence."[60] Page apparently accepted this notion.

In 1970 Page purchased Crowley's old Boleskin House near Loch Ness in Scotland to "go up and write in." The property was in total disrepair, and Charles Pace was hired to restore the estate. The house was believed to be haunted by demons. Page said:

> Strange things happened in that house that had nothing to do with Crowley. The bad vibes were already there. There were two or three owners before Crowley moved into it. It was also a church that was burned to the ground with the congregation in it. And that's the site of the house. [Lord Fraser] . . . was beheaded there and sometimes you can hear his head rolling down. . . . So that sort of thing was there before Crowley got there. Of course, after Crowley there have been suicides, people carted off to mental hospitals.

Asked about Boleskin's attraction, Page replied, "The unknown. I'm attracted by the unknown, but I take precautions. I don't go walking into things blind."[61] Stories were told of footsteps in the night and chains being dragged about the house, tales that Page refused to discuss or joke about. Following Crowley's example, Jimmy relaxed by climbing the mountainsides near the famous lake, "No, I haven't seen the monster but its definitely there," he said.

Page amassed a huge collection of Crowley first editions and manuscripts. To house the material, he financed an occult bookshop in London. It was named after Crowley's "A Journal of Scientific Illuminism *Equinox.*" He explained the store as ideal because it enabled occult literature to be located in a single location. Page no longer owns the shop.

Page made the acquaintance of the underground filmmaker Kenneth Anger at a "magick" auction. Anger was known for *Hollywood Babylon*, a muckraking book on the sex lives of movie stars. As a avant-garde director he had produced *Scorpio Rising* and *Fireworks,* both focusing on male sexuality. One student of the occult found his later film, *The Inauguration of the Pleasure Dome,* to be an attempted "expression of Crowley's religio-magical philosophy of Thelema in terms of light, colour and sound."[62] In Crowleyan circles he was admired for uncovering the erotic murals in the "chamber of nightmares" at the Abbey of Thelema; the Italian police had whitewashed the art work following Crowley's expulsion. Anton LeVey of the Church of Satan was an associate; Anger used him and Bobby Beausoleil in *Invocation of My Demon Brother,* a film scored by the Rolling Stones' Mick Jagger.

Anger asked Page to write a sound track for an occult movie to be shot in Egypt. *Lucifer Rising* featured Beausoleil in the title role.(Beausoleil came to notoriety for his participation in the homicidal escapades of the "Manson Family"; he was subsequently convicted of first-degree murder.) An actor and musician, he played lead guitar and sitar for the Magick Powerhouse of Oz, a San Francisco rock band. Anger had planned to use the eleven-piece unit in the film until he encountered superstar Page.

During a 1975 layoff for Plant to recover from a holiday accident, Page supposedly completed a dirge-ridden shadowy instrumental at Boleskin. He compared the composition to Michael Oldfield's "Tubular Bells" sound track to *The Exorcist.* "I wanted to create a timelessness, so by using a synthesizer I tried to change the actual sound of every instrument, so you couldn't say immediately 'that's a drum or a guitar." Key to it all is to come up with something timeless."[63]

Producer Anger was not happy with Page's "timelessness"; he had expected sixty minutes of music and had not gotten it. Beausoleil reentered the project from a prison cell. "One thing Bobby does have is time to devote to it," noted Anger. The fate of the film and the soundtrack remain a mystery.[64]

*Led Zeppelin III*'s original pressing had Crowley's motto, "Do What Thou Wilt," inscribed into the inner part of the master. "Untitled" released in November of 1971 contained "Stairway to Heaven." The closing verse included, "And if you listen very hard/ the tune will come to you at last." Backwarding the seemingly religious "Bolero"-like revealed a host of messages. Audiologist Michael Walker remarked, "You produce a song that forward is a spiritual song, and then on the backside you make something that's just the opposite." Magick is theory and practice?

About that time Graham Bond, who believed himself the illegitimate son of Aleister Crowley, committed suicide by leaping into the path of an oncoming train. The British organ player of blues had once led a band by the name of Magick.

Selected portions of these events would eventually enter into the pop and evangelical press. Led Zeppelin's publicity people tiptoed around this issue, and Page's responses about "magic" were increasingly coy.

This eclectic account does not answer the satanism question. The messages are clearly there as well as the theoretical duality. "Christianity, suggests Robert Hunter, "insists upon the theology of God and the Devil, absolute Good and absolute Evil, Heaven and Hell, the Spirit and the Flesh."[65] In the minds of most observers there was little doubt about which side of the duality Page was on. In the wake of John Bonham's tragic death Led Zeppelin disbanded in 1980. The total riddle surrounding "Stairway" has not been resolved. Was the song an exercise in crowlenization or a subliminal satanic plot? Page and Plant provide conflicting stories. Page prior to scoring "Stairway": "We want to try something new with the organ and acoustic guitar building up and building up, and then the electric parts. I'm really looking forward to doing it. . . . I can't really say any more in case it doesn't work out." Plant afterward: "Page had written the chords and played them for me. I was holding a paper and pencil and for some reason, I was in a very bad mood. Then all of a sudden my hand was writing out words: 'There's a lady . . .' I just sat there and looked at the words and then I almost leaped out of my seat. Looking back I suppose I just sat down at the right moment." Page on the same session, "I'd written the music over a long period, the first part coming at Bron-Y-Aur one night. The other parts came together piece by piece . . . [Plant] had 40 percent of the lyrics together almost immediately. Then we all threw in ideas . . . and the song and the arrangement just came together."[66] Technically, the composition could not have been quite this spontaneous.

Crowlenization as a technique is quite purposeful. "They made many many takes of 'Stairway,' before they came up with a finished product," says Walker. The method is complicated and prearranged. The reverse material must be done originally, and then be phonetically transposed so the reverse and forward recording are intelligible as sentences. The word "Satan," he states, "is easy as 'um-um there's' is the audible palindrome." "Revolution #9" was a much easier task due to the garbled nature of the entire album cut.

Upon cursory examination the Crowley-Page connection has merit. The inclusion of Anger makes the circumstantial mystery even more intriguing. However, the historical web is too vague to support the New Christian Right's satanism conspiracy theory.

Two members of Led Zeppelin, including Page, deny involvement in black magic or devil worship. Page's fascination with Crowley is undeniable, but which aspects? The writings of "The Beast" are obscurantist to the point of incomprehensibility. Backwarding was a Crowleyan exercise the purpose of which involves a higher ritualistic consciousness. This does not *ex post factum* imply satanism, unless the dualism notion is introduced. Hell is the antithesis of Heaven. Even accepting this Crowleyan view, one arrives at a Scotch verdict: the satanic plot is not proved.

Led Zeppelin spawned imitative heavy metal bands trading on the black magic motif. Black Sabbath's *Heaven and Hell,* according to Ozzy Osbourne, "is about this guy name Aleister Crowley." Ozzy included "Mr. Crowley" on his *Blizzard of Oz* album.

Following in Wyman's footsteps, Congressman Dornan provided the media with a list of alleged "backmasked" songs:

Group:    Pink Floyd
Album:    "The Wall"
Song:     "Good Bye Blue Sky"

Going backward in the song you hear, "Congratulations you have just discovered the secret message. Please send your answer to Old Pink in care of," then the rest is too fuzzy to understand. An album goes gold when you sell a million and goes platinum when you sell 2 million, they have sold 38 million copies.

Group:    E.L.O.
Album:    "Face the Music"
Song:     "Fire on High"

Going forward at the beginning of the song, you cannot understand, but when you turn it backward, it says, "the music is reversible, but time . . . turn back, turn back, turn back."

ELO plays hop scotch with these records. One of their songs when played backward, talks of the mighty water fall, then the next album that came out, had a song on it called, "The Water Fall."

Song:     "Elderooo"

Going backward it says, "He is the nasty one, Christ your offernal. Oh where are dead men, everyone who has the mark, live."

Group: Styx
Album: "Paradise Theatre"
Song: "Snow Blind"

These words going backward, say "Satan move through our voices."

Group: Black Oak Arkansas
Album: "Rauch and Roll"
Song: "When Electricity Came to Arkansas"

Going backward, these words say, "Satan, Satan, Satan, Satan, Satan. He is got God. He is God." In a live concert the lead singer started yelling "Natas, Natas, Natas." Backward this says Satan. But this is the first time anything going backward makes sense as far as the spelling is concerned.

Group: Led Zeppelin
Album: Led Zeppelin IV (Untitled)
Song: "Stairway to Heaven"

On this one song there are many messages:

"I live for Satan"
"The Lord turn me off"
"There is no escaping it"
"Here's to my sweet Satan"
"There's power in Satan"
"He will give you 666"

Isn't it strange that here are so many messages? This is a relatively quiet rock song. What is their purpose?

Group: Blue Oyster Cult
Song: "We're Kissin in Dallas"

These words going backward say, "My name is Satan"

Group: The Cars
Album: "Candy-O"
Song: "Shoo-Be-Doo"

These words say "Satan," repeated approximately 11 times.
[Press Release: 4 June 1982.]

Several state legislatures took these allegations quite seriously. Bills appeared in the California, Colorado, and Arkansas statehouses requiring a warning label on backmasked recordings. In February 1983 the Arkansas Senate approved such a bill 86-0; it was vetoed by the governor. "Thrown out after it became known to the press," reported Michael Walker. "They got on him, saying 'This is crazy.'" Crazy or not, the campaign continued.

National and state legislative measures intensified the local antirock bonfires. The Reverend Rusty Mayfield of Topeka's Evangelic Gospel Church organized a three-day exorcism, "Hammer and Fist." On the last night 150 young people gathered and destroyed 3,000 records. "The music that's coming out now," he repeated, "has basically a Santanic element." Mayfield pointed to "PTL" show to support his contention.

Some of the rally-goers related tales from the pages of the *Exorcist*. Lori Rice told NBC: "I was always listening to rock music, and I began to hear voices in the night. I had one summer I just couldn't go to sleep because of the voices were talking to me. . . . Voices that were telling me I wouldn't live very long. I believe that it came from Satan that was using records to get to the young people." In panic, she dumped the albums into a sack. "I looked over at the sack," she recalled, "I began to see all these green things, I'd never seen anything like that."

The decade-old "Stairway" was number one on the record incendiary chart. The Reverend Luis Gallo attracted 300 youths to a record-burning ceremony in Miami. The pastor of the Baptist Gethsemane Church began the purification rite by replaying "I Live with Satan" reversed from Led Zeppelin's acclaimed classic. A frenzy ensued as the throng clapped and cheered while records were smashed and melted in steel drums.

"Rock musicians are being used," exclaimed a Maryland evangelical, "by Satan to spread his evil world." To demonstrate he played a tape of "Stairway." Crowlenization was stimulating Led Zeppelin sales. As had been the case with Woody Guthrie and the Beatles, the fundamentalist Right jumped to some provocative but unsubstantiated conclusions.

The McCarthyites and Noebel had ideologically misrepresented the Communist party's use of folk music in the 1930s and 1940s. Their wild accusations, which occasionally had a factual basis, were so broad as to lack any semblance of credibility. The New Christian Right's assertions, again, were unconvincing except to other believers in their strain of ultra-conservative theology. A fairly persuasive case based on circumstantial evidence could have been presented *if* the proponents had done their homework. Theoretician Larson's *Rock* is illustrative of just a few historical inaccuracies.

In their treatment of satanism some antirock partisans, especially ministers, took some liberties with the names, places, and events. Larson, the most knowledgeable of the group, indicated Led Zeppelin's drummer John Bonham died in Aleister Crowley's Boleskin House: "The residence is said to be haunted by a death curse." In truth, Bonham died from an adverse reaction to 40 measures of vodka at Page's "new" residence, the Old Mill House on Mill Lane in Windsor, miles away from Boleskin House. Larson also writes, "Bonham known to associates as 'the Beast'"; the drummer's nickname was "Bonzo," as Larson states a page earlier in *Rock*.[67] (Bonzo, of course, was the costar of several Ronald Reagan films.) "Most observers, Larson claimed, "attributed the band's break-up to Page's satanic obsession." Others pointed to a series of deaths and mishaps around the heavy metal stars. "No, that is bullshit," retorted Plant. "You can be anything, or do anything, and you don't have to affect your friends by what you do."[68]

Simply tying Page via the Boleskin House to Crowley does not explain backmasking. Crowley was a complete mystery to the American public. "The wickedest man who ever lived" was Hitler, not some obscure Englishman. "Noted for murders," as Larson charged of Crowley, was more applicable to Jack the Ripper. Crowley was accused of many outrages, but never homicide. A more telling point was raised by curious Led Zeppelin mavens: "How do you play the record backwards?" This technological question did more harm than any objective analysis of the revelations of "The Beast" and Page's understandings of them.

Bryant Gumbel on "Today" closed a discussion of backmasking, cynically with: "It is subject to interpretation."

David Sachlebein's three-hour presentation, "Rock 'n' Roll: Soul Control," left University of Maryland undergraduates skeptical. "It's the most ridiculous thing I've ever heard," said one freshman. Another felt the backmasking segment was biased: "He put the idea into everybody's heads that there was something there." A Sachlebein supporter guardedly said, "Even without the backwards stuff, there's enough poison in the regular frontwards lyrics to kill you." Talking to a *Sun* reporter, the evangelist asserted, "Whether you believe in backmasking or not, it's clear that rock's message is not the message of Jesus Christ."[69] A majority of rock musicians and industry people would agree with the last half of the statement.

Popular music was entertainment, not theology. Allegations of satanic messages sold more records than born-again musicians. "Bizzers" agreed that Dylan's "serve somebody" salvation albums and tour were economic disappointments. The Reverend Maris Brady's observation that young people will buy records "to find out what the hidden message was" had merit, and was a conclusion shared by a number of artists and record-company publicity poeple.

British music critic Gary Herman stated, "Black magic, satanism and the occult are merely fertile sources of shock imagery for bands devoid of any superior resources with which to get themselves noticed."[70]

Ozzy Osbourne, then with Black Sabbath, acknowledged that the widely reported santanism of the band was hype rather than conviction. More recently, Osbourne mused, "I just like to have fun." He is having fun. A *Circus* interview was illustrative. Discussing Crowley, Osbourne said, "That man was the phenomenon of his time." He was unfamiliar with any of Crowley's voluminous writings. "I don't have to be, I can feel it," Osbourne answered.

    *Circus*: Crowley is said to have sold his soul to the devil."

Ozzy: Yes I feel like I've met him. I feel that I was a servant of his once.[71]

Osbourne's answer has at least two meanings. *Newsweek*: "Ozzy Osbourne liked to bite off the heads of birds." His wife: "Ozzy's isn't into Satanism or the killing of animals." Fans fully expect an animal sacrifice at an "Oz" concert, and local humane societies send observers, who leave content. "It's almost like a comic book with music," in the view of a label executive.[72]

Satanism by the mid-1980s became an overt marketing ploy. Iron Maiden released *The Number of the Beast*. *Metal Blade* by Slayer numbered it's record sides "6" and "66." Dio's *The Last in Line* features a goat's head and other demonic symbols. The album evoked the anticipated reaction from KMLB (Monroe, Louisiana). Charles Malley, the station manager complained, *Billboard*: The ad for the new Dio album was sickening. . . . The demonic figure towering above the masses with both hands brandishing the symbol of Satanic worship was one of the most graphic examples we have seen."[73]

Satanism was rapidly becoming the shock-rock of the decade, thumbing its product at the New Christian Right. On *Piece of Mind*, Iron Maiden backmasked a message between two cuts. Said lead singer Bruce Dickinson; "It's one for the Moral Majority."[74] Styx, on the Dornan backmasking list, placed a sticker on *Kilroy Was Here*: "By order of the Majority for Musical Morality, this album contains secret backward messages." The inside liner notes spoke of a mythical Dr. Righteous, who through his cable television network was able to ban rock and roll. The song "Heavy Metal Poisoning" opened with "What the devil's goin on." On the cut Styx backmasked "*annuit coeptis novus ordo seclorum*," the inscription from the U.S. dollar bill.[75] ELO released *Secret Messages*. As usual record executives ducked the issue, citing the "artistic freedom" of artists. John Kalodner of Geffen Records deviated from the pack, saying, "The bands aren't perpetrating evil on society . . . the more parents are offended by it, the more the teenagers want it." Ozzy Osbourne's wife and manager observed, it's a "marketing campaign we invented for him. He doesn't take it seriously." This was directly from Jimmy Page's strategy: "I'm no fool; I know how much the *mystique* matters. Why should I blow it now?" A broadcaster believed, "They're just blowing smoke." The pun out of the way, he continued, suggesting the heavy metal demographic limited its airplay; working-class adolescents were an insignificant speck in the marketing strategies of time buyers.

"Stairway" was a staple on AOR-FM stations. It surpassed "Hey Jude" and "Bridge over Troubled Waters" as a universal play. Led Zeppelin fit the stations' format. More contemporary practitioners of heavy metal appeared on the basis of chart position. Ironically, the more publicity a group received for satanic messages, the higher the airplay possibilities. "If they

were really serious," wondered a deejay, "why invite all of the media attention?" Privately, a West Coast publicist mused, "There's a whole new generation buying Led Zep albums. You can't buy that kind of interest," Officially, Atlantic, distributor of Swan Song, says, "They're not discussing
the matter."

The antirock seminars continued. Guests on the "PTL" blasted the
devil's music. The conspiratorial flavor was abating "It's recognized as a
problem by everyone." Baptist minister Jeff R. Steele told *Billboard*, "But
at the same time, I sincerely believe more damage is being done by the top
40 than by all this stuff put together. . . . [It] does more damage than all the
Ozzy Osbournes and AC/DCs put together.[76]

Antirock ultraconservatives experienced a setback when in 1983 Interior
Secretary James Watt banned rock concerts from U.S. Park Service hold-
ings. In part his memorandum read, "It is imperative that we get entertainment that will point to the glories of America in a patriotic and
inspirational way that will attract the family." On 6 April 1983, Watt applied the profamily directive in the District of Columbia: no rock music
during the Fourth of July celebration on the Mall, "We're not going to
encourage drug abuse and alcoholism as was done in the past years. It's
going to be the military people with their patriotism, and Wayne Newton."
The Beach Boys were unwelcome because they attracted "the wrong element, and you couldn't bring your family, your children, down to the
mall." Watt had again provoked controversy, as was his wont.[77]

The Beach Boys, despite some drug-related problems, were publicly perceived as the epitome of "wholesomeness," (The term is inaccurate, as was
much of the coverage of the entire media event; rock has always been
ambiguously rebellious, ranging from *Blackboard Jungle* to some vidclips
on MTV.) The group was one of the few members of the rock community
who did benefits for Republican candidates. During the 1980 presidential
primaries, they performed a fundraising concert for the aspiring candidate
for the nomination, George Bush. Only Bob Larson had attacked the band
since the 1960s; the Colorado minister charged them with providing a
"launching pad" for "TM and occultic mysticism into the mainstream of
America." Other than in fundamentalist circles this was old news now
forgotten.

The ensuing storm of criticism found Watt claiming ignorance of the
band. "Obviously, I didn't have anything to start with. . . . I've learned
about the Beach Boys in the last twelve hours," he said. Douglas Baldwin,
Watt's press person, tried to put the best face on the situation, saying the
Beach Boys were not mentioned in the guiding memorandum.

Predictably, acerbic Democrats like Congressmen Downey and Miller
rejoiced in Watts folly, but the most telling criticism came from the Reagan
administration itself. "It's an unfortunate action since my wife and kids . . .

went to see them last year and had a wonderful time," said Michael Deaver, White House chief of staff, adding, "Anyone who thinks they are hard rock would think Mantovani, my kids grew up with their music playing jazz." "I like the Beach Boys," stated Mrs. Reagan. Vice-president Bush predictably echoed the sentiment: "They're my friends, and I like their music." The ban was lifted. The interior secretary was handed a plaster foot with a large mock bullet hole through it at the White House. Independence Day found cabaret singer Wayne Newton drawing half the number of people the Beach Boys would have attracted.

Watt's attempt to prohibit rock was farcical. He picked on the wrong band. Inadvertently, he dampened the Right's antirock campaign and enboldened some groups to give albums such titles as *Secret Messages* (ELO) or *Number of the Beast* (Iron Maiden).[78] The war against rock seemingly subsided but there were still skirmishes. "It doesn't make any difference," said the Reverend Mark Muirhead while leading a "Record Smash" in suburban Baltimore. "Pornography through the airwaves" should cease," he demanded as some 1,500 albums were destroyed. This incident received little media coverage.[79]

The fascination with backmasking was fading as the focus shifted to the two M's of 1984: MTV and Michael Jackson. MTV was accused of purveying sexual violence to its viewers (see chapter 7). The administrators of Bound Brook High School in New Jersey objected to the Michael Jackson look, and confiscated white and black sequined gloves and studded belts. They claimed the "look" was dangerous—the dress codes of the 1950s revisited.

Michael Jackson's religious commitment to the Jehovah's Witnesses was unquestioned. He was wholesome and pious, and was compared positively to previous pop idols such as the Beatles by the mass media. Evangelical talk-show guests objected to his influence on adolescents. "Is he a proper role model?" they asked.[80] (This issue was raised by many observers. Sociologist Asa Hilliard rhetorically wondered "why Michael Jackson's role model is Peter Pan; why he cuts his eyebrows and has nose jobs. . . . Is this the role model we want for our children?") Jerry Falwell provided an authoritative answer: "[He] . . . sets a bad role model . . . My ideal is not because Michael may be a sissy, that he has found a formula that sells and makes millions and millions of dollars, you say you can't fault him for that. I think rather you can when so many young poeple see what he is and what he's doing and think that's for me. I think the end is bad." Jackson was a poor villain, especially after being praised by Reagan for his contributions in combating teenage alcohol consumption.

The political Right viewed rock and roll as a Kremlin tactic to subvert U.S. youth. The New Christian Right colored the music as an antifamily satanic conspiracy. In both instances they were preaching to the converted. The FCC was no longer a major participant in the battle between good and evil. Congress avoided major "social issues" and had little patience with subliminal demonic messages. Ironically, the ultraconservatives appeared to grow in numbers, but their ability to censor the nation's music had diminished dramatically since Spiro Agnew's Las Vegas "drug-song" speech. Three decades of battle against Stalinism and Satanism was ending with Falwell's "sissy," only to be revived in 1985 by the "Washington Wives."

The religio-political Right's apparent pullback may be a lull before another fire storm or merely the reaction to a more realistic definition of the situation. "We're not angels," said Bruce Dickinson. "We don't go to church every Sunday. On the other hand, we don't spend time messing around worshipping the devil."[81] Iron Maiden's lead singer summed up the state of the so-called rock culture. The rock of the 1980s had become more entertainment than participation. Star-studded "No Nukes" concerts and "Live-Aid" featured "names" not messages. The Clash, Tom Robinson, and other socially active artists were yesterday's shooting stars. Joan Baez could not land a recording contract. Dylan, the "bard of a generation," dismissed music video, the medium of the 1980s, with "I'll watch it for, you know, as long as my eyes can stay open.[82] The music industry is counting on the "rock culture" to keep its eyes and ears open.

## NOTES

1. Gary B. Rush, "Toward a Definition of the Extreme Right," *Pacific Sociological Review* 6 (Fall 1963): 73.
2. Frank Zappa, "The Oracle Has It All Psyched Out," *Life,* 28 June 1968, p.85.
3. Quoted in "Segregationists Would Ban All Rock, Roll Hits," *Billboard* 7 April 1956, p. 130.
4. Quoted in "Segregationist Wants Ban on 'Rock and Roll,'" *New York Times,* 30 March 1956, p. 39. Also see "Deep South R&R Hassle," *Billboard,* 7 April 1956, pp. 20, 133; "Jim Crow Chief Hits at Rock and Roll," *Melody Maker,* 13 May 1956, p. 7.
5. "Segregationists Would Ban All Rock, Roll Hits," p. 130.
6. Jere Real, "Folk Music and Red Tubthumpers," *American Opinion* 7 (December 1965):24. See R. S. Denisoff, *Great Day Coming: Folk Music and the American Left* (Urbana: University of Illinois Press, 1971), pp. 151- 63.
7. Quoted from "The Children of Bobby Dylan," *Life,* November 1965, p. 44; "Rock 'n' Roll: Message Time," *Time,* 17 September 1965, p. 102.
8. David A. Noebel, *Communism, Hypnotism and the Beatles: An Analysis of the Communist Use of Music* (Tulsa, Okla.: Christian Crusade Publications, 1965), p. 10. For other explanations of Beatlemania, see Evan Davis, "The Psychological Characteristics of Beatle Mania," *Journal of the History of Ideas* 30 (April-June 1969): 273-301.

9. David A. Noebel, *Rhythm, Riots, and Revolution* (Tulsa, Okla.: Christian Crusade Publications, 1966), p. 112.

10. Bob Larson, *Rock and Roll: The Devil's Diversion* (McCook, Nebr.: Bob Larson, 1966), p. 19.

11. David A. Noebel, *The Beatles: A Study in Drugs, Sex and Revolution* (Tulsa, Okla.: Christian Crusade Publications, 1969), p. 21.

12. Gary Allen, "That Music: There's More to It Than Meets the Ear," *American Opinion* 12 (February 1969): 49.

13. Phillip Abbott Luce, "Are the Beatles Termites? The Great Rock Conspiracy," *National Review,* 23 September 1969, pp. 959, 973.

14. "The Anti-Rock and Roll Crusade: An Interview with a Real White Panther," *Creem* 2:9.

15. There has been very little research conducted in this area. In the *Federal Register* of 10 May 1984, the Office of Adolescent Pregnancy was encouraging a study of "suggested causes of the increase in adolescent premarital sexual relations." One causal variable listed was rock music.

16. There is little incentive for an artist or a recording company to release a record that will not receive media play, thereby insuring its failure. Consequently, most so-called controversial songs have emanated either from established stars such as the Rolling Stones, Bob Dylan, and Prince, who can rely on album sales regardless of media. Jimmy Buffett's "Why Don't We Get Drunk (and Screw)" or the Tubes' "Don't Touch Me There" enjoyed a word-of-mouth popularity, as did Bob Bare's "Drunkin' Druggin' and Watchin' TV."

17. Quotations from "The Doors: The Fire's Still Burning," MTV, 1 July 1984.

18. John Burks, "Jackie Gleason Is Really a Great Man," *Rolling Stone,* 17 May 1969, pp. 1, 6.

19. Noebel, *Beatles,* pp. 25-26.

20. Quoted in Dorothy Townsend, "Graham Links Lure of Rock Music to Religious Search," *Los Angeles Times,* 30 December 1970, p. 3.

21. Quoted in "The New Rebel Cry: Jesus Is Coming!" *Time,* 21 June 1971, p. 59.

22. David A. Noebel, "One Christian's View," *Christian Crusade Weekly,* 11 April 1971, p. 1.

23. Billy James Hargis, "U.S. Takes to 'Superstar,'" *Christian Crusade Weekly,* 5 March 1972, p. 1.

24. Quoted in David Batterson, "Lennon as Lenin," *Creem* 4 (November 1972):33.

25. Jerome Rodnitzky, "Book Review: The Beatles," *Popular Music and Society* 1 (Spring 1972): 178.

26. Luce, "Are the Beatles Termites?" p. 959.

27. Quotations from Bruce Buursma, "Conservatism of Last 12 Years in Religion Continuing Historian Martin Marty Says," *Toledo Blade,* 31 January 1981; J. Milton Yinger and Stephen J. Cutler, "The Moral Majority Viewed Sociologically," *Sociological Focus* 15 (October 1982): 293; Martin E. Marty, "Fundamentalism Reborn: Faith and Fanaticism," *Saturday Review,* May 1980, pp. 37-42.

28. "*Penthouse* Interview," March 1981, p. 152.

29. Ron Powers, "The New 'Holy War' Against Sex and Violence," *TV Guide* 18 April 1981, pp. 8, 10. Also James Mann, "Books and TV—New Targets of Religious Right," *U.S. News and World Report,* 8 June 1981 p. 46.

30. Bob Larson, *Rock* (Wheaton, Ill.: Living Books, 1983) p. 125.

31. Quotations in "Rock, Soap Operas Called Sex Turn-Ons" *Los Angeles Times,* 8 March 1970, p. D.15. Bob Larson cites this study at length in *Rock and Roll,* pp. 154- 55.

32. Quotations in "War Declared On Rock Music," *Sentinel Tribune,* 26 November 1975; Mike Royko, "Syncopated Beat Gets Blame," *Chicago Daily News,* 27 November 1975.

33. Larson qualified his statement: "Christian music should be primarily designed to touch the head and the heart. When it only appeals to the hip and the heel the spiritual benefit is diminished." *Rock and Roll,* p. 101. The antirock stance, especially record burnings, is opposed by many mainline Christians. See Richard D. Mountford, "Does the Music Make Them Do It?" *Christianity Today,* 4 May 1979, pp. 20-23; James M. Pennington, "Rock Music—Love Ad Infinitum, Ad Absurdum," *Christianity Today,* 8 July 1977, pp. 20-21.

34. Quotations in "Sex-Rock Assailed By Rights Leader," *Cleveland Plain Dealer,* 16 January 1977, p. A-24; Jean Williams "Sex-Oriented Lyrics, Titles Stir a Storm," *Billboard,* 25 December 1976, pp. 1, 19.

35. *Federal Register,* 10 May 1984.

36. "Today," NBC-TV, 6 July 1982. Mountford, "Does the Music Make Them Do It?" pp. 20-22, reflects views expressed by many ministers. Also, August through November 1981 issues of *Contemporary Christian Music.*

37. "War Declared on Rock Music."

38. "Aural Sex: The Rise of Porn Rock," *Human Behavior,* July 1976, p. 66.

39. "Rock 'n' Roll Poisoned the Minds of This Generation, Preacher Claims," *Sentinal Tribune,* 1 October 1980, p. 1.

40. Quotations in K. L. Woodward and David Gates, "Giving the Devil His Due," *Newsweek,* 30 August 1982, pp. 72-74. Also L. A. Zurcher, Jr., and R. G. Kirkpatrick, *Citizens for Decency: Anti-Pornography Crusades as Status Defense* (Austin: University of Texas Press, 1976).

41. Larson, *Rock,* pp. 45-46.

42. Ibid., p. 41.

43. Charles White, *The Life and Times of Little Richard* (New York: Harmony Books, 1984). Also Vernon Gibbs, "Sex and God and Rock and Roll," *Village Voice* 10 August 1982.

44. Quotations in Tom Zito, "Rock Is Unrighteous?" *Rolling Stone,* 19 February 1981, pp. 9, 12, 16. Also Steven Rabey, "Rock 'n' Roll Bar 'b' Que," *Contemporary Christian Music,* August/September 1981, p. 15.

45. Quotations in Zito, "Rock Is Unrighteous?" p. 16; William H. Inman, "Rally Against 'Demon Rock' Offends Some," *Sentinal Tribune,* 12 October 1981, p. 2; "Album Burners Have No Sympathy for the Devil," *Toledo Blade,* 29 April 1982.

46. Terrance Stanton, "Open ACTS," *Cablevision,* May 1984, p. 22.

47. Quotations in Jennifer Kerr, "Lawmakers Weigh Subliminal Messages in Rock Recordings," *Oakland Tribune,* 28 April 1982, pp. 1, 9; Joe Quintana, "The Devil and Rock 'n' Roll: Sacramento Faces the Music," *Los Angeles Herald Examiner,* 28 April 1982, pp. B-1, B-9.

48. Quoted in Joe Rassenfoss, "Church, Political Leaders Say the Evil Lurks in Lyrics—Do They Know of What They Speak?" *Kansas City Star* 3 June 1982, pp. 1B, 6B.

49. Quoted in Paul Kendall, *Led Zeppelin: A Visual Documentary* (London: Omnibus Press, 1982), n.p.

50. Michael W. Walker and Raymond G. Daniloff, "On the Controversy Surrounding Backward Messages in Rock Music," paper presented at the American Speech-Language-Hearing Association National Convention, Cincinnati, Ohio, 18 November 1983.
51. Emphasis added. "One Plus One Plus One Is Three," *Rolling Stone* 15 November 1969, p. 6.
52. This account is a synthesis of numerous Crowleyan accounts of the ritualist's concepts of pertinent experiences. There exist as many views of Crowley as there are writers on the subject. See John Symonds and Kenneth Grant, eds., *The Confessions of Aleister Crowley: An Autobiography* (New York: Hill & Wang, 1969); John Symonds, *The Great Beast* (London: MacDonald, 1951); Peter Haining, *The Anatonomy of Witchcraft,* (New York: Taplinger, 1972), pp. 69-73; Francis King, *Sexuality, Magic and Perversion* (N.J.: Citadel Press, 1972).
53. Huxley doesn't mention the experience in his influential *Doors of Perception,* a countercultural best seller in the 1960s. Jim Morrison named his band from the title; see King, *Sexuality, Magic and Perversion.*
54. The Master Theorion (Aleister Crowley), *Magick in Theory and Practice* (New York: Castle Books, 1929).
55. Francis King, ed., *Crowley on Christ* (London: C. W. Daniel, 1974), pp. 14-15.
56. Venetia Newall, *The Encyclopedia of Witchcraft and Magic* (New York: Dial Press, 1974), p. 59; *Encyclopedia of Occultism and Parapsychology,* p. 203.
57. Philip Norman, *Shout! The Beatles in Their Generation* (New York: Fireside Book, 1981), p. 291.
58. Quoted in Bill Harry, *The Book of Lennon* (New York: Delilah Books, 1984), p. 159. Also see George Martin, *All You Need Is Ear* (New York: St. Martin's Press, 1979), pp. 203-5.
59. Quotations in Cameron Crowe, "Zeppelin Rising . . . Slowly," *Rolling Stone* 12 August 1976, p. 23; John Hutchinson, "Robert Plant: Into the Light," *Record,* September 1983, p. 11; Ritchie Yorke, *The Led Zeppelin Biography* (New York: Methuen, 1976), p. 183.
60. Symonds and Grant, *The Confessions of Aleister Crowley,* p. 675.
61. Quotations in Cameron Crowe, "Led Zeppelin: Jimmy Page and Robert Plant," *Rolling Stone,* 13 March 1975, p. 37; Crowe, "Zeppelin Rising," p. 23.
62. *Sex,* p. 150.
63. Mike Houghton, "Led Zeppelin's Jimmy Page—from Sessions to Super Stardom," *Circus,* 28 October 1980, p. 34. The film has not been released.
64. "Anger Recruits ex-Manson Musician," *Circus,* 17 March 1977, p. 58.
65. Robert Hunter, *The Storming of the Mind: Inside the Consciousness Revolution* (Garden City, N.Y.: Anchor Books, 1972), p. 87.
66. Quoted in Yorke, *The Led Zeppelin Biography,* pp. 103, 115.
67. Larson, *Rock,* pp. 152-53.
68. Hutchinson, "Robert Plant."
69. Quotations in David Simon, "Satan Called Soul in Control of Rock and Roll," *Baltimore Sun,* 30 March 1983, p. B-1.
70. Gary Herman, *"Rock 'n' Roll Babylon"* (New York: Perigee Books, 1982), p. 161.
71. "The Land of Oz: A Talk With Mr. Osbourne," *Circus,* 26 August 1980, p. 26.
72. Quotations in Cathleen McGuigan, "Not the Sound of Silence," *Newsweek,* 14 November 1983, p. 102.

73. "Letters to the Editor," *Billboard,* 4 August 1984, p. 10.

74. Quoted in Ralph Kisiel, "British Rock Group Iron Maiden Plans Toledo Show," *Toledo Blade,* 4 September 1983, p. D1.

75. Stephen Holden, "Serious Issues Underlie a New Album from Styx," *New York Times,* 27 March 1983, pp. H27-H28.

76. Quotes in Ethlie Ann Vare, "Satanic Image Questions Industry's Metal Morals," *Billboard,* 14 April 1984, p. HM16; Crowe, "Zeppelin Rising," p. 9.

77. Quotations in "Wants Wayne Newton and Army Band Instead of Beach Boys," *Sentinel Tribune,* 6 April 1983, p. 1.

78. Quotations in Bill Thomas, "Bad Vibrations Sway Watt on Beach Boys," *Baltimore Sun,* 8 April 1983, pp. A1, A5; Matthew C. Quinn, "Watt's Ban on Rock Music Strikes Sour Notes" (UPI), *Sentinel Tribune,* 7 April 1983, p. 1; "James Watt: Bad Vibrations," *Newsweek,* 18 April 1983.

79. Craig Hankin, "Heaven Can Wait," *Rock and Roll Confidential,* March 1984, pp. 5-6.

80. See Tom Shales, "Androgynies Analogous to Aimless TV," *Satellite TV Week,* 12 August 1984 pp. F8, F9; Jim Miller, "The Tour, the Money, the Magic," *Newsweek,* 16 July 1984, p. 70.

81. Kisiel, "British Rock Group Iron Maiden Plans Toledo Show."

82. Quoted in Kurt Loder, "Rolling Stone Interview: Bob Dylan," *Rolling Stone,* 21 June 1984, p. 24.

# 9

## "Who Knows?" The Demise of
## the Rock Culture?

Forecasting trends in the record industry is akin to predicting the weather. This is particularly true in the mid-1980s. There are many imponderables.

Segments of the 1960s New Left portrayed rock music as a useful tool for revolutionary activity. John Sinclair of the White Panther party, and MC-5 manager, argued that rock has psychopolitical effects upon the unconscious minds of youthful audiences. Because of the loose and spontaneous nature of much writing on the sociopolitical impact of music during the 1960s, it is difficult to present a nice, neat, clear-cut typology or continuum of ideological perceptions.

The "street" is the alternative life-style so widely publicized during the late 1960s. Theodore Roszak characterized this life-style as a counterculture in opposition to the dominant one. The group was young, white, middle class, and Protestant or Jewish. Charles Reich described carriers of Consciousness III as persons who for a few years will "pulse to music, know beaches and the sea, value what is raunchy, wear clothes that express their bodies, flare against authority, seek new experience, know how to play, laugh, and feel, and cherish one another."[1] To which he might have added "smoke" and in some cases "take dope." Both chroniclers of the new life-style made popular music its focus. Academician Roszak's approach to popular music was not overly enthusiastic. He acknowledged the vital role it played in the lives of young people; he found its potential for molding a counterculture questionable. He admitted: "I find this music difficult to take. . . . I fear I tend to find much of it too brutally loud and/or electronically gimmicked up . . . the pop music scene lends itself to a great deal of commercial sensationalizing: the heated search for startling new tricks and shocks."[2] This is the traditional "opiate-of-the-masses" posture taken by those who opposed the advent of rock and, indeed, criticized the Beatles as political opportunists. The late Phil Ochs, a major proponent of protest songs, had outlined a similar sentiment in the liner notes for a Jim and Jean album some four years earlier: "Many grew their hair down to their wallets and jumped on the Beatle bandwagon in true hands-across-the-sea spirit. Palms upward as usual . . . discotheques spread like fungus. Many were moved to proclaim a new era of culture for the masses."[3] Prior to his metamorphosis in Hollywood, Ochs violently opposed the "overwhelming blare of drugged speakers." The Left's position on rock music was not totally negative. John Sinclair interpreted rock music as the *geist* (life force) for its achievement.

Until John Lennon championed his cause, Sinclair meant little outside the Detroit area. Abbie Hoffman, in *The Woodstock Nation*, discussed him as a *cause célèbre*, but Sinclair never became a household word. In the Detroit-Ann Arbor area, home of the University of Michigan, Sinclair was both political guru and martyr. He was a prime catalyst in the Ann Arbor underground scene, one of the founders of the Detroit-based White Panther party and a self-styled rock promoter and manager. He served part of a ten-year sentence in a Michigan penitentiary for the possession of two marijuana cigarettes. In the music world he is best known for his early tutelage of the MC-5.

Sinclair, like his philosophical contemporary, Timothy Leary, was a verbose pamphleteer who has treated many subjects in rambling essays. One of his favorite themes was the political significance of rock and roll. As do most political manifestos, Sinclair's tracts touch upon many metaphysical levels and can be appreciated by the most anti-intellectual, while possessing some attraction for the academically inclined. At the simplistic level, Sinclair's worldview was predicated upon the belief that a combination of rock music and drugs has created a new "energy force" that is both humanitarian and political. This force in turn is communicated by liberated rock-and-roll bands to "the people," who respond to the acts by creating even greater degrees of cosmic force, which in time will destroy the dominant or existent "death" culture. Rock music is that force. At a higher plane, Sinclair, as did the German dialectians, assumed that an independent force, rock music, has inherently "political" effects at every level of consciousness. In the Sinclair model, rock and roll is the advanced or vanguard power that creates consciousness.

In one long autobiographical paper Sinclair recited his conversion to the "new music" at the screening of *Blackboard Jungle*, which he saw seven times.[4] The purity of "Rock Around the Clock," he claimed, was corrupted to the point that the music transmitted false consciousness. Only the advent of mind-expanding drugs alterd this course. "We started gobbling all that good LSD," he writes, "and got turned on to the rest of the world, and at the same time we started hearing and feeling an incredible new music in the air."[5] Although rock music remained an overall microcosm of the contradictions of the "death culture," it was being liberated by Dylan, the Beatles, and the Stones. These performers, by their music, added to the sensate power of drugs and helped to create a "new people's culture" or "a wholly organic expression of a people's life-style" antithetical to the values of "Amerika."

> While we were off our feet lying on the floor trying to get our heads together, the greedheads and vultures of the dealth culture moved in on us and ripped us off for our music and the pure force of our energy and love and started using them against us, and we didn't realize it until the rip-off was almost complete. And then we said . . . we might as well go along with this, it isn't what we wanted but it's what's happening now and we might as well flow with it until it runs itself out, because it's too big and too powerful for us to fight it and besides this is all we've got, if we don't take this, shit, we might not get anything we want.[6]

Organic power, according to this view, was terminated or temporarily sidetracked by the overt repression of the "new community." In defense the alternative culture must band together and mobilize against the oppressors. Music and the rock concert, at the Grande (Detroit), would once again be the consciousness-expanding weapons.

In an earlier manifesto Sinclair described the interaction between audience and the performer as central to his thesis. Star quality and profit were negations of this posture in that a star or a profiteer was above the new people's culture. Stars and entrepreneurs, he contended, are the minions of the ruler of the death culture:

> These fucking PIGS! They've made our music and our celebrations into cheap consumer products, they've destroyed the use-value of our culture and converted it all into dollars and cents, anti-feeling and anti-sense, all in the name of profit and greed, and most of our people don't even know what they're missing because the pigs did this so fast that it's the only thing most of us have ever known—concerts where you sit down in a seat all night and watch the S*T*A*R*S.[7]

The solution to this problem in part was to return to the simplest communal "happening" where energy blared from giant speakers to the audience, who responded with even greater force.

In "A Letter from Prison" Sinclair outlined the "energy transmission" of the communal rock-and-roll concert:

> The stage show grew directly out of the music, all of the dope we were smoking, and out of our culture and our collective history. As the music got more frantic the stage show got farther out, and the people responded wildly

and it got more and more wild. It was a beautiful demonstration of the principles of high energy performance. The performer puts out more, the energy level of the audience is raised, and they give back more energy to the performers, who are moved to the audience and sent back, etc. until everything is total frenzy.

This process changes in the people's bodies that are molecular and cellular and which transform them irrevocably just as LSD . . . does. The transformation may last only as long as the performance, but with repeated exposure the transformation becomes *permanent, and you can never bring those people back down* to television consciousness again.[8]

Implicit in this argument is the assumption that participants must be of the same communal group or culture. Sinclair argued that the "capitalists" and "imperialists" are attempting to exploit the new community.

If the people of the rock and roll culture, the people of Woodstock Nation, continue to consume and support everything the pigs hand them, the capitalists and rock and roll imperialists will determine the future of our culture just as they have determined its recent past. If, on the other hand, the people of the rock and roll culture start to get themselves together and work out solutions to their problems and unite with their bands and workers and diggers and start implementing these new solutions, the people will be able to recapture the control of their own culture and move for righteous revolutionary change.[9]

The manifesto went on to urge bands and performers to play more benefits, more "free gigs for the people." The funds derived from these benefits should be used to further expand the institutions of the alternative culture.

One of the structures of the alternative culture would be a people's record cooperative that would record, produce, package, and market records by local bands. Sinclair argued, however, that bands might begin with established recording companies in order to make themselves the coopting of the musicians. He still feels rock music is a powerful force, but he is much more cautious about its ultimate influence upon the culture. Despite this switch in emphasis, Detroit still appears as the capital of loud working-class bands that specialize in glorifying and replicating the early sounds of rock and roll. The Detroit image of rock and roll was not universally shared outside the Michigan area. Many rock fans looked upon acts from the region as oddities, an attitude that several bands (Iggy and the Stooges and Ted Nugent) capitalized upon.

Segments of Sinclair's worldview were in fact shared by many of the street people. Music was presented as a form of generational conflict and the dawning of a new consciousness or culture by segments of the student protest movement and other youth enclaves. This belief thrust the street community into direct confrontation with the popular-music industry.

Sociologist J. Milton Yinger writes, "Undoubtedly rock music has been most powerfully counterculture . . . the chief ritual of a new life; it is community; it is religion." This musical counterculture—"sound, lyrics, volume, artifacts, audience, set and setting"—compose a value system or a definition of the situation.[10] Woodstock was the model.

The importance of Woodstock in any examination of rock culture cannot be overestimated because as *Time* correctly observed, "The spontaneous community of youth that was created at Bethel was the stuff of which legends are made; the substance of the event contains both a revelation and a sobering lesson"[11] Woodstock generated an ethos, a mythology, that lent support to the most ardent proponents of the dawning of a new community as well as to its many opponents. The Woodstock Music and Art Fair was almost a spontaneous unplanned event. It was originally scheduled to be held some 15 miles from Woodstock, in the hamlet of Wallkill, whose main claim to fame was the residence there of Bob Dylan. The aroused residents of Wallkill banded together into a Concerned Citizens Committee to keep the "dope-smoking hippie hordes" away. They were successful in their efforts, and there was some question as to whether the three-day event would be held at all.

The concerned citizens of Wallkill were not alone in their opposition to the festival. Mark Kramer, correspondent for Liberation News Service, the underground version of the Associated Press, filed a story titled "The Rock Imperialists" that condemned Mike Lang and Artie Kornfeld of Woodstock Ventures as rock investors who "look hip and talk hip" but were in effect exploiting the youth culture and the "revolutionary energy of rock." So the rock imperialists," he wrote, "deliver the goods. When you want a banana, United Fruit sells a good banana. And when you want a rock festival, Woodstock Music and Art Fair, Inc., sells a good rock festival—at $7 a day."[12]

After some five weeks of haggling, the festival was moved to Bethel and billed as an Aquarian Exposition—three days of peace and music in White Lake, New York: 15, 16, and 17 August. Handbills distributed in New York City announced, "To Insure Three Days of Peace & Music We've Left Wallkill and Are Now at White Lake." The handout went on to thank "the people of Bethel for receiving the news of our arrival so enthusiastically." This was a slight exaggeration of the situation. The citizens of Bethel were no less happy about the location of the affair than those of Wallkill. Their protests, however, were not as effective. A judge refused to grant an injunction after the promoters pointed out that only 60,000 people were expected and then promised to deal with all security, sanitation, and traffic problems. Given the incorrect crowd estimate and other unforeseen events, nearly all of these assurances would not be kept. New York City off-duty policemen scheduled to provide security were refused permission to moonlight. A hundred members of the Hog Farm, a New Mexico commune, led by Hugh Romney (Wavy Gravy), were enlisted to deal with health, sanitation, and other problems.

On the night before 15 August, half of the expected 60,000 were already camped on the grounds, and many more were on the way. The early arrivals were the vanguard of the street community. As press accounts reiterated, they were very much into the "oppositional life-style." Those who came after were in search of an experience, a happening. The next day a crowd of 200,000 people was milling about on Max Yasgur's thousand acres, which he had rented for the weekend for the reported amount of $50,000. Another 50,000 to 200,000 persons, depending on which crowd tally is used, soon joined them.

From the beginning the affair was serendipitous. Not even the most optimistic promoter could imagine an estimated million people clogging up the highways trying to reach the festival. Because 186,000 tickets has been sold, Woodstock Associates expected 200,000 people, maximum. As *Rolling Stone* commented, "No one was prepared for what happened and no one could have been."[13] Lines of cars stretched for 20 miles from the fair; the fences surrounding the Yasgur farm collapsed, allowing thousands of gate crashers to mingle with those who had paid eighteen dollars for the three days. One promoter labeled it a "financial disaster." The sanitation facilities, 600 portable toilets, were overtaxed and many ceased to function. The water supply proved inadequate, a situation made more desperate by heavy rainstorms and various illnesses, 300 cases of which were believed to be related to adverse drug reactions. By the night of 15 August, as journalists and spectators duly noted, Woodstock was the third largest city in the state of New York, minus any formal organization. All the while, the parade of entertainers, ranging from folksingers to the high-energy theatrics of Jimi Hendrix and the Who, continued, interrupted only by Chip Monck, the unofficial master of ceremonies.

It was Monck who best outlined the situation at Bethel the first day. To the assembled throng he said: "We're turning a little of the responsibility back onto you. We have the ability to gather this many people here and now it's also our responsibility to take care of ourselves in the midst of a phenomenon. And it's a responsibility no one ever had." He continued, "There are a hell of a lot of us here. If we are going to make it, you had better remember that guy next to you is your brother." Jerry Hopkins as well as other journalists have repeatedly reported this *gemeinschaft* or communal aspect of the gathering. "Everywhere there was a sense of 'family,' a sharing, a forthright mutual concern."[14] Woodstock was the antithesis of individual enterpreneurship and exploitation. One does not make a profit from his brother or sister.

On 16 August Monck announced to the crowd that Woodstock Ventures had ceased selling tickets. Woodstock was now entirely in the unsuspecting hands of the celebrants, not the management. In this announcement much of the "love-in" festival ideology was born. Festivals from that point on were to be gatherings of the people united by joy and music. As many participants assert, this image was more a contrivance of the media than a reality. The first day's rain drove off a considerable number of people that night, and mud and the lack of sanitation forced others to leave. Many were *not able* to withdraw. Still, Woodstock transcended the most farfetched dreams of nineteenth-century utopian-anarchist writers who saw salvation in the death of God and the state, who believed that once the masses are free, they will create a new culture. At Woodstock this appeared to happen, despite the structural anomie. By its apparent success, Woodstock became the model for future festivals, as well as the 1960s version of Rousseau's ideal state of nature. As the *Life* editorial concluded, "Everybody remembered. Woodstock made it."[15] Woodstock, in the vernacular, "blew a lot of minds." Only the Radical Right, with its usual distaste for anything associated with drugs or sex, and the New Left objected to the festival.

The Left was not happy with Peter Townshend's pushing Abbie Hoffman off the stage while he was trying to make a "free-John-Sinclair" speech. A *Rolling Stone* correspondent would later remark, "That's the relationship of rock to politics."[16] Hoffman left the affair to write *Woodstock Nation* in five days, applauding the political potential of youth while denouncing the rock stars and promoters. A more typical reaction is provided by Joseph Sia:

> The big thing was being there and taking part in a festival where everyone shared what he's had. In any crowd this large you expect some misfortune. There were three deaths and two births over the weekend—far below the usual statistics for a city of half a million people. . . . Where was the violence that was supposed to accompany any large gathering of young people? What the straight world failed to understand was that these young people, wet, tired, hungry, simply were not interested in fighting. They had come to a remote, peaceful setting to get together and rap, and to listen to the supersounds of their favorite superstar rock groups.[17]

Sia's argument echoed most of the press and media reports from Woodstock. The wanton savagery predicted by the media had not occurred. Indeed, many newspapers, including the August *New York Times*, took highly positive editorial positions after the affair was over, although they had originally opposed it.

Analyses of Woodstock generally centered around the peaceful nature of the gathering and the theme of youth as a new social force. Psychologist Rollo May portrayed it as "a symptomatic event of our time that showed the tremendous hunger, need and yearning for community." Paul Williams, founder of *Crawdaddy*, noted in a promotional blurb for Warner Bros., "Old World crumbling, new world being born, Woodstock a festival of getting together, celebration of birth, not the first and scarcely the last but every time you're born it feels like a whole new life. . . . Peace be with you brother till we meet again." Ellen Sanders, contributor to *Saturday Review* and the Los Angeles *Free Press*, saw it as

> a three-day live-in where food, shelter and joy were shared. Authority was missing in action, hundreds of thousands of young people suddenly realized they could have it any way they wanted. A choice was made; genuine peace, love and humanity prevailed, It worked. Joyously, profoundly, we were all touched by one another en masse for the duration of a festival after which nothing could ever be the same."

Greil Marcus of *Rolling Stone* indicated it was a "foundling of something new, something our world must now find a way to deal with. The limits have changed now . . . the priorities have been rearranged, and new 'impractical' ideas must be taken seriously. . . . This is just the beginning—or the end—and we must now sit down and figure out how to make it work." *Life*, a mirror of middle-class values, reported "Woodstock had been a total experience, a phenomenon, a happening, a high adventure, a near disaster and in a small way, a struggle for survival."

Not all voices were affirmative. Barry Farrell, in a review for *Life*'s special issue on the festival, cautioned that while the fair was "a victory for music and peace," it was also "a display of the authority of drugs. . . . It was groovy, as the speaker kept saying, but I fear it will grow groovier in memory, when the market in madness leads on to shows we'd rather not see."[18] To this Hoffman added, "It never ceased to amaze me how groups, instead of imitating our . . .[political] model and trying to rip-off Woodstock Ventures again or the Fillmore or Columbia Records, tried instead to devour us."[19] Woodstock was all of these things and more. It became a standard of comparison no less utopian than Rousseau's world of the noble savage. It was the prototype, as Marcus urged, for future events. The festival also created a form of generational consciousness that implied a superiority of purpose absent in other sectors of society.

The erosion of the rock culture began as the litter was being cleaned up on Yasgur's farmland. In less than a year two of the Woodstock Nation's idols would have overdosed: Jimi Hendrix and Janis Joplin. Few of the acts artistically survived the seventies. Bill Graham bitterly said, "Woodstock was the beginning of the end."

Woodstock commercialized the rock culture. The Rolling Stones' "free" concert presented at the Altamont Raceway in California was the last nail in the coffin of the rock culture of the sixties.[20]

*Rolling Stone*, in the December issue of 1969, ran a banner headline proclaiming, "FREE ROLLING STONES: IT'S GOING TO HAPPEN! After a series of planning mishaps the event took place on a dusty auto racetrack near Livermore, with 300,000 people in attendance. During the chaotic afternoon, a young black man, Meredith Hunter, was stabbed to death by one of the Hell's Angels who had been hired to keep order at the affair, as they had done at the Be-In. In all, four persons died—one more than Woodstock—and a number of injuries and discomforts were endured. Even a performer, Marty Balin of the Jefferson Airplane, was felled by a Hell's Angel. A good deal of Consciousness III was contradicted that day, when it became clear that the entire event had been staged to allow the Rolling Stones' management to film a *Woodstock*-like movie. The film, *Gimme Shelter*, including the murder scene, was released a year later. The headline of the underground San Francisco paper, *Good Times*, summed up the general reaction to Altamont: "Mick Jagger Used Us for Dupes," a lead quotation attributed to a member of the Hell's Angeles.

Altamount had the same impact upon the Woodstock Nation as the "trashings" and bombings did on the increasingly disillusioned New Left. The big chill was settling in.

Entering the 1970s James Taylor was on the cover of *Time*. Taylor, a middle-class songwriter saved from the sinking Apple venture, appealed primarily to white female college students with his sensitive love ballads. He was not charismatic on record or stage. With an elaborate publicity campaign manipulated by Norm Winter, Elton John was touted as the "savior" of the 1970s. A cynical Hollywood observer commented, "The press and the radio were so desperately looking for a super hero. . . . You couldn't have bought that kind of publicity. The timing was right." *Los Angeles Times* writer Robert Hilburn acknowledged there was "little to dig one's artistic teeth into." Record company executives and fans waited for a distinct, identifiable new sound or trend. None emerged, although there were some false starts and prophets. Socially significant subtrends were touted and hyped. Most ended up in the cutout bins at chain department stores throughout the nation. Jimmy Cliff and Bob Marley, proponents of the politically laced Jamaican reggae sound, were supposed to be super-stars. It did not happen. The controversial Sex Pistols and other "punk" acts received a wave of press coverage. Broadcasters and record buyers did not follow the "Rock Critics Establishment" in New York. Renaming the sound "New Wave" could not save it.

The commercial failures of the 1970s may be attributed to the rise of the apolitical "Me Generation." The values of the "culture of narcissism" may explain the temporary success of Kiss and disco. Both were fantasies and escapes from Watergate, the Vietnam experience, the everyday pressures of school or job, lack of fuel, inflation, alienation, and a political system that seemed not to work. The film *Saturday Night Fever* was the *Blackboard Jungle*, *Easy Rider*, and *Big Chill* of the 1970s. The antihero in *Fever* negated reality on the dance floor in disco contests.

The "Disco Disaster," as Christgau termed it, put rock on the back burner and the demographics were all wrong for the record industry. A character in the *Big Chill* flicks his turntable. When asked about his choice of music, "You mean you still listen to that music?" he quickly replies, "There is no other music." The sound track and a sequel did quite well on the 1980s charts.

The *Big Chill* generation did not disintegrate. The "Happy Together" tour featuring four 1960s rock acts sold out the country. Survivors of the socially conscious decade—the Dead, Stones, Starship—did fairly well. Still the self-gratification of the 1970s was solidifying into the conservativism of the 1980s. Robin Gibb of the Bee Gees said, "Flower power was the most destructive period in music. The music itelf wasn't that bad, just what it represented. People thought that to live in a lovely world they had to prop themselves up with a lot of ugly drugs." "I no longer go for a message that hammers on one's head," recalls composer Marc Dorfman, "because that quickly wears thin. Music should be entertaining."[21]

Lee Abrams, whose firm was a major player in the rock scene, predicted in 1980: "I would say from a musical standpoint, the fanaticism . . . is dying down." Kent Burkhart, the architect and popularizer of disco radio, added, "In the past year or year and a half we have been in a period of what you could term contemporary nostalgia."[22] Some critics would call this a self-fulfilling prophecy. The Atlanta consultants would receive a good deal of blame for the apparent decline of the rock culture. *Newsweek*'s Jim Miller in a state-of-the-music article would write: "Today such restlessness is confined to the margins of America's youth culture—and is shut off the airwaves by the timid technocrats manning our brave new world of computer print-outs." His counterpart at *Time*, Jay Cocks, wrote, "The kids who grew up in the rock generation found an identity, and a voice in their music. Their kids have yet to find a sound of their own."[23]

There is a fragmentation in concert tours and broadcasting. Los Angeles and other metropolitan centers exhibit a small but vocal "punk rock subculture" akin to the London club scene of the mid-1970s.

Music video introduced new and old sounds. Unfamiliar faces and sounds appeared on MTV. Most were from the British Isles, where video clips were regularly prepared for the BBC's "Tops for the Tops" and then exported to the European market. A majority of the acts were British; many were totally unknown to U.S. audiences. For lack of a better descriptive phrase "new music" entered the lexicon, an umbrella term designed to cover a plethora of musical fusions and artists.

The sounds that some called the second "British invasion" were difficult to define. The term *androgyny* appeared in the pop-culture vocabulary and applied to Michael Jackson, Boy George of Culture Club, and Annie Lennox of the Eurythmics. These were the leaders of the "new music."

Jim Sullivan of the *Boston Globe* aptly demonstrated the problems of "new music" when he wrestled with a definition:

> [It] . . . encompasses a wide array of musical styles and philosophies. There's new technology at work (preeminently synthesizers and drum machines); there's fascination with the darker, turbulent side of romance; there's a rediscovery of older pop idioms such as rockabilly. Motown soul, Jamaican ska and reggae; there's fertile stylistic cross-pollination, such as the merger of African rhythms and traditional American pop forms. . . . At best, New Music is about creating something fresh, about risk and adventure. It's music that moves one's spirit.

Stephen Holden in the *New York Times* merely termed it a "multiplicity of styles." The "new music" was in fact more defined by its practitioners than its sound. Greg Geller of RCA aptly noted, "The English groups are younger and they sound fresher." Lee Abrams said, "By 1982 New Music was breaking left and right, with or without air play. We had to react or fade away." Radio, especially "Hot Hits," played what listeners saw on their cable systems. (see chapter 7).[24]

Most of the publicity fell on the shoulders of the androgynous *troika*: Jackson, Boy George, and to a much lesser extent Lennox. All enjoyed cover stories in the nation's weekly newsmagazines. CBS's "Face the Nation" had Boy George confronting the Reverend Jerry Falwell of the Moral Majority: "The illusion that I'm promoting homosexuality is obviously rubbish," Boy George told Leslie Stahl. "I'm 6-foot guy. I'm very much a man . . . do your thing." Michael Jackson has refused comment on the issue. One Tufts University psychologist saw this as an appealing quality. David Elkind told a reporter, "Kids are so surfeited with sex that these androgynous guys are almost a relief . . . [Jackson is] the lost boy of Never-Never Land."[25]

While few psychographic studies are available, it does appear that Jackson and Culture Club appeal to demographic extremes. The "Victory tour" attracted the youngest segment of the MTV audience and their parents. Culture Club's numbers are in the same range. As with previous teen idols, there is a massive merchandising industry surrounding Michael Jackson and Boy George, ranging from white sequined glove to one-issue full-color magazines that naturally include wall posters. The more gentlemanly Duran Duran appears to enjoy support from a similar taste public.

The multidimensional aspect of "new music" cannot be called a trend in the sense of Presley's rockabilly strains or the Beatles' distinctive Mersey sound. It's a cast of characters with as many roots and musical influences as video clips. By 1985 much of the heralded "new music" was getting old. It faced an antithesis: neo-heavy metal.

"There is a continuing oscillation of superficial values, waves that sweep the country one in reaction to another," said psychiatrist Burton Conn. In the best Newtonian fashion heavy metal was a response to "new music," symbolized by Billy Idol's black-leather studded glove in contrast to Michael Jackson's white hand cover.[26] MTV's exposure of neo-heavy metal bands has appeal to a white-male, under-21 demographic. The heavy metal of the 1980s is a far cry from the works of Steppenwolf, Deep Purple, or the premier act, Led Zeppelin. ("Beat" writer William Burroughs coined the term *Heavy Metal Meal*. The Fugs named its publishing company Heavy Metal.)

David Gans perfectly captures the ethos of the 1980s version of "power rock."

> It is a fundamental conceit of Heavy Metal that teenagers are a great oppressed underclass, forced to take out garbage, load dishwashers and do homework with little to sustain their spirits but cable TV, video games and the vile, repellent and loud form of entertainment known as Heavy Metal.
>
> Met is nominally a style of music, but music is virtually beside the point. What's important is that the performers, staging, graphics, and sound be as vile, repellent and loud as possible—because the payoff is not aesthetic satisfaction. The true purpose of Heavy Metal is to piss off parents, irritate teachers, take one's mind off roaring rivers of hormones, and antagonize shopping mall security personnel—those oppressors whose true purpose is to snuff out fun and abridge teenage freedom.[27]

Other observers tend to agree. "Heavy metal has always appealed especially to frustrated male working class rage," noted Dave Marsh, now of *Radio and Records. Newsweek* characterized the mavens: "The fans imitate the heavy metal dress of their idols—sleeveless T-shirts, leather jackets, studded leather wrist bands—and in concerts, they will shake their fists in unison above their heads as they scream the lyrics along with the band."[28]

Certainly heavy metal has a solid following in the so-called Rust Belt. But in the 24 November 1984 *Billboard* only three metal groups have albums in the top 30; none in the teens or above. This is not surprising because heavy metal appeals to a specific part of the youth audience, a segment of the 23 million households wired by cable into MTV. Deborah Frost suggested in a *Rolling Stone* review that groups such a Quiet Riot, Motley Crue, and Twisted Sister are in the *fantasy* business. Quiet Riot's Kevin DuBrow agrees: "They pay their money, they're escapists, they want to feel they're part of *something*. That's our job to give it to them. We're entertainment." Frost adds that MTV provides "the fantasy accessories that give the average American alien metal fan a sense of belonging to *something*."[29] That "something" is the social glue that unites the black-leather concert set. Metal rites occur at crowded arenas rather than festivals. Outside the industrial, heavy-manufacturing auto and steel states there are insufficient numbers to justify mass outdoor concleaves. Not to mention obtaining permits for such gatherings. The satanic image of metalists would surely provoke community opposition. Even in Toledo, Ohio, a bastion of high-power music, only one of three concert venues will accept the likes of Black Sabbath or Quiet Riot. In the Midwest some broadcasters are predicting a decline in the popularity of the genre. Some call it "a self-parody." Others point to an "oversaturation" of heavy metal or just plain "overkill."

The neometalists are backing away from the concept that established them in the rock world. Robin Crosby of Ratt calls its power sound "pop metal." "Old heavy metal is boring," he said. "I know because we used to be into it. But we dropped that heavy-metal look and all the bondage gear. What we're really after is a mass audience." From Rudy Sarro of Quiet Riot: "We consider ourselves an American hard-rock band. We're melodic. We play melodic songs very loud." The Scorpions' Herman Rarebell adds: "We're not the typical head-banging, heavy-metal band. . . . We have melody and not just hard, crashing, rattling guitars all the time." When groups disassociate with the sound that made their careers, it is a sign the genre is in trouble. It is also possible they have been reading reviews of their concerts and albums in the music press. Little of it has been stellar.[30]

Cable operators may have an input. Few agree with the New Christian Right's or Ted Turner's description of MTV clips as "satanic" or "trash," but they are tired of adult subscribers' complaints regarding the content of the service. "Turns" or termination of the service is always a concern.

Turner attempted to counter MTV with the Cable Music Channel. After a month's exposure of the "PG" fare the Atlanta cable mogul had fewer than 400,000 households, compared to MTV's reported 23 million. MSO people, like advertisers, look at numbers. Even CNN, the Turner all-news channel, reported the music video outlet would not survive. (Some observers implied Turner's motives were more egoistic than economically sound.) And it did not; after thirty-four days CMC was no more.

The notion of a rock culture in the 1980s appears slim. There may be taste publics generationally tied to segments of a fragmented music scene much less visible than in the Woodstock period. Apple computer inventor Steve Wozniak found out the hard way. "I just *had* to give them that enjoyment again, like another *Star Wars* movie," he told *Record* magazine. The result was the 1983 Memorial Day US Festival held in the hot dry mountains near San Bernardino in California. Wozniak lost $10 million when only half of the anticipated 600,000 attendees braved the arid desert environment to hear Van Halen, the Clash, Ozzy Osbourne, U2, and others. Law-enforcement officers labeled the festival "an absolute mess." There were two fatalities and 145 arrests, and 135 people were treated for serious injuries. David Lee Roth, reportedly "party'd out," incited the milling throngs with jeers like "More people have been arrested today alone than all weekend last year. You guys are a bunch of toady motherfuckers!" Us was more Altamount than Woodstock. Wozniak's promoter, Barry Fey, was prophetic in May when he observed, "I was at Woodstock, there's not gonna be anything else like that, so why go?"[31] There was no US festival in 1984. A promoter involved in festivals in Cleveland and Michigan's Speedway Jam, lamented, "Wozniak killed the outdoor concert forever."

Kent Burkhart's prediction of growing conservativism in the 1980s has proved correct in politics and music. Congressman Thomas Downey, a 35-year-old, said, "Much of what I feel about government was shaped during the late '60's. These feelings are not shared by younger members who were not molded by the Vietnam experience." The 1980s may come to be called the "Survival Generation." As one bank executive in his twenties noted, "Given the recessions and high inflation through the '70's that sense of existential security has evaporated and forced us to focus on survival."[32]

Musically a similar trend can be observed. One university student wrote: "Most of the people who I talk to who grew up with the early groups say they still prefer listening to their favorites, while not caring too much for the new groups." David J. Bruehrer, a Bowling Green State University upperclassman, commented, "Is there a 'rock culture' today? The answer would have to be a qualified no. . . . I don't believe that Culture Club and Duran Duran represent a 'rock culture' today. But, rock and roll, with its inherent potential for reaching the young and capturing their attention, is capable of most anything. So, who knows?"

In *Solid Gold*, published a decade ago, this writer looked to the basic roots of U.S. popular music. Country and black music were the choices for upward mobility in the late 1970s. The picks were partially correct in that the *Saturday Night Fever* and *Urban Cowboy* crazes did take place, and bland crossovers from both genres continue to penetrate the trade charts. These wells seem dry with "modern country" and "urban contemporary."

The rock music idiom has come full circle from the 1950s. So has the music audience, and radio broadcasting formats. CHR stations, many successfully challenging AOR, are mirror images of Storz's Top 40 affiliates. MTV, with its emphasis on single clips and power rotation, owes some of its programming philosophy to Storz and McLendon, despite the computer printouts of psychographic data and audience targets. Heavy metal, with its drugstore satanism and teen fantasies of Kraft-Ebbing, create the symbolism of generational conflict in a manner "Elvis the Pelvis" only hinted at.

The new player in the game, which is only just under way, is music video. MTV is an important component in the music and motion-picture industries. As of the mid-1980s Bob Pittman's narrowcasting critics notwithstanding, has worked. But the future is fraught with more questions than answers. Music video in the United States is an entirely new ballgame. There are no historical or empirical benchmarks by which to measure success or failure. The legality of the exclusives enjoyed by MTVN is in the judicial system. The viability of music video channels geared to the *Big Chill* generation is a shaky and unproved proposition. The number of music channels a cable system will or can carry is another open question, as is advertising support as well. Here Pitman is probably correct in predicting that cable is capable of supporting only *two* pop/rock stations. There will be a shakeout if the proposed Discovery Music Network and VH-1 go after the same demographic. Only time will tell. As the Bowling Green student aptly noted, "Who knows?"

## Notes

1. Charles Reich, *Greening of America* (New York: Random House, 1970), pp. 169-70.
2. Theodore Roszak, *The Making of a Counter-Culture: Reflections of the Technocratic Society and Its Youthful Opposition* (Garden City, N.Y.: Doubleday, 1969), p. 291.
3. Phil Ochs, liner notes, Jim and Jean, *Changes* (Verve Folkways, FT 3001).
4. John Sinclair, "A Letter from Prison," *Creem* 2 (n.d.). Also see John Sinclair, *Guitar Army* (New York: Douglas, 1972).
5. John Sinclair, "Liberation Music," *Creem* 2 (n.d.): 19.
6. Ibid., p. 20.
7. Ibid.
8. Sinclair, "A Letter from Prison."
9. Sinclair, "Liberation Music," p. 21.

10. J. Milton Yinger, *Countercultures: The Promise and Peril of World Turned Upside Down* (New York: Free Press, 1982), p. 145. Also Dick Hebdige, *Subculture: The Meaning of Style* (New York: Methuen, 1979).

11. "The Message of History's Biggest Happening," *Time*, 29 August 1969, p. 32.

12. Mark Kramer, "The Rock Imperialists," *The Fifth Estate*, Fall 1969, p. 7.

13. Greil Marcus, "The Woodstock Festival," *Rolling Stone*, 20 September 1969, p. 17.

14. Jerry Hopkins, *Festival! The Book of American Music Celebrations* (New York: Collier Books, 1970), p. 140.

15. "The Great Woodstock Rock Trip," *Life* (special edition), 1969, p. 4.

16. "It Was Like Balling for the First Time," *Rolling Stone* 20 September 1969, p. 24.

17. Joseph J. Sia, *Woodstock 69: Summer Pop Festivals* (New York: Scholastic Book Services, 1970).

18. Barry Farrell, "Gloria! Donald! Countermiracle at the Great Stones Rock Show," *Life* (special edition), 1969.

19. Abbie Hoffman, *The Woodstock Nation* (New York: Vintage Books, 1969), p. 130.

20. Stanley Booth, "The Stones at Altamount," *Rolling Stone* 13 September 1984, pp. 25 ff. Also Robert Santelli, *Aquarius Rising: The Rock Festival Years* (New York: Delta Books, 1980).

21. Quoted in Dolores Barclay, "Message Less Important in Music of '70s," *Toledo Blade*, 16 May 1979, p. 30.

22. Quotations in "Staying in Tune with the Times," *Broadcasting*, 25 August 1980, p. 56.

23. Quotations in Jim Miller, "Is Rock on the Rocks?" *Newsweek*, 19 April 1982, p. 107; Jay Cocks, "Rock Hits the Hard Place," *Time*, 15 February 1982.

24. Quotations in Jim Sullivan, "Triumph of the 'New,'" *On Campus*, March 1984.

25. Quotations in "Jackson's Mr. Clean Image Good for Kids," *Sentinel Tribune* 14 August 1984, p. 8.

26. Quotations in Mark Sauer, "Sex-Crossed Superstars," *U.S. Press*, 2 October 1984, p. 6.

27. David Gans, "Twisted Logic (I'd Sat Severely Bent)," *Record*, December 1984, p. 37.

28. Quotations in Cathleen McGuigan, "Not the Sound of Science," *Newsweek*, 14 November 1983, p. 102.

29. Deborah Frost, "Heavy Metal Rears Its Ugly Head Again," *Rolling Stone* 27 September 1984, pp. 83-84.

30. Quotations in Ralph Kisiel, "Holy Headache! Heavy Metal Has Returned," *Toledo Blade*, 25 November 1984, pp. F1-F2.

31. Quotations in John Mendelsohn , "US Festival '83: No More in '84," *Record*, August 1983; Steve Pond, "Violence Mars US Festival," *Rolling Stone*, 7 August 1983, p. 46; Steve Pond, "Wozniak: $20 Million Lost on US Festivals," *Rolling Stone*, 1 September 1983, p. 45; Kurt Loder "The US Festival: Money Talks," *Rolling Stone*, 26 May 1983, p. 55. See John G. Fuller, *"Are the Kids All Right?"* (New York: Times Books, 1981).

32. "Here Come the Baby-Boomers," *U.S. News and World Report*, 5 November 1984, pp. 68-69.

# Epilogue

The glitter returned to the gold in 1984. The number of gold and platinum wall trophies increased by 20 percent over 1983. CBS researchers, awaiting the official RIAA figures, pegged the value of shipments—record and cassette—at some $4.464 billion as contrasted to the peak year of 1978, which was set at $4.1 billion. (CBS figures *usually* parallel those of the industry trade association but are released a month earlier; the estimates proved too high.)

While music moguls rejoiced, a closer examination of the figures reveals a two-edged sword. Michael Jackson's *Thriller* fueled the beginnings of the recovery in 1983 almost singlehandedly. Jackson was the "engine" while most of the boxcars were from the MTV tracks. The big sellers in 1984 were established artists, crossovers, and sound tracks. Sound tracks outdistanced the two top sales years combined, 1978—*Saturday Night Fever* and *Grease*—and 1980. Five sound tracks led by *Footloose* sold some 10 million units. The success of at least two, *Footloose* and *Eddie and the Cruisers*, can be directly traced to video exposure. Prince's *Purple Rain* adds another 10 million to the sound-track derby. As RSO and MCA once painfully discovered, sound tracks can be highly capricious in the music marketplace.

Black crossovers, nine of which reached the platinum peak, included Lionel Richie's 1983 release *Can't Slow Down* at 10 million units; Tina Turner with 3 million albums; the Jacksons' disappointing—for them—*Victory* did 4 million in sales, as well as the Pointer Sisters along with Chaka Khan. Of the nine original 1984 black million-unit sellers, only four were studio sets; five were sound tracks.

Heavy metal acts in the "broadest sense of the classification," like Van Halen at 3 million, and the Scorpions with two platinums led the ten acts into this exalted category in sales. Heavy metal, according to some observers, has become a parody of itself kept alive by the visual potentials of the genre. Bob Pittman agreed, cutting heavy metal acts aired on MTV. "We've pulled way back on heavy metal," he said, because they appeal "only to a heavy metal audience." He elaborated, "People either love it or hate it, and people who hate it, hate it with a passion." The irritation factor is dreaded

447

in broadcasting. The reason for the cutback was reportedly a 25 percent drop in the network's ratings. Despite 1984's being its first year free of red ink, the outlet's numbers, according to A. C. Nielsen, declined from a healthy 1.2 to less than 0.9 in 1984. Dee Snider of Twisted Sister commented, "Back to the road"—an exposure device much less effective than MTV. PolyGram's Randy Roberts summarized the industry's reaction: "We are very concerned."[1] It had reason to be. The *Billboard* album chart of 30 March found only the Jimmy Page and Paul Rodgers fusion group, the Firm, listed in the top-twenty slots.

Seasoned performers did well. Huey Lewis and the News, Bruce Springsteen, Cars, John Couger Mellencamp, Van Halen, Tina Turner, and Prince were hardly newcomers without a few gold records hanging in their dens. Only Cyndi Lauper's *She's So Unusual*, a staple on MTV's power rotation, can be labeled as a new addition.

The first platinum album of 1985, released in January, traditionally a poor sales month, was John Fogerty's *Centerfield* with a pure Creedence Clearwater Revival sound of the 1960s. Many CHR stations with their "immediacy" orientation began expanding their playlists to include material from the past decade at least. There is little speculation of a revival.

Women rockers like Madonna, Cyndi Lauper, Sheena Easton, and Tina Turner have generated a good deal of media attention, including a *Newsweek* cover story. Sociologist Jack Levin, however, told *USA Today* their "lyrics are oriented to the past, not to the future—not even to the present."[2] Record companies can take little solace from remarks of that nature.

A darker cloud surfaced in March 1985. Country music sales began to drop drastically, except for a few superstars. Country and symphonic music were the two categories unaffected by the "crash of '79," and both increased their market share in the early 1980s. "I'm so lonesome I could cry" is a line from a famous Hank Williams song. It sums up the feelings of a number of country music artists, talent agents, and music publishers in Nashville.

Big-name country stars are not selling records or filling concert halls the way they did in the early 1980s when the rest of the music industry was going under or suffering in the recession of 1979. At that time the major labels counted on country sales to provide revenue when rock and pop artists could not even give their albums away. Most of the kids were playing Pac-Man at that time, not buying records. But country fans remained loyal. The record industry association, RIAA, which monitors sales, indicates that country enjoyed a 20 percent market share.

The numbers are currently dropping, and significantly. Artists like Crystal Gayle, Mickey Gilley, Barbara Mandrell, Don Williams, Conway Twitty, and others are all selling fewer than 150,000 units—a 60 to 70 percent drop. A number-one hit single averages 80,000 sales.

Crystal Gayle's Warner Bros. album *Cage the Songbird*, containing two number-one singles, has sold only 80,000 copies, barely the break-even point for the company. Twitty's *By Heart* was down to 150,000; he is usually in the 400,000 bracket. A number of other top sellers are not breaking the 100,000 barrier. Gilley's *Too Good to Stop Now* peaked at 70,000. Charley Pride suffered a similar numerical fate with *Power of Love*. The biggest loser was Ronnie McDowell, whose *Greatest Hits* album sold only 40,000 albums. Crossover stars like Eddie Rabbitt and even Waylon Jennings, with cable television exposure, are equally feeling the economic pinch. The current crop of superstars like Alabama, Willie Nelson, Hank Williams, Jr., and the Statler Brothers seem still to be piling up the gold records and selling out venues.

There are numerous explanations for this decline in country music. One Nashville insider said, "Most of country isn't country anymore." Don Reid of the Statlers noted, "Too many country singers want to be pop." Chet Atkins has echoed this sentiment for several years. Despite the fact, one of the worst offenders in this area, as with Sylvia, is RCA. Traditional country fans seem to be turned off by these pop-oriented music city performers.

Alabama's Randy Owen, one of the acts still in the gold-record category, explained the success of the group: "If there is a secret of our success, touring, is that we go to small places. We sell 9,000 to 10,000 tickets. We go back there year after year. Those people appreciate the fact that we come and see them. And that's our kind of people. . . . We can do that for as long as we want to do it." The bottom line for the group, Owen noted is, "We don't target a product to go to a particular market." Country fans appear to like this approach.

One popular explanation for the setback is the conditions in the farm economy. "Farmers are 99 percent country music-oriented," observed Harry Peebles of the International Country Music Buyers Association (ICMBA) to *Billboard*. This view does not totally cover the situation; the Country Music Association (CMA) estimates that a majority of fans live in urban and suburban areas. Blaming the agricultural crisis may be somewhat misleading. Other insiders indicate the problem is more internally generated. Veteran promoter Lon Varnell told *Billboard*, "What we need to do now is hold on to what we've got." "There are too many people," wrote David Skipper of Loretta Lynn Enterprises, "playing ostrich and sticking their heads in the sand."[3]

And still another view is that while the rock resurgence was fueled by MTV, the Nashville Network (TNN) does not have the same mass exposure or sales punch. TNN claims to have sold over 1.1 million albums, but many retailers dispute the figure. One record company executive suggested that TNN misses both ends of the demographic scale. Traditionalists and teens do not tune in the network.

Nobody seems to have a solution. In fact some city moguls of country music refuse to acknowledge that a problem exists, in typical Nashville fashion. They hope the situation will solve itself. If history is any teacher, it will not. Ironically, the country music executives seem to have learned little from their counterparts in New York and Los Angeles who said the same thing in 1979.

VH-1 aired on New Year's Day 1985 at 6 P.M. (EST) while most of the country was mesmerized by the annual bowl games. Some saw the MTV Network's effort to tap into the 25-plus market as a definite gamble. Ted Turner's crusade to clean up music video lasted thirty-four days, going off the air with a meager 350,000 households; MTV bought him out. Comparisons were inevitable, although Bob Pittman insisted to CNN, Turner's all-news network, "The only similarity between Cable Music Channel and either of our two music networks is that they both use videos somewhere in the mix. I think everything else was completely different." VH-1 started with a potential viewership of 3.5 million, some ten times Turner's audience. June is predicted to see an expansion of two million more households. Bob Roganti, vice-president and general manager of advertising sales, projected "7 to 10 million" by the end of 1985. Madison Avenue exhibited mixed reactions to the new music station. "MTV mushroomed primarily because it became a word-of-mouth situation," said Ira Tumpowsky of Young and Rubicam. He doubted VH-1 could repeat the "I Want My MTV" campaign because of the older audience, programming, and format. Another observer suggested that MTV "tapped into an ignored television market, 18-to-24-year-olds while VH-1's demographic target is the most sought after," and "there are a vast number of different ways to reach . . .[the] 24-to-49 age bracket."[4] This observation raised the key question. The cherished 25-plus market has not yet established itself as a reliable consumer of music video. Only time will tell if MTVN's second musical attempt will follow in the footsteps of the flagship satellite channel.

At the April NARM convention in Hollywood, Florida, the RIAA released its official numbers. Domestic labels shipped some $4.37 billion of cassette and record product, surpassing the banner 1978 peak. The unit figures, however, were less than those of 1977-78. In dollars LPs and EPs declined by 8 percent from the previous year. Prerecorded cassettes showed the largest gain, 32 percent from 1983. The mini-Walkman craze contributed greatly to the increase. This phenomenon is predominantly visible in the pre-21 age group.

The national successes of 1984 may be mercurial. As the usually optimistic trade paper *Billboard* notes, "Throughout the year, no one suggested that the recording industry was returning to previous rates of growth." *Rolling Stone* added, "What seems to be happening is a sort of rock Reaganomics as the richest part of the record business pulls rapidly away from the rest of it."[5]

The year 1985 may mark a new beginning for the record industry. Regardless, few observers see future conditions as exhibiting the same potentials for growth as occurred in past decades. The merchandising, promotion, and telecasting of MVs is an entirely new ball game. How it will turn out nobody really knows. The music business is engrossing because of its chief characteristic: suspense.

### Notes

1. Quotations in Jefferson Graham, "Heavy Metal on the Outs at MTV," *Rolling Stone*, 11 April 1985, p. 16; Tony Seidman, "MTV Cuts Back on Airtime for Heavy Metal Vidclips," *Billboard*, 23 February 1985. p. 3.
2. Quoted in Dan Sperling, "Explicit Hits Have Some Folks All Shook Up," *USA Today*, 14 March 1985, p. 3D.
3. Quotations in Ed Morris, "Country Promoters, Agents Face Tougher Marketplace," *Billboard*, 16 March 1985, p. 76. Also "Letters to the Editor," *Billboard*, 30 March 1985, p. 10.
4. Quotations in Tony Seidman, "VH-1 Off to Fast Start, Says MTV," *Billboard*, 30 March 1985, p. 30. Also Jill Marks, "Laid-Back Launch," *Cable TV Business*, 15 February 1985, p. 10.
5. Adam White, "Talent Almanac 1985," *Billboard*, 22 December 1984, p. TA-3; John Pareles, "Work Hard, Play Hard," *Rolling Stone* 3 January 1985, p. 136.

# Bibliography

Unlike *Solid Gold*, in which notes were used exclusively to identify printed material for quotations, this volume includes major sources in the notes. Consequently, it would be redundant to rehash the state of the literature. Those seeking further bibliographical and evaluative information are directed to my *Sing a Song of Social Significance* (2d ed., 1983), especially the closing three chapters. Dean Tudor's *Popular Music: An Annotated Guide to Recordings* (1984) contains a fairly substantial list of books (not articles) dealing with popular music. Social scientists will find George Lewis's "The Sociology of Popular Music: A Selected and Annotated Bibliography," *Popular Music and Society* 7, no. 1, to be quite helpful as a starting point. It is well to remember that all bibliographies are dated the moment they are typed or word processed.

There are several works that I have found to be most helpful in dealing with the music industry on an everyday basis. These are Brock Helander, *The Rock Who's Who* (1982); Mike Clifford, *The Harmony Illustrated Encyclopedia of Rock* (4th ed., 1983); Arnold Shaw, *Dictionary of American Pop/Rock* (1982); and especially Harvey Rachlin, *The Encyclopedia of the Music Business* (1981), and Sidney Shemel with M. William Krasilovsky *This Business of Music* (2 vols.). *The Rolling Stone Rock Almanac: The Chronicles of Rock & Roll* (1983) is a nice historical compilation, although most significant events in the music business are omitted. Ehrenstein and Reed's *Rock on Film* (1982) is the current definitive work on film and contemporary music. Broadcasting, unfortunately, has not received equal treatment as of this writing. Philip K. Eberly's *Music in the Air: America's Changing Tastes in Popular Music, 1920-1980* (1982) is the best, but hardly complete, effort to date.

Despite the proliferation of rock and pop music books since the early 1970s, only the biographical sphere seems to have noticeably improved. For further observations, again, see *Sing a Song of Social Significance* (2nd ed.).

# General Index

A & M records: artist development at, 103-6; artist management at, 72; company integration at, 162; crash of '79 at, 110, 117; cutouts at, 226; distribution practices at, 218, 219, 220; publicity at, 208-9. *See also* Record companies/industry; names of artists and executives

A&R (artists and repertoire) director, 82-87. *See also* Producer/production; Record companies/industry

ABC (American Broadcasting Company), 98-99, 241, 382

"ABC Rocks" (television show), 371

Acid rock, 165-66

Advertising, 120-21, 128-29, 134, 199, 202, 290, 350-51, 353, 358, 369, 370

*Advertising Age* (journal), 353

AFTRA (American Federation of Television and Radio Artists), 233

Album covers. *See* Art

Albums on radio. *See* AOR

Alligator Records, 87-88

Altamont concert, 439

American Association of Sex Educators and Counselors (AASEC), 402-3

"American Bandstand" (television show), 16, 26, 91, 236, 237-38, 334, 339, 346, 347, 354, 380, 395

American Federation of Television and Radio Artists (AFTRA), 233

*American Opinion* (journal), 381, 383, 393, 394-95, 399

American Society of Composers, Artists, and Publishers (ASCAP), 8, 16, 236

AOR (album-oriented rock), 133-34, 138, 142, 150, 248, 253-55, 257-59, 284, 356. *See also* Narrowcasting

Apple record label, 89, 93, 101. *See also* Beatles

Arbitron (ARB) ratings, 128, 199, 241, 252, 261, 356

Ariola records, 117, 220

Arista records, 71, 220

Art work, 147, 168, 187-97, 344-45

Artist(s): contracts, 56-59, 62; cutouts and, 227; development of, 103-6; discovery of, 37-38; editorial control for, 165; life style of, 43-44; management of, 37, 69-74; motivation of, 40-44; MTV and, 342-43, 361-62, 363-65; process to stardom for, 37-38, 44-59, 75; product promotion by, 68-69; reviewers and, 308-9; social characteristics of, 59-62; touring of, 54, 57-58, 62-69. *See also* Artistic freedom; Producer/production; name of artist, singing group, and recording

Artistic freedom, 159-60, 169-72, 249, 422

Artists and repertoire (A&R) director, 82-87. *See also* Producer/production; Record companies/industry

ASCAP (American Society of Composers, Artists and Publishers), 8, 16, 236

Asylum records, 177. *See also* WCI

Atari video games, 132, 134

Atlantics, 71, 82, 99, 117, 218, 219. *See also* WCI; names of artists and executives associated with company

Audience. *See* Demographics; Esoteric/exoteric audiences; Market/marketing; Sales, record

Backmasking controversy, 406, 407-10, 424. *See also* Crowley, Aleister; Satanism

*Baltimore Sun* (newspaper), 355, 363

Bands: equipment for, 45-46, 50, 51; material for, 46-48, 50; starting, 44-45; working, 42-52, 69. *See also* Big Band era; name of band

Bartlett chain, disk jockeys in, 241

Beast of 666. *See* Crowley, Aleister; Page, Jimmy

"Beat Room" (television show), 347

jockey, 232, 233-36; drug lyrics controversy and, 275-84; FCC and, 271-84; free-
form, 246-51, 253; in early 1980s, 133-34;
influence on record sales of, 178; marketing and, 112, 119-20, 134, 178; MTV compared to, 232, 349-50, 355, 356, 357, 358;
politics and, 255-56, 273-74; superstars
and, 255; technology and, 236; tip sheets
for, 245, 263-64; Top 40, 240-41, 243,
247, 251, 253; during World War II, 12-13.
*See also* AOR: CHR: Drugola; Market/
marketing; Payola; Program directors;
Taping controversy; name of consultant,
disk jockey, and programmer
*Radio and Records* (magazine), 201, 256, 258,
323, 325
Radio Corporation of America. *See* RCA
*Radio Only* (magazine), 256, 260
*Rag* (magazine), 303
Ratings. *See* Drugola; Payola; name of rating,
e.g. Neilsen, Arbitron; name of artist and
recording
RCA (Radio Corporation of America): country music on, 449; crash of '79 at, 110;
cutouts at, 227; distribution practices at,
211, 213, 215-16, 218, 219, 220; home office location of, 161; as a major recording
company, 81-82; print media and, 309;
record release of, 90, 309; returns policy
of, 117; superstars at, 96-97; video discs,
106. *See also* Record companies/indus-
try; names of artists and executives associated with company
"Ready, Steady, Go" (television show), 335,
347-48
Rebellion, rock as a symbol of, 13-15, 17, 18
*Record* (magazine): refusal to print Dave
Marsh column, 69, 163
Record burnings, 404-5, 406, 419-20, 427n33
Record clubs, 211-12
Record companies/industry: artist development by, 103-6, 143; attacks on, 132-33;
bureaucracy of, 162; cutbacks in, 3, 21,
110-12, 117, 119, 150; cutouts and, 158,
224-27; definition of, 79; distribution
practices in, 158, 211-24; East coast/West
coast offices of, 161-62; fads in, 28-29;
FCC and, 279-83; film industry and,
125-26, 149-50, 166; as a gamble (success/
failure), 80, 160, 451; independent, 87,

88-89; major, 80, 81-87, 88; marketing by,
80, 158, 179-210; mergers of, 98-99, 126,
MTV as rescuer of, 143, 144, 353, 357-60,
445; NARM relations with, 124; new directions for, 143; in 1950s, 7-8; in 1970s,
28-29; in 1980s, 28-29; presidential role
in, 158-59; print media and, 291, 296,
316-23, 324-25; problems of, 32; pro-
ducers/production in, 158, 159, 163-77;
record releasing by, 89-93; specialty,
87-88; staff loyalty in, 168; structure of,
161-62; types of, 81-82. *See also* A&R director; Contracts; Demographics; Depression of '79; Management of artists;
Superstars; Taping controversy; name of
company/label
Record releasing, 89-93, 97-98, 113-14,
131-32, 245, 426n16. *See also* Market/
marketing; Sales, record
Record returns, 108-10, 117
*Record* (magazine), 321
*Record World* (magazine), 178, 319, 325
Recording acts, 56-59
*Red Channels* (magazine), 378-79
Reggae music, 29, 106, 107-8. *See also* names
of artists and singing groups
Releasing, record. *See* Record releasing
Renting, record, 137-38
Reprise Records, 71, 99, 219. *See also* WCI
Returns, record, 217
Reviewers, 290, 304-16, 362-63. *See also*
name of reviewer
Rhythm and blues music, 8, 15, 28, 84,
85-86. *See also* Rock and roll music
RIA (Recording Industry of America): an-
nouncement of Osmonds' ten gold rec-
ords, 341; consumer preference figures by,
224; dispute about sales figures of, 319-20;
drugola investigation by, 267; FCC ruling
on drug-lyric controversy and, 277; sales
and shipment figures of, 4, 127-28,
144-45, 148, 447, 448, 450; taping controversy and, 116, 130, 146, 321. *See also*
Gortikov, Stan
*Rock* (magazine), 163, 264, 289, 290, 303, 401
*Rock and Roll Confidential* (magazine),
269-70, 311, 320
Rock and roll music: acid, 165-66; attitudes
about, 5, 6, 8-9, 10; audience for, 8, 27;
cable television and, 443-44; communism

# Index of Names of People
# and Singing Groups

# Index of Recordings/Video Clips